Pasargardae

A   N

• Tepe Yahya

M E L U H H A

Strait of Hormuz

OMAN

Sutkegendor •

E
M
I
R
A
T
E
S

Gulf of Oman

Buraimi •

Jebel Hafit •

• Bat

M
A
K
K
A
N

OMAN

Bahrain
through the ages
the Archaeology

Bahrain
through the ages
the Archaeology

Edited by Shaikha Haya Ali Al Khalifa
and Michael Rice

KPI

London, New York, Sydney and Henley

First published in 1986 by KPI Limited
14 Leicester Square, London WC2H 7PH, England

Distributed by
Routledge & Kegan Paul plc
14 Leicester Square, London WC2H 7PH, England

Routledge & Kegan Paul Inc
29 West 35th Street, New York, NY10001

Routledge & Kegan Paul
c/o Methuen Law Book Company
44 Waterloo Road
North Ryde, NSW 2113
Australia

Routledge & Kegan Paul plc
Broadway House, Newtown Road,
Henley-on-Thames, Oxon RG9 1EN, England

Produced by Worts-Power Associates
Design by Pengilley Designs

Set in Cheltenham typeface
by Typesetters (Birmingham) Limited
Smethwick, West Midlands
and printed in Great Britain
by Dotesios Printers Limited,
Bradford-on-Avon, Wiltshire

ISBN 07103 0112-X

List of Contents

Editorial Note

This volume is based on the papers delivered at the archeological sessions of a conference organized in Bahrain on the initiative of the Government of the State of Bahrain, in December 1983. The story of the Conference is told elsewhere. The administrative effort was enormous and we should like to record here our thanks to the following Ministry of Information personnel without whose assistance neither the Conference nor this book would have been possible: Mr Ebrahim Noor, Mr Mohamed Ghiloom, Miss Zubaida Miradi, Mr Ahmed Abassi, Mr Mohamed Almeer, Mr Mahmood AlDoy, Mr Hassan Juma and Miss Leila AlMahmeed.

The papers are substantially the texts of the lecturers delivered at the Conference, adapted to printed form with the minimum of changes other than the standardization of spellings for place and proper names. The transliteration of place names etc. is that generally adopted in Bahrain.

Bibliographical references supplied by the authors have been consolidated into one comprehensive bibliography. The papers at the Conference dealing with the history of Bahrain in the immediately pre-Islamic, and the Islamic period up to the present century, will be the subject of a second volume of the Proceedings. Some of these papers and others have been published in *Al-Watheeqa*, the journal of the Bahrain Documentation Centre.

Introduction

It is a great pleasure for me to introduce this book on the first part of the Proceedings of the Bahrain Historical Conference, which was held in Manama in December 1983.

The Conference was judged, by those who took part in it, to have been a resounding success. Certainly we in the Government of Bahrain were delighted at what was achieved during the week the Conference took place. I would now like to take this opportunity to set down formally, the record of the planning and organisation of the Conference for it was, to the State of Bahrain and I hope for the study of the history of that region of which Bahrain is a part, an important and productive event.

The decision to organise the Conference was taken by the Cabinet in the knowledge that 1983 was the two hundreth anniversary of the arrival in Bahrain of the Al Khalifa family and their supporters. His Highness Shaikh Isa bin Sulman Al Khalifa is the tenth member of the family to rule the State and it was decided that a conference which reviewed and set into a modern academic perspective the rich and complex history of Bahrain would be a fitting way to celebrate the bi-centenary. The event was seen as one in which all the State's citizens could participate and from which even future generations would draw some benefit.

The Ministry of Information was responsible for the organisation and administration of the Conference. Mr Michael Rice was appointed by the Ministry as General Secretary for the Committee and under his guidance Ministry staff, headed by Mr Ebrahim Noor, issued the invitations, answered the numerous and varied enquiries, dealt with the day to day running of the Conference as well as the follow-up with the historians and researchers once the Conference was over – all in all an enormous undertaking.

The Prime Minister, Shaikh Khalifa bin Sulman Al Khalifa therefore set up a Ministerial Committee with responsibility to plan the Conference in detail. The Committee was appointed in 1980 and thereafter met throughout the ensuing two and a half years, before the Conference took place. The Conference itself, entitled, 'Bahrain through the Ages' was held from 3–9 December 1983.

The Ministerial Committee met under the distinguished Chairmanship of Shaikh Abdullah bin Khalid Al Khalifa, the Minister of Justice and Islamic Affairs, himself a well-known historian of Bahrain. The other members were Mr Yusef Shirawi, the Minister of Development and Acting Minister for Cabinet Affairs, Dr Ali Fakhroo, Minister of Education, and myself as Minister of Information.

The Committee was assisted by an academic committee whose members were Shaikha Haya Ali Al Khalifa, the Director of Antiquities and Museums, Dr Ahmed Abu Hakima, Dr Kaml Selibi, Dr Mustafa Najar and Dr Ali Aba Hussein.

Invitations to participate in the Conference were sent to all those scholars in the Arab world and beyond it who were known to be interested in studies relating to Bahrain and the Gulf region. Those invited were asked to indicate the subject on which they wished to give a paper; the only condition imposed by the Ministerial Committee was that the subject proposed should be relevant to Bahrain's history.

The response was remarkable and very pleasing. More than one hundred scholars indicated that they wished to participate; their countries of origin represented most of the Arab world whilst others came from southeast Asia, India, Pakistan, Western Europe, the United States and Canada.

So considerable was the interest in the Conference that it was at once apparent that its proceedings would have to be divided, with some discussions taking place simultaneously. Approximately half the participants attending the Conference were archaeologists and ancient historians; they thus constituted a coherent group and represented one section of the Conference whose deliberations were of common interest. The balance of the Conference was divided into those whose interest lay in historical studies relating to Bahrain from the time of the Revelation of Islam to the seventeenth century, whilst a third group was concerned with the emergence of the modern state of Bahrain, post-1783. There was a special session devoted to architectural studies.

In the event approximately one hundred and twenty scholars attended the Conference. There was wide public interest in it, stimulated by extensive coverage in Bahraini media before and during the Conference. Members of the public who were interested in the deliberations of the Conference were invited to attend some of the sessions.

The opening Ceremony at Bahrain's Sheraton Hotel was performed by His Highness the Amir. The Prime Minister, the Crown

Prince, Ministers and invited guests were in attendance. His Highness wished that every participant in the Conference be presented to him, a gesture which was greatly appreciated by those who were thus enabled to meet him.

In addition to the sessions of the Conference held every day, morning, afternoon and, sometimes extending into the evening, the participants were able to visit most of the Island's important archaeological sites. Of these visits the outstanding was perhaps the monumental site at Barbar which the Department of Antiquities had re-excavated and specially prepared for the Conference so that participants could see for themselves what is, with little question, the most imporant archaeological site in the entire Gulf region.

Several important publications, on archaeological and historical topics, were made available at the Conference and distributed to the participants. A handsome commemorative medallion in gold was struck specially and presented to all those who took part.

At the inaugural session of the Conference, following the opening Ceremony, I was able to make a significant policy statement on behalf of the Government of Bahrain, concerning the Government's care of the State's historic and cultural heritage. This is the substance of what I was able to say.

When we started planning for the Conference, we were well aware of the richness of Bahrain's history and heritage. We also believed that not enough information about that history and heritage had been made available to individual citizens or to scholars who were interested in the history of this region. The Conference, therefore, itself was seen as providing a forum of discussion amongst scholars, eventually calculated to generate academic interest amongst students and visitors interested in the history of Bahrain.

The Government of Bahrain had undertaken the mammoth task of convening this forum of the most distinguished historians and archaeologists from the conviction that they would augment the wealth of knowledge about our heritage. But to take practical steps to preserve that heritage the Government has embarked on an ambitious programme for the restoration of historic buildings and the preservation of archaeological sites.

Initially, in this four-year budget, we have planned an expenditure of one million dinars for such projects. Concern for the heritage of the past is not a new departure, however, for many years ago we undertook the restoration of the Khamis Mosque, which is one of the earliest Islamic monuments in the Gulf, and now we have started the re-excavation of the great monument at Barbar. This comes from a period almost contemporary with that of the Pharaohs in Egypt and demonstrates how high a culture flourished here so long ago.

We have also undertaken to preserve for future generations

many traditional Bahraini houses, a witness of our concern to protect the State's historic architecture. The Saidi House in Muharraq was the first project in this programme. We have since completed the restoration of the Shaikh Isa House in Muharraq also and we hope eventually to take over other houses in Bahrain.

In 1983 we started the renovation of the old Law Courts Building in central Manama. Although relatively recent in its history, this building represents a most interesting period of Bahraini architecture. It is now open to the public and will become our museum of the contemporary and the traditional ways of life. Another major conservation challenge to us is represented by the forts which are so distinctive a part of our historical heritage. The Bahrain Fort, for example, we know has been rebuilt many times and the present structure rests on top of an earlier Islamic fort. We must undertake renovation of that building into a monument that will reflect our concern for the history of Bahrain. Abu Maher Fort was renovated four years ago, and now stands as a beautiful monument overlooking the coastguard harbour.

Our efforts in the restoration of historic sites face two other challenges: the promoters of modern building techniques and those contractors who employ the most ingenious methods of taking destructive shortcuts. These are often the real enemies of conservation policy. Equally, a lot of the new products available for preservation work have not been properly tested and if used could in fact accelerate decay and deterioration. After all, not long ago concrete was quite conscientiously used in the conservation of historic buildings.

As challenging as the preservation of the forts is the preservation of the fields of burial mounds for which Bahrain is so famous. The mounds are particularly difficult to preserve because, to give an idea of the magnitude of the task facing us, we really need to preserve entire mound fields, involving tens of thousands of burial mounds. This of course is extremely difficult to do, the more so as we have two very urgent projects going through the mound fields at this moment. Both projects represent the continuing development of Bahrain as it has been undertaken through the ages; the old and the new must continue to exist alongside each other. The Bahrain–Saudi causeway, which is the biggest architectural challenge in the history of Bahrain, is passing through the Sar site, whilst Hamad Town, the new Government Housing Project, is being built on an adjacent mound field.

It is an irony that new townships are being built alongside our most extensive historical monument. We have to deal with the problem urgently and complete the excavation of the mounds in time for the township and the causeway to be finished. The buckets and brushes of archaeologists have to beat the bulldozers of the contractors. At the end of the day, more than half a million dinars will have to be spent to excavate and research these mounds. Many excavation teams from friendly countries are busy on this project.

Archaeological discoveries are most rewarding for the researches of the expeditions which are working throughout the State. But their results have to be protected from atmospheric pollution once they are out of the ground. Our first museum was a large room on the ground floor of Government House. opened in 1970, at the time of the last major archaeological and historical conference to be held in Bahrain. The museum has since grown in size, in presentation techniques and in the preservation of its contents, since it moved to its present site in 1974. We have recently allocated land and appointed architects for a new National Museum, which we are committed to build at an estimated budget of about thirteen million dinars. The treasures of Bahrain will find a new safe home very soon.

The Government of Bahrain is determined to undertake the task of preserving the history and heritage of this country for future generations and it will do it scientifically, because we know that it is a problem that should not be left to amateurs.

The Conference represented the most important gathering of scientific and academic skills ever assembled, to bring to bear the light of research and analysis on Bahrain's past. It is revealing to consider the extent of Bahraini studies in the years which intervened between the Conference held in 1970 and that held in 1983. At the earlier conference there were just seven papers which related specifically to Bahrain; in 1983 that number had increased to one hundred and sixteen, with evidence of deep and committed interest in our country's past now being demonstrated in centres of learning and research throughout the world.

This book will, I know, represent a valuable source of information and research material for many years to come. It represents the record of a most memorable and worthwhile event in the scholarly history of Bahrain.

TARIQ ALMOAYED
Minister of Information,
The State of Bahrain

Shoreline changes in Bahrain since the beginning of human occupation

PAUL SANLAVILLE AND ROLAND PASKOFF

The coast of Bahrain, especially in the main island, is presently undergoing a rapid evolution hastened by human intervention. The northern part of the island, in particular the northern shoreline exposed to the so-called *shamal*, a north wind, is severely eroded. As a consequence, the southern part of the island receives sediments carried by the littoral drift and aggradation is taking place along the shoreline.

This evolutive trend is not a recent one. Old defensive structures against marine erosion, such as groynes and walls, are found on the coast of the northern part of the main island which has been populated, irrigated and cultivated for several millennia.

Bahrain also shows clear evidence of sea level variations which combined their effects with wave and current actions.

GEOMORPHIC EVIDENCE OF SEA LEVEL VARIATIONS

During the last interglacial period, between 125,000 and 80,000 years B.P., sea level probably was about 4 to 5 m above the present one. Only the central part of the main island, an anticline structure of Eocene limestones, emerged from the sea. The surrounding coastal plain was submerged with the exception of the rocky highland of Sar Hamalah which was a small island, fig. 1. Along the internal edge of the western lowland, Doornkamp *et al.* (1980) drew attention to the presence of beach sediments at the foot of a former subdued cliff. For instance, near Mamlahat al Mamtalah, cross bedded conglomerates, characterized by well rounded pebbles and marine fauna, crop out where the western slope of the central anticline breaks abruptly. Conglomerates were truncated by continental erosion during the last glacial regression.

Likewise, not very far from the road from Awali to Zallaq, the bottom of a wadi reveals Eocene limestones unconformably covered by consolidated sands including marine shells and pebbles (Dar Kulayb). At Malakiyah, a well classified sandy deposit, horizontally

1 Relief and geology of Bahrain

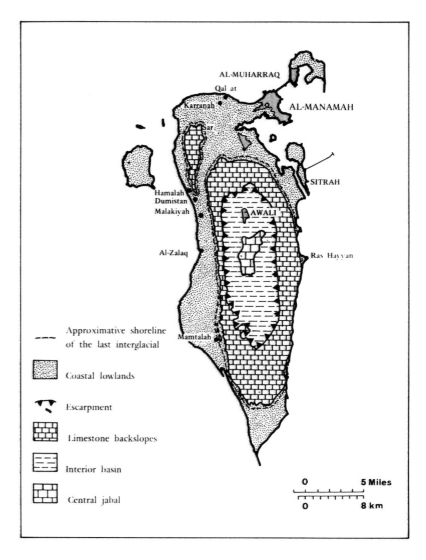

AL-MUHARRAQ

Qal at

Karranah

Sar

AL-MANAMAH

SITRAH

Hamalah
Dumistan
Malakiyah

AWALI

Al-Zalaq

Ras Hayyan

Mamtalah

⎯ ⎯ Approximative shoreline
      of the last interglacial

Coastal lowlands

Escarpment

Limestone backslopes

Interior basin

Central jabal

0   5 Miles

0   8 km

bedded, several decimeters thick, can be observed in a similar position. Farther north, around Durmistan, comparable marine sediments are found. They crop out on a large surface and, because they were bulldozed for road construction purposes, good exposures are available: they display Eocene limestones at the bottom, and above, separated by an unconformity, cemented quartzose sands, 1 m thick, sometimes rich in shells, with a duricrust at the top (Durmistan formation). A very similar deposit appears on the seashore itself at Al Aqariyah.

Thus, strong field evidence supports the idea that a former shoreline was located at about + 5 m in the western coastal plain, fig.

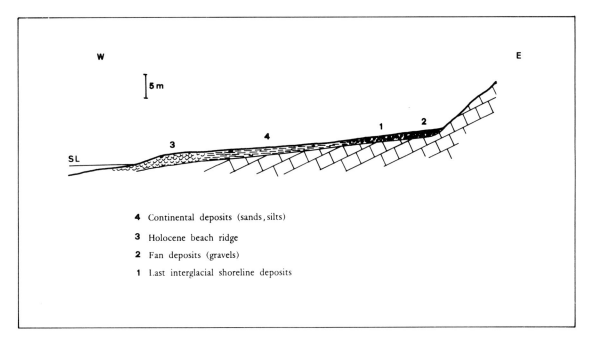

W

5 m

E

SL

3

4

1

2

4 Continental deposits (sands, silts)

3 Holocene beach ridge

2 Fan deposits (gravels)

1 Last interglacial shoreline deposits

2. No absolute dating is available for it, but we agree with Doornkamp *et al.*'s suggestion (1980) that it probably dates back to the last interglacial period. However, we also assume that it was preceded at a similar level by one or more older Quaternary transgressions.

At the time of the deposition of the Durmistan formation, the main island of Bahrain was reduced to its central part separated by the sea from the Sar Hamalah highland. It was inhospitable and uninhabited: topography was rugged and no fresh water was available since the present day coastal lowland was entirely submerged.

Afterwards, an important regression took place and almost the entire Gulf emerged. At that time Bahrain was part of the Arabian subcontinent (Kassler, 1973) and the coastline was located farther south, where the Gulf of Oman is today. Interstadial transgressions probably occurred during the last glacial period. Beach deposits dating back to 32,700 to 44,300 B.P. are reported by Sayari and Zötl (1978) on the Island of Malul and a − 22 m level dated at 26,700 years B.P. is described by Kassler (1973) in Qatar. Up to now, nothing similar has been found in Bahrain.

Sea-level at the end of the postglacial transgression approached its present position and reached + 2 m in Bahrain according to field observations and radiocarbon datings.

On the eastern coast of the island, Holocene beach deposits are widespread (Doornkamp *et al.*, 1980). The best exposure can be observed at Ras Hayyan where a former rocky islet is now linked with

2 Cross-section of the west coastal plain of Bahrain

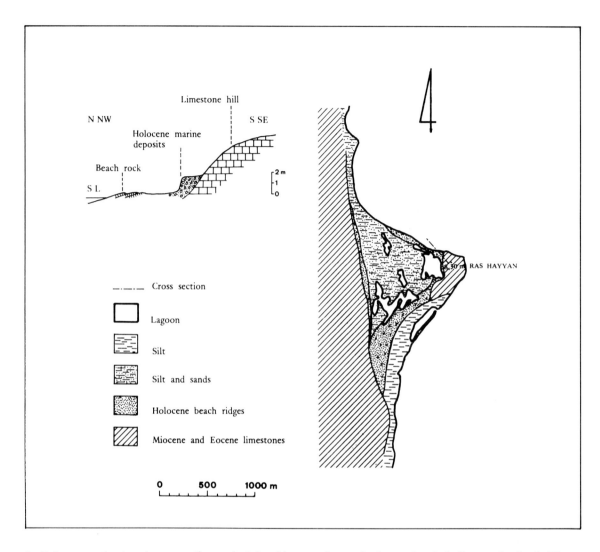

3 Holocene marine deposits at
Ras Hayyan

the main island by a twin tombolo made of shelly sands, fig. 3. These sands point to a sea level about 2 m higher than the present one. Today, they are partly cemented in beach-rock in the intertidal zone and suffer erosion. Four radiocarbon datings performed at Birmingham yielded ages between 6,670 and 6,940 years B.P., one sample we got at + 1.70 m was dated at 5,070 ± 160 years B.P. (J. Evin, Ly-2872). Consequently, in Bahrain, there is undoubted evidence of a shoreline which ran about 2 m higher than the present one between 7,000 and 5,000 years B.P., corresponding to the top of the Flandrian transgression.

Comparatively, in Abu Dhabi, after a detailed field study of the sabkha and a large number of radiocarbon datings (34), Evans *et. al.*

(1969) concluded that present sea level was reached 7,000 years B.P. by the postglacial transgression whose top at + 1 m was attained around 4,000 years B.P., tardily if compared with Bahrain.

From the western coast of Bahrain, Doornkamp *et al.* (1980) got four radiocarbon datations, with two cross checking datings on each of the four samples. Three samples coming from an area drastically reworked by the wind, about 1 m above present sea level, yielded ages ranging between 4,230 and 4,900 years B.P. (samples 001, 012 and 034). The fourth sample was collected from further within the same area (Mamtallah), more or less at present sea level, which, according to field observations and aerial photograph analysis, has been filled up by marine deposition more recently: 3,130 ± 130 and 3,330 ± 180 years B.P. were the two results for this sample. In the Mamtallah area, the 1/25,000 scale topographic map clearly shows three former coastal barriers made of coarse shelly sands separated by troughs with finer sediments. They are the result of progressive marine deposition during the last 3,000 years.

Finally, on the northern coast, west of Qal'at al-Bahrain, in particular at Karranah, above the present day large intertidal zone (1,800 m wide at low tide) there exists a corrosion marine platform developed in limestones, with patches of weakly cemented shelly sands including fragments of pottery. Again we have here evidence of a postglacial sea level 0.80 to 1 m higher than the present one, but absolute dates are not available.

ARCHAEOLOGICAL EVIDENCE OF HOLOCENE SEA LEVEL VARIATIONS

Archaeological excavations on coastal sites, because they give a detailed stratigraphy and a precise chronology, are very useful for understanding shoreline changes during the last millennia. From this point of view, our collaboration with the French archaeological team currently carrying out research at Qal'at al-Bahrain was highly fruitful and we gratefully acknowledge the help of Monik Kervran, head of this team, who gave us full support.

According to Larsen (1980), excavations made by Bibby (1969) at Qal'at al-Bahrain revealed, in layer 29, at 1.5–1.9 m above present average sea level, cemented marine sands, here called *farush*, including pre-Barbar ceramics dating back to 2,400–2,300 B.P. These marine sands are evidence of a beach which is contemporaneous with human occupation of the site of Qal'at al-Bahrain. They were found again here and there in the course of Kervran's team's excavations.

For instance, beneath the Islamic fortress, square F52 displays the following section from bottom to top, fig 4a:

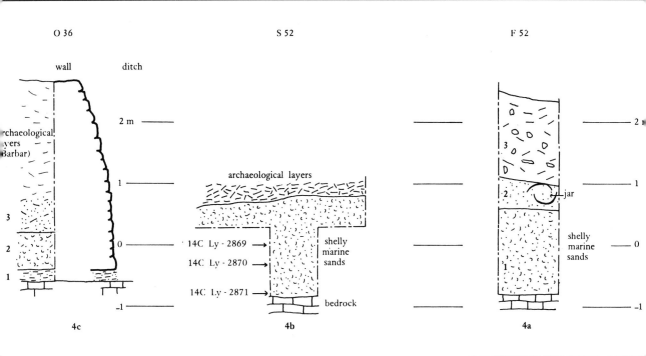

4 Cross sections in Kervran's excavations at Qal'at al-Bahrain

3. an archaeological layer pointing to occupation dating back to the Neo-Babylonian epoch (VIIth–VIth century B.C.)

2. sands, partly man-reworked, in which an undated funeral jar was found

1. shelly marine sands, unequally cemented

0. a bedrock of Eocene limestones

Marine sands are found up to + 0.60 m above the present average level of high tides. This figure is calculated on the basis of a 2.20 m high tide. Consequently, they clearly indicate a sea level at least 0.50 m higher than the present one.

Farther east, square S52 gives a rather interesting profile. Archaeological layers cover marine sands which are 0.85 m above the present average high tide level. Owing to a drilling which reached the bedrock through more than one meter of marine sands, shells were collected at three different levels and subsequently dated by J. Evin at Lyon. Results are in good accordance with stratigraphy; fig. 4b:

top: 3,030 ± 120 years B.P. (Ly-2869)
middle: 3,260 ± 160 years B.P. (Ly-2870)
bottom: 3,430 ± 120 years B.P. (Ly-2871)

The marine sands visible in square F52, fig. 4c, have not yet been dated. However, taking into account their altitude, their facies and the stratigraphic relationship with the archaeological layers, they look like those of square S52. These coarse shelly sands (frequently including entire shells of Gastropods), thick (1 m and more) and homogeneous, are an indication of deposition in the upper part of the intertidal zone. Radiocarbon datings point to a slow sedimentation, probably related with a progressive rise in the sea level. Water rolled and worn potsherds, hard to identify, have been found; one of them could be Kassite (second millennium B.C.).

In 1982, south of the Islamic fortress, M. Kervran unearthed a ditch, 7 m wide at its base, limited by a twofold wall made of limestone blocks and still 3.20 m high, which is more recent than the Barbar period. At its base the ditch was excavated into a Holocene beach. Behind the wall, in square O36, beneath the archaeological layers of the Barbar period, the following strata are found from top to bottom, fig 4c:

3. man-reworked shelly sands
2. unequally indurated beach sands
1. greenish clayey sands

The calcareous bedrock is found here at − 0.10 m and the top of the Holocene beach is at about 0.20 m above the average high tide level. Given their facies, the clayey sands may represent a deposit in the lower part of the intertidal zone and the beach sands a deposit in the upper part. Absolute dates are not available.

Moreover, just in front of square S52, on the present beach, the remnants of an old jetty are noticeable. On top of them, at + 0.58 m above the average high tide level, patches of dead Polychet Annelids – probably *Pomatoleios* sp. (J. Laborel determination) – are preserved. The same Annelids live today 1 m below in the middle part of the intertidal zone, a fact which indicates that at the time the dead Annelids were alive, sea level was about 1 m higher than it is today. The dead Annelids yielded a radiocarbon age of 4,350 ± 160 years B.P. (J. Evin, Ly-2867). If this is true, the jetty is very old, dating back prior to the Barbar period, because it appears that it was restored with pinkish cement before the growth of the dead Annelids took place. No archaeological dating is available for the jetty which in fact was probably a groyne erected when sea level and shoreline positions were close to the present one. However, a progressive sea level rise accounts for the damage which led to the restoration of the jetty.

Some data given by Larsen (1980) can be added to these observations. In a section located at Al Wasmiyah, eolian sands cover shelly sands which indicate a beach deposit, subsequent to a high sea level, corresponding to the Barbar I period (about 2,100 B.C.). On the other hand, rolled and worn Kassite ceramics were found at a distance between 63 and 74 m from the present shoreline and about 1.20 m above the high tide level, but the stratigraphic context of these findings is not entirely clear. It seems that in this area Neo-Assyrian and Neo-Babylonian materials are lacking. Only Hellenistic materials are present. Larsen's view is that sea level was higher than today at the beginning of the first millennium, during the Neo-Assyrian and Neo-Babylonian periods.

SEA LEVEL VARIATIONS IN BAHRAIN DURING THE LAST MILLENNIA

Using the available stratigraphic and chronological data, let us now try to draw a curve summarizing sea level variations in Bahrain during the last millennia, fig. 5.

The top of the Flandrian transgression that followed the last glacial regression is dated at between 7,000 and 5,000 years B.C. At that time sea level reached about + 2 m, and in the northern and western part of the island the coastal plain was narrower than today.

Then, sea level fell but we do not know if this fall was progressive and regular or if, in fact, it is the result of minor oscillations, as suggested by the study of the old jetty at Qal'at al-Bahrain. At that time, the sites of Ubaid in the southwest sabkha were inhabited.

Given the radiocarbon datings of our British colleagues and those we got from the Annelids of the old jetty at Qal'at al-Bahrain on one hand, taking into account the beach deposit with ceramics older than the Barbar period, corresponding to layer 29 of Bibby on the other hand, around 4,300 years B.P. sea level was at about + 1 m and the shoreline was off shore if compared with its present position. A site occupied prior to the Barbar period was then undergoing wave erosion and the jetty of Qal'at al-Bahrain itself was damaged.

It is up to archaeologists to discover the northern extension of the city during the Barbar and Kassite periods but, at that time, sea level had probably fallen, maybe down to the present datum since remnants of houses were found at this height in square S52.

Afterwards, in the second half of the second millennium, sea level slowly rose. Between 3,430 and 3,030 years B.P., it reached about + 1 m (square S52). The beach includes many fragments of ceramics dating back to older periods as can be seen in square S52, and here and there along the coast west of Qal'at al-Bahrain in patches of shelly sands unequally consolidated. The top of the positive oscillation of the sea level could correspond with the Kassite period or may be its end. The ditch of Qal'at al-Bahrain, called 'dry dock' by Bibby and recently studied again by Monik Kervran, may have been

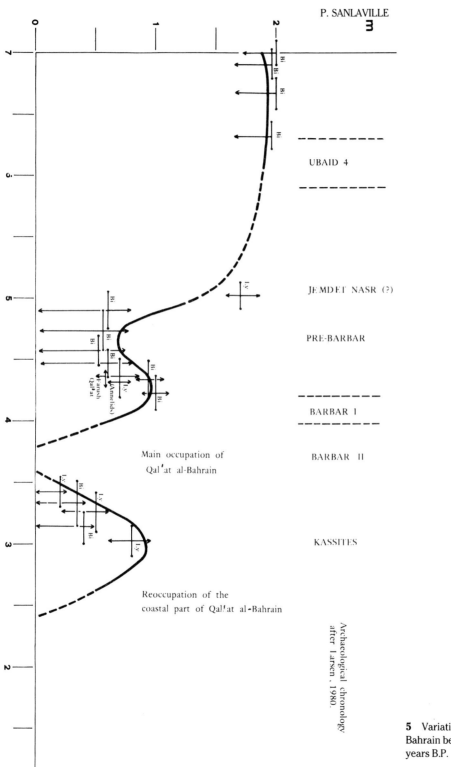

5 Variations of the coastline in Bahrain between 7,000 and 2,000 years B.P.

excavated at that time, as a higher sea level allowed it to be flooded at least at high tide.

The excavations in square S52 have shown that sea level fell to its present position, and in the Hellenistic period the datum was the same as now. In fact, more data are still needed. We do not know if shoreline variations took place later but we think that the shoreline was located farther north when the Islamic fortress was built up.

We do not know the exact causes of sea level variations in Bahrain (eustatism, local neotectonics, general movement of the Arabian plate, hydroisostatic response to the postglacial transgression). Direct correlations with neighbouring areas are hazardous. For instance, in Abu Dhabi, according to Evans *et al.* (1969) sea level was at + 1 m around 4,000 B.P. In Qatar, shells of *Cerithium* collected into a barrier corresponding to a sea level at + 2 m (Perthuisot, 1977) were dated: three assays gave coherent results ranging from 3,930 to 4,340 years B.P. (Taylor and Illing, 1969). At Ras Tanurah, shells at about + 2 m gave less concordant ages ranging from 3,380 ± 180 to 4,670 ± 190 years B.P.

In fact, more field data and more radiocarbon datings are necessary for a better picture of sea level variations around the Gulf in the Holocene. As far as Bahrain is concerned there is no doubt that appreciable sea level oscillations took place during the last millennia, having an important impact on harbour activities and land cultivation in the coastal plain through water table variations.

Variation in holocene land use patterns on the Bahrain Islands: construction of a land use model

CURTIS E. LARSEN

INTRODUCTION

Archeological research on Bahrain over the past several decades has centered on the excavation of tombs and major settlement sites on the north coast of the island. The great number of tombs covering the upland slopes of the island piqued the curiosity of workers a century ago (Durand 1879) and continue to interest a great number of scholars (Bibby 1954, Cleuziou *et al.* 1981, Ibrahim 1982, Frohlich 1982, 1983). Excavations at Qal'at al-Bahrain over the past thirty years by first the Danish Expedition (Bibby 1957, 1969), and more recently by the French Expedition (Kervran *et al.* 1982) have demonstrated the long and complex archeological record for the islands. The excavation of temple structures at Barbar (Mortensen 1956, 1970) and at Diraz (McNicoll and Roaf n.d.) has lent additional data to place Bahrain in a secure archeological context.

Bahrain was the trading and ritual center of the kingdom of Dilmun during the late third and early second millennia B.C. It succeeded the earlier Dilmun settlements on the mainland in this role at a time when direct long distance trade between Mesopotamia and the Indus Valley waned following the end of the Akkadian empire (*c.* 2250 B.C.). Extensive research by Masry (1974), Oates (1976), Oates *et al.* (1977), Potts (1983b), and Piesinger (1983b) shows that eastern Arabia was a locus for Mesopotamian trading as early as the fifth millennium B.C. Trading continued, apparently unbroken, throughout the fourth and early third millennia B.C. By the close of the third millennium, however, settlement and political emphasis shifted from the mainland to the island. Whether this shift was triggered by demographic changes taking place on the mainland or by the progressive dessication of lakes and rivers in the Arabian interior is still unclear (Larsen 1980, 1983). Bahrain-Dilmun subsequently became not only an exporter of its long-standing luxury item, pearls, but the center of the copper trade. Its mercantile exchange network linked the mining areas of Makkan (Oman) with the lucrative markets of Meluḫḫa

(Indus Valley) and Mesopotamia (Oppenheim 1954, Gelb 1970, During Caspers 1972b, 1979, Hansman 1973).

By 2000 B.C., Bahrain had changed from a sparsely-settled island, to a thriving offshore trading center that linked the nearby mainland settlements near Dhahran and Qatif with the distant island of Failaka near Kuwait. This well-defined cultural and political unit delivered goods and raw materials from the east to the city states of southern Mesopotamia (Larsen 1980, 1983, Piesinger 1983b, Potts 1983b).

This period of increased trading marked Bahrain's first development as a trading center. This development occurred during the Isin and Larsa dynasties of Sumeria, at the onset of the second millennium B.C. By the Old Babylonian period (1800–1595 B.C.), Bahrain-Dilmun had lost its former importance, at least as judged by the less frequent mention of Dilmun in contemporary historic texts (Oppenheim 1954, Larsen 1980, 1983). Although archeological evidence suggests that the Dilmun settlement on Failaka island persisted well into the second millennium B.C. (Kjaerum 1983), its counterpart on Bahrain was apparently diminished prior to the Kassite period (1595–1200 B.C.) in Mesopotamia. Dilmun, whether located on the islands of Failaka and Bahrain, or on the Arabian mainland, was not heard from again until the fourteenth century B.C. when trade in dates was mentioned in a pair of Kassite period letters from Dilmun (Cornwall 1952, Oppenheim 1954, Bibby 1969). This time, however, the historical and archeological evidence portrayed Bahrain-Dilmun as a minor trading center in the Gulf exporting dates to Mesopotamia (Oppenheim 1954, Larsen 1980, 1983).

Following the Kassite period trade, Bahrain-Dilmun did not appear as a significant economic or political entity until the mid-first millennium B.C. , when it became involved with struggles between the Neo-Assyrian empire and the Sealand of southern Mesopotamia. Conflicts between 711 and 605 B.C. featured Dilmun, but as only a peripheral component to the Mesopotamian sphere of influence. Dilmun continued in this role during the subsequent Neo-Babylonian empire in the north, until it, in turn, was succeeded by the Achaemenid dynasty of Persia in 539 B.C.

Bahrain remained an important offshore trading location throughout the remainder of the first millennium B.C. when it was featured in Greek descriptions of the Arabian coast during the fourth century B.C. and later in connection with the Chaldean trading center of Gerrha on the Arabian coast that competed with Seleucid sea trade in the Gulf (Arrian 1933, Pliny 1969, see Potts *et al.* 1978 for a review). Although later historic mention is rare, Bahrain seems to have maintained its identity as a trade center well into the early first millennium A.D. At least we know that pearls continued to be associated with the island in Parthian times (Nodelman 1960) and that it later was related to the trade network of Sasanian Persia until the beginning of the Islamic era (Taylor 1856, Schoff 1912, Vine 1937, Whitehouse and Williamson 1973).

Bahrain attained its second major peak of development as a trading center in medieval Islamic times. Beginning in the early twelfth century A.D., the island became linked with a growing maritime trade network that culminated with the kingdom of Hormuz in the fifteenth and sixteenth centuries A.D. The extent of this medieval development was only superseded in recent times with the advent of the petroleum economy of the past half century.

From Bahrain's inception as an offshore trading center in the third millennium B.C., the island's position and artesian water resources have underwritten its recurrent development as a maritime trade center that has expanded and contracted with the economic influences of the Arabian Gulf region. Thus, for at least four thousand years, Bahrain has been a recurrent center for trade and development along the east Arabian coast. These patterns of economic change have left a related spatial array of archeological remains on the surface of the island. These surficial archeological data extend the present emphasis on individual archeological site excavation to one that examines the past land use and settlement patterns on Bahrain. Land use and settlement patterns, in turn, provide a model for relating the arrangement of the archeological sites to a broader series of economic and environmental conditions.

The island can be differentiated by land use zones that reflect on the economic framework for past settlement. Land use studies promise to form a future base for more complete and informed archeological survey, excavation and research. This paper, based on more extensive work (Larsen 1980, 1983), shows briefly the geo-archeological framework for settlement on Bahrain, the variations in the extent of land used for settlement during the past 6,000 years, and presents a model to explain the settlement history of the island.

GEO-ARCHEOLOGICAL CONTEXT

The main island of Bahrain is an elongated geologic dome, fig. 6, formed by the folding of late Tertiary limestones and dolomites (Willis 1967, Brunsden et al. 1979, Larsen 1980, 1983, Doornkamp et al. 1980). The dome is surrounded on its periphery by a narrow coastal plain ranging in width from a few hundred meters to ten kilometers. The coastal plain is widest on the north coast of the island where it rises gently from sea level to an altitude of about ten meters at its intersection with the dip slope of the dome. This altitude serves as the inland limit to the coastal plain in all but a few areas. A veneer of Pleistocene and Holocene marine and terrestrial deposits

6 Geological Map of the Bahrain Islands. (Larsen 1983, copyright University of Chicago, with permission)

7 Potentiometric Map of Water in the Alat and Khobar Aquifers. (Larsen 1983, copyright University of Chicago, with permission)

(See p. 28–9)

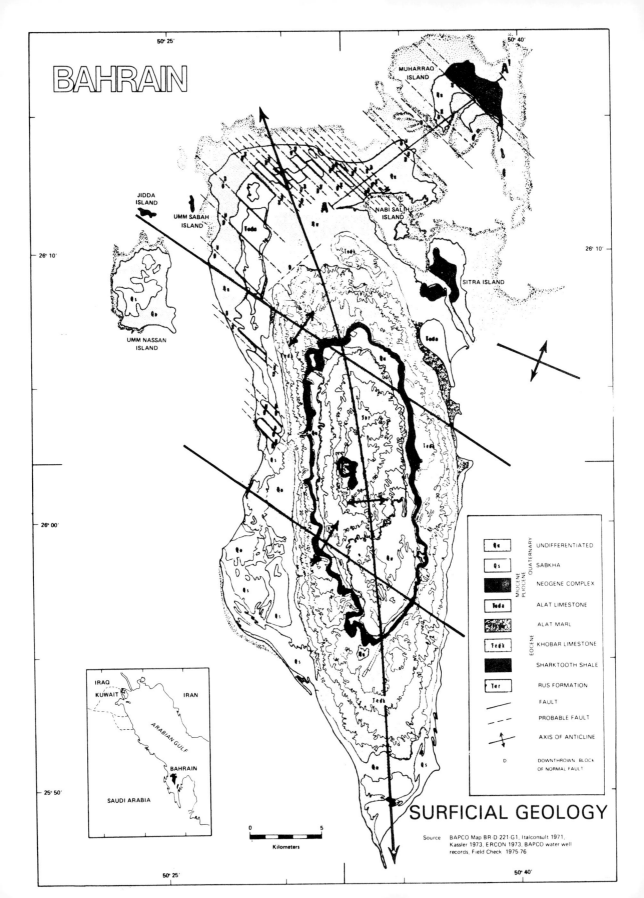

BAHRAIN

JIDDA ISLAND

UMM SABAH ISLAND

UMM NASSAN ISLAND

MUHARRAQ ISLAND

A'

A

NABI SALIH ISLAND

SITRA ISLAND

26° 10'

26° 10'

50° 25'

50° 40'

26° 00'

25° 50'

50° 25'

50° 40'

Qa		UNDIFFERENTIATED
Qs	QUATERNARY	SABKHA
		NEOGENE COMPLEX
Toda	MIOCENE PLIOCENE	ALAT LIMESTONE
		ALAT MARL
Tedk	EOCENE	KHOBAR LIMESTONE
		SHARKTOOTH SHALE
Ter		RUS FORMATION
		FAULT
		PROBABLE FAULT
		AXIS OF ANTICLINE
D		DOWNTHROWN BLOCK OF NORMAL FAULT

SURFICIAL GEOLOGY

Source: BAPCO Map BR·D 221·G1, Italconsult 1971,
Kassler 1973, ERCON 1973, BAPCO water well
records, Field Check 1975 76

IRAQ

KUWAIT

IRAN

ARABIAN GULF

BAHRAIN

SAUDI ARABIA

0   5

Kilometers

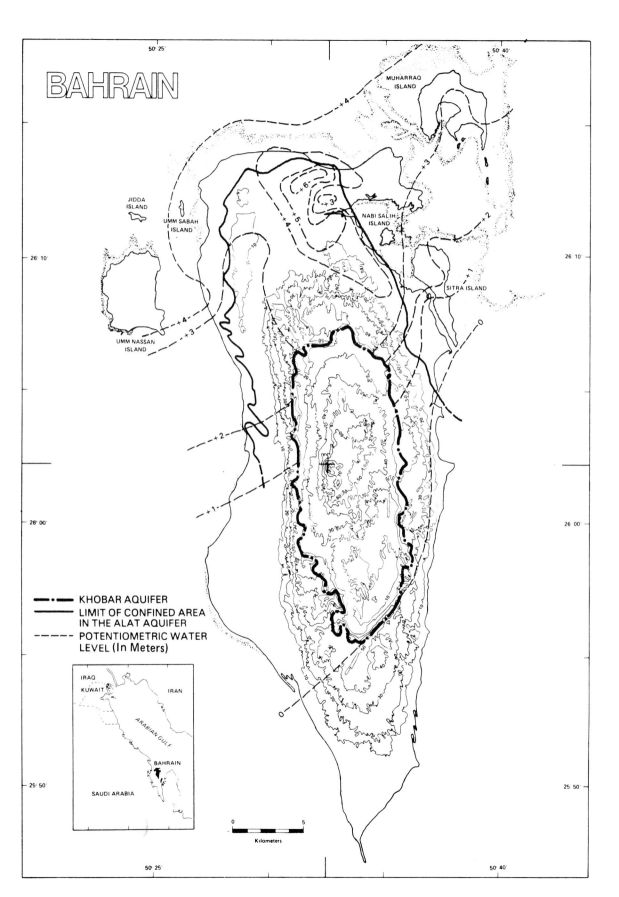

covers the plain. These deposits range from limestones to marine and eolian sands. Colluvial and alluvial sediments derived from slope erosion on the dome are deposited as coalescent fans at the intersection of the dip slopes with the coastal plain. Soils developed on these sediments have formed the productive agricultural lands of Bahrain.

Agriculture and settlement are critically dependent on the distribution of artesian water. The water, in turn, is influenced by the geologic structure of the underlying rocks and the periodic recharge of the subsurface aquifers by precipitation. The sedimentary formations of eastern Saudi Arabia dip gently to the east. Late Tertiary rocks that crop out at the surface east of Riyadh dip beneath the gulf, but appear at or near the surface at the geologic domes at Bahrain and Dhahran. Rainwater entering the porous and permeable late Tertiary limestones at the surface in Saudi Arabia is transmitted downward and eastward along the regional dip of the sedimentary formations (Wright 1967, Italconsult 1971). Water stored at depth in the various aquifers is under hydrostatic pressure and reaches the surface along fractures in the surrounding rocks, or where the aquifers are exposed at the surface around geologic structures.

Bahrain is an example of these hydrological conditions. Figure 7 shows a potentiometric map of the islands (Italconsult 1971, Larsen 1980, 1983). The map shows the theoretical altitudes to which artesian water is expected to rise in artesian springs or drilled wells. Contouring of observed data points defines a theoretical surface that reflects the distribution of hydrostatic pressures in the underlying aquifer. Artesian water is distributed diagonally across the main island of Bahrain following a northeast-southwest trend. The greater potential water levels (+4 m) occur along the northwest coast of the main island. The potential altitude of the spring levels decreases from +4 m in the north to near sea level in the south. An anomalously high zone of potential water levels and greater spring flow is located on the north coast of the island. Here spring and well levels reached an altitude of +6 m in 1971 (Italconsult 1971). This anomalously high pressure zone marks an area of intensely fractured and faulted rocks, see fig. 6. Fractures allow the interconnection of the near surface aquifers with deeper subsurface artesian aquifers, providing copious water flows. Figure 8 shows the modern settlement pattern of Bahrain to mirror this water distribution. The majority of modern settlements located in the islands are contained approximately within the +6 and +1 m potentiometric contours. Population is similarly distributed. Population decreases rapidly away from the urban centers of Manama and Muharraq (see Larsen 1983:9). Villages, reflecting population density, are closely packed along the north coast. The arrangement of villages is directly related to the number and location of

8 Modern Settlement Distribution in Bahrain. (Larsen 1983, copyright University of Chicago, with permission)

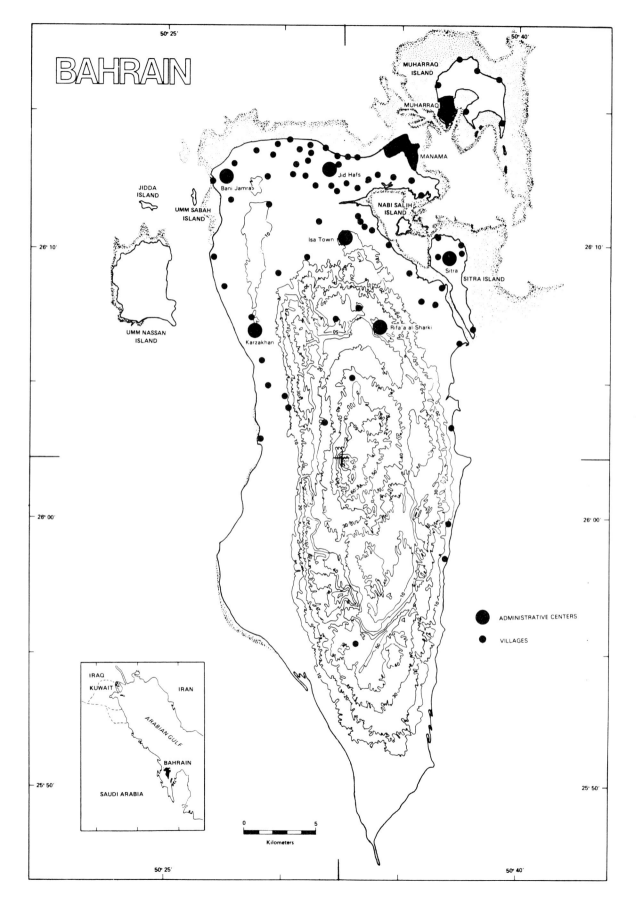

artesian springs in this same area (see Larsen 1983:119). Artesian water flow, springs, villages, and population all closely mirror the underlying fault and fracture zone.

The geohydrological framework to Bahrain provides a powerful organizing device for examining the historical and archeological settlement patterns for Bahrain. Faulting along the north central coast has given rise to an artesian center about which settlement has been located over the past 6,000 years.

A TIME-SPACE PERSPECTIVE OF SETTLEMENT

Changes in settlement area can be reconstructed from the composite array of archeological sites shown in figure 9. This map shows the combined results of surface surveys carried out by the Danish and British Expeditions to Bahrain as well as those of my own survey work in 1975 and 1976 (see Larsen 1983:26 and Appendix II). Dating the periods of occupation for these sites, based on ceramic collections (Larsen 1983: Appendix I) provides a chronological control to past settlement. This, coupled with the geo-hydrological framework to the settlement distribution described above, provides a time and space perspective of Bahrain's settlement history. Figure 9 shows archeological sites to be concentrated along the north coast of the island, in association with the artesian center, fig. 7. When the time ranges for the occupation of each site are considered as a function of distance from the north coast of the island, fig. 10, a clear variation in the extent of land occupied over the past six thousand years is apparent. Settlement has expanded away from and contracted to the artesian center on the north coast at discrete intervals.

The earliest period of expansion occurred between 5000 and 4000 B.C. as evidenced by the presence of Late Ubaid and Group D flint sites along the southwest coastal plain of Bahrain and at a distance of about thirty km from the north coast. An apparent absence of later occupation sites dating to the late fourth and early third millennia B.C. suggests that contemporary settlement was sparse at this time and was confined to the north coast.[1]

Settlement spread rapidly to the south again during the late third and early second millennia B.C. By this time, the major activity of Dilmun had shifted from the mainland to the island. A maximum in the area of land occupied was reached during Barbar II times, c. 2000 to 1800 B.C. (City II of Bibby 1969). This maximum corresponds with the development of Bahrain-centered Dilmun as a coherent cultural area linking the Arabian coast with Failaka island. It also coincides with the height of the copper trade in Isin-Larsa Mesopotamia. By the late second millennium B.C., settlement had contracted once again to the artesian core on the north coast, paralleling the reduced mention of Dilmun in historic texts. This period of reduced land use is

9 Archeological Site Map.
(Larsen 1983, copyright University of Chicago, with permission)

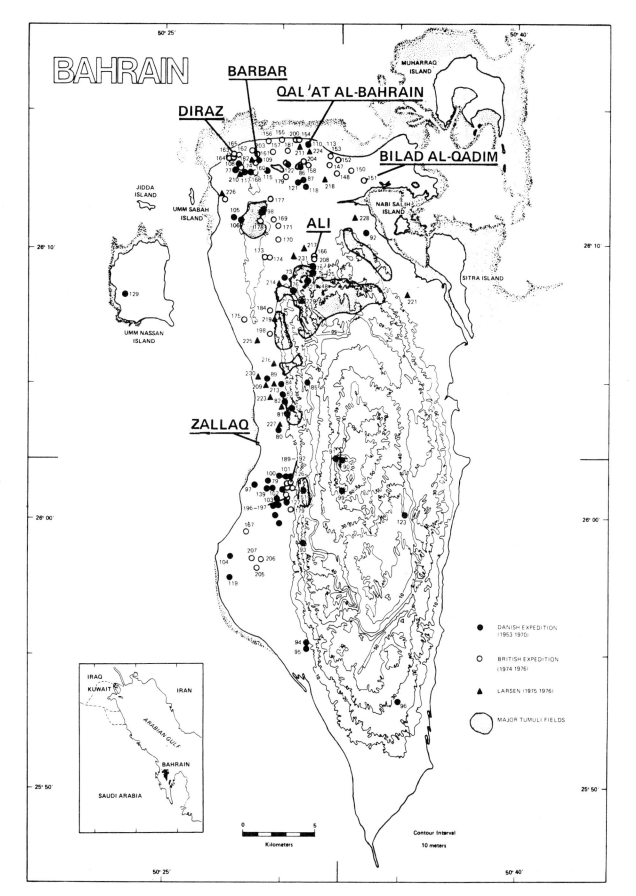

BAHRAIN

DIRAZ

BARBAR

QAL 'AT AL-BAHRAIN

BILAD AL-QADIM

ALI

ZALLAQ

MUHARRAQ ISLAND

JIDDA ISLAND

UMM SABAH ISLAND

NABI SALIH ISLAND

SITRA ISLAND

UMM NASSAN ISLAND

DANISH EXPEDITION (1953 1970)

BRITISH EXPEDITION (1974 1976)

LARSEN (1975 1976)

MAJOR TUMULI FIELDS

IRAQ
KUWAIT
IRAN
ARABIAN GULF
BAHRAIN
SAUDI ARABIA

0   5
Kilometers

Contour Interval
10 meters

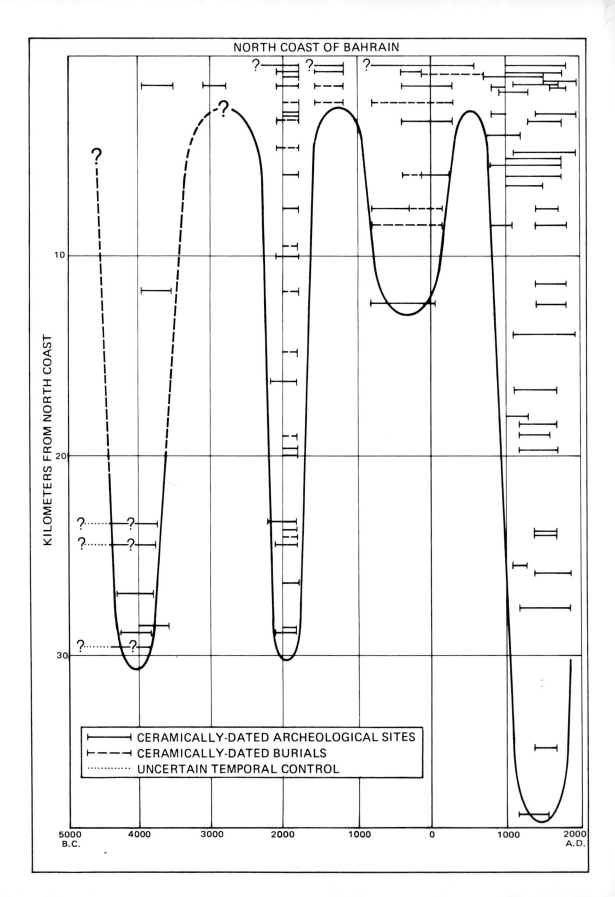

NORTH COAST OF BAHRAIN

KILOMETERS FROM NORTH COAST

├──┤ CERAMICALLY-DATED ARCHEOLOGICAL SITES
├- -┤ CERAMICALLY-DATED BURIALS
├······┤ UNCERTAIN TEMPORAL CONTROL

5000 B.C.   4000   3000   2000   1000   0   1000   2000 A.D.

reflected in Kassite period accounts of Dilmun as an exporter of dates in the fourteenth century B.C. and the cessation of Dilmun's role as the copper exporter to the north.

During the first millennium B.C. settlement spread southward once again, but this time to little more than ten km from the north coast. This expansion began with the growth of the Neo-Assyrian and Neo-Babylonian empires in the north and continued into the early first millennium A.D., including the periods of Greek through Parthian influence in the Gulf. This resurgence was also followed by a contraction of settlement to the north coast during the mid-first millennium A.D. This time, however, diminished settlement and land use corresponded temporally with the Sasanian empire in Persia, a period known for increased and widespread maritime trade elsewhere in the Gulf.

A fourth period of expanded settlement began with the Islamic era and reached an apparent maximum during late medieval times. It was during this period that Bahrain became firmly incorporated in the Arab maritime trade network eventually centered at Hormuz. Figure 10 shows medieval Islamic archeological sites to have been located nearly forty km from the north coast. In reality, agricultural settlements spread only as far as those during the previous Barbar II occupation at the beginning of the second millennium B.C. Those medieval sites located farther to the south represent special purpose defence structures or perhaps hunting camps.

When based on the archeological record, Islamic period sites began to be abandoned in the south of the island during the post medieval period. Settlements south of the village of Zallaq, fig. 9, were abandoned in late Islamic times (A.D. 1500–1750). Durand (1879), for example, noted that date gardens had been abandoned on Bahrain prior to his visit in the late nineteenth century. Abandonment of agricultural lands and villages were presumably related to cultural-ecological changes. This trend has only been reversed during the past fifty years as the result of increased development and population growth associated with the modern petroleum-based economy in the Gulf region. Variations in settlement and the area of land utilized on Bahrain have been functions of both changing economic conditions and variations in precipitation over the past six thousand years (Larsen 1980, 1983). Each of the three later periods of settlement and land use expansion shown in figure 10 coincided with periods of maritime trading in the Gulf when Bahrain was featured as an important integral center. No direct comparison can be made with the earliest period of expansion, however. Although traders from southern Mesopotamia were active along the Arabian coast in Ubaid times, it is doubtful that such trading can be compared with the developed maritime exchange networks that began to expand in the third

10 Land Use Variations Based on Settlement Sites and Tombs. (Larsen 1983, copyright University of Chicago, with permission)

millennium B.C. Clearly, the increased economic importance of Bahrain in the trading system created the necessity for increased areas of settlement as population grew, in part, amplified by the influx of outside groups. The development of outlying lands was spurred on by increased precipitation during periods when increases in surface runoff supplied water to areas outside the effective range of artesian springs (Larsen 1983). Among these areas were the colluvial and alluvial fans formed at the intersection of the coastal plain with the western slopes of the Bahrain dome. These fans were seasonally replenished by fresh sediment carried and deposited by wadi systems draining the dome. Increases in precipitation and runoff also allow dry farming to be carried out on these soils at higher altitudes above the coastal plain.[2]

Settlement and land use variations on Bahrain have been episodic. These can be related to a variety of cultural, economic, and natural environmental changes affecting the islands and the region, but they do not yet provide sufficient insight into the land use potential of Bahrain as a whole. Such a definition for land use can be important for developing future site survey strategies on Bahrain.

A LAND USE MODEL FOR BAHRAIN

Archeological research efforts centered on the sites along the north coast do not furnish a sufficient body of data to gain an understanding of the land use or settlement system of Bahrain. In fact, current emphases on Gulf trade and ceramic chronology detract from the mundane data necessary to understand Bahrain as an agricultural system that provided a base to its past settlement. The finite land area of Bahrain and its circumscribed environmental boundaries allow it to be examined in a more straightforward theoretical manner. In fact, Bahrain lends itself well to the land use concepts and model presented by von Thünen (1875) in the early nineteenth century – a model that has since become a classic base to land use and central place theory among geographers.

Bahrain's land use patterns can be envisioned as a series of discrete and specialized zones, presented by von Thünen in a simplified theoretical manner for land use differentiation in an isolated state. The model defined zones of land distributed concentrically about an urban market center. The zones of land use ranged from very narrow bands of intensively farmed lands near the central city through increasingly wider zones of more extensive cultivation, culminating with a zone of ranching or herding. Von Thünen defined his isolated state as follows:

1. The state was cut off from the rest of the world and was surrounded by waste land on all sides.

2. It was dominated by a single large city which acted as the only urban center.

3. This city was located in the midst of a broad and featureless plain of assumed equal fertility.

4. The farmers shipped their produce to the central city in return for manufactured goods.

5. Farmers transported their own produce to the central market along a system of converging roads of equal quality and with transportation costs directly proportional to the distance from the urban center

6. Profit by all farmers was maximized and was adjusted automatically to the needs of the central market.

Thus von Thünen's model was not only contained with a closed system, but also depended upon ideal economic conditions. In real geographic settings concentric land use zones are clearly not inevitable (Lösch 1940, Haggett 1965, Haggett *et al.* 1977). Indeed, few geographic areas can approximate such ideal or homogeneous physical settings. In addition, isolated market controlled economies do not exist in the modern world.

Bahrain is and has been historically linked with world trade networks. This automatically eliminates it from von Thünen's ideal closed system. Yet other useful parallels can be drawn from his model. For example, Bahrain is influenced by a single large city that acts as the sole urban market. While not located in the center of a featureless plain of equal fertility, Manama can be viewed in a modified semi-concentric land use ring system characterized by land use zones radiating outward from a coastal city (see Haggett 1966:162). The main island of Bahrain is neither broad nor featureless, but its coastal plain represents a skewed approximation of such conditions, albeit differentially watered by artesian sources. In pre-industrial times Bahraini farmers marketed their produce along a network of trails that converged on the urban center. A lack of mechanized transport in the past approximates near constant transportation costs. Therefore, a majority of von Thünen's assumptions can be applied to pre-industrial Bahrain in a very general way.

Even though simple, the model gives a basic theoretical understanding to land use systems on the island. Haggett (1966:166) however, warned that the concept of the isolated state could only be of limited value in modern land use studies because of its direct derivation from von Thünen's nineteenth century estate records. Therefore it has been encouraging to note that both Smith (1976) and Plattner (1976) have used similar generalized models as explanatory devices for understanding changing socio-economic patterns in modern underdeveloped countries. But, it is precisely the nineteenth and pre-nineteenth century view of Bahrain we wish to obtain. This gives the model an added importance and mirrors Grotewold's (1959) conclusion that the theory in itself is not faulty, but rather no longer fits the *modern* economic world of industrial societies.

Bahrain should be seen conceptually with the port city of Manama ringed by semi-concentric zones of intense gardening featuring dates and vegetables as the dominant crops. Although the economic demand for dates has decreased in modern times, both dates and vegetables continue to represent the leading local cash crops in the Manama market (Government of Bahrain 1975). Beyond this zone lie successively broader concentric zones devoted to more extensive agriculture. While some herding is still carried out in the outlying areas of Bahrain, this is only a minor practice today.

A first impression of the von Thünen model shows cultivation to decrease in intensity with increasing distance from the market center. Grotewold (1959) pointed out that this was only an apparent condition and was based as much on market demand and price. Thus, extensively cultivated crops were not rigidly excluded from areas near the market center, but were conditioned by other economic factors. Other useful observations have been made by Chisholm (1962) who considered land use zones as a series of steps rather than as continuously graded. From his work in Sicilian villages, he noted that crops like grapes and citrus fruits were most characteristic of the inner land use zones while other fruits were found in the next successive zone away from the center. Less perishable crops were located at still greater distances from the market. Chisholm found that zonation in land use zones also occurred on a smaller scale. Concentric land use zones were present around individual villages and farms as well. The labor devoted to cultivation decreased with increasing distance from the individual village or farm. One kilometer was found to be a critical commuting distance for the distribution of fields about villages.

A similar relationship was reported for Bahrain in Larsen (1983:96) based on a sample of fifty-one villages. In Bahrain, the mean distance to the farthest garden maintained by local villages was found to be 0.97 km. Such distance relationships reflect a minimization of effort on the part of farmers that is found at a variety of scales, from village to state levels. Rural population on Bahrain, as an example, decreases exponentially with increasing distance from the urban center at Manama (Larsen 1983:9). This demonstrates the largest scale example of such central-place oriented settlement and economic trends on the islands.

Distribution of population about the city of Manama is not a simple economic function of that city as the market center. The villages of Bahrain reflect the decrease in population away from the city center (Larsen 1983:112). Villages are more densely packed nearer the city than in the countryside. The location and density of villages, however, directly parallels the number and location of artesian springs on the island (see Larsen 1983: figs. 15 and 20). Clearly then population and land use on Bahrain are directly biased by the distribution of artesian water. While economic factors are undisputed variables in the settlement and agricultural development of the island, the fortuitous location of artesian springs on the north coast of the island serves as the overriding influence on land use. Thus, any use or adaptation of the von Thünen model for Bahrain must be tempered by the distribution of artesian water.

In von Thünen's original work from the early nineteenth century (von Thünen 1875), he included a detailed summary of his empirically-determined land use zones, as well as the relative area and distance of each zone from the central city. These are presented in tabular form in Table 1 (adapted from Haggett *et al.* 1977:205).

The data in Table 1 represent the dietary and societal needs of

Table 1

VON THÜNEN'S ISOLATED STATE MODEL

Zone	Percent of state area	Relative distance from central city	Land use Type	Main marketed produce	Production System
0	<0.1	<0.1	Urban industrial	Manufactured goods	Urban trade center
1	1	0.1–0.6	Intensive agriculture	Dairy products and vegetables	Intense dairying, no fallow garden system with heavy manuring
2	3	0.6–3.5	Forest	Firewood	Sustained-yield forestry
3a	3	3.5–4.6		Grain, fodder potatoes	6-year crop rotation, no fallow
3b	30	4.6–34	Extensive agriculture	Grain	7-year crop rotation, 1 yr. fallow
3c	25	34–44		Grain, animal products	3-field system: (1) grain, (2) pasture, (3) fallow
4	38	44–100	Ranching	Animal products	Stock-raising
5	–	beyond 100	Waste	None	None

Source: Haggett et al. 1977

northern Germany and not Bahrain. Yet, in this preliminary stage of model development, these concepts can be transposed into a useable framework for the island. Consider for example figures 7 and 9. Figure 7 shows the potentiometric surface for the Khobar aquifer. The surface shows a decrease in hydrostatic water pressure from north to south with the +1 m potentiometric contour passing through the southwest coastal plain. Figure 7, on the other hand, shows the southernmost clusters of archeological sites to fall within this same area. These sites show evidence of Barbar II phase and medieval Islamic occupations. While we know that artesian water levels have been falling in Bahrain over the past several millennia (see Wright 1967, Italconsult 1971, Larsen 1980, 1983, Doornkamp *et al.* 1980), this portion of the island seems to have been the southern limit to settlement.

The exact functions of these outlying settlements is not yet clear. Certain Barbar period sites along the southwest coast (site 104, for example) were characterized by large oyster shell middens and were probably pearling camps (Nielsen 1954). Others, such as sites 78, 98, 102, and 126, yielded serrated flint sickle blades (Larsen 1983:31). These do not directly indicate the harvesting of grain, but this suggestion is certainly possible. Therefore, until the important Barbar II settlement site at al-Wasmiyah (site 97) is excavated and displays contradictory evidence, we should consider grain cultivation as a possible use for this portion of the island in the early second millennium B.C.

Like the earlier Barbar period sites in this part of the island, few concrete data are available to describe the function of medieval Islamic sites found in this same vicinity. Archeological excavation strategies have not yet focused on settlements in this part of the island. The most important historical clue to grain cultivation on Bahrain comes from Portuguese reports at the beginning of the sixteenth century A.D. Afonso de Albuquerque (see Bent 1890) reported that the island was noted for horse breeding, its fruits, and its barley crop. From this reference it is possible to suggest a more extensive agricultural system for Bahrain than has been discussed before. Although this single mention is not corroborated by other sources, it seems reasonable to project this report of barley cultivation into the few centuries preceding de Albuquerque's visit.

If we can assume the concepts of von Thünen to have validity for Bahrain, the southernmost late medieval settlement sites probably were agricultural settlements devoted partially to the extensive cultivation of grains, including barley. Here too, a lack of focused data collection from the southern archeological sites prohibits a firm functional identification.

With a knowledge of these three coincident findings, (1) the artesian limit, (2) the southern settlement limit during Barbar II times, and (3) the southern limit to late medieval settlement, it is possible to derive a proportional concentric ring model for Bahrain based on von Thünen's data in Table 1.

By allowing the southernmost settlements on the coastal plain to represent the outer limit of von Thünen's zone 3c, the border to his area of extensive agriculture, the distances from the market center to the other zones can be calculated by simple proportionality. Here, however, there can be no direct comparison beyond a general grouping of intensive and extensive agriculture, and a pastoral zone. Table 2 is an adapted version of von Thünen's model for Bahrain, based on the southernmost settlement sites along the southwest coast. The ancient market center, for the purpose of the model, is the walled third millennium B.C. city site at Qal'at al-Bahrain. This makes the model applicable for earlier periods. Since Manama was not mentioned in historic accounts until the fourteenth century A.D. (Rentz and Mulligan 1960) the ancient city is a useful choice for archeological studies.

The distance from Qal'at al-Bahrain to the southern settlement area was found to be twenty-five km. This compared to von Thünen's theoretical limit of forty-four (dimensionless units), provides a proportional conversion factor of 0.57 to be applied to von Thünen's relative distances shown in Table 1.

Table 2

MODIFIED VON THÜNEN MODEL FOR BAHRAIN

Zone	Relative Distance from market center (in kilometers)	Land-use type	Marketed products	Production System
0	<0.1	Urban	Manufactured goods	Trade center
I	0.1–0.35	Intensive agriculture	Dates, vegetables, citrus fruits	No fallow gardening with heavy manuring
II	0.35–2.0	Intensive agriculture	Dates, vegetables wood for fuel	As above
IIIa	2.0–2.6	Extensive agriculture	Dates, grains, fodder	Transition to fallow-field system
IIIb	2.6–19.3		Grains with subordinate date cultivation along coast	Rotated crops
IIIc	19.3–25.0		Grains, animal products	Rotated crops, including pasture
IV	>25.0	Herding	Animal products	Pastoralism

The modified concentric ring model for Bahrain is shown graphically on figure 11. The zones of intensive agriculture (zones I and II) form only a small semicircular area of land about the ancient port city. Zone IIIa, which marks the transition to more extensive agricultural practices is only a narrow band closely related to the zones of intensive agriculture. The greatest agricultural land area on the main island is contained within zone IIIb, the theoretical zone of the greatest extensive cultivation. This zone includes the modern outlying agricultural villages of the island and tends to fall within the +2m potentiometric contour shown in figure 7. Zone IIIc includes the southernmost Barbar II phase settlements at al-Wasmiyah, site 97. Zone IV includes the Barbar II oyster-shell middens at Ras al-Jazayir, site 104 (Nielsen 1954) and the Late Ubaid site at al-Markh, site 167 (Roaf 1976). Sites 94 and 95 (fig. 9) are found still farther to the south, but these Islamic period sites appear to have been special purpose outposts on the southern coasts unrelated to the land use model.

This land use model is highly simplistic and reflects only the most theoretical case for the agricultural lands on Bahrain. It does not take into consideration, for example, the prevalence of date gardens along the north coast of the island in zones I and II, as well as along a narrow strip along the western and southwestern sea coasts. Clearly dates have been a major agricultural crop in all portions of the first three land use zones. It is common, however, to intercrop fruits, vegetables, and nuts in the date gardens of the north coast, a reflection of the intensity of cultivation in the gardens closest to Qal'at al-Bahrain. This intensity in the cultivation of intercrops in the date gardens has been observed to decrease along the southwest coast, but no quantitative data are at hand to bolster the case.

This nineteenth century model based on a single German estate has provided an early theory for the study of central places among geographers. Over the past century and a half the role of central places, and in particular, the decreasing population and other economic gradients associated with increasing distance from urban centers has been shown (Haggett *et al.* 1977:191–230). Thus, whether the variables to be considered are those related to economic markets or simple energy harvesting networks, the case for decreasing demand on the surrounding environment as a function of increasing distance from the central organizing force seems clear.

SUMMARY AND CONCLUSION

The history and archeology of Bahrain have frequently been examined from a perspective of ancient trade and the islands' strategic position for maritime trade in the Arabian Gulf. These are major factors in Bahrain's development and evolution into the modern state. The focus of archeological excavation has centered on the

11 Modified von Thünen Land Use Model for Bahrain.

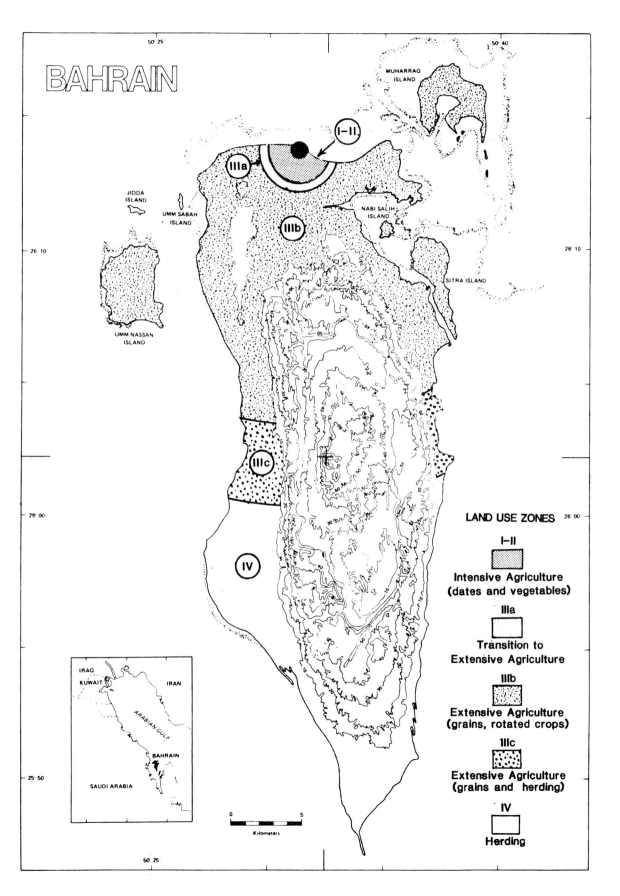

BAHRAIN

MUHARRAQ
ISLAND

I–II

IIIa

JIDDA
ISLAND

UMM SABAH
ISLAND

NABI SALIH
ISLAND

IIIb

26 10

SITRA ISLAND

26 10

UMM NASSAN
ISLAND

05

IIIc

26 00

LAND USE ZONES

26 00

I–II

Intensive Agriculture
(dates and vegetables)

IV

IIIa

Transition to
Extensive Agriculture

IIIb

Extensive Agriculture
(grains, rotated crops)

IIIc

Extensive Agriculture
(grains and herding)

IRAQ

IRAN

KUWAIT

ARABIAN GULF

BAHRAIN

25 50

SAUDI ARABIA

IV

Herding

0   5

Kilometers

50 25

major stratified sites on the north coast of Bahrain and on tombs. Both categories are under increasing danger of destruction as the suburbs of Manama spread outward with increases in population and ongoing economic development. New housing and roads rapidly encroach upon four to six thousand years of archeological evidence for settlement which used and reused the north coast of the island. Excavation of stratified settlement sites, especially at Qal'at al-Bahrain, has provided a chronological framework for dating the ceramic artifacts from the island. The results of the current salvage excavation of tombs, for example, gives a much needed view of the early population of Bahrain. Our view of other parts of the island, and its function as a cultural and environmental whole remains obscured by other archeological priorities.

Land use variations on Bahrain have been examined over the past several years and have shown spatial difference in the areas of land used by settlement over the past six thousand years (Larsen 1980, 1983). Figure 10, for example, shows episodic changes in land use. Settlement and agricultural lands expanded and contracted not only about the ancient urban market center at Qal'at al-Bahrain, but about an artesian center located on the northeast coast as well. This region is marked by a great number of artesian springs which are located along geologic fractures and faults in the same location. Settlement has used this artesian center as its environmental pivot point. The ancient urban center, in turn, developed in this zone of greatest artesian pressure, spring number and water flow. A hierarchy of villages has developed from this same environmental framework.

The land use model for Bahrain identifies four theoretical zones of land use on the main island. These range from zones of more to least intensive agricultural, and by analogy, cultural activity on ancient and historical Bahrain. By comparison with modern population-distance relationships with Manama we can view ancient Bahrain in a similar framework. In its periods of most extensive development during Barbar II and late medieval times, population and settlements were spread in decreasing numbers from north to south in response to both market conditions at Qal'at al-Bahrain and the artesian gradient for the islands. During periods of minor development, such as the Kassite period, a similar but less pronounced distance relationship probably occurred, but only in the northern portion of the island. Population and settlement fluctuated with Bahrain's involvement in Gulf trade. It expanded to its maximum extent during favorable environmental periods when greater precipitation allowed development of dry farming areas along the colluvial-alluvial fans and on the southwest coastal plain.

This changing pattern of land use and population distribution fluctuated as shown in figure 10. When the least favorable developmental conditions existed settlement and agriculture contracted to the dependable artesian core of the island along the north coast where agricultural production was not at risk. When economic and environmental conditions were in phase, settlement expanded to the south. The timing of such changes in settlement and land use were described earlier in Larsen (1980, 1983). The development of a formal land use model for Bahrain is presented here for the first time. The concentric-ring model, fig. 10, has been developed from the writer's data and has been extrapolated in places. In spite of this, it is founded, albeit simplistically, in the more secure realm of central-place theory.

The model is presented as a means to view Bahrain, and in particular ancient Bahrain, as an economic whole. The agricultural framework upon which Bahrain has depended for survival over the past several thousand years has depended, in turn, on the land. This important component is often overlooked by scholars more involved with research on Gulf trade. The land use model allows us to understand Bahrain as a unit in a trade system and to understand variation from the developmental histories of other areas of the Arabian Gulf.

Most important to future research on Bahrain, this model presents a framework for the potential functional differentiation of settlement sites on the island. It allows archeological investigations of southern and central parts of the island to be planned in advance. The types of data to be recovered and the specialists needed to interpret them can be chosen early in the research strategy rather than as afterthoughts. We need, for example, to understand Bahrain's operation as a settlement system. This can only be accomplished by fuller understanding of sites in outlying areas and their functions.

The model forms a theoretical construct to be enhanced or discarded as new data dictate. At the present, it serves as a context for incorporating the archeological site data from Bahrain. The concentric ring model, fig. 11, as well as the episodic variation in settlement and land use shown in figure 10 are examples to be followed in the investigation of other Arabian Gulf areas. The timing of episodic changes in settlement from other areas can be compared to Bahrain for timing. Differences in settlement and land use expansion among the various areas may indicate real changes in local economies or environmental systems that are presently not available to the archeologist.

In short, the land use model, or realistically, models presented here, serve as tools for researching not only Bahrain, but other parts of the region as well. In their weakest points, the constructs shown in this paper can provoke future revisions in land use and settlement analyses. In the best case, Bahrain can be used as an archeological model for the rest of the Gulf region.

Author's Note: Figures 6–10 are the copyright of the University of Chicago.

1. The only clear early third millennium archeological evidence from Bahrain is a single Jemdet Nasr polychrome potsherd recovered from the temple I levels at the Barbar Temple (Mortensen 1970). This find points to a possible nearby settlement dating to 3000 B.C., but the temple I occupation levels themselves belong to the late third millennium B.C. (Larsen 1983:245–48).

2. The relationship of the colluvial and alluvial fans with the coastal plain is discussed in detail in Larsen (1983:192–95).

The human biological history of the Early Bronze Age population in Bahrain

BRUNO FROHLICH

Few archaeological sites in the world provide as extensive research opportunities for archaeologists and anthropologists as those on Bahrain Island. It was an early center of trade and economic growth in the Arabian Gulf. Trade connections with adjacent areas of the Arabian Gulf, Mesopotamia and the Indus Valley began in prehistoric times and have continued to the present. Many archaeological sites representing various stages in the development of human societies are present on the island. Recently developed methods, techniques and multi-disciplinary approaches make it possible to reconstruct same aspects of the ancient history of the Bahrain people who were so important to early trade and communication among Near Eastern countries. Data from such research helps to clarify the process of societal development and decline. This study, concentrating on the origin and development of Bahrain burial mounds, is based on human skeletons and architectural features from excavations by (1) the Arab Expedition to Bahrain in 1978–1979 (Ibrahim 1982 and Frohlich 1982), (2) the Directorate of Antiquities and Museums in 1981, 1982, and 1983 (Frohlich 1983), and (3) skeletal material from various Danish archaeological expeditions to Bahrain (Bibby 1970).

Large tumuli, or burial mounds, are a common sight in many countries. For example, Bronze Age burial mounds are frequently encountered in Scandinavia and northern Germany (Worsaae 1849 and Glob 1971). Prehistoric burial mounds occur in North America (Thomas 1849 and Griffin 1967), China (Chang 1971), Siberia (Rudenko 1970), southeastern Europe (Filov 1934), and France (Le Rouzic 1932). Closer to Bahrain, burial mounds dating to the third and second millennia B.C. have been identified in eastern Saudi Arabia (Bibby 1970, Potts *et al.* 1978, Zarins nd, and Frohlich *et al.* nd.), Oman (Frifelt 1975b and de Cardi 1976), and Qatar (de Cardi 1978). Yet few places, if any at all, have more, or certainly more concentrated mounds than Bahrain, fig. 12.

12 Bahrain Burial Mounds
located between Ali Village and
Hamad Town. Maximum height
approximately 210 cm, maximum
diameter approximately 1800 cm

The large number of mounds in Bahrain has stimulated much speculation regarding their origin (Mackay *et al.* 1929, Cornwall 1943b and 1946a, Bibby 1970, Larsen 1980 and 1983, Lamberg-Karlovsky 1982, Frohlich 1983, During Caspers 1984 and Zarins *et al.* nd.). So far, my data suggest that these mounds were a local development, a product of the people living in Bahrain during the third and second millennia B.C. They represent an architectural development that changed little, or not at all, in its basic configuration over time. Any changes that did occur seem to have been caused by accessibility to better techniques and, possibly, increased societal economic strength. Significantly, the study of mound materials yields results producing an unparalleled opportunity for investigating the biological and cultural history of people who occupied the western shore of the Arabian Gulf during the third and second millennia B.C.

PREVIOUS WORK

The first reported excavation of a Bahrain burial mound was conducted in 1878–1879 carried out by E. L. Durand (1880). Between this earliest excavation and 1981, approximately 310 burial mounds have been excavated by various teams (Durand 1880, Smith 1890, Bent 1890 and 1900, Jouannin 1905, Prideaux 1912, MacKay *et al.* 1929, Cornwall 1943b, 1944 and 1946a, Bibby 1954 and 1970, Glob 1954a, Cleuziou *et al.* 1981, Ibrahim 1982, and Frohlich 1982). Since 1981, the Directorate of Antiquities and Museums in Bahrain has been conducting a major salvage excavation of burial mounds south of Ali Village at the new city development, Madinat Hamad. The number of excavated mounds at Hamad Town exceeds four hundred (as of the 1982/1983 excavating season); thus the total number of excavated mounds has more than doubled between 1981 and 1983. Fortunately, during the 1978 to 1979 excavations carried out by the Arab Expedition and the 1981 Bahrain Directorate of Antiquities and Museums excavations, a standardized data collection was developed making it possible to combine information from various seasons and sites.

BURIAL MOUND TYPES

Although several types of burial mounds have been defined by previous investigators, these researchers have been handicapped by the limited number of excavated tombs upon which classifications have been based. Excavations since 1978 have permitted the definition of three types of tomb architecture: (1) Early Type burial mounds; (2) Late Type burial mounds; and (3) Below Ground Type burial complexes.

The first two types were based on a sample of 328 excavated burial mounds (Table 1). Early Type burial mounds were mounds containing chambers without cap-stones (n=192), fig. 13. Late Type burial mounds were defined as mounds containing chambers with cap-stones (n=122), fig. 14. Of 328 mounds, 14 were either of an intermediate type or they were not classified (Table 1).

Metric dimensions and variations between the two groups are seen in Table 2. All metric variables showed statistically significant

Table 1

BAHRAIN BURIAL MOUNDS
BASIC STATISTICS

	Early Type Mounds	Late Type Mounds	No Data	Total
MOUNDS	192	122	14	328
MAIN CHAMBERS	192	122	14	328
SUBSIDIARY CHAMBERS	89	44	–	133
OTHER CHAMBERS*	0	28	–	28
TOTAL	281	194	14	489

*Other chambers than the main chamber found inside the ringwall(s).

The statistics include data from the Arab Expedition (1978–1979) and Excavations by the Directorate of Antiquities and Museums, Bahrain (1981–1983).

13 Early Type burial mound. Burial chamber located inside the ringwall. No capstones cover the chamber. Mound (New City no 29) excavated by the Directorate of Antiquities and Museums northeast of Hamad Town

14 Late Type burial mound. Burial chamber located within the ringwall. Capstones cover the chamber. Mound (S-18) excavated by the Arab Expedition to Bahrain (1978–1979) (Ibrahim 1982 and Frohlich 1982)

differences between the Late Type and the Early Type when the 'Student's t-test' was applied, except for one variable. This anomalous variable was the magnetic compass direction of the long axis of the burial chamber (Table 2). Additionally, all metric variables, except for one, were significantly larger in the Late Type as opposed to the Early Type. Only one variable, *maximum width* of the burial chamber, was larger in the Early Type. This was due to the more round and round/squared configuration of chambers in the Early Type as opposed to the rectangular configuration of Late Type chambers, figs. 13 and 14, and Table 2).

Below Ground Burial Complexes were clusters of chambers placed below the present ground surface that were not covered by distinct or well-developed mounds, fig. 15. This classification was

Table 2

'EARLY TYPE' AND 'LATE TYPE' MOUND DIMENSIONS

Variable	Mean	S.D.	Sample Size	Maximum	Minimum
EARLY TYPE					
BURIAL MOUND:					
DIAMETER	726	170	176	1280	300
HEIGHT	68	20	90	170	25
RW. DIAMETER	511	137	185	960	190
RW. HEIGHT	30	9	183	78	10
CHAMBER:					
MAX. LENGTH	146	23	189	245	71
MAX. WIDTH	85	17	189	138	45
MAX. HEIGHT	49	13	190	84	11
DIRECTION	79°	16	191	117°	35°
LATE TYPE					
BURIAL MOUND:					
DIAMETER	925	252	118	2265	400
HEIGHT	142	39	106	250	40
RW. DIAMETER	597	141	113	1030	270
RW. HEIGHT	43	15	115	100	15
CHAMBER:					
MAX. LENGTH	178	36	120	303	94
MAX. WIDTH	70	9	122	100	50
MAX. HEIGHT	83	20	121	145	40
DIRECTION	76°	15	118	130°	45°

All dimensions are in cm

Student's t-test: All variables, except one (magnetic direction of the burial chamber) are significant different (P=0.00). 'Late Type' variables are larger in all cases, except one (max. width of the burial chamber).
Multivariate statistics (Mahalanobi's D square) shows significant difference (P=0.00).

15 Below Ground Burial
Complex. Complex located east of
the burial mounds south of Sar
Village. Excavated by the Arab
Expedition to Bahrain and by the
Directorate of Antiquities and
Museums (Ibrahim 1982, and
Mughal 1983)

based on the 1978 to 1982 excavations of 587 burials in the Sar Burial
Complex (Ibrahim 1982, Frohlich 1982, and Mughal 1983).

A chronology of the cultural materials has yet to be developed
for the region, so no reliable dating method is available to establish
the time-span of the mounds. Based on construction features and
geographical location, however, I suggest that the so-called Early
Type mounds are the oldest, followed by Late Type mounds, and,
finally, by Below Ground Burial Complexes. A tentative time-span
estimate would be from 2500 B.C. to 1800 B.C.; this estimate is based on
discussion with archaeologists familiar with Bahrain pre-history,
although it should be emphasized that few agree upon the same
estimate.

Both the Early and Late Type burial mounds contained either a
single burial chamber or multiple burial chambers. They had, either
one ringwall or a complex system of interactive ringwalls, most often
found in association with multiple burial chamber systems. They may
also have single or multiple subsidiary burial chambers located
outside the ringwall systems. Most importantly, however, they all
conform to the same general construction pattern – central burial
chambers surrounded by ringwalls, fig. 14.

Variation existed within the three types. However, a clear understanding of this variation must await further data analysis. For comprehensive descriptions of construction features and cultural finds, consult Ibrahim (1982) and Mughal (1983).

Only one body, with few exceptions, was placed in each grave chamber. It appears that all were primary burials. A body was placed in a semi-flexed position on its right side with its long axis oriented toward the northeast (and the legs toward southwest), fig. 16. The hands were placed either in front of or below the anterior part of the cranium.

Not all the burial chambers have yielded human skeletal remains, however. This observation had caused some concern in regard to the reconstruction of the demography, where it was assumed that every burial chamber had been constructed with the interment of one human being in mind. In order to understand and explain the presence of empty chambers, two possibilities are observed: (1) no interment of a human body took place; or (2) no human bone fragments were observed because of an almost complete decay of the biological matrix or the excavator missed the observation by lack of experience. So far, we have only observed one case supporting the first possibility, e.g. no human body has been interred, which could be observed by the presence of animal bones but no human bones (Frohlich 1982). In all other cases it is believed that the recording of an empty chamber is partly or in full caused by the lack of training in observing smaller pieces of human skeletal remains. In order to verify this hypothesis, the discharged material from the sieving process of twelve 'empty' burial chambers was searched by me during the Sar excavations in March 1984. In nine out of the twelve cases it was possible to identify small fragments of human bones; the three remaining cases were doubtful since the exact location and identification of the sifted material was in doubt. Furthermore, it was clear that the people with extensive experience in excavating burial chambers obtained a much higher frequency of chambers with human skeletal remains than people with little or no experience. These observations do not solve the problem, however. An extensive project involving chemical analysis of the chamber deposit including and excluding skeletal material was initiated during the excavation of burial mounds in the Dhahran area, Eastern Province in Saudi Arabia (Frohlich *et al.* nd) and in the Sar burial mound field in Bahrain. Hopefully this will add more data and results so that this important problem can be solved. Until then, the evidence available strongly suggests that all but a few of the burial chambers had been used for the interment of at least one human body.

A total of 191 (53.7%) burial chambers (not including subsidiary burial chambers) had a single alcove located at the northern or

Table 3

ALCOVE LOCATION AND SKELETAL POSITION

Alcove Location	n	%	Skeletal Left	Position ** Right
NO ALCOVE	165	46.4	0	38
ONE ALCOVE (NORTH)	112	31.5	0	61
ONE ALCOVE (EAST)	42	11.8	19	0
TWO ALCOVES (NORTH AND EAST)	33	9.3	0	9
OTHER (IRREGULAR)*	4	1.1	0	1
TOTAL	356	100.1	19	109

*Three chambers contained one alcove at the center of the northwestern longwall, and one chamber contained four alcoves.
**The recorded numbers of skeletons with known position are less than the recorded number of alcoves because of either a high decay of the skeletal material and/or disturbance by thieves and/or animals.

eastern corner of the burial chamber, or had two separate alcoves, one located at each of these two corners. Where only one alcove was present in the eastern corner, the deceased was always placed on its left side. When there were other alcove configurations or when no alcoves were present, bodies were always placed on their right sides, Table 3 and figs. 16 and 17. No skeletons were found in the sitting position reported by Durand (1880), Prideaux (1912) and Mackay *et al.* (1929). Where skeletal material was found arranged in positions other than those described above, it could be explained by subsequent robbery attempts or displacement of bones by animals.

Animal bones, mostly of sheep and goats, were located adjacent to human skeletons or along in alcoves. Cut and burn marks were present on the animal bones. Presumably, these bones were the remains of food that accompanied the dead.

SEX VARIATION

At the present stage of my research (Summer 1983), the sex of 133 skeletons have been determined: 81 were males, and 52 females, Table 4. These skeletons included those from the Moesgård Museum in Denmark (n=37), individuals recovered by the Arab Expedition (n=55, not including 37 skeletons from the Sar Burial Complex), and those from the Bahrain Directorate of Antiquities and Museums excavations (n=224), Table 4.

16 Deceased person placed on its right side in a semi-flexed position. Alcove in lower left corner (north). Chamber excavated by the Directorate of Antiquities and Museums. Mound B-North 12, chamber no. 1

17 Deceased person placed on its left side in a semi-flexed position. Alcove is in upper left corner (east). Chamber excavated by the Directorate of Antiquities and Museums. Mound B-north 6, chamber no. 2

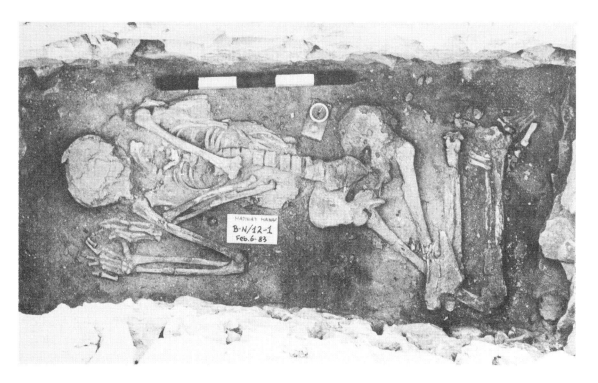

Table 4
SEX AND AGE DISTRIBUTION

Excavated by:	Adults			Infant	Child	Subadults Total
	Male	Female	Unkn			
Arab Expedition (1)	12	11	24	8	0	55
Bahrain Directorate of Ant. & Museums (2)	56	33	110	16	9	224
Total:	68	44	134	24	9	279
Danish Expeditions (3)	13	8	11	5	0	37
TOTAL:	81	52	145	29	9	316

Notes:
(1) 1978–1979, does not include skeletal material from the Sar Burial Complex
(2) 1981–1983
(3) 1954–1975

The proportion of males in the sample is significantly different from the expected 50% (p=greater than 0.01) (Blalock 1972), but this discrepancy can be explained by the relatively small number of sexed skeletons. Only 133 (47.8%) of 278 adult skeletons potentially available for examination have been studied. When the reconstruction and analysis of material presently under way at the Smithsonian Institution has been completed, the number of adult skeletons will increase significantly. With additional skeletons, the number of males should approximate the number of females.

The distribution of mounds with male skeletons and those with female skeletons appeared to be random. Neither were there any statistically significant differences in mound or chamber sizes between those containing male skeletons when compared with those containing female skeletons, Table 5.

AGE COHORTS

At this preliminary stage of analysis all skeletal material has been divided into three age cohorts: infants (0–1 yr.), children (1–18 yrs.), and adults (more than 18 yrs.). Future age-at-death analyses including microscopic age determinations, will permit more refined aging of adults (Ortner and Putschar 1981). Age determination based on the skeletal material from the 1978–1979 Arab Expedition suggests that there was a large number in the forty to fifty age category (Frohlich 1982).

The Arab Expedition excavations revealed the presence of small subsidiary burial chambers outside the ringwalls of some mounds (Ibrahim 1982). Yet no skeletal remains were found in these sub-

Table 5

MALE AND FEMALE STATISTICAL DATA

Variable	Mean	S.D.	Sample Size	Maximum	Minimum
MALES:					
BURIAL MOUND:					
DIAMETER	865	180	49	1340	525
HEIGHT	139	38	40	205	46
RW. DIAMETER	602	126	50	980	375
RW. HEIGHT	38	13	48	70	15
CHAMBER:					
MAX. LENGTH	169	34	55	260	109
MAX. WIDTH	72	11	56	115	57
MAX. HEIGHT	75	22	55	125	30
DIRECTION	82°	40	55	356°	56°
FEMALES:					
BURIAL MOUNS:					
DIAMETER	827	185	28	1400	500
HEIGHT	127	42	22	181	50
RW. DIAMETER	561	127	26	780	270
RW. HEIGHT	37	12	26	60	17
CHAMBER:					
MAX. LENGTH	166	34	32	257	125
MAX. WIDTH	76	14	32	120	58
MAX. HEIGHT	74	23	32	125	28
DIRECTION	78°	17	31	119°	45°

All dimensions are in cm

Student's t-test and Mahalanobi's D squared do not show any significant difference between selected architectural variables when metric variables from mounds with male skeletons are compared with metric variables from mounds with female skeletons.

sidiary chambers (Frohlich 1982). The more recent excavations (1981 to 1983) at Madinat Hamad yielded, for the first time, subadult skeletal remains in the subsidiary burial chambers, fig. 18, (Lowe 1982). These finds demonstrated that all age cohorts were represented in the burial mounds. Excavations in 1982 and 1983 by the Bahrain Directorate of Antiquities and Museums further increased our sample of infants and children, all of which were associated with subsidiary burial chambers.

Presently, 133 subsidiary burial chambers have been identified, Table 1, and 25 contained subadult human skeletons that could be assigned an age at death. These 25 skeletons may be increased somewhat when the bones are fully restored.

18 Subsidiary burial chamber located outside the ringwall. Child skeleton is placed on its right side in a semi-flexed position. Chamber excavated by the Directorate of Antiquities and Museums. Mound B-north 70, chamber no. 3

In addition, there is a possible correlation between the age of subadults ranging from newborn to approximately fifteen years, and the maximum length and width of subsidiary burial chambers. An association between tomb chamber dimensions and age-at-death suggests possible application of subsidiary burial chamber dimensions for estimating age-at-death when well preserved human skeletal remains were not identified during excavation. Also, this finding suggests that subsidiary burial chambers were constructed for specific individuals after their deaths.

The frequencies of skeletons in the three age cohorts are seen in Table 4. When skeletons from the Danish Expeditions and the Arab Expedition are added to those of the 1981–1983 excavations, the number of skeletons reaches 278 adults (88.0%), 29 (9.2%) children, and 9 infants (2.9%), Table 4. These data deviate somewhat from the mortality rates reported by Hassan (1981) and Ortner (1981), in which the subadult mortality rate was approximately 45%, including a 10% infant mortality rate. These rates approximate those of primitive human societies in the modern world where it has been reported that about half of the Southwest African !Kung (Howell 1979) and South American Yanomama (Neel and Weiss 1975) die before the age of fifteen years. The low Bahrain rate is explained by the poor preservation of subadult skeletons in subsidiary burial chambers – only 25

(18.8%) of 133 subsidiary chambers contained well preserved human skeletal remains.

If one assumes, however, that subsidiary chambers all contained one subadult, the resulting mortality frequency approximates more closely the rates reported by other researchers. Out of 489 burial chambers, 133 were subsidiary chambers, indicating a 27.2% subadult mortality rate, Table 1. (We would have expected a higher frequency, e.g. closer to 40%. One explanation may be that some skeletons with an age of death between fifteen and eighteen years have been found in the main chambers, indicating that adulthood in ancient Bahrain began about fifteen. If one includes these burials in the subadult age category, the subadult mortality rate will be much closer to the mortality rates found in other contemporaneous societies in the Middle East.)

STATURE

Based on stature estimates from a total of 68 individuals, the average living stature for males was 170.4 cm. (n=43) and for females 162.4 cm. (n=25). Stature for this burial mound population was greater than other contemporaneous Middle Eastern populations (Frohlich 1982). For example, an Early Bronze Age sample from Bab edh-Dhra in Jordan yielded stature estimates of 164.8 cm. and 154.7 cm. for males and females, respectively (Frohlich and Ortner 1982). Corresponding figures for the Keratas sample in Anatolia were 166.3 cm. and 153.5 cm. (Angel 1970).

POPULATION DEMOGRAPHY

The question of the origin of the Bahrain burial mounds has been explored by several investigators. Mackay *et al.* (1929) concluded that because there was such a large number of mounds some may have been used by people from mainland Arabia, and Bahrain Island may have been used as a sacred burial place. Cornwall (1943b and 1946a) suggested that the practice of building burial mounds derived from southern Arabia, or more specifically, Yemen, from which it gradually spread to other adjacent areas. Cornwall also suggested that the mounds were used primarily as a final interment place for male warriors and that the skeletons represented only a small fraction of the population (Cornwall 1946a). Lamberg-Karlovsky (1982) more recently discussed the origin of the mound burial tradition, commenting on the large number of Bahrain burial mounds. He concluded that the skeletons were a result of the burial of people who lived in adjacent Arabian Gulf areas.

Common to all these ideas is that they lack an appreciation of the demographic factors contributing to the development of burial areas. Larsen (1980 and 1983) has counted approximately 172,000 burial mounds on Bahrain Island. Considering the possibility that later time periods, although represented by a small number of mounds, may be present, about 150,000 burial mounds are tentatively assigned to the 2800 B.C. to 1800 B.C. time period (Frohlich 1983). The Arab Expedition and excavations in 1981, 1982, and 1983 showed that 489 burial chambers have been found in 328 excavated burial mounds, Table 1. This represents an average of 1.49 individuals per mound. The number of the dead in mounds would, therefore, be 150,000 times 1.49 – a total of 223,500 individuals. Life expectancy, based on a preliminary analysis of mortality rates, has been estimated as between thirty-five and forty years. This value is higher than estimates derived from other Old World (Hassan 1981 and Angel 1971) as well as New World prehistoric populations (Ubelaker 1974).

The time span during which the mounds were used is the most unreliable item in these calculations. So far, no investigator has arrived at a satisfactory time span upon which most archaeologists can agree. In fact, opinions range from one thousand years (2800 B.C. to 1800 B.C.) to as little as two hundred years (2000 B.C. to 1800 B.C.). Samples for radiocarbon dating have been submitted recently for analysis, and the results should provide a better estimate of the time range associated with the burial mound tradition in Bahrain. Until these data are available, my calculations will use time spans ranging from two hundred years to one thousand years to account for all possibilities, Table 6.

With a life expectancy of forty years at birth, a population size of 44,700 persons will produce 223,500 deaths in two hundred years. With a life expectancy of thirty-five years at birth, a population of 7,823 persons will result in 223,500 deaths in one thousand years. Intermediate values are also shown in Table 6. When using any of

Table 6

POPULATION ESTIMATES

| Time span | Life Expectancy | |
	35 years	40 years
200 years	39,113	44,700
500 years	15,645	17,880
1000 years	7,823	8,940

Reference: (Ubelaker 1978) $P = N/(M \times T)$
where P = average living population size
        N = number of deceased persons (223,500)
        M = $1/e_o$
        e_o = life expectancy (35 and 40 years)
        T = Time span (200, 500, and 1000 years)

these estimates, the large number of burial mounds can easily be explained by the number of individuals who occupied Bahrain Island as suggested by settlement pattern data. (The number of burial mounds is well within the range expected given the estimates of population density during any of the periods thought possible for the burial mound tradition.)

For example, the Qal'at al-Bahrain tell, located on the north central coast of Bahrain Island, measured approximately 134,000 m². The tell contained the remains of a walled city dating to approximately the same time period as the burial mounds (Bibby 1970, Hawkes 1974, and Larsen 1980 and 1983). Allowing 20 m² per person, the average population sustained inside the city walls was 6,700, a number close to the 6,918 to 8,335 value obtained by Larsen (1980). Although there are no data available for calculating the ratio between the number of people living in Bahrain Island cities and people in rural areas, some ideas of this ratio can be obtained from other sources (Weber 1899). It can be assumed that between 10% and 40% of the entire population lived in urban areas, while 60% to 90% lived in rural areas. When the data were applied to the 6,700 person Qal'at al-Bahrain urban population, an upper population estimate for the entire population would be between 67,000 persons (10% urban) and 16,750 persons (40% urban). Yet, this only considers one urban Bahrain settlement, namely Qal'at al-Bahrain. Most recently (Khalifa 1984), a contemporary settlement, east of the Sar burial mound field, has been located. Carbon samples for dating purposes are presently being analysed by the Smithsonian Institution and compared with similar samples collected from the adjacent burial mounds in the Sar area; so far, the cultural finds strongly suggest coeval existence between the Sar burial mounds and this newly found settlement.

Several assumptions have been made when calculating these demographic figures: the population was assumed to be stable, no migration took place, and the male to female ratio was equal. These assumptions, of course, are unrealistic, especially if mound building spanned one thousand years (Frohlich 1983). However, the estimates provide an approximation of what might be expected and can be further evaluated as more data become available. Also, it is clear from present data that the expected number of skeletons and the many burial mounds can be explained by a population limited to Bahrain Island.

It should be noted that these estimates do not include data from the Below Ground Burial Complex 1.5 km. south of Sar Village (Ibrahim 1982 and Mughal 1983). Data from newly excavated burials, located inside the modern Hamad Town construction site, assigned a tentative code name 'UBF', also were omitted. Thus, it is likely that there will be an increase in the total sample of Early Bronze Age burials when more Below Ground burial complexes are found and excavated. Although the number of burials is likely to increase, there is no existing evidence that requires us to assume that the dead were anything other than inhabitants of Bahrain Island.

The huge number of known burials on Bahrain Island is not unique. Similar living and burial population estimates were seen in the Early Bronze Age cemetery at Bab edh-Dhra in Jordan. Electromagnetic surveys and excavations in Jordan have yielded relatively reliable estimates of the number of dead that can be expected to be found. The number obtained is about 250,000, a total which would have been produced by a living population of 6,000 over one thousand years (Frohlich and Ortner 1982, and Ortner 1983). Therefore, the large number of burials found in ancient cemeteries is a normal expression of long time periods and low life expectancies. It does not require any elaborate hypotheses of bodies being brought from foreign lands. What makes the Bahrain burial mounds so unusual is the remarkable vista presented by thousands of burial mounds extending as far as the eye can see. This sight, which is so impressive, has dominated archaeological interpretations based on impressionistic assessments of cultural features instead of quantitative analysis of excavated materials.

As a final caution it must be emphasized that this is a preliminary analysis of the human skeletal material from Bahrain. As additional material is obtained from other geographical areas the picture will become much clearer. The analysis of skeletons from Bahrain Island is only part of a research program that includes human skeletons and related data from sites in Jordan (Bab edh-Dhra), Saudi Arabia (Eastern Province), Turkey (Keratas), Egypt (Early Dynastic), and Oman. In addition, the temporal and geographic scope of this research will be expanded in the foreseeable future. The Early Bronze Age skeletons will be compared with skeletal samples from other time periods in both Bahrain and Jordan. Electromagnetic prospecting for Bronze Age cemeteries is currently taking place on Failaka Island in Kuwait, and skeletal material from the Eastern Provinces of the Kingdom of Saudi Arabia is presently being studied. This data will allow comprehensive study of major cultural and demographic transformations in the ancient Middle East. It will also contribute to a better understanding of population interaction, including gene flow, and the developmental role of particular population centers in what all agree is a pivotal geographical area in the evolution of western civilization.

The results of this ongoing research can be summarized in the following statements:

1. A minimum of 172,000 burial mounds are located on

Bahrain. Approximately 150,000 of these mounds are tentatively associated with the Early Bronze Age (2800 B.C. to 1800 B.C.). There are also below ground burials associated with this and other time periods.

2. Two distinct mound types are defined. Early Type mounds excluding cap-stones and Late Type mounds including cap-stones.

3. Most burial mounds consist of a central stone burial chamber surrounded by a stone ringwall. A few burial mounds contain more than one burial chamber inside the ringwalls and some have more than one surrounding ringwall.

4. Most burial chambers contain one skeleton. Most burials are primary interments.

5. Typically the body rests on its right side, with the body axis toward the northeast. All are semi-flexed. Alcoves may be located in the north and/or east corner(s). When one alcove is located in the east corner, the body is always placed on its left side in a semi-flexed position.

6. Males and females, as well as all age cohorts, are represented in the burial mounds. Subadults are placed outside the ringwall(s) in subsidiary chambers, and adults are placed inside the ringwall(s).

7. Mortality rates are similar to rates found in other contemporary societies in the Middle East, although there is a higher fequency of older people in the Bahrain burial mounds.

8. The development of the Bahrain burial mounds is a local development. Demographic analysis, in combination with an evaluation of settlement patterns, suggests that additional Bronze Age underground burials may be found on Bahrain.

Dental anthropological investigations on Bahrain

KAREN HØJGAARD

INTRODUCTION

Bahrain, with its fascinating history elucidated by abundant written evidence from 3000 B.C. until now, with about 172,000 burial mounds and magnificent ruins, certainly claims to be explored.

I fully agree with Bruno Frohlich when he writes that at least some of the answers concerning the origin of the ancient Bahrainis and of the mounds can be found by analyzing the human skeletal remains from those mounds.[1]

Bones tell tales; physical anthropologists are now studying the skeletons and to complete their work, dental anthropological investigations ought to be performed on every single tooth found in the excavations.

Teeth are often the most well preserved part of the body and as both genetic and environmental factors are stamped on them, they can help us to acquire knowledge of ancient peoples, their possible affinities and their way of life.

Perhaps in the future dental anthropologists will be able to contribute a little to the solution of the questions discussed by Bruno Frohlich and C. C. Lamberg-Karlovsky.[2]

It has been a great pleasure for me to examine some of the tooth material from Bahrain, and here I shall summarize some of the results and demonstrate the lines of approach.

MATERIAL

Teeth and jaws from twenty-five burial mounds near Ali excavated by the Danish Archaeological Expeditions to the Arabian Gulf, under the direction of Professor P. V. Glob have been examined. They date to *c.* 2000 B.C. Judging by the dentitions, the remains of 29 adult individuals were represented in this material. Details are published in the *Scandinavian Journal of Dental Research*.[3]

Teeth and jaws from Janussan excavated by Dr. J.-F. Salles have also been investigated.[4] They date to *c.*500 B.C. This material consisted of the remains of the dentitions from seven graves.

Estimated by the teeth and jaws five of the graves contained 4 adult individuals and 1 infant aged eleven. The remaining two graves contained tooth germs (the crown of the tooth calcified in the jaw) and jaw fragments corresponding respectively to 5 and 14 buried babies.

In addition to these studies of mine, I have only been able to find one article in the literature dealing with teeth from Bahrain made on material apparently deposited in Shiraz.[5] Teeth and bones from Diraz East and Ali East are investigated. They date to *c*.500 B.C.

According to the author one tomb from each place was excavated. The tomb in Diraz East contained the remains of 36 individuals: 14 children, 1 adolescent and 21 adults. The tomb in Ali East contained the remains of 117 individuals: 53 children, 4 adolescents and 60 adults. There is no information in the article about measurements of these teeth or details about their morphology, fig. 19a, b, c.

METHODS
The following scheme was used in my investigations:

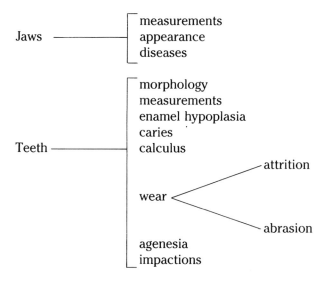

The bad condition of the material hindered a thorough description. The detailed results are published elsewhere; the results in broad outline are as follows.

RESULTS
The jaws were well proportioned and delicately built. To my surprise all were marked by a pronounced ante mortem loss of especially the molars. The molars were also missing in quite young individuals, a

long time before wear could have spoiled the teeth. Could the teeth have been removed? Or were they exfoliated due to inflammation after attacks of caries? I took radiographs of all the specimens in the hope of finding some cracked tips of roots left behind, a thing unfortunately often seen in a dental practice in the procedure of extractions. I found at least four tips of roots still in the jaws.

In literature, dental extractions are first mentioned about 800 B.C.,[6] as far as I have been able to find out. The Bahrainis thus appear to be the first people in the world known to have carried out dental extractions.

So far no forceps have been found in Bahraini soil, but I think an 'extractor' could have been used, such as the one Aristotle (384–322 B.C.) spoke of. Geoffrey Bibby has kindly given me a picture of two pointed ancient objects excavated on Bahrain, compared with two modern elevators utilized daily in Danish dental practices, fig. 20a, b.

Carious lesions and the unbearable pain these caused must have been the reason for these numerous extractions. From written sources we know that their food was rich in soft carbohydrate. Dilmun was famous for its cultivation of fine sweet dates.[7] The Bahrainis made jam, cakes and beer from the dates and had raisins and figs.[3] The finding of many baking ovens disclose that bread was also part of their nourishment.[8]

Jarman's description of the material deposited in Shiraz also mentions a wide-spread ante mortem loss. Bruno Frohlich has told me that the same is true of the extensive newly excavated material from the burial mounds.

The teeth showed Caucasoid but not Mongoloid traits; they were small and well-formed with bright white enamel. Only a few had severe enamel hypoplasia; it was only seen in the three Iron Age individuals in the material from Ali, but many had attacks of caries. No small fractures, 'chipping', along the border of the masticating surface were seen like those found on the teeth of Umm an-Narians.[9]

Mottled enamel caused by too much fluorine in the drinking water was not noticed. The fame of Bahrain's wells was justly founded. Excessive fluorine in the water is still not often found here according to the World Health Organization.[10]

As in all ancient populations wear of the teeth was already heavy early in life. Of particular interest is the peculiar wear of the lingual surfaces of some upper incisors which was also found on the material in Shiraz. It does not look like the wear found in native women in for example Greenland from softening strips of leather by pulling them between the front teeth. Previously, I have suggested it might be caused by twisting rope or yarn using the front teeth as a tool.

In the meantime I have been working with the striation due to

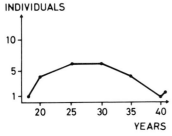

Diagram showing approximate age distribution for the adult Bahrainis from Ali, 2000 B.C.

different microwear of teeth seen in a scanning electron micro-scope.[11] I think that if the teeth with the queer wear were examined in this manner, some telltale striae might be revealed. So S.E.M. examinations ought to be performed on these teeth, now in the Smithsonian Institution and at Shiraz, and on teeth found in the future with that particular wear.

The average age-at-death for the material from Ali determined by the wear of the teeth was 25–30 years.

The majority of the material from Janussan consisted of tooth germs and a few fragments of jaws of babies, so my usual scheme for investigation was of little value here. However, dental anthropological examinations could reveal the minimum number of buried babies and assess their approximate age-at-death which was impossible from the destroyed or even missing bones in these graves.

Five infants had been buried in a jar at the age of about 30, 9, 6, 4 and 1 month respectively. A basin contained 14 infants buried at the ages of about 35, 24, two at about 12, 9 and the remaining 9 between 6 and 0 months; disintegration prevents greater accuracy. Unfortunately, the tooth germs did not suggest why all these babies died. The teeth are perfectly formed and the mineralization of the enamel is sound.

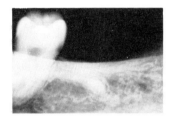

19a, b, c Young Bahraini individual from Ali, 2000 B.C. The mandible shows excellent healing after loss of molars. The radiograph shows a tip of a root still in the jaw

Written sources describe epidemics spreading at that time. Thucydides wrote about a great plague which broke out in Athens in 430 B.C. when the Peloponnesian states and their allies had invaded Attica. It was said that the malady had its origins in Ethiopia, whence it descended into Egypt and Libya.[12] Is it possible that it also affected Bahrain?

DISCUSSION

In the introduction I mentioned that future dental anthropological investigations might contribute a little to our knowledge of where the first Bahrainis came from. The method is to apply odontometry.

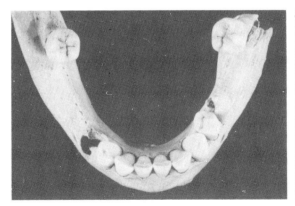

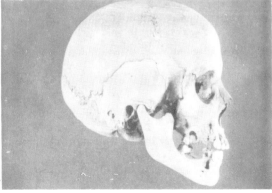

In addition to the dimensions of all measurable teeth from any necropolis on Bahrain and from the wider area of the Gulf it is also necessary to provide information about hereditary genetic morphological traits. For example,

Maxillary incisor teeth
1. Shovel shape
2. Median lingual ridges
3. Incisor rotation or winging
4. Marginal interruption grooves
5. Lingual tubercles.

Canine teeth
6. Canine distal accessory ridge

Maxillary molar teeth
7. Cusp number
8. Carabelli's trait
9. Metaconule variation
10. Protoconule variation
11. Paramolar cusp
12. Third molar presence

Mandicular molar teeth
13. Cusp number
14. Groove pattern
15. Variation in cusp 6
16. Variation in cusp 7
17. Protostylid variation
18. Paramolar cusp
19. Third molar presence
20. Three-rooted first molars

When the total number of teeth are described in this manner from each excavated site with representative sample sizes and the bones from the same places are also analyzed, multivariate and cluster analyses will without doubt reveal patterns of relationship.[13]

Despite the small samples I have described, the measurements of the permanent teeth from Bahrain of 2000 B.C. are compared to the nearly contemporary teeth from Umm an-Nar to show what can be done, Table 1.

Differences in mean crown diameters between the samples were evaluated by the t-test and significant differences would have been shown in the table.

As can be seen there are no significant differences between the means in the sixteen possible tests, so the groups might have been derived from the same gene pool. The lack of homogeneity in the scanty material, however, prevented further conclusions.

The measurements of infants' teeth from Bahrain and the Gulf area are given in Table 2.

The tendency towards smaller teeth in populations closer to us in time does seem to be present, but again the number of individuals examined is depressingly small.

At the moment the most obvious site investigated on the eastern side of the Gulf suitable for comparison is Timargarha. J. R.

20a, b Two pointed instruments from ancient Bahrain – perhaps elevators? At the sides elevators from a modern dentist's practice

Table 1

MEAN CROWN DIMENSIONS OF PERMANENT TEETH FROM BAHRAIN (2000 B.C.) AND UMM AN-NAR (2500 B.C.)

	Mesiodistal diameter						
	Bahrain[1]			*Sig.*	*Umm an-Nar*[2]		
	x	*(n)*	S.D.	*level*	x	*(n)*	S.D.
Maxilla							
I 1	8.52	(7)	.89	n.s.	8.80	(5)	.90
I 2	6.30	(6)	.38		5.65	(1)	–
C	7.41	(10)	.45		6.50	(1)	–
Pm 3	6.28	(2)	–		6.53	(6)	.29
Pm 4	6.82	(3)	.35		6.82	(3)	.67
M 1	10.24	(12)	.40	n.s.	10.25	(9)	.36
M 2	9.34	(5)	.47	n.s.	9.22	(3)	.60
M 3	9.43	(4)	.99		9.28	(2)	–
Mandible							
I 1	5.47	(7)	.52		–	(0)	–
I 2	5.90	(7)	.45		5.90	(1)	–
C	6.66	(8)	.46	n.s.	6.50	(5)	.62
Pm 3	6.92	(5)	.75	n.s.	6.53	(13)	.24
Pm 4	6.72	(4)	.60	n.s.	6.92	(6)	.46
M 1	–	(0)	–		11.30	(26)	.46
M 2	10.33	(3)	.92	n.s.	10.50	(20)	.42
M 3	10.33	(6)	.51	n.s.	10.76	(11)	.66
	Buccolingual diameter						
Maxilla							
I 1	7.08	(7)	.30	n.s.	6.90	(5)	.89
I 2	5.87	(6)	.32		5.35	(1)	–
C	8.10	(10)	.41		6.90	(1)	–
Pm 3	7.90	(2)	–		8.33	(6)	.55
Pm 4	8.68	(3)	.76		8.48	(3)	.98
M 1	11.19	(12)	.38	n.s.	11.43	(9)	.61
M 2	10.26	(5)	.47	n.s.	10.43	(3)	.86
M 3	10.21	(4)	.91		9.23	(2)	–
Mandible							
I 1	6.07	(7)	.46		–	(0)	–
I 2	6.29	(7)	.45		5.90	(1)	–
C	7.45	(8)	.73	n.s.	7.09	(5)	.44
Pm 3	7.27	(5)	.73	n.s.	7.20	(13)	.47
Pm 4	7.42	(4)	.75	n.s.	7.78	(6)	.67
M 1	–	(0)	–		10.34	(26)	.49
M 2	9.45	(3)	.60	n.s.	9.59	(20)	.46
M 3	9.73	(6)	.54	n.s.	9.67	(11)	.40

1. Højgaard (1980b).   2. Højgaard (1980a).
n.s.=not significant.

Table 2

COMPARATIVE DATA FOR DECIDUOUS CROWN DIMENSIONS OF PREHISTORIC POPULATIONS NEAR THE GULF

Mean mesiodistal diameters (in mm)

	Bahrain			Timargarha[1]			Bahrain[2]		Umm an-Nar[3]		Kish[4]	
	500 B.C.			1400–850 B.C.			2000 B.C.		2500 B.C.		3000 B.C.	
	x&S.D.	(n)		x&S.D.			(n)	x	(n)	x	(n)	x
Maxilla												
i one	6.61 0.46	(12)	n.s.	6.60 0.29	(4)							
i two	5.45 0.48	(8)	n.s.	5.38 0.52	(6)							
c	6.35 0.32	(3)		6.84 0.53	(9)		6.80	(2)	6.85	(1)		
m one	7.26 0.44	(9)	n.s.	7.58 0.59	(8)				7.30	(3)		
m two	8.67 0.12	(9)	xx	8.98 0.35	(8)				9.02	(3)	9.76	(5)
Mandible												
i one	4.04 0.30	(7)	n.s.	3.95 0.42	(4)							
i two	4.62 0.12	(5)		4.67 0.38	(3)							
c	5.30 0.39	(3)		5.99 0.29	(7)		6.00	(1)			6.20	(2)
m one	8.35 0.59	(11)	n.s.	8.27 0.36	(13)				8.42	(4)	8.15	(11)
m two	9.49 0.05	(3)		10.13 0.40	(14)		10.36	(1)	9.98	(4)	9.56	(16)

Mean buccolingual diameters (in mm)

	Bahrain			Timargarha			Bahrain		Umm an-Nar		Kish	
Maxilla												
i one	5.19 0.18	(12)	n.s.	5.18 0.30	(4)							
i two	4.70 0.28	(8)	n.s.	4.89 0.25	(7)							
c	5.53 0.24	(3)		5.38 0.39	(9)		6.12	(2)	6.10	(1)		
m one	8.11 0.46	(9)	x	9.09 0.34	(8)				8.45	(3)		
m two	9.04 0.45	(9)	x	9.81 0.45	(9)				9.74	(3)	9.48	(5)
Mandible												
i one	3.71 0.16	(7)	n.s.	3.75 0.35	(4)							
i two	4.46 0.32	(5)		4.40 0.36	(3)							
c	5.07 0.24	(3)		5.47 0.37	(6)		5.88	(1)			5.70	(2)
m one	7.20 0.33	(11)	n.s.	7.02 0.48	(13)				6.99	(4)	6.90	(11)
m two	8.38 0.25	(3)		8.92 0.42	(13)		9.98	(1)	8.51	(4)	8.58	(16)

1: Lukacs (1983).
N. Pakistan
2: Højgaard (1980b).
Bahrain
3: Højgaard (1980a).
Umm an-Nar
4: Carbonell (1958)
Mesopotamia

n.s.=not significant.
x=significant at 1% level.
xx=significant at 5% level.

Lukacs, who has studied the material, has done fine work in his studies of teeth from India and Pakistan.[14] The few statistical comparable tooth groups in Table 2 show too many differences to lend any support to a belief in derivation from the same gene pool.

I hope the future will give us sufficient material to disclose the possible origin of the first Bahrainis.

One thing is clear:

Future archaeologists and dental anthropologists will find well cared-for teeth from the present age, even if the dates still are sweet and delicious on Bahrain. In 1980 24 dentists were practising on Bahrain and 16 health centres with two dental chairs in each were under construction; more dentists and dental auxiliaries were being trained.

1. Frohlich, B., 'The Bahrain Burial Mounds', *Dilmun*, Journal of the Bahrain Historical and Archaeological Society, 11, 1983.

2. Lamberg-Karlovsky, C. C., 'Dilmun: Gateway to Immortality', *Journal of Near Eastern Studies*, 41, 1, 45–50, 1982.

3. Højgaard, K., Dentition on Bahrain, 2000 B.C. *Scand. J. Dent. Res.*, 88, 467–475, 1980b.

4. Boucharlat, R. & Salles, J.-F., 'The history and archaeology of the Gulf from the 5th century B.C. to the 7th century A.D.: A review of the evidence', *Proceedings of the Seminar for Arabian Studies*, 11, 65–94, 1981. Lombard, P. & Salles, J.-F., La Nécropole de Janussan (Bahrain). Maison de l'Orient. Lyon 1983.

5. Jarman, S., 'Bahrain Island: Human skeletal material from the first millennium B.C.', *Bulletin of the Asia Institute*, Shiraz, 2–4, 19–40, 1977.

6. Weinberger, B. W., 'Did dentistry evolve from the barbers, blacksmiths or from medicine?' *Bull. Hist. Med.*, 2, 8, 965–1011, 1940.

7. *The Assyrian Dictionary*, Vol. 1, A, part II, 1968.

8. Frifelt, K., Personal communication.

9. Højgaard, K., Dentition on Umm an-Nar (Trucial Oman), 2500 B.C. *Scand. J. Dent. Res.*, 88, 355–364, 1980a. Idem, 'Dentition on Umm an-Nar, c. 2500 B.C.', *Proceedings of the Seminar for Arabian Studies*, 11, 31–36, 1981.

10. Barmes, D. E., *Oral Health Situation Analysis*, Bahrain. W.H.O. 1981.

11. Højgaard, K., 'S.E.M. (scanning electron microscopic) examination of teeth from the 3rd millennium B.C. excavated in Wadi Jizzi and Hafit', *South Asian Archaeology*, in press, 1983. Idem, 'Various Aspects of Ancient Teeth from the Gulf', *Proceedings of the Seminar for Arabian Studies*, 14, 1984, in press.

12. Patric, A., 'Diseases in Antiquity: Ancient Greece and Rome', in, Brothwell, D. & Sandison, A. T., *Diseases in Antiquity*, Springfield, 1967.

13. Rathburn, T. A., 'Morphological Affinities and Demography of Metal-Age Southwest Asian Populations', *American Journal of Physical Anthropology*, 59, 47–60, 1982.

14. See bibliography.

India and Bahrain:
A survey of culture interaction during the third and second millennia

JAGAT PATI JOSHI

When C. J. Gadd published his classic paper on the 'Seals of Ancient Indian Style found at Ur' in the *Proceedings of the British Academy*, Vol. xviii 1932, little did he realize that one day seals of the Persian Gulf type would also be found in India. It was only thirty years later, in the early sixties, that S. R. Rao was able to publish in 1963 'A Persian Gulf Seal from Lothal' in *Antiquity*, Vol. xxxvii, No. 146, p. 96. This laid the foundations of studies in the chronology of the Indo-Gulf trade relations.

The two decades which have elapsed between that find and the present have not been without consequence, both in India and in Gulf countries. A tremendous amount of field work and its publication has been achieved. Between 1977 and 1979 Qal'at al-Bahrain was excavated by Monik Kervran *et al.* (Bahrain 1982). In the later 1970s, Rafiq Mughal explored the island of Bahrain and located a number of sites belonging to the fourth and third millennia B.C., each providing definite evidence of Indo-Bahrain trade; detailed publication is awaited. Equally, in India some important publications considered the problem of Indo-Gulf trade of the protohistoric period. In 1973 S. R. Rao published *Lothal and the Indus Civilization*. In 1976 Shashi Asthana wrote the *History and Archaeology of India's contact with other countries (from earliest times to 300 B.C.)*. In 1981 Shereen Batnagar came out with the *Encounters: The Westerly Trade of the Harappan Civilization*. There are also some extremely penetrating papers, that by Dr. Dilip K. Chakrabarti, 'External trade during the Harappan Period', and another by Jim Shaffer, 'Harappan External Trade: A Critical Assessment', both presented in November 1977 at the seminar entitled 'The Indus Civilization: Problems and Issues', held at the Indian Institute of Advanced Studies, Simla, though not yet published.

But one should not think that research in the archaeology of the Gulf countries only began as late as that. Serious studies in the archaeology of Bahrain started as far back as 1959 with the Danish

Archaeological Expedition from the University of Aarhus, under Professor P. V. Glob and T. G. Bibby. Year after year until 1972, they excavated a number of sites, publishing yearly reports in the journal *Kuml*. In 1972 Bibby published his very popular archaeological monograph on the archaeology of Bahrain, entitled *Looking for Dilmun*. These works add to the information published in 1929 by Mackay, in the proceedings of the British School of Archaeology, which was based on some survey work, and some recent work published in both Arabic and English on the archaeology of Bahrain in *Al Watheeka*.

The corpus of writing on the archaeology of this island reflects the great importance that the world of scholarship attaches to it. We in India have special interest in the archaeology of Bahrain for one very special reason: India had a large trade network with Mesopotamia, much of which appears to have passed through Bahrain, which is generally identified with Dilmun, the Holy Land where the Sun Rises, of the ancient Mesopotamian texts (Kramer, *Expedition*, Vol. VI, No. 3, 44ff).

The third and second millennia B.C. witnessed the growth and flowering of some great Bronze Age cultures from Mesopotamia to the Indo-Pakistan sub-continent, particularly from the Euphrates, via Makran, Sind and Gujarat, up to the Saresvati Valley. In this Bronze Age phenomenon, Bahrain and the Persian Gulf played the vital role of the 'half-way house', transmitting cultural cross-currents from the east to the west. In any study of the Bronze Age cultures of South Asia and West Asia, the role of Bahrain is very significant in terms of trade connections and exchange of ideas.

It is common knowledge that in South Asia, the Indus Valley Civilization, which flourished from 2700 to 1900 B.C. (chronology based upon MASCA calibrated dates) ranks very high. It covers an appreciably larger area than either Early Dynastic Egypt or the Sumerian. Like the other Old World civilizations, the Indus Civilization grew from the skilful utilization of fertile valleys. The general characteristics of the civilization include grid-iron layout of the cities, elaborate drainage systems and a kind of semi-pictographic script.

Since 1977 considerable work has been going on both in India and Pakistan on the Indus Civilization. At the moment our knowledge of the extent of the culture is derived from an area starting from Sutkegendor in Makran in the West to Alamgirpur (Meerut district) and Hulas (Saharanpur U.P. district) in the east, and from Manda (Jammu district) and Rehman Dheri in Pakistan, to Diamabad in Maharashtra. In addition to Moenjo-Daro, the important excavated sites are Harappa, Balakot and Allahdino in Pakistan and Kalibangan, Manda, Surkotada, Lothal and Daimabad in India.

The Indus Valley Civilization has widespread West Asian contacts which have been discussed by scholars at great length. The Sumerian textual references to Dilmun (Gulf area), Makkan (Makran) and Meluḫḫa (Sind) are very important; the Harappan artifacts found in various parts of West Asia, and some of the artifacts of West Asian origin found in India, assume great significance in the appreciation of cultural contacts and the trade mechanism over the entire area during the period of the Indus Valley Civilization.

The geographical position of Bahrain island, reinforced by its natural features – artesian springs in the coastal area, a deep belt of cereal and date cultivation, and harbours – makes it an ideal half-way house for international trade from India to Mesopotamia.

Needless to say, the straight roads, defence walls and system of weights might be reminiscent of Harappan influence; it should be borne in mind that a number of seals bearing Harappan motifs have been found in Bahrain. Rafiq Mughal's discovery of Harappan seals from Kajjor and Buni is definite evidence of Indus-Bahrain contacts. The fire altars at Barbar may be compared with fire altars discovered at Lothal or Kalibangan (a square brick lined pit containing many animal bones having cut marks). The discovery of an unworked ivory may suggest an Indian origin. The discovery of a Bahrain-type round seal from the Harappan port town of Lothal, a terracotta Sumerian-like head and a terracotta model of an Egyptian mummy from the same site suggest definite links. In 1982 on the Gulf coast Tosi discovered a potsherd with two large fish-shaped Harappan characters flanking another linear character. It is the first tangible evidence of Indus earthen pots being taken to such a far off place.

The items of trade included copper, silver, carnelian, ivory, timber, tin, tortoise shell, 'fish eye', pearls and cloth. A total of forty-two items have been listed so far.

Besides the West Asian type of copper pins found at Harappa, Chanhudaro, Manda and Banawali, the presence of Reserved Slip Ware of the type found in Khabur Valley in Syria and at the Harappan sites of Moenjo-Daro, Surkotada, Lothal and some sites of Kutch further suggests a close trading link around 2300 B.C., the time of Sargon of Akkad. The cylinder seals from Kalibangan and Moenjo-Daro also add to evidence for West Asian contacts although they might not have come from Bahrain Island.

In the context of Indo-Gulf trade Dales (1969) feels that the Kulli people, who co-existed in the hills as contemporaries of the Harappans, played the role of middlemen in the Indus-West Asian trade which generally passed through Bahrain. However, except for a painted storage jar from Balakot, which has a poor counterpart in Bahrain, nothing tangible of Kulli culture, recorded from eighty Kulli sites, has been found in the Gulf area and port towns of the Indus people.

In a recent article on pottery and other objects from the Gulf of Oman published by Cleuziou in *South Asian Archaeology* 1979 (Berlin), edited by H. Hartel, we have definite examples of Harappan pottery types, such as dishes-on-stand, basins, storage jars, etc. These pots link up with Tosi's discovery of an inscribed potsherd.

To conclude, we have a sufficiently large amount of archaeological data to show Indo-Bahrain cultural and commercial contacts in the third millennium B.C. Nevertheless, much work remains to be done to clarify the picture, emerging steadily but as yet still very hazy and somewhat disjointed. We, therefore, would very much like to initiate joint expeditions to make this picture complete.

The prehistory of the Gulf: recent finds

JACQUES TIXIER

Thanks to the activities of international archaeological missions established at the request of interested countries, amongst whom I should like to thank the oficials of the Ministry of Information at Qatar for their help, our knowledge of the prehistory of the Gulf, particularly in the southwest, has increased greatly in the last decade. It is now possible to take stock of this; here I shall examine these latest discoveries in chronological order together with the problems that they inevitably raise.

PALEOLITHIC

As far as I know, there is no real evidence for Paleolithic tools on the Saudi coast, at Bahrain or in the United Arab Emirate.

At Qatar, the provisional classification put forward by H. Kapel has broken down. There is no definite Lower Paleolithic. A flourishing 'Mousterian' flint industry has been found on numerous sites, particularly in the region of Al Khor; on superficial examination, in fact one might think it amounted to a Middle Paleolithic culture. But more searching examination, particularly the excavations of M.-L. Inizan, have resolved this problem. What we actually have are stone collections of the Ubaid period. Nevertheless, the Paleolithic could, geologically speaking (P. Gehin), have existed at Qatar. Systematic work over six seasons has not provided any results.

NEOLITHIC

For convenience we shall deal under this heading with those sites which, although they do not give us any evidence for the production of food, still fall within the Neolithic context of the Near and Middle East at this time. All the information about Qatar at this period I owe to M.-L. Inizan of the French Archaeological Mission at Qatar.

The oldest industrial complex seems to be one of 'blades and bladelets' (the Arrowhead Blade culture of H. Kapel). These assemblages always include a large number of unretouched pieces: cores, blades, flakes, waste of a characteristic type with an economy of knapping which proves that these are workshops where each core has produced only a few regular blades (1 to 3) designed to be transformed into points with a tang and parallel retouch by pressure flaking. A few scrapers are found. These points, few in number, characteristic of the pre-ceramic Neolithic, appear in the Levant from the beginning of the eighth millennium B.C. and continue for about two millennia. No dwelling sites are known and no organic material has been found which would allow C14 dating; but geological evidence does not rule out this probable link.

As there is a considerable distance between Qatar and the Near East and no connecting route has yet been traced, we do not know with any certainty where these people came from, nor anything of their way of life or what became of them.

On the other hand it has been possible to date to the middle of the sixth millennium a new site at Shagra in the southeast area of Qatar. Work is still in progress but the site consists of a 'hut' made of small slabs of Tyrrhenian sandstone, dressed or simply stacked and made up of two 'rooms' within an oval measuring 5 × 3 m. The site yielded remains of fish, marine molluscs and a flint industry, with mostly leaf-shaped pieces made by percussion and tanged arrowheads made by pressure flaking. There is also a series of small pestles, pock-marked, cup-shaped and grooved stones.

This is the oldest 'building' in this part of the Gulf. There is no pottery. This small group of people, deriving its livelihood from the sea (close by at the time) can be compared (but not hastily identified) with those sites already known which have produced bi-facial arrowheads before the presence of Ubaid pottery at Qatar.

These latter are well known thanks to three excavations in the region of Al Khor; two habitation sites and one burial, all three dated to the fifth millennium. The burial is a sunken pit in which the bones of a young woman, previously cremated, were deposited (Khor FPP).

The two other sites share similar assemblages of stone tools, made up basically of bifaces knapped on the spot. Sources of raw material – good quality flint in the form of large blocks, unique in the region – were very close. One of these sites is a simple establishment with organized hearths (Khor P), the other, more complex, comprises a large workshop for production of bifaces, a single bifacial arrowhead and very little pottery; there is a painted vase with a rounded ledge with holes inside the rim, very characteristic of Ubaid III–IV, a stone vessel, grinding material and very few adornments. The cooperation of J. Desse and M.-L. Inizan proved, thanks to ultrafine sieving, that this was a beach fishing camp where sparidae were also dried, while the study of the marine molluscs (M. Chouquert) show that these were consumed on the spot, cooked over fires made from driftwood on which there were traces of burned barnacles (Khor FB).

There was no indication of the domestication of animals or cultivation of plants, but there was a direct connection to the Ubaid world whose trade, if not its occupation area, extends as far as the west coast of the Qatari peninsula.

Were these people then Ubaidians? or aboriginal peoples enjoying a trade relationship with Mesopotamia or with the many sites known along the length of the Saudi coast and present also on Bahrain? Was the 'fish industry' for export to distant lands? Were the bifacial flints, which might very probably also have been exported, been tools connected with the boats? What sort of navigation and what sort of fishing were practised?

One thing is clear: according to the preliminary results of pollen analysis and the geological weathered strata the climate was distinctly more humid in the sixth and fifth millennia B.C.

CAIRN BURIALS

The excavations of B. Midant-Revnes have provided us with precise knowledge of inhumation practices at Al Khor in a collection of eighteen cairns (on the edge of the sabkha like the sites with Ubaid pottery and not far from them). A pit was dug in bed-rock, the body was always placed on its side with kneews drawn up; a grave holding one, two or several individuals only some of whom have ornaments at the wrists, ankle or neck made of sea shells, obsidian beads; the grave was then filled with earth or small rocks (sometimes crowned by a circle of flat slabs) then topped by a cairn. However there is nothing at all to allow us to date this group, which has not provided any pottery. These funerary monuments are quite certainly pre-Islamic and could be much older still. The mystery must remain until C 14 can give us a date or until some fossil can provide a date for guidance.

Other than certain new points in Barbar pottery a site of the Kassite period, on an island near Al Khor, a real 'factory' for the manufacture of the purple dye obtained from sea shells is the only really new feature. But, by then, we are already well into the Protohistoric.

To summarize: a Prehistory of this region of the Gulf which seems to us to be recent but rich in human groups mobile and of many kinds, is also rich in problems for debate. One of the greatest riddles remains the absence of large scale monumental architecture at Qatar, between Bahrain and the United Arab Emirates.

The Gulf in Prehistory

JOAN OATES

Undoubtedly the most unexpected discovery in Gulf archaeology in recent years was the identification of a type of prehistoric pottery, known to archaeologists as Al Ubaid after a small site just west of Ur where it was first excavated, and previously associated solely with Iraq and adjacent areas of Syria and Iran. The discovery of this very distinctive painted pottery in 1968 in the Eastern Province of Saudi Arabia, some seven hundred km. south of Ur, aroused great interest and led archaeologists to search for comparable material in other regions in and bordering on the Gulf, in particular in Bahrain and Qatar. In the Eastern Province some forty sites were identified (Burkholder and Golding 1971, Bibby 1973, Masry 1974), situated for the most part along the better-watered coastal areas, well south of Kuwait, and inland near Hofuf. Many of these consisted of little more than a surface scatter of chipped stone together with a few painted sherds; four were larger mound sites. Soundings were carried out at three of the latter by Dr. Abdullah Masry (1974). Recent surveys have failed to add to this original corpus of sites (Potts *et al.* 1978). However, two sites were subsequently identified in Bahrain (Roaf 1974, Oates 1978) and five in Qatar (de Cardi 1974, 1978, Inizan 1980). No material of this type has yet been found south or east of Qatar. At the same time neutron activation, petrographic and electron microprobe analyses, carried out on sherds from Bahrain, Qatar and the Eastern Province, have shown that of the Ubaid sherds tested both the plain and painted examples appeared to derive from Mesopotamia, often quite specifically from southern Mesopotamia (Oates, Davidson, Kamilli and McKerrell 1977). A chaff-tempered coarse red ware, found in Qatar and in the Eastern Province, seems to be of local manufacture, but is found only in association with the imported Ubaid ceramic. In other words, there would appear to have been no local tradition of pottery manufacture at this time, and the apparently local pottery was either made by Ubaid 'visitors' from Mesopotamia themselves or inspired by contact with them.

A glance at the bibliography shows that in the last decade much has been written about these exciting discoveries, while little new Ubaid material has been found in the Gulf area since the comprehensive studies of the late 1970s. It might well be asked, therefore, whether any further comment is justified. However, the recent publication of the 1946–49 excavations at Eridu (Safar, Mustafa and Lloyd 1981), a publication long awaited and now much welcomed by the scholarly world, provides an appropriate moment to re-assess the chronological attributions of the Gulf Ubaid and the period of contact with Southern Mesopotamia.

The importance of Eridu lies in the fact that it is the sole site so far excavated to have provided a lengthy sequence of material attributed to the Ubaid period, very approximately the fifth millennium B.C. (uncalibrated radiocarbon years). Of course, no stratigraphic sequence is ever a 'complete' sequence, but Eridu provides the only sequence in which all known phases of the Mesopotamian Ubaid are represented. Unfortunately, with the exception of the cemetery, the material comes essentially from soundings, i.e. without significant lateral and, therefore, genuinely informative distribution. Nonetheless, and despite the many important discoveries concerning Ubaid Mesopotamia made in recent years, especially from rescue operations in the Diyala basin near Jebel Hamrin (*Sumer* 1979), the stratigraphic sequence established almost fifty years ago at Eridu continues to remain the sole basis for any typological analyses of Ubaid materials.

The Ubaid period is conventionally divided into four phases, based on the temple sequence at Eridu about which some information has been available since 1948 (Lloyd and Safar 1948, Oates 1960); the new volume greatly expands our knowledge of this material and, for the first time, provides information about the so-called Hut Sounding. This is of especial importance, since the latest levels of the Hut Sounding almost certainly post-date the latest levels in the temple sequence (Temples VI–VII), and thus chronologically extend the existing Ubaid sequence at the site. The levels are grouped as follows:

	Temple Sequence		*Hut Sounding*
Terminal Ubaid	–		I–II
			III–V
Ubaid 4	VI–VII	cemetery	VI–VIII
Ubaid 3	VIII–XII		X–XIII
Ubaid 2	XII–XV		–
('Hajji Muhammad')			
Ubaid 1	XVI–XVIII		
('Eridu')			

The correlation of the Hut Sounding with the temple sequence is far from certain. Both excavations, as we have already mentioned, were no more than soundings, and functional differences would be expected within any ceramic group, dependent on context. That is, one would expect to find different types of pottery in a temple and in a private house. Thus it is possible that the differences in the pottery from the Hut Sounding and the temple precinct may be entirely functional, not chronological. However, there are sufficient similarities among the published examples to suggest the approximate contemporaneity of Temple VI, the cemetery and Hut Sounding levels VI–VIII. Moreover, the cemetery would appear to be contemporary with level V, and possibly also levels IV–III. Although the excavators consider Temple VI also contemporary with levels III–V, an examination of the published evidence shows that the most persuasive parallels lie between the immediately preceding levels in the Hut Sounding (VIII–VI) and the cemetery and Temple VI.

Type	*Hut Sounding*	*Cemetery*	*Temple Sounding*
1	I–III (V)	–	–
3	VII–VIII	+	VI
6	I–VII	–	–
8	I–V	+	–
9	V–VIII (III–IV)	most common type	VI
10	VII–VIII (III)	–	VIII–IX
14	(II, VII)	+	VI
20	IV–VII (II)	+	VI

1		3		6		8		9		10		14		20
H.S. I	II	III	IV	V	VI	VII	VIII	cemetery		T.S. VI		VIII–IX

The well-known 'soup plate' (fig. 21:9), for example, the 'most common type in the cemetery' (Safar *et al.* 1981: 158) occurs also in Temple VI; a few specimens, unfortunately not illustrated, are reported from Temple VIII. In the Hut Sounding this very distinctive type appears in large quantities in levels VI and VII, is common in V and VIII, but rare in levels III–IV. No specimens are reported from levels I–II. It is also relevant that whereas the cemetery 'soup plates' are usually elaborately decorated on their flange-like rims (*ibid.* figs. 75–6), those from H.S. levels VI–III are ornamented solely with solid bands of paint, a characteristic feature of the very latest Ubaid ceramic (*ibid.* figs. 129–30).

Beaker type 3 (fig. 22) is found in H.S. levels VII–VIII *only*; it is a common cemetery type; indeed strikingly similar painted examples

21 Pottery from the Hut
Sounding at Eridu, after Safar,
Mustafa and Lloyd 1981, Fig. 127

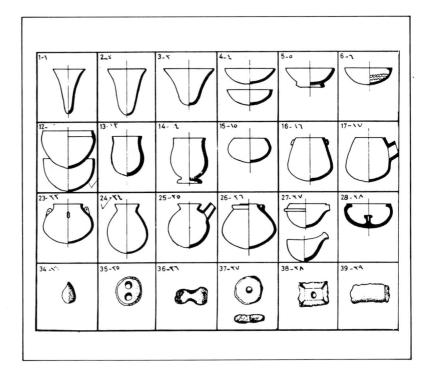

22 Al 'Ubaid sherds from the
1973–74 season at Al Markh,
Bahrain

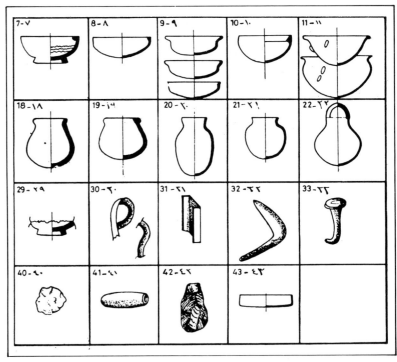

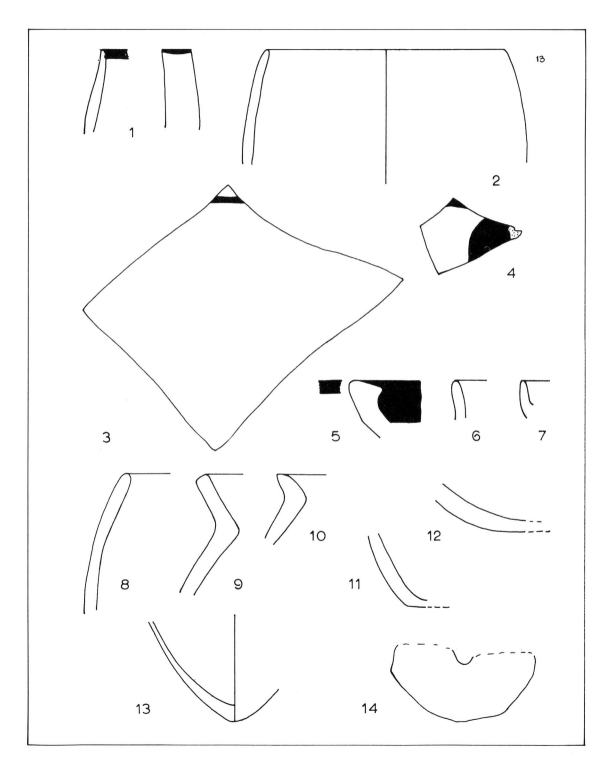

are illustrated from the cemetery and H.S. VI (*ibid.* fig. 78:13; fig. 130:1). An elongated, unpainted beaker, unknown from the temple sequence or the cemetery, is found in H.S. levels III–I, with a single specimen in H.S. V. Also very characteristic of the end of the Ubaid period is the wavy combing (type 6) which is found in the Hut Sounding from level VII onwards, but is not reported from Temple VI. Present evidence from both Ur and Eridu indicates that the wavy combing and the single wide bands of painted decoration, often associated with it and more especially with type 8, are criteria of the last known phase of the Ubaid assemblage (*ibid.* 262; Oates 1976, 28; 1978, 44; *pace* Adams and Nissen 1972, 99). Such pottery is character-istic of Woolley's Ur-Ubaid III (1956, 87–9, and pl.17; note that the earlier Ur-Ubaid II=Ubaid 4), and is common in the final phase of Ubaid occupation at sites like Warka (Boehmer 1972, pls. 44, 47, 57) and Tell 'Oueili (Adams and Nissen, 1972, fig. 79).

A re-examination, in the light of the Eridu report, of the Ubaid material published from the Gulf area in general confirms previous attributions. The earliest pottery of all comes from the unexcavated site of Halilih near Bušehr. Here there are sherds of unequivocal Ubaid 2 attribution; the closes parallels lie with the site of Hajji Muhammad and with Eridu levels XV–XIV.[1] By contrast with the evidence from sites on the western side of the Gulf, petrographic and thin section analysis of sherds from Halilih, carried out by Dr. Diana Kamilli, has revealed that although some are possible Mesopotamian imports, others show a local or non-Mesopotamian character (M. Prickett, pers. comm.). At both Dosariyah and Ain Qannas in the Eastern Province, Hajji Muhammad types also occur, but in associa-tion with more standard Ubaid ceramics, a characteristic feature of early Ubaid 3 first recognized at Ras al 'Amiya (Stronach 1961). Un-fortunately, it must be noted that it is difficult in the new Eridu volume to identify the precise chronological distribution of particular ceramic types owing to the illustration in the report of a number of sherds that would appear to be late survivals, certainly out of context and perhaps derived from *libn* or levelling fill (e.g. the very character-istic Ubaid 2 types illustrated from Temple VIII, in particular fig. 83:14, a very distinctive Ubaid 2 type; also, *inter alia*, 7, 9, 18, 20, while number 8 is a type generally considered characteristic of Ubaid 1 levels; indeed there is not a single sherd on figure 83 that would be out of place in a *pre*-Ubaid 3 horizon). Thus not all the sherds illus-trated from a particular level necessarily belong there. The stratifica-tion of sherds on multi-period mud-brick sites must always be open to qustion; one would have hoped at Eridu for the recovery of a greater number of complete, and therefore more reliably stratified, vessels.

The three sites excavated by Masry would all appear to have

been occupied by the early Ubaid 3 phase. Among the earliest types illustrated by him are the Hajji Muhammad bowl from the surface of Ain Qannas (Masry 1974, fig. 18), a bowl fragment which at least superficially resembles the 'ladles' known from a Late Samarran/ 'Transitional' context at Choga Mami (*ibid.* fig. 66:1; Oates 1968, pl. 12), and a very distinctive type from the earliest level (8) at Abu Khamis (*ibid.* fig. 90:1) that is especially characteristic of early Ubaid material at Choga Mami (Oates 1983; 1976, fig. 2) and at Eridu of level XIII. Hajji Muhammad-like decoration is found on what appears to be a 'tortoise vase' at Dosariyah (Masry 1974, fig. 39:2); complete examples of this type, known also at Ras al Amiya, Choga Mami – and even Tell Brak in northeastern Syria, are found as late as Eridu Temple VIII (Safar *et al.* 1981, figs. 73, 82:9). A very distinctive bowl fragment from an upper level at Abu Khamis is also very closely paralleled in Temple VIII (Masry 1974, fig. 77:3; Safar *et al.* 1981, fig. 82:11). In other words Ain Qannas, Abu Khamis and Dosariyah were all certainly occupied during Ubaid 3 and conceivably as early as late Ubaid 2; there is no published pottery from these sites necessarily later than Ubaid 3. In Qatar, the site of al Da'asa would appear to date from approximately the same time (Oates 1978, 42–4), though the overall quantity of pottery recovered is far less than from the Eastern Province sites.

Ras Abaruk (Qatar) and Al Markh (Bahrain) are undoubtedly of later date (Oates 1978, 44), the pottery in many ways resembling that from the Hut Sounding (fig. 22; Roaf 1976: fig. 7). Also found in the later levels of the Hut Sounding are the very distinctive banded jar rims (e.g. Safar *et al.* 1981, fig. 130:31, level V and fig. 132:39, 42, level II) which are characteristic of the very latest Ubaid pottery at Warka and Ras Abaruk (de Cardi 1978, fig. 4:2–4). It is in relation to this post-Ubaid 4 or 'Terminal Ubaid' phase that the recent publication of the Hut Sounding material is perhaps of greatest value, in providing for the first time its stratigraphic confirmation.

In conclusion, it now seems clear that the contact between Ubaid Mesopotamia and areas bordering the western side of the Gulf and Bahrain dates from perhaps as early as the end of Ubaid 2, was most evident during Ubaid 3, probably continued during Ubaid 4, and came to an end at the very end or 'terminal' phase of the Mesopotamian Ubaid. Up to now no Uruk materials have been recovered in the area of these sites. It must be emphasized that this contact with Ubaid Sumer, though it continued over this fairly lengthy span of time, was essentially intermittent. The Gulf sites, including the mound settlements of the Eastern Province, show for the most part only ephemeral traces of impermament occupation. Al Markh and Ain Qannas provide very important clues to the local context of the period of Ubaid contact, in demonstrating that the indigenous aceramic flint sites both *precede* (Ain Qannas) and *succeed* (Al Markh, Roaf 1974) the Ubaid-related settlements. Of particular importance in this respect is the recent recognition that Kapel's (1969) flint types A, C and D, previously thought to have had very different chronological distributions, all occur together, and in association with Ubaid pottery (Inizan 1980).

Since the existing evidence strongly suggests that all the Ubaid pottery in the Gulf was actually manufactured in Sumer, whatever its date, one can only conclude that its presence represents a repeated pattern of movement *from* Sumer to the Gulf, whether for trade, the exploitation of marine resources, or some other unknown purpose. The absence of Ubaid material on known overland routes, in particular the Wadi Batin, makes it equally clear that this movement was by sea. The paucity of settlement debris makes it unlikely that any large number of people was involved, or that they stayed in the Gulf for prolonged periods. A seasonal pattern of exploitation suggests itself, with fishermen and/or merchants sailing down the Gulf, and returning after relatively short intervals. This interpretation is supported not only by the ceramic analyses so far carried out and by the ephemeral and limited nature of the archaeological sites, but also by the fact that no local potting tradition developed – at least the aparently local coarse ware occurs only in association with the Ubaid ceramic and was presumably made by or in response to the needs of the foreign visitors, and the tradition of pottery manufacture disappears when this Mesopotamia contact is lost. This interpretation, moreover, makes sense in the general context of the now well-attested pattern of Ubaid exploitation of natural resources in other regions on the Mesopotamian periphery. Whether the cessation of contact between Sumer and the Gulf was the result of natural causes, such as rising sea level, changing trading or fishing patterns, or some political process, remains to be established.

1. I am very much indebted to Miss Martha Prickett for copies of the drawings of the Halilih sherds.

Some aspects of Neolithic settlement in Bahrain and adjacent regions

Those of us privileged to inspect the monumental architecture of the temples and public buildings which illustrate the quality of life on Bahrain during the third millennium B.C. must surely have reflected upon the island's earlier inhabitants whose presence is so poorly attested. It was at a Conference held in Bahrain in 1970 that the discovery and subsequent identification of Ubaid pottery in the Eastern Province of Saudi Arabia was first made known (Burkholder and Golding, 1971). Since then sites associated with Ubaid-type pottery have proliferated and their general distribution in Qatar and the Eastern Province (Oates 1978, map, fig. 1) point overwhelmingly to the likelihood of comparable material having once existed on Bahrain but, apart from the late and post-Ubaid occupation deposits at al-Markh, no settlements of the period have so far been recognised. Nor is there much prospect of recovering such evidence in the normal course of field survey. Given the choice, the early hunter-gatherer would almost certainly have headed north, attracted by the incidence of fresh water from springs, both inland and offshore. It is however precisely in that part of the island that the land surface has been progressively disturbed by man who has used it intensively for burial purposes, agriculture, mineral extraction and more recently in the course of industrial and urban development. Such land-use obviously narrows the field for the archaeologist and short of some startling chance discovery of Ubaid levels within a site of later date the outlook seems unpromising. Even within the area of the ruinfield of Diraz which encompasses the well of Umm es-Sejur, surely an obvious target for the early settler, the Ubaid period is represented by only a single surface sherd.

It was speculation along these lines that prompted this note on some aspects of neolithic settlement in the southern sector of Bahrain and adjacent regions, in particular, site location and function and, since some of them are aceramic and consist only of a scatter of flints, a brief re-appraisal of the late Holger Kapel's important classification based on Qatar's lithic industries seemed called for in the light of recent excavations.

In 1954 reconnaissance by a Danish team located a dozen aceramic flint sites on Bahrain of which two were found in the northwest, three lay near Jebal Dukhan and the remaining concentration occurred to the south of the Zallaq-Awali road (Glob 1954a, map, p. 94). One site (no. 27) consisted only of a scatter of chippings regarded as a flint-worker's output in the course of a few hours' work but the debitage had the merit of illustrating various stages in the production of barbed and tanged arrowheads (Glob 1954b, fig. 4, d-h). In the same area two other sites (nos. 4 and 29) yielded evidence of early agricultural activity in the shape of flint sickle blades (Glob 1954b, fig. 5, d-h) and a few kilometres south of al-Markh yet more barbed and tanged arrowheads were collected from the sabkha (Site no. 2070, Roaf 1976, 159).

At the time of their discovery many of these surface sites were difficult to date; some of the material was regarded as belonging to a Middle Paleolithic flake culture while other artifacts were ascribed to the neolithic period (Glob 1954b, 112). The search for flint sites then switched to Qatar where Kapel's exploration provided a wealth of surface material which he categorised in four main Groups A–D on the basis of their typological and technical character (Kapel 1967). The A-Group, which included material found on a number of sites around Khor on the northeast coast, was regarded as probably the oldest. The B-Group comprised blade-arrowheads including a number found together on a site in the southeast in a context with a C14 date of 5020 ± 130 B.C. (Kapel 1967, 17). The C-Group, characterised by scrapers and awls, was thought by Kapel to be ancestral to the D-Group which included a variety of pressure-flaked tools of which the barbed and tanged arrowheads were subsequently recognised as being identical to those found in association with Ubaid-type pottery on various sites in the Eastern Province, western Qatar and at al-Markh.

With the D-Group securely related to settlements of the Ubaid period it is necessary to refer briefly to the chronological modifications which can now be made to the classification in the light of recent discoveries. Undoubtedly the most important of these has been the association of A-Group implements with pottery of Ubaid 3–4 on the French Mission's excavations near Khor, which has placed that lithic industry firmly in the latter part of the fifth millennium B.C. The site, identified as a workshop producing flake tools and bifacially retouched pieces, had the added interest of being contemporary with a stone cist containing a cremation accompanied by a few Ubaid sherds, the first burial of this period identified in Qatar (Inizan 1980b, 51–97).

The lowered dating of the A-Group calls for a general re-assessment of the related assemblages. Thus the ascription of one of Bahrain's lithic industries to the Middle Palaeolithic must be increasingly in doubt and the same may apply to some of the artifactual assemblages in the Eastern Province of seemingly Late Palaeolithic date, notably the massive implements of Sawwan Dira and Sawwan Dhabatiyah around the Jabrin Oasis which bore a close resemblance to those of the A-Group (Masry 1973, 89). In view of the relation of the Khor A-Group and Ubaid 3–4 ceramics it is also worth noting that so far surveys in the Jabrin region have yielded only a single Ubaid-type sherd (Adams, Parr and Mughannum 1977, 29).

It remains to consider the relation of the other three Groups. An occupational sequence – admittedly intermittent – established on the large settlement of Ain Qannas in the al-Hasa region is particularly relevant (Masry 1973, 96 ff.). There, two distinct lithic assemblages were identified in aceramic levels: the earlier, which was comparable to the Qatar B-Group, being restricted to the lowest levels (12–14), while C-Group implements appeared above (levels 6–11) and were in turn overlaid by an occupation of probably short duration containing both D-Group tools and Ubaid 2 pottery. Recent excavations by the French Mission at Zghaïn al-Bahath on the edge of an inland depression in western Qatar where Kapel had found many flint sites have shown the B-Group to be the oldest assemblage (Potts nd.). C-Group scrapers certainly cannot be regarded as necessarily occurring only in aceramic contexts as both C- and D-Group implements have been found together with Ubaid-type pottery at al-Da'asa and Ras Abaruk 4 in western Qatar (Smith 1978b, 105) and throughout the occupation at al-Markh. The distinction between the two Groups could well have technical rather than temporal implications arising from the use of certain types of tools for different kinds of specialised activities.

The location and occupation debris found on all three of the last named sites reflect the exploitation of marine resources, and although al-Markh now lies over a kilometre from the sea, environmental studies showed that it had originally been located on the eastern edge of a small and sparsely occupied island separated from the west coast of Bahrain by a channel which later silted up to form an area of sabkha (Roaf 1976, fig. 6).

The only structural features noted at al-Markh were a number of shallow pits and a fish-midden some ten metres in diameter whose size surely points to some activity – most probably fish-curing – carried out on a more than purely domestic scale. The pits had been dug into the sand and a few were lined with either shells or fish-bones while others had been filled with bones, shells and flints in ashy layers which alternated with clean sand. A similar alternation of debris layers and sand was observed in the build-up of the midden and would lead to the conclusion that the site had probably been used on a season basis. The first phase of occupation, dated to *c*.3800 B.C. by association with pottery assigned at the earliest to Ubaid 4 and possibly later (Oates 1978, 44), was probably partially contemporary with that of Ras Abaruk 4. An intriguing feature, noted both there and also at al-Da'asa but to a much lesser degree, was the care with which even undecorated sherds had been repaired and in several instances re-used, the broken edges being ground down to serve as rims. An obvious inference is that Ubaid-type pottery may not have been easy to replace and there was no evidence of any local product to take its place. There is, in fact, some doubt as to whether pottery was used in the later phase, a contingency with implications for the dating of some aceramic sites which could thus be either pre- or post-Ubaid (Roaf 1976, 160).

Although no qualitative difference was evident in the lithic industries of al-Markh 1 and 2, both being comparable to Groups C and D, nine times as much flint per cubic metre was recovered from the later deposits. This was interpreted as due in part to a fundamental change in the subsistence pattern. The earlier inhabitants had relied largely on the exploitation of inshore resources comprising small to medium-sized fish combined with the gathering of molluscs, mostly venerids and pearl oysters, as a readily available addition to their diet. The later deposits, on the other hand, contained the bones of much larger fish together with dugong, mammal and goat, and it has been suggested that breakages resulting from the heavier work of scaling and gutting the catch and butchering the animals could explain the greater quantity of flint tools discarded.

Changes in the subsistence base may also have been accompanied by new fishing techniques (Roaf 1976, 150). The earlier inhabitants probably relied largely on nets and traps perhaps laid out across the channel separating al-Markh from the main island, the latter operated in much the same way as the arrow-shaped *hadhra* which are so distinctive a feature around Bahrain's coasts. These traps are currently made of palm stems staked out in such a manner that the fish swimming in on the tide are trapped as it recedes. During the later occupation when more substantial fish including some carnivorous species were caught some form of raft or boat would no doubt have been required for retrieving them from the traps and light craft such as the *hagariyah*, built of palm stems lashed together and enclosing a narrow deck, may have been employed for that purpose (Bibby 1972, 209). Like the *shashah* currently used for inshore fishing along the Batina coast of Oman, these craft have a limited buoyancy and need to be dried out when waterlogged. Presentday craft are however sufficiently sturdy to take an outboard engine and the recent introduction of expanded polystyrene in the decking is an adaptation likely to guarantee their future use (Facey and Martin 1979, 152). Given the existence of more sophisticated boats in the Ubaid period (Howard-Carter 1981, 216, note 33) and the emphasis placed on piscatory temple offerings, fish-curing, which is known to have been practised in the third millennium (Crawford, 1973, 233), may have provided earlier migratory communities around the Gulf with a readily exchangeable product.

On the small coastal encampment of al-Da'asa in western Qatar nearly sixty pits were uncovered during excavations in 1973, many either filled or lined with burnt stones (Smith 1978a, Pl. XIII and plan, fig. 4). As at al-Markh, their high density on the shore of this sheltered bay is best attributed to fish-curing. The reasons for the lining or inclusion of stones in their fill is uncertain but one possibility is that they may have served to consolidate the soil thus making it easier for whole fish impaled on small stakes to be dried initially in the wind. Larger fish could have been split but left on the bone or strung up in strips to dry, both methods still used in some regions of the Gulf. As an additional preservative, of practical use where the catch had to be transported, the dried fish might have been lightly smoked and analysis of the charcoal from one of the pits showed that it had contained a non-woody fuel, probably either dung or grass.

Al-Da'asa was occupied at an earlier date than al-Markh to judge by its pottery which included sherds decorated in the style of late Ubaid 2 or early Ubaid 3. It would thus be approximately contemporary with Dosariyah, the largest of the Eastern Province coastal settlements, where Ubaid pottery was found together with a coarse red ware of local manufacture, and it is relevant to note that three small fragments of a similar ware occurred at al-Da'asa. The lithic assemblage comprised mostly scrapers, points and cutters while querns and a group of six domestic implements including a pounder, hammer and rubber-stones, and a piece of coral which probably served as a grater were found undisturbed near post-holes of a shelter. While the inference is that grain was either cultivated or collected, no firm evidence of agriculture was obtained.

Ubaid pottery was also noted on three other locations: a coastal encampment to the south and on two sites to the north at Bir Zekrit and Ras Abaruk (Site 4). No excavations were undertaken at Bir Zekrit but its position on two small promontories overlooking a gap in the plateau marked it as an ideal 'kill-site' into which gazelle, whose bones were found in the occupation of Ras Abaruk 4, could easily have been stampeded and slaughtered (Smith 1978c, 107–116).

The remaining site lay on a plateau in the middle of the narrow Ras Abaruk peninsula. The quantity of flint debris as distinct from tools – mostly scrapers and cutters – suggested that the encampment

had been occupied seasonally by people who had lived off both the
sea and the land to judge by the fish-bones, shells and animal bones,
including gazelle and equid, in their domestic debris. Several hearths
could be distinguished within the area examined but no trace was
found of activities comparable to those carried out at al-Da'asa and
al-Markh. It had originally been thought that tools of Middle
Palaeolithic type found on the site might represent an earlier occupation (Smith 1978b, 82) but the results obtained at Khor now suggest a
dating more in keeping with that of the pottery which included sherds
of Ubaid 4 and later thus indicating some degree of contemporaneity
with al-Markh. The Ras Abaruk peninsula has attracted seasonal
migrants from Ubaid times onwards and it is relevant in the wider
context of Bahrain's history to mention that Barbar pottery was
uncovered during a geomorphological examination of the silts in the
depression adjacent to the neolithic settlement (de Cardi, 1978, fig. 3,
p. 33). Comparable material has also been collected from Hvar Island
and it would be surprising if no trace of earlier settlers was eventually
found there.

The recognition of Ubaid-type pottery on widely scattered
locations around the Gulf soon prompted investigations as to where
it had been manufactured. At the instigation of Dr Joan Oates,
relevant sherds from both al Da'asa and Ras Abaruk 4 were examined
with comparable material from al-Markh and the Eastern Province by
neutron activation and petrographic analyses. The important results
of that research are by now well known and both the plain and
painted sherds can be regarded as south Mesopotamian products,
while in a sample of sixteen sherds from al-Da'asa studied against a
control group from Ur, nine almost certainly came from there (Oates,
Davidson, Kamilli and McKerrell 1977; Oates 1978, 47).

Pottery was not the only foreign commodity reaching the Gulf
settlements during the Ubaid period. At Dosariyah, Khursaniyah and
Abu Khamis, as well as the inland site of Ain Dar, a small but
significant number of obsidian blades, knives and beads have now
been recorded (Masry 1973, 75). Although obsidian occurs in the
Hadhramaut, it is more likely that these objects were made in central
Anatolia and distributed from there through southern Mesopotamia
along with the ceramics of that region (Crawford 1978, 129). No
similar material has yet been found in either Bahrain or Qatar but
other exotica from those areas include a couple of carnelian beads
from al-Markh and al-Da'asa and several of amazonite from the latter
site and Ras Abaruk 4, the nearest source of both minerals being
India. All these objects have the advantage of being compact and
extremely durable, qualities which no doubt made them particularly
convenient as ancillary exchange goods transported possibly with
pottery to the larger settlements along the Gulf which may have

served as coastal entrepôts in a series of 'down the line' exchanges. Ubaid pottery, particularly the plain ware, may not have much aesthetic appeal, but it would undoubtedly have been of practical value to the fishing-hunting-herding communities whose needs were not met by a local product until the appearance of a coarse red ware at Dosariyah. That ware, hand-made within a basketry frame, was technically inferior to the imported pottery but excavation showed that it comprised 80% of the ceramics at Abu Khamis by the early fourth millennium B.C. (Golding 1974, 22) when, to judge from al-Markh, Ubaid pottery was becoming scarce.

The identity of those who carried cargoes of pottery from southern Mesopotamia on the first stage of its distribution remains obscure (Oates *et al.* 1977, 23): it is certainly difficult to envisage either seafaring merchants or fishermen from Ur encamped at al-Da'asa or the Eastern Province sites without either their own weapons or tools and as yet no trace of such essentials has been found. Instead, the stone tools of al-Da'asa were identical to those at al-Markh and the Arabian sites in the Ubaid period and show no affinity with those of southern Mesopotamia.

One final point: in the location-pattern now emerging in the coastal region between Dosariyah and Abu Khamis the major settlements are seen as surrounded by a number of much smaller encampments, though it is as well to note that the latter were in some cases located within a radius of up to forty kilometres from the larger sites (Masry 1973, 78 and 191). The small encampments have been interpreted as 'special function' sites frequented by reason of their proximity to such natural resources as clay, limestone and tabular flint. If the latter was as widely traded as is thought then trace-element analysis of flint tools found in the Eastern Province might be expected to establish the relation between the larger settlements and the working-sites surrounding them as well as giving some indication of the tool types to be associated with known flint deposits and their areal dispersal.

Early maritime cultures of the Arabian Gulf and the Indian Ocean

MAURIZIO TOSI

The conquest of the ocean, a place of immense resources and a way of communication, was a process of slowly accumulating knowledge of an alien element, as the sea was extraneous to the primordial evolution of *Homo sapiens*. For the first navigators it was like venturing into outer space and only a body of accumulated experience, strengthened by tradition, would have ensured survival at sea. The initial stages were the result of the process of physical and cultural adaptation in the coastal populations, developing through the course of millennia parallel to the formation of agricultural economies in the inland regions from cultivation of plants and raising of animals. Nevertheless, while in the last thirty years the origins of agriculture have been the object of extensive research carried out in just about every region in the world, the conquest of the ocean has remained one of the least comprehensible chapters in prehistory. Somehow archaeology has not yet developed adequate research strategies in this area, contrary to that which has been achieved for the cultural and ecosystemic transformations which brought about the Neolithic revolution. Many still maintain that the primary development of seacraft came about as a by-product of the first urban and agrarian based societies of the Middle East, in the fourth and third millennia B.C., primed by elite demand for exotic goods from distant lands. The rather sporadic archaeological evidence suggests, however, that the rapid progress of navigation in this period was possibly due to the slow pre-existent build-up of skill among those coastal populations extraneous to the development of the rural societies as they were tied to a different model of adaptation. The most ancient evolution of seacraft, taken as a whole of knowledge and techniques directed at controlling the sea and its resources, took place in four geographical centres which have a largely parallel history: the North Sea, the Mediterranean, the Erythraean Sea and Insulindia. At the base of its development everywhere there were populations of Late Palaeolithic hunters and gatherers, who during the first part of the

Holocene, between 14,000 and 7,000 years ago, had adapted themselves to living off the exploitation of the coastal and marine biomass. The sea could provide sustenance equally as constantly and surely as the practice of agriculture and it required fewer adjustments for Palaeolithic technology. The progressively increasing body of accumulated knowledge allowed the technological load to be stored in men, before it was in objects, and so this change shows up as barely visible in the archaeological record. The conjoining of these two ways of life occurs rather late, but it precedes the emergence of urban and statal societies. This was established after 5000 B.C. when the formative period agrarian economy in the arid regions between the Nile, the Indus and Central Asia came of age. A close-knit network of rural villages, started off safely in the sedentary occupation of land in a spiral of growing accumulation, spread through this vast territory. The soldering of the coastal economies accelerated the development of both societies: the fishermen were able to acquire the technology of metal and pottery; the farmers gained access to trade with distant countries which in a short time transformed their own spectrum of subsistence resources. Of the four areas in which prehistoric seacraft developed, the Erythraean Sea which with a ring of water around the Arabian peninsula connects the great centres of eastern civilization between Egypt, Mesopotamia, southern Iran and the Indus valley, is naturally the first to be seen in history, documented already in the cuneiform texts of the third millennium B.C. The particular conditions prevailing in the area retarded every process of political and economic integration with inland centres based on agri-pastoral economy. Between the Red Sea and the Gulf, the coasts of the Indian Ocean are a single desert. The mouths of the few large rivers become dispersed into intricate deltas covered with mangroves or sandbars which divide the sea from the land. Here, more than elsewhere, physical barriers have, until recent times, isolated the two processes of adaptation consolidating them into dialectically opposing forms of life even if they tended towards integration.

This dichotomy has influenced the progress of studies. Archaeological research in the Middle East has evaded the already poorly visible remains of the Indian Ocean's populations of prehistoric fishermen, with the result that this aspect has remained unknown. We are obliged to proceed on the analogy of the scanty references made in the Egyptian, Cuneiform and Greek sources which are not only too late to offer direct indications, but they are also distorted as terms of urban societies. For the Greeks, to whom we owe the most accurate evidence, from Herodotus to the geographers of the Roman era, the coasts of the Erythraean Sea were inhabited by poor and backward people with no interest in commerce, scornfully united under the name *Ichthyofagoi*, the fish-eaters, so emphasizing a form of life directed to the sea. And yet these same sources testify to the skill of the navigators which permitted communications between Africa and India through a chain of settlements continuing along the desert coasts of Arabia. In reality, a history of the most ancient oceanic navigation cannot be compiled on the basis of analogies with indirect and posterior information, written by populations which, although more culturally developed, were largely marginal with respect to this particular form of life. Primarily we should instead base our research strategies on archaeological data collected in the places where the *Ichthyofagoi* and their predecessors lived, along the coasts of Arabia, Baluchistan, the Horn of Africa and the Red Sea. Research on one hand, should be directed towards the reconstruction of the processes of adaptation to the marine eco-system over the entire post-Pleistocene span, on the other hand, to documenting the forms and times of contact with regions with an agricultural economy to evaluate the effects of integration and resistance in the cultural fabric of the coastal populations. This research approach is based on the indirect observation of phenomena which we presume to be closely linked to a human population's relationship with the sea. The history of navigation, therefore, should be divided up into a spectrum of effects, extracting it from the mutations visible in the otherwise

23   Prehistoric Coastal Sites between Oman and Baluchistan: open circles represent aceramic settlements; black triangles indicate sites with Harappan pottery

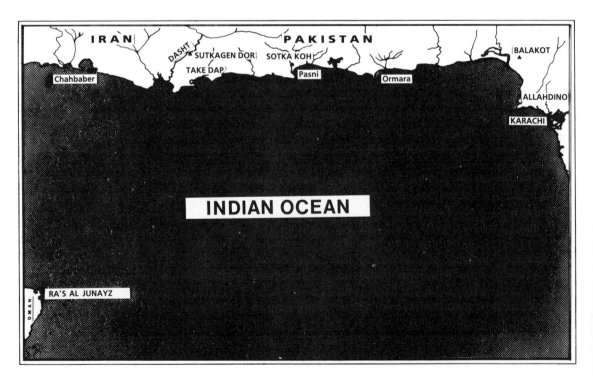

unprofitable archaeological record and using the data relative to the diet, the structure of the settlements, the technology of fishing and the funerary rituals.

ANCESTORS OF THE ICHTHYOFAGOI IN PREHISTORIC TIMES

The first long term project dealing with this subject has been set in motion. The study is centred on the prehistoric cultures along the Oman coastland, a region that historically played a dual role, acting as a hinge between Asia and Africa as well as the oases of inland Arabia and the Ocean. Through the excavations of some settlements and the intensive exploration of approximately six hundred km. of coast between Muscat and Dukhum, the first systematic reconstruction of the history of the seafaring peoples from between 5000 and 2000 B.C. is being attempted.

This chronological period corresponds to the emergence and first expansion of urban civilizations in Southwestern Asia. Somehow the parallel evolution of the maritime societies along the northern seaboard of the Indian Ocean, and the eastern Arabian littoral in particular, are to be viewed against the background of those hegemonic formations, as an alternative process of adaptational development. A selective drive from early post-Pleistocene times towards an intensified exploitation of maritime resources would have eradicated by the fourth millennium B.C. different economic traditions along the coastal deserts of the Indian Ocean (Tosi 1983; Biagi *et al.* 1984: 43–44).

Three Italian institutions have come together for this project: *The Istituto Universitario Orientale* of Naples, the *Centro Studi e Ricerche Ligabue* of Venice and the *Istituto Italiano per il Medio ed Estremo Oriente* of Rome, supported by the Ministry of National Heritage and Culture of Oman. After about five years of fieldwork it has been possible to isolate twenty or so prehistoric sites and a group of these at Ra's al-Hamra, a promontory situated thirteen km. to the east of Muscat, has been under excavation for four seasons. The settlements were formed by curvilinear groups of wood and reed dwellings, standing on the edge of the cliff in order to better exercise control over the different ecosystems exploited by the fishermen-gatherers. Across an area of a few square kilometres, closed in by the mountains and the Ocean, there is interwoven a mosaic of diverse ecosystems, of land, coast and the sea, ensuring all year round a broad range of resources to the human population. Fishing is favoured by the coast's configuration: the base of the continental platform narrows in correspondence with the promontory and large banks of plankton are trapped against a submerged calcareous barrier cutting the continental shelf in an almost continuous line between Fahal island and Ra's al-Hamra. The exploitation of plankton, during the winter months, causes masses of fish to gather in the immediate vicinity of the promontory.

In the fourth millennium B.C. population developed along the span of the explored coastline with small family groups set apart on the various promontories and the islands closest to the coast, a scheme suggestive of the descriptions of the *Ichthyofagoi* related in the Greek sources. The economy comprises forms of coastal and open sea fishing as well as the gathering of molluscs along the sand floor exposed at low tide. The identification of fish remains has provided the first series of data on the seafaring capacities of the prehistoric *Ichthyofagoi*. W. Torke from the University of Tubingen has identified among the fish remains species of small and large dimensions which would require the contemporary adoption of different techniques. Fishing with nets ensured a catch of small sardines and herrings as well as their predators ranging in weight from one to fifteen kilograms. Among the larger fish we can cite types of tuna, mackerel and barracuda which could only be captured with a hook and line from boats, considering that some specimens weighed over forty kilograms. The technocomplex remained aceramic at least for the whole fourth millennium B.C. with a lithic industry specialized in jasper and quartzite. The fishing kit evident across the archaeological record included weights for the nets made from notched pebbles as well as steatite and shell hooks. At close quarters these tools recall a morphology diffused since the Late Palaeolithic but the resemblance could be more formal than real if we recall the model of development storing the information more in man than in the tool. The contacts of the agricultural societies in the outside world is attested by mammalian remains: a small percentage of their bone remains has been identified by H. P. Uerpmann from Tubingen as belonging to domestic species of goats and cattle. These are animals which do not live in the wild state on the Arabian Peninsula and so they must surely have been imported in previous centuries from Iran or the Near East. The use of small capriovines and bovines by the *Ichthyofagoi* is confirmed by Greek sources describing domestic animals adapted to forage enriched by fish meal.

The most direct information on the cultural complexity of these distant forefathers of the *Ichthyofagoi* is probably to be derived from the numerous graves discovered at Ra's al-Hamra and under excavation under the direction of S. Salvatori. In the death ritual the fishermen reveal the intensity of their ideological bond with the sea, the result of a long process of adaptation which renders them as more similar to historical Polynesians than to their contemporaries in the protourban Middle East. The dead are placed on one side in a shallow pit under a covering of limestone blocks and smooth river pebbles. The link with the sea is evident in the frequent orientation of the head towards the water, in the use of *Macrocallista* valves held in the hand in front of the face, in the marine turtle remains placed with the dead, and in some cases, the head of this animal has been placed directly alongside that of the man. Burial was probably accompanied by a funeral meal, the remains of which were also placed in the grave; among these we have not only found the most significant indications as to their dietary habits but also dolphin bones and those of large marine mammals and the jawbone of a dog which is the most ancient so far confirmed in the scanty archaeological documentation of the Arabian Peninsula.

The excavations at Ra's al-Hamra have indicated that the process of development of the coastal societies in the fourth millennium B.C. was as complex as that based on agriculture and it is derived from a parallel trajectory of post-Pleistocene adaptation. The possibility that an equally bold specialization was attained elsewhere on the Erythraean Sea on the basis of analogous ecological relationships in the continuous contacts among coastal populations should not be excluded.

Even if this young project does not define in detail the cultures of the fishermen who populated the Indian Ocean initiating the conquest of it, these first discoveries indicate the path to be followed in order to begin writing the history of the most ancient Oceanic navigation on the side of *Ichthyofagoi*.

This picture of two autonomous systems in equilibrium alters in the following phase, corresponding to the maximum expansion of protostatal societies in the entire Middle East, from the beginning of the second half of the fourth millennium B.C. The development of trade will lead to increasingly bolder forms of integration between the two economic forms and their relative technological heritages. The result will be the emergence of Oceanic seacraft which combines metallurgy and dietary resources from the agrarian societies with knowledge of the sea, that of the fishing societies.

EFFECTS AND PRODUCTS OF PROTOHISTORICAL TRADE ALONG THE COASTS OF ARABIA

The rather poor archaeological evidence suggests that maritime communications between the centres of the development of urban society in the great alluvial plains and the coastal populations of the Indian Ocean intensified even in the course of the fifth millennium B.C., preceding by at least a millennium the birth of the first states in lower Mesopotamia. The indicators of movement in the two directions of trade are marine shells and pottery. The former spread over all the continental hinterland from the end of the sixth millennium to be worked as ornaments. The Predynastic pottery of Upper Egypt, on the contrary, appears on the Red Sea from the Badarian period around 4500 B.C., marking the beginning of a process of functional integration of the two axes of north-south communication, the Nile and the Red Sea, between the Mediterranean and the countries of the Horn of Africa. There is evidence of contact between Mesopotamia and the Arabian coasts as far back as the fifth millennium B.C. as attested by the hundreds of sherds painted in the al-Ubaid style found in small fishing settlements on the east coast of Saudi Arabia and in Qatar. Neutron analysis of the trace elements present in the Saudi sherds has revealed a spectrum of content identical to that of the Mesopotamian examples, revealing the common origin of the clays. Rafts, catamarans and reed vessels were the boats of this period as suggested by the rock graffiti along the banks of the wadis leading from the Nile to the Red Sea. These boats ensured river communications on the Nile as well as the Tigris-Euphrates so that journeys along the coasts of the Gulf would have developed as a simple extension of the already very active axes of riverine trade. So for a good part of the fourth millennium metal was not to be at all widespread in the manufacture of tools and the construction of hulls was limited to the use of light materials or whole trunks. Ethnographic analogies demonstrate however that these boats, even the simplest types like the Arab *shashas* of palm stems, can stay at sea for months, travelling along the coast in stages of thirty to fifty kilometres, fig. 23.

The continuous establishment of small groups of fishermen along the coasts of the Erythraean Sea ensured forms of contact, also continuous, between remote regions differing in ecology and in history but able to interfere in the development of agriculture with the transportation of seed and small animals. The short distances which separated the fishing settlements could be covered easily by reed canoes. In this way, since every centre was in regular contact with its neighbours a continuous bridge was formed along the Arab coasts which put Africa and Asia in communication like a chain of small rings. The bones of goats and cattle from Ra's al-Hamra are direct evidence in the archaic age of this passage of animals from one region to another, with the consequent alteration of ecological equilibria in the receiving territory. With the advance of navigational techniques the rings of the 'chain' uniting the two continents could have become increasingly wider until already at the end of the third millennium B.C. the seacraft of the Indian Ocean might have been able to join, in a single voyage, the extremes of the trade system. Interference of maritime trade in the conditions of agrarian production in prehistoric times was postulated around 1950 by the American geographer Carl O. Sauer, but his precursory theories were set aside also for the lack of empirical data. The first indications have emerged for the intensification of bioarchaeological studies and the discovery of the remains of African plants in the Oman peninsula and

Baluchistan. Palaeobotanist L. Costantini has in fact isolated imprints of sorghum (*sorghum bicolor*) in unbaked clay bricks from the buildings datable to around 3000 B.C. at Hili 8, an agricultural settlement in the oasis of Buraimi. Sorghum is a summer crop originating in the Ethiopian-Sudanese region; at Hili it was cultivated together with two species of wheat (*Triticum dicoccum and T. aestivum*) and barley (*Hordeum distichum and H. vulgare*) which represent the products of the winter harvest. The presence in this same context of date pits and jujube seeds would confirm the full activity of an intense agriculture with the rotations of harvests characteristic of an oasis economy. In Baluchistan sorghum is widespread at the beginning of the second millennium and appears in the site of Pirak, near Sibi, together with rice, indigenous to the Gulf of Bengala and southeast Asia and with winter graminaceous crops of local origin in a synthesis which was to remain characteristic of Indian agriculture.

If at the beginning of the third millennium B.C. sorghum was already an integral part of the complex system of the ecological and social relationships that would lie at the basis of the Arabian oases, it is logical to suppose that its introduction into the region had taken place much earlier. Our attention, therefore, is further concentrated on the fishermen of the fifth and fourth millennia B.C. whose culture we glimpse in the Ra's al-Hamra excavations. The prehistoric *Ichthyofagoi* laid the basis for the transformation of prehistoric agriculture in the Middle East and the Indian sub-continent derived from the integration of domesticated species in different centres from their plan of origin. On the other hand archaeology's research strategies cannot be planned on the basis of the accidental discoveries of rare finds originating in remote regions. Contact should be evaluated in term of its effects on the transformation of single cultural complexes and the material bases of economy. The development of archaeological research even in small sample areas along the entire coastal span, from the Horn of Africa to the Indus delta will permit the definition of modes and times of evolution of early seafaring populations. To date an opposing line has been taken, favouring the indications of the ancient sources in order to determine the history of these distant and diverse populations. In reality when, around halfway through the third millennium B.C., the Mesopotamian texts mention the countries beyond the 'Lower Sea' a network, as we have already seen, of trade capable of conveying exotic products along the corridors of the Red Sea and the Persian Gulf had already been active for at least two thousand years.

THE MARITIME COMMERCE OF THE FIRST STATE SOCIETIES IN THE INDIAN OCEAN

The supplying of prestige goods such as ornaments of exotic metals

and stones, rare plants and animals were for the protostatal societies
of the Middle East as important as the resources for primary production. It was not so much a demand of consumption as a sign of
prestige. Ceremonial pomp assured the continuing aggregation of a
population around the dominating élites. It was therefore the
supreme responsibility of the sovereigns to remain guarantors to
their people for the availability if not the submission of distant lands
which produce such goods. Thus Hatshepsut (1490–1468 B.C.), the
Queen of Egypt at the time of the eighteenth dynasty, will glorify her
stature as supreme ruler with a large expedition to the land of Punt to
gather the incense tree, described in minute ethnographic detail in
the reliefs of the Der el-Bakhri temple at Thebes. Punt had already
been mentioned in texts from the fifth dynasty in the area of the
Pyramids (2700–2500 B.C.) and which should be located towards the
mouth of the Red Sea, 1,000–1,200 km. further south than the
maritime ports of Upper Egypt. Hatshepsut does not hesitate however to obtain new credit with her expedition emphasizing the sub-
jection of a country producing an exotic aroma essential to the
practice of the cult.

An identical need, in Mesopotamia, led to the compilation of a
text by Sargon, founder of the Akkad dynasty in lower Mesopotamia,
where a clever synthesis expressed all his pride in the new capital
city and the benefits of commerce with exotic overseas countries.

The text may date back to 2300 B.C. and has come to us in a
bilingual version, in Sumerian and Akkadian, probably compiled six
hundred years later in Old Babylonian times. Here is the Akkadian
version according to H. Hirsch:

MA me-lukh-kha MA
ma qan^{Ki}
MA dilmun^{Ki}
in gar-ri-im
si a-ga-dè^{Ki}
ir-ku-us

'. . . made the Meluḫḫa ships, the Makkan ships, the Dilmun ships tie
up alongside the quay of Agade.'

The names of the countries Meluḫḫa, Makkan and Dilmun
designate coastal regions which for the Sumerians were aligned as a
single route in the Lower Sea. Sargon's text mentions them all
together for the first time as parts of a single compartment in the
geography of his time. Perhaps the most appropriate image is that of
an upsidedown funnel which narrows from the Erythraean Sea until it
flows into lower Mesopotamia, conveying goods and products from a
much broader area towards the major centres of production and consumption. The location of the three countries is partly spoilt by the
falsely linear perspective with which the Sumero-Akkadian tradition

represents them. Any attempts to identify them on the basis of textual data with different coastal regions of the Indian Ocean has remained largely hypothetical. Archaeological research in the Arab states of the Gulf have supplied the first indications with a certain foundation.

The closest to Mesopotamia was Dilmun which from the island of Failaka in Kuwait to the Sumerian ports, extended along the entire Arab coast to the Qatar Peninsula. In Sargon's era, Dilmun entered a period of maximum cultural and economic prosperity. Its political centre was located in the northern part of the island of Bahrain. The al-Ubaid pottery found in Saudi Arabia proves that all this region had been in contact with Mesopotamia since the fifth millennium B.C. The same geographical proximity contributed to continuity and intensity of trading, but in spite of the cultural and political magnificence of its great neighbour, Bahrain, it developed altogether original character-istics in all the manifestations of its material culture. And yet for the Sumerians, and for the Babylonians after them, Dilmun remained the land of promises, chosen by the gods as the home of the immortals, and before all others that of Utnapishtim, survivor of the Deluge whom Gilgamesh tried in vain to persuade to reveal his secret of an impossible survival. Dilmun would have developed as a commercial enclave linking Mesopotamia with the broadening corridor of coastal and hinterland countries adjoining the Arabian Sea. Archaeological remains suggest great economic vitality at the end of the third millennium B.C. in all the Gulf islands, from Failaka to Bahrain. Towards the end of the third millennium B.C. the list of goods which Dilmun exported to the Near East, through the cities of Lower Mesopotamia would lead to the supposition of the confluence of different geographic regions according to commercial inclinations which Bahrain has preserved up until the present day.

Makkan emerges from the sources as the land of copper and diorite, the stone *par excellence* of Mesopotamian artists, in which they carved the major masterpieces of archaic plastic art. With the same pride as Sargon, Gudea, Lord of Lagaš around 2200 B.C., initialled one of the sculptures which represented him, a reminder that the stone comes from Makkan. Geological evidence and archae-ological discoveries combine to place the principal centre on the Oman Peninsula. Relations with Mesopotamia are active until the end of the fourth millennium B.C. when pottery and ornaments from the first monumental graves of Oman faithfully imitate typologies from the Jemdet Nasr period (3100–2800 B.C.). For the protostatal culture of Mesopotamia this is the period of major expansion: the Jemdet Nasr models are again encountered with equal resemblance from northern Syria to southeastern Iran. Oman, Iran and Syria were soldered together by a great trade circuit which for two thousand kilometres conjoined the course of the Euphrates to the entire length of the

Gulf. Once again the antiquity and the intensity of contacts would not
have impeded a fully autonomous cultural development in the most
marginal region. In the course of the third millennium a rural
economy affirmed itself in Oman which integrates into the intensive
agriculture of the first oases, the raising of camels, probably initiated
by hunters, on the fringes of the desert and the intensive exploitation
of coastal and maritime resources. In northern Oman, for the first
time the integration of oceanic fishermen with the agrarian populations of the interior came about in the early part of the third millennium B.C. with the increasing stabilization of local exchanges and the
definition of specialized economic compartments. Such sharp division of activities at a subregional level certainly represented a
patterned control of resource scarcity, ultimately driving Arabia into
becoming the only hyperarid region in the world to develop an
independent source of capital. The new Bronze Age fishermen were
indeed different from their Late Stone Age predecessors still living at
Qurum in the fourth millennium B.C. A greater affluence in goods and
types of nourishment appears as the immediate character. The most
remarkable example of the new conditions comes from the earliest
site to be excavated in the Oman peninsula: the island of Umm an-Nar
a few miles to the east of Abu Dhabi. First a Danish and later an Iraqi
expedition have brought to light the remains of a large compound of
square-plan houses on stone foundations, with marked evidence of
maritime activities (Thorvildsen 1962; Frifelt 1975: 359–366). The
houses of Umm an-Nar are not the ephemeral structures of Ra's al-
Hamra, but true permanent buildings, overlooked by more impressive
funerary towers built in limestone blocks on the edge of a slightly
higher marine beach line. Here the fishermen were buried collectively, probably in keeping with a social division according to kinship
groups. The ritual no longer has the marked ties with the sea world of
the burials of Ra's al-Hamra, while it is very close to the graves
excavated in the various Bronze Age centres of the interior, along the
oases belt. As expected, the most marked difference with the earlier
complexes is represented by the economic integration to the
agricultural hinterland. The community of fishermen could avail itself
of goats, camels, cattle and probably also wheat and barley which
could not be produced along the sandy shales of the coastland, but
had to complement the sea diet (Hoch 1979). Pottery was in current
use and craft activities included a small metalsmith workshop with
slags and casting moulds. It appears that Umm an-Nar was some kind
of a centre for the coastal region between Abu Dhabi and Dubai,
inhabited by small groups of fishermen spread by seasonal patterns
of occupation along the flat off-shore formations in sea-to-brackish
environments. An example of these minor sites has been recently
excavated by Dr al-Tikriti at Ra's Ghannada (personal communica-

tion), some sixty km. northeast of Abu Dhabi. The graves at Umm an-Nar yielded ornaments of precious stone from Afghanistan such as lapis lazuli.

Meluḥḥa was certainly the most distant of the countries beyond the sea. The list of its products which were embarked there is among the richest and most varied and comprises precious stones (chalcedony, cornelian and lapis luzuli) copper, gold and other prized metals, ebony, the wood of sissoo, the gis-ab-ba 'sea wood' (maybe mangrove), cane, peacocks and roosters. The texts also speak of ships, skilled sailors and sophisticated inlaid furniture. These are the products of an involved society in control of resources common to regions of northeastern India. The most obvious explanation to all seemed identification with the Indus Civilization. The whole Baluchistan coast was occupied by people with a culture identical to that of the alluvial plains of Sind with a chain of settlements endowed with fortification systems, each situated several kilometres from the coast on the banks of the rivers which penetrate most deeply to the interior of Makran. A similar occupation is again encountered on the eastern extremity of the Harappan culture, in the crown of settlements which surrounds the Khatiawar peninsula. The period of maximum expansion is placed astride 2000 B.C., corresponding to the height of the Neo-Sumerian era in Mesopotamia, when references to maritime trading with Dilmun, a point of confluence for the countries of the Lower Sea, frequently recur in the texts of Ur. To complete a picture of the total control of the routes of the oceanic funnel north of Dilmun, from the Indus Civilization now comes the

24 Harappan inscription incised on shoulder of painted jar found at Ra's al Junayz, Oman

very recent discovery of a Harappan inscription at Ra's al-Junayz, an inlet on the corner of Arabia facing the Pakistani coast, by the Italian Archaeological Mission in Oman, fig. 24.

Four picture-writing characters are incised on a sherd which was found, together with other diagnostic material including pottery and metal, on the surface of a Bronze Age site. This locality occupies an even more strategic position in the coastal route which unites Karachi to the Horn of Africa along the coasts of southern Arabia. Associated with Harappan material, the pottery corresponds to the Wadi Suq culture which extended all over the Oman peninsula in the first centuries of the second millennium B.C. This type of pottery has been found in association with Harappan fragments even at Hili 8 among Period III layers, radiocarbon dated to 1950 B.C. More recently Wadi Suq graves have been found at the northern tip of Masira island, thus extending the evidence of its maritime control all over the Omani coastlands. The existence of a port or simple Harappan mooring at the Arabian mainland, would rather confirm the intensity of trade relationships with this region. It is probable that this is the first of the moorings after the six hundred kilometres of open sea which separate India from Arabia. Once Ra's al-Junayz had been reached the voyage towards Africa could be continued along the coast without expanses of open sea.

Although it is still too early to draw conclusions from such a recent discovery, it seems increasingly likely that the Indus Civilization contributed more to oceanic seacraft than any of the other protourban civilizations of the Middle East. Besides the technological and economic achievements it had in common with Egypt and Mesopotamia, . . . the Indus Civilization controlled in plenty the most indispensable of all natural resources for seacraft: the trees that would produce the planks to assemble ocean-going large vessels. The resources of India and the skill of the Arabian fishermen were combined and brought together once the growth of the Indus Civilization transformed it into a powerful system of dominance over large portions of the Subcontinent and across the Arabian Sea, pushing for the rare resources of Oman and the peninsula. The early efficiency of this transmaritime trade network greatly impressed the memory of the agricultural civilizations of Mesopotamia and Egypt, that remained marginal to it. Notwithstanding the successful Arabian integration of economic compartments, the world of plants and the world of fishes remained throughout the ancient history of the Middle East essentially alien to each other, never experiencing the forms of intensive intersection we shall see in the Mediterranean basin.

Echoes of this early Indian thalassocracy have come to us today in a memory distorted by the geographical distances that confused the contemporary records. Archaeology confirms this with the presence of the most typical products of the Indus Civilization, steatite seals with picture-writing inscriptions and their imprints on clay pottery which was found all along the axis of the Gulf and the Euphrates corridor: at Yahya in Southern Iran, in Bahrain, in Failaka, and the Mesopotamian centres of Umma, Eshnunna and Nippur. On the other hand, in the Indus Civilization territory, to date no Mesopotamian product has emerged and in the same country of Dilmun up until the threshold of Sumeria proto-Indian presences are clearly dominant.

With the name Meluḫḫa the Mesopotamian sources would not have indicated a single territory or a particular political unit so much as the whole funnel of the Erythraean Sea, already unified in the Greek sources as the land of the *Ichthyofagoi*. The ships of Meluḫḫa moored at the quay of Agade would have perhaps come to meet on the Horn of Africa, with Egyptian ships heading for Punt. The rediscovery of this Bronze Age thalassocracy over the Indian Ocean and its long development along the Arabian coastlands perhaps represents one of the most exciting perspectives to be opened up by archaeology in the coming years.

The origins of the Dilmun Civilization

GEOFFREY BIBBY

Far and away the largest single archaeological site in Bahrain (and with the exception of the Hellenistic site of Thaj in Saudi Arabia the largest site in the Gulf) is the tell of Qal'at al-Bahrain. The tell, measuring some 300 by 600 metres, comprises the remains of a considerable city, occupied at many periods over the past four to five thousand years. Below Portuguese, early Islamic, Hellenistic, Neo-Babylonian and Kassite levels there lie the remains of a fortified city of the Barbar culture, which has been identified as the culture of that land of Dilmun which played so large a role in the cultural, religious and mercantile life of the Sumerians around the turn of the second and third millennia B.C. The tell was excavated by the Danish Expedition regularly for a dozen or so years in the 1950s and 1960s, and less regularly in the 1970s. These excavations traced the course of the fortification wall of this Barbar (or 'Early Dilmun') period around the greater part of the perimeter of the tell, but only within the northern run of the wall, closest to the sea, did we find substantial remains of streets and houses of this period. And only here did we find occupational levels *earlier* than the construction of the city wall, levels which thus represent the earliest traces of civilization in Bahrain.

Accordingly in the middle sixties we returned to the north wall, and excavated a fairly extensive area of some 180 square metres within the wall down to bedrock – and indeed beyond. For we discovered that the bedrock here was composed of *farush*, the limestone conglomerate that forms between high and low tide. It contained quantities of potsherds, and, breaking through it, we found further layers of sand and *farush*, with occupation debris, continuing for over a further half metre before we reached sterile green clay.

The object of the excavation was to determine in more detail the characteristics of the levels associated with the city wall, which we had called City 2, and of the levels anterior to the building of the wall, which we called City 1; to establish whether there was any break between the two; and to discover what, if any, foreign influences existed which could give a line on the origins of the first settlement on the site. It is the results of this excavation which are presented here.[1]

Figure 25 shows the area of the excavation, with the city wall forming, as it were, the backdrop. There are two gates through the wall, at different levels. The upper one is Hellenistic, and immediately beneath that the City 2 levels commence, continuing down until the construction level at the foot of the wall. Everything below that is City 1. The total height shown is six metres, and our datum point is another metre further down, the present-day high water mark. The whole area was dug with considerable care, and thirty levels were distinguished, all fortunately reasonably horizontal. The pottery from each level was, of course, kept separate, and all small finds were plotted in in three dimensions. A schematic diagram, fig. 26, shows the significant pottery by level, and the most important small finds at the exact levels at which they were found.

25 The city wall at Qal'at al-Bahrain

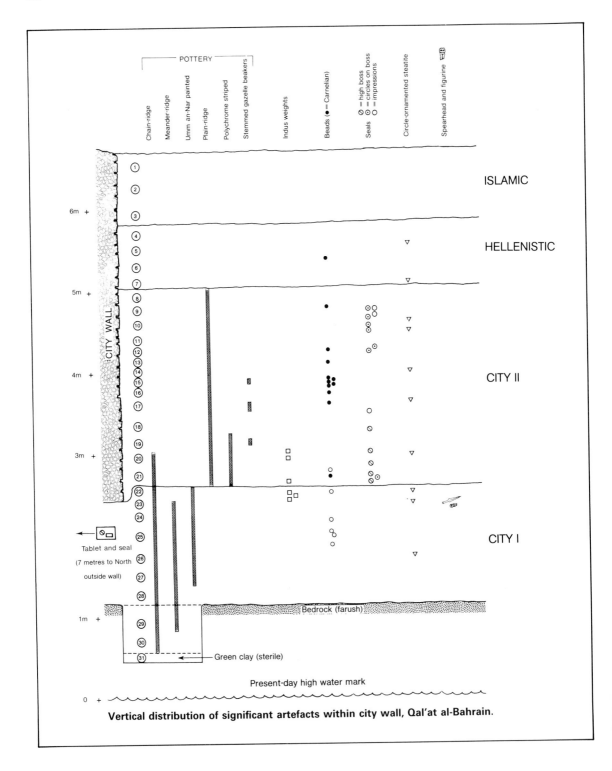

Vertical distribution of significant artefacts within city wall, Qal'at al-Bahrain.

Of the small finds one of the most interesting groups comprises six weights of Harappa-culture type and standard, fig. 27. They were found in the last two levels of City 1 and the first three levels of City 2. The significance of this will be discussed below.

26   Vertical distribution of significant artifacts within the city wall, Qal'at al-Bahrain

Beads proved interesting and perhaps significant. Eighteen were found in all, scattered evenly through the levels of both cities. But the five beads found in the City 1 levels were of turquoise, or of turquoise-coloured faience, while throughout City 2 they are, with one exception, of carnelian.

The most important group comprises the round stamp seals. Twelve were found here, in addition to three impressions, and all occurred in City 2, none in City 1. Significantly, the upper six were of the type found in the second temple at Barbar and in large numbers on Failaka, the shallow-bossed type with four dotted circles on the reverse and somewhat Mesopotamian designs on the obverse. The six lower seals, of which the first three occur in the very first level of City 2, are of another type, with a high boss and designs comprising entirely animals. Only one of these bears the four dotted circles on the reverse, and it is otherwise of the same type as the rest of the group. We should remember, perhaps, in this connection that the dotted circle is the dominant motif on the steatite bowls of Early Dilmun, and figure 26 shows the ten fragments of circle-ornamented steatite found scattered evenly through City 1 and City 2.

We found copper in fairly large quantities at all levels, mostly in corroded scraps, but near the top of the City 1 levels there was a fine socketed spearhead, and close to it a terracotta female figurine, of Mesopotamian type, and resembling closely those ascribed by Woolley to Larsa or Ur III times, fig. 28.

Turning now to the pottery, we note that the main character-istic of City 1 and City 2 is that very much of the City 2 pottery is red ware decorated with parallel ridges, while City 1 has ware of much the same type decorated with regularly squeezed and depressed ridges, the pattern that we have called 'chain-ridge'. We had met both characteristics before, at the Barbar temples and elsewhere. But here we find chain-ridge ware present from the very earliest level under the *farush* up through the whole of City 1, and in the first two levels of City 2. There it overlaps with the plain-ridge ware, which commences sharply with City 2, not being found earlier.

Mixed with the chain-ridge ware and plain red sherds of City 1 there was some 50% of other wares, buff, straw-coloured, often greenish-white. They are of types, with practically no neck and sharply out-turned rims, which we find in the Umm an-Nar ware of the Oman peninsula. More clearly typical of Umm an-Nar ware are large globular vessels decorated with raised ridges in what one might call a meander pattern, while most unmistakable of all is the painted ware,

27 Weights of the "standard of Dilmun"

28 Spearhead and figurine from the upper levels of City I

with its black-on-red chevrons and drooping triangles, fig. 29). As will be seen from the diagram, this Umm an-Nar ware occurs throughout City 1, and terminates sharply with the building of the city wall. There is no Umm an-Nar ware in City 2.

Together with the plain-ridged 'Barbar' pottery a new type of painted ware commences with City 2, a polychrome ware with broad horizontal stripes of black and orange-yellow on a cream slip. It is seen most clearly on an almost complete vessel now in the Bahrain National Museum. At a later stage in City 2 we find very fine stemmed goblets decorated with running portraits of gazelles.

Looking at this assemblage, what conclusions can we reach? There would appear to be a definite discontinuity between City 1 and City 2, in that the people who built the city wall used a different type of painted pottery, introduced seals and carnelian, and so on. Yet the innovations and disappearances are only superficial changes in a basic identity of pattern. For example, the 'hole-mouth' jars of City 2, which comprise about half of the total pottery, are identical with those of City 1, while the general shape of the chain-ridge vessels is a clear precursor of the plain-ridge ware of City 2. It is not, apparently, the culture that changes – it is the outside influences upon the culture.

29   Painted Umm an-Nar sherds from City I

At the close of City 1 and with the beginning of City 2 it is clearly Harappan influence that plays the chief role. The carnelian can have come from nowhere else, and the Harappan weight system is clearly taken over *in toto* – in fact the Harappan weight system is known to the Sumerians of Isin-Larsa times as 'the standard of Dilmun'.[2] The seals that commence with City 2 are not Harappan seals. They are of a different shape, though a shape that does occur three times at Moenjo-daro – perhaps intrusive from Dilmun. One can, however, say that they are 'Harappan-inspired'. Two, of the early type, even bear inscriptions in the Harappan script, while most of the rest bear an animal in the chief, often a bull, though never a humped bull. Mesopotamian influence is conspicuously slight. There is only the terracotta female figurine from the uppermost levels of City 1. A so-called 'Amorite tablet' has been given considerable prominence in the chronological discussion, but it was found outside this area, seven metres to the north outside the city wall, in the layers that slope steeply down to what must have been the beach north of the wall. It was found together with one of the seals bearing Harappan script, and, to judge by the pottery found with it, would lie most happily in the first three levels of City 2.

When we come to City 1 the most obvious foreign influence is that of Umm an-Nar. There is clearly a considerable Umm an-nar influence here, but City 1 is not an Umm an-Nar settlement. Some of the best-known Umm an-Nar pottery types, like the black-on-grey painted ware and the hanging jars, are absent from Bahrain, while the most conspicuous feature of City 1, the chain-ridge ware, is absent from Umm an-Nar. In fact, Umm an-Nar appears rather to be a very strong intrusion in an indigenous culture. There is as yet very little to indicate where we should seek the origins of this indigenous culture. But two surface sites to the north of Hofuf oasis in Saudi Arabia, which we investigated in 1969, produced pottery which is very plausible as a forerunner of the hole-mouth jars, and could well suggest that we should look to the mainland of East Arabia for the origins of the Dilmun culture.

Let us now review what we have. We should not exaggerate City 1. Perhaps to call it a city at all is a misnomer. We have no evidence for more than a small collection of stone houses along the shore, perhaps nothing bigger than the little fishing village of Umm an-Nar itself. It was a settlement of local people, but with very strong connections with what we may well call Makkan, perhaps even incorporating a trading-post of Makkan merchants looking for outlets for their copper to the north. Certainly the large number of corroded scraps of copper found in the sand of City 1 suggests that copper was abundant.

Clearly one would like to know more about this settlement, to dig further south, up from the beach levels which are all that have as yet been found. An attempt in 1978 ran straight into a walled water-channel which we at first thought might be a harbour. Later investigations by the French team have apparently tended to show that it is rather a much later moat to the landward side of the Islamic palace or fort on the present foreshore. It might even have been both. But clearly one should find the other side of this excavation, and dig deeper.

However that may be, obviously something happened at the end of City 1. What it was we do not know, but it was clearly associated with a break in the Umm an-Nar connection and with establishment of contact with India and the Harappan culture. Undoubtedly more capital is poured into the coastal settlement. A very massive and very extensive wall is built, apparently enclosing an expanse very much bigger than the built-up area. Seals and weights are introduced, and there appears to have been some reciprocal contact with Mesopotamia. For the same early seals as now appear here are also found at Ur.[3]

As time goes on, contact with Mesopotamia deepens, as the seals begin to reflect the Mesopotamian glyptic repertoire. Looking outside this small hole in the ground on the north coast of Bahrain we can see temples being built at Barbar, the thousands of burial mounds arising, and the settlement on Failaka developing.

There remains the question of chronology. When did all these things happen? Here the evidence is still unfortunately scanty. The late type of seal appears quite firmly anchored in Isin-Larsa times, about 1900 B.C. The 'Amorite tablet' and the female figurine, we are told, cannot be earlier than Ur III, perhaps 2100 B.C. But they can hardly be later than this either, unless City 2 lasted an incredibly short time. After all, the early type of seal is dated at Ur, with some uncertainty, to the Akkadian period. A personal view would put the building of the city wall at the beginning of Ur III or in late Akkad. When City 1 began depends on the date given to Umm an-Nar, and that is still a subject of disagreement. But a time in late ED III, perhaps 2400 or 2500 B.C., would seem to fit the facts, and the early pottery has a very ED III 'feel' to it.

We should have liked, of course, to push the beginnings of civilization in Bahrain back to 2600 B.C., the traditional date of Gilgamesh. But you cannot have everything . . .

1. The excavations were carried out by mag.art. Else Roesdahl, assisted by Svand Bue-Madsen, in the years 1964 and 1965. The preliminary reports appeared in *Kuml* 1965 and 1966.

2. See T. G. Bibby: '. . . according to the standard of Dilmun,' in *Kuml* 1970.

3. See C. J. Gadd: 'Seals of Ancient Indian Style found at Ur,' in *Proceedings of the British Academy*, 1932, 190.

'The island on the edge of the world'

MICHAEL RICE

At the Third Conference in Asian Archaeology, held in Bahrain in 1970, I presented a paper which reviewed some of the then relatively familiar, more or less archaeological, evidence for a connection between Sumer and Egypt effected through the Gulf route in high antiquity.[1] I also dilated on some less familiar material, like the curious similarity between the silhouettes of Osiris and the male Eridu figure. My observations were then quite kindly received; I have been prompted therefore to repeat the journey, but this time to take with me as my guides some texts which seem to me to point to a variety of interesting directions in the exploration of that misty hinterland, lying somewhere between myth and reality, which surrounds the prospect of contacts between the Sumerians and the Egyptians at the end of the fourth millennium, a contact in which the Gulf people may have been involved. My guide books are rather cumbersome documents: they include the Pyramid Texts[2] (which, incidentally must surely be acknowledged as the supreme literary expression of the collective unconscious), the inscriptions of the Horus Temple at Edfu,[3] which, though Ptolemaic in date probably incorporate much earlier material and, like some of the Pyramid Texts, descend from Predynastic times. I have also drawn on another corpus of inscriptions at Hermopolis,[4] which may also contain early records of recollections of the Egyptian people.

I would like to suggest that these texts (and no doubt others unknown to me) may contain evidence that the Egyptians preserved, however faintly, memories of an island, far distant towards the east, on the edge of the world, where the first and most crucial acts of creation occurred and where the first and second generations of gods had their home. This island, the Egyptians believed, played a profound part in the experience which contributed to the ideology of the Pharaonic state as well as to its very foundation. But in considering the island as the place of beginnings, and as the Egyptians envisioned it, it may be appropriate first to recall how their distant contemporaries, the Sumerians spoke of Dilmun, the paradisial and pristine nature of which is central to what follows here.

In the Sumerian texts which celebrate Dilmun, several epithets are customarily attached to it, in which it is represented as a paradisial place where the gods dwell and in which various acts of creation are induced. The epithets employed include 'the Land of Crossing', 'the Land where the Sun Rises'[5] (for the land is sited in the Sea of the Rising Sun) and throughout its literature particular emphasis is placed on Dilmun's purity:

> The Land Dilmun is a clean place,
> That place is clean, that place is bright[6]

Par excellence, Dilmun is a pure place, perhaps even *the* pure place. Dilmun was 'the Land of Pure Decrees' Meskillag, and one of its tutelary goddesses was Ninsikilla, the Lady of Pure Decrees.[7] I shall return to this aspect of its reputation further.

Now let me call in evidence three quotations from the Father of Egyptology himself, Flinders Petrie. Writing in the magazine *Ancient Egypt*, which he founded to popularize the study of Pharaonic civilization, he wrote of the alien, non-Egyptian influences which he, like others, felt could be detected in the late predynastic cultures:

> The strong Mesopotamian suggestions of the design have, as we noted before, no exact parallel in the East. They seem rather to belong to a people of Elamite or Tigrian origin and ideas who had progressed on their own lines. The presence of shipping as an important factor would be against their having come to Egypt across the Arabian desert. The probability seems that they branched off to some settlement in the Persian Gulf (such as the Bahreyn Islands) or on the South Arabian coast and from their second home had brought its style and ideas into Egypt.[8]

In another article, charmingly called 'The Geography of the Gods', in which he examines the geographical origins and associations of the principal divinities of Egypt, he writes:

> The general diffusion of the worship of Hathor and her identification with many other deities or genii points to her belonging to the dynastic people, as already stated.
> The movement of the dynastic people appears to have been by sea round from the Persian Gulf and up the Red Sea into Egypt.[9]

Later, in *The Making of Egypt*, he returned to the same theme.

Speaking of the 'Falcon tribe' which he believe had conquered Egypt prior to the beginning of the First Dynasty, Petrie says:

> This falcon tribe had certainly originated in Elam, as indicated by the hero and lions on the 'Araq knife handle'. They went down the Persian Gulf and settled in 'the horn of Africa'. There they named the 'Land of Punt', sacred to later Egyptians as the source of the race. The Pun people founded the island fortress of Ha-fun which commands the whole of that coast, and hence came the Punic or Phenic peoples of classic antiquity.
>
> Those who went up the Red Sea formed the dynastic invaders of Egypt entering by the Qoceir-Koptos road. Others went on to Syria and founded Tyre, Sidon and Aradus, named after their home islands in the Persian Gulf.[10]

The third quotation is separated from the earlier ones by some twenty-odd years; in between them Petrie was responsible for sending Ernest Mackay to Bahrain, to review the grave mounds. No hint of the Master's concern for Sumero-Egyptian origins, however, appears in Mackay's rather staid report.[11]

Petrie, it will be observed, speaks of the prospect of Gulf as well as Elamite influences being present in pre-dynastic Egypt with considerable assurance, which might indeed be taken for an expression of certainty. What is not clear is why he considered that the Gulf islands were involved at all, though earlier nineteenth century commentators seem often to have believed that the Egyptians and the Sumerians had either a common origin or were influenced in their formative periods by some other, third party. Evidently Petrie saw the people of the Gulf islands as fulfilling this role.

Another scholar, of a time slightly earlier than that in which Petrie was writing, who toyed with the idea that Bahrain might have had some special, insular significance to the Egyptians was Cecil H. Smith of the British Museum. In a discussion following the presentation of a paper by Theodore Bent to the Royal Geographical Society on his visit to Bahrain in 1889, Smith suggested that 'To Nefer', the Egyptian name for the land of Punt, one of the most frequent loci cited in later times as the home of the gods, might in fact mean 'the holy island'.[12] Earlier still, in the first scholarly analysis of ancient Dilmun in modern times, Rawlinson in his commentary on Durand's report 'On the Antiquity of the Bahrain Islands' in 1880 observed that 'Tilmun' might convey the meaning 'The Blessed Isle'.[13]

Baumgartel, who analyzed the predynastic period exhaustively, believed that the 'original home of the Naqada II people' was not far distant from that of the Sumerians.[14] She also suggested that the late predynastic kings were descended from the Naqada II people.

From the very earliest times the Egyptians seem to have maintained the idea that many of the beliefs and events which characterized their 'culture' – to employ a term which of course they would not have recognized – had their origins, in their pristine form, in a far distant island. One of the most frequent symbols for the first land to emerge at the creation is the Primaeval Hill or Mound. This is sometimes explicitly insular in character: thus in the Pyramid Texts Utterance 484 speaks of 'the Primaeval Hill in the midst of the sea'.[15] The land here is specifically a sea-girt island and not a hillock of mud revealed by the withdrawal of the waters of the inundation which has so often been described by Egyptologists as the first land to appear at the Creation. The primaeval place was the Island of Rest, or Peace.[16]

The Island of Peace was associated with the Rising Sun, in which capacity it was 'the Island of Flame'.[17] It was the Divine Emerging Island which appeared from the Abyss of primaeval waters, personified as *Nun*, the oldest of the gods, according to some theologies.[18] In this context the primaeval hill sometimes was called Ta-Tanen;[19] Tanen was the god of the Primaeval Mound in Memphite theology and is clearly a precursor of Ptah. From the Island of Flame (or Fire) came, in the very beginning, *Hike*[20] the personification of the vital essence which to the Egyptians was the basis of life. The island was a magical place far distant to the east beyond the limits of the world, a place of everlasting light where the gods were born. As King Pepi remarks 'I go up this eastern side of the sky where the gods were born' (PT Utterance 264).[21] In the great incantation which forms Utterances 273/4, in which the deified King leaps into Heaven and consumes the other gods in a celestial cannibal rite, the text proclaims the magical nature of the Island of Fire:

> The King is the Bull of the Sky,
> who conquers at will,
> who lives on the being of every god,
> who eats their entrails
> Even of those who come with their bodies full of magic
> From the Island of Fire.[22]

The gods are said 'to give an island' to the justified Osiris and Egyptian legend spoke of 'Middle Island',[23] an unknown, distant locality which was reached only by the boat of Anty, the Ferryman, who carried passengers to the island like Sursunabi, Ziusudra's ferryman, who carried Gilgamesh to Dilmun.[24] Anty plays a somewhat equivocal role in the dispute of Horus and Seth for when the tribunal hearing the evidence of the two gods' contention decides to remove its hearings to a remote and distant island, Anty the ferryman is instructed not to provide Isis with a passage to the island. The goddess bribes Anty however and, by a deplorable piece of trickery, secures the verdict in favour of her son, Horus, at the expense of Seth. Seth incidentally was Lord of Asia and particularly of lands to the east of Egypt.[25]

One of Horus' titles is 'Horus of the Land of Sunrise'.[26] He is often saluted as Horus of the Horizon (Harakhte) in which, according to Frankfort, the horizon signifies the land of light, the mountains to the east of Egypt, at the eastern edge of the earth.[27]

There were many ferrymen who feature in the Pyramid Texts; various of them are associated with regions to the east. Thus Utterance 359 observes:

> O Re, commend me to the ferryman of the Winding Waterway, so that he may bring me his ferryboat . . . in which he ferries the gods . . . to the eastern side of the sky.[28]

The island was repeatedly identified as a place of reeds;[29] the land there was marshy. One of its names, as we learn from the Book of the Dead, was the Field of Reeds of the Blessed. This, too, is said to be located on the eastern edge of the world.[30] Both the Egyptians and the Sumerians sustained the most affectionate memories of their earliest shrines or temples, which were built of reeds. Thus, the Edfu temple, in its innermost recesses reproduces the archetypal reed shrine in stone;[31] the Sumerians, on the other hand, immortalized in their poetry Ziusudra's reed hut, to the walls of which Enki whispered the warning of the Deluge to come.[32] Enki's most ancient shrine at Eridu probably recalled a reed-built prototype.[33]

At the creation, according to the Edfu inscriptions, the creator spirits brought into existence a number of sacred places of which the first two were 'the Mound of the Radiant One' and 'the Island of Re'.[34] Others included the High Hill, the Oil-Tree and the Place of Ghosts.[35]

The land contiguous to the original island was called *Wetjeset-Neter*.[36] Other names by which the island was known in the beginning, as well as the Island of Peace, were the Island of Trampling and the Island of Combat.[37] The island first lay in darkness surrounded by the primaeval waters called *Wa'ret*.[38] Its original inhabitants and sovereigns were Falcons.[39] Horus is, of course, the supreme Egyptian Falcon, the same Horus who was saluted as Lord of the Land of Sunrise.

Adjacent to the *Wa'ret* were several sacred places: the *pay-lands*.[40] These included the Island of Fury.[41] The island was the site of the archetypal temple and is to be recognized as the Homeland of the Early Primaeval Ones.[42]

According to the Hermopolitan myths the Sun-God himself was born in a pool which existed on the primaeval island.[43] In the Edfu texts the island itself is called the *Pool which came into existence at the Beginning*.[44] The island was the nucleus of the world. The gods who emerged in this period were the Most Aged Ones of the Primaeval Time.[45] The pool stood on the edge of the island; it was surrounded by reeds.[46] The island was known to be the realm of the Falcons.

It seems that the island was associated with the idea of the death of an early generation or company of the gods; the gods were killed, it appears, in some form of battle.[47] The island may have become their tomb.[48] The falcons who were the island's original rulers became associated with its funerary customs, thus recalling the early generation of gods who met their deaths there.[49] The idea of islands as numinous places and their funerary nature seem thus singularly ancient.

The lands in the vicinity of the island were known, as we have seen, as *pay*-lands. The Creator brought them into existence by drying up the water around his place of origin and so exposing the land.[50] He went on to create the world.

Then the Creator, who is now revealed as Tanen, together with the Falcon, seems to have made a journey through the *Wa'ret* which took in some of the *pay*-lands.[51] They appear to have set out on their journey from the island.[52]

The island is the place of the Ancestors.[53] In the Edfu tradition the Ancestors came from places far distant from Edfu itself, which is concerned to present itself as the home of the Egyptian people.[54] Indeed, the assumption of such Ancestor gods as their own was part of Edfu's campaign in asserting its claim to be recognized as the Egyptian homeland.

The original temple of the Falcon is recognized as originating in the Blessed Island of the Child.[55] The temple itself is identified with the primaeval sacred mound, the Divine Emerging Island. The Primaeval Mound is, as we have seen, identical with the Pure Land, one of the most frequently employed epithets of Dilmun.[56]

I cannot resist drawing attention to one other curious parallel, or coincidence, if you prefer it. One of the most frequently repeated glyphs in the iconography of, for example, the Gulf seals is the foot or footprint, a symbol which indeed also appears in Mesopotamia in the earliest times.[57] In Egypt, by contrast with Mesopotamia and the Gulf, the hieroglyph which represents the foot is shown in profile; it means 'place' or 'position' and also represents the consonant 'b'.[58] However there is a special usage of the hieroglyph in the Pyramid Texts (though employed very rarely, according to Gardiner) where it appears as a compound.[59] The compound consists of the foot with a jar from which water is pouring. The meaning here, according to Gardiner, is 'Pure', 'Clean', as in Utterance 513.

'Be pure: occupy your seat in the Bark of Re: row over the sky and mount up to the distant ones: row with the imperishable stars, navigate with the Unwearying Stars'.[60]

One of Enki's shrines is described as 'the clean place'.[61]

The associations of the foot, water, the meanings 'place' and 'pure' and the idea of distant journeying (albeit to the far-off stars) is compelling, at least to one who started out on this voyage through the Egyptians' perceptions of their island connections.

It will be said, perhaps with reason, that I am making a Cosmic Mountain out of a Primaeval Molehill. The archaeological evidence to supplement my textual references is slim enough, that I readily admit.

But the study of early Gulf cultures, in which Bahrain-Dilmun plays so essential a role, will, I have no doubt, produce evidence in years to come which will bear upon these issues. It may even be that the common denominator between the Sumerians and the Egyptians will prove to be the people who became the Dilmunites. I suspect that the texts' concern with the *pay*-lands, the process of their drying up, the wanderings of Tanen and the Falcon and the repetition of the island motif might represent the memory of a disturbed and precarious period in the people's history, when they were living perhaps around the perimeter of the al-Rub al-Khali or in its vicinity. We know that late neolithic populations flourished there and that lacustrine conditions persisted well into late prehistoric times around the edges of what is now the Empty Quarter.[62]

Whilst, as several scholars have suggested, the Mesopotamian mace may have played a part in the eventual conquest of the Two Lands by the Falcon princes from This in Upper Egypt, there is no evidence for an invasion or anything like it in the period immediately before the Unification.[63] In the light of later history it seems more likely that what Mesopotamian influences there are in Egypt and, perhaps, what recollections there may be of the Primaeval Island in the Egyptian consciousness, were implanted by relatively small bands of men, traders perhaps or refugees from a dying environment, or, conceivably, both. It probably only needed one of them to be an exceptionally accomplished and persuasive raconteur for his stories of life in the far distant land of the sunrise to make a profound, even a lasting impression, on his hearers, particularly if his audience were the able chief of a lively congeries of tribes and his close associates.

Finally, the mention of the power of story-telling prompts the recollection of the Enchanted Island, of which the Shipwrecked Sailor told so marvellous a tale.[64] He had been voyaging to the mines (where were those mines located, one asks, that he had to sail to them?) when a storm destroyed his ship and, alone of his companions, he was cast up on the shores of a lonely island. There he was most graciously received by the island's divinity, a human-headed serpent of a notably kindly disposition, who was bedecked in gold and lapis lazuli. The serpent-king introduced himself as one of the rulers of Punt. This is, so far as I am aware, the only occasion when Punt is identified as an island. The serpent-king declined the offer of the sacrifice of asses, which, rather surprisingly, the sailor proposed to him. Well he might refuse it, if Punt proved to be located in East Arabia, for the asses of the Hasa province have long been celebrated.

When the sailor eventually left the island he was loaded with treasures by the generous serpent. To anyone familiar with Dilmun's customary merchandise the gifts make interesting reading for they are all products for which the island's trade was later celebrated:[65] perfumes, ivory, rare woods and, very strikingly, baboons, though what an Egyptian was to do with such animals in which his own land abounded is not clear. The sailor was also presented with hunting dogs. This too is interesting in the Anubis, who, in certain of his manifestations was undoubtedly a hound, is proclaimed as 'Anubis who presided over the Pure Land' (PT.U 437).[66] Since Anubis is a god of the dead, in several forms, this utterance seems to link a funerary divinity with the Pure Land of myth. The serpent-king returned the sailor safely to the Residence of the King of Egypt, which he reached after *a sea-voyage of two months*. Even in the Middle Kingdom, when this engaging story was first written down, magical islands in far-away seas still exercised a fascination for the Egyptians.

Though the picture is still as misty as ever, I believe there may be some points emerging on that distant eastern horizon which may repay further consideration. It would be foolish indeed to assert that *all* references to islands in Egyptian religious or mythological texts must refer to Dilmun. Indeed I do not suggest that any are precise references nor that the island did not exist in the dimension of myth more often than being fixed anywhere on the earth's surface: rather I suggest that the recollection of a sacred island, which may have become Dilmun, was a direct inheritance or was handed on to the Egyptians by a third party. Then it was conflated with the natural tendency of a riverine people to think in terms of the great waters of their river withdrawing to reveal an island at the beginning of the sequence of creation.

I may be piling fantasy upon speculation but it seems to me difficult to identify any island with a reputation for special sanctity, of great significance as burial place, lying far away to the east of Egypt which so precisely matches the required topography as does Bahrain. If Bahrain is Dilmun, as most of us will recognize, the Sacred Pure Land of later Sumerian myth, then Bahrain's topography, its central mountain, pool, reed lined shores and proximity to Arabia's sabkha may be more than merely suggestive in the context of the earliest Egyptian mythologies and, perhaps, of something more than myth.

1. Rice, Michael, 'The Wilder Shores of Dilmun' 3rd Conference in Asian Archaeology, Bahrain 1970, unpublished.

2. Faulkner, R. Q., *The Ancient Egyptian Pyramid Texts*, Oxford, 1969.

3. Reymond, E. A., *The Mythical Origin of the Egyptian Temple*, Manchester University Press, 1969.

4. Reymond, *op. cit.*

5. Pritchard, J. B. ed., *Ancient Near Eastern Texts*, Princeton, 1955, 'The Deluge'.

6. Pritchard, J. B., *op. cit.* 'Enki and Ninhursaq'.

7. *Ibid.*

8. Petrie, W. F., *Ancient Egypt*.

9. Petrie, W. F., *Ancient Egypt*.

10. Petrie, W. F., *The Making of Egypt*, 1939.

11. Mackay, E., 'Bahrain and Hammamiyeh', *British School of Archaeology in Egypt*, Vol. 47, London, 1929.

12. Smith, Cecil H. in J. T. Bent, 'The Bahrain Islands in the Persian Gulf', *Proceedings of the Royal Geographical Society*, Vol. 12, 1890.

13. Rawlinson, H. C. in Durand E. L., 'Island and Antiquities of Bahrain', *Journal of the Royal Asiatic Society*, Vol. XII.

14. Baumgartel, E. J., *The Cultures of Prehistoric Egypt*, Vol. II, Oxford, 1960.

15. Faulkner, *op. cit.*

16. Reymond, *op. cit.*

17. *Ibid.*

18. Rundle Clark, R. T., *Myth and Symbol in Ancient Egypt*, New York, 1959.

19. *Ibid.*

20. *Ibid.*

21. Faulkner, *op. cit.*

22. *Ibid.*

23. Rundle Clark, *op. cit.*

24. Pritchard, *op. cit.*, 'The Epic of Gilgamesh' Old Babylonian version.

25. Te Velde, H. *Seth, God of Confusion*, Brill, Leyden, 1977.

26. Frankfort *Kingship and the Gods*, University of Chicago Press, 1948.

27. *Ibid.*

28. Faulkner, *op. cit.*

29. Rundle Clark, *op. cit.*

30. Kees, H., *Ancient Egypt A Cultural Topography*, Chicago, 1961.

31. Reymond, *op. cit.*

32. Pritchard, *op. cit.* 'The Deluge'.

33. Reymond, *op. cit.*

34–55. *Ibid.*

56. Kramer, S. N., *Sumerian Mythology*, New York, 1961.

57. Porada, 'Remarks on seals found in the Gulf States', *Artibus Asia*, Vol. XXXIII, 1971.

58. Gardiner, A. *Egyptian Grammar*, 3rd edition, Oxford.

59. *Ibid.*

60. Faulkner, *op. cit.*

61. Kramer, *op. cit.*

62. McClure, H. A., 'The Arabian Peninsula and Prehistoric Populations'. Field Research Projects, Coconut Grove, Miami, Florida, 1971.

63. *Cambridge Ancient History 1*, Part 1 'Prolegomena and Prehistory', Cambridge, 1970.

64. Erman, A., *The Literature of the Ancient Egyptians*, Methuen, 1927.

65. Leemans, W. F., *Foreign Trade in the Old Babylonian Period*, Brill, Leyden, 1960.

66. Faulkner, *op. cit.*

Burial mounds near Ali excavated by the Danish Expedition

KAREN FRIFELT

When the Danish Archaeological Expedition started work in Bahrain in December 1953 its first priority was not excavation of the grave-mounds. True, it was the number of the mounds – at that time on the basis of air photographs roughly calculated at 100,000 – that pro-voked the expedition. To quote from its first report: 'The presence of this enormous number of burial-mounds on an island which measures no more than thirty miles from north to south and only a third of this from east to west is one of the riddles of history, a riddle which was made more mysterious by the fact that not the slightest sign of prehistoric habitation had been found on the island. The solution had therefore been given that the numerous burial mounds showed that Bahrain had been used as a prehistoric burial island by the inhabitants of the Arabian mainland.'

The suggestion that Bahrain was a vast necropolis for the sur-rounding lands came from Ernest Mackay who in 1925–26 made a comprehensive investigation, opening thirty-four or thirty-five tumuli near the village of Ali, some of them among an outstanding group of about twenty, the 'Royal Tombs', up to 12 m high. He was, however, not the first to call attention to the island. In 1878–79 Captain Durand had opened one of the smaller and one of the largest mounds at Ali, and in 1889 Mr and Mrs Bent repeated this *modus operandi*, again at Ali. In 1903 the Belgian A. Jouannin made a short examination of one of the big Ali mounds, and in 1906–07 Colonel Prideaux tunnelled nine big Ali mounds besides about sixty of the smaller ones in the near surroundings. In 1940 P. B. Cornwall excavated thirty mounds, but he chose the southernmost group on the island, Umm Jidr, which had not been examined before, at least not in recent times. His graves, however, were not different from the other third millennium graves further north, as was noted by T. G. Bibby who visited the site a few years after Cornwall. All these qualified excavators had in due time produced reports. Some of their conclusions have proved wrong, but their observations are valuable. During the years also many of the smaller mounds had been opened by amateurs, while on one occasion two big Ali tumuli were examined by officers from the English ship Sphinx (in the late 1880s).

For the Danish expedition the main purpose was not looking for settlements that could explain the burial mounds, but to obtain comparative material – first and foremost pottery – and to get a firsthand knowledge of the construction. Five mounds were carefully chosen and excavated during the first campaign: two in a group west of Sar confirmed what was known from previous excavations, they were of the characteristic Bahrain type, one with a stone chamber and two side-chambers – alcoves – and the second one considerably larger with two-storied chambers and an entrance shaft, both good representatives of types used during the Barbar/Dilmun civilization. The three remaining mounds from this first campaign were different in appearance: wider and not so regularly circular. They were located in a group on the Manama-Budaia road, but as they dated to the Iron Age they do not concern us here, except to point out that this campaign already made it clear that the burials covered several periods, a point that has tended to be forgotten during later discussions on the origin of the enormous burial fields. The excavations were published in *Kuml* the following year.

Few mounds, apart from occasional rescue digs, were excavated during the following Danish campaigns, with one exception and that was partly a rescue operation. In the tumulus field south of Ali bulldozers were making serious inroads, and during the 1962–63 campaign it was decided to examine as many as possible before they disappeared. This was an extensive and planned project comprising some forty mounds.

In 1959–60 four mounds south of the Budaia road and two near Sar were excavated and a rescue dig was done on a mound north of the Budaia road at the turnoff for the Portuguese Fort. These seven graves belong to the Iron Age and have not yet been published. A rescue operation was also undertaken in 1959 at Buri where a bulldozer had opened a mound containing at least three stone graves. Only one was left for examination, with a skeleton in flexed position and a red ridged Barbar vessel. A similar mound at Umm Jidr was opened in 1965 by amateurs and finished by the Danish team. Here too was a skeleton *in situ* – flexed position – while the accompanying vessel, found in an alcove, was a red 'grave-vessel' with rounded bottom and ribbed neck. These two graves are mentioned in a brief note in *Kuml* 1966. During our winter campaign of 1961–62 two of the large mounds at Ali were examined as a sort of rescue dig since bulldozers had started quarrying around their edges. They were only partly excavated, but in both of them tunnels by previous disturbers were located. In one of these two black-on-red painted goblets and three small eggshell-thin red bowls had been left behind. The operation has been briefly mentioned in *Kuml* 1964.

In the 1960s amateurs were very active in the mound fields. I shall mention only the work of two of them – the opening of nearly fifty mounds from several different mound fields – because they have been published with descriptions, measurements and grave goods by Elisabeth During Caspers in 1980. In 1979 a group of French archaeologists, S. Cleuziou, P. Lombard and J.-F. Salles excavated five 'Barbar' mounds at Umm Jidr, these too have been published. Finally there is the large project started in 1977 by Bahrain's Department of Antiquities on the Sar burial field, one of the most extensive on the island. The causeway between Bahrain and Saudi Arabia that looked like a disaster for the burial mounds may have contributed immensely to their study. Many hundreds have been carefully excavated, and the first report has already been published by one of the excavators, Moawiyah Ibrahim.

And now to the mound field south of Ali and our campaign there, fig. 30. Two areas, about one kilometre apart, were chosen, the two excavated groups, A and B, numbering forty-one mounds. Group here means a selection of mounds within a smaller part of the dense mound field. Group A was located 3–400 m southeast of the southernmost of the large Ali mounds. Of the nineteen mounds excavated here a few had already been partly removed, while the rest were chosen because they appeared intact in an otherwise badly disturbed area. Except for maybe one or two they had, however, been broken into, possibly in prehistoric times, and at least partly plundered. The mounds were rather low, less than 2 m high, most of them in fact less than 1.50 m, but with a large diameter, generally about 10 m, but several of them considerably more, up to nearly 20 m. The burial chambers covered by sand and gravel were as a general rule built of large roughly cut blocks in three to six courses with smaller stones in between to tighten the walls. Most of the chambers were over 2 m long, never under 1.50 m, and many were easily 1 m wide and 1 m high. The orientation was approximately east-west, with entrance, if any, in the west end. All the chambers except one had alcoves, generally one or two at the east end, but in one case there were no less than four side-chambers, two at each end. They may have been used for gifts or provisions, but only in two of them was a pot found. Large capstones roofed the chamber, smaller ones the alcoves. The floor was on the limestone rock, though never dug into it, and fine sand or gravel had been scattered over it. In the chamber with four alcoves both floor and walls had been plastered. A ringwall at the foot of the mound was located in only one case – but I shall return to this question.

The remains of the dead were badly preserved, only in one

grave could it be ascertained that the body had been placed in a flexed position. It is, however, reasonably certain that no grave from the beginning was empty, usually a few human bones were found. In about half of the chambers animal bones were collected, and in the few cases where it has been possible to have them analyzed they have proved to be from goat, always young animals.

With the extensive disturbance and robbery of the tombs it is difficult to get a reliable picture of the gifts and their location in the chambers, but a certain uniformity is indicated. Most of the graves had contained copper/bronze though generally only scraps are preserved, but in one case a plain finger-ring and in another the point of a dagger or spearhead were collected. Ostrich eggshells were a common feature, they were always found shattered, but several had traces of ornamental painting. Small baskets coated with bitumen were apparently a regular component of the furnishings. Only pieces of bitumen with reed impressions were left, too small to attempt reconstruction, but by analogy with the Sar finds the conclusion may be permitted. The regular use of bitumen makes one speculate on its source. Was there a seepage known in Bahrain or possibly in the Eastern Province of Saudi Arabia or was it part of the trade with Southern Mesopotamia? At least three tombs had contained alabaster vessels, only one was complete, a small conical bowl. Three other graves had fragments of ivory, too small to identify their use. Two well-furnished burials had a 'seal' made of seashell, like a stamp seal of Dilmun type, with the natural spirals forming the obverse. On one of them a half-hearted attempt had been made to incise an unidentifiable figure among the spirals. Gold was found in only one tomb: a small link of four spirals. Otherwise jewellery was represented by no more than a carnelian bead or two left in some of the graves.

Pottery always accompanied the dead, and when it is missing in four of the chambers it is clearly due to disturbance. The 'grave-vessel' of fine buff or red ware with round base was present in most burials, fig. 31. One well provided tomb (with the gold link and an alabaster vessel) had four of them. It is the commonest form of pottery in the mounds, also outside the Ali field, but rarely found in the settlements. Five of the Barbar vessels with cream slip and built-in strainer were recovered, quite remarkable, since they have not often been found in graves, except for the 'Royal Tombs' of Ali. The type is not too frequent in the settlements either. It is known in the Barbar temple through several phases: Temple Ia and b and IIa, occasionally also later, but it was by no means ever common (personal communication from Peder Mortensen). Red-ridged Barbar vessels occur, but never the chain-ridge ware. One painted sherd from a large jar of fine well-fired orange ware with black festoons and a chequer pattern, fig. 32, has no parallels in Bahrain, but is at home

30 Air view of Ali among its gardens and south of the village part of the burial field with thousands of pinprick mounds. The two groups excavated during the Danish campaigns are indicated. The "enclosure" between the village and the Buri road is the site of the "Royal Tombs", but there are also several sizeable mounds south of the road. The two white dots indicate "Royal Tombs" partly excavated by Professor Glob (not included in this paper). – The photo is by courtesy of Bapco and was taken in 1952 before the devastation of the mounds became serious

31   Six "grave-jars": the three on
top come from Group A, the two
larger vessels from the same
grave; the ware is buff to light
orange and only the one on the left
shows traces of a red coating,
outside and inside of the neck. In
the bottom row vessels from
Group B: one jar of brick-red ware
and one buff with purple coating.
The squat jar with flat base is of
friable brown ware with purple
coating and is characteristic of the
Group B graves

32   Overseas import: sherd from
large vessel of orange ware with
black painting on cream slip,
known in the Indus culture, and
found in a Group A grave at Ali

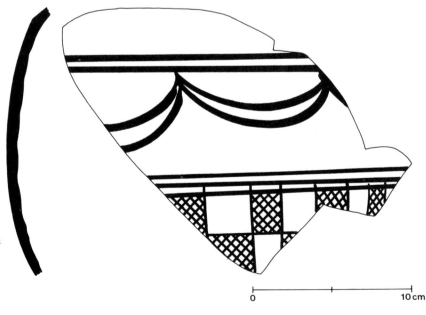

in the Harappa culture, known from several sites in the Indus valley, while a similar sherd is found in the Harappan levels at Balakot (personal communication from George Dales).

Though weapons, jewellery and other valuables had been picked out and removed by intruders before us enough was left to justify the name of rich graves for this group.

Group B was located about one kilometre southwest of the Group A graves. Between the two groups a wide area had been completely at the mercy of bulldozers that had razed to the ground all the mounds found there. A water pipeline crossing the field towards Ali had become the borderline for the devastation. East of that the plain was empty, while to the west the mounds had not been disturbed in modern times. Twenty-two tombs were excavated here, a fraction only of this dense mound field. They are more unassuming than those in the first group, not much lower perhaps, but the diameter is here only about 7 m or even less. The chamber was considerably less than 2 m long, built of medium to small, usually unfashioned blocks in three to four courses and covered with moderately sized capstones. As a general rule there were no alcoves, a few graves had one or even two, but hardly more than a niche. Here too the floor was the bedrock with sand or gravel scattered over it. Though on the whole more modest and more poorly constructed – some of the chambers had partly collapsed – these graves had the additional detail of a ringwall at the foot of the mound. One of our sections indicated that this wall had originally been visible after the completion of the mound, though it was now more or less covered with sand and gravel. The apparent lack of ringwall in the first group might be explained by the thick deposits that had here among the dense mounds washed down during the centuries, covered the old surface and the low surrounding wall and, incidentally, made the mounds appear lower than they were built, fig. 34.

It was obvious that for some reason the bones – both human and animal – were better preserved here. In two graves the dead was found in situ, in flexed position. The animal bones are probably from goat (they are presently being analyzed at the Smithsonian) and some show traces of burning. It is quite likely that the better preservation is due to less disturbance which again might be explained by the lack of valuables among the grave gifts. Yet some of the chambers had been broken into, and of course we cannot know what has been removed from them, but the overall impression is that these burials have always been poorly furnished. Only one among them had evidence of copper/bronze: small rodshaped pieces.

For the rest the gifts were restricted to pottery, and it was a modest selection, fig. 31. The 'grave-jar' with round bottom here usually had a grooved neck and a preference for purplish-red paint

33 Comparison between Dilmun grave ware and the Suq culture of Oman: Top left, jar of orange ware with red coating from Group A at Ali; top right, buff jar with cream slip and black lines from Wadi Suq. Bottom left, cup or goblet from Hamala North in Bahrain (after During Caspers 1980) of brick-red ware with plum-red decoration; bottom right, fragments of vessels of black-on-buff and black-on-red from the Suq culture

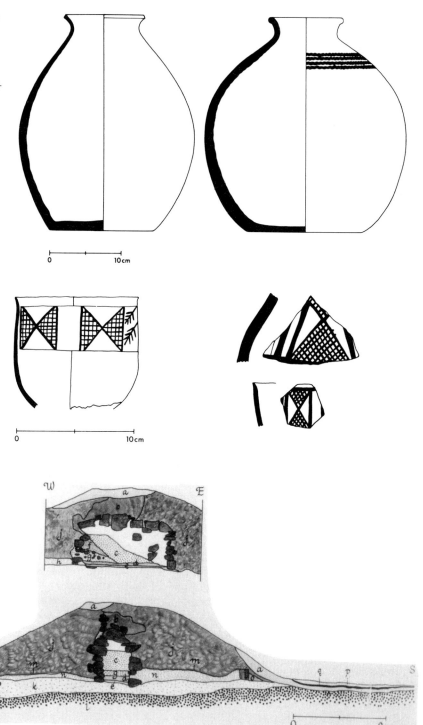

that covered the vessel all over, even the inside of the neck, but it was not so common in the burials here. A small squat jar of friable brown ware with flat base, rounded body, short neck and plain rim, often with a purple slip, is characteristic for this grave group. It is also known from the Sar excavations and from some of the graves examined by amateurs published by During Caspers, but not reported from the Qal'at al-Bahrain or from the Barbar temples.

The obvious difference between our two grave groups calls for an explanation. There are two, or rather three, possibilities: the difference may be chronological, it may be social – or both.

Let us take the rich Group A first, the one closest to the Ali 'Royal Tombs', not just in distance, but in contents as well: alabaster, ivory, carnelian, metal, ostrich eggshells, and among the pottery, strainers. Julian Reade in his study (1978) on the Ali Tombs suggests a dating to Isin-Larsa as likely for most of them. To this I can add that E. During Caspers' Hamala North tomb with its Ali affinities includes a small goblet of fine red ware with black cross-hatched butterfly motif which I believe I can match with one from the Suq-Sunaysl graves in Oman, dated by me (1975) to about 2000 B.C., fig. 33. When I was looking for comparative material for the Wadi Suq grave complex I became aware of the resemblance of some of the painted Barbar pottery – plum-red with black horizontal bands – as well as some of the potshapes to the Suq material. From the rich grave group (A) under discussion I shall draw attention to a large jar with rounded body and low centre of gravity, a form also known among the Suq pottery. The Harappan sherd from the same group of graves need not contradict a dating around 2000 B.C. and I would be inclined to date Group A a little earlier than the big Ali Tombs. To state my reasons for this I must turn to the report on the Sar burials by Moawiyah Ibrahim, published 1982.

Based on the construction Dr Ibrahim describes several grave types, one of them a 'mound with a single chamber built above surface' – to which the two groups here discussed belong. If I understand Dr Ibrahim rightly, he believes that his other types go back to this 'basic' form. In a more developed type the mound has a central burial connected with subsidiary burials each of which is surrounded by a more or less complete ringwall. This, according to Dr Ibrahim, is a transition to his 'Burial Complex', where apparently the mound has been abandoned and we have subterranean stone cists with ringwalls, often interconnected, the graves very close together. These have several things in common with the Wadi Suq graves: they are subterranean, have ringwalls, one end of the grave is often connected with the wall, and as already mentioned, there are also similarities in the grave goods, though steatite seals which in Bahrain are not

34 Long N.-S. and short E.-W. section through mound 46 in Group B at Ali

a Concentration of loose stones and earth, light brown

b Very loose stones and earth with plant roots, dark chocolate brown

c Extremely fine loose irregular particles, crystalline, light grey

d Compact brown clay with fragments of human bones

e Coarse sand and gravel with dark brown fragments of animal bones, some burnt

f Coarse aggregated particles of sand and gypsum with small stones, sloping E

g Very loose stones and gravel with bone fragments at the bottom

h Fine brown sand

j Brownish-grey coarse sand and gravel with gypsum formation obscuring details

k Brown-white gypsum and large stones (destruction of level 1)

l Limestone rock

m Lower limit of coarse gravel

n Medium light brown sand and stones

o Fine compact brownish sand and gravel without gypsum

p Very fine compact greybrown clay

q Dark brown aggregated loam

Interpretation: a at the foot of the mound is washed-down clay, while b is the filled-up robbers' hole and g may be a disturbed layer from the same intrusion, c and f are deposits from the slow destruction of the limestone blocks, o is an accumulation behind the ringwall suggesting that its stones originally were visible at the foot of the mound, m is the old surface while p is material recently deposited by water, and q indicates an old growth of grass; d and e are old deposits that have filtered through the walls and covered the burial.

uncommon in the Burial Complex have not been found in the few Wadi Suq graves excavated so far.

It looks now as if we shall end by having all the Barbar/Dilmun graves crowding each other around the beginning of the second millennium B.C., and the old suggestion of Bahrain as a necropolis for the surrounding countries, including Mesopotamia, has recently been voiced again. I do not, however, think there is any support for this idea in the burials or their equipment. To sum up my own views on the chronological question: accepting the Ali 'Royal Tombs' as Isin-Larsa, the Burial Complex from Sar might be the graves of the common people from the same period, while my Group A with the rich graves would be slightly older, possibly within the period of Ur III. My Group B with the poorer graves might be still earlier, and this I base partly on the squat brown jar and partly on the purple paint neither of which, as far as I am aware, is known from the other grave groups mentioned above. The type with a single chamber under mound (with or without alcoves) seems to account for the main part of the mounds in Bahrain, but may, as Dr Ibrahim points out, have continued side by side with the developed forms. Whether it accounts also for the burials from Bibby's City 1 remains a question – at least the chain-ridge ware so characteristic of that period has not been found in any of the known graves.

These views which agree in the main with the chronology proposed by my colleagues from Moesgård are suggestions only and future investigations may alter the picture. It is unlikely that Bahrain should not have been occupied all through the third millennium and even earlier (Ubaid pottery has been found), though the principal sites may during the older period have been located on the mainland, in the Eastern Province of Saudi Arabia. However, in connection with City 1 on the Qal'a Umm an-Nar pottery was found, closely similar to that known in the Oman peninsula about the mid-third millennium. And recently the Department of Antiquities under Shaikha Haya al Khalifa in its continuing excavations of mounds has turned up pottery of the Umm an-Nar type, while third millennium graves different from the known Dilmun graves have come to light. Bahrain has used an anniversary in its recent history to take stock also of its prehistory – there is no doubt that both are growing.

Author's Note. – The examination of the Ali mounds was begun by P. V. Glob and carried on by Peter Crabb and Grith Lerche to whom I am indebted for plans and information.
The drawings are by Elsebeth Morville and Orla Svendsen.

Dilmun – A trading entrepôt: evidence from historical and archaeological sources

GERD WEISGERBER

Dilmun's role as a trading station in an international network of trade in the third millenium B.C. is generally recognized.[1] Trading partners have been identified as Makkan and Meluḫḫa, the present-day Oman Peninsula and cultures in the Indus Valley. This interpretation is gaining acceptance and in the course of the following article will be considered the basis of further discussion.

The article will show that the position of Dilmun should be reconsidered in the light of recent archaeological discoveries and interpretation of historical sources. How should the term 'trading emporium' be defined? Is it simply a flourishing market and transfer point? Is it a market for quality goods, existing at a time when such markets were not free ports – as we known for Sumer? Long-distance trade was controlled by the temples and ruling authorities; according to the level of culture pertaining, equally bureaucratic. However, it is exactly this bureaucracy which we have to thank for the historical records regarding Dilmun's long-distance trading activities.

Long-distance trade has been repeatedly viewed in the last decades from the viewpoints of archaeology[2], history[3] and anthropology[4]. Each of these aspects can be differently weighted in importance or viewed in combination with each other. Here I have chosen the archaeo-historical aspect, which reflects the state of source materials. Two examples are given, which illustrate the theme of the paper.

The island of Dahlak is situated in the southern Red Sea, lying off the coast of Eritrea and the harbour city Massaua.[5] Dahlak is the largest island of a coral archipelago; the surface is bare of vegetation other than a single stand of acacia trees in a basin. Although the island has an area of 750 km^2, there is no water available other than that provided by the sparse rains. Earlier inhabitants made their living through pearl-diving and turtle fishing; today the island is virtually uninhabited. In earlier periods, this barren island played an important role in overseas trade, due to its geographical location in the Red Sea. Ruins of a large settlement (town?) and six large grave-fields with inscriptions in Kufi and Nashi lettering attest to this previous important role. The remains date from 327 H/939 A.D. to H/1235 A.D. with a peak in the fourth and fifth centuries – (1000–1200 A.D.). The number of inscriptions has parallels in such grave-fields as Assuan or Cairo; at the height of its prosperity Dahlak was an independent sultanate. Historical records do not exist and no archaeological studies have been carried out up to now; epigraphic data provides the actual calendar periods referred to above. Although little is known about Dahlak, there can only be one explanation of the economic basis for settlement – control of shipping in the Red Sea. Whether this control was carried out as an independent sultanate, or under the jurisdiction of Asmara, is a question which may never be clearly answered. Another aspect is which of the shipping lanes were controlled – the North-South and South-North traffic, or traffic between Eritrea and Yemen. Whatever the case, the town's inhabitants were prosperous enough to be able to afford inscribed gravestones, made of imported solid stone, although the water supply was provided only by rain-water cisterns. The profits were more likely the takings from customs duties and tariffs of the shipping trade than peacefully gained proceeds from market trading.

Dahlak is an interesting example of profiting from an advantageous geo-strategic situation; and an example of how quickly an attained standing is reduced to nought.

One of the most fascinating examples of long-distance trade is the silk trade between China and the Western World.[6] Almost everything known about the subject is based on written sources. Roman materials contain reports on the regular traffic to India and Sera (China) from the early first century B.C. on.

At the end of the second century B.C. silk was first introduced to Persia; during the Parthian Wars the Romans became acquainted with this Persian silk, as the Silk Road continued up to Palmyra in Syria. Enormous quantities of the costly material flowed into the Roman Imperium, as long as China reigned over the Western Countries (East Turkestan) – up to 1 A.D.. During the seventy-five years interregnum alternative routes were searched out; a southern route ran to India and in the interregnum some one hundred and twenty Roman ships sailed yearly to Indian ports. Arikamedu is a well-known harbour on India's East Coast, with large amounts of Roman Arretine pottery.[7] This fact documents Lamberg-Karlovsky's 'Central Place Trade' theory. Enforced longer periods of stoppage, due to waiting for the monsoon winds, led to many Roman sailors and traders remaining in India. Numerous Roman finds are known between India and China; on the other hand, Indian finds in the Roman Western World have the character of occasional 'souvenirs'. Trade goods – for which all these adventurous voyages were made – can no longer be archaeologically determined.

Roman ships sailed directly to China in 166, 226 and 284 A.D. However, the number of Roman finds in Eastern Asia in this period are few; they increase beginning with the fourth century. Trading expeditions were frequently carried out by Byzantines and Sassanids. However, the only permanent remaining traces are gold coins in oases in Mongolia and Northern China. Without the evidence given by the coins a long period of trade along the Silk Road would not be documented. The coins also indicate that there were periods in which the northern land route between east and west Asia was preferred – or perhaps was indeed the only route open to traffic.

One thing can be determined regarding the silk trade over land routes: the Chinese exporters never made contact with the final buyers. The farthest point reached by a Chinese ambassador, Can Ying, was probably the Iranian Coast. Here he was detained by the Parthians. Usually the silk was passed on to the Bactrians in Pamir. Other than silk, no other East Asian trade goods arrived in the West. The direct and frequent contacts of Western seafarers do not seem to have led to trade in other articles than silk with the West. As previously mentioned, Roman seafarers left many traces of their presence in India and China.

Relating to the problem here discussed, this fact is of basic importance; whatever prevailing conditions may have been, Roman seamen left cultural remains in trans-shipping and final ports, attesting their physical presence. On the other hand, only silk – out of all other possible trade goods – seems to have been transported back to home ports in the West, with the exception of some few souvenirs.

In the order of reference Dilmun, Makkan, Meluḫḫa, are known on many cuneiform tablets from the middle of the third millenium B.C. Their fluctuating importance for providing Mesopotamia's raw materials has been discussed by various authors.[8] This standard view can be differentiated; among other aspects, archaeology in the Gulf and East Arabian areas has made much progess in the last decade, throwing new light on conditions prevailing.

Around 2500 B.C. Dilmun is first referred to as a supplier of wood, by Urnanshe, King of Lagaš.[9] His successors, Lugalanda and Uri'inimgina (before 2350 B.C.) dispensed various textiles, resins, oil and silver out of the state storehouses to merchants of Lagas. The merchants were to trade the goods in Dilmun for copper and other wares, such as onions, linen, resin and bronze 'marine spoons'. It is known that at this time single ships sailed from Elam to Lagas; the written sources would however imply that Mesopotamian merchants carried out overseas trade with Dilmun, or indeed, may even have been the original initiators of such trading systems.

During the succeeding Old Akkadian Period (2334–2193 B.C.) the Mesopotamians were no longer the only traders to visit Dilmun. The seas were open to all countries and seafaring merchants from the distant lands of Dilmun, Meluḫḫa and Makkan tied up at Akkad's quay, during Sargon's reign (2334–2279 B.C.). Copper was shipped directly from Makkan; people from Meluḫḫa are mentioned in written sources as interpreters and seamen. During the reign of Gudea of Lagaš, copper, diorite and wood were delivered from Makkan and Meluḫḫa delivered rare woods, gold, tin, lapis lazuli and carnelian to Lagaš. Naramsin warred against Makkan; Mesopotamia strove for predominance in the area.

The Ur tablets (Ur III Period, 2112–2004 B.C.) testify that the Gulf was no longer an open sea. Ships travelled to and from Ur and Makkan, bringing produce from Makkan – onions, goats, oil, wood, reed and copper. Dilmun is now scarcely used as a port of call. During trips to Makkan, obviously products of Meluḫḫa were loaded: some copper and mainly rare woods, such as Sisso wood. There are no records indicating that ships from Meluḫḫa docked in Sumer, or that Sumerian seafarers were themselves in Meluḫḫa.[10] Ships from Makkan did not sail to the north. It appears that one or more trading centers in Makkan were visited during the voyages where Makkan wares – chiefly copper – and luxury items from Meluḫḫa were bartered. Therefore it appears that many wares referred to in the written sources as 'Makkan goods', actually were materials originally brought from Meluḫḫa. Through trans-shipment in Makkan, these goods were then later referred to as coming from Makkan; the same confusion occurs later with materials from Dilmun. It is important to stress this point of confusion, as older discussions of trade-routes and the location of Makkan based their conclusions on the fact that Sisso wood was presumed to come from the Makran coast and Meluḫḫa. Even at present, the trading center used by the Sumerian merchants in Makkan – where goods from Makkan and Meluḫḫa were bartered – is not known. A cogent premise for the location of such a port – or landing place – would be a site on the southern Gulf Coast in the United Arabian Emirates. The period of Sumerian sea traffic to Makkan covers approximately one hundred years, so that it is difficult to estimate what kind of archaeological remains could be found or expected.

At the end of the Ur III Period, in the reign of Ibbisin (2028–2004 B.C.), the point of interest changed again and his ships dropped anchor at Dilmun.

It is clear that the merchants sailing to Makkan also visited Dilmun, probably to obtain fresh water. About 2000 B.C. (Old Babylonian Period, 2017–1712 B.C.), the inhabitants of Dilmun had apparently been able to utilize their strategic position on the sea lanes. The island rose from a simple refuelling station to a merchant power, controlling the sea traffic in the Gulf. The island Failaka in the north was taken over as part of the control network. 'Control' should be understood as meaning that no Sumerian merchants could sail directly to Makkan, as they had done in the previous ʿcentury. Merchants from Makkan and Meluḫḫa could no longer sail directly to Sumer, without stopping at Dilmun. It seems as if Dilmun had taken over the function of an emporium; merchants coming from the south-east had to unload their wares at Dilmun. Dilmun's merchants then transferred these to traders from the north; the lucrative transit trade was completely in the hands of Dilmun's merchants. Of course contacts between people of Mesopotamia and Makkan and Meluḫḫa staying in Dilmun were taken up; the Dilmun traders however were sure to secure their part of transit profits. The wares themselves from the south and ('invisible wares' of the) north remained the same; however more ivory and tortoiseshell was exported to Sumer.

This period was the height of Dilmun's prosperity; wares from various cultures were traded on the island. Both the goods and the foreign merchants trading in Dilmun's markets influenced forms of trade. The cuneiform characters had been taken over from the Sumerians, but the system of weights used in barter derived from the Indus Valley culture.[11] Spreading out from Dilmun, this system of weights became very popular and was used as far away as Ebla in Syria. Merchants are pragmatists and each exchange leads to profit.

Dilmun is mentioned for the last time in written records, during the reign of Samsu'liluma in the year 1744 B.C., with the entry . . . '12 measures of purified copper from Alasia and Dilmun'. With this notice, the new supplier of copper is also mentioned; Alasia (Cyprus) would control the Mediterranean and Near Eastern market for copper for the next millennium. Alasia's rise did not occur in isolation; obviously a lengthy series of crises led to the collapse of the existing system in the East. Unlike Dahlak, Dilmun did not cease to exist; Tukulti-Ninurta refers to himself as 'King of the Upper and Lower Seas' and ruler over Dilmun and Meluḫḫa. However, Meluḫḫa and Makkan are no longer referred to in written records in the old sense.

Do the events in the Gulf reflect experience, such as those illustrated at the beginning of this report for Dahlak and the Silk Road? The answer seems to be 'Yes'; just as on the island of Dahlak, the inhabitants of Dilmun seemed to have taken advantage of their favourable geographic situation. At a time when it was possible to make use of a political situation the Dilmun merchants developed a power base for their own profit within a network of international trade relations. As in the case of Dahlak, such a position was very sensitive to changes in political and economic conditions, leading to the relapse of Dilmun into a subordinate role. In Dilmun/Bahrain the natural living conditions were so propitious that both before and after the rise to power larger settlements continued to exist.

Drawing conclusions from the history of trading silk over sea-routes, where cultural remains of the peoples involved in trading can be found at the market settlements, the question arises: is this the case for Dilmun/Bahrain?

Text analysis showed that direct trade contacts between Makkan and Meluḫḫa and Sumer existed from the middle of the third millennium. These contacts were broken by the rapid rise of Dilmun to a monopoly trade center. As a consequence, there should be relatively few physical remains of the Makkan and Meluḫḫa merchants in Mesopotamia. The physical geography of Mesopotamia has also changed considerably since ancient times – the coast has continually been built up into the Gulf and rivers have changed their courses. From the viewpoint of archaeology it can be stated that often no cognizance was taken during earlier excavations of the existence of a few 'unusual' sherds. It is therefore not surprising that few remains bear witness to the presence of foreign merchants on Mesopotamian soil. The actual wares traded have long since vanished, or been re-worked, or – as in the case of lapis lazuli – cannot be directly ascribed to sea-trade. Only the written sources tell us about the existence of foreigners in Mesopotamia: 'interpreters from Meluḫḫa', 'Meluḫḫa village'.[12]

The period in Eastern Arabia in which Makkan rose to a position of main trading area for a large assortment of wares is better documented. The people from the East – Meluḫḫa – and from the North – Sumer – dropped anchor in Makkan. Sumerian remains are few in number, due to the 'invisible goods' (which leave no material archaeological traces). Additionally the Sumerian sailors did not have to wait for the monsoon winds in order to return to home ports, so that their stay in Makkan would not be as long as that of the merchants and seamen of Meluḫḫa. More recent archaeological researches in East Arabia have brought to light many finds which are related to the presence of Indus valley people. In the settlements of Hili 8[13] and Maysar-1,[14] both of which have been investigated, Indus Valley pottery is frequently found. Seals with Indus Valley script and typical iconography[15] indicate influences in Makkan down to the level of business organization. Marks identifying pottery in Makkan were taken from those used in the Indus Valley, including the use of the signs on pottery used in the Indus Valley.[16] The discovery of a seaport – which may be ascribed to the Harappans – at Ra's al-Junayz on Oman's East Coast by an Italian Expedition[17] would seem to indicate that trade routes should be viewed in a more differentiated fashion than has been done up to now.

It should be presumed that several routes existed: in addition to the route through the Straits of Hormuz, with landings at the (politically acceptable) ports, it can also be postulated that landings were made on the East Coast of Oman and further transport of goods carried out overland to the northern Coast. This route would explain the large number of Harappan remains in the Oman Interior Basin area. Whether it is better, in the sense of marine navigation, to land first on the Arabian East Coast and later to sail through the Straits of Hormuz, is a question which can be answered by those having a knowledge of prehistoric seafaring.

Although Meluḫḫa and Makkan disappear from Mesopotamian written records from the late second millennium, the archaeological records testify to the existence of both peoples and their connections as far as Dilmun. The finds have not yet been exactly correlated with specific trade periods. However it is clear that such finds do document these connections at the beginning of the second millennium, as proved by the find at Ras al-Junayz and the seals discovered at Maysar-1 (Oman) and Al-Hajjar (Bahrain). With the end of Harappan culture, the Western Countries are no longer ports of call;[18] Makkan lost contact with the East and the islands of the north. The period of cultural and economic climax, which was supported by people of the Indus Valley, declined in Makkan and Bahrain. The simultaneous redirecting toward the West, for example copper provided by Alasia in Cyprus, led to Makkan being shut off from Mesopotamia's development for almost the next one thousand five hundred years. Contacts and influences prevailed however in Bahrain, as this island lies in the sphere of influence of Mesopotamia. Bahrain would nevertheless never again control the Gulf in later periods.

1. For general information see Geoffrey Bibby, *Looking for Dilmun*, London, 1970; James D. Muhly, Copper and Tin, *Transactions of the Connecticut Academy of Arts and Sciences*, New Haven, Connecticut, vol. 43, 1973, p. 155–535 and 46 1976, 77–136.

2. Carl C. Lamberg-Karlovsky, 'Trade mechanisms in Indus-Mesopotamian inter-relations', *Journal of the American Oriental Society*, vol. 92, 1972, 222–229; M. E. L. Mallowan, 'The mechanics of ancient trade in western Asia, Reflections on the location of Magan and Meluhha', *Iran*, 3, 1965, 1–8.

3. Gerd G. Koenig, 'Frahbyzantinische und sassanidische Munzen in China, Geld aus China', Führer des Rheinischen Landesmuseums Bonn Nr. 108, Köln 1982; A. L. Oppenheim, 'The Seafaring Merchants of Ur', *Journal of the American Oriental Society*, vol. 74, 6–17.

4. Reviewed by R. C. McAdams, 'Anthropological Perspectives on Ancient Trade', *Current Anthropology*, vol. 15, 1974, 239–258.

5. Giovanni Oman, 'The Islamic Necropolis of Dahlak Kebīr in the Red Sea', *East and West*, vol. 24, 1974, 249–295.

6. Further reading in the vol. cited under no. 3.

7. R. E. M. Wheeler/A. Gosh/Krishna Deva, 'Arikamedu: an Indo-Roman Trading-station on the East Coast of India', *Ancient India*, vol. 2, 1946, 17–124.

8. Kurt Jaritz, 'Tilmun-Makan-Meluhha', *INES*, vol. 27, 1967, 209–213; J. Gelb, 'Makan and Meluhha in Early Mesopotamian Sources', *Rev. d'Assyr. et d'Archeol. Orientale*, vol.

64 1970, 1–8; Romila Thapar, 'A possible identification of Meluhha, Dilmun and Makan', *Journal of the Economic and Social History of the Orient*, vol. 18, 1975, 1–42; more complete bibliography in G. Weisgerber, 'Archaologische und archaometallurgische Untersuchungen in Oman', *Allgemeine und Vergleichende Archaologie-Beitrage*, vol. 2, 1980, note 1.

9. My citations of cuneiform texts are based on a manuscript by Wolfgang Heimpel to appear soon in a final publication volume of our archaeological work in Oman.

10. Elisabeth C. L. During Caspers, 'Sumerian Traders and Businessmen residing in the Indus valley cities. A Critical Assessment of the Archaeological Evidence', *Annali dell'Istituto Orientale di Napoli*, vol. 42, 1982, 337–379.
Elisabeth C. L. During Caspers, 'Harrapan Trade in the Arabian Gulf in the Third Millennium B.C.', *Mesopotamia*, vol. 7, 1972, 167–191; *ibid.* 'New archaeological evidence for Maritime Trade in the Persian Gulf during the late Protoliterate Period', *East and West* NS, vol. 21, 1971, 9–20; *ibid.*, 'A short survey of a still topical problem: The third millennium Arabian Trade Mechanism seen in the light of the recent discoveries in Southern Iran', *Acta praehistorico and archaeologica*, vol. 3, 1972, 35–42.

11. T. G. Bibby, '. . . efter Dilmun Norm', *Kuml*, 1970, 345–353; Michael Roaf, 'Weights on the Dilmun Standard', *Iraq*, vol. 44, 1982, 137–141; M. P. Hendrickx-Baudot, 'The weights of the Harappa-Culture', *Orientalia Lovaniensia Periodica*, vol. 3, 1972, 5–34.

12. Simo Parpola/Asko Parpola/Robert H. Brunswig, 'The Meluhha Village. Evidence of acculturation of Harappan Traders in the Late Third Millennium Mesopotamia?' *Journal of the Economic and Social History of the Orient*, vol. 20, 1977, 129–165. The complex problem of trade and archaeological evidence cannot be seen better than at Kultepe. The Assyrian Trading Outpost is only seen in the texts: 'If the tablets and their sealed envelopes had not been found, in fact, we might never have suspected the existence of a merchant colony' (T.Ozguc, 'An Assyrian Trading Outpost', *Scientific American*, 1962, 97 ff.) Cited after Lamberg-Karlovsky 1972.

13. Serge Cleuziou, 'Preliminary report on the second and third excavation campaigns at Hili 8', *Archaeology in the United Arab Emirates*, vol. 2/3, 1978/79, 30 ff.

14. Gerd Weisgerber, '. . . und Kupfer in Oman', *Der Anschnitt*, vol. 32, 1980, 62–110; *ibid.*, 'Mehr als Kupfer in Oman', *Der Anschnitt*, vol. 33, 1981, 174–263.

15. See note 14.

16. Gerd Weisgerber, Makan and Meluhha – 3rd millennium copper production in Oman and the evidence of contact with the Indus valley. Paper read in Cambridge 1981 and to appear in South Asia Archaeology 1981.

17. Maurizio Tosi, A possible Harappan Seaport in Eastern Arabia: Ra's al-Junayz in the Sultanate of Oman. Manuscript.

18. This idea first put forward by John Hansman, 'A periplus of Magan and Meluhha', *Bulletin of the School of Oriental and African Studies*, vol. 36, 1973, 554–587; *ibid.*, 'A further note on Magan and Meluhha', *idem.*, vol. 38, 1975, 609–610.

Dilmun and Makkan during the third and early second millennia B.C.

SERGE CLEUZIOU

The differences between the archaeological assemblages of Bahrain and the Oman Peninsula were very soon recognized by the Danish excavators in the Gulf (Bibby 1970a: 295–98) who proposed to consider them as the Dilmun and Makkan countries of the Mesopotamian texts. At this early stage of research, the culture of Dilmun was matched to Mesopotamian assemblages[1] while the links of Makkan with the chalcolithic cultures of Baluchistan and the Indus valley civilization were emphasized. Some relations between the two main archaeological areas of the Gulf were of course traced, but remained very weak.[2] There is somewhere between Bahrain and Abu Dhabi a border between cultural assemblages, but the study of their relations remains difficult, although according to historical texts these relations were clearly important. Attempts to break this situation have recently been made by D. Potts (1978: n.d.), and we would like to suggest some more links here. One of the obvious problems in such a matter is the weakness of our chronological frame, at a time where a difference of fifty years is certainly highly significant in the chronological record. Despite the efforts of the Danish team (Bibby 1967, Mortensen 1970) and others (Potts 1978: n.d., Larsen 1977), and certainly due to the large technical and financial investments required by the excavations of Qal'at al-Bahrain or the moundfields of Ali and Sar, the chronology of Dilmun is not settled yet on the firm basis we need. For instance, the duration and absolute dating of the best known period, city II, remains unclear while a huge amount of material has been recovered from Qal'at al-Bahrain, Barbar, Diraz and the moundfields. Most of the third millennium occupation remains unknown and the presence of late fourth/early third millennium, sometimes claimed (Mortensen 1970: 395 and fig. 3) is still questionable. In the meantime, the work of several teams in the Oman Peninsula has brought to light a complete sequence, from late fourth to early/mid second millennium B.C. I do not intend to fill the gaps in the archaeological record of Bahrain from a nearby but different area, but simply to propose a tentative interpretation according to what we know for the time being.

1. A CHRONOLOGY AS SEEN FROM 'MAKKAN'

Let us first consider the archaeological sequence of the Oman Peninsula as it emerges from recent work, mainly that of the French archaeological mission at Hili 8 near al Ain in the Emirate of Abu Dhabi. The archaeological sequence of this site is still unique in Eastern Arabia as it encompasses the whole time-span from the late fourth to the early second millennium B.C. Earlier periods are out of this paper's focus, but they do exist in the al Ain area as well as along the Oman Sea coast, along the Omani mountains and in the Western Province of the Emirate of Abu Dhabi. A better knowledge of these periods is of paramount importance for a better understanding of the origins of the third millennium cultures, but we shall leave this question aside.

Our sequence deals only with settled farming/herding communities of the piedmontane area between the Omani mountains and the sand desert, to which can be matched several settlements on the Gulf and Oman Sea coasts. Since the beginning, the settlement at Hili 8 has a full developed farming and herding economy, mainly date palms, fruits and cereals (Cleuziou and Costantini 1980, 1982); sheep, goat and cattle (Cleuziou 1982). For the purpose of this paper,[3] we shall summarize the sequence as follows.

a) PERIOD I

The ceramic assemblage is very limited. It includes brown unpainted pottery which can be related to the 'Jemdet Nasr' horizon of the Oman Peninsula, as it is known from the Jebel Hafit cairn burials (Frifelt 1970) and the possibly later 'beehive graves' (Frifelt 1975b) together with black on red painted pottery. The main architectural feature of the third millennium settlements in Eastern Arabia – i.e. a solid base tower – is already present. If we assume some relation between these towers and the social structure, we must probably admit some continuity too in the social organization throughout the whole millennium. Chronologically, this period can be related to Jemdet Nasr or Early Dynastic I in Mesopotamia. Several authors have emphasized cultural parallels with Mesopotamia (Frifelt 1970, During Caspers 1971a) and it is needless to reconsider them here. But other links should not be dismissed, such as those with Southeastern Iran/ Baluchistan, according to the presence of black on red painted pottery, or the ones to the south with Eastern Africa as they can be traced by the occurrence of sorghum among the cultivated cereals (Cleuziou and Costantini 1980, 1982). These links should not all be interpreted in the same way. At present, south-eastern Iranian and

African connections remain unclear, while the commonly accepted idea for the relations with Mesopotamia is trade, in the light of Sumerian and Proto-Elamite long distance trade as it is known during the Jemdet Nasr period. One should notice however that the items traded are unknown. They can only be suspected according to the potentialities of the area, but for instance, we have not been able to recognize, on archaeometrical data, if copper was already exported.

b) PERIOD II, PHASE IIa TO IIc
This period starts with an important transformation on the site. The solid base tower is rebuilt and surrounded by a ditch. This is accompanied by the introduction of plano-convex mudbricks in the architecture. Pottery is still scarce in IIa and IIb and includes almost exclusively a fine black on red painted ware, but orange/buff sand tempered ware painted in black appears in IIb and becomes dominant in IIc, a phase which is marked by an increased importance of pottery use. This orange/buff pottery will continue until the end of the third millennium B.C. and forms our 'domestic ware'; it includes mainly small jars, pots and storage vessels. Some shapes have counterparts in the settlement pottery at Umm an-Nar, which was certainly occupied at this time. 'Umm an-Nar type' collective burials start with the beginning of the period, like tomb M excavated by our mission at Hili (Vogt n.d.). In terms of Mesopotamian chronology, it would broadly correspond to Early Dynastic II and III. It is noticeable that according to archaeometrical studies (Berthoud 1979), Omani copper is present in significant quantities in Greater Mesopotamia as early as Early Dynastic II, and becomes dominant during Early Dynastic III (Susa D 'vase à la cachette', Royal Cemetery at Ur).

c) PERIOD II, PHASES IIe TO IIg
It is considered for the purpose of this paper as a single period, while phase IIe is clearly separated from IIf according to the pottery. We have omitted here the phase IId of our sequence, the material found in the deposits of this phase being probably a mixture of IIc and IIe.[4] Fine ware almost disappears from the settlement and becomes restricted to funerary deposits. Domestic ware is rather different from the former period. C14 dates range from 2470 ± 150 B.C. for IIe to 2200 ± 110 B.C. for IIf[5] and we would like to suggest a very broad contemporaneity with Akkadian period (IIe) and Ur (IIf), 2000 B.C. being a *terminus*. It is the time of the largest 'Umm an-Nar type' graves, like Hili round structure (Frifelt 1970) and grave A at Hili North (Cleuziou and Vogt 1983). Among the grave assemblages, black on red painted wares remain predominant, but their shapes and decorative pattern differ slightly. Black on grey and incised grey wares comparable to Bampur IVc to VI occur, as well as the small globular 'suspension

vessels' characteristic of the area. All the known third millennium settlements (Hili, Bat, Maysar, Amlah, etc. . . .) were occupied at that time, and this seems to correspond to the main development of copper mining activities at Maysar.

d) PERIOD III
It completely differs from previous periods according to funerary customs, settlement pattern and pottery assemblage. K. Frifelt (1975a) mentioned it for the first time and I have tried a first interpretation (Cleuziou 1981). New discoveries enhance every year the importance of this period, which should no longer be considered as a kind of 'terminal Umm an-Nar'. It is represented all over the Peninsula by burials, both collective and individual like those of Shimal, Qattarah, Wadi Suq, Wadi Sunaysl, Maysar 9, etc. . . . while settlements are still badly known, the only proper excavation being the poorly preserved top layers at Hili 8. The wares of this period, mainly red or buff slipped buff ware with black or violet painting, are known as 'Wadi Suq' ware among the archaeologists working in the area. Chlorite production is also very distinctive (Cleuziou 1981: 287) and D. Potts (n.d.) has recently suggested the term 'late série récente' to fit in the classification proposed by Miroschedji (1973).[6] Available C 14 dates point towards the early second millennium B.C.[7] and I shall propose a broad contemporaneity with Isin-Larsa and Old Babylonian periods in Mesopotamia.

To summarize, the settled community at Hili 8 appears fully developed since around 3000 B.C., at a time where Mesopotamian influence seems obvious. It continues until c. 2000 B.C. with no major breaks. The appearance of 'Umm an-Nar type' burials by 2700 B.C. and their generalization all over the Peninsula can be considered as a period of integrative process (during the second quarter of the third millennium) followed by a period of maturity, from c. 2500 to 2000 B.C. Important changes occur at the beginning of the second millennium, with what is usually called the 'Wadi Suq' period. This frame is admittedly very crude, with still a lot of question marks and many points to be explained. What was the role of copper mining and exportation in the 'integrative process'? What is the meaning of the change around 2000 B.C.? How long did the new cultural assemblage last and why did it disappear? etc. . . . Much more information is necessary to answer these questions, and the issues discussed below clearly depend on these answers. But let us now match this imperfect tool with what is known of surrounding areas.

2. MAKKAN AND THE NEAR EASTERN WORLD
Oman Peninsula/Makkan lies half way between the two main civilization centres of the third millennium Middle East: Mesopotamia and

the Indus valley, and can be considered in the same evolutionary trends as other communities in the same situation in the Indo/Iranian borderland: Tepe Yahya, Shahdad, Bampur, Shahr-i-Sokhta, as it has been done in a first attempt by Lamberg-Karlovsky and Tosi (1973). Broad cultural relations with this area can now be traced as early as 3000 B.C. They have been emphasized in many papers since B. de Cardi's excavations at Bampur (de Cardi 1968). The aim of most of these papers, to quote among others Tosi (1976), Hastings and others (1975), Frifelt (1975a) was to find links between both sides of the Strait of Hormuz in order to establish the Eastern Arabian chronology with the help of supposedly better known data, namely the Tepe Yahya and Bampur sequences! We are now in a rather different position and can compare our sequence with other ones in order to establish and interpret relations not only chronologically but in terms of, say, historical relations.[8] We are very quickly facing a lot of unanswered questions, for instance the presence of the same black on grey and incised grey ware. Was it made on both sides of the Strait of Hormuz? Was it traded from south-eastern Iran to other areas? Possible East Arabian imported vessels can also be found on the Iranian side, like a pot of early period IVA at Tepe Yahya which can be related to our phase IIe, or possibly IIf at Hili (Potts n.d.). We will not list all these parallels here (see Cleuziou forth., Potts n.d.). They just attest that two neighbouring areas were interconnected. Only the reverse would really be surprising.

It is much more interesting to turn to the Indus Valley. To my knowledge, the earliest artifact pointing to some Indus relationship is a 'thumb nail' impressed sherd of phase IIc at Hili 8 (Cleuziou 1978/79, fig. 23 no. 1), a very early date indeed for such an item. All other objects linked to the Indus Valley appears in late third millennium and mainly early second millennium contexts. For the late third millennium, these include 'thumb nail' impressed sherds from Maysar 1 (Weisgerber 1981, fig. 77), a Harappan influenced three faced seal from Maysar 1 (Weisgerber 1981, fig. 54), incisions on pottery rims at Maysar and Hili, and two etched carnelian beads from grave A at Hili North. Most of these objects however seem to be local in fabrication (if we except the etched beads). This is also the case of several black on red vessels of fine ware at Hili North, bearing palm leaves and in one case pipal leaves decoration. At present, the most likely is an increasing influence of Harappan civilization on Eastern Arabia during the last two centuries of the third millennium. This influence seems to strengthen during the early second millennium where proper Harappan objects are found all over the Oman Peninsula: a cubic stone weight at Shimal, sherds of Harappan storage jars on several sites including Hili 8 (period III), Maysar and Ras al-Junayz. One of the sherds of Ras al-Junayz bears a Harappan inscription and

Tosi (forth.) has emphasized the importance of this discovery for the knowledge of Harappan control over the Oman Sea. The recent discovery of Wadi Suq material by Weisgerber on the Masirah Island backs this viewpoint. In this respect, further comparisons of the Wadi Suq assemblages with other areas also under strong Harappan influence at the same time, like Gujarat, could be a promising subject of research. It is rather clear that Eastern Arabia was submitted to increasing Harappan pressure around 2000 B.C., and that it was under some strong Harappan influence during the early second millennium.

If we now turn to the west, there seem to be some discrepancies between archaeological and historical records. The importance of Mesopotamian relations during the early third millennium B.C. has already been noticed. In turn, the first mention of *Makkan* in the texts is the well known inscription of Sargon of Akkad according to which he 'made the boats from Meluḫḫa, the boats from Makkan and the boats from Dilmun tie up alongside the quay of Agade'. This is later followed by the raid of Naram Sin against Makkan. The relations even seem to increase in the later periods, according to Gudea and Ur Nammu's texts, and economic texts of Isin-Larsa and Old Babylonian periods. Archaeological records however would more or less give an opposite idea, with a lowering Mesopotamian influence. Various authors have solved this contradiction by interpreting the official texts as testimonies of an attempt to reconquer lost influence or, at least during the Akkadian period, as an illustration of Akkadian imperialism. Later texts deal with purely commercial relations. Whatever the truth behind the texts, it seems obvious that these economico-political expeditions or this trade did not alter the material culture of 'mature Makkan' in a significant way, contrary to what happened in the incipient earlier period. The only possible question is that of Umm an-Nar, where Mesopotamian-like pottery is found on the settlement during ED III and possibly Akkadian period.

To summarize, the cultures of Eastern Arabia shift from Mesopotamian influence in the early third millennium B.C., directly reflected by the archaeological remains, to a Harappan influence around 2000 B.C., the latter being less evident, probably due to the emergence of a mature local culture during the third millennium. We can hypothesize that the sharp cultural changes during the early second millennium B.C. are linked to that pressure, but cannot demonstrate it at that stage of research.

3. MAKKAN AND DILMUN

What about the relations between the two neighbours? Here again, we are left with unsolved archaeological problems, and most of the similarities will be used only in ascertaining the chronological frame. The occurrence of Umm an-Nar-like pottery was the first evidence found by the Danish excavators in the 'farush' or pre-city I levels at Qal'at al-Bahrain (Bibby 1970: 377). The main comparison was recognized in the jars with a rim strongly bent outwards and vertically cut, many of these being decorated with applied ridges. They usually wear applied ring bases to a round bottom. Such features do exist at Umm an-Nar, and to a lesser extent at Hili 8 during phase IIc. A few painted sherds were also present in the 'farush' levels (cf. Larsen 1980, fig. 43h) which are similar to Umm an-Nar but cannot be ascertained to any particular period in the evolution of fine ware as evidenced from Hili 8. Umm an-Nar-like painted pottery was also found in graves at Buri, which can be matched to sherds of phases IIa-c at Hili 8 and to a pot found at Tawi Silaīm in the Omani Sharqiyah by B. de Cardi (de Cardi and others 1977: fig. 3 no. 1). This globular shape can be related to the second period defined in that paper from the archaeological sequence in Makkan, but it is not a very safe criterion. On the other hand, no sherd of the 'chain ridged pottery', already present in the pre-city I layers, has ever been found in Eastern Arabia. These similarities are interesting chronological features, but probably do not tell us that much. Rims strongly bent outwards and vertically cut are found in the Gulf area: in Bahrain, in the Oman Peninsula, as evidenced from Umm an-Nar, Hili and some sherds from surface collections at Wadi Far I (Hastings and others 1975: fig. 10 ff) or Wadi Ithli 4 (Hastings and others 1975: fig. 20 F), but also on the Iranian side where the shape is present from Tepe Yahya IVC to IVA. This may represent a kind of interregional item, without significance for proper relations between two particular areas.

Black on red painted wares with Umm an-Nar affinities are also quoted from city I at Qal'at al-Bahrain, but again cannot be compared exactly to Eastern Arabian examples. A more detailed study may even be necessary. We know enough material now from this area during the late third millennium B.C. to cease to rely on the argument that the material is similar because it is painted black on red and start to trace differences. We could very soon define three groups: Bampur, Tepe Yahya and Eastern Arabia, and only the small amount of material restrains us from making a fourth group with Bahrain. In other words, we cannot compare sherds from city I to early rather than to late fine ware in the Umm an-Nar tombs, a difference of at least two or three centuries! To complete the story, painted black on grey ware or incised grey ware are absent from Bahrain[9] (but this is meaningless according to the small amount of fine ware ever found) and the type of jars of pre-city I which could be compared to Umm an-Nar seems to continue during city I (Larsen 1980: fig. 46a-c, g). The message is clear: information is too weak to support precise conclusions.

Let us now turn to the main bulk of information available from Bahrain: City II, Diraz, Barbar, the moundfields and al-Hajjar cemetery. Even such an enumeration is hazardous because it assumes contemporaneities which are not obvious. According to Potts (n.d.) an unpublished cuneiform tablet of basal City II is 'of post Ur III date, i.e. Isin-Larsa'. This would definitely put City II in the early second millennium B.C., that is contemporary with the fourth period outlined in that paper for Eastern Arabia: the Wadi Suq period. But should such a dating be accepted for 1) the Barbar temple and 2) for all of the hundred thousand or more tumuli datable to City II? In order to be safer, we will briefly examine these different locations separately.

From Qal'at al-Bahrain comes a single chlorite vessel of 'late série récente', but out of context. To my knowledge, this is the only item which can be directly related to Eastern Arabia on that site.

The settlement of Diraz has yielded several copper items which can be compared to items from Oman Peninsula. One is a socketed spearhead of a type which does not seem to appear before the Wadi Suq period. The others are long celts of a type known from several 'Umm an-Nar type' burials but until now absent from Wadi Suq contexts (al-Takriti A. 1975, *Bahrain National Museum* no. 2, 5, 6).

The Barbar temple has also produced several pieces of evidence. A very high date has been established for it by Mortensen (1970), but there seems to be a common agreement to consider now that temples II and III should be contemporary with City II, while temple I should be contemporary with late City I or a transition to City II. Among the painted sherds found in temple II and III, one at least recalls very clearly late Umm an-Nar fine ware (Mortensen 1970: fig. 6 bottom right) while Larsen (1980: 311) quotes 'a sherd identical to black on red painted graveware from the Wadi Suq' originating from temple III. Reference is given to Frifelt (1975a: fig. 22d), indeed a very distinctive type of Wadi Suq pottery.

Several kinds of items come from the gravemounds. Socketed spearheads are reported from Ali (Bibby 1954: 136). Steatite vessels of the 'late série récente' have been found on various occasions (for instance *Bahrain National Museum* 160, 161, 162) but hemispherical bowls of the 'série récente' also occur (Ibrahim 1982) together with a third type of vessel, a tronconical beaker with the whole body covered with incised horizontal lines with the exception of the bottom, decorated with oblique lines. Such objects have been found at Hili (Frifelt 1975a: fig. 17e) and grave A at Hili North, and seem to be found only in the later graves of Umm an-Nar type, namely the very end of the third millennium B.C.

This is a rather disappointing inventory, but at least it confirms the chronological setting of the main expansion of Bahrain settlements and tumuli: the very end of the third millennium B.C. and mainly the early second millennium B.C. There is little to tell about the shape of the copper objects, except that they can be matched to

Eastern Arabian objects of the same period: late third millennium B.C. for the long celts and early second millennium for the socketed spearheads. But the chlorite vessels have very probably been imported from Eastern Arabia. I have already advocated that 'later série récente' was produced in the Oman Peninsula and exported all over the Gulf where it is found not only in Bahrain but also at Tarut (Zarins 1978b: pl.71 no.136, 246), Failaka (*Kuwait, Dept. of Antiquities* n.d.: fig. 32), Bender Bušehr (Pezard 1914: fig. VIII) and Ur (Woolley and Mallowan 1976: pl.100 no. 6). The Khudra graves and recent work at Maysar in the Sultanate of Oman confirm this idea, according to the great amount of items found there. The same may probably be true for the 'série récente': more than sixty items were found in the excavated half of tomb A at Hili North. At least we can say that chlorite items were traded from Makkan to Dilmun.

If we look now for Bahrain related objects in Eastern Arabia, the inventory is even poorer. Only one Gulf seal is reported, from an unsafe context at Mazyad (see Cleuziou 1981: fig. 8). Of some interest, but different, is a cylindrical suspension vessel from the Wadi Suq graveyard of Maysar 9 (Vogt 1981: fig. 56). It is decorated with stylized caprids. This vessel has a good parallel, decorated with geometrical pattern in black on red, coming from a grave of site I at al-Hajjar (*Bahrain National Museum* no. 176). They are both variants of a well known series found in Isin-Larsa period in various Mesopotamian sites, which is usually decorated with engraved scenes. The two vessels are again a good chronological link, while the seal can really be considered as an import.

Several objects found in the Wadi Suq period graves at Qattarah near al-Ain are of interest. These are four small gold or electrum plaques in the shape of animals worked by *repoussé* technique, which were probably sewn onto clothes. I have suggested (Cleuziou 1981: 289) a comparison with a small copper figurine also sewn onto clothes found during an amateur excavation at Hamala in Bahrain (During Caspers 1980: fig. 4b). The style of the representations is admittedly puzzling and we have no argument to decide whether they may represent an import from Bahrain to East Arabia, or the reverse, or an import to both countries from some other place. From the Qattarah grave also comes a small silver figurine of a bull with a body worked in *repoussé* and a cast head. This tiny beautiful object was also sewn onto clothes (see Cleuziou 1978/79: 44 top). These similarities have been put in question by E.C.L. During Caspers (1982: 542) who relates the object from Hamala to a Harappan origin and prefers an Iranian inspiration (Luristan) for the Qattarah examples. I personally wonder why a Harappan origin is to be excluded also for the Qattarah examples.

This review cannot be concluded without quoting the three

sided seal of al-Hajjar, similar in shape and partly in decoration to the example found at Maysar. They both reflect a Harappan influence rather than a local interaction, possibly in the same way as the animals already quoted.

To summarize, archaeological evidence of relations between Bahrain/Dilmun and Oman Peninsula/Makkan is presently rather weak and we certainly cannot understand the international relations through the Gulf area without the help of 1) Mesopotamian texts and 2) the increasing discoveries of Harappan related objects.

4. OF TEXTS AND GOODS

It may seem strange to emphasize this opposition of texts versus objects, but this corresponds in some way to what each area has to offer to modern archaeologists: lost perishable goods (see Crawford 1973) but clay inscribed texts for Mesopotamia, and a wide range of raw material transformed by skilful craftsmanship but vanished texts (on perishable support?) for the Indus. To a lesser extent, the Bahrain/Oman Peninsula belongs to the same type of – admittedly rather artificial – opposition. We have a lot of written evidence for Bahrain, or better say Dilmun, including cuneiform writing in Bahrain itself, and increasing evidence for the occurrence of exportable goods in the Oman Peninsula and the fact that they were exported. Archaeologists are clearly more at ease with the second type of evidence than with the former. But how can we match both?

The strong Mesopotamian influence in the Oman Peninsula during the first and part of the second period defined in this paper is not attested in any written document. At the same time, nothing is known of the archaeology of Bahrain, except . . . one Jemdet Nasr sherd (Mortensen 1970: fig. 3) from the temple I at Barbar and a Jemdet Nasr or EDI stamp seal from grave 1 at al-Hajjar 1 (Rice 1972: 68), both clearly out of context. But a lot of evidence comes from unfortunately uncontrolled excavations on Tarut island[10] where material ranging from Jemdet Nasr to ED III is recorded (Potts n.d.; Rashid 1972; etc. . . .). The fact that all the material recorded there and published is of Mesopotamian origin, or at least strongly influenced, is however to be taken with care. Only Mesopotamian-like objects have been emphasized, and maybe recorded.

A rather puzzling problem is raised by one of the most famous items exchanged during the mid-third millennium B.C.: chlorite vessels of the 'intercultural style' (Kohl) or 'série ancienne' (Miros-chedji). They have been found in dozens at Tarut, while not a single sherd is reported from Bahrain. Should we admit as commonly accepted an early dating for these items (ED II and ED IIIa) and con-sider that Bahrain's occupation post dates ED IIIa? This was possible until the demonstration by D. Potts that at least part of these objects have to be dated to Akkadian times, if not later (Potts n.d.; see also Potts 1978: 38). There must be some reasons beyond chronology to explain this absence in Bahrain. I am afraid this may simply be the lack of convenient data.

How far Dilmun was integrated in the Mesopotamian area at that time is unclear, but it probably remained a particular country, be it or not the 'Land of Paradise'. It is only in the time of Ur-Nanshe that it appears as trading goods to Mesopotamia. Significantly enough, the exotic goods involved are not those that Dilmun can offer, and the copper from Dilmun referred to in a pre-sargonic text (Leemans 1960: 116) can safely be considered as a copper of Omani origin, according to what we know from archaeometrical studies.

The development of the proper Dilmun assemblage starts somewhere during Late ED III or Akkad period. It includes a special type of ceramics easily recognizable by their paste (red with white inclusions) and several distinctive features such as for City I and pre-City I the chain-ridged decoration. The occupation of Bahrain island gives an impression of gradual extension, but it remains to be demonstrated to what extent until the end of Akkadian times this is more than an impression (see Larsen 1980: 96). This is a period of full development in the oases of Eastern Arabia according to the evidence of phase IIe at Hili and some other sites.

Historical texts on the other hand tend to indicate a strengthening of Mesopotamian pressure in the Gulf under Akkadian rule. One can discuss the reality of Sargon's claim of power over Dilmun and Naram Sin's conquest of Makkan. Conquest of the world, both real and mythical outside Mesopotamia, was part of the duties of an Agade King, and Dilmun in some way belongs to both geographies. Tying up again the boats of Meluḫḫa, Makkan and Dilmun to the quays of Agade is certainly the sign of an economic interest for the Gulf countries, and it coincides with a strong pressure on the Iranian plateau as well. But did such an interest include conquest and direct power? This is another question that archaeology cannot at the moment help to solve. Moreover, this is a period where Mesopotamian objects become almost non-existent in Eastern Arabia. If we had ignored the texts, we would have described the situation as the emergence of a well defined, and maybe 'brilliant' cultural entity,[11] and the same may even be applied to Bahrain.

By the end of the third millennium B.C., Bahrain reaches a peak in its occupation and civilization, and becomes the middleman between the Mesopotamian entity to the west and the Harappan power to the east. This is the time where gravemounds develop on a wide scale, which is still a challenge to archaeologists. The interpretation of these gravemounds *is* questionable and no convincing argument has really been settled in favour of one or another interpretation. I do not intend to enter this discussion here, but from its solution will clearly depend our understanding of the evolution of the area around 2000 B.C. Emphasis has been put on the Mesopotamian aspect of several pottery shapes which were used as a chronological argument from Cornwall (1946a) to During Caspers (1980), a view recently criticized by Lamberg-Karlovsky (1982). We have probably more than 'scraps' to link the material of tumuli to City I or City II, but the highly specialized (and standardized) aspect of the tumuli assemblages recently re-emphasized by Lamberg-Karlovsky (1982: 49) is obvious. It must be noticed that specialized funerary material also appears in 'Umm an-Nar type' collective burials during the second part of the third millennium. This is probably a general tendency on the Iranian plateau as well at the same time. In this respect, the high similarity of settlement and funerary assemblages in the Oman Peninsula during the early second millennium B.C., i.e. at a time where Bahrain moundfields reach their apogee, may be of some interest to notice and interpret.

The most obvious importation from Eastern Arabia to Bahrain (chlorite vessels) is widely associated with this production, circulation and use of these specialized items. But at the same time, we know from the texts that Dilmun took part in the copper trade from Makkan to Southern Mesopotamia, and at least in this instance textual, archaeological and physico-chemical evidence agree in demonstrating the importance of this trade. Whatever the relation between economy and ideology ('funeral business' at least) in Bahrain – and it would be interesting to know at least something about it – Dilmun's power extends all over the Gulf, from Failaka to Qatar, and everything demonstrates that it was in a position to control all relations throughout the area. At that same time, Harappan tradesmen do not seem to appear any more in Mesopotamian records (Parpola and others 1977). This coincides to some degree with the strengthened influence of the Harappan world over Eastern Arabia, and the strong cultural changes occuring there around 2000 B.C.

Mesopotamian pressure in Akkadian times, perhaps competing with Indus interest, did not foreshadow the development of local cultures in the Gulf. These cultures seem to have taken benefit of favourable factors like mineral resources (Eastern Arabia) and increased water flow due to higher sea-level favouring land use in Bahrain (Larsen 1980: 179, 217–18, 243) and maybe Eastern Arabia as well. Trade, possibly or probably accompanied by political pressure, is certainly to be recorded among these favourable factors.

Later, in Gudea's time and Ur III dynasty, trade seems to have been a Mesopotamian venture, with direct relations between Sumerian merchants and resource areas. To which extent the rise of Dilmun as the sole middleman in Gulf trade, the Harappan influence in Eastern Arabia and the appearance of Wadi Suq culture are linked is a major problem. By 2000 B.C., we may consider that Eastern Arabia was included in Harappan control over the Arabian Sea while Dilmun had seized the role of official intermediate between this area of influence and the Mesopotamian world. This situation was to last until major changes occurred, namely the end of City II and the end of Wadi Suq period, which seem to coincide with the end of Harappan civilization and the beginning of a long crisis in Southern Mesopotamia. But this would be the subject of another, much more speculative paper.

1. Even before the first Danish excavations, the material excavated in the tumuli had been rather accurately dated with the help of Mesopotamian parallels by Cornwall, in his unpublished PhD. thesis.

2. Bibby compared the material of Umm an-Nar graves to pre-City I material from the very first campaign at Umm an-Nar.

3. The proper sequence is still under elaboration, and we request the reader to consider the periods proposed here as a convenience for our demonstration, not as a definite one.

4. This does not mean that IId is a phase of transition and is probably due to the difficulties of separating contexts in the field. Further analysis may lead to a division of phase IId into two phases related to IIc (early IId) and IIe (late IId). But deposits related to IId are difficult to interpret, and we may also never reach a proper conclusion.

5. Calibrated dates for MC 2265 (3900 ± 100 B.P.) and MC 2262 (3690 ± 90 B.P.). Accordingly, these dates are slightly higher than the historical horizon to which I proposed to relate these phases, but this is an unusual discrepancy in the use of calibrated dates and should not be overemphasized. For a list of C-14 dates at Hili, see Cleuziou 1978/79: 68, or Cleuziou and Costantini 1980, table 1.

6. If we want to keep Miroschedji's terminology, I think we had better keep the new label in French and call it 'série tardive'.

7. One date has been obtained at Hili 8: MC 2259, 3520 ± 90 B.P., that is after calibration 1990 B.C. ± 110.

8. We should of course keep in mind all the problems already mentioned. Because of the long timespan and the large geographical area considered, our information may be considered too scarce to allow any attempt of that kind.

9. There is only one sherd quoted, from Horat (Larsen 1980: 96). It is interesting to notice that a good collection of black on grey sherds was found at Tarut (Masry 1976: XLVI).

10. The history of discoveries at Tarut is reviewed in Zarins. Forthcoming publication of the results of excavations at al-Rufaya may help to clarify the situation.

11. One may of course play the reverse game, which has been a favourite of archaeology, and advocate that the destruction of the first round tower at Hili, which happened at the end of IId or somewhere in IIe, or the deep layer of ashes covering one floor of IIe, are related to an Akkadian invasion, as may be also the apparent decline or disappearance of Umm an-Nar during the Akkadian period. But up to now, I see no serious reason to consider such arguments.

Death in Dilmun

C. C. LAMBERG-KARLOVSKY

The burial mounds of Bahrain have been the subject of both renewed research and new debate. The pioneering work of Mackay (1929) and Cornwall (1943a), among others, was substantively advanced by Bibby (1954, 1969), whose Danish team provided the fullest understanding of the 'Dilmun Civilization'. Within the past years two significant publications have greatly advanced our understanding of the archaeology of Bahrain in general, and the vast burial grounds in particular. The exemplary publication of Larsen (1983) on the geoarchaeology of Bahrain and Ibrahim (1982) on the excavation of numerous burial mounds adds a new dimension to our understanding of Gulf archaeology. Additionally, Potts (n.d.) has presented the first systematic attempt to provide a relative chronology for the Gulf area.

In 1982 I published an article amplifying the earlier views of Mackay (1929) and Cornwall (1943a), (*contra* Bibby 1969: 18), which suggested that:

> **1.** there is an insufficient indigenous settlement pattern (i.e. population) of this date to account for the enormous number of graves in Bahrain and the adjacent Eastern provinces of Saudi Arabia, and that
> **2.** these tumuli represent an elaborate funerary cult reflected in Sumerian literature referring to Dilmun (Lamberg-Karlovsky 1982: 46).

With increasing research on, and excavation of, these burial mounds scholars have been consistently increasing the number of burials present on the island. Suggestions have ranged from:

Cornwall (1943b)	50,000 tumuli
Bibby (1969)	100,000 tumuli
Larsen (1983)	172,013 tumuli
Ibrahim (1982: 1)	'double the number of Bibby's estimate'

Since 1878 Europeans have, on numerous occasions, carried out excavations of the tumuli mounds on Bahrain. The first such work was undertaken by E. L. Durand (1880: 189–201). Finally, after over one hundred years, we are, for the first time, presented by Professor Moawiyah Ibrahim and his colleagues, with a comprehensive publication detailing the results of the tumuli excavations of the Arab Expedition at Sar el-Jisr, Bahrain. Prior to this publication we lacked an adequate typology of these burial mounds and an understanding of their construction technique, as well as an understanding of the archaeological context of associated material and skeletal remains. The Arab Expedition is to be warmly congratulated for making the results of this expedition available in an exemplary and timely fashion.

Dr. Ibrahim in his monographic report on the results of his expedition does not directly confront the issue of whether the burials incorporate the dead of surrounding geographical areas or exclusively represent the burials of an indigenous population. He does, however, imply that all five types of burial tombs belong to the same culture 'within a long time period' and that they were 'built by specialists' who were 'centrally organized'. From a study of the funerary objects Ibrahim concludes that 'many seem specifically made for burial purposes' and when confronted with tombs lacking human skeletons but with rich funerary remains (i.e. S-100 with ostrich shells, bronze nail or drill, basket coated with bitumen, animal bones) he advances the notion that 'the possibility existed that this tomb was dedicated to one who died outside his homeland.' He also alludes to the frequent occurrence of fragmentary burials and suggests that some mounds were for 'family burials.'

The question of whether the burial mounds of Bahrain are the exclusive cemeteries of an indigenous population or, as I recently proposed (Lamberg-Karlovsky 1982), whether they include the burials of peoples from surrounding areas is directly addressed in the provocative article by Dr Bruno Frohlich (1983), the physical anthropologist on the above mentioned Arab Expedition. Dr Frohlich (1983: 8) concludes his study, based on the techniques of archaeological demography, in the following manner:

> The data, does however, suggest one important factor; it is *not necessary* to explain the large number of burial mounds by 'importing' the dead from surrounding geographical areas. The size of the island, the number of people it can support, is assumed to be such that it may be necessary to look for *more* burials in order to explain the known, settlement patterns *Mutatis mutandis*!

Two points, of which Dr Frohlich is fully aware, make this conclusion premature. Firstly, there is a lack of data concerning the distribution of settlement and structures on Bahrain. The lack of data and research on the carrying capacity of the island, as well as settlement pattern, prohibits an adequate estimate of population size. In the absence of the above data it is difficult to explain how Dr Frohlich concludes that one needs 'to look for more burials in order to explain the known, settlement pattern'. Secondly, Dr Frohlich bases his conclusions on calculations of average life expectancy, derived from a study of the burials, which he believes to be between 35–40 years. Thus, if the life expectancy is 35 years and the tumuli represent a time span of 500 years a population of 10,500 would be sufficient to produce 150,000 dead persons. The use of life table calculations are not without interpretive difficulty. Life table calculations present averages and means as a substitute for population structure, assuming that the population is stationary without fluctuation in birth rate, male-to-female ratio, and mortality rates: in short without variability during a defined time span.

Dr Frohlich's work is nevertheless of extreme importance and will undoubtedly provide an archaeological demography of what clearly appears to be the largest prehistoric cemetery in the ancient Near East. Even if it is conclusively shown that the burials are exclusively of an indigenous population several important factors require further consideration. In order to emphasize these I have compiled the following summary of the Arab Expedition's excavations of the burials and tumuli of Sar el-Jisr.

Totals of Burial Mounds Excavated
    155 mounds excavated
     27 mounds without human burials
     33 mounds without artifacts/ceramics
   17.4% mounds without burials
   21.2% mounds without artifacts/ceramics

Type I
Mound with a single burial built above surface
     35 mounds with single burial
      7 mounds without human burial (6 with artifacts/
          ceramics
     14 mounds without artifacts/ceramics
    20% mounds without burials
    40% mounds without artifacts/ceramics

Type II
Mound with a single burial cut into bedrock
      4 mounds excavated
   100% mounds with human burials and artifact/ceramics

Type III
Mound with central burial connected with subsidiary burials
            38 mounds excavated
             0 mounds with subsidiary burials (multiple burial)
            23 mounds with single burials
            15 mounds with no burials (12 with artifacts/ceramics)
         39.5% mounds with no burials
             4 mounds without artifacts/ceramics
         10.5% mounds without artifacts/ceramics

Type IV
Mound provided with shaft entrance
It should be noted that this type of mound-burial is similar to that of
Type III, both contain stone semicircles built against the ringwall to
incorporate subsidiary burials.
            17 mounds excavated
             9 mounds with single burial
             3 mounds with multiple burials
             1 mound without burials
             4 mounds cited only as human bones present, unable to
                distinguish whether single or multiple burials
             1 mound lacked artifact/ceramics, also human burial
          5.8% mounds without burials and artifact/ceramics
         17.6% mounds with multiple burials

Type V
Burial Complex
This 'Burial Complex' consisted of an incompletely excavated area of
32 five-by-five meter squares consisting of more than 1,000 interconnected burials. The possibility of other burial complexes of this type,
in adjacent and unexcavated areas, is stated as being distinctly
possible (Ibrahim 1982).
    The excavators state that over 200 burials of this type were
uncovered, however, in their published tables only 42 graves are
reported upon (Ibrahim 1982: Table V).
            32 single burials
             2 multiple burials
             8 with no burials (4 contain artifacts/ceramics)
         23.5% burials contain no human remains
            15 burials contain no artifacts/ceramics
         46.8% contain no artifacts/ceramics

Mackay (1929)
            34 burials mounds excavated
            13 burials mounds without human burials
         38.2% burial mounds without human remains

Cornwall (1943)
>   30 burial mounds excavated
>   12 burial mounds without human remains
>   40% burial mounds without human remains

COMMENTARY

From a study of Ibrahim's (1982) published tables several distinctive features can be pointed out that are of signficance.

1. The greatest number of interments are *single* burials. In fact, only 5 interments within the 155 mounds and 200 burials of the 'Burial Complex' contained multiple burials, and these multiple burials never exceeded 4 dead. Type III, identified as having a central burial area with subsidiary burials around the outer ringwall, in fact contained not a single subsidiary burial!

2. In the aggregate 17.4% of the burial mounds contained *no* human burials. Type III, which appears to be the most labor intensive construction, has 39.5% of the burial mounds without human burials!

3. A total of 21.2% of the burials contain *no* artifacts. At times artifacts are placed in tombs which lack human burials, and conversely, human burials are often interred without artifacts.

4. The presence of both adults and children is noted in the tombs. The former appear to dominate numerically. However, tomb S-267.3, a Type IV burial mound, is one of the richest in terms of material remains and is reported to be that of a child. It has been assumed that the recovery of wealthy child burials indicates that status is ascribed at birth, not achieved during life (Shennan 1975). This hypothesis, although suggestive for the mound burials on Bahrain, requires further research.

5. The burials on Bahrain do not contain the wealth of material culture evident in the tombs of Kish (Mackay 1925; Moorey 1978); Xabis: Shahdad (Hakem 1972) or Ur (Woolley 1934), to mention only three third millennium cemeteries. The ceramic types found in the burials on Bahrain, some said to be produced for specific funerary purposes (Ibrahim 1982), are all of indigenous Dilmun type. The absence of foreign material in the tombs is notable. Only a very few lapis lazuli (less than a dozen), and agate beads were recovered. Similarly only 7 burials of hundreds excavated by Ibrahim (1982) contained steatite vessels. These vessels were all of the type designated by de Miroschedji (1973) as 'série récente' having the characteristic 'dot-and-circle' motif at Susa, Yahya, Oman, and Abu Dhabi. Exceptional for its being a 'foreign' object is a single etched carnelian discoid bead from tomb S-267.3 – long regarded as an Indus type artifact (During Caspers 1972a).

In 1977 the author had the good fortune to excavate a tumulus burial south of the Dhahran airport in Saudi Arabia from which an etched carnelian bead was also recovered. Over 1500 tumuli litter the landscape here. The excavation of this mainland tumulus mound (208-95) is architecturally similar to Ibrahim's S-100 (Type I). (Potts, *et al.* 1978: 9).

It is of interest to point out two 'Persian Gulf' seals recently recovered from burial mounds by Ibrahim (1982 Fig. 50: 4–5). Both seals are of 'glazed steatite' and depict stylized bulls. The 'glazing' of steatite seals to produce a white surface 'glaze' (probably produced by heat treatment) is characteristic of both Akkadian and Indus seals; the period of maximum Indus-Mesopotamian contact (Lamberg-Karlovsky 1972). Additionally, the contouring of the bull's neck with a series of concentric rings is *precisely* like that of the bulls on Indus seals (see for example Marshall 1931: Vol. III Pl. 107, 109, 118, 123, 126, 139, etc.).

In addition to the above Bibby (1954) recorded the recovery of ivory artifacts and numerous ostrich shell-cups; the former an import, the latter, most likely, a locally available commodity. The thirteen burial mounds from which Ibrahim (1982) recovered copper/ bronze artifacts do nothing to eliminate the generalization that the tombs contained limited wealth and very few foreign resources.

DISCUSSION

Tainter (1978: 106–7) has confidently stated that Binford's (1971) ethnographic cross-cultural survey of burial practices confirms 'beyond serious contention the argument (still rated sceptically by some) that variability in mortuary practices must be understood in terms of variability in the form and organization of social systems, not in terms of normative models of behavior.' More recently, Hodder (1982: 195–98) has emphatically stated that there is every reason to be sceptical of the social reconstructions of cemetery evidence. Hodder concludes:

> . . . that many aspects of social organization . . . are not expressed in burial, whereas some aspects are . . . but that what is represented depends on attitudes to death structurally related to attitudes in life. Because of the dominant role of these attitudes, the aspects of societal organization which are represented in burial may be ideals picked out from practical social relations or even in contrast to them, reverting and distorting.

Where does this leave us in attempting to understand the largest prehistoric cemetery known in the Old World? Clearly the detailed presentation of the data, as begun by Ibrahim (1982), is obligatory.

The analysis of the Bahrain burials according to regional patterning, within-cemetery patterning, and within-grave patterning still awaits a detailed final publication. It is abundantly clear, however, that the accumulation of facts alone does not provide an understanding of or give a meaning to their significance.

Thus how are we to explain the fact that Dilmun, which Sumerian myth relates from the beginning of time, was given fresh water and made a flourishing emporium by Enki for his consort Ninhursag, where Enki placed Ninsikil, 'the pure lady' and Enshag 'the fair lord' to reign, and which Sumerian literature pictures as a 'paradise', contains a cemetery which is as impressive for its size as its *beigraben* are unimpressive. There is not a hint in the tombs for the existence of what the written texts suggest: a flourishing trade entrepôt trans-shipping gold, copper, copper utensils, lapis lazuli, ivory objects, inlaid tables, pearls ('fish-eye'), and beads of semi-precious stones to Mesopotamia (for a comprehensive listing see Pettinato 1972). A materialist analysis of the tombs on Bahrain would scarcely support the view that 'Dilmun emerges as the trading power par excellence in the Gulf, securing direct lines of supply from Meluḫḫa and Makkan and effectively eliminating them as threats to her monopoly over the sea trade with Sumer' (Potts 1978: 46).

Given the fact that most of the tumuli on Bahrain have been looted it still appears that mortuary ceremonialism did not include the placing of great wealth in the tombs. The construction of the tombs does however represent a very considerable investment of labor. It is equally difficult to comprehend why almost a quarter of the tombs lack human burials. The distribution of tumuli mounds extends to the Arabian peninsula in the vicinity of Dhahran and the al-Hasa Oasis. Potts (1983b: 16) has recently reiterated the view initially expressed by Cornwall (1944: 117–19): that the region of al-Hasa 'was well within the cultural boundary of late third/early second millennium Dilmun' (Potts 1983b: 16). Cornwall also observed, and commented upon, what Ibrahim's (1982) published tables of excavated tombs further attest: the fact that many tombs were constructed that 'contained not a single human bone – or anything else' (Cornwall 1944: 122). These vacant tombs may have been commemorative tombs, to serve as a home for the spirit of one who died in more distant lands. Alternatively, as repeatedly commented upon by Kramer (1963: 147–49; 277ff.) and Jacobsen (1976: 112ff; 1970: 108) Dilmun was intimately related to Sumer, particularly at the religious and spiritual levels and it is not inconceivable that commemorative and/or actual burials of Sumerians took place on Dilmun which the Sumerians regarded as a 'Paradise' or 'Abode of the Blessed' where mankind is given 'life like a god' and 'breath eternal' (Lamberg-Karlovsky 1982, see also Kramer 1963).

Lastly, it must be said that within archaeology the belief remains that patterns in death reflect patterns in the life of a society. Current interpretations of burial data, at whatever scale, are invariably concerned with explanation in terms of social behavior. In the manner of vulgar materialism cemetery organization is equated to social organization (Alekshin 1983). This approach, however, if applied to the tumulus mounds of Bahrain would fail to distinguish the class structure and the concomitant complexities within the political and economic organization which simply must have characterized this extensive commercial entrepôt. The almost egalitarian nature of tomb 'wealth' belies the complex social stratification which must have existed; while the differential labor invested in small as against large tombs tells us little of the role played by the entombed. A materialist approach to these burials, whether by archaeological demography or a study of wealth and resource distribution in the tombs, fails entirely to comprehend the cognitive element of meaning in terms of concepts, symbolic principles and ideologies. It is clear that the mortuary ceremonialism of *both* Dilmun and Makkan (Oman-Abu Dhabi) emphasized the construction of large sepulchre stone chambers for the deceased. The *large* tombs that characterize these two cultures stand in physical contrast to the mortuary practices of the rest of the prehistoric Near and Middle East. In both size and number of tombs nothing in the Near East compares to the sepulchres of Dilmun and Makkan. Interpretations of their meaning must include an investigation of their attitudes to death and the way in which these belief systems were integrated within their social environment. A promising point of departure in comprehending the symbolic principles and ideologies toward death (and Dilmun) are contained in Sumerian literature; which, in spite of the relative absence of archaeological remains in the tombs, at least suggests the *possibility* that Dilmun was place for burial where immortality could be obtained (Lamberg-Karlovsky 1982).

Dilmun and Makkan share the mortuary practice of constructing large sepulchre chambers. The types of tomb construction however differ, as does the fact that the tombs of Dilmun are single burials while those of Makkan (Oman and Abu Dhabi) are true collective tombs (Frifelt 1976; Cleuziou 1977).

The differences between the collective burials of Makkan and the single burials of Dilmun allow us to suggest a number of hypotheses. Though burial behavior may distort and invert, as it masks the wealth of Dilmunites seen in their minimal grave goods, it does not totally hide. Cemeteries may be territorially organized and bounded or they may be scattered and diffuse. The cemeteries of Bahrain (Dilmun) and those from Abu Dhabi to Oman (Makkan) are territorially bounded, located in proximity to settlements. It has been suggested by Saxe (1970) and more fully reiterated by Goldstein (1976) that bounded cemeteries are consistently associated with corporate groups characterized by lineal descent. The corporate group's communal rights over restricted resources (land) are maintained by links with their common ancestors.

We further suggest that the differences between the collective burials of Makkan and the single burials of Dilmun reflect a differential cohesiveness of the corporate groups and a concomitant difference in the cultural complexity that characterized both areas. Thus the collective burials represent a tighter bond within the corporate groups: communal tombs containing families, clans, etc. (Recently at Hili, in Abu Dhabi, Cleuziou has excavated a single tomb containing at least one hundred burials (personal communication).) The individual tombs of Dilmun represent a breakdown of earlier close kin groupings. These differences reflect, in turn, different patterns of economic organization. The individual tombs of Dilmun reflect not only a breakdown of corporate kin groupings but an increase in social stratification, where personal status is achieved rather than as in Makkan ascribed through kin alignments and corporate ownership of kin lands.

Let us turn now to the relative absence of wealth in the tumuli of Bahrain. The placing of luxury items in a burial is tantamount to the removal of capital from circulation within a society. The removal of capital from circulation provides a continuing incentive for the production of more commodities in order to replace those lost through interment with the dead. The interment of luxury commodities serves the dual purpose of symbolically enhancing the status and rank of the deceased family as well as stimulating the need for continuous production. Thus a pre-industrial rank-society involved with *production* (Sumerian Ur) differs from a pre-industrial rank-society involved with *commerce* (Dilmun). A pre-industrial society involved with commerce, particularly of unfinished products, is ill-served by the elimination of goods by burial. In a dominantly commercial society, involved in the trans-shipment of *unfinished* goods, both rank-status and profits are manifest in the *circulation* of goods not in their elimination by burial. Capital and status are developed on Dilmun not through cyclical production of elite goods and their deposit in human burials but through success in commerce and the continual circulation of goods. The absence of elite goods on Bahrain becomes more comprehensible with such an interpretation. One may now fairly ask how status and wealth on Bahrain, in the absence of elite goods in burials, is shown. I would answer this by suggesting the notion that success in commerce brings both profit and wealth. Wealth is, in turn, evident in the burials not through the disposal of capital, that is in the material remains deposited in the tombs, but in the costs of labor-value in constructing the tombs. The status and wealth, the tangible evidence of one's success in commerce and/or agricultural production on Bahrain, is evident in the differential labor costs in the construction of tombs. It has long been known that the tombs on Bahrain vary greatly in size and complexity. The large tumuli mounds of Ali 'are stupendous, the least of them as high as a three storey building' (Bibby 1969: 18). The three attempts at excavating these large 'Royal Tombs' undertaken by Prideaux, Mackay and Bibby recovered little in terms of material remains, perhaps due to earlier looting. Nevertheless, the absence of material remains in the tombs is compensated for by a display of wealth evident in the different labor costs of constructing these earthen covered stone sepulchres.

This paper has attempted to point out (1) the relatively high percentage of tombs on Bahrain that lack either human burials, material remains or both; (2) the relative impoverishment of material remains in the tombs; (3) the ideological significance of Dilmun and the Sumerian world order; (4) the paradoxical situation between the texts of Sumer stressing the commercial importance of Dilmun and the absence of wealth in their tombs; and (5) the distinction between Dilmun's single graves and Makkan's collective tombs. It has also suggested a series of hypotheses which may shed light on the above points; namely, (1) single burials as opposed to collective burials are suggestive of a greater social stratification resulting from the breakdown of communal corporate group ownership; (2) societies involved with a primary emphasis upon production, as opposed to those primarily involved with commerce, are more likely to dispose of capital in their burials. Societies more involved with a commerce of unfinished goods are benefited by continual circulation of goods for exchange value; (3) personal wealth and status, first evidenced exclusively by material remains (private capital) in tombs later becomes manifest in the exploitation of labor value in the construction of status monuments and the reduction and/or elimination of capital in tombs. As the past is vastly different from the present so in death people often become what they were not in life. The easily observable may be insignificant and indeed may obscure complex patterns of interrelationship. The enormous number of Bahrain tumuli cannot fail to be observable. This paper seeks to explore that which is far from self-evident or observable: their meaning and structure within the social organization of Dilmun.

The Barbar Temple:
stratigraphy, architecture and interpretation

H. H. ANDERSEN

INTRODUCTION

When P. V. Glob in 1954 became aware of the large tell at Barbar, he followed in the footsteps of E. L. Durand from 1878. Both paid attention to a large socket stone, protruding from the tell. As the surface finds indicated to Glob that the tell originated from the Bronze Age, he decided to start excavations. He then discovered remains of stone-built temples from the third millennium.

This tell and a smaller one a little northeast of it were investigated between 1954 and 1961. P. Mortensen and the author were responsible for most of the field-work but other research delayed publication. As this situation has now changed, we can today give a description based on recent studies.

Through this work it became obvious that our conception of the archaeology of the temples had to be revised. The well-known sequence of three temples, Temple I–III, was confirmed but the conception involved a stratigraphical mistake of the uppermost horizon, the correction of which had far-reaching consequences. The error was due to the fact that the relevant horizon had been plundered and in this way escaped direct recognition.

It is then necessary to use new arguments for the three temples which assume new forms and become more complicated, because we have to suggest five building stages (Ia–b, IIa–b and III). Another important result of the re-study was the detection of another temple, the so-called NE-Temple.

As we are going to show there is clear evidence in the stratigraphy of the tell for a sequence of three temples, but first we will deal briefly with the general structure: a 'high temple' with a double stepped platform, an upper square one and a lower oval one, and two wing-structures, a basin to the west and an enclosure to the east. This is paradigmatic for Temples I and II, whereas Temple III just seems to consist of a single square platform. The existence of the NE-Temple adds to this picture the idea of a double-temple.

It is interesting to note that the temple well at the southwest corner goes through five individual building-stages following the five stages of the temple.

The ruined state of the temple is due to demolition in connection with the re-buildings but also to plundering of later times, especially damaging to Temple III and parts of Temple II and the NE-Temple.

STRATIGRAPHY

Three very distinctive horizons of the square platform from the main section constitute our three temples, fig. 35.

Temple Ia is indicated by its retaining walls (C–D), placed on subsoil (A). The platform is solid and covered by plaster (F).

Temple Ib presents an enlargement of this platform, using the same floor-level. Its retaining walls (G–H) are, however, placed at a higher level.

Below and around the square platform, we have the oval platform but its retaining walls are not visible on this section. It is important to point out that the bottom-layer of Temple I was artificial, a layer of clay (B) with many foundation deposits.

Temple IIa establishes a new platform. Its retaining walls (K–L) were placed at a still higher level, and a floor of large slabs covered the solid platform. Here, we also see a foundation wall (O), sunk below the floor, with remains of a wall (P) which belongs to a building on the platform. Its counterpart (Q) used the retaining wall as a foundation.

The oval platform is now figuring through one of its retaining walls (T) and, to the south, a stairway (U). The surface of this platform (V and S) coincides with the foot of the upper platform.

Temple IIb retains the upper platform of its predecessor, but the lower platform has been enlarged through a new retaining wall (X and R).

Temple III, finally, established a third platform above Temple II. The retaining walls (Z and AA) were again placed at a higher level and a third floor-level (AC) was created but nowhere preserved. Vast

35 Temple I–III, section

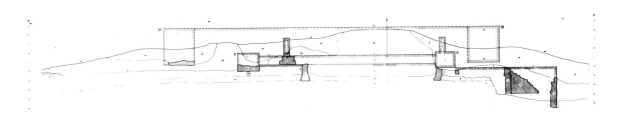

layers filled up the platform and all surrounding remains of Temple II were covered.

The robber-holes (AD–AF) reflect walls that have now disappeared but our projections can all be documented. In this way our three temple-horizons are clearly demonstrated.

Northeast of this main tell was a smaller tell. Its stratigraphy can now be interpreted as reflecting another double stepped platform-temple, fig. 36.

On the subsoil (H) was placed the lower platform (I). Only its eastern retaining wall was observed, reflected by a robber-hole (F). A huge gypsum-layer (A) established a foundation for the upper platform (J). Its top-level was not preserved. The retaining walls (C) were heavily plundered and foundation walls (B) inside the platform had totally disappeared. From the foundation walls we deduce a building upon the platform. A large robber-hole (D), finally, from top to bottom of the tell, indicates a centrally placed, deep-lying structure, presumably the main sanctuary of this temple.

ARCHITECTURE
Temple Ia presents a rectangular upper platform, fig. 37. The sides are 23–25 m long and 15–17 m wide. The fully preserved northern retaining wall was 2 m high. Local stone with clay as mortar was used as building material.

Temple Ib was first recognized during the re-study and no excavation was aimed directly at the understanding of phase b. The outline of its upper platform may have been trapezoid. Again local stones were used but now with gypsum as mortar. The obverse was plastered.

The platform was solid, apart from a perhaps symbolic room in the southwest corner of Temple Ia. On the gypsum-floor several rooms were built, en suite along the sides, a single room in the centre. This was definitely a cella; at one end the typical altar-podium was found. Appurtenances of the cult appeared in the open areas between the rooms. The lower platform of oval or semi-circular shape is only known from fragments but there is no doubt of its existence.

36 NE-Temple, section

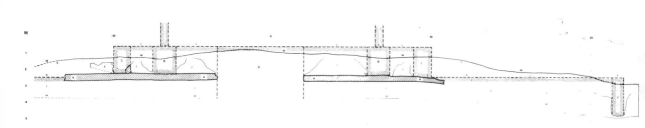

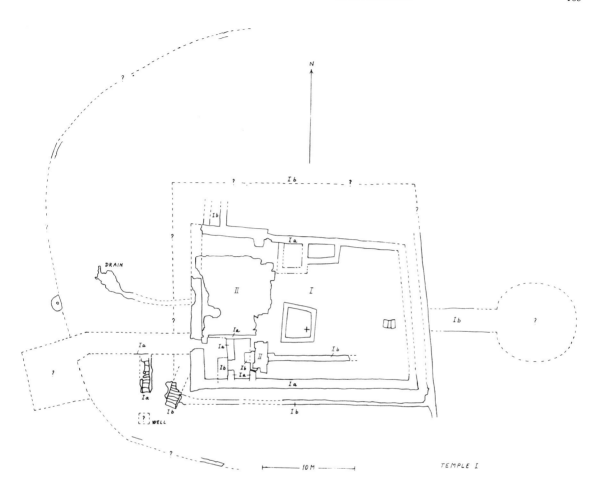

37 Temple Ia–b, plan

The same applies to the wing-structures, although of the enclosure only a ramp (Ib) could be documented and of the basin parts of a staircase (Ia), both leading to the respective structures which are such striking features of Temple II.

The temple well itself was not found either but two shafts with steps led down through the lower platform, exactly where all later wells were situated. These structures belonged to Temple Ia and b respectively.

Finally the topographic situation of Temple I should be briefly described. It was placed on a low mound sloping down towards a depression in the southwest where a freshwater spring was gushing.

Temple II, a replica of Temple I, was the best preserved temple, fig. 38. Finely worked limestone, perhaps from Jidda Island, created the temple's new look. We shall deal with it in four parts: the upper platform, the lower platform, the basin and the enclosure.

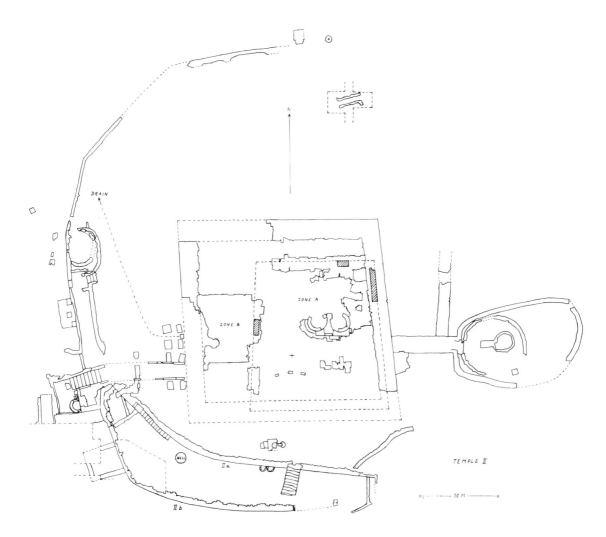

38 Temple IIa–b, plan

1. The upper platform remained trapezoid, measuring 26 × 24½ × 27 × 25 m. A solid ashlar wall 2 m high formed the retaining wall, but only 40% of the flight was preserved. The new floor-level was covered with slabs and comprised two areas, A and B, B lying a little lower than A.

Partly standing on foundation walls, partly on retaining walls, a special wall surrounded A, indicating the proper sanctuary, either as a trapezoid court or building, one side 15 m, the other ones 18 m each. Inside were found series of remains belonging to the cult and dominated by a centrally placed, double circular altar. The western area, B, was occupied by rooms, partly secondarily built, but the wider continuity was broken.

2. The lower platform, the half part of an oval figure or adapted

to the ground as a semi-circle, presents two retaining walls in a sequence, a and b, the latter phase 58 m broad. The long axis measures more than 70 m. The northern walls were low, the southern ones much higher, because of different ground levels, fig. 39.

The oval wall IIa was preserved to the south, 3½ m high, ending to the west at the basin, to the east at a transverse retaining wall. Sideways a stairway led down to a well at the foot of the wall and a frontal one also appeared. Plastered local stones were used for the wall.

The oval wall IIb was partly plundered. Ashlar masonry brought this new wall into stylistic harmony with other Temple II walling.

On top of this platform an altar appeared to the south. The well was rebuilt by a shaft through the enlargement, established by the

39 The successive retaining walls of the lower curved platform of Temple IIa and IIb. Here to the south the walls still stand in places to their original height of 3–4m. Above and to the right rose originally the upper platform and the actual temple buildings

Temple IIb platform. Thus the well could be operated from the top of the platform.

North of the basin was a small oval enclosure, measuring 6 × 4 m, and a short stairway belong to Temple IIa, a podium with a triple-altar to Temple IIb as well as a number of upright stones on plinths. A double wall with a bottom layer of ashes appeared to the north.

Sections in all directions gave qualified evidence of the fact that the lower platform was covered when Temple III was built.

3. The basin appeared at the foot of the oval platform to the west as a chamber sunk below ground level, enclosing a freshwater spring. It was connected with the upper platform by a staircase and appeared as a subterranean structure, 6 m long and 4–5 m broad but much rebuilt. Thus it discloses a final phase in the long history of Temple II. It must have been roofed and was covered when Temple II was demolished.

We can discern a room-partition, an eastern antechamber, giving admission to a deep western room, the proper basin. This measured 4 × 2½ m high ashlar walls. The water stood 1½ m high. Large subterranean channels lead out into the surroundings. A water-cult was indicated by the interior, a cylindrical cistern and a stone jar with holes, the latter placed upon a high socle.

A staircase, 15 m long and almost 2 m broad, with about 30 steps, leads from the basin to the upper platform, an ascent of 7 m height. Only the lowest eight steps were preserved and again a single one, exactly on the surface of the lower platform. This step happens to be the threshold-stone of a gateway and passing through this the processions moved down through the lower platform to the basin. In the opposite direction from the gateway the staircase was free-standing, leading to the upper platform. At the foot of the retaining wall it was flanked by a double line of eight great socket stones.

4. The enclosure to the east of the temple was dedicated to large-scale sacrifices, attested by massive deposits of dark, grey, powder-like layers, covering the eastern area. A ramp connected the enclosure with the upper platform. Several building-stages are known, two of them successive, both belonging to Temple II. An older enclosure was circular and on the plastered floor was placed an altar-structure. The latest enclosure was a large oval one, 15 × 9 m, with an altar-block in the southern area. The uppermost phase of the ramp belongs to this enclosure and a road leads from the ramp in a northern direction. Like the basin the sacrificial enclosure fell victim to the building of Temple III.

To the east of the enclosure we discovered parts of a large sub-terranean channel.

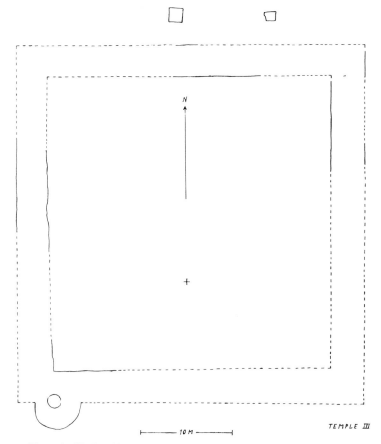

TEMPLE III

|——— 10 M ———|

Temple III, fig. 40, was so damaged by stone-plundering that the excavators misinterpreted the basic structure. It was explained as an 'enclosing, outer wall' surrounding a ceremonial mound which covered a deserted temple site. Actually this very wall was the retaining wall of a right-angled, square platform, measuring 38 × 38 m, elevated on the covered remains of Temple II. 3½ m broad, this wall was built of a mixture of gypsum and limestone blocks, with huge boulders at the rear. Two large socket stones to the north may have flanked a now disappeared stairway. The old well was rebuilt, now looking like an apsis, protruding from the southern retaining wall. The new well-shaft was placed on top of the preceding one of Temple IIb.

The floor had totally disappeared. Lying well above the tell-surface, it would give a minimum height of 4 m, Temple III then rising to the double height of its predecessors, now as a perfect square but without wing-structures. Instead of that we have through the NE-Temple the conception of a double-temple, fig. 41. Altogether this presents a remarkable break with the tradition.

40 Temple III, plan

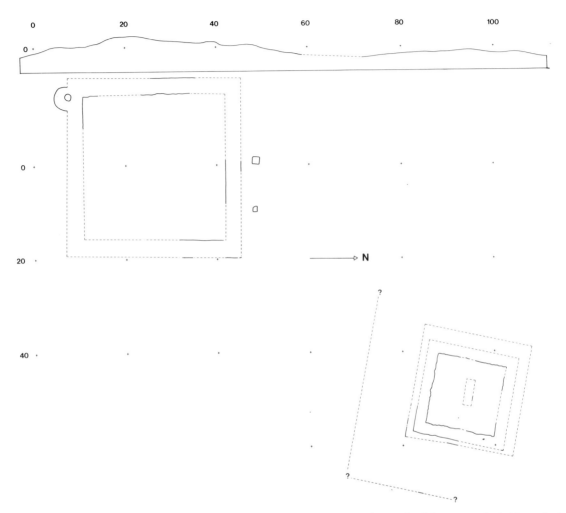

41 Temple III and NE-Temple, situation plan, above contour of the double tell

The NE-Temple also appeared as a double stepped platform but very little is known about the lower platform, fig. 42. The upper one, however, was a perfect square, standing upon a thick foundation layer (A) of gypsum, measuring 24 × 24 m. Upon this foundation two square walls had been built, an outer one and an inner one. The outer walling (C) was the retaining wall, measuring 19 × 19 m. The inner walling (B) was a foundation wall, measuring 15 × 15 m. Upon this wall we must imagine a building on the floor of the upper platform.

A robber-hole (D) in the centre went through the whole tell. We may here see evidence of a former structure, sunk well below the surface but excavation came to an end before clear evidence of the sense of the structure was obtained. Maybe the L-shaped staircase of the sacred well at Umm es-Sejur gives an idea of the sanctuary which we can imagine here.

In spite of the plundering of almost all the walling, enough remains to postulate a height of 2 m for each platform. This reveals a structure comparable with Temple III.

INTERPRETATION

Dedications were never found. Therefore the interpretation of the Barbar Temple has to rely upon the architecture and in a wider sense upon the identification of Bahrain with Dilmun and a general background in the Sumerian culture.

Considering the architecture of Temple I and II, the oval temple, we may speak of a provincial Sumerian style with traditions going back to temples like the one of Al-Ubaid which was dedicated to the mother goddess, Ninkurzag. Local features would then be the stone architecture, the axes of orientation, the interior of the sanctuary etc.

Considering the spiritual tradition, the myth of 'Enki and Ninkurzag' would point to three deities which must have been important to a cult-centre in Dilmun, the divine pair, Enki and Ninkurzag, and Enki's son Inzag.[1] Enki and Ninkurzag's connection with Dilmun is rooted in the mythical idea of this country as their divine province. Inzag later appears as the patron-deity of Dilmun.

The clue to our problem may be given by some striking features of the Barbar Temple. The temple was situated at a freshwater spring, indicating the numinous power which gave the impulse for the cult at Barbar. Over this spring was built a basin and we know that a water-cult took place here. If we in this case want to draw a conclusion, the

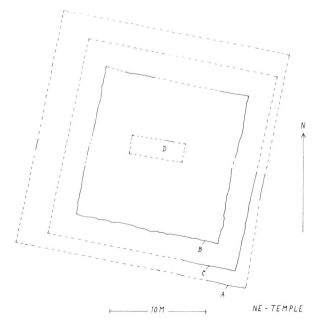

N

10 M   NE - TEMPLE

42 NE-Temple, plan of the upper platform, the walls (B and C) indicated through outer outlines

most obvious interpretation would be that this unique structure represents an 'apsu'. The temple-apsu is well known from the texts but it has been extremely difficult to identify in excavations.[2] As the special dwelling of Enki, the god of the subterranean freshwater ocean, also called 'apsu', this deity then is reflected in an outstanding way. As a deep, quiet, hidden place the apsu is the abode of Enki as the god of wisdom. He there administers the 'mes'[3] and as the Lord of the Apsu he is also the god of the springs which dispense freshwater and fertility.

The power of water to cleanse made Enki a prominent god of purification and lustration magic. The holy ablutions which took place in the apsu of the temple yielded the life-spending power of its water and from this point of view we can imagine what his worshippers had to do when they moved down from the 'high temple' of Barbar to the 'watery deep' where Enki was the master.

Confronted with this sphere of Enki, we would like to draw attention to another specific feature of the architecture of our temple, i.e. the clay-layer at the bottom of the whole structure. The myth of 'Enki and Ninmach' explicitly refers to 'the clay above the apsu', from which, according to this myth man was created by Enki, Ninmach (another name for Ninkurzag) and Nammu (Enki's mother). The

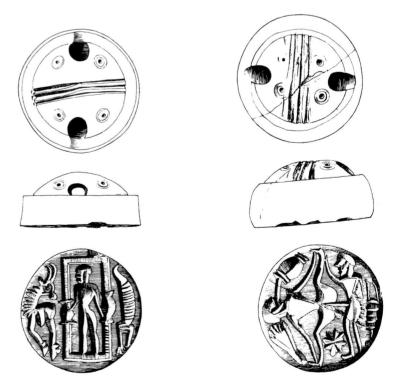

43 Seal-engravings depicting Enki

clayish foundation of the Barbar Temple may be an expression of this idea and it looks definitely more ritual than functional.

It may also be mentioned that a Nippur hymn refers to a temple of a god of wisdom in Dilmun in this way: 'In the temple of Shag-namsar (i.e. benefactor of wisdom) which is in the mount of Dilmun, in the temple of the holy stylus.'[4]

Enki himself is in our opinion depicted at least on two seals found at Barbar, fig. 43. One shows Enki in his apsu,[5] one shows him celebrating a 'sacred marriage'. The myth of 'Enki and Ninkurzag' is concerned with Enki's incestuous sexuality as a repeated motif. Our scene would then show Enki and Utto, with Enki taking his pleasure of Utto intoxicated by the wine he had given her.[6]

The stairway leading to the apsu also led to the sanctuary of the upper platform. It may of course have been dedicated to Enki but his consort goddess, Ninkurzag, may have been worshipped here too and the double altar might reflect the cult of a divine pair.

On Temple III and the NE-Temple it is difficult to make any comments. The proper sanctuaries had disappeared but the changes of the architecture may imply new tendencies in the cult. As an example we can here mention the growing importance of Inzag.

1. Also Inzag's consort goddess, Lakhamum (P. B. Cornwall, *Dilmun*, 1944, 158ff), Erua (M. Jastrow, jr., *Die Religion Babyloniens und Assyriens I*, 1912, 117), Meskilak and Nin-insina (D. O. Edzard, in: H. W. Haussig, *Wörterbuch der Mythologie I*, 1965).

2. Cf. the L-shaped, sunk chamber in the so-called 'Steinstifttempel' in Uruk (H. Lenzen, *Vorlaufiger Bericht über di . . . Ausgrabungen in Uruk-Warka*, XV, 1959, 15ff).

3. 'You (i.e. Enki) have placed the numinous power ('me') of your chosen shrine, the apsu, the sublime sanctuary, over all numinous powers' (K. Oberhuber, *Die Kultur des alten Orients*, 1972, 58).

4. An Assur-fragment gives E-karra (i.e. Quai-Temple) as name of a Dilmun-temple (P. B. Cornwall, *Dilmun*, 1944, 53).

5. Cf. an Akkadian representation of this motif (H. Frankfort, *Cylinder Seals*, 1939, pl. XVIII, k).

6. We here follow a special interpretation of the myth (T. Jacobsen, *Before Philosophy*, 1949, 171).

The Barbar Temple:
its chronology and foreign relations reconsidered

PEDER MORTENSEN

Shortly after Professor P. V. Glob had started excavations at Barbar in 1954 he suggested a third millennium date for the site. His argument for this – supported by Geoffrey Bibby – was primarily Mesopotamian parallels to some of the more outstanding copper objects found during the first two years of excavation: some of the weapons, the handle shaped as a man, and the bull's head. Although a few prominent European and American archaeologists, pointing to Roman and Parthian parallels to the red-ridged pottery and the ashlar-built walls, suspected the temple at Barbar to be much later, the date given by Glob and Bibby has since been generally accepted.

Some years later, in 1970, an attempt was made to date the individual phases of the temple complex. Referring to a sherd of a polychrome Jemdet Nasr jar found in a layer north of the first temple and to the deposit of conical clay goblets known from the foundation of the earliest temple, I suggested an Early Dynastic I date for Temple I. The construction of the second temple which at the same time was assumed to be the first oval temple at Barbar was, with some uncertainty, dated towards the middle of the third millennium. With reference to the stamp seals the third temple was noted still to be in use towards 2000 B.C.

This fairly long sequence was supported by evidence published by Elisabeth During Caspers (1971b; 1974). But more recently a short chronology indicating an Ur III-Isin-Larsa date for the three temples has been suggested by Daniel Potts (1978 and 1983a) and by Curtis E. Larsen (1983). Larsen's conclusions are based primarily on an examination of a ceramic sequence from Ras al-Qal'a for which he has traced a number of useful Mesopotamian parallels, and on a correlation between the sequence of Ras al-Qal'a and the Barbar temples.

In the meantime, however, our conception of the architectural development at Barbar has been modified and revised at a number of essential points as a consequence of H. Hellmuth Andersen's recent work on the stratigraphy of the temples at Barbar. The first temple has now been subdivided into two phases, Ia and Ib, and Temple IIa and IIb can be separated from what was previously thought to be part of temple III. A preliminary re-examination of the ceramic sequence and of other pieces of evidence useful in dating the Barbar temples will therefore be presented here.

One of the difficulties in dealing with the pottery from Barbar is that ceramics from Temple II and III deposits are mixed with sherds from earlier phases. This is especially the case with materials found within the temple terraces, which to a great extent are filled up with soil from earlier constructions. A casual acquaintance with the pottery from Barbar might in this way leave a false impression of typological stability – or lack of change – within the sequence. The ceramic evidence presented here is therefore based on seven samples of pottery from Barbar, deliberately chosen from contexts that can be clearly defined:

1. *Phase Ia* is represented by ceramics found within the first temple platform and sealed off by the terrace floor.

2. *Phase Ib* by a sample from occupation layers north of the platform.

3. *Phase IIa* by pottery from layers deposited in front of the south wall of the oval platform during the time when the temple was in use.

4–5. *Phase IIb* by two samples from layers accumulated within the eastern oval, and outside the southern terrace wall, respectively.

6. *Phase III* by sherds from occupation layers on the western side of the temple, outside the large, square terrace wall and probably representing a rather late phase in the development of the third temple.

7. *The NE-temple* is represented by a sample of pottery found below the terrace floor.

The typical Barbar pottery is a sand- and lime-tempered ware, hard fired, but in the early phases rather brittle. The firing has often been irregular, resulting in colours ranging from bright red to greyish. There is a tendency towards darker red and brownish wares in the later part of the sequence, i.e. in Temple IIb and III.

The chain-ridged ware is restricted to Temple I, whereas the ordinary ridged Barbar ware, in a great range of varieties, occurs throughout the sequence, although it represents less than 4% of the materials from Temple III.

A plastic decoration consisting of small knobs or of vertical or wavy bands added across the horizontal ridges is restricted to pottery from Temple I. A few pink and orange ware sherds appeared in Temple I which also produced a number of buff sherds with a fine purple or plum-red slip.

44 Red Barbar ware, Diagram showing the development of hole-mouth jars and goblets from temple Ia to III

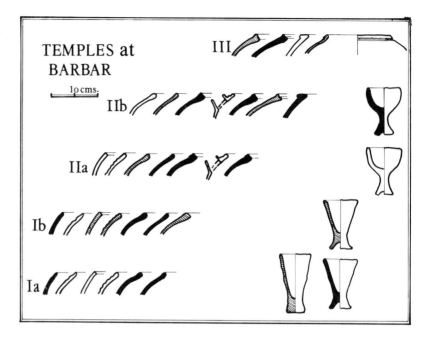

TEMPLES at BARBAR

10 cms.

III

IIb

IIa

Ib

Ia

It is remarkable that buff ware sherds, compared to the local Barbar ware, is rare, representing 3% of the ceramic assemblage from Temple Ia and less than 1% from Ib and II. Only in the late sample from Temple III, 29% of the sherds are buff.

The development of a selection of ceramic types at Barbar can be illustrated as follows: The first diagram, fig. 44, shows a series of goblets and profiles of hole-mouth jars arranged in horizontal rows by temple phases, starting at the bottom with Temple Ia. The most common types are shown in black, the less common are filled in by hatching, and types represented only by a few examples are shown in outline. The frequency of the individual types can thus be followed vertically from bottom to top. Characteristic of the hole-mouth jars shown in this plate is a development from plain or slightly rounded rims in Temple Ia and b to rather elaborate thickened or flat rims in IIb and III. A few globular jars with a short spout appear in IIa and b. The temporal distribution of the goblets, as shown to the right, is already well known, starting in Temple I with conical beakers, some of which have a solid foot, and ending with open, half-globular goblets in Temple IIb.

The next diagram, fig. 45, shows a series of bowls to the left, and to the opposite a selection of rim-profiles of large cooking-pots and pithoi, most common in IIa and b.

The development of the rim-profiles of the classical Barbar jar with a vertical neck is illustrated in fig. 46. The high-necked collars

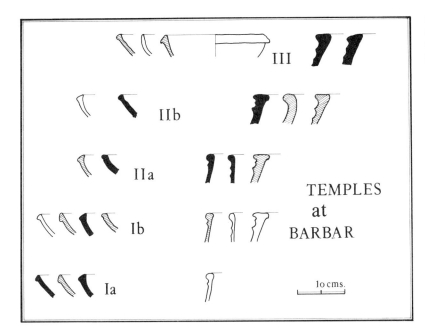

III

IIb

IIa

TEMPLES
at
BARBAR

Ib

Ia

1o cms.

45 Red Barbar ware. Diagram showing the sequential development of bowls, cooking pots and pithoi

with a plain or triangular rim are typical for the early phases, whereas Temple IIb, and especially Temple III are characterized by shorter collars with thick triangular lips often heavily drawn down along the outside of the rim.

As previously mentioned the distribution of buff ware sherds at Barbar, fig. 47, is characterized by an almost complete gap in Temple II, and by a remarkable discontinuity in types from Ib to III. In Temple III a number of new shapes appear in buff ware as well as in the local red or reddish brown ware.

Painted pottery is rare, and most of it is a simple, local imitation of the ridged ware, painted in black, sometimes on a creamish or white slip or wash. There are, however, a few pieces of imported painted pottery. From Temple I comes the Jemdet Nasr sherd previously mentioned. I think it must have found its way into this place from an earlier activity at the site, perhaps in connection with the well. Found in Temple I layers, and restricted to Ia and b are also a few painted sherds of Umm an-Nar type. An interesting sherd decorated with an opposed semi-circular pattern, characteristic of the Wadi Suq phase in Oman, was found in a Temple II context north of the temple.

It has previously been pointed out, first by Geoffrey Bibby and since by Curtis E. Larsen, that there is a close resemblance between the pottery from the Barbar temples and City 2 at Ras a-Qal'a. But after the ceramic sequences from City 1 and 2 at Ras al-Qal'a have

46   Red Barbar ware. Diagram
showing the sequential
development of collared jars

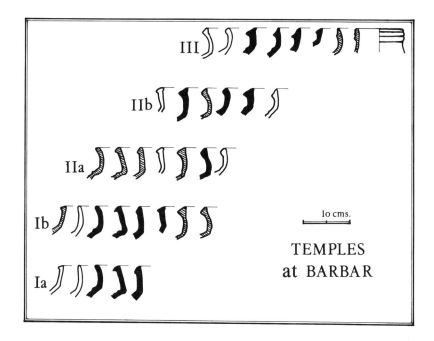

been re-examined by Flemming Højlund, it is now possible, based on
his observations, to correlate the Barbar temples more exactly with
the sequence at Ras al-Qal'a, fig. 48. The presence of both chain-
ridged and ridged wares, characteristic of Temple I, is only paralleled
at City 2 A. The materials from Barbar IIa is closely related to the 2 B-
phase at Ras al-Qal'a, and the late sample from Barbar III seems to be
similar to late City 2 or 3 A, whereas the pottery from the NE-Temple
at Barbar typically seems to fit in approximately at the end of Temple
IIb – before City 2 F at Ras al-Qal'a.

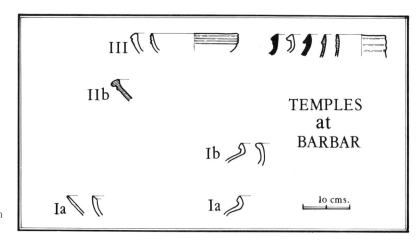

47   Barbar buff ware. Diagram
showing the sequential distribution
of some characteristic shapes

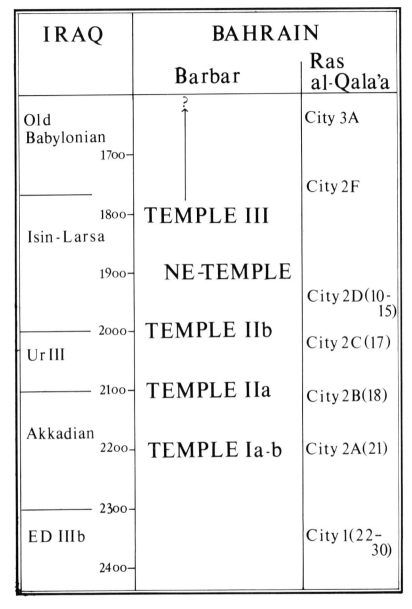

IRAQ	BAHRAIN	
	Barbar	Ras al-Qala'a
Old Babylonian		City 3A
1700		
		City 2F
1800	TEMPLE III	
Isin-Larsa		
1900	NE-TEMPLE	
		City 2D(10-15)
2000	TEMPLE IIb	
Ur III		City 2C(17)
2100	TEMPLE IIa	City 2B(18)
Akkadian 2200	TEMPLE Ia-b	City 2A(21)
2300		
ED IIIb		City 1(22-30)
2400		

48 Chronological table showing the correlation between Mesopotamia and phases at Barbar and Ras al-Qala'a

In a wider perspective there are on a general level some similarities between ceramics from Barbar I and IIa on the one side, and Akkadian and Ur III pottery especially from Nippur, and from the Diyala and Hamrin regions in Mesopotamia on the other side. More specific parallels can be pointed out between a number of types from Temple IIb and the Isin-Larsa phase at Ahmad al-Mughir and other sites in the Hamrin plain, and between the pottery from the

NE-Temple at Barbar and sites in Susiana, especially the Simashki-phase at Farukhabad, dated roughly between 2100 and 1900 B.C.

The foreign relations of Barbar are perhaps more clearly visible within other groups of finds of which only a few shall be mentioned here because of their possible chronological implications.

In his article H. Hellmuth Andersen has briefly touched upon the altar stones with holes erected in the courtyard of Temple II. Heavy wear along the edges of the holes originally led P. V. Glob to suggest that the stones might have been used when tethering animals for sacrificing. Professor Edith Porada has kindly pointed out to me that similar stones, originally functioning as anchors, were found erected in temples at Ras Shamra and Byblos. A variety of shapes were found along the Mediterranean, but those most similar to the stones from the Barbar date to the last centuries of the third millennium. Almost identical anchor-stones have been found in Egypt where they have been used secondarily in connection with bull offerings, e.g. at Saqqara in front of the tomb of Mereruka, dating to the Sixth Dynasty.

Other hints towards the date of Temple IIa at Barbar are given by some of the objects found below the floor of this temple, possibly placed there as foundation deposits. The cylindrical alabaster jars are similar to jars from the third millennium found widely spread over the Near East from Egypt to Mesopotamia. The facetted rim-profile of the tallest jar is, however, not only rare, but is in Egypt restricted to the Fifth and Sixth Dynasties. A cylindrical alabaster jar with an identical rim has been found at Ur in an Akkadian context.

In his paper on the metal objects from Barbar, Dennis Heskel has pointed towards a number of similar copper objects found in Syria, Mesopotamia, and Iran. In the present context, however, I shall touch briefly upon the most famous object from Barbar, the bull's head of copper, also found below the floor of temple IIa. This head is traditionally compared with similar Early Dynastic heads from the Royal Cemetery at Ur, and from Khafajah, Al Ubaid and Tello. But in my opinion the most striking stylistic feature that can be paralleled in Mesopotamia is the very characteristic way in which the horns of the bull are shaped: when seen *en face*, they describe a low curve out and then almost meet again over the head of the animal; but instead of meeting they turn into an approximately parallel final course. Comparing these horns with the horns of bulls and bullmen depicted on Mesopotamian cylinder seals there is no similarity to the rather low and open horns of the Early Dynastic periods, but there are a number of close stylistic parallels from Late Akkadian and – to a slightly lesser extent – from Ur III cylinder seals.

Another chronological tie between Temple IIb at Barbar and a number of other sites at Bahrain and along the coast of the Arabian Gulf is the first appearance of the typical Dilmun seals. With one exception the stamp seals found at Barbar are of type 1 A in Poul Kjærum's terminology. They appear at Ras al-Qal'a in City 2 C, and at Failaka in phase IA in a context dated by imported cylinder seals to the transition between Ur III and Isin-Larsa. Finally, one seal of Kjærum's type I B, dated to the Old Babylonian period, was found at Barbar in Temple III occupation layers.

In conclusion we are left again with a fairly long chronology for Barbar, assuming that the temples cover a period of roughly six to seven hundred years. The ceramic correlations with Ras al-Qal'a and Failaka are now clear. There is not yet an exact fixpoint for the building of Temple I, although we believe that the temple was built by the middle of the Akkadian period. But it must be emphasized that the early temples at Barbar seem to reflect archaic traditions expressed in the architecture as well as in the pottery and in the tradition of scattering votive goblets over a large area in the interior of the temple terrace.

The foundation deposits of Temple IIa indicate an Akkadian or early Ur III date, and the Ur III-Isin-Larsa date suggested for Temple IIb is supported by two radio-carbon dates which, calibrated, give an age of 2035 B.C. and 2070 B.C. $\pm$ 100 years. The NE-Temple and the third temple were probably founded in the middle of the Isin-Larsa period. But the recent ceramic analyses of pottery from Temple III occupation layers in relation to Flemming Højlund's comparative studies of the second millennium pottery from Failaka and Ras al-Qal'a have surprisingly given the Third – and unfortunately very little known – Temple at Barbar a life of possibly three hundred years in the second millennium, throughout the Old Babylonian period down towards the beginning of the Kassite era in the Gulf.

The Barbar Temple: the masonry

BRIAN DOE

At the Barbar temple site there are three stone built temples super-imposed one above the other. This illustrates successive rebuilding as the earlier structures fell into disrepair, a characteristic of the Sumerian temples found in Mesopotamia.

Temples I and II are approximately the same in size but Temple III, covering a larger area above Temple II, has been robbed of stone and only portions of its large foundations, square socketed bases at the northern entrance and the circular well head remain.

Temple I lies completely beneath the floor of Temple II. It was surveyed during the original excavation, when it was seen to have been built in comparatively small stones and had a plaster floor. By contrast, Temple II was built in large squared masonry and the floor was paved.

The types of masonry, the method of construction and the workmanship of the cut stone, the ashlar facing stone of the southern perimeter wall and the Apsu chamber suggest that a technological change took place during the time between the building of Temple I and Temple II. It is also apparent that the use of small stones con-tinued, probably for economy, in parts of the later temple.

This early development in the type of stone masonry apparently bridges the technical gap between the use of clay blocks and of stone as a building material. The use of collected stones of a suitable size led to the discovery and quarrying of stone, a technique which also required the manufacture of the stone blocks and their transport to the site.

This is the only temple with Sumerian religious and architec-tural affinities so far known to have been constructed in stone. The limestone used for Temple II is thought to have been quarried and shipped from the nearby island of Jedda and from a quarry on Muharraq Island.

At Barbar stone was used for the foundations, walls and flooring of a temple by people who were apparently unused to stone masonry

but who, from their building technique, could have been familiar with clay brick construction and therefore understood the need to build in level courses.

Temple I has been partly excavated, but except for a portion of its plaster floor, now exposed on the northwest corner, it has been covered over and lies beneath the floor of Temple II. The north wall of Temple I was seen to be of roughly hewn small stones, uncut blocks of random size and coursed. This type of walling is usual when good stone is not plentiful or available, and could have been used by builders without a stone building tradition. Similar stone work, to be seen in the construction of the tomb burials at Sar, points to the availability of stone in the area.

THE MASONRY OF TEMPLE II

Examples of well cut masonry are evident in the finely cut stonework and edging of the foundations, noticeable particularly in the exposed walling on the east and north walls, fig. 49. Here the large rectangular cut stone of foundation walling and portions of the superstructure remain *in situ* on the east side and on the smaller superstructure on the west side of the temple, where there remains an example of well cut paving slabs, laid on plaster screeding.

This ability in cutting stone was not apparently fully exploited and structural strength was realised more by the size of the stones, some perhaps in weight up to two tons, than by the building method. One must admire the ability with which such heavy stones were transported and placed in position.

In certain of the walls there was no apparent attempt at regular

50 Fine squared paving in the foreground laid in single line with breaking joint.
Immediately behind are remains of the plaster floor of Temple I.
Beyond are the remains of foundations of Temple III which was built above Temple II

bonding and the sheer weight of each stone provided stability. However some courses of stones were laid across the thickness of the wall thus binding the sides together. The necessity for horizontal courses was clearly understood but the need for alternate 'breaking' or offset vertical joints for lateral strength was not fully appreciated. On occasion the joints continue almost vertically through several courses. This suggests that while the need for a regular size and shape was appreciated by the stone cutters the builders were inexperienced in the method of bonding.

A similar characteristic is seen in the fine paving on the west side of the platform of Temple II, fig. 50. Here slabs are laid with a straight joint, or course, in one direction and regular offset joints in the other. Elsewhere the paving is not so evenly squared.

Fine cut stone blocks were also used on the south oval wall and also for the walling of the Apsu on the west side.

In this walling, of a later phase of Temple II, it is noticeable that where a square cut stone does not fit the adjacent stone, a piece is cut out of that stone or another small piece of stone is inserted during building operations. This characteristic is seen in 'solid' stone walling and also in the ashlar facing of the southern oval 'platform' wall. Here the ashlar facing stone used in conjunction with solid masonry walling suggests an economy in the use of large blocks.

The use of thinner stone slabs as a facing in conjunction with larger blocks, is noticeable also in the masonry walling of the Apsu, fig. 51. Again the horizontal joint or course was maintained for stability although vertical joints do not alternate with regular frequency and in certain places stones have been cut to fit the

51 The Apsu, the stone chamber built over the holy well or spring. This view from the ceremonial staircase faces the west wall and illustrates the masonry workmanship

adjacent stone. This suggests the method of construction was not fully appreciated, and as stone sizes were not standardised there had to be instances of 'on site' cutting to fit stone together.

It may be noted that the large Umm an Nar tomb at Hili, now 'reconstructed', shows that certain ashlar facing slabs have been cut to fit together in a similar manner. Whether there were contemporary associations with the work at Barbar may only at this stage be suggested, although 'Umm an Nar' pottery is known in Bahrain not only at Qal'at al-Bahrain, but, it is understood, has been found in quantity at the Hamed Town excavations.

A collapse of part of the north wall of the Apsu due to an erosion of subsoil and pressure from the weight of sand, made it possible during the reconstruction to see the size and thickness of stones, for this wall incorporates rectangular blocks as well as thinner ashlar facings, particularly noticeable on the upper courses.

Probably the masonry in the Apsu and the masonry on the western end of the southern oval wall were contemporary, for this outer wall also shows the two sizes of masonry, fig. 52. It may be noted that this stone is different in texture and colour from the wall and foundation masonry of the Temple II platform and may have come from different quarries, for it was built at a later phase of construction.

52 Masonry at the western side of the southern oval wall. The technique of placing the stones on level courses and the chisel marking by the mason after building appears to show the use of the left hand

The faces of the ashlar masonry on the western end of this oval wall show signs of chisel finish, to produce a level surface. From the slanting chisel marks, which in places extend across adjacent blocks, this work seems to have occurred in situ, after the wall was built.

The inner terrace wall which follows an oval perimeter is built of random sized uncut stone laid roughly in courses. The staircase is built in similar stonework. This wall is considered to belong to Temple II, replacing a similar oval wall to the platform of Temple I, and probably reusing the stones. Although coated with juss plaster this stonework appears comparable with the stonework of the north wall of Temple I, the earliest temple. Thus this inner oval wall and staircase are of the same period – and provided the southern oval wall for the terrace of an earlier phase of Temple II, fig. 53.

The walls of the oval 'sacrificial' area on the east side are built of uncut random size stone similar to the walling of the earlier period. A ramp of cut stone leads up to the floor of Temple II.

Of the rectangular cut stone platform or altar with two circular plinths on the paved floor of Temple II it may only be said that here the masonry cutting and fine finish show the hand of a master craftsman, fig. 54.

Masonry blocks similar to the Temple II stonework have been observed lining some of the old wells of the northern oasis areas of Bahrain. It is of interest that evidence of early stone plundering of this Temple may have been in the first millennium B.C. At Janussan, east of Barbar, certain dressed stone built tombs have been constructed with large squared and chiselled masonry blocks. Their sizes and chiselling, similar to the masonry blocks remaining in the walling on the east side of the Barbar Temple II platform, suggest this was their origin.

53 The southern oval wall with behind the inner terrace wall and staircase in uncut stone. Behind the circular altar is the modern protective facing to the floor level of Temple II

54 The double circle 'altar'? or plinths on the paved floor of Temple II

ENVOY

The Sumerian influence, apparent in the design of the first two temples, appears to show in the use of small stone to replace clay blocks in Temple I, but the use of cut stone in Temple II suggests the craftsmen who built this may have come from elsewhere, where there was a tradition of building in stone.

The masonry technique at Barbar is similar in many respects to masonry found in the area now thought to have been Makkan. From here, quarrymen and masons, experienced in the construction of circular tombs and rectangular dwellings as at Umm an Nar, inland Buraimi and Oman may have been brought to Bahrain, ancient Dilmun, for the building of Temple II at Barbar, and perhaps other buildings.

The study of masonry technique in itself remains merely a guide but may be considered relevant evidence only when used in association with other dateable material.

'The land of Dilmun is holy . . .'

GEOFFREY BIBBY

I have taken my title from the best-known of all the references to Dilmun in the cuneiform corpus, the passage from the commencement of the myth of Enki and Ninhursag. You all know how it goes on – how Dilmun is a land where the lion kills not, and the wolf does not devour the lamb, a land where the sick say not 'I am sick', and the old man says not 'I am an old man'. Dilmun is a blessed land, where natural ills and sickness and death do not exist. That this description of Dilmun lies behind the Biblical story of the Garden of Eden may well be true, and there have been attempts to construe Dilmun as the Sumerian Eden and as the Sumerian Paradise. The Danish Sumerologist, Bendt Alster, has recently pointed out that this is going much too far.[1] He quite rightly states that the idea of an Eden, a land where man lived in bliss before all the curses of civilization were heaped upon him, is completely foreign to the Sumerians, who considered civilization to be a blessing bestowed upon mankind by the gods; and that Paradise, a place of eternal happiness beyond death, was equally outside their philosophy. This, I think, we must accept. But we must not throw out the baby with the bath water. We are left with some very specific statements, that Dilmun is a pure land, a Holy Land, a land immune to the ills to which flesh is heir.

But if Dilmun was a Holy Land to the Sumerians, did they do anything about it? Mackay's old idea, that the stupendous number of burial mounds on Bahrain must mean that people from outside the island were brought here for burial, has recently been revived by Carl Lamberg-Karlovsky.[2] Quite apart from the fact that there are serious faults with his mathematics, this is simply not tenable. Even with the most optimistic view of the number of persons buried in the mounds, even aided by the sensational discovery of the large burial complexes on the edges of the mound fields, and even with the most pessimistic view of the length of time that the mound fields were a-building, it is still impossible to deduce a population figure higher than the number of people who were living quite happily on Bahrain a hundred years ago, under probably more adverse climatic conditions than prevailed four thousand years ago. And Alster has pointed out, very truly, that burial overseas is an idea that would have been abhorrent to the Sumerians – and that, had they indulged in it, we should find it recorded in the tablets.

There is, of course, another possible Sumerian course of action. For hundreds and thousands of years pilgrims have sought the holy places of their faith in order to increase their chances of Eternal Life – and normally do not stay to be buried there. Was Dilmun a place of pilgrimage in the ancient world? There again the answer is clearly No. If it had been so, it would have been recorded. We know of only two Sumerians who came to Dilmun for purposes other than trade, Ziusudra and Gilgamesh. And while one admittedly settled here, he specifically did not die here. Anyway, both are very clearly portrayed as exceptions to the general run of humanity.

But is it perhaps wrong to look for holiness brought in from outside? Did Dilmun receive its reputation for holiness because it was holy to the Dilmunites? This is worthy of serious consideration. Because there are some very odd things about Bahrain, archaeologically speaking.

The most striking of these oddities, of course, are the burial mounds. Once we have come over the initial shock of seeing these unending thousands of mounds we rather tend to take them for granted. They just are there. But you can not just dismiss the largest burial field in the world like that. And from one point of view the size of the population that built them is immaterial. Whether they were built by a small population over a large number of centuries or by a large population over a small number of centuries, one thing is clear –that the population spent a large part of its available wealth and energy burying its dead. Looking at the burial practices of other contemporary peoples one can only compare the Dilmun preoccupation with death and the afterlife with that of Egypt. We know in Egypt – because the Egyptian climate has preserved the written records – how sophisticated was the religion that manifested itself in an elaborate care for the dead. Can we postulate a similar sophistication in Dilmun's religious life? We are at least forced to postulate a comparatively large corps of professional tomb-builders continually at work raising the stone chambers and the mounds. And it was not merely time they were willing to devote to the dead, it was also space. The mound fields cover a very appreciable amount of at least grazing ground. We can see today the quite impossible dilemma of the Antiquities Department, where it is impossible to extend a town, or build a new one, to expand a garden or build a road, without destroying a whole raft of burial mounds. That this situation was also reached in antiquity is strongly suggested by the burial complexes on the edges of the mound fields. They are just as elaborate as the mounds, just as monumental with their ring walls and stone chambers, but they did use less ground, which apparently was then beginning to be in short supply.

But it was not only death that interested the Dilmunites. When in 1953, just thirty years ago, we started looking for the settlements of the mound builders we found a promising tell at Barbar. We dug it, and found a temple. Just how imposing a temple it was, even by Mesopotamian standards, we now know from the excavators. We dug a mound close by to the northeast – and found another temple. Some years later the British expedition dug another apparent settlement not far away to the southwest – and found another temple. And half a mile away, at Umm es-Sejur, we had already dug what was traditionally supposed to have once been the largest well on Bahrain. It was a very cursory reconnaissance dig, and all we found, apart from a very considerable quantity of large fine squared blocks of cut stone lying jumbled below water level in the centre of the hollow, was a little underground chamber approached by a staircase and containing a very finely made well, with a wellhead formed of one single immense block of chiselled stone. And the sacred character of the well was shown by the decapitated statues of two rams found on the stair. I am more than half convinced that Umm es-Sejur, when it is dug, will turn out to be a temple that can well have outshone Barbar. So there we have four temples, all found almost casually while looking for something else, and all dating to the time of the mound builders, to the centuries around 2000 B.C.

Now, I do not know what it all means. But it does seem as though the ratio of temples to settlements is just as unusual as the ratio of burial mounds to settlements. In fact in the northwest corner of Bahrain nothing has been found *but* temples. They are very different, the one from the other, but two at least of them are fundamentally associated with fresh water. It makes one wonder whether *all* the fresh-water springs of Bahrain were holy springs, whether the people of Dilmun themselves believed that their abundance of artesian water was due to the especial favour of Enki, the god of the waters under the earth. Did they believe that they were a Chosen People, blessed in this world and the next? Did the Sumerians believe that Dilmun was a Holy Land because the people of Dilmun told them so?

1. B. Alster, 'Dilmun, Bahrain, and the alleged Paradise in Sumerian myth and literature', in *Dilmun. New Studies in the Archaeology and Early History of Bahrain*, ed. D. T. Potts, Berlin (1983).

2. C. C. Lamberg-Karlovsky: 'Dilmun: Gateway to Immortality', *Journal of Near Eastern Studies*, 41, 1982.

Bahrain and the Arabian Gulf during the second millennium B.C.: urban crisis and colonialism

CHRISTOPHER EDENS

The second millennium of the Arabian Gulf constitutes an enigmatic episode in the history of the region, a virtual blank between two long periods of great vitality. As in analogous cases in the history of western Asia, much scholarly attention is paid those periods about which a great deal may be said, while considerably less effort is expended on 'dark ages'. The present study grapples with the second millennium 'dark age' in the Arabian Gulf, in the belief that social and economic changes of considerable historical significance occurred during this period, and that therefore the period will reward amply any study.

The paper is divided into two parts. The first section, descriptive in intent, provides a review of the available archaeological evidence of occupation around the Gulf during the second millennium; relevant Babylonian textual materials are included here. The second section, more synthetic and speculative in nature, provides an interpretation of the patterns found in the evidence reviewed in the first section. The theoretical bias of this section is that of world systems and interregional economic structures acting in time; this framework is the most appropriate for a region such as the Gulf.

Before proceeding with the review of evidence, the meaning of the term 'second millennium' must be defined. Contrary to what, strictly speaking, is implied by the term, the second millennium refers to the period c.1800/1700 to 800/700 B.C., i.e. the period of time between the better documented Early Bronze Age and Iron Age occupations throughout the Gulf. One may draw fairly firm limits of periodization at these two points, wherever one is in the Gulf. The second millennium defines a social historical unity *vis-a-vis* preceding and subsequent periods rather than an arbitrary slice of time.

REVIEW OF EVIDENCE

The leitmotiv of the Arabian Gulf during the second millennium B.C. is an obscurity of occupation, with only a very few exceptions. In this section of the paper these exceptions will be reviewed. In this review of evidence, Bahrain takes pride of place, due both to the occasion of the present volume and to the centrality of Bahrain to an understanding of the Gulf during this millennium. The theme of a Kassite horizon provides the thread on which other areas of the Gulf are strung in order of significance, followed by areas of whch little definitive may be said. The distinct case of Bušehr, the only relevant occupation on the Iranian coast, complete the *tour d'horizon*.

BAHRAIN

The ceramic content and dating of the late third millennium occupation of the Qal'at have been thoroughly discussed in Larsen's recent study (Larsen 1983). Larsen assigns an Isin-Larsa date to the City II occupation on the basis of converging lines of evidence. During the period of time represented by the Qal'at City II, settlement on the island was both extensive and urban: some fifteen Barbar II sites occur, extending far down the west coast; the Qal'at was a walled town of about 18 ha.; and other large 'urban' settlements also existed, e.g. at Diraz. Babylonian texts indicate that this apogee of third millennium occupation on Bahrain was coeval with the peak of trading relations with Babylonia, a trade which revolved around copper trans-shipped from Oman.

Larsen's review indicates a probable eighteenth century B.C. date for the end of City II, a conclusion entirely congruent with the disappearance of direct or indirect textual references to the Gulf trade at this time (Leemans 1968). The subsequent occupation at the Qal'at, City III, is Kassite in general character, for which a fourteenth-thirteenth century B.C. date seems most plausible. In other words, a gap in occupation, spanning three or four centuries, occurs at the Qal'at.

This Kassite[1] presence on Bahrain is attested only by the Qal'at itself, by a surface scatter of sherds near Barbar village (apparently since destroyed by cultivation), and by a very limited number of mortuary contexts, notably at al-Hajjar, Diraz, Sar and Buri (cf. Larsen 1983 for a listing of sites on Bahrain, to which may be added Mughal 1983: 64). In terms both of number and distribution of settlement, the Kassite period on the island marks an episode of retrenchment, a condition also reflected in amount of burials attributable to this time.

At the Qal'at, Kassite levels appear to be almost as widely spread through the site as are Barbar levels. Kassite repairs or rebuilding on the city wall are attested in the northern and western exposures (Bibby 1965: 103; 1966: 147; 1970 *passim*), while a Kassite construction in the southeastern part of the site seemingly represents a modest contraction of the area contained within the city walls along the southern edge of the site (Bibby 1965: 107). Occupation levels are associated only with the southern stretch of the exposed city wall (Bibby 1965: 107), although Kassite debris and pits occurred near the north wall (Bibby 1958: 155–6). Unfortunately none of these Kassite loci have been reported with any detail. Indeed, the only section of the Kassite occupation at the Qal'at which has received a degree of attention has been the so-called warehouse of the central sounding.

The central sounding contains a rectangular building 21.5 by 16.5 m in dimension, separated from what may be a second similar building by a wide street (12 m across) and from a third by a narrow alley (cf. Bibby 1970: 344). The main building consists of a total of eight chambers arranged symmetrically around a central passage, four rooms to a side, with entrance to the building from the west. The walls of the building are uniformly massive, the exterior walls being c. 1.5 m thick and interior ones only slightly less formidable; construction is of dressed stone, with plaster floors. Bibby has termed the building a warehouse on the basis of its contents, a description which fits neatly with expectations engendered by readings of two of the few Kassite documents referring to Dilmun (Cornwall and Goetze 1952). The function of the building, however, seems more complicated.

The contents of the building have been described in an abbreviated fashion in several preliminary reports and in Bibby's popular account. These descriptions permit an outlining of the notable materials from the structure. The depositional matrix directly on the floors of the building is described variously as being a highly bituminous or carbonized material (Bibby 1965: 103; 1970: 346) several cm thick (Bibby 1967: 90). Such deposits evidently refer to primary occupational activities within the building. Over this primary deposit is a fill sequence, some of which appears to be immediately post-occupational (e.g. the putative roof-fall; Bibby 1965: 106), while other elements may post-date Kassite occupation by a considerable time (e.g. the collapsed masonry in which the silver hoard was found; Bibby 1965: 102). These fill episodes contain materials which have no association whatsoever with the Kassite building (e.g. the silver hoard and a 'bathtub' burial), but also contain a certain amount of material which probably or definitely do belong with the building. Unless explicitly judged otherwise, the materials reported from the Kassite building are here considered to belong with the building. In any case, most of the objects are stated to derive either from the floor deposit or from immediately above this deposit, and in all likelihood are either genuinely associated with the floor or are from an upper story of the building.

The materials may be discussed under six headings: organics, metal, stone, ceramic, glyptic, and epigraphical. One feature of note: with the exception of two bones found in a jar set into the floor of a room (Bibby 1967: 91), no faunal remains are reported.

Organics: These include, in addition to bitumen, wood impressions, woven palm mats, date pits, and an unidentified grain (Bibby 1965: 102–3, 106). The first two items presumably derive from architectural elements, whereas the remaining two are contents of a pair of rooms. In one case, the date pits are said to have formed a pile on the floor, and it was from these pits that the single radiocarbon determination was derived.

Metal: Metal objects were found in at least two loci of the building. In one instance both weapons (a pair of spear points) and tools (a hoe blade), all of copper/bronze, were found in the fill directly over the primary deposit (Bibby 1965: 103). These implements are not illustrated or otherwise described.

Stone: Stone objects are limited to a cube of uncertain function found in the corner of a room, around which were several cobbles of a 'reddish-purple' stone (Bibby 1967: 91), and a large number of 'hammerstones' in the alley just north of the building (Bibby 1965: 106). In addition, some red ochre was found in one of the rooms of the building.

Ceramics: The ceramics are described only in reference to the '100 meter section', for which the Qal'at Kassite suite of forms and wares is presented (Bibby 1958: 155, 160, fig. 7; 1970: 136–138; see now Højlund, this volume). The Kassite assemblages are dominated by a range of pedestal bases, corresponding to the Kassite goblets (Nippur I types 46A and 47), a simple bowl (Nippur I type 43C) which occurs more rarely, and lids. The Qal'at pottery thus formally and qualitatively resembles Babylonian Kassite assemblages very closely. The fabric of these vessels is thick and coarse, of a 'honey' or 'caramel' color, and usually sand tempered. The latter feature marks a significant variation from Babylonian wares, which are characteristically tempered with chaff. In addition to this fabric, a poorly described red ware also occurs in the Kassite repertoire (Bibby 1967: 91), seemingly as a minor element.

Glyptic: No seals of any kind are reported as occurring in Kassite deposits at the Qal'at. However, at least three sealings do come from the Kassite building; one sealing from the fill over the primary deposit (Bibby 1965: 106) and two from the primary deposit of a single room (Bibby 1967: 91). Unfortunately, these materials have not been published or otherwise assessed. Two cylinder seals from the al-Hajjar graves are pertinent here. Made of faience (?) and iron ore (?), they are ranged by Porada with the Nuzi style and fourteenth-thirteenth century respectively. The latter seal is noteworthy in its stylistic discrepancies from its Mesopotamian referents, elements of which discrepancies perhaps align the seal with the earlier Gulf seal tradition (Rice 1972: 70–71).

Epigraphical: Two complete tablets and at least that number of fragments are reported from the central building; Bibby, in his popular account, puts the total number of pieces at six to seven (Bibby 1970: 347). One fragment was recovered from a secondary context while the remainder came from a primary context within a single room (Bibby 1965: 103; 1967: 91). As with the sealings, the tablets have not been published, although Bibby does characterize one as a school text, and another as an administrative text (Bibby 1970: 347). The name of Kastiliašu is legible on one of these tablets (K. Nashef, oral communication at the conference). In addition, the recent French expedition recovered a stone block bearing the name of Burnaburiaš from the Early Islamic fort in the northern part of the Qal'at. Mention of another piece of epigraphical material relevant to Kassite Tilmun is appropriate here: the 'shoe' found by Durand in the last century. The inscription on this stone refers to the tribal or geographical designation Agarum, which also occurs in several texts from Failaka (Glassner n.d.).

The variety of materials contained within the structure is more than Bibby's hypothesis of a date-storing warehouse will comfortably accommodate. The key to the question of function rests in the nature of the administrative apparatus found within the building (notably sealings and tablets) and in the character of the neighbourhood surrounding the building. Of the latter, only hints are available in the absence of further excavation – the walls of the other buildings seem quite as massive as those of the first, perhaps indicative of a public or otherwise wealthy quarter of the city – while the former will require the skill of specialists in assessment of the evidence. Meanwhile, Bibby's hypothesis may be broadened to a more general attribution of an administrative function of the building. In any event, the Kassite, i.e. Babylonian, nature of the City III period in Bahrain must be stressed, certainly in its ceramics and literacy, and seemingly also in its seals.

The date and duration of the Kassite occupation on Bahrain is uncertain. At present, only three lines of evidence may be brought to bear on the subject, each of which is ambiguous or otherwise limited – the ceramics from the Qal'at, the radiocarbon date from the 'warehouse', and the textual references in Kassite sources which mention Tilmun.

The Kassite ceramic assemblage from the Qal'at appears best to fit a later Kassite date, i.e. roughly 1400–1100 B.C., on the basis of comparison with Nippur (McCown and Haines 1967, Franke 1978) and Babylon (Reuther 1926, Strommenger 1964), as well as other sites (e.g. Aqar Kuf, the recent Hamrin excavations, etc.). Such comparisons must be used with extreme reservation, however, since the later Kassite and post-Kassite periods are two of the least understood in

Babylonian ceramic history, while earlier Kassite materials are virtually invisible. Moreover, an appeal to commonalities with Nippur and Babylon, while pragmatically intelligible, may be completely specious, given the strong probability of regional as well as temporal and functional variability in ceramic assemblages within Babylonia. The use of a sand temper distinguishes the Bahrain material from most of the straw tempered Babylonian ceramics. This contrast perhaps implies a local, or certainly non-Babylonian manufacture of the Bahrain Kassite pottery, a conclusion which should also warn against a facile comparison with Mesopotamian assemblages.

The single available radiocarbon date of a Kassite context at the Qal'at falls at 1180 ± 110 B.C. (K-827), uncorrected. Applying the most recently compiled calibration tables (Klein *et al.* 1982), this determination corresponds to a 95% confidence interval of 1670 to 1120 B.C. with a 'central tendency' of 1490 B.C. This single date does not help specify the chronology of the Kassite horizon more closely.

The available epigraphical evidence, restricted though it may be, suggests a more limited range of two centuries. The texts from Bahrain itself refer to a Burnaburiaš and to a Kastiliašu. The former is presumably Burnaburiaš II (1359–1333 B.C.), since the older Burnaburiaš reigned prior to the Kassite conquest of the Sealands and thus before his presence on Bahrain was geographically possible.[2] The latter is probably Kastiliašu IV (1232–1225 B.C.). Although an equation with Kastiliašu III is possible, thus occurring just after the conquest of the Sealands by Ulam-buriaš early in the fifteenth century, such an assignment is unlikely since Agum III (?) also campaigned in the Sealands in the following generation, indicating that the area was unlikely to have been firmly controlled by Ulam-buriaš, and so was unsuitable as a base for immediate expansion further south.

A few pertinent references to Tilmun are extant in sources from Babylonia. The earliest of these is the cylinder seal inscription published in this volume by J. Reade. This inscription refers to a Sukkanakku of Tilmun whom Reade dates to perhaps 1420–1410 B.C. A second and allied source is the pair of letters found at Nippur, also discussed by Reade. These texts make implicit reference again to a governor of Tilmun during the second half of the fourteenth century.

Other Babylonian sources mention Tilmun without implying a political connection between the two. A later copy of a text of Kurigalzu I (*c.*1400 B.C.) lists Tilmunite dates (asnê) as going to a temple of Ištar (Ungnad 1923). Assuming that this does not refer to a locally grown variety of date, Kurigalzu was adhering to an old tradition of the consumption of Tilmunite dates in cult settings (cf. Sigrist 1977: 174). A handful of texts from Nippur mention Tilmunites in Babylonia or Kassites in Tilmun (see Nashef 1982: 261 for citation). Although undated, these texts may be presumed to fall in the century between the reigns of Kurigalzu II and Kastiliašu IV inclusive, the period into which some 90% of the dated Nippur sources fit (Brinkman 1976: 37 and n.11; and more recently 1983). Lastly, the royal titulary of the Assyrian Tukulti-Ninurta I (briefly in control of Babylonia after 1225 B.C.) mentions both Tilmun and Meluḫḫa. Although the presence of the latter place name urges caution in accepting Tukulti-Ninurta's territorial claim at face value, the fact that his incursion into Babylonia put to an end the rule of Kastiliašu IV, who seemingly is named on a tablet from the Qal'at itself, lends a great deal of credence to Tilmun as a part of the Assyrian holdings (cf. Brinkman 1972: 276).

Two things stand out from the discussion of the textual evidence for Tilmun. First, the available sources span the two centuries between roughly 1420 and 1220 B.C. fairly evenly. Relations between Tilmun and Kassite Babylonia during these two centuries seem to have been regular, involving transference of both people and objects. Second, Tilmun apparently was under the political control of Babylonia for these two centuries, as shown by references, oblique or outright, to Babylonian governors of Tilmun neatly spanning both centuries.

Political control of Tilmun by Babylonian governors entails the existence of some form of colonialism on the island. Whatever its precise nature, colonialism helps account for the Babylonian nature of the material culture of this period on the island, though some local elements are barely perceptible.

The date of the Qal'at City IV occupation is somewhat less obscure. Salles' review of the problem indicates a seventh-fifth century B.C. date of the 'palace' and immediately subsequent vestiges (Salles 1982; see also Lombard this volume). This chronology leaves yet another long gap of four centuries or more in occupation. Some of this gap will probably be filled eventually, given textual references to Tilmun during the eighth century by Assyrian kings. But however this gap is to be filled, City IV marks a new stage for the Gulf – the redevelopment of local regional ceramic traditions, coeval with those of Iron Age Oman, which define new cultural distinctness from surrounding regions, even while in close interaction with them.

FAILAKA

The Danish excavations at Failaka are only now being published, with notices on the ceramics, architecture, and glyptics having appeared (Kjaerum 1980, 1983; Højlund 1981, 1983; Pollard and Højlund 1983). Additional notes have appeared for individual items found more recently (e.g. Ferrara 1977). These notices indicate that Barbar, Kassite and post-Kassite occupation levels occur in the two excavated second millennium sites on the island. Højlund's ceramic

studies, supplemented with architectural and stratigraphic information, indicate that breaks in occupation occur between each of these
major phases of habitation. However, the sites, particularly F-3,
apparently represent classic examples of spiral stratigraphy with
sectors of the site experiencing cyclical settlement and abandonment. This situation makes the apparent ceramic breaks of uncertain
import. Nonetheless, in view of occupational history both in Bahrain
and in southern Babylonia, a hiatus of settlement during the several
centuries between the early Old Babylonian and the later Kassite
occupations is not unreasonable. A similar gap between Kassite and
post-Kassite levels is less certain.

The sites F-3 and F-6 are fairly small (each under a hectare) and
were differentiated in function throughout the second millennium,
with F-6 containing a 'palace' complex and F-3 private architecture
and various special activity areas (e.g. Barbar period kilns). While
Kassite occupation of F-3 is definite, such an occupation of F-6 is less
sure (cf. the contradiction on this point in Højlund 1980, 1983); post-
Kassite levels may have the reverse assignment.

As with Bahrain, the dating of the Kassite and post-Kassite
phases is far from evident. The large number of Mitanni-style seals
would urge a date in the fifteenth-fourteenth centuries B.C., i.e.
roughly comparable with that suggested above for the Qal'at City III.
The Kassite ceramics of F-3 are not yet well enough published to
enter the discussion usefully. The post-Kassite dating of the last
occupation on F-6 presumably rests again on glyptic evidence,
although the published ceramics are entirely compatible with a
Kassite dating as well. On the whole, the combination of available
ceramic and glyptic indices fit most comfortably with a date broadly
identical with the date for City III, with a somewhat later occupation
also occurring on one site.

Kjaerum indicates a basic stylistic continuity from the older
third millennium Gulf seal tradition to major elements of the later
second millennium corpus on Failaka, exclusive of the cylinder seals.
The validity of this suggestion is enhanced by the cylinder seal
published by Ferrara, which presents a combination of Kassite
inscription and execution with a Gulf tradition repertoire of motifs.
Such a combination of traditions on a cylinder seal calls to mind the
al-Hajjar example. The meaning of this stylistic continuity and
'hybridization' is uncertain in the face of the disruption and
discontinuity of other traditions, most obviously of ceramics.

QATAR

The only side definitely assignable to the second millennium in Qatar
lies on a small island in the bay of Khor, excavated by the French
mission in the early part of this decade (Edens 1981, 1982). The site

consists of a small series of structures visible on the surface and a small shell midden, these features being the only contexts which yield any depositional depth. The ceramics of the site appear to conform to the Kassite assemblage at Failaka (Højlund 1983) and correspond well to certain elements of the Kassite assemblage at Babylon (Reuther 1926: 13; Abb. 1c, 7, 9; cf. Strommenger 1964). The Qatari assemblage also contains a sand-tempered red ware as a minority fabric. The same ambiguities in dating as face Bahrain and Failaka are present in Qatar as well. The single available radiocarbon determination falls at 850 ± 70 B.C. (Gif 5898), which corresponds to a 95% confidence interval of 1225 to 810 B.C. with a 'central tendency' of 1020 B.C. This date tends to support a date slightly later than City III, but again a single determination cannot be given a great deal of credence by itself.

The content of the midden is dominated by a single species of marine gastropod which, like its near relatives in the Murex family from the Mediterranean, produces a fast purple dye. The high relative frequency and absolute abundance of the gastropod, and the physical state of these shells in the midden, converge to suggest that the Khor site was in fact specialized in the production of purple dye. The overwhelmingly Kassite character of the ceramics of the site – both in fabric and in form – suggests further that the occupants of the site were closely associated with Babylonia of the later second millennium, either directly or, less likely, indirectly through Bahrain. The use of purple dyed cloth in Kassite and post-Kassite Baylonia is well known through textual evidence (cf. Aro 1970). Given this new site in the Gulf, there is no longer any reason to assume, *a priori*, that textual references to marine dyes implies relations to the west (cf. Oppenheim 1967 for just this assumption at a slightly later date). In sum, the archaeological and textual evidence for Babylonian involvement in the Gulf during the second millennium indicates that this involvement went well beyond a simple traffic in dates.

SAUDI LITTORAL

Zarin's recent excavations in the Dhahran tumuli field has produced a significant sequence of tomb deposits, two parts of which fall between the Barbar and Iron Age horizons. The earlier of these, occurring in a single tomb, is ceramically Kassite, and bears close resemblance to mortuary materials on Bahrain. A radiocarbon date for this deposit falls in the middle of the second millennium when corrected, but has a large standard deviation (Zarins *et al.* n.d.). The second part of the second millennium materials is aceramic in nature, identified by a variety of metal, stone and other materials. Zarins suggests that these deposits may refer to the Ahlamu or comparable peoples. Possibly related are a series of deposits with a coarse shell-tempered ceramic, stratified below Iron Age materials. Such ceramics are found on at least one coastal site (Zarins *et al.* n.d.). Potts (1982a) has summarized the Iron Age occupation of the Eastern Province.

The presence of second millennium occupation in the Jabrin area is suggested by a ceramic style which is usually placed in the third millennium, the so-called dark-faced hole-mouth material. While this style is undoubtedly a third millennium product, a radiocarbon determination from a sounding in the Jabrin area indicates that the ware may extend to the end of the second millennium (a date of 1100 ± 85, although whether this date is reported corrected, or what half-life is used is unclear; Adams *et al.* 1977: 29). As before, a single date by itself has limited significance particularly when a clearly first millennium ceramic form occurred on the same site in a cist grave (Adams *et al.* 1977: 29; Bibby 1973: 48). Bibby (1973: 59) also reports a socketed spear point from a tomb in the region, which he would date to the second millennium; given the revised dating of Omani metal (Lombard 1981), however, this assignment is uncertain. The subject of second millennium occupation in the Eastern Province clearly needs further clarification.

GREATER OMAN

As in the littoral regions to the north, occupation in greater Oman is undocumented from the second millennium, i.e. between the so-called Wadi Suq horizon and the Iron Age. The end of the Wadi Suq may be dated, somewhat conventionally, to 1800 or 1700 B.C., and the beginning of the Omani Iron Age to *c.*800 B.C. These chronological limits correspond perfectly with the second millennium of this review – a thousand years of negative evidence. The only hint of occupation during these thousand years comes from a series of radiocarbon dates published by Frifelt for Hili, two of which pertain to surficial features which perhaps post-date the Wadi Suq horizon (Frifelt 1969: 174); the determinations fall at *c.*1800 and 1550 B.C., corrected. A third determination, from Bat, falls at *c.*1600 B.C., and may also refer to a post-Wadi Suq feature (Frifelt 1979: 584). The ceramic and other materials associated with the dated features at Hili and Bat are not described; moreover, one cannot exclude the possibility that the Wadi Suq actually terminates further into the second millennium than conventionally thought. Such a revision would not seriously alter the hypothesis of a profound economic shift to camel pastoralism, with its attendant absence of substantial architecture, during the second millennium (cf. Cleuziou 1981).

LIYAN

Pézard's excavations at Bender Bušehr in the early part of this century indicate occupation dating to both the end of the third and end of the second millennia (Pézard 1914). The earlier occupation shows relations with the Gulf, Malyan and Susa, thus forming an important Elamite link into the Gulf economic system. The later occupation is attested principally by dedicatory inscriptions which date to both the thirteenth and the twelfth centuries B.C., but the greater part of which belong to the middle of the latter century (cf. König 1965 *passim*). A correlation with the post-Kassite occupation at Failaka, where Elamite style seals are reported (Kjaerum 1980), is possible.

DISCUSSION

The patterns of occupation in the Gulf reviewed above may be summarized in the following two points:

1. A chronologically and materially well defined Kassite horizon occurs along the southern shores of the upper and central Gulf, with occupation focused on northern Bahrain. A date of the fourteenth-thirteenth centuries B.C. and a condition of colonialism are suggested for this horizon. A second, Middle Elamite, horizon is present at Liyan.

2. Both the Kassite and the Middle Elamite horizons occur within the framework of long-term gaps of documentable occupation and local cultural traditions, gaps which basically span the second millennium as defined here. Some continuities are dimly perceptible in the ceramics of Saudi Arabia and in elements of glyptic style, particularly at Failaka. The significance of these continuities in the face of disruption of other cultural expressions remains to be elucidated.

Each of these observations singles out patterns in which the Gulf region corresponds to wider patterns in the history of the second millennium in neighboring regions of the Near East. These wider patterns are the interregional phenomenon of an urban crisis at the beginning of the second millennium on the one hand and the establishment of administrative control over foreign parts toward the end of the second millennium on the other.

URBAN CRISIS

The urban crisis of the end of the third millennium refers to the widespread, interregional, and progressive retrenchment or even collapse of urban life during the final centuries of the third millennium and the beginning centuries of the second. The far-flung and fertile commercial and cultural links which had related such disparate core regions as Babylonia, Elam, Central Asia, and the Indus seem largely to have dissolved, reflecting the increased isolation of non-urban communities. As a part of this dissolution of links between these four core areas, the nature of societies which oriented themselves toward these links, either as suppliers of traded materials or as nodes on transportation and communication routes, also altered. Reflected in their settlement patterns, the changes in these peripheral or inter-stitial societies are manifested as virtual or complete abandonment of visible settlement.

Biscione's analysis of the Central Asian urban crisis serves as a useful model for three core areas – Central Asia itself, the Indus, and Mesopotamia, although in the latter case the qualities found in the first two are greatly muted. Biscione (1977) finds a three-fold shift in settlement pattern to have occurred between Namazga V and Namazga VI times. These changes are summarized as follows:

1. a shift of the geographical center of settlement eastward from the Kopet Dagh to the river deltas and oases to the east;

2. a reduction in the average size of settlements along with a disappearance of settlement size hierarchies, i.e. settlements become more uniformly small; and

3. an increase in the aggregate settlement area.

More recent survey, notably in the lower Murghab delta, requires some modification of Biscione's model. The Gonur oasis settlement system is urban and hierarchical in nature, dominated by Gonur-depe and by several lesser centers; Sarianidi (1981: 173) suggests that Gonur-depe was the focus of settlement in Margiana during Namazga VI times. This continuation of settlement hierarchy should not disguise the fact that a smaller proportion of Namazga VI settlement in the lower Murghab delta is urban (put at about 30 ha or more) than had been the case along the Kopet Dagh in Namazga V times. Namazga VI settlement systems continue to appear non-urban and non-hierarchical in the other settlement clusters to the east of the lower Murghab. Thus urban crisis in Central Asia was not a complete abandonment of urban life, but rather was a complex mix of reduced urban life, expanded rural settlements, and of population expansions into previously unsettled regions.

Comparable changes occurred in the greater Indus region, although here again different areas underwent different changes. The best studied settlement changes are in the Hakra/Ghaggar system, Haryana, and Gujarat. These three areas, together with vaguer assess-ments of settlement in Sind and Punjab, confirm a picture of significant reduction of urbanism and of overall numbers of sites in the Indus heartland (cf. the Hakra/Ghaggar pattern; Mughal 1982) combined with expanded numbers of more uniformly small sites in formerly peripheral areas (cf. Possehl 1980; Gupta 1982). As in Central

Asia, these changes probably do not reflect a demographic collapse, but rather a complex redistribution of populations and their aggregates. The disruption and eventual disappearance of urbanism in the Indus region correlates with the disappearance or profound alteration of the appurtenances of an urban political order (writing, systems of weights and measures, unified glyptics).

The Babylonian pattern is qualitatively similar, in that both the degree of urbanism and aggregate settlement size declined in once densely populated areas to the advantage of other areas within Babylonia. However, the degree of urban collapse experienced in other regions never occurred in Babylonia, and an urban tradition was maintained throughout the second millennium. Indeed, the urban crisis along the Nippur-Warka stretches of the Euphrates is present only as a steepening rate of decline of urbanism following the Old Babylonian period, occurring within the longer-term trend of declining urbanism after the ED II/III peak (Adams 1981: 138). An analogous observation holds for the Ur area as well (Wright 1981: 330), where peak urbanism occurred just before the collapse. In Akkad, the amount of urban occupation actually increased somewhat through the second millennium, due principally to enlarged occupation at Babylon and to the 'artificial' establishments at Dur Kurigalzu (Aqar Kuf). The patterns observable in aggregate settlement show similar subregional complexity, with peak occupations occurring at different times in different parts of Babylonia (generally correlating well with the patterns of urbanism); a shift occurred from south to north in the relative center of aggregate settlement, though the Nippur-Warka axis remained the focus of settlement in absolute terms during the second millennium.[3] In sum, the urban crisis in Babylonia is best regarded as an abbreviation of urbanism within an attenuated settlement hierarchy as part of a very long term process rather than as a crisis and transformation of more limited duration as seen in the previous two core areas.

This formulation, however, does disguise a very sharp event in the south of Babylonia, i.e. the cessation of literate political administration and possible abandonment of cities (perhaps even Nippur; cf. Gibson 1980: 199) in the latter part of the eighteenth century B.C. The settlement pattern, perceived in chronological ceramic units of several centuries, does not reveal the full complexity of the urban crisis as a process, much less transform that process into history. This fact has obvious implications for the barely emergent complexities of the Indus and Central Asian cases.

Elam, the fourth core area, shows a pattern of change strongly divergent from the others according to Carter's (1971) study. Through the end of the third millennium and the first half of the second, the urban element in Elam declined to the advantage of towns, while the village element remained relatively stable; the aggregate settlement size expanded during this time. With the Middle Elamite period in the second half of the second millennium, these trends reversed: urbanism expanded to unprecedented levels (for much the same reasons as in Kassite Akkad – the artificial establishment at Dur-Untash), while villages and towns both declined in importance. In keeping with the previous trend, aggregate settlement size increased. On the whole, Elam stands apart as a region which escaped the broad urban crisis, putting that crisis off until the end of the second millennium.

Malyan and the surrounding Kur river basin, the ancient Anshan, constitutes the best known of the peripheral or interstitial societies. Following an episode of seeming total abandonment in the mid-third millennium, the Kaftari settlement pattern in the Kur valley consisted of a very large urban center at Malyan surrounded by a large number of small rural sites (Sumner 1981). Later in the second millennium a sharp contraction in settlement occurred, as measured by the size of Malyan itself, by the total number of sites and by the average site size. Furthermore, two distinct ceramic traditions (Qaleh and Shoga-Taimuran) existed contemporaneously, marking off two distinct regions within the valley (Jacobs 1980). The Middle Elamite horizon in the Kur river region appears only at Malyan, in this context of reduced and segmented population.

Elsewhere in and around the Iranian plateau comparable settlement collapses are evident: various valleys or sections of the Zagros, the Indo-Iranian borderland, the Gorgan plain, and 'Turan' (including Shahr-i Sokhta) show some variation on the theme. These instances may vary considerably among themselves, but their overriding commonality is evident – a decline in urban, aggregated or settled life in the earlier part of the second millennium. The settlement chronologies for various areas of the Gulf, reviewed above, fit the extreme of the pattern perfectly well.

The patterns of relative deurbanization and population shifts in core areas, of disappearance or fundamental alteration of administrative apparatus in these core areas, and of sharp discontinuities of settled life in peripheral areas coincide with radical reorientations of commercial and other ties between regions. The source areas and entry points of industrial metals imported into Babylonia best indicate the latter reorientation. In contrast with the third millennium paradigm, when copper had southern sources and both copper and tin entered Baylonia via the Gulf or Elam, during the second millennium both metals entered Babylonia from the north or west with the sources of copper also lying in those directions (cf. Muhly 1973 *passim*). The Aegean oxhide copper ingot at Dur-Kurigalzu (cf. Brinkman 1974: 401) stands as a synecdoche of this new paradigm.

Such paradigmatic shifts carry political connotation, since control over means of production as well as means of destruction then favored northern over southern Babylonia, and the autonomy of northern from southern Mesopotamia. At the same time, the paradigmatic shift eliminated elite expropriation of surplus both from local production for exchange and from trans-shipment of goods. In essence, the urban crisis is a surface representation of the disintegration of the third millennium 'world economy' described by Kohl and others.

The causes of the disintegration of the third millennium pattern are difficult to grasp in detail, and in any case this task falls beyond the purview of this study.[4] Several observations are nonetheless relevant, as they pertain to the Gulf of the second millennium.

The geographical and chronological pattern of the urban crisis makes unlikely external forces, such as climatic change, as sufficient causal agents, even while some exogenous change can be documented for some regions (e.g. NW India). Rather, urban retrenchment in core areas must be analyzed in terms of the interregional structures emergent by the end of the third millennium together with more local economic and political historical conditions. The intersection of these two levels of analysis is most clearly seen in Babylonia.

At the local level within Babylonia, the progressive salinization of soils and declining agricultural productivity in the south, the consolidation of political power to the north and the use of water by this power as a political weapon against the south, the concurrent population growth in the north with its newly increased demands drawing off water before it reached southern users, and the westward shift in the course of the Euphrates away from the old centers were intertwined factors promoting the urban crisis of the south. These factors may all be situated within Gibson's model of the deleterious result of centralizing management of irrigation and agricultural production (Gibson 1974).

In Babylonia the local conditions intersect with interregional structures via the vehicles of trade. Edens (n.d.) has argued that the third millennium Gulf trade evolved in the direction of greater structural dependence by the societies connected one to the other by the trade, due principally to the change in location within those societies of the consumption of the materials provided by the trade. As an example, copper was an elite or 'precious' commodity through the first half of the third millennium, and was consumed within elite settings. Later in the third millennium and into the second, copper became an industrial metal and was applied more broadly to such things as agricultural production. Thus for Babylonia the changing structure of trade emphasized, both directly and indirectly, centralized agricultural production and centralized manufactories such as textiles, since production had come to depend increasingly on control of metals as means of production and since agricultural and manufactured goods were exported in return for metals. The trade accelerated the articulation of irrigation works and bureaucratic management of those works, ultimately finishing in the agrarian disaster of the early second millennium.

Although evidence for other core areas is largely lacking, analogous processes may have occurred in these areas as well. Fairservis (1967) has postulated environmental degradation due to social pressures as the reason for the Harappan decline, a thesis which fits well the present argument; the status of Harappan commerce, on the other hand, remains controversial (cf. Shaffer 1979). The Central Asian situation is even less evident. Elam's settlement history differs from the other core areas in ways pertinent to the argument. Carter suggests that the location of settlement during the late third millennium reflects external control of Susiana so as to exploit the commercial potential of the region; later in the second millennium, under autochthonous rule, settlement location shifted to an agrarian pattern (Carter 1971: 178–181, 184). Also pertinent, both Elam and Akkad experienced their own settlement collapse and agrarian disaster at the end of the second millennium, immediately after political florescence, a repetition of the process nearly a thousand years later.

At the same time, change of the social location of trade affected peripheral and interstitial areas more sharply than core areas, although in differing ways. The ever expanding demand for Omani copper by Babylonia may have consumed charcoal at a rate faster than replacement of vegetation, leading to deforestation of the Omani mountains, extensive alteration in local hydrologic conditions, and an end to copper production. Weisgerber (1980: 119) has suggested a similar account for the demise of early Islamic copper production in Oman, although correlation with local political events makes this account tendentious. Bahrain, grown fundamentally dependent on controlling the Babylonia-Oman exchange and on urban consumption of imported foodstuffs (Edens n.d.), was squeezed from both sides. The general failure in Oman combined with the related reoriented paradigm in Babylonia to dissolve Tilmun's economic foundation.

The nature of the population in the Gulf left in the wake of the urban crisis is largely unknown. A major economic orientation throughout the Arabian peninsula was surely a pastoralist one, based most probably on the newly domesticated camel. In the context of the present discussion, pastoralism must be viewed as an escape mechanism for previously settled oasis or mixed farming-herding populations faced with newly arisen pressures. On Bahrain and in the better-watered oases of the adjacent littoral, cultivation must have continued, even if on a scale much reduced from Barbar period levels. But as with pastoralists, such cultivators are scarcely visible in the material record. In any case, the urban crisis of the end of the third millennium has the effect of diminishing and dispersing populations in the circum-Gulf region.

KASSITE COLONIALISM

Colonialism in the pre-modern world is a concept difficult to define with any rigor and even more difficult to translate into archaeological terms, as recent attempts at both exercises show (e.g. Finley 1976 and Branigan 1981 respectively). Finley is surely correct in pointing to land, labor, and metropolitan relations of production as critical variables for analysis of kinds of colonialism (Finley 1976: 184), but the sorts of information needed to understand these and other variables in the present analysis are sorely lacking, even for metropolitan Babylonia under Kassite rule. Patterns of the material record, as presently perceived, allow only interpretation heavily hedged about with qualifications and deliberate obfuscation. Indeed, identification of the Kassite horizon in the Gulf as colonialism itself rests fundamentally on the few textual hints reviewed above; the Kassite ceramics of the period corroborate this claim only in that they do not contradict it. In sum, one may at best sketch the outlines of Kassite colonialism in the Gulf from the few available hints and suppositions without being able to flesh interpretation out into a full account.

Expansionary state structures were not uncommon in the Late Bronze Age of the Near East. Egyptian occupation of Nubia and of Syro-Palestine during the New Kingdom provides the clearest examples of such state expansion, here along two highly distinct lines (cf. Kemp 1978). Babylonia and Elam provide two further instances. These latter two cases are highly similar one to the other, and are more akin to the Egyptian colonization of Nubia than to the militarism in Syro-Palestine.

Elamite expansion into Fars is evident in material and epigraphical finds at Malyan, Tul-e Spid, and Bender Bušehr (Liyan). In the case of Malyan, Middle Elamite ceramics occur only at this center and not in the environs of the Kur valley. The Middle Elamite occupation is characterized by a massive architectural complex with which are associated epigraphical and glyptic material, and apparently also storage facilities for various kinds of materials. all these elements being consistent with an administrative function for the building (cf. Carter and Stolper 1976). This occupation of Malyan occurs within the context of the urban crisis described above. At Bušehr the nature of the Elamite occupation is less clear, as is the nature of local populations, although again the public nature of the epigraphical remains suggest the Elamite presence as a political and cultic function. In sum, the end of the second millennium on the Iranian plateau saw a Middle Elamite expansion to the south and southeast, an expansion which involved the transference, indeed imposition, of the political and administrative apparatus of the Elamite kingdom in areas which immediately prior to this expansion had been outside the sphere of Elamite materials.

The Middle Elamite expansion shares a number of characteristics with the Kassite expansion into the Gulf. These commonalities may be divided into two groups: those pertaining to the 'metropolis' and those relating to the 'colony'. Regarding the first, expansionism in both instances occurred in the midst of political revivals. These revivals were marked at home by higher concentrations of urban space, by general building programs, and by restoration of temples. Such activities in Babylonia started in the final part of the fifteenth and widened in the fourteenth century B.C. Re-establishment of bureaucratic administration in the south of Babylonia also occurred at this time. All of these changes occurred soon after unification of Babylonia under Kassite rule early in the fifteenth century. In Elam, where relevant political history is less clearly understood, such activities are evident by the beginning of the thirteenth century B.C. (see the historical review in Stève *et al.* 1980). Political revival was also evident in dealings with foreign polities, manifested in political treaties, commercial and diplomatic relations, and military campaigns. In the latter regard, relations between Babylonia and Elam continued in the time-honored mould of hostility, exemplified by the successes of Kurigalzu II and of Sutruk-Nahhunte I respectively.

The second group of commonalities, that pertaining to the colonized region, is more diverse. Both expansionary episodes occurred in the context of the settlement collapse provided by the urban crisis. In both cases, the metropolis had enjoyed close relations with the colonized area at the end of the third millennium, being political federation in the case of Elam, and commercial ties in the case of Babylonia. Each kind of relation entailed a certain degree of acculturation or cultural integration. And in both cases colonialism involved bureaucratic administration and incorporation into the political arrangements of the respective metropolies.

The close structural parallelism of these two cases suggests that colonialist expansion was one of the standard diplomatic, commercial and military options open to successful and emergent great power dynasties in the Near East of the later second millennium. Egyptian expansion into Nubia early in the Eighteenth Dynasty provides a third, well documented, case which exhibits many of the characteristics of the previous two, particularly regarding metropolitan conditions and anterior relations with the colonized region (cf. Kemp 1978, W. Adams 1984). Colonialism as a regular part of foreign relations may be one of the manifestations of the new militarism based on horse and chariot, and of the social conditions promoted by this novel means of destruction; these new attitudes are clearly evident in Egypt and Babylonia, as well as in regions further north. As such, colonialism was a proper part of the internationalism in the greater Near East of the Late Bronze Age.

While this sketch of a comparative account of Late Bronze Age colonialism may help remove surprise at finding such a phenomenon in the Gulf it does not go far toward revealing its nature. In contrast to the Nubian case, where the nature of Egyptian colonialism is revealed both by archaeological and by textual evidence, the nature of Kassite colonialism in the Gulf is largely intangible. At present, one may best approach an elucidation of Kassite colonialism by the roundabout elimination of the unlikely, thus leaving as likely the residue of possibility.

Although not colonialism properly speaking, trading colonies or commercial factories are an historically important reason for the implantation of a population in a foreign locale; the Old Assyrian establishment at Kanesh is of course the Assyriological 'type specimen' of such factories. 'Trade colonies' may not in fact be distinguishable from colonies *sensu stricto*, as shown by the Portuguese installation at Hormuz in the early seventeenth century A.D. Trade, and control of strategic locations through which trade flows, must therefore be considered as a possible orienting axis of the Kassite expansion into the Gulf.

Since the third millennium Gulf trade was so strongly oriented around the metal traffic, the shift of paradigms presented above suggests that a Gulf trade of the second millennium was structurally unimportant. This *a priori* argument must be balanced against the factual observation that Kassite Babylonia had access to lapis lazuli independent of interference by its major fourteenth century B.C. competitors, and therefore through a southern Iranian or an Arabian Gulf route. Lapis, as the Amarna correspondence clearly shows, balanced gold as the medium of royal gifts, and therefore assumes a central importance to Babylonian economic life (cf. Edzard 1960). Other indications of a Gulf trade, whether direct or indirect, are few. Marine shells are present in second millennium contexts in many Mesopotamian sites, although few of these instances have been even summarily described (Susa, Babylon, Nuzi, and al-Rimah stand out). These shells, many of which belong to the Indo-Pacific biotic province, are direct indicators of exchange links which reached, if not passed through, the Gulf. Unknown are the materials which might have accompanied these shells. Furniture made of *mesu*-wood, a commonly imported item of the third millennium trade, appears in a

handful of Kassite texts from Nippur (collected in Chicago Assyriological Dictionary M, 237). Leemans (1968: 216) has supposed the
later Old Babylonian references to such objects to be heirlooms; such
a construction of the Kassite instances, some centuries later, is still
possible, though much less credible. However, imports of *mesu*-wood
need not have come through the Gulf, as the wood may also have
come overland from the Indo-Iranian borderlands. Lastly, the red
ochre found in the Qal'at may have originated in Hormuz Island,
another small indication of traffic through the Gulf.

These few indications of trade, mostly indirect or ambiguous,
permit a conclusion of the existence of a Gulf trade, but they do not
permit a reasoned assessment of that trade. Giving more weight to
the *a priori* than to the equivocal concrete, the trade seems to have
been desultory, with little structural importance. Consequently,
control over a Gulf trade was not a major factor in the initial Kassite
colonization of the Gulf, nor was it an important focus for the
organization of that colonization.

Ironically, trade through the Gulf seems to have revived considerably just prior to the end of the period considered in this study.
A later copy of an inscription of Simbar-Šipak (1026–1009 B.C.),
founder of the Second Sealands Dynasty, describes a throne made of
mesu-wood and inlaid with gold (Goetze 1965). In this case access to
new supplies of *mesu*-wood may be implied. At a slightly later date,
when the Assyrian Shalmaneser III (858–824 B.C.) established effective
control over the southernmost parts of Babylonia on behalf of
Marduk-zakir-sumi I, the tribute extracted from the southern tribes
included many items which may have been traded through the Gulf –
ivory, elephant hides, *mesu*-wood, ebony, incense, etc. – as well as
those which most certainly did not, such as iron.[5] In any case, one
must agree with Brinkman (1968: 197–198) that, judging from the
variety of the tribute, the southern tribes controlled a large-scale and
extensive trade by the end of the ninth century B.C. All of this correlates very well with literary evidence of Tilmunite ability a century
later to give over to Assyria 'tribute' which included copper (presumably originating in Oman), a complete return to third millennium
symmetries. These fragments of evidence point to the conclusion,
only slightly speculative, that the Gulf trade had revived considerably
by the end of the second millennium.

While the unimportance of trade as a motive for Kassite colonialism leaves a wide range of motives still possible, several observations point to extraction of surplus or production of commodities as
central to the Kassite occupation. The incorporation of Tilmun into
the Kassite administrative structure, indicated by the titles used in
the texts above, suggests analogous incorporation of Tilmun into
Kassite relations of production. These relations centered on land, on

taxes of agricultural production, and on labor obligations, where lands were held by the crown or granted to other formal institutions or to individuals. These relations of production, if extended to Tilmun, imply forcible extraction of agricultural surplus by bureaucratic coercion. Such a hypothesis conforms well both with the physical evidence of the Qal'at and with the concern expressed in the pair of Nippur letters for Aḥlamu predation, stores of dates and transfer of personnel. The Kassite installation in Qatar also easily fits this model. The royal interest within Babylonia in dyes and dyed textiles was strong, and perhaps amounted to a royal monopoly (Arnaud 1970: 74). Accordingly, a *Kassite* extractive industry of purple shellfish dye in the central Gulf implies either an enterprise under royal commission, or a similar but 'extra-legal' enterprise undertaken by semi-autonomous tribal groups from southern Babylonia. The ceramic differences with Bahrain indicate that, in any event, the Qatari extractive industry was not operated out of Bahrain. These considerations show that while Kassite activities in the Gulf were multivarious, they were all oriented around direct extraction and expropriation of products, agricultural or marine, local to the Gulf.

CONCLUSION

The second millennium in the Arabian Gulf was dominated, in a social historical sense, by two structures whose bounds lay well beyond the shores of the Gulf itself. These two structures, the urban crisis and colonialism, were really part of a wider sequential dynamic involving the disarticulation of third millennium social realities followed by the emergent reintegration leading up to the first millennium pattern of empire. Brinkman identifies Kassite Babylonia as the region's first national state (Brinkman 1974: 397), of which Tilmun for a time formed a part. This later second millennium pattern adumbrates that of the first millennium, when Mesopotamian empires incorporated surrounding lands, including Tilmun. The second millennium pattern is therefore a pivotal one in the long-term history of the Near East, marking a radical shift in the mechanisms of interregional integration. Bahrain's history over these three millennia captures in microcosm the essence of this western Asian history.

Acknowledgements

I wish to thank Jacques Tixier for inviting me to participate in the Mission Archéologique Française à Qatar excavations at Khor Ile, and through him the CNRS, Ministère des Affaires Etrangères (both of France), and the Ministry of Information, Department of Antiquities (of Qatar) for funding. I also wish to thank Geoffrey Bibby, Karen Frifelt and especially Flemming Højlund for permitting me to examine some of the ceramics from the Qal'at and from Failaka now housed at Moesgård. Juris Zarins very kindly informed me of the recent highly relevant finds in the Dhahran tumuli fields. C. C. Lamberg-Karlovsky has provided many years of encouragement, and financial support.

1. The term Kassite may bear at least four meanings: 1) an ethnic and linguistic designation either inside or outside Babylonia; 2) a political dynasty within Babylonia; 3) a period of time in the social history of Babylonia; and 4) the artistic and industrial products of 3), with particular reference to ceramics and glyptics. In the present study, the term 'Kassite' never carries the first connotation. For the remaining three designations, context of usage makes the intended meaning clear in most cases without going to pedantic extremes.

2. The regnal sequence and chronology for Kassite and post-Kassite Babylonia used in this paper follows Brinkman (1976 and 1968 respectively). Some alteration of both sequence and chronology may prove necessary (most recently, see Brinkman 1983).

3. The comparison in settlement histories of Akkad with more southerly sections of Babylonia is based on comparison of the following tables with Adams 1981:

aggregate hectarage				proportion of size class			
size class	Ur III	O.B.	Kassite	size class	Ur III	O.B.	Kassite
≤4.0 ha	35	68	64	≤4.0 ha	.11	.11	.09
4.1–10	30	51	81	4.1–10	.09	.08	.11
10.1–20	110	151	115	10.1–20	.33	.25	.16
20.1–40	0	30	73	20.1–40	.00	.05	.10
>40	158	309	402	>40	.47	.51	.55
totals	333 ha	609 ha	735 ha				

These tables are derived from Adams (1972) and Gibson (1972) in a manner analogous with that used by Weiss (1975) for the earlier periods. The size of occupation at Aqar Quf is put at 20 ha. for the Ur III and Old Babylonian periods and at 180 ha. for the Kassite period, and the size of Babylon at 12, 60 and 120 ha. for these periods respectively. The Aqar Quf figures are based on the description and map of the area given in Adams 1972 (site 047). The Babylon figures, on the other hand, are largely speculative. Since these two sites comprise a large proportion of the urban space during the Kassite period, room for error is considerable. Furthermore, the inclusion of Babylon emphasizes the urban proportion since the hinterland to the west of the city was not surveyed. Finally, these tables are not directly comparable with Adams 1981 since different summing procedures were used. Lack of space prohibits a full discussion of the derivation of the tables and of the assumptions underlying them. The tables must, in any case, be considered as a very rough indication of areal settlement trends.

4. Two major features of the urban crisis are the seeming shift to pastoralism in core and peripheral areas with attendant population movements on the one hand, and the wave-like progression of the crisis in space and time on the other. These features may in fact be causally related, in the fashion well-known from numerous 'barbarian invasions' at various times in Old World history. The progression of the crisis ran from east to west over the span of several centuries centered on c.2000 B.C., following regional radiocarbon chronologies. This observation emphasizes the obvious fact that the crisis was a process of some duration rather than an event.

5. The use of *mesu*-wood as an indicator of interregional contacts is greatly complicated in the first millennium by the growing of the tree in Mesopotamia at least as early as the ninth century B.C. by Assyrian kings (for a recent review, see Maxwell-Hyslop 1983). The presence of the tree in Babylonia proper by the end of the eighth century B.C. makes the wood extremely equivocal as an indicator of trade during most of the first millennium.

The chronology of City II and III at Qal'at al-Bahrain

FLEMMING HØJLUND

For some years I have worked on a publication of the second millennium pottery from the Danish Excavations on the island of Failaka in Kuwait, and with the permission of Geoffrey Bibby and Karen Frifelt, I made a brief study of the pottery from the Qal'at al-Bahrain stored in the Prehistoric Museum. I have also had the opportunity to familiarize myself with the pottery from the Barbar Temples, while Hellmuth Andersen and Peder Mortensen were studying this material. My purpose was to see if I could recognize pottery assemblages in Bahrain comparable to the periods defined for Failaka. The main result of this preliminary investigation is a sub-division of Bibby's City II into six periods and City III into two periods and a demonstration of occupational continuity on the Qal'a from City II to City III, i.e. from the third millennium till at least about 1500 B.C. and probably throughout the second millennium B.C.

The first period, *City IIA*, fig. 55, is characterized by plain jar rims (1), slightly triangular jar rims (2), plain hole-mouth rims (3), slightly thickened hole-mouths with a bevelled front and a shallow groove on the upper surface (4), yellow jars with red painted wavy lines (5–6), large bottom-less cylinders with sharp ridges (7), and plates (8). All, with a few exceptions, handmade in red, sand-tempered wares. Ridged bodysherds are far more numerous than chain-ridged. A few wheelmade, light buff rims (9–10) are the remnants of an important part of the potter of City I, which has obvious Mesopotamian parallels as Curt Larsen has pointed out, besides the similarity to Umm an-Nar referred to by Bibby.

 City IIA pottery is found for instance in layer 21 in Bibby's trench south of the North Wall, which has also been dealt with by Curt Larsen. *City IIA* pottery compares well with pottery from *Barbar Temple Ia and b*.

In *City IIB* we find triangular rims with a convex upper surface, a

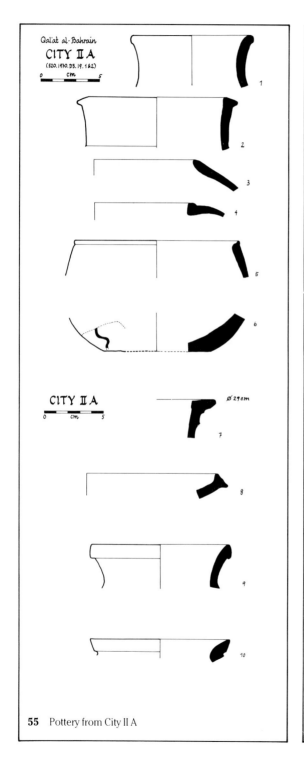

55   Pottery from City II A

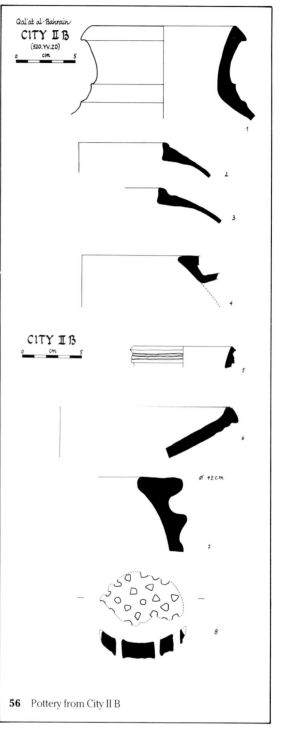

56   Pottery from City II B

pointed lip and a tall, splaying neck (1), thicker hole-mouth rims with a concave bevelled front (2–3), spouted hole-mouth jars (4), red burial pots with striated rim (5), large yellow plates (6), ribbed pithoi (7), and sieve-necked jars (8), fig. 56. The yellow jar with painted red wavy lines and the cylinder continues from *City IIA*.

City IIB pottery is found for instance in Bibby's layer 18 and it compares well with *Temple IIa*.

Very typical of *City IIC* pottery (fig. 57) are still thicker hole-mouth rims with a concave bevelled front, sometimes with two shallow grooves, a moulded upper lip and 1–3 ridges on the upper surface (1–2). The high-necked version of the jar with triangular rim (3) still occurs, but a lower neck is introduced. The large yellow plate with a ringbase continues (4–5), as do spouted hole-mouths, pithoi, yellow jars with painted red wavy lines, red ware burial pots with striated rims, cylinders with sharp ridges, as well as a new type of cylinder with no ridges, but with clear marks of scraping on the surface.

City IIC pottery is found in Bibby's layer 17 and it compares well with *Temple IIb*. It is typologically contemporary with, or perhaps a little earlier than *period 1A* pottery in Failaka.

City IID (fig. 58) has some low-necked jars with thick triangular rims (1), but the majority have smaller and more rounded triangles (2). The hole-mouth rims with moulded upper lip and ridges continue (3), as do the large yellow plates, the spouted hole-mouths, the red ware burial pots with the striated rims, the cylinders with sharp ridges and the scraped variant without ridges (4), the yellow jars with the painted red wavy lines and the pithoi.

City IID pottery is found for instance in Bibby's layers 10–15 and has a good resemblance to pottery from *Failaka 1A*.

Between *City IID* and *F* there is at the moment a gap. It is my impression that there is pottery in the Qal'a material which typologically could fill in this gap, but during my short study I have not succeeded in finding this kind of pottery in safe stratigraphic relation to *City IID and F*.

City IIF (fig. 59) is characterized by elongated and smoothed triangular rims (1–2), slender, pointed, 'up-turned' hole-mouth rims (3–4), a few moulded, ridged hole-mouth rims with a convex front (5), plain jar rims with a thickened lip (6), plates and bowls in several variations, some showing Mesopotamian influence (14–16) and quadrangular rims (17–18).

In *City IIA–D* the potters worked with the hand technique and used the fast wheel only for small painted cups and beakers. In *City*

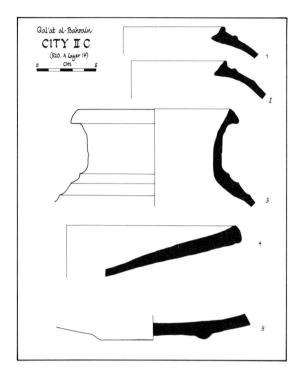

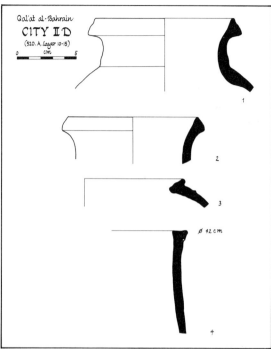

57   Pottery from City II C

58   Pottery from City II D

59   Pottery from City II F

60   Pottery from City III A

IIF, however, we find several larger shapes (7–10) made on the fast wheel and nearly always painted (11, 13) or decorated with very fine ridges on the shoulder (12).

City IIF pottery has a close resemblance to that part of the *Failaka 3A* pottery which follows the Barbar tradition. On the other hand, it is an interesting fact that *City IIF* lacks the Babylonian shapes, which are found on Failaka in *period 3A*.

In *City IIIA* we find again the elongated, smoothed triangular rim (1) and the plain jar rim (2), plus a few hole-mouths, all in handmade technique. Most of the inventory is, however, wheelmade, such as quadrangular rims of different sizes (3–5), three-ribbed jar rims (6), bowls with striated, incurved rim (7), grooved hole-mouths (8), beakers with button bases (9–11), string cut bases and ring bases (fig. 60). While the Mesopotamian origin of these shapes is obvious, no similar assemblage has so far been published from Mesopotamia to my knowledge. As the following discussion will show, this assemblage must be dated to *Late Old Babylonian or Early Kassite*, which is still a Dark Age in Mesopotamia.

The finely sand-tempered wares of these Mesopotamian shapes are not typical of Mesopotamian pottery, but resemble in some respect the wares used for the wheelmade Barbar types in *City*

Qal'at al-Bahrain
CITY II F
(420. Layer 15)
0 cm 5

CITY II F
0 cm 5

CITY II F
0 cm 5

Qal'at al-Bahrain
CITY III A
(420. Layer 14)
0 cm 5

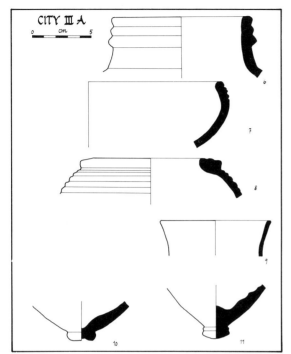

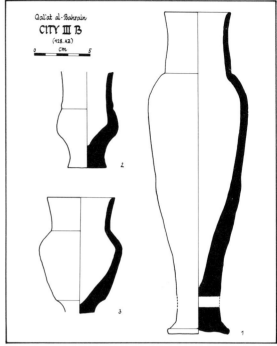

60   Pottery from City III A

IIF, a fact that may indicate local continuity also in the production of wheelmade pottery.

City IIIA has very close resemblance to *Failaka 3B* and to a late phase of the *IIIrd Temple* at Barbar.

City IIIB has again a number of Mesopotamian shapes (fig. 61): tall goblets (1), turnip shaped goblets (2–5), bowls with straight or wavy sides (7), and lids (6). The quadrangular rim (8) may relate to similar shapes in *City IIIA*. Band rims (11) are four and triangular rims (10), which have nothing to do with the triangular Barbar rims, but have Mesopotamian origins. A coarse stump base (12) and pithoi also occur (13). Again the wares are mostly of a sand-tempered variety that indicate a local continuity in pottery production from *City IIIA*.
City IIIB resembles *Failaka 3C*.

An important fixpoint for the establishment of an *absolute chronology* for this relative sequence is the beginning of the *Failaka* settlements (fig. 62). This has been dated by Poul Kjærum to around 2000 B.C. from the evidence of the cylinder and stamp seals. *City IIA and B* should consequently be put in the *Ur II* and the *Akkadian period*. How far back *City IIA* can be pushed is rather uncertain. Room should, however, be made for an Akkadian dating of *City I*.

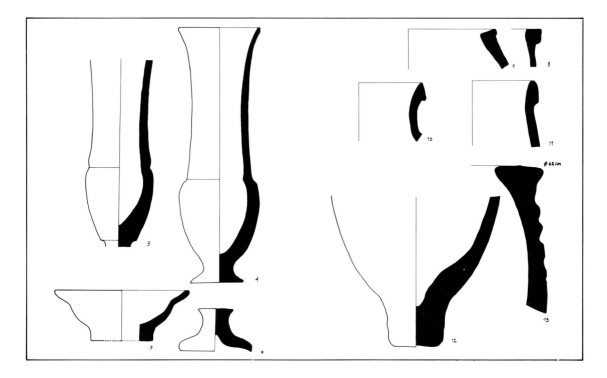

61   Pottery from City III B

If this dating of *Early City II* is confirmed by future investigations, we must conclude that the so-called *'Amorite Tablet'* has been
found out of context. It is dated philologically in the Isin-Larsa period
and was found with City IIA pottery.

The next fixpoint is the large quantity of Old Babylonian pottery
in *Failaka 3A*. Indeed, a jar of the most diagnostic *period 3A* type has
been found by B. Hrouda in the Isin Tell in a grave also containing a
tablet dating to 1752 B.C. *Failaka 3B* and *City IIIA* must consequently
be placed in *Late Old Babylonian* or *Early Kassite*.

A *terminus ante quem* for *Failaka 3C* and *City IIIB* is given by the
Mitanni seals found with *period 4* pottery in Failaka. These seals
cannot, according to Kjærum, be dated later than the fourteenth
century.

It should be noted that nothing just like the *period 4* pottery
from Failaka, which is very Mesopotamian in both shape and ware has
been identified in the Qal'a. It seems that City IIIB shapes continue in
the Qal'a during the rest of the second millennium and into the first
millennium, where they at some point in time are supplemented by
new types, such as a proto-type of the so-called 'snake-bowl'.

On the diagram the periods showing obvious Mesopotamian
influence in pottery production, have been emphasized with circles.
The sharp decline in the frequency of Mesopotamian pottery at the

beginning of City II is naturally not to be explained by a severing of relations with that area. On the contrary, it may be a reflection of the development of Bahrain as the centre of a politically independent state slowly taking control of the trading between the Southeast and Mesopotamia. By the end of the Ur III period the Arabian Gulf was apparently so completely the Dilmunite Gulf that they could safely put up trading stations on Failaka, right on the borders of Mesopotamia.

62 The Chronology of City II and City III at Qal'at al-Bahrain

Iron Age Dilmun: a reconsideration of City IV at Qal'at al-Bahrain

PIERRE LOMBARD

All historians and archaeologists working on Bahrain's antiquity are familiar with the many Mesopotamian historical texts referring to Dilmun in the first millennium B.C.[1] They generally realize what discernment and carefulness these numerous mentions of post-Kassite Dilmun require in their interpretation. Nevertheless, they induced some scholars to commonly speak of 'Assyrian' and 'Neo-Babylonian' periods in Bahrain.[2]

In our opinion, a too strong application of the Mesopotamian chronological and cultural framework, often ill-adapted to the local archaeological evidence, is rather unfounded.[3] One knows that the cultural impact of an Empire, or of a ruling dynasty is not easily measurable by the archaeologist on the field and, actually, these terms often appear artificial. In Bahrain they finally obliterated Dilmun's identity in this period and have led specialists to rather neglect Bahrain's relation with neighbouring Arabian, and more generally Near-Eastern areas during the Iron Age.[4]

Today it is essential that a reconsideration of the archae-ological documents of this period take the recent local or regional research into consideration, in order to estimate Bahrain's cultural position between, on the one hand, the traditional Near-Eastern centres of the Fertile Crescent, and on the other hand the centres of influence recently brought to light in the Arabian Gulf area.

The present contribution wishes to briefly propose some research orientation in that direction, based on results gathered from the only excavated settlement site from this period.[5]

CITY IV AT QAL'AT AL-BAHRAIN

Iron Age archaeological levels have been essentially uncovered at two different places on the tell of Ras al-Qal'a: (1) in the strati-graphical sounding 518 carried out in the inner courtyard of the Portuguese Fort (still unpublished, except for a brief study by C. Larsen);[6] (2) in the large excavation 519, situated South of the Fort

63 Excavation 519 at Qal'at al-Bahrain (Danish Archaeological Expedition). The City IV buildings

64 Bronze situla from a bath-tub coffin (City IV). Bahrain National Museum

and which will interest us here. The impressive structures discovered there by the Danish Expedition are still difficult to interpret today, fig. 63. This monumental complex, served by a narrow alley, was immediately considered to be a very important building, perhaps the Palace of Uperi, the historical king of Dilmun in the time of Sargon II.[7] This rather seductive hypothesis was later hinted at by G. Bibby himself who proposed then to consider these structures as *residences of very wealthy or prominent citizens*.[8] As a fact, and in spite of an apparent adaptation of the Mesopotamian 'reception suite' patterns,[9] it seems more reasonable today to avoid the somewhat subjective term of 'palace', which usually implies a political and an economic function, not really demonstrated in the present case.

Scholars have debated the date of these buildings at length.[10] On the one hand, they are later than the Kassite period in so far as they are clearly constructed above the City III warehouse, which destruction is dated by radiocarbon from 1180 ± 110 B.C., suggesting the fourteenth century B.C., according to corrected data. On the other hand, the stratigraphy reveals this place was later re-used as a kind of rubbish dump during the Seleuco-Parthian period (City V in the Danish sequence). This quite lengthy chronological interval is fortunately bracketed by intrusive burials earlier than the Hellenistic City V: the famous 'bath-tub coffins' which have been dated by Glob from the seventh century B.C.[11]

THE BATH-TUB COFFINS

This uncommon discovery merits closer examination; in fact it appears as a precious *terminus ante quem* for City IV, particularly because the buildings discussed earlier had not yielded a true occupation layer.

In many respects, the date suggested by Glob seems rather early. His position was based on conoid stamp-seals in chalcedony which were associated with at least two of these burials. As a fact, they illustrate a well-known type, representing a worshipper before an altar or symbols, and commonly represented in Mesopotamia in the seventh and sixth centuries B.C.[12] Nevertheless it appears that this type of seal persisted in some areas through the Neo-Babylonian period down to Achaemenian times;[13] for instance, many similar impressions are preserved on datable tablets of this time.[14]

Other elements plead for a slightly later date. The only undisturbed coffin yielded several bronze implements, of an evident use. There is a shallow bronze dish, a situla with a loop handle, fig. 64, a handled strainer, fig. 65 and a hinged ladle. In other words what is usually called a 'wine-set'. This particular kind of material has been recently reviewed by R. Moorey, and his conclusions are quite helpful for the dating of the Bahrain specimen.[15]

The strainer belongs to a well-known type whose functional part is hemispheric and whose handle is decorated with a duck's head; according to Moorey, this type cannot be earlier than the fifth century B.C.[16] Convincing parallels can be found, for example, in the Syro-Palestinian area and, in fact, all belong to fifth century B.C. or at least late sixth century B.C. contexts. In addition to similar pieces from Till Barsip in North-Syria,[17] one must emphasize the complete set discovered at Neirab, near Aleppo: it is very similar in style and composition to the Bahrain specimen.[18]

Turning now to the method of burial, fig. 66, earthen sarcophagi appear in precisely these same regions of Levant, Syria,[19] and especially Mesopotamia where they are represented in different periods.[20] On the contrary, this burial custom remains highly unusual in the Dilmun area, given the present state of research. In addition to some graves supposed to have been found at Karzakan, in Bahrain,[21] the only attested cemetery of this kind was excavated south of Dhahran, and is said to be very similar to the one from Qal'at al-Bahrain.[22] This very scarce occurence seems to indicate it was a burial custom foreign to the inhabitants of Iron-Age Dilmun. Of course, future research should indicate whether we are in the presence of a local assimilation, or if this burial custom is the result of a limited foreign population's settling on Bahrain in the mid-first millennium B.C.

65 Bronze strainer from a bathtub coffin (City IV). Bahrain National Museum

THE BUILDINGS' OCCUPATION

According to the excavators, the destruction layer, 1.50 m thick, lay

66   Clay bath-tub coffin from Excavation 519 (Bahrain National Museum)

directly on three successive floors, whose excavation revealed practically no occupation material, except the snake-bowls discussed later.[23] An examination of the documents kept at Moesgård, Denmark confirm this situation, rather common in big monuments: as a fact, the few objects discovered must be related to the looting of the intrusive coffins (for instance another bronze situla with a loop handle, and perhaps a bronze mirror; the stratigraphical position of the latter is not clearly established, however). Among the scarce material from this layer, I nevertheless noted some fragments of stone vessels, one of them apparently coming from an area far from the graves, fig. 67. Without doubt they resemble the Iron-Age artifacts of the Oman Peninsula from where they were probably imported.[24] Unfortunately, we know from the latest French excavations in the United Arab Emirates that these items are not in fact good chronological indicators: they appear, for example in the successive archaeological layers at Rumeilah (Al-Ain oasis, Abu-Dhabi Emirate), without any apparent evolution of style or decoration.[25]

THE 'SNAKE-BOWLS'

67   Fragments of stone vessels, City IV (nos 1–3), and 'snake-bowls'. (Forhistorisk Museum, Moesgard. Denmark)

About forty vessels of this kind come from two different places in Excavation 519; the diversity of the shapes and sizes, fig. 67: 4–10, is wider than indicated by the plate originally published by G. Bibby.[26] The most revealing group was found in the entrance room of the westernmost building. Fourteen of these deposits were unearthed

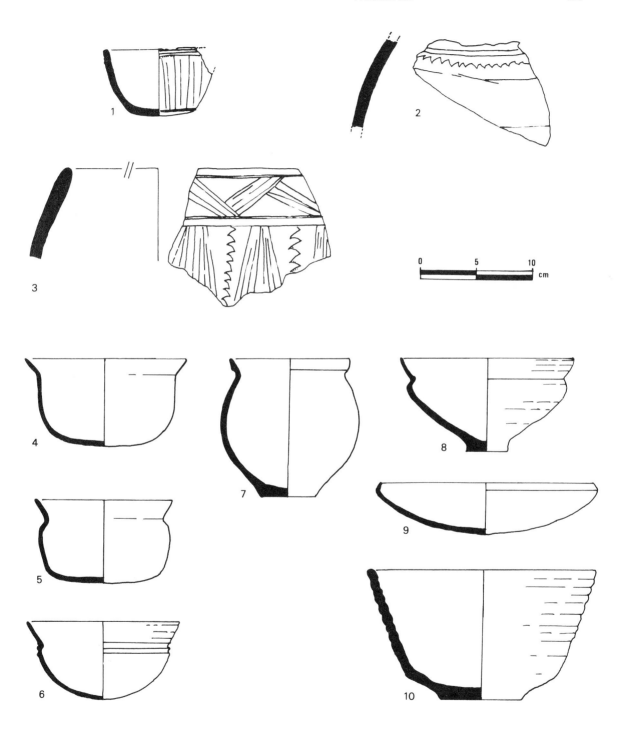

near a square limestone base of a pillar, laid down in pits in the floor layer. Several of these vessels contained the skeleton of a snake, often coiled around a semi-precious stone.[27]

My purpose is not to discuss here the meaning of these deposits or to emphasize this evident memory of Gilgamesh's epic,[28] but rather to examine their eventual interest for chronology. It is generally considered that these bowls are contemporaneous with the buildings in which they were found.[29] Their stratigraphical position, however, must be interpreted with care. We know other evidence of hiding: the silver hoard from City IV was also found in 1962 in a pit dug in the floor layer.[30] Now the intrusive nature of this finding seems demonstrated: in all probability, it is contemporaneous with the bath-tub coffins.[31]

A typological examination of the shapes must provoke similar caution. The carinated specimen, fig. 67: 6, recalls both the typical Achaemenian 'cream-bowls' form Pasargadae or other Iranian sites,[32] as well as the Nimrud Palace Ware[33] which has been put forward in connection with it.[34] As the whole discovery of these snake-bowls seems contemporary, and in spite of a great variety in the shapes, one must admit a convergence of several regional traditions which remains of course to be explained.[35] Let us add that the pinkish pottery with white lime grits of specimens reproduced, fig. 67: 4, 5, suggest that they should be considered as local products. This ware, which curiously recalls the one from Barbar period, is frequently attested among the material associated with the bath-tub coffins.[36]

CONCLUSIONS

The term City IV actually covers a somewhat complex and confuse layer. Reviewing first millennium archaeology at Bahrain at the Lyon Meeting, in June 1982, J-F. Salles has already proposed to break City IV in two different phases:

– a phase 'a', represented by the buildings layer;
– a later phase 'b', represented by the intrusive burials;[37]
I definitely share this proposal, which, unfortunately, does not attribute any date for the first phase.

The present review has stressed the complexity of the stratigraphy. Between the Kassite warehouse of City III, apparently burnt down at the end of the fourteenth century B.C. and the intrusive bath-tub coffins (for which we propose a fifth century B.C. date), the impressive buildings of Sounding 519 are today stil difficult to place in the chronology, for lack of a real occupation layer. Given the present state of research, we must admit that the scarce material collected (especially the snake-bowls) does not provide definitive chronological indices and there is no conclusive evidence that it corresponds to the period of occupation of the buildings.

1. Cf. mainly: Campbell-Thompson *et alii*, 'The British Museum excavations at Nineveh 1931–32', *L.A.A.A.*, XX, 1933; 99–105; Cornwall, *Dilmun, the History of Bahrain Island before Cyrus*, unpublished Ph.D., Cambridge (Mass.), 1944, 83–102; Oppenheim, 'The seafaring merchants of Ur', *Journal of the American Oriental Society*, 74, 1954, 16–17; Kessler 'Zu den keilschriftlichen quellen des 2./1. jahrtausends v. Chr. über Dilmun', *in* Potts, ed., *Dilmun, New Studies in the Archaeology and Early History of Bahrain*, Dietrich Reimer Verlag, Berlin, 1983, 148–153; Oates (D.), *in this volume*.

2. For example, Rice, 'The grave complex at al-Hajjar, Bahrain', *Proceedings of the Seminar for Arabian Studies*, 2, 1972.

3. C. Larsen (*Holocene land use variations on the Bahrain Island*, unpublished Ph.D., Chicago, 1980, 64), too, deplores this constant reference to the Mesopotamian chronology; however, he underlines the fact that '*these primary sources (. . .) provide the only available view of Bahrain, albeit from the vantage point of observers belonging to the major forces in the greater regional system*'.

4. I consider here the term 'Iron Age' to cover broadly the first half of the first millennium B.C. This denomination appears quite suitable because it avoids any reference to a particular area. It is used with the same meaning in the Oman Peninsula (*Cf.* Boucharlat, 'Les périodes préislamiques récentes aux Emirats Arabes Unis', in Boucharlat et Salles ed., *Arabie orientale, Mésoptamie et Iran méridional, de l'Age du Fer au début de la période islamique*, Editions Recherche sur les Civilisations, Paris, 1984, 191–195). It similarly squares with Potts' *Early Hasaean* of Eastern Saudi Arabia ('Northeastern Arabia in the Later Pre-Islamic era', *ibid*, 119).

5. I wish to thank here Geoffrey Bibby for his welcome and help at Moesgård Museum. Our discussions about the material of City IV at Qal'at al-Bahrain have allowed the present review.

6. Larsen, *op. cit.*, 34, 318 ff.

7. G. Bibby, *Looking for Dilmun*, Hardsmondworth, 1972, 179.

8. *id. ibid.*, 361.

9. *Cf.* D. Oates' contribution in this volume.

10. Glob, 'The ancient capital of Bahrain', *Kuml*, 1954; Bibby, *Looking . . .*: 178–182; Larsen, *op. cit.*, 320–321; Salles, 'Bahrain hellénistique: données et problèmes', in *Arabie orientale . . .*, 155–156.

11. 'A neo-babylonian burial from Bahrain's prehistoric capital', *Kuml*, 1956, 173.

12. Porada, *The collection of the Pierpont Morgan Library* (Bollingen Series XIV), Washington, 1948, pl. CXX et CXXI.

13. *id. ibid.*; 96; Von der Osten, *Ancient oriental seals in the collection of Mr. E. T. Newell*, Chicago, 1934, 9.

14. Zettler 'On the chronological range of neo-Babylonian and achaemenid seals', *Journal of Near Eastern Studies*, 38, 1979, 257 ff.

15. 'Metal wine sets in the ancient Near East', *Iranica Antiqua*, XV, 1980, 181–197.

16. *id. ibid.*, 186.

17. Thureau-Dangin et Dunand, *Til-Barsib*, Geuthner, Paris, 1936, pl. XIX, 1, 3.

18. Abel et Barrois, 'Fouilles . . . effectuées à Neirab', *Syria* IX, 1928, fig. 4, p. 198.

19. Mainly at Megiddo (Lamon et Schipton, *Megiddo I*, Chicago, 1939, fig. 87, p. 76).

20. At Nimrud (Oates, 'Nimrud 1957, the Hellenistic Settlement', *Iraq*, 20, 1958, pl. XXVII, 13, 14); at Babylon (Reuther, *Die Innenstadt von Babylon (Merkès), Wissenschaftliche Veröffentlichung der Deutschen Orient-Gesellschaft*, Leipzig, 47, 1926, Tf. 62; 93); at Nippur (McGuire Gibson, *Excavations at Nippur, 11th season*, Oriental Institute Chicago Monographs, 22, Chicago 1975, fig. 63, p. 87); at Sippar (Haerinck, 'Les tombes et les objets du sondage sur l'enceinte de Abu-Habban', in L. De Meyer ed., *Tell ed-Der III*, Leuven 1980, pl. 5 et 7); at Tell al-Laham (Safar, 'Soundings at Tell al-Laham', *Sumer* 5, 1949, pl. V, a-c).

21. Personal communication from Shaikha Haya Al Khalifa, Director of the Department of Archaeology and Museums, State of Bahrain.

22. Potts, 'Northeastern Arabia in the Later Preislamic Era', in *Arabie orientale . . .*: 109.

23. Bibby, *Looking . . .*: 167, 178.

24. Bahrain Island does not possess any soft stone like chlorite or steatite. F. Tarawneh (*A report on al-Hajjar excavations, Mound 1, Season 1970*, n.d.: 5) has suggested that such vessels could have been carved on Bahrain, from rough material imported from the Oman Mountains. Today however, the very close similarity of shape and decoration makes this hypothesis rather unsafe. On the Omani production, *cf.* Lombard, 'Iron Age stone vessels from the Oman peninsula. A preliminary note', *Proceedings of the Seminar for Arabian Studies*, 12, 1982, 39–48.

25. Boucharlat et Lombard, 'Fouilles de Rumeilah, Oasis d'Al-Ain, U.A.E.', in *Arabie orientale . . .*: 238; *id.*, forthcoming.

26. Bibby, *Looking . . .*, fig. p. 180.

27. Glob, 'Snake sacrifices in Bahrain's ancient capital', *Kuml*, 1957, 114 ff; Bibby, *Looking . . .*, fig. p. 180 et pl. 17a.

28. During a famous episode of this historical epic, the Snake steals the Pearl (the so-called 'Flower of Immortality') got by Gilgamesh in Dilmun, and therefore achieves immortality instead of the Sumerian hero (*cf.* the translation by Labat, in *Les religions du Proche-Orient*, Fayard-Denoël, Paris, 1970; 221).

29. Bibby, *Looking . . .*: 180.

30. Bibby, 'Arabian Gulf Archaeology', *Kuml*, 1964, 102.

31. Krauss, Lombard and Potts, 'The silver hoard from City IV, Qal'at al-Bahrain' in Potts ed., *Dilmun . . .*, 1983, 161–166.

32. Stronach, *Pasargadae*, Oxford University Press, 1978, fig. 106, 13; Haerinck, 'Les tombes . . . de Abu-Habbah', pl. 6: 4, pl. 12: 12–14.

33. Oates, 'Late Assyrian Pottery from Fort Shalmanezer', *Iraq*, XXI, 1959, pl. XXXVII; 59.

34. Salles, 'Le Golfe Arabe dans l'Antiquité', *Annales d'Histoire de l'U.S.J.* (Beyrouth) 1, 1981, 17.

35. A Mesopotamian component is likely. One may nevertheless consider with some caution the comparison proposed by Salles ('Bahrain hellénistique . . .', note 6) with Oates, 'Late Assyrian Pottery . . .', pl. XXV.

36. Krauss, Lombard et Potts, *op. cit.*, 161; Larsen, *op. cit.*, 322–323.

37. Salles, 'Bahrain hellénistique . . .'; 156.

MAR-TU and the land of Dilmun

JURIS ZARINS

*Another future line of research [in southern Mesopotamia] is
the survey of the Southern Desert beyond the great dunes. It is
there that direct evidence of nomadic people must be sought.
(Wright 1981: 336, 338).*

INTRODUCTION

Buccellati remarked a number of years ago that a people known as
the MAR-TU seemed to be connected with the island of Dilmun in the
Gulf. He concluded that it seemed difficult to see how one could combine whatever we know about the MAR-TU with the possibility of
their coming from an island (Buccellati 1966: 249). In this respect, he
was echoing the sentiments of Landsberger who earlier had suggested that there was a connection between the Arabian peninsula
and the MAR-TU (Landsberger 1954: 56, n. 103). Since these statements of a number of years ago, much has been learned about the
historical and archaeological situation in the Gulf (now see Potts, n.d.
in press). Even more recently, the broad sweep of survey across the
Arabian peninsula has enabled researchers to more accurately fit
within a larger framework the results of the Gulf discoveries. As a
result of these developments, largely within the decade of the 1970s,
we can perhaps put forward a hypothesis which could help to explain
the apparent association of MAR-TU and the land of Dilmun.

THE PROBLEM

From the Ur III (2112–2004 B.C.) and Isin-Larsa (2025–1763 B.C.)
periods, we have a number of textual sources which suggest that an
ethnic group of people called MAR-TU were associated with the land
of Dilmun – the first of three entities found to be trade partners with
Mesopotamia from at least 2500 B.C. (the others being Makkan and
Meluḫḫa). From Drehem, a city near Nippur, we note the occurrence
in two texts (dated to AS 2–2044 B.C.) (CST 254 and TRU 305) of a
colophon which reads 'MAR-TU (and) Diviners coming from Dilmun'

(or MAR-TU Diviners coming from Dilmun) (Buccellati 1966: 249). In a text from Isin, dated to Šu-ilišu (1984–1975 B.C.) (BIN IX 405) manufactured leather objects are made for 'Dilmun and the MAR-TU' (Buccellati 1966: 250). In addition, other evidence suggests that the MAR-TU were associated with (sea) fishing (Civil 1961; Buccellati 1966: 90). Thus, Buccellati and later Gelb concluded that the MAR-TU existed in the south in the area of the Gulf as far as Bahrain (Gelb 1968: 43; 1980: 2). Finally, this linkage is suggested by a text from Eshnunna, a Mesopotamian city on the Diyala river. In this text most likely dated to Išaramašu (c. 1970 B.C.) MAR-TU are arranged by segmented lineage affiliation (babtum). The total states that twenty-six MAR-TU are e-lu-tum-me, a term perhaps best translated as meaning 'trustworthy' or 'reliable' vís-à-vís the local Eshnunna officials. One MAR-TU from the lineage of Bašanum is said to be a-ab-ba-ta or 'from the sea(lands)' or the land across the sea (Gelb 1968: 43).

THE MAR-TU AND THE ARCHAEOLOGICAL RECORD

The third and second millennium B.C. literary record has suggested that the people living in the open steppe west of the Euphrates river were nomadic and barbaric:

> A tent dweller (buffeted?) by wind and rain . . . the one who digs up truffles at the foot of the hill . . . who does not know how to bend his knee (i.e. respect authority), who eats uncooked meat . . . who in his lifetime does not have a house, who in the day of his death will not be buried . . . who knows not barley . . .
> .(Buccellati 1966: 92–93; Liverani 1973; Kramer 1963: 164).

From approximately 2500 to 1950 B.C. they were labelled as MAR-TU (westerners) by the sedentary populations of the Tigris-Euphrates Valley. As such, these people would then seem to share certain characteristics with other pastoral nomads such as strong kinship bonds, impermanent dwellings, distinctive technology, movement to procure pasturage (usually along seasonal lines) and water for herds, trade networks and interaction with agriculturalists or sedentary populations, and an ideology in which domesticated animals are viewed as the main subsistence strategy.

But the MAR-TU and other pastoral people have long been viewed erroneously by researchers who have suggested that they lived in a harsh and desert-like environment, and thus were saddled with an impoverished part-culture which would have left behind little or no record of their passing (witness the remarks by Woolley and Lawrence 1914–15: 20, 27, concerning the Sinai). Anthropological study of pastoralists in the past has yielded claims that pastoralism appeared relatively late on the scene. It was almost always viewed in the light of the development of the historical state (Sahlins 1968: 33; Lees and Bates 1974; Adams 1974; Possehl 1977; Krader 1981: 499). Consequently, reconstruction of the MAR-TU and other pastoral societies in the Near East has been generated by an appeal to the historic record (see e.g. Buccellati 1966; Brinkman 1968; Kupper 1957; Posener 1940).

While we propose to define briefly the archaeological dynamics of a pastoral group called the MAR-TU, they invariably formed part of a larger entity which can be dubbed here conveniently a 'pastoral nomadic technocomplex' (Clarke 1968: 338–343). (Similarly, today we can recognize the Rwala and Murra as smaller sub-units of a larger cultural/linguistic group known as camel Bedouin). This larger entity lies in a region south of the 250 mm isohyet, as suggested by Buccellati (1966: 239) and can be considered to be divided into two sub-categories: 1) the western area including the Sinai and the Negev south of Beersheba, and 2) the eastern area encompassing all of Jordan east of the Jordan Valley environs, southern and eastern Syria, western Iraq, and north-central Saudi Arabia. The evidence generated to date best fits a time-block covering four millennia – 6000–2000 B.C.

Observation of material remains within this region has been anything but systematic and thorough. It began as the result of explorers first crossing the Negev in the second half of the nineteenth century (Palmer 1871; Trumbull 1883). Serious archaeological work in the western area can be said to have begun only with the work of Glueck in the 1950s (Basor 1955–65 passim; Glueck 1955: 122) and augmented by more recent work in the 1960s and 1970s. A recently concluded three-year survey and excavation at Bir Resisim in the central Negev has added immensely to our data base (Cohen and Dever 1978, 1979, 1980). Palmer was the first to describe the extensive cultural material from the Sinai (1871: 139–142, 257–258, and passim) followed by Holland (1870) and later Currelly (1906). More recently , work in the 1970s has been concentrated both in the south Sinai, centering on the plutonic outcrops, and north Sinai around the Jebel massifs.

The smaller western area can perhaps be contrasted with the much larger eastern one which is of more relevance here. In this area work lagged behind and it was not until the 1920s that observers began to note the same nomadic technocomplex in both eastern Jordan and western Iraq (Maitland 1927; Rees 1929; field 1960) – an area dominated by the Harrat al Rajil lava field (Helms 1975: fig. 1). The densest number of sites studied to date appears to center on the road from Azraq to Rutba with additional sites extending into southern Syria (Field 1960: 60–67). The full extent of this techno-complex is suggested by Poidebard's aerial survey (1934: pl. CXL) which shows quite clearly that this cultural technocomplex extended even across the Euphrates to the Jebel Sinjar area. Most recently, work has concentrated in both the eastern arm of Jordan (Betts 1982) and south Jordan (Henry *et al.* 1981, 1983). Within the last decade, the Saudi Arabian survey program has significantly increased our scope and understanding of this technocomplex. The recovery of the cultural remains in northern and central Saudi Arabia has enabled us to obtain a truer picture of the range and variability of the culture. In northernmost Saudi Arabia (an extension of the Harrat al Rajil lava field) material is plentiful (Adams and Parr 1977: pl. 4). Other centers of this technocomplex include the Wadi Sirhan and the Jowf-Sakaka basin (Parr, Zarins *et al.* 1978; Zarins 1979). In the northwest (Midian) other dense groupings occur, notably in the Tabuk basin and along the Red Sea coastline (Ingraham, Johnson *et al.* 1981: 68ff). The southern border of the technocomplex is ill-defined perhaps due to shifting cultural zones. Nevertheless, aspects of this technocomplex have been identified in the central and western Nejd (Zarins *et al.* 1979; Zarins *et al.* 1982) and the western and southern Hejaz (Zarins *et al.* 1980; Zarins *et al.* 1981).

In relation to the specific archaeological record of the techno-complex and its relation to the MAR-TU, perhaps the following observations can be made. Historically, the early MAR-TU from at least the ED III period have been associated with the western borderlands and specifically in the Jebel Bishri area in east-central Syria. It was in this locality that the Akkadian kings and later the trade expeditions encountered these pastoral people (summary by Buccellati 1966: 235–242). Survey work in the 1960s confirmed Poidebard's earlier evidence of stone circle complexes and kites in the Jebel Bishri area (Buccellati, personal communication). It would be a mistake, however, to restrict their presence to this region or insist that this was their natural homeland as some have done. Rather it is our contention that the archaeological data suggests that the MAR-TU were, in fact, to be found in a wide arc fronting Mesopotamia (and Dilmun!) from central Syria to northeast Saudi Arabia, fig. 68.

THE ECOLOGY

Under current conditions, camel pastoralists organized in tribal groupings dot the countryside in varying degrees of intensity. The archaeological record described above, in contrast, has confirmed that the culture under review here abandoned the area and that most sites were either not re-occupied at all or only in much later historical periods. This creates a problem in trying to define the transition between the earlier nomads (Helms calls them 'indigenous proto-Bedouin' (1976: 26) or 'paleo-Bedouin' (1982)) who left behind the archaeological record described above and the appearance of the Bedouin camel-herders (Ahlamu?, Hapiru?, Shosu?) accustomed to

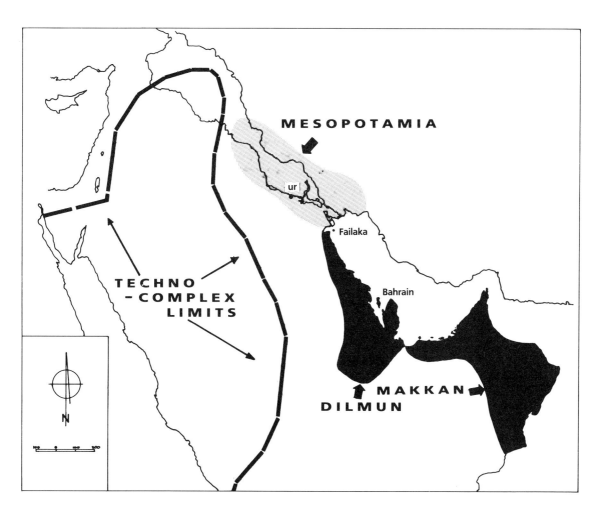

68 The Pastoral Technocomplex in relationship to Mesopotamia, Dilmun and Makkan

fighting as rider warriors (Dostal 1959). The latter have left behind a different type of archaeological record (for further details and a suggested model, see Zarins *et al*. 1980: 20–23; Zarins *et al*. 1981: 28–31; Zarins *et al*. 1982). To examine the changes that occurred within the region defined above, a brief understanding of the ecological factors that shape the area today must be contrasted with a proposed reconstructed environment.

The largest part of the area under consideration lies within the Saharo-Sindian phyto-geographical zone (Zohary 1952: 202). The bulk of the region is a vast tableland sloping west to east and is extremely arid (80% receiving less than 200 mm of rainfall). Intermittent wadi flow occasionally gives way to sheet and flash flooding and local depressions such as the Dead Sea, Wadi Sirhan, Ain Azraq, and the Jowf-Sakata basin occasionally retain large volumes of water. The climate today tends toward the extreme Mediterranean type with winters mild to cold and short and rainy. The summers are long, hot and dry. Thus, the present-day landscape is dominated by features typical of the arid climate such as exposed rock, abrupt scarps, mesas, pinnacle rocks with intervening flat-floored wadis filled with detritus, open plains, gravel flats, dune formations, and pans (Thompson 1975: 1–23; Schyfsma 1978; Zarins et al. 1979: 11).

The study of this region in terms of discerning a different landscape based on altered climatic conditions has lagged considerably as would be expected. Nevertheless, within the last fifteen years, evidence has been accumulating from different sub-areas of the region to support our assumptions. Quoting one authority: 'These findings generally agree with the results of other authors who have studied the Iran-Iraq region, and have concluded that the post-Pleistocene climate becomes more humid and can be subdivided into drier and more humid periods . . .' (Diester-Haas 1973: 222; cf. Nützel 1976: fig. 5). In East and North Africa, the evidence also suggests a modest but significant increase in precipitation in the Holocene (Butzer 1971: 581–585; Butzer et al. 1972; Edmunds and Walton 1980; Gabriel 1978: 28–29). Butzer was perhaps the first to coin the phrase 'Neolithic Wet Phase' based on work in the Nile Valley, and he defined a complex moist interval beginning c. 7000 B.C. interrupted by drier spells and terminating in stages between 2900 and 2350 B.C. (Butzer 1959: 76; 1976: 32). The most recent syntheses generally confirm such earlier work (Alayne Street and Grove 1979: 99; Haynes 1980: 70).

More recent investigations within our specific region support such data in its broader applications (Neev and Emergy 1967; Hukreide and Wiesemann 1968; Henry et al. 1981; Lloyd 1980; Marks and Scott 1976: 44–48; Moore 1979; Horowitz 1980: 249–50; Hanihara and Sakaguchi 1978). Recent work in Saudi Arabia has also reinforced this documentation on active Holocene humid phases (McClure 1976; 1978: 262; Kinsman 1968; Masry 1974; Zarins et al. 1979: 10; Hötzl et al. 1978: 205, 232; Garrard et al. 1981; Zarins et al. 1982). For the larger Arabian peninsula then, (including Bahrain), a summary profile, Table 1, as generated by Larsen (1980: 216–230 and Table 5) and Hötzl and Zötl (1978: 303 and Table 50) suggests a complex fluctuation of climatic conditions alternating between moister and drier peaks during the early Holocene terminating c. 2200 B.C.

FAUNA

This pastoral complex depended on domestic animals for its existence and there has been a tremendous amount of work carried out in the past to define in the Fertile Crescent which species were first domesticated and in which regions they predominated. Up to the present, little has been collected from the technocomplex in actual

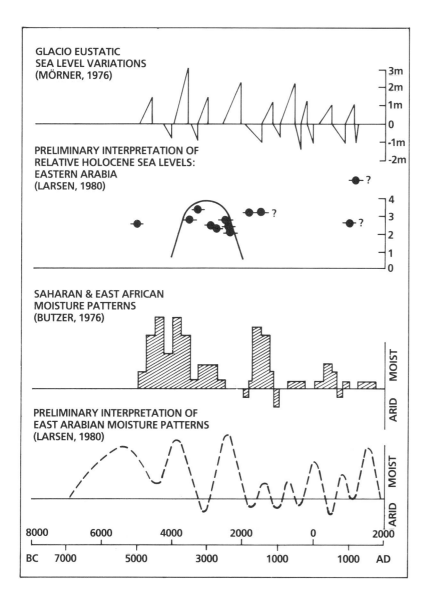

paleo-zoological data, but linguistic and artistic material has helped in more or less defining the species involved. Hunting continued to play an important role (especially during phase A) to judge from the rock art (Zarins 1982) and objects such as the Hunters' Slate Palette.

Summary of Near Eastern, Early Holocene, Moisture Patterns (after Larsen 1980)

OVICAPRIDS

Domestic sheep are well attested from the mixed farming zones from at least 8500 B.C. (summary by Wapnish and Hesse, in press) and by the PPNB, domestic sheep were a mainstay of the mixed zone farming cultures (Clutton-Brock 1978). Both domestic sheep and goat remains are attested from our cultural area from at least the Chalcolithic period (Henry *et al.* 1983; Gaillard *apud* Dubertret and Dunand 1954–5; D. Hakker *apud* Beit-Arieh 1974: 153, n. 5; Cohen and Dever 1978: 37; 1979: 254).

BOVIDS

Domestic cattle are traditionally regarded as deriving from wild Anatolian stock (Mellaart 1975: 98; Perkins 1969) but recent investigations would appear to indicate that domestic cattle may have been present in northeastern Africa as early as 7500 B.C. (Wendorf and Schild 1981). This would be an attractive possibility in explaining the quick spread of cattle pastoralism across northeastern Africa to all of Saharan Africa as well as northern Arabia. Both long-horned and short-horned varieties are known from actual sites (Lernau 1978: 85; Gaillard *apud* Dubertret and Dunand 1954–5). Saudi Arabian rock art also prominently features long-horned cattle (Zarins 1982).

EQUIDS

Equid domestication is perhaps the most difficult to detect and is probably the most controversial. The native equid of Southwest Asia, *E. hemionus*, turns up within our technocomplex region as a game animal in Late Pleistocene and early Holocene contexts (Zarins 1976). It appears to have never been truly domesticated (Zarins 1978c: 16–17) although it may have been used in cross-breeding experiments and most likely tamed (Zarins 1976: 116ff., 189ff.; Littauer and Crouwel 1979: 24–25; Clutton-Brock 1978: 100). The wild ass, *E. asinus*, possibly a native of both North Africa and Southwest Asia, appears as a domestic in a late Egyptian pre-Dynastic context. Possibly the domestic form spread quickly throughout southwest Asia via our pastoral technocomplex as it is found at Tel Gat in EB I context and at Arad in EB II context (Lernau 1978: 85–86). The representations of Old Kingdom date in the Sinai are well known. Horses and hybrid forms are known only from historical sources (see below).

CAMEL

The camel, like the equids, is a source of considerable controversy due to the question of Bedouin origins (Dostal 1959; Mikesell 1955; Ripinsky 1975; Bulliet 1975). The animal has been found in our cultural area since at least the mid-Pleistocene (Zarins 1978a) and its remains are known from the Neolithic well into the Late Bronze Age, but there has been a reluctance to ascribe domestication to any of these remains (B. Hesse, personal communication). Its earliest possible attested domestic form appears to be found in the United Arab Emirates datable to the early third millennium B.C. (Hoch 1979:

613; J. Tixier, personal communication; H.-P. Uerpmann, personal communication; Zarins 1982). From this southeastern area of the peninsula, the domestic form spread northward and the pastoralists, facing increasing aridity, began to utilize the animal *c.* 2000 B.C. (Zarins *et al.* 1980: 23–25). Unfortunately, from the crucial second millennium B.C., texts mentioning such groups as the Ahlamu (Cornwall 1952), Shosu (Giveon 1971), and Hapiru (Greenberg 1955) give no indication of camel use.

MATERIAL REMAINS

The technocomplex described above in terms of the ecology and the fauna, has yielded archaeological data which can be classed as follows: 1) structures, 2) lithics, 3) ceramics, and 4) rock art. The most ubiquitous of the structural remains are what we refer to as 'stone circles'. Many sites within this large region can consist either of simple, single 'homesteads' or multiple chains covering several kilometers. Different construction techniques throughout the region suggest multiple sub-phases of occupation over time (confirmed to some extent by the ceramics and lithics). Many sites have appended 'corrals', separate animal pens, large central areas, or possible defensive walling enclosing the multiple joined circles (see Betts 1983). Future analysis of excavated sites such as Bir Resisim may lead to defining kinship groups within these sites (Cohen and Dever 1981). Tumuli, another prominent group of remains, are sometimes found interspersed among the stone circles or built along prominent ridge-lines. In the latter case, they often have appended 'tails' i.e. small piles of stones in a line behind the main tomb. These also may relate to kinship relationships. Kites, one of the more spectacular features of the technocomplex, are low, long stone walls which converge into a small circular head. Many are grouped together in chains and often form interlocking structures covering ten–fifteen kms. (Helms 1981: 38ff.). First noted from the air in the 1920s, (Maitland 1927), they may be game traps for gazelle, equids, and ostrich. They have been noted from the Sinai to the Jebel Sinjar. Stone pillars usually found in clusters unassociated with tombs or living sites, have also been found spread across the region. One of the more spectacular sites has been found in northern Arabia (Zarins 1979). These pillar sites appear to have clear cult associations and possible astral alignments.

Lithics from these sites can, on occasion, be very profuse. Two principal periods can be discerned although considerable overlapping probably existed. The earlier phase (*c.*6000–4000 B.C.) is dominated by PPNB types principally burins, blades, and some projectile points (Garrod 1960; Betts 1982: 28ff.; Adams *et al.* 1977: 34ff.), the later phase, *c.*4000–2000 B.C., by fine bifacially retouched arrowheads, tabular flint fan scrapers, and canaanean blades (Ronen

1970; Beit-Arieh 1983: 44; Parr *et al.* 1978: 38).

Ceramic materials are not common at many sites, rare at others, and in sites in the southern region of the technocomplex, no ceramic materials have been found. Certainly the sites of the western region can be dated more securely by virtue of ceramic types found in the Palestine farming communities (Cohen and Dever 1980, 1981; Beit-Arieh 1983: 44). This ceramic material first appears in the Chalcolithic and continues through the Early Bronze Age to the Middle Bronze Age I period when the sites are abandoned. Ties with southern Palestinian towns and the Egyptian Empire are also well attested. From southern Jordan and northern Saudi Arabia, Chalcolithic and EB I ceramic vessels, while rare, have been attested. Metal items appear to be restricted to Phase B of the complex and have been recovered both from survey and excavation.

The rock art can provide a contemporary view of some of the most essential elements of this prehistoric culture – an invaluable human dimension to a culture dominated by stone structures and lithics. The earlier phase perhaps coincides with the earlier lithic tradition. Based on rules of patination and superimposition, the early simple outline style correlates well with the PPNB tradition. Principal sites include Kilwa in what is now northern Saudi Arabia (Rhotert 1938) and the Har Harif massif in the Negev (Anati 1955: 32–33). Within central and northern Saudi Arabia this style is quite widespread and noted particularly at Jubba, Hanakiya, and other sites in the Jowf-Sakaka basin. This style seems to have extended southward along the higher elevations of western Saudi Arabia to Taif and even south of Abha (Zarins *et al.* 1980, 1981; Zarins 1982).

The later phase of the rock art (*c.* 4000–2000 B.C.) has been labelled the 'Hunting and Pastoral Phase' by Anati (1962). The principal sites are again to be found in Saudi Arabia. In the Bir Hima/Najran area (Anati 1968; Zarins *et al.* 1981), at Jubba in the great Nefud (Parr *et al.* 1978), the Jowf-Sakaka basin (Parr *et al.* 1978), and Hanakiya near Madina (Courtney-Thompson 1975; Zarins 1982) a new style has been devised. It is dramatically different from the earlier simple outline style. The human figures in many cases are drawn nearly lifesize, and details in dress, body features, and composition have been refined. The style involves not merely outline pecking but also interior modelling. The main animal depicted is the bull with accentuated long horns and other animals present include the ibex, oryx, ostrich, camel, and fat-tailed sheep. To the north of Saudi Arabia, parallels for this rock art phase are to be found in Wadi Rajil near Jawa in eastern Jordan (Hunt 1976: 24–29) and in the Negev where Anati describes three different styles for this phase (1962: 213). More recently, similar material has been found on sandstone boulders in western Iraq in a tributary of the Wadi Hauran (east of Rutba) (Tyráček and Amin 1981). The Hunters' Palette (probably from Hierakonpolis) illustrates the clearest parallels to this artistic style and its themes and style fit comfortably within the rock art repertoire of the fourth millennium B.C.

LINGUISTIC CONSIDERATIONS AND THE MAR-TU

For our purposes here, we would like to concentrate on the Phase B aspect of the technocomplex as expressed in the eastern sub-region. In fact, we want to focus on the culture when the precipitous decline of this way of life had already begun. From a mere trickle of historical information *c.* 2500 B.C. the accounts reach a peak *c.* 2000–1900 B.C. when the impetus towards the sedentary zone was clearly strong (Buccellati 1966: 253ff.). As we have suggested earlier, we know that the sedentary people of the Mesopotamian valley called these nomadic pastoral people the MAR-TU and that between 2500–2000 B.C. they began to increasingly infiltrate the Mesopotamian cities (at least as perceived by the official scribes) (Liverani 1973: 104–106). As climatic conditions deteriorated in the region to the west and south, cuneiform records increasingly describe the people, name them, and their products. Under the Ur III empire, their contribution to the Sumerian state can be traced by the examination of receipt and delivery texts, principally at Drehem (Buccellati 1966: 284–300). A separate series of texts indicate that the Ur III kings waged military campaigns against these people, confiscating animals and taking prisoners (Lieberman 1969: 58ff.; Buccellati 1966: 290; Gelb 1973: 79). From this body of evidence, we can conclude that the MAR-TU appeared to be principally dependent on ovicaprid and cattle herding and notably developed their own special breeds of sheep including the gukkal – the fat-tailed sheep. Equids are also well-known and include the wild ass of the steppe (*E. hemionus*), the horse, and various hybrids. Infiltration into Mesopotamian society was peaceful and conformed to the classical anthropological pattern. The poor fled to town looking for work (soldiers, workers, servants, couriers) and the rich (sugagum, abu Amurrim, rabiānum MAR-TU) for socio-political reasons. (See the discussion of a certain MAR-TU named Naplanum in the Ur III Drehem texts and his relationship to Naplanum, the first King of Larsa, Buccellati 1966: 319.)

It would be our conclusion then that these pastoral people of the west were first seen as a geographical entity coming from the hamad region and infiltrating Mesopotamian society – not along a single contact point nor just in a small restricted time period. Thus, in the anthropological sense, they bridged both societies by being in contact with their homeland, in raiding and trade, as well as by infiltration as explained by Rowton's concept (1974) of 'enclosed nomadism'. We feel, based on the archaeological evidence presented above, that this process began at least as early as 6000 B.C. – our phase A – when the early pastoralists interacted with the settled communities of Syria, Palestine, and later Mesopotamia. This hypothesis is confirmed when writing appears on the scene (as in the Sumerian case). For example, the newly discovered Ibla texts mention the MAR-TU principally in connection with metal daggers (Pettinato 1980: 9 and commentary) and prisoners of war (Pettinato 1981b: 120, see text TM 75G. 309). (Note also the MAR-TU name Iblanum as meaning man from Ibla, Buccellati 1966: 155, 246.) We have virtually no historical material from Palestine unfortunately to document this interaction (see the archaeological implications of the MB I however, Dever 1971). However, a detailed study of the ceramics from the South Sinai suggests a close interaction pattern with the southern urban zone of Palestine and the Egyptian Delta (Amiran *et al.* 1973; Beit-Arieh 1981). Similarly, the historical records from Old Kingdom Egypt describe the same phenomenon of the people from the western region of the technocomplex (Negev/Sinai) infiltrating the Egyptian Delta. The following describes the Aamu nomads from the *Instructions to Merykare* (Tenth Dynasty, *c.* 2130–2040 B.C.):

> The wretched Asiatic (Aamu), bad is the country where he lives, inconvenient in respect to water, impracticable because of many trees, its roads are bad on account of the mountains. He does not settle in one single place, for the (lack of) food makes his legs take flight. Since the time of Horus he has been at war. He does not conquer, nor yet can he be conquered. He does not announce the day of fighting . . . (Posener 1971: 534; Thompson 1974: 142).

From the early second millennium B.C. we have a much wider body of evidence dealing with the MAR-TU. This is due to the greatly increased numbers of MAR-TU escaping the hamad and entering the settled zones. As early as Šu-Sin year 4 (2034 B.C.) we see that a large defensive wall was being built in central Mesopotamia for the express purpose of keeping out the MAR-TU (the MAR-TU wall (called) the one which keeps Didanum away, Buccellati 1966: 92). Unfortunately, by the early reign of the succeeding king, Ibbi-Sin, things had changed:

> Reports that hostile MAR-TU had entered the plains having been received, 144,000 gur grain (representing) the grain in its entirety was brought into Isin. Now the MAR-TU in their entirety have entered the interior of the country taking one by one all the great fortresses. Because of the MAR-TU I am not able to provide . . . for that grain . . . (Jacobsen 1953: 40).

The newcomers were able to over-run the settled zone precisely because of earlier infiltration which had been peaceful. The earlier MAR-TU were incorporated into the Ur III bureaucratic structure and undoubtedly numerous leaders had residences in the settled zones as well. By the time of Naplanum and his successors, these MAR-TU had effectively taken over the socio-political structure of the alluvium in the south (Išbi-Erra, 2014 B.C., speaks in a year 4 date that he destroyed MAR-TU cities (Buccellati 1966: 39)). According to the year date of Ibbi-Sin 17, some of these MAR-TU apparently came from the Gulf region: 'The year the MAR-TU, the powerful south wind who, from the remote past, have not known cities, submitted to Ibbi-Sin, the king of Ur.' (cf. also Gelb's views, 1961: 36).

MAR-TU AND DILMUN

The installation in the alluvium of MAR-TU rulers inevitably led to the MAR-TU assuming greater and greater power in the bureaucratic operations of the states as well. At Ur, where in the Ur III period, Buccellati states the number of MAR-TU was surprisingly low (1966: 321), in the following decades the city became a dependency of Larsa and its MAR-TU dynasty. A brief perusal of UET V (texts datable to Gungunum-Sumuel, 1932–1866 B.C.) provides at least sixty MAR-TU names (Gelb 1980: 553ff.). Oppenheim's review of UET V suggests that Ur apparently served as a focal point and port for foreign trade, specifically with Dilmun (Oppenheim 1954: 8, n. 8). A number of texts describe this activity as traders called *alik Dilmun* sailed to Dilmun and exchanged goods. A number of texts (e.g. UET V 286, 297, 549 and 796) clearly demonstrate that individuals with MAR-TU names were involved in the trade (e.g. in UET V 297 a certain Zubabum; in UET V 549 a person named Milkudanum; and in UET V 796 Alazum). This then is a clear link between Dilmun and the MAR-TU – a hypothesis already formulated from a number of literary texts and Ur III economic records (see above). Surely this link must have involved not only high Ur officials and private investors but also naval personnel (see the summary by Leemans 1960: 23–56).

A very illuminating text, probably from Ur, and dated to the tenth year of Gungunum (1923 B.C.) has been described by Hallo (1965: 203). This text is a mercantile agreement involving certain staples perhaps traded to Dilmun. The name of the obligated partner is Ha-tin-DINGIR-i-ba-nu-um son of Ap-ka-lu-um. While Hallo feels that both names have reasonable Akkadian etymologies (Hallo 1965: 202 and nn. 30–32) he does note that neither occurs in the OB onomasticon. Rather, it appears that both names are MAR-TU. As suggested by Hallo himself (Ibid, n. 32), the first name could read Ha-tin-ILI-i-ba-nu-um. MAR-TU names from Mari and Tell Asmar provide some parallels (see HTN names in Huffmon 1965: 205–206; Gelb 1980:

586; for i-ba-nu-um, see Gelb 1980: 589). The second name Ap-ka-lu-um has a parallel MAR-TU name Ap-ka-nu-um (Gelb 1980: 565). The link of the MAR-TU in this text with Dilmun is confirmed by the 'Persian Gulf' seal impression on the tablet (Buchanan 1965; see below).

From Susa, we have a text which Lambert dates to the early Isin-Larsa period on palaeographical grounds (1976: 71). While the entire text appears to resemble the Ur business contracts, we reproduce only the obverse here:

obv.	10 ma-na urudu (x?)	Ten minas of copper
	iti e-la-ma-tum	(in) the month of Elamatum
	ki A-ab-ba	from Appâ? (cf. UET V 5)
	ki Mi-'il'-ki-il	(and) Mi-il-ki-il
	dumu Tè-im-^{d}En-za-ag	son of Te-im-^{d}En-za-ak
	é?-ki-ba-(x–x)	the e-ki-ba . . .
	šu-ba-ti	received.

The majority of names in this text are MAR-TU. Mi-il-ki-il recalls both an identical name in Gelb's compendium (1980: 623) and the name in the Bahrain text (see below, ILI-mi-il-kum). Another man, possibly the investing merchant in this text, also has an obvious MAR-TU name of the -anum type: Mi-il-ku-ma-nu-um. Two MAR-TU names from the *alik Dilmun* texts at Ur are similar: Mi-il-ku-da-nu-um (UET V 549) and Mi-li-ik-i-li-a (UET V 491) (for other similar parallels, see GELB 1980: ix and 624). Two of the three witnesses in this transaction also have MAR-TU names: A-hu-ma (MAD 3, p. 165; Gelb 1980: 557) and possibly Mi-nu-up-DINGIR (so far un-attested). Two key facts ally this text to Dilmun. First, the tablet is again sealed by a circular impression of a 'Persian Gulf' seal (Lambert 1976: fig. 1) which also associates it with the YBC 5447 text described above. Secondly, Mi-il-ki-il is described in the text as the son of one Tè-im-^{d}En-za-ag. This name clearly incorporates the titulary deity of Dilmun, Inzak, a name known from both the Durand stone found on Bahrain (^{d}In-za-ak) and other Mesopotamian sources (see Leemans 1960: 141, n. 2 and UET V 286). In the I-L Sumerian story, *Enki and Ninhursag*, Enki says that ^{d}En-za$_6$-ag will be the Lord of Dilmun (Kramer 1944: 58). In two letters written from Dilmun and found at Nippur (Ni 615 and Ni 641), the god Inzak is clearly stated to be the principal deity of Dilmun (Cornwall 1952: 144–45; the name is written in the Kassite letter, *c.* 1370 B.C. as ^{d}In-zag$_x$ (SAG) and ^{d}In-za-ag). Since the assumption is that the man came from Dilmun (reinforced by the Gulf seal impression) and his son bears a MAR-TU name, it would seem that MAR-TU were to be found in Dilmun as actual residents during this period. This would certainly closely tie the MAR-TU and Dilmun. In UET V 716 is another reference to an inhabitant of Dilmun, a certain Me-a-ti-a-nu-um (Oppenheim 1954: 15). The name seems to be clearly MAR-TU in origin, being another -anum name (Gelb 1980: 622 Ma-ti-DINGIR? or p. 619 Ma-a-nu-um?). The evidence of the Nippur letters (cited above) prompted Cornwall to remark that 'Dilmun appears as a land with a population of Semites still not very far removed from the life of the Arabian deserts . . .' (1952: 141). It would appear then that the evidence provided above ties in the MAR-TU with Dilmun both as inhabitants and engaged in trade with Mesopotamia.

In 1932, Gadd published a well-known article in which he examined a group of seals which Mortimer Wheeler in 1958 labelled 'Persian Gulf seals' (Wheeler 1958: 246). Of Gadd's original eighteen seals, *sixteen* were found at Ur (Bibby 1958: 243), perhaps again confirming the role of Ur as a port in overseas trade. Within the last two decades we have obtained a better picture of the distribution and origin of these 'Persian Gulf' seals and it would appear that the most popular circular style coincides with the rise of the I-L period in Mesopotamia. The largest number of seals have come from Failaka (Kjaerum 1980) and in the Gulf they have often been called Dilmun seals. A large number have also come from Bahrain (Bibby 1958) with a smaller number from Eastern Saudi Arabia, the U.A.E., Oman, and the Indus Valley. (An unpublished seal with very close parallels to the Failaka examples, was found in I-L context at Ischali in the Mesopotamian Diyala region (A. 17007 Chicago; Buchanan 1965: 206, n. 14). The vast bulk of the Gulf seals are from the Ur III-I-L periods and seem to be localized in the Gulf region, prompting authorities to conclude that the seals indeed represent the Dilmun type. Thus, returning to YBC 5447, Buchanan suggests the Gulf seal on the tablet indicates an origin from Failaka and the adjoining mainland area (1965: 208; 1967: 107). A similar argument can be used in discussing the Susa tablet (Lambert 1976). (For the latest summary on the Gulf seals, see Potts n.d.) It seems clear in summary that the MAR-TU were linked to Dilmun in a political sense (rulers in southern Mesopotamian towns), commercial agents in Mesopotamia (alik Dilmun), and inhabitants of Dilmun itself (Susa Tablet, UET V 716).

A neglected part of the over-all pattern however involves the more recent archaeological developments in the Gulf and Saudi Arabia. Within the area of the northeastern portion of the Arabian peninsula itself, the same process of sedentarization and 'seepage' was occurring. The southern MAR-TU not only infiltrated southern Mesopotamia, but also the entity known as Dilmun. It would appear to be safe to say that Dilmun as a historical entity probably also goes back to at least our Phase A (*c.* 6000 B.C.) with the onset of the southern Ubaid culture's involvement in the East Arabian littoral (Masry 1974; Oates *et al.* 1977: 228, 232). Again, the city and area of Ur are prominently mentioned. From this period onward, a sedentary presence was established along the East Arabian littoral which has never departed. This sedentary focus reached a peak during the ED Mesopotamian period as affirmed by the survey and excavation of such mainland sites and areas as Jabrin oasis, Al Hasa oasis, Abqaiq, Dhahran, and Tarut Island (summarized by Potts n.d. and Piesinger 1983a). The ceramics and other objects from this region during these periods reveal very close connections with Mesopotamia (e.g. in the use of bitumen for waterproofing). In contrast, as we indicated above, our pastoral technocomplex also extended into central Saudi Arabia perhaps south of Buraydah/Anezah. It seems certain then that the eastern littoral of Arabia was not only a focus of attention from Mesopotamia but also by the early MAR-TU pastoralists of the hamad to the north and west. (Similarly, we have shown above that the Sinai pastoralists interacted both with the southern Negev urban areas and the Egyptian Delta.) Without recounting the evidence here, we feel that Dilmun as an entity stretched from Failaka as far south as the U.A.E. and included both Bahrain and the East Arabian littoral, fig. 68. This concept is echoed as late as the classical Arab period when historians such as Yaqut defined Bahrain as the continental eastern littoral of Arabia from Basra to Oman (Burrows 1928: 3). One explanation then of the MAR-TU being in Dilmun would be that of infiltration as in the Mesopotamian example. The difference would be that this process in the case of Dilmun was largely a 'silent' one.

Once again, let us return to the ecological argument which we cited in the case of Mesopotamia. During the last three–two hundred years of the third millennium B.C. progressive dessication was setting in in the Arabian-Syrian hamad, a strong factor in accelerating the MAR-TU towards the well-watered alluvium. To the south, similarly, as progressive dessication set in, accompanied by ecological and socio-political problems, the settled zone was forced to retreat to a few sites along the coast, and Dilmun became principally identified with the offshore occupation of Failaka and Bahrain. With the resurgence of occupation, principally during the I-L period, (labelled on Bahrain as City II or Barbar II), we see a coinciding of views: MAR-TU occupation of the southern Mesopotamian plain and the intimate association of the MAR-TU with Dilmun during the I-L period. This viewpoint is also buttressed by the on-going excavations of tumuli both on Bahrain and at Dhahran. In both cases, the Barbar II occupation of the tumuli seems the largest and most extensive. Similarly on Failaka, the archaeological evidence from seals and ceramics suggests for F. 3 and F. 6 a primary occupation during the I-L period (Højlund 1981: 37–38; Kjaerum 1980: 45; Potts n.d.). The MAR-TU seepage theory is further buttressed by Buccellati's observation that the MAR-TU in the north soon became known as the Ahlamu

(1966: 243, and n. 44). Similarly in the south the Kassite letters of *c.* 1370 B.C. speak of the Ahlamu and their impeding the normal operations of the Dilmun authorities (Cornwall 1952).

Finally, a number of textual sources from the Dilmun region confirms our thesis that the MAR-TU were intimately connected with the region. A number of inscribed objects have been found in the F.3 and F.6 settlements on Failaka (see Government of Kuwait n.d. pls. 46, 53, 64, 82). One steatite bowl fragment from F.3 of probable I-L date lists a number of names which are now fragmented. One complete name reads [m]Ia-mi-ú. This names appears to be a MAR-TU name with such parallels as Ia-mu-ú-a and Ia-mi-i-la (Gelb 1980: 603). Other inscriptional material must await publication. From Bahrain, we have the well-known Durand stone discovered in 1879. The attached cuneiform inscription reads é-gal ri-mu-um ìr [d]In-za-ak lú a-ga-rum. The name Ri-mu-um may have MAR-TU parallels with examples such as Ri-ma-an, Ri-ma-nu-um, Ri-ma-tum and Ri-mu-[d]IM (all RIWM names, Gelb 1980: 633). A-ga-rum has fewer parallels, but possibly MAR-TU Ha-gu-ra, Ha-gi-rum (Ibid, p. 583; Huffmon 1965: 190 HGR). (Oppenheim feels the text may belong to a late OB or Kassite time period, and thus belong to the realm of the Ahlamu, 1954: 16, n. 27. For a later vision on Hajar, see Yaqut in Burrows 1928: 10.)

The final piece of textual evidence is a small cuneiform tablet found at the base of City II in the Qal'a excavations on Bahrain (Bibby 1969: 350–356). We first saw the tablet in 1971 and subsequently Gelb provided a transliteration of the text which consists of three individual names and one patronymic. Based on the palaeography, Gelb considered the text to belong to the early I-L period (1980: 2). The text also reproduced by Brunswig and Parpola (n.d., p. 10) has no obvious obverse and reverse and no indication as to use or purpose:

AYO 881   obv.?   [m]I-zi-ta-am-bu
                    dumu I-a-bi-na-im
           rev.?   [m]I-a-bi-na-im
                    [m]DINGIR-mi-il-kum

ILI-milkum may be considered as related to the name Milki-il found on the Susa tablet quoted above and Milik-ilija in the Ur I-L text UET V 491. In any case, all of the names in this small text are clear MAR-TU names. Thus, we have come full circle from the MAR-TU mentioned in the Tell Asmar text who is a-ab-ba-ta, the MAR-TU mentioned in the I-L Ur texts, especially the 'Gulf' sealed texts, the Failaka MAR-TU name and finally MAR-TU names from Bahrain itself. These new texts clearly indicate then that the MAR-TU were associated with Dilmun, something that Buccellati had hinted at in 1966.

We may finally note that precisely at the time the I-L period in

Mesopotamia was being re-shaped by MAR-TU pastoralists, a re-surgence of trade took place with Dilmun as suggested by the cuneiform evidence reviewed by Oppenheim and the recent archae-ology of the East Arabian littoral, Failaka, and Bahrain. Surely this trade was facilitated by the over-all control which the MAR-TU enjoyed both in an official capacity as rulers of southern Mesopo-tamia and as unofficial couriers of culture between the hamad region to the west and the cultural centers of Dilmun. This would, we suspect, account for the texts linking the MAR-TU and Dilmun in the cuneiform literature of the early second millennium B.C. Why this arrangement ended, not to be resumed until the very late second millennium B.C. is a matter for speculation and another study elsewhere.

The shell seals of Bahrain

HAYA AL KHALIFA

Man's disposition leads him to imitate nature. He imitated nature and so planted seeds to provide himself with food all the year round. Thus he attained agricultural abundance. He also gained knowledge of fire and how to control it; the sun was a natural resource that inspired him. And if we ask the question 'what were the natural resources that inspired man to mark his personal property before the invention of writing?' the answer would lead us directly to seals. But what were the natural resources which man exploited to acquire these seals? In my opinion, they were sea shells.

In 1977, the Directorate of Archaeology and Museums of the State of Bahrain, in conjunction with the Arab Archaeological Mission, nominated by the Arab League, undertook to excavate the burial mounds of Sar, near the Causeway between the Kingdom of Saudi Arabia and the State of Bahrain. In tomb 116 we found one of these shell seals, but it was classified as a shell ornament, fig. 69.

In the following season, on the site of the Sar cemetery, the Arab Archaeological Mission found shell seals with deliberately carved engravings of various motifs, in addition to the natural helicoidal form. We thus became convinced of their identity. After reference to the shell collection of the Directorate of Archaeology and Museums, finds which had been discovered in previous excavations of stone tombs, it transpired that some of them were classified as 'shell ornaments' while others were classified as 'imitations of Dilmun seals'. Later on, more such seals were discovered in burial grounds of other sites (al-Muqashsha', Kerakan, Sar,[1] 'Isa Town, Hamad Town), the total amounting to twenty-nine seals. If we add to that two seals from the cemetery of Ali (Excavations of the Danish Mission[2] and another one from the excavations of Umm Jidr (French Mission[3]), the total of known seals of this kind is thirty-two, in addition to three more of whose identity we are uncertain but which will be discussed later in detail. Other forms of sea shell which resemble these seals, but have one longitudinal hole through their tops were excluded as

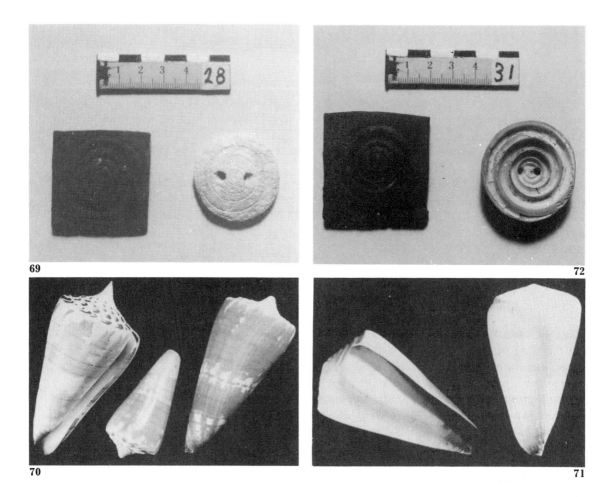

69   A shell seal from tomb 116, Sar burial mounds

70,71   Examples of the shells used for seals

72   The internal spiral found on some shells

they were considered to be ornamental sea shells and not seals. A collection of these was found in some of the cemeteries which I mentioned earlier. Moreover Cleuziou found in the cemetery at Hili (U.A.E.) four like them.[4]

The craftsman's choice of sea shells from the Conidae species to make his seals was excellent. They are distinguished for their variety, unique beauty, shiny colours, smooth surface, and the size and thickness of their bases. This is in addition to the helical interior form and the sharp edges which the craftsman can obtain at the base of the sea shell from the inside by accurately sawing it to make it suitable for use as a seal. Nature has provided him with another pattern at the back of the seal which is another spiral shape protruding in some sea shells and non-existent in others. The craftsman added to the back of the seal one horizontal suspension hole or two pierced longitudinally.

The following species of shell were probably in use: figs. 70, 71

1. Conus Generalis Maldivus
2. Conus Virgo
3. Conus Flavidus
4. Conus Terebera Thomasi

As it is difficult, at present, to classify these seals methodically in a chronological sequence, I have therefore attempted to classify them in accordance with the development of the inscriptions carved on the obverse and the reverse of the seal. The seals were divided into two groups. The first of these is divided into two categories whilst the second is divided into three categories. This classification is not definitive but a first step which will assist us to identify them. It may be possible in the future to transfer a seal from one category to another or transfer one group of these seals to follow another or to precede it. No doubt the current archaeological excavations in the burial mounds will provide us with more information about the stylistic features of these seals.

The first group is divided into two categories:-

Characteristics of the first category
The craftsman sawed the shell just above the base where thickness varies from one shell to another. Then he polished the obverse, reverse and sides of the shell on smooth stones. Thus the obverse of the seal appears as if the spiral shape was engraved on it by nature. The craftsman, thanks to his instinctive intelligence, noticed that this natural spiral shape varied in minute details from one shell to another. This distinctive feature made him choose this very kind of shell for making the seals. The craftsman also noticed that sometimes there was a natural glossy coat covering the obverse of the seal including the internal spiral where the sharp edges protrude and kept it from wear by usage, fig. 72.

The Edge of the Seal
The craftsman scraped and rubbed smooth the side edge of the seal until it formed its required circular shape. But it is advisable to point out other details: the thickness of the side edge varies from one seal to another. However, that this does not necessarily accord with the size of the shell, for some large seals have small side edges whilst some other small seals have large side edges.

The part of the side edge adjacent to the face of the seal sometimes slopes inwards, sometimes outwards; it may be straight from top to bottom. At other times it is grooved in the middle in the form of a furrow or alternatively in that of two convex arcs. These variations in the side edge of shell seals are similar to those found in chlorite seals.

73

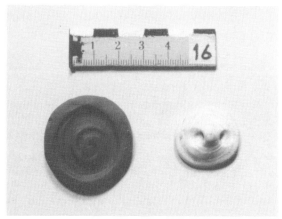

74

73 The reverse of a seal whose apex is pierced by two longitudinal holes

74 A Type Two seal whose tip often has raised natural ornament

The Reverse of the Seal
Variations in the reverse of the shell seal depend upon the type of shell used for the making of the seal and the modifications the craftsman made by rubbing it on smooth stones so that it would take on the required shape. Thus, different types of reverse were evolved. Below, we outline the features of some of them:

Type One
The reverse of this type of shell seal consists of a half circle covering the whole of the reverse and it rises slightly from the edge to the centre point. The reverse of the seal has a natural recessed pattern of a spiral, which ends at the apex in a circular shape on each side of which it is pierced by two longitudinal holes; fig. 73.

Type Two
The reverse of this type consists of a pyramid-like cupola covering the whole of the seal's reverse and ends at the apex with a sharp tip which is drilled horizontally. This tip has a raised natural ornament, but it may often be missing, fig. 74.

Type Three
The reverse of the shell seal of this type comprises a small hump in the middle; sometimes it is flat while at other times it is rounded. It is drilled horizontally from both sides and in one case there are two opposed horizontal holes, fig. 75.

Type Four
The reverse of the shell seal of this type consists of a small pyramid in the middle a few millimetres away from the side rim. Its base is drilled horizontally while its head rises to a sharp point, fig. 76.

75

76

77

78

Type Five

The reverse of the shell seal of this type is completely flat and is in the shape of a disc pierced by two longitudinal holes. There are seventeen seals of this group in the possession of the Directorate of Archaeology and Museums, fig. 77.

The Second Category

The craftsman has chosen shells which were smaller in size than those of the first category and the same technique as before was employed to prepare the shell as a seal, fig. 78. The obverse of the seal shows a raised natural spiral shape, whose sides are sharp whilst the lateral edge is circular and quite thin in which there are two horizontal holes. The reverse of the seal is flat rising slightly at the apex.

Probably this shell had a sharp tip which was cut off, making the interior spiral appear, from above, as a small circle at the centre of

75 The small hump in the middle is characteristic of Type Three seals

76 The head of a Type Four seal rises to a sharp point

77 A typical example of a Type Five seal, the reverse pierced by two longitudinal holes

78 Animals' bodies are represented by lightly drilled holes forming adjoining circles

the seal's reverse. Four cavities were engraved, surrounded by four circles each one in a corner while a frame of etched dots resembling a string of pearls encompass these circles.

Since there are only three seals in this category, it is difficult to make a judgement about their nature. It may be that this classification is the appropriate one, but it is also possible that they represent the latest phase in the development of shell seals. It is also possible not to classify them as shell seals but as earrings or part of a necklace. This becomes more probable because two of them were found in one tomb.

THE SECOND GROUP

This group, as far as the method of engraving is concerned, is divided into three categories:-

Category One

The reverse of the seal and its edges correspond completely with those of category one – group one. As for the obverse, the craftsman left a small part of the natural spiral shape in the middle of the seal. The remainder is a flat space on which the craftsman engraved simple motifs such as lines resembling the rays of the sun extending from the spiral shape almost to the rim of the seal. In another seal, ten circular depressions surrounding the spiral shape were cut, fig. 79. In yet another there are six with four more grouped to form a four-legged animal.

Category Two

This has almost the same details of category one but two or three animals, one of them upside down, are cut on the obverse, fig. 80. The bodies of these animals are cut in the shape of adjoining circles, created by lightly drilled holes, whilst the hands, feet and horns are straight lines. Yet it is difficult to determine what these animals are. The subject-matter of the seal has parallels with the chlorite seals but there is a difference in the method of engraving. There are four seals in this category.

Category Three

The seals in this category represent the peak of artistic quality in shell seals. Sizes are either large or medium. The reverse has a rounded or flat hump bored horizontally and the side edge is flared. As for the obverse, the craftsman used only the middle part of the natural spiral shape as an important motif. He used, also the method of overlapping drilled holes to depict the bodies of the animals. In seal number 23 there are, in addition to the natural spiral shape, two animals facing in opposite directions and between them a hollowed-

79

80

79 Ten circular depressions surround the spiral shape of this seal

80 Animals' bodies are represented by lightly drilled holes forming adjoining circles

out circle which, perhaps, represents the full moon. There is also a crescent and a sun or a bright star, and three circles which perhaps represent three stars.

Seal No. 29 – lines radiate from the natural spiral shape possibly representing the sun's rays; and there are three animals, one of which is upside down.

Seal No. 1 – six horizontal lines emerge from the natural spiral shape with one line placed perpendicularly to them; also an animal, and a sun or a bright star, fig. 81.

Seal No. 15 – the craftsman put great effort into the cutting of this seal where he has added to the natural spiral shape. Horizontal lines emerge from the natural spiral shape and are cut by a perpendicular line. There is an engraving of an animal, probably a gazelle, with two long horns and in front of it a circular depression which perhaps represents the full moon.

The artistic unity which is demonstrated by the flat circular chlorite seals has been preceded by the gradual evolution and development of the shell seals and there are general similarities, and continuity, between the motifs of the shell seals and the chlorite ones.

DISCUSSION

● Shell seals, until now, have not been found in areas of domestic occupation or temples but only in the cemeteries. Equally, they were not found in the earliest city, or in strata underneath it which would suggest that they date to an earlier period than the first city.

● Shell seals were found in numerous different types of burials such as those of Hamad Town, which bear a resemblance to the burials of Umm Al-Nar and Hili, that is, the burials of Area B.S. in Hamad Town which were considered a transitional period between the earlier burials and those of the Barbar period; the individual burials of the Barbar period in Sar, Hamad Town, Isa Town, 'Ali, Umm Jidr, Karzkan; the multiple burials in Sar and the tombs of Al-Hajjar and Al-Muqashsha' hewn in the rock in the form of a *serdab* in which the burial chamber had been re-used in several different periods. Does this mean that these shell seals were in continuous use for a long period of time? Or were they re-used and kept in later periods than when they were made?

● These seals were discovered in tombs in cemeteries which were disturbed or in tombs which were re-used. It is, therefore, difficult to determine their date or even to associate them with the archaeological finds discovered with them in the tombs, such as pottery. It is also not easy to ignore the parallels of the elements of the shell seals, other than the natural ones or those added by man, in order to deduce a chronological development of the methods of carving found in them.

● The craftsman used a borer with a curved head for cutting the seals. This explains why the animals appear devoid of their natural form. They consist of drilled holes closely linked with each other. This artistic style was common in the early cultures of the Near East such as Jemdet Nasr.

● It is possible that the craftsman found that the limited natural patterns of the shell seals did not meet the purpose required of them: i.e. establishing private ownership, in view of the limitations of their natural decoration. The increase in the demand for the seals was, perhaps, the result of the expansion in inter-regional trade over short distances and probably over long distances too. Also therefore, the craftsman added other motifs inspired by nature and faith.

● These inscriptions could represent religious scenes or tribal symbols, namely what the bedu call the mark (WASM), which they use to indicate private ownership.

● Perhaps the spiral shape inspired the potter in decorating the pottery of Barbar period which is characterised by raised and incised rings.

● We notice that the maker of the shell seal adopted the natural spiral shape which centres the interior part of the shell as a principal

81

83

82

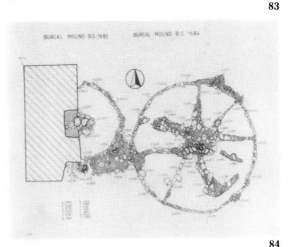

84

motif for the seal; then he added other different motifs. This same practice is followed in some of the flat circular chlorite seals where the craftsman chose principal motifs which he cut in the middle of the seal and surrounded with other motifs.

● The craftsman chose animal forms and heavenly bodies for engraving on these seals and excluded human beings.

● It may be noted that the depictions of two or three animals, one of them upside down, (mountain goats, cows, bulls, goats and gazelles) have parallels in the flat circular chlorite seals. There are many examples, figs. 82–83, such as one seal from Failaka[6] and two seals from Sar and seals 319, 320, 324, 340 at Bahrain National Museum.[7] The examples of this continuity are many. For instance, eight or ten stars engraved in a circular arrangement, and the drawing of the

81 Horizontal lines emanating from the natural spiral shape of the shell enhance its decoration

82,83 Animals carved to decorate the seal

84 Some of the tombs at Hamad Town were constructed like the sun and its rays

spinning wheel in the shape of a gazelle's head might represent the cardinal and secondary points or a sun whose rays take the shape of gazelle heads.

● The craftsman chose certain features to engrave on the shell seals such as the crescent, the round drilled depressions which perhaps represent the stars whilst the spiral shape could represent the galaxy or the sun. I do not exclude the gazelle being the symbol of the sun for we in the Arabic language still use the gazelle as a metonymn for the sun. Moreover, it has been confirmed, through excavations in the burial mounds, that their owners had beliefs relating to the sun. They tried continually to make their tombs face east-west with a slight inclination toward north east or south east according to the inclination of the sun in the seasons of the year. Thus we were able to determine the season in which each tomb was built. Some of the tombs were designed like the sun with rays, fig 84, (Hamad Town: B.S. Tomb No. 1684).[8] Thus, the heavenly bodies in general and the sun in particular played a major role in the lives of the owners of these seals and give us a not insignificant idea of the subjects and ideas which engaged their minds. Anyone who ascribes the religious concepts of this area to the religious concepts of Mesopotamia is at fault because all the archaeological evidence indicates a local community progressing towards its own ideological independence, dictated by its own capabilities and the development of its circumstances.

SUMMARY

The study of shell seals found in Bahrain's burial mounds, will shed a light on the historical and artistic development of the seals in Bahrain in particular, and the Middle East in general, in ancient times. It is most probable that this area was one of the most important centres for producing seals.

If we assume that these shell seals are the origin of the flat circular chlorite seals, some of whose subjects bear similarities to the seals of Mesopotamia, the Indus Valley, Syria and Cappodocia (i.e. Anatolia) or even Egyptian scarabs, then the inscriptions of the shell seals represent the distinctive character of their owners before their area was exposed to external influences. These antiquities indicate a local society which marched along the road to progress by depending on its circumstances and the development of its own capabilities, especially the development of ancient maritime trade. Moreover, the characteristics of the shell seal motifs and the methods of crafting them and the choice of the appropriate shells available in the Gulf environment have all succeeded in moulding an independent artistic and intellectual personality.

I hope I have succeeded in shedding some light on the importance of the study of the art of engraving on shell so that it may be treated as an art of its own and take its distinctive place among the ancient arts; perhaps this art was the origin of arts in general from which man deduced form, sculpture and engraving.

1. Ibrahim, M. 1982 *Excavations of the Arab Expedition at Sar el-Jisr, Bahrain*, 157 No. 1–4.

2. Bibby, T. G. 1964 'Arabian Archaeology', *Kuml*, 107.

3. Cleuziou, S. 1981 *Fouilles à Umm Jidr (Bahrain)*, Edition A.D.P.F.; Paris 27–28.

4. Cleuziou, S., Lombard, P., Salles, J. F. 1977–79 *The French Archaeological Mission 1976/77, Archaeology in the United Arab Emirates*, vols. II and III, Department of Antiquities and Tourism Al-Ain (Arab edition). (Fig. 17: 1).

5. Bosch, D. & E. 1982 *Seashells of Oman*, 127: 129–130.

6. Kjaerum, P. 1980 'The Stamp and Cylinder Seals (Failaka)', *Journal of the Jutland Archaeological Society*, Denmark, Publication XVII, Vol. I: I 1983, P123, No. 294.

7. Ibrahim, M. 1982 *Excavations of the Arab Expedition at Sar Al-Jisr*; Mughal, M. R. 1983 *The Dilmun Burial Complex at Sar: 1980–82*, No. 3, Directorate of Archaeology & Museums (Bahrain).

8. Directorate of Antiquities and Museum 1981/3 Unpublished report from Hamad Town (Bahrain), Directorate of Antiquities and Museums.

Susa and the Dilmun Culture

PIERRE AMIET

The Susian plain has traditionally been identified by the inhabitants of Mesopotamia with the kingdom of Elam, a formidable neighbour but also indispensable ally in relations with the Iranian plateau, which is rich in primary materials not found in the alluvial plains. Susa was therefore the gateway to this plateau, and the meeting place of two rival worlds which disputed her possession. Thus her history is punctuated by alternate annexations, by the mountain people of Elam in present-day Fars,[1] of which Anshan was the capital, and the Mesopotamian powers, anxious to secure such a key position. So it was that in the Uruk period, at the beginning of historical tradition, Susa had become a part of the Mesopotamian world and of a Sumerian-type culture, while afterwards, during the period contemporary with Jemdet-Nasr and Early Dynastic I, it became a part of the Proto-Elamite world of the southeastern plateau, which stretched at least as far as what is now Seistan. Indeed we know that Proto-Elamite writings have been found as far afield as Shahr-i Sokhta, in the Hilmand delta. After the collapse of the Proto-Elamite civilisation, Susa was again linked with Mesopotamia throughout much of the third millennium, to such an extent that she too obtained her copper by the sea route from Oman, the land of Makkan, and no longer from the rich plateau. This period saw the birth of the mountain civilisations which do not seem to have been dependent on any permanent sites; this leads one to suppose that they were in large part the creation of nomadic peoples who were not herdsmen but artisans, making a living from the exploitation of metals, in Luristan, and of stones such as chlorite, in southeastern Iran. I am tempted, in consequence, to see a link between these people and the Biblical Kenites, also nomadic craftsmen; they were able to create specific cultures, based on highly individual artistic traditions. And beyond the highlands of Iran was born the great urban civilisation of Harappan India, from that time onwards an equal partner of the Mesopotamian civilisations. A complex trading system then developed within Iran, parallelled by the maritime traffic round the coast. It is significant that the name of Dilmun now makes its appearance in Sumerian literature, as a vital trading post on the 'Lower Sea'. From this time her culture becomes a part of the particular context which I have just outlined.

The travelling craftsmen working in chlorite and serpentine seem to have originated in eastern Iran, to judge from the evidence of the Tepe Yahya excavations, which revealed the existence of a workshop producing art forms which represent an original culture. This means that the influence of trading connexions with distant lands, frequently emphasised during recent years, is not the only factor involved; the influence of particular cultures, often difficult to locate precisely, must also be taken into consideration. I agree with P. de Miroschedji,[2] that the artefacts characteristic of what may be termed the chlorite culture can be divided into two groups.

The first, 'ancienne', extends without any noticeable development over at least three centuries, from Early Dynastic II up to and including the Akkadian period. The second, 'récente', is contemporary with Ur III and perhaps with Isin and Larsa. Evidence of the first group has been found scattered from Harappan India to the Syrian frontier at Mari. Oddly enough, the bulk of the evidence has not been found in eastern Iran, the presumed place of origin, but in the island of Tarut,[3] which must have belonged to Dilmun. As a result, the problem is to know whether this place was simply a staging post or actually a creative centre. I think we can, however, agree on a primary origin in southeastern Iran, associated with a people who were not content merely to transport their wares from these distant parts; their workshops too must have been portable, and established in particular at Tarut. More precisely, we may suppose that such workshops were in operation as far as and including Mesopotamia, where they became subject to local influences, adopting, for example, the Sumerian motif of the lion-headed eagle.

Like a number of Mesopotamian towns, Susa has yielded substantial evidence of this 'chlorite culture', whether it arrived by the same sea route as the Oman copper, imported by Dilmun, or by the land route across Fars. We cannot be certain, but, when we consider that at this period in the middle of the third millennium Anshan seems to have been deserted, it is more likely that the chlorite and serpentine vases reached Susa by sea. They were not purely exotic products, because the presence of local copies in a bitumen compound[4] implies a closer affinity between the people of Susa and those who initiated this culture. It is hardly possible to be definite, but we should note that this is only a first example, to be repeated several centuries later in different circumstances.

The empire of Akkad, through its policy of expansion, especially southwards towards the countries of Makkan and Meluḫḫa must have been responsible for an increase in maritime trade at the end of the first period of the chlorite culture, an end which may have been brought about by this empire. From the victory proclamations of the kings of Akkad we also learn that the city of Anshan had been re-established, as the capital of a revitalised political ally: Elam itself. Nevertheless, this State seems initially to have played only a modest role, as one among other principalities. In addition, the import by Ur[5] and Eshnunna[6] of inscribed objects typical of the Harappan culture provides the first reliable chronological evidence. It is certainly possible that writing developed in India before this time, but we have no real proof. Now Susa had received evidence of this same civilisation,[7] admittedly not all dating from the Akkadian period, but apparently spanning all the closing years of the third millennium.

To the evidence so far must be added the head of a statuette[8] which differs from all the others found in some quantity at Susa and which are related to the Mesopotamian tradition. This head, on the other hand, with its long straight nose like a cylinder halved lengthwise and a 'careened' chin with a beard indicated by simple incisions, is so closely related to the sculptures of Moenjo-Daro that we may reasonably consider it to be an import. If such is the case, the most probable route for its transport was by sea, even though imports from Central Asia suggest that land routes also converged on Susa.

These links were strengthened at the end of the third millennium, reaching a peak at the beginning of the second. This is the second period of chlorite vases, consisting of large numbers of bowls, either undecorated or simply marked by a line of little incised circles, just like the little flasks with square bases, which are found from Susa to Turkmenia and even Bactria, which was newly colonised at that time by people come both from India and the West. The complexity of their cultural links makes identification difficult. From this time onwards there existed a whole collection of cultures in eastern Iran, or even what might be called Outer Iran. Some evidence of these has been found at Susa: compartmented copper stamp seals, axes, grooved columns, and a necklace of material identical or comparable with those of Tepe Hissar and Turkmenia. On the other hand, it is still difficult to identify the 'birthplace' of the chlorite vases, assuming that there was only one; because, from the time of Level IVA, Tepe Yahya no longer housed a workshop providing evidence of a locally-based production of objects carved in this stone. However there is ample evidence of vases of the recent group at Tarut, whence they could have been exported towards Mesopotamia: for example, the votive bowl of the merchant Shesh-shesh at the time of Shu-Sin in Ur III.[9] Likewise the vases found at Susa could have been imported via a 'maritime merchant' such as Urniginmu,[10] who dedicated a collection of arms at the time of Shulgi. We may postulate that the people who distributed the vases of the recent group were at least established in islands like Bahrain, though we cannot say that these islands were centres of production. A little later, however, a distinctive group including piriform vases with fairly dense linear decoration seem definitely to have been made in Oman, as demonstrated by S. Cleuziou.[11] These are good examples which show that the settlements established along the sea routes were not merely devoted to trade over long distances, but were capable of producing original cultures.

Besides the statuette head already mentioned, Susa received from Harappan India a cylinder seal of steatite bleached by firing, and a stamp seal of green serpentine, distinguished, apart from the inscription and the bull decoration, by its disc shape and its sheep bell shaped like a large knob with a central groove. It does not seem unlikely that such stamp seals served as models for those described as 'Gulf' or Dilmun type, which are found in large numbers from Bahrain to Failaka. The most archaic of these stamp seals,[12] generally of steatite or serpentine bleached by firing, have been incorrectly dated to the beginning of the third millennium, following the discovery of one in the disturbed Level IVB at Tepe Yahya. At the present time even those stamp seals similar in shape to the Indian and whose crude decoration allows classification as of archaic type do not seem to antedate the Akkadian period, but their context on the Bahrain sites is not yet properly understood. Most of these stamp seals, forming what might be called the classic group, have the shape of a thick disc; on the reverse, recessed, is a semi-spherical sheep bell in light relief, the base pierced, decorated with a central band and four small incised circles.

B. Buchanan has published a tablet dating from the reign of Gungunum of Larsa, in the twentieth century B.C., which carries the impression of such a stamp seal.[13] The date so revealed has been wholly confirmed by the impression of a stamp seal from the same group, fig. 85, found on a Susa tablet of the same period.[14] It is, in fact, a receipt of the kind in use at the beginning of the Isin-Larsa period, and mentions a certain Milhi-El, son of Tem-Enzag, who, from the name of his god, must be a Dilmunite. In these circumstances we may wonder if this document had not been drawn up at Dilmun and sent to Susa, after sealing with a local stamp seal. This seal is decorated with six tightly-packed, crouching animals, characterised by their vague shapes, with legs tucked under the bodies, huge heads and necks sometimes striped obliquely. The impression of another seal of similar type, fig. 86, depicts in the centre a throned figure who seems to dominate the animals, continuing a tradition of which examples are known at the end of the Ubaid period in Assyria.[15] This shows to what extent an archaic type of iconography can be deceptive.

85 Susa, seal impression on a tablet of the beginning of the second millennium, Louvre Sb 11221

86 Susa, impression of a stamp seal on a sealing, Louvre MDAI, 43, no. 240

87   Susa, stamp seal from the Gulf, Louvre, MDAI, 43, No. 1716

88   Susa, stamp seal from the Gulf, Teheran Museum, MDAI, 43, no. 1717

89   Susa, stamp seal from the Gulf, Teheran Museum, MDAI, 43, no. 1718

90   Susa, cylinder seal from the Gulf, Louvre, MDAI, 43, no. 2021

91   Susa, cylinder seal from the Gulf, Teheran Museum, MDAI, 43, no. 1975

Four Dilmun-type stamp seals have been found at Susa;[16] one of which has been damaged, with the loss of the engraved face. These all belong to the classic group, with a sheep bell cut in a semi-spherical shape, decorated with a band across the centre and four small incised circles. The simplest, fig. 87, depicts two goat-type animals crouching head to tail, inside and outside an oval. The saucer-shaped incised eyes, striped necks and general attitude are typical. The second seal, fig. 88, incomplete, shows an animal tamer wearing a skirt and grasping with one hand a stylised goat, similar to those on the first seal, with its feet bound; this too has links with a very ancient tradition, noted at Susa on impressions of cylinder seals of the Uruk period. With the other hand the personage holds a large object, of a kind noted on several Failaka seals,[17] and which we tentatively identify as some kind of architectural feature or shield.

The theme of the master of animals occurs again on the last stamp seal, fig. 89, where this personage, naked and very thin, has a stylised head shaped like a narrow arch, with indentations to mark the nose and mouth. It is a very typical stylisation, often observed on Dilmun seals. The subdued animals have bound feet, and surround a square object on which the tamer stands. As elsewhere, when animal heads emerge from a similar shape, one may imagine it to represent a cage or hut.[18]

Two Susa cylinder seals must also be considered as Dilmunite imports,[19] from the fact of their resemblance to similar rare objects found on the islands of the Gulf. Like the stamp they are made of steatite, which in one case has been fired and turned a whitish yellow. This last cylinder seals depicts a divinity who can be identified by his horned tiara, fig. 90. He wears an unevenly chequered robe which falls in angular folds to cover the body. A pair of gods identical to this are depicted on a Failaka cylinder seal.[20] This personage is attended by a naked man, and alongside are two tamers grasping a pair of crossed animals, like those depicted on a Dilmunite stamp seal in the Louvre (AO 26501). The other cylinder seal, fig. 91, is very like a new one published by P. Kjaerum.[21] It shows three figures, with highly stylised

heads in the form of notched arches, in low relief. They wear boldly chequered skirts. One is seated; the other two, standing with backs turned, hold an enormous feathered arrow, and one of them extends a hand towards a stylised goat like those on the stamp seals.

This group of seals is smaller than that of Ur, but we may properly add to it another, figs. 92–95, very different group, which includes stamp seals made from a bitumen compound, the material preferred for those Susa cylinder seals which I described not long ago as of 'popular' type.[22] They should be considered primarily as Anshanite, as they are found almost exclusively at Tell-i Malyan.[23] To sum up, these cylinder seals seem fully representative of the unified cultures imposed on their linked states by the kings of Anshan and Susa, mainly in the nineteenth and eighteenth centuries. Their 'popular' character is the more significant because it suggests that this culture was not merely confined, as in former times, to the intellectual élite of scribes conversant with the Elamite language. The decoration of the cylinder seals is characterised by crude workmanship and frequent recourse to rough hatching. Now this type of workmanship is seen again on six stamp seals found at Susa,[24] notable for the material of which they are made: a bitumen compound. Their design too is manifestly inspired by that of the Dilmunite stamp seals. The simplest, somewhat drum-shaped, bear two crossed lines on the reverse, divided by four stars. The most elaborate has a convex reverse side, and depicts a tamer with three heavily hatched animals, fig. 92. Three simpler stamp seals bear the image of a woman shown full-face, squatting with legs apart, possibly on a stool, fig. 95. This theme too continues a very ancient tradition, illustrated on seals contemporary with the foundation of Susa.[25] There is also evidence for a woman in this position on at least one Bahrain seal,[26] though here she is shown with a man lying beneath her. The Anshanite character of these seals, which have nevertheless all been found at Susa, suggests that we should expect to find many more at Tell-i Malyan, where excavation has been prematurely interrupted. It can be assumed that they illustrate the profound affinity

93 Susa, stamp seal made from a bitumen compound, Louvre, MDAI, 43, no. 1722

92 Susa, stamp seal made from a bitumen compound, Louvre, MDAI, 43, no. 1720

94 Susa, stamp seal made from a bitumen compound, Louvre, MDAI, 43, no. 1726

95 Susa, stamp seal made from a bitumen compound, Louvre, MDAI, 43, no. 1725

between the Elamite people who migrated to Anshan and Susa and the Dilmunite people. By analogy, such a deduction would tend to confirm that, in the middle of the third millennium, it was also due to their close links with the Dilmunite people that the Susians too copied in a bitumen compound the art of the chlorite carvers, who had migrated to eastern Iran as well as to the islands of the Gulf. This is only a hypothesis advanced to show what new perspectives on the diffusion of the Dilmun culture have been opened up by the material found at Susa.

1. We admit, with François Vallat, *Suse et i'Élam*, Paris, 1980, that Elam proper corresponded to the plateau of Fars with its capital at Anshan. We think, however that it probably extended further north into the Bakhtiari Mountains.

2. Pierre de Miroschedji, 'Vases et objets en stéatite susiens du Musée du Louvre' *Cahiers de la D.A.F.I., 3* 1973, p. 9–79.

3. Juris Zarins, 'Typological Studies in Saudi Arabian Archaeology', *Atlal, 2* 1978, p. 65ff.

4. Pierre Amiet, *Elam*, Auvers sur Oise, 1966, fig. 124. 'Archaeological discontinuity and ethnic duality in Elam', *Antiquity, LIII*, 1979, pl. XX-b.

5. C.-J. Gadd, 'Seals of ancient Indian style found at Ur', *Proceedings of the British Academy, XVIII*, 1932.

6. Henry Frankfort, 'Tell Asmar, Khafaje and Khorsabad . . .', *OIC, 16*, 1933, p. 50, fig. 22.

7. L. Delaporte, *Musée du Louvre. Catalogue des Cylindres orientaux . . .*, vol. I, 1920, pl. 25 (15), S.299. P. Amiet, *Glyptique susienne. MDAI, 43*, 1972, vol. II, pl. 153, no. 1643.

8. P. Amiet, 'Contribution à l'histoire de la sculpture archaïque de Suse', *Cahiers de la D.A.F.I., 6*, 1976, p. 57 et pl. XI (1–2).

9. P. Amiet, *Antiquity, LIII*, 1979, pl. XXI-a.

10. P. Amiet, *Elam*, 1966, fig. 177.

11. S. Cleuziou, 'Les deuxième et troisième campagnes de fouilles à Hili 8', *Archéologie aux Emirats Unis, vol. II–III*, 1978–79, p. 28 (3.3).

12. Edith Porada, 'Remarks on Seals found in the Gulf States', *Artibus Asiae, XXXIII(4)*, 1971, p. 331, s.

13. B. Buchanan, *Studies in honor of Benno Landsberger*, Chicago, 1965, p. 204, s.

14. P. Amiet, 'Antiquités du Désert de Lut', *RA, 68*, 1974, p. 109, fig. 16. Maurice Lambert, *RA, 70*, 1976, p. 71–72.

15. P. Amiet, *RA, 68*, 1974, p. 109, fig. 17.

16. P. Amiet, *Glyptique susienne. MDAI, 43*, 1972, vol. II, pl. 159, no. 1716–1719.

17. *Archaeological Investigations in the Island of Failaka, 1958–1964*. Kuwait Government Press, fig. 81.

18. *Op. cit.*, fig. 86.

19. P. Amiet, *Glyptique Susienne*, 1972, vol. II, pl. 125, no. 2021 et pl. 173, no. 1975.

20. *Archaeological Investigations in the Island of Failaka, 1958–1964*, fig. 71.

21. Poul Kjaerum, *Failaka/Dilmun. The Second Millennium Settlements*. Vol. 1: 1. R *The Stamp and Cylinder Seals*. Aarhus, 1983, no. 373.

22. P. Amiet, *Glyptique susienne*, 1972, p. 239, s.

23. W. Sumner, 'Excavations at Tell-i Malyan, 1971–72', *Iran XII*, 1974, p. 172, fig. 12.

23. P. Amiet, *Glyptique susienne*, 1972, vol. II, pl. 159, no. 1720; 1722–1726.

25. P. Amiet, *La Glyptique mésoptamienne archaïque*, 2nd ed., Paris, 1980, pl. 115, s., no. 1541; 1545 ('insecte'); 1578 B top right; 1579–1581.

26. Peder Mortensen, *Kuml*, 1970, fig. 8.

The Dilmun seals as evidence of long distance relations in the early second millennium B.C.

POUL KJÆRUM

The many seals recovered during the archaeological excavations in Bahrain[1] and on the island of Failaka in Kuwait[2] have revealed the existence of a specific glyptic province on the two islands, possibly also comprising the east coast of the Arabian Peninsula.[3] It arose around the beginning of the second millennium and extended into the early Kassite period.[4]

In the pre-Kassite period stamp seals were almost the only kind of seals present in the area, and the two islands have now yielded about five hundred specimens. Most of these are of the same basic shape: a unifacial stamp seal with a usually circular obverse and a domed reverse of variable height and diameter. Only a minor, though distinct group is bifacial.[5] The unifacial seals with domed reverse have been divided into two separate groups characterized by the ornament on the reverse.

In type I the only ornament is one or two grooves diagonally across the dome, while in type II the same design is augmented with circles, as a rule four, arranged symmetrically around the grooves or lines, fig. 96. Buchanan has termed the latter type *Tilmun-type*,[6] and the term is worth retaining since it is diagnostic for the Dilmun area in its most prosperous period – the first half of the second millennium.

The difference between the types may seem small and insignificant, but it is in fact accompanied by a major change in style as well as in motifs. In type I the design is dominated by animal figures and symbols of various kinds, while the Dilmun seals are characterized by ritual scenes involving people, gods, cult objects and animals.

The transition to seals of Dilmun type seems to have taken place during the Ur III period towards the end of the third millennium. This date is indicated by finds of seals in the early style IA in context with two cylinder seals of post-Akkadian and Ur III style in two Failaka tells and by carbon-14 datings from Barbar temple II to 1975–2025 and 1945–1965 B.C.,[8] containing seals of the same early Dilmun style.

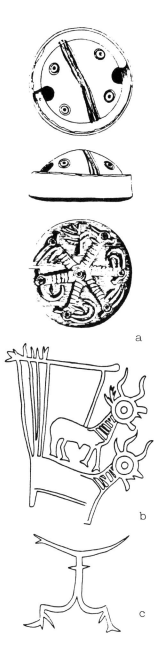

96   a: Dilmun seal from Barbar, b: Harp, Failaka no 267, c: Table, Failaka no 166, d: Acrobat, Failaka no 43, e: Bucranium, Failaka no 298, f: Double Animal, Failaka no 260, g: Volute Standards, Failaka no 14. Scale 3:2

The date is further indicated by a carbon-14 date from F6 on Failaka to 1770–1870 B.C. (Pearson Cal.) related to seals of the later style IB, and further by the dated impressions on tablets from Susa and Ur, the latter dated to the 10th year of Gungunum (*c*. 1923 B.C.).[10] Though there are clear indications that the Dilmun type succeeds type I,[11] it is also apparent from a certain hybridization of motifs and engraving techniques that there is a chronological contact between them. This is particularly marked on Bahrain where e.g. no less than about 18% of the Dilmun seals have motifs of type I character whereas this applies to only two (0.5%) of the Failaka seals.[12] Circumstances suggest that the development of the Dilmun seals took place on Bahrain, though the motifs to a great extent were inspired from outside.

The rich and varied imagery of the seals has already, through the few examples published, given reason to suggest the existence of connections with Mesopotamia, Syria/Anatolia and India.[13]

The comprehensive material now published has confirmed the existence of these relations and the multiplicity of elements and motifs makes it worth while to consider the intensity of the different relations and to a certain extent also to reflect on the nature of these.[14]

INDUS

Unambiguous evidence of contact is found in the occurrence of Indus script on a Dilmun seal from Failaka,[15] though combined in a manner which according to Parpola is not present in the Indus area, but is characteristic of Indus inscriptions on seals from Mesopotamia and the Gulf area.[16]

While the background for the script is evident, the origin of the water carrier on a seal from Mazyad in Oman and one from Ur is not quite so certain, although the similarity of the figure to the corresponding Indus script character is striking. Derivation from Indus has previously been suggested, but there the figure occurs only in script and is never, as the two Dilmun and the Syrian representations, characterized by stars, which are extremely rare among the Indus symbols, and never attached to the water carrier.[17]

As suggested by Edith Porada,[18] the Astral Waterman on these seals may be related to Syrian representations of Aquarius, though it is highly deviant in execution. After all, the water carrier with a yoke on his neck was probably an everyday phenomenon and associated with stars an immediately understandable astral symbol, and so, as in Egypt, preferred in Dilmun to a more exotic figure.

The many bull representations on the Dilmun seals have also been considered Indus-related, but apart from a few occurrences such as the one on the above-mentioned seal with Indus script, they are integrated in motifs foreign to the Indus repertoire (cf. below). Finally Edith Porada[19] has drawn attention to the similarity between the radial motifs consisting of animal protomes which occur in numbers on Failaka as well as in Bahrain, fig. 96a, and in Anatolia and Indus. The latter is unique, however, and the similarity is purely formal, but the design could, chronological circumstances permitting, have been inspired by the Dilmun motif. By and large, the script is the only certain 'motif' common to the Indus and Dilmun seals, but affords in itself incontrovertible evidence of a connection between the Gulf and the Indus culture continuing until the beginning of the second millennium, further strengthened by one more unifacial stamp seal with Indus script found on Failaka, and of course also by the Dilmun seal from Lothal.[20] Apparently, however, the influence did not transcend the commercial plane, and the two seals may be a testimony of Indus residents on the island.

MESOPOTAMIA

If the evidence of connections with India is scarce, the merchants and seamen from the Arabian Gulf seem to have felt at home in southern Mesopotamia and Elam, to judge from the wealth of Dilmun seals and the commercial agreements found in Ur and Susa.[21] But these seals did not penetrate further north and west.[22]

As Gadd has already pointed out, the motif repertoire of the Dilmun seals is dominated by Mesopotamian imagery, an observation which the subsequent great increase in the amount of material has not invalidated. The dress and the horned crown of the gods, bullmen, monkeys, standards of various kinds, harps with taurine sound-boxes, fig. 96b, erotic scenes and many other features, manifest not only close contact, but also a deeper, spiritual affinity.

In this respect, Dilmun does not differ from other cultural areas close to Mesopotamia. There too, a Mesopotamian heritage is the cornerstone of the artists repertoire, and as here combined with elements taken from elsewhere and naturally dominated by themes and motifs reflecting local culture and religion. The most ordinary and characteristic ritual motifs of the south Mesopotamian repertoire of the period in question – the Isin-Larsa-Old Babylonian period – are, however, not present, or they are just implied in a few themes, and the south Mesopotamian influence may not be direct in spite of the obvious close contact between the two neighbouring cultures.

The common Babylonian imagery must therefore – however powerful its influence – take second place in the present article, which seeks to plot Dilmun relations to more limited cultural areas.

THE LEVANT

The influence from the glyptic art of the Levant is in some respect

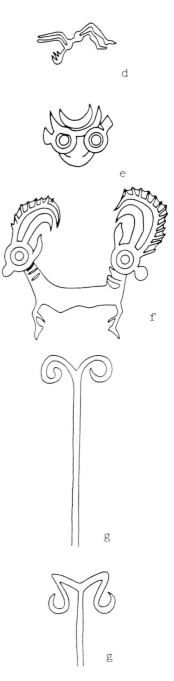

d

e

f

g

g

97   Failaka no 163 Impression

98   Failaka no 162

more tangible than the Babylonian, as it comprises a number of single figures as well as composite figures and themes, represented on Dilmun seals, but unknown in contemporary Mesopotamian art. This is not the place to give a full presentation of elements and motifs common to the Levant and Dilmun, and I shall confine myself to a few selected examples. In a series of seals from Failaka, tables are a central element in the design. They are all characterized by a concave top, resting on a moulded column which bifurcates into two curved legs with bull's hooves, fig. 96c, or, exceptionally, human feet.[23]

Undoubtedly they represent tripods with a column of three rods bound together with a ring, reproduced as a moulding. Tables of a similar construction are in the Syro-Cappadocian area a common occurrence in seal designs and other artistic representations from Isin-Larsa-Old Babylonian times. In basic principle and main form, they all correspond closely to the tables on the Failaka seals and some are quite identical, as e.g. the table on a late eighteenth century ivory relief from Ebla,[24] the relief stele from Alalakh[25] (though with legs sculptured in relief) and on several seals.[26]

Outside the Levant, tables of this specific type are only known from one Old Babylonian seal, belonging to Shu-Sin's governor in Umma,[27] while the rare occurrences of tables in Mesopotamia and Elam are of a different form. Whether these tables were copied from pictorial representations or from actual tables is uncertain. Tables of this kind may have been an article of trade and may have been part of the ritual equipment in both areas. The common themes in which they occur indicate, however, that they served the same ritual purposes both in Dilmun and Syria.

As would be expected various forms of banqueting scenes predominate, fig. 97, with single or antithetic gods drinking from cups by a table covered with bread and/or other kinds of food.[28] More remarkable is the placement of the table on a podium or altar, and bullmen or men with or without palm fronds in their hands flanking the table, as known from both areas.[29]

In a single case the table is used for a gymnastic performance,[30] with acrobats doing handstands from the column, fig. 96d. Though this rather bizarre motif is unique, the posture of the acrobats resembles Syrian renderings of the same figure, as is also the case with acrobats on a Dilmun seal from Ur.[31]

While the table is a kind of furniture without any specific symbolism, though connected with ritual performances, other images with a Levantine background are purely symbolic.

This applies to standards characterized by in and out-turned volutes, fig. 96g, which are interpreted as highly stylized palms and are found in both Syrian and Cappadocian imagery. They are faithfully copied on Dilmun seals, the only difference being that they are often topped with an astral symbol, usually a sun-disc, in the Levant, while they are always plain in the Dilmun seals.[32] The human head or a mask on a staff belongs to the same category, fig. 98. It is only represented on a single Dilmun seal from Failaka; though it differs in details from the more numerous Syrian and Cappadocian render-ings,[33] the placing of a human head on a podium as a symbol, equivalent to an emblem or a standard, seems indicative of a common spiritual concept.

A series of abstractions and of *pars pro toto* renderings of animal forms also relate the Levant with Dilmun. A distinct abstrac-tion is the double animal, consisting of two animal foreparts, joined at the belly, fig. 96f. In the Dilmun area it occurs only in the form of antelopes, in the Levant also in that of a lion.[34]

Bulls' heads or bucrania are numerous, often with crescents, fig. 96e, or exceptionally a sun disc between the horns defining them as celestial symbols. Their context is usually ritual, placed on altars, between drinkers or held by gods or bullmen.[35]

Related to these are the frequently occurring antelope and occasionally taurine protomes. Edith Porada has already drawn attention to the agreement between the Dilmun seals' radial composi-tions with animal heads and necks and Anatolian compositions of the same character, though with griffin heads.[36] This observation may be extended to whorls of protomes and heads connected by ribbon-shaped necks, found in both areas.[37] In Dilmun alone the protomes are also attached to the corners of altars, and it is remarkable that these often form part of drinking scenes,[38] and it may be a local variation of the Levantine motif: drinking by a bull altar, fig. 99.

These abstractions of animal forms occurring in common are manifestations of one side of an animal cult which finds other expres-sions in the art of both areas, but is foreign to Babylonia in the period in question. So animals occur in connections and also in renderings which characterize them as idols and also as attributes to deities.

In a number of scenes, animals – usually bulls and antelopes – are placed on altars or podia,[39] figs. 100, 101 and in other ritual performances the place of altars or standards is taken by serpent monsters – single or entwined – or antelopes, which certainly must be conceived as idols,[40] figs. 101, 102.

As attributes, fig. 103, serpents are held in the hands of deities and antelopes and bulls form the thrones of gods,[41] fig. 105. The animals found in these contexts are usually naturalistic, i.e. in the same form as the animals on the seals in general, but a few are clearly characterized as idols by wearing the horned crown of the gods,[42] fig. 104. The same themes are found in the Levant, in a form which, although divergent, contains so many common elements that a con-nection seems certain. Thus we find the bull on the altar, with or

99   Failaka no 174 Impression

100   Failaka no 83 Impression

101   Failaka no 82

102 Failaka no 126

103 Failaka no 206

104 Failaka no 89 Impression

105 Failaka no 204

without a bird on its back, as a frequent combination.[43] Frequently found too, is the altar on a bull's back, gods combined with vertical snakes,[44] and finally the god on an animal throne, often, as here, combined with a bird, or drinking and surrounded by animals.[45]

A final example of the western relations is the scene with drinkers which Buchanan[46] (and later Porada) has already shown to be a motif common to Dilmun and Syria. This motif which has its ancestry in Early Dynastic and Akkadian art, occurs in both places in large numbers in various contexts, either as single drinkers by an altar or as antithetic drinkers, drinking from the same jar or individual jars, fig. 99, and as mentioned above also in connection with altars characterized by animal symbols.

The motifs of the seals and the distribution of the actual seals indicate a net of connections from the Dilmun area in the Arabian Gulf to near and more remote areas. As a diagnostic form for Dilmun, the distribution of the actual seals shows that the connections with the Indus culture were still upheld in the beginning of the second millennium, which is further confirmed by the Dilmun seal and other stamp seals with Indus script from Failaka, whereas the occurrence of motifs like the water carrier and protome-radial are debatable. Other influences from the Indus cannot be traced in the Dilmun motifs.

The Oman connection has been established with only one seal from Mazyad, mentioned above, but this is a grave-find which may mean that the Dilmun merchant himself died there during a mission.

The finds of Dilmun seals in Eastern Saudi Arabia, however, where also pottery of Barbar type has been found, may indicate that the eastern part of the peninsula was an integrated part of Dilmun and not be just a testimony of relations. The largest group of Dilmun seals outside the Gulf are – naturally enough – from the neighbouring cities of Ur and Susa and their environs. Further north and west the Dilmun seals, however, did not penetrate.

Apart from the more general Mesopotamian motifs, it is motifs from the Levantine area, Syria and Anatolia, which have found greatest favour in Dilmun imagery. This influence is so strong and of such a nature that it cannot solely be due to relations like trade and sporadic personal contacts of various kinds. A form like the table with taurine legs may, of course, be an imported object which has gained acceptance, but all the other elements, whether single figures or themes, are of a ritual or religious nature and must reflect spiritual phenomena common to both Dilmun and the Levant. The animal cult, for instance, cannot merely be a reproduction of something seen abroad or copied from a pattern book. Our view of art as something primarily aesthetic, not necessarily having an understandable content, is relatively recent. The motifs of the seals must indicate a local conceptual reality. The contact between the two areas must therefore have extended beyond the mere mercantile intercourse which had been carried on for several centuries before the advent of the Dilmun seals.[47]

In association with the first demonstration of a connection between Dilmun and Syria based on seal imagery, Buchanan concludes: 'It seems possible that around 2000 B.C. the Persian Gulf merchants had a relationship, other than one involving trade, with some ethnic element in Syria (merchants or colonists)'.[48] Certainly, the massive change in seal motifs at the transition between the third and the second millennia, with the Dilmun seals gaining absolute dominance, can hardly be regarded as a mere vagary of fashion.

The transition was not, however, followed by any break in continuity in other areas of material culture. The Dilmun seal itself seems to be a development of the preceding seal of type I; a few Dilmun seals still exhibited the old motifs, and both ceramic and architectural traditions continued. It was also the traditional, material culture with its early origins in Bahrain which was carried over with the colonization of Failaka, with the appearance of the early Dilmun seals.

The imagery which dominates these seals therefore hardly reflects a massive change in the basic make-up of the population, but rather a displacement towards population groups with Mesopotamian and especially Levantine cultural background, which must have formed a powerful new ethnic element of western origin, attaining dominance in Dilmun around the turn of the millennium.

1. Ibrahim 1982, p. 37 ff. with further references Mughal 1983, p. 83 ff. with references.

2. Failaka 1983.

3. Golding 1974, p. 19–32.

4. Kjærum 1980.

5. Failaka 1983, nos. 336–366, and Roaf 1976, Ibrahim 1982, pl. 60: 1.

6. Buchanan 1965, p. 206.

7. Failaka nos. 368–369.

8. Mortensen 1970, p. 293, and same in this volume. Copenhagen C14 lab. no. K 1575–76.

9. Copenhagen C14 lab. no. K 2124.

10. Buchanan 1965, p. 206, for stylistic definitions cf. Kjærum 1980.

11. Bibby 1957, p. 140, and same in this volume.

12. E.g. Ibrahim 1982, fig. 50/4–5 and Failaka nos. 253–254.

13. Gadd 1932, p. 200, 210; Buchanan 1965, p. 207, Porada 1971, p. 335.

14. The background of the motifs on the Dilmun seals will be further evaluated by me in the text volume to the Failaka seal catalogue, forthcoming.

15. Failaka 1983, no. 279.

16. Brunswig 1983, p. 106.

17. Legrain 1951, no. 628, Cleuziou 1979, fig. 8, Parpola 1984, p. 187.

18. Porada 1971, p. 335 with reference also to the Egyptian rendering of Aquarius as a water carrier.

19. Porada 1971, p. 335.

20. Failaka 1983, no. 319, Rao 1963, pp. 96 ff.

21. Gadd 1932, Amiet 1972, nos. 1716–1719, same 1974, pp. 108 ff., Lambert 1976, pp. 71 ff.

22. The seal from Ishchali, mentioned by Buchanan 1965, p. 206 may not be a Dilmun seal according to Ratnager 1981.

23. Failaka 1983, nos. 43, 163–169.

24. Matthiae 1980, p. 14.

25. Woolley 1955, pl. LII A.

26. Brett 1936, no. 64, Porada 1966, p. 248 and Alalakh 1982, no. 22 with references.

27. Yale 1982, no. 652.

28. Failaka 1983, nos. 163–165, and e.g. Matthiae 1980, p. 14.

29. Failaka 1983, 163 and 166, e.g. Woolley 1955, pl. LII A. Failaka 1983, nos. 166–167, cf. e.g. Ward 1910, fig. 839, Contenau 1922, pl. XXVI: 180, Alalakh 1982, no. 22 with references. Hazzidakis 1934, pl. XXX: 3b.

30. Failaka 1983, no. 43.

31. Legrain 1951, pl. 37, fig. 624, Alalakh 1975, no. 111 with ref. and for the posture on the Ur seal cf. Ashmolean 1966, no. 892.

32. Alalakh 1975, no. 76.

33. Seyrig 1960, pp. 233–241, Alalakh 1975, no. 140, Yale 1982, no. 1180–81 with a complete list and ref.

34. Bahrain: Qala no. 520 ADP, Failaka 1983, nos. 81, 255, 260, compare e.g. Ashmolean 1966, no. 854, and Porada 1966, p. 251.

35. Failaka 1983, nos. 69, 72, 93, 176, 184; Buchanan 1965, p. 207 and Porada 1971, p. 335. Also Lefébure 1906.

36. Bahrain: Mortensen 1970, fig. 8; Failaka 1983, nos. 1, 3 and Porada 1971, p. 335.

37. Failaka 1983, nos. 2, 22 and 175. Alp 1968, no. 76, e.g. Kültépé I, 1952 pl. LXIX and Kültépé II, 1962, 606A.

38. Failaka 1983, nos. 170, 173–175.

39. Failaka 1983, nos. 78–89.

40. same nos. 122, 82 and 126.

41. same e.g. nos. 81, 179 and 186, 204.

42. same nos. 88, 89.

43. e.g. Porada 1966, pl. XVII: 81, a and XVIII: k and 244 ff.

44. same: pl. XVII: b and p. 245, e.g. Porada 1947, p. 64 and 122 (and no. 738). Ozgüc 1968 pl. XXVII: 1.

45. CANES nos. 879, 894 and Ozgüc 1965 nos. 70, 74.

46. Buchanan 1965, pp. 204–209.

47. Pettinato 1981.

48. Buchanan 1965, p. 207.

ABBREVIATIONS

Alp 1968	*Zylinder-und Stempelsiegel aus Karahöyük bei Konya*, Ankara
Alalakh 1975	Dominique Collon: *The Seal Impressions from Tell Atchana/Alalakh*, Neukirchen
Alalakh 1982	Dominique Collon: *The Alalakh Cylinder Seals, BAR International Series 132*, Oxford
Amiet 1972	P. Amiet: *Glyptique Susienne*, vol. I–II, Mem. de la Dèlègation Archéologie en Iran XLIII, Paris
Amiet 1974	P. Amiet: *Revue d'Assyriologie*, vol. LXVIII: 2, 97 ff
Ashmolean 1966	Briggs Buchanan: *Cat. of Ancient Near Eastern Seals in the Ashmolean Museum*. Vol. I, Oxford
Bibby 1957	T. G. Bibby: *Kuml*, Journal of the Jutland Arch. Society, Århus, 128 ff
Bibby 1969	T. G. Bibby: *Looking for Dilmun*, New York
Brett 1936	H. H. v. d. Osten: *Ancient Oriental Seals in the Coll. of Mrs. Agnes Baldwin Brett*, OIP XXXVII, Chicago

Brunswig e.a. 1983   Brunswig, Parpola and Potts: 'New Indus related Seals from the Near East', in
                     Dilmun, Berliner Beiträge zum Vordern Orient, Berlin
Buchanan 1965   Briggs Buchanan: 'A Persian Gulf Seal', *Studies in honor of Benno
                     Landsberger*, 199–209, Chicago
Cleuziou 1979   Serge Cleuziou: 'Oman Peninsula in the early Second Millennium' in Hartel
                     (ed.) *South Asian Archaeology*
Contenau 1922   Georges Contenau: *La Glyptique Syro-Hittites*, Paris
Failaka 1983   Poul Kjærum: *Failaka/Dilmun, The Second Millennium Settlements, The
                     Stamp and Cylinder Seals*, vol. 1: 1, Jutland Archaeological Society Publ.,
                     XVII: 1, Aarhus
Gadd 1932   C. J. Gadd: 'Seals of Ancient Indian Style', *Procs. of the Brit. Academy*, vol.
                     XVIII, 191–210
Golding 1974   M. Golding: *Evidence for Pre-Seleucid Occupation of Eastern Arabia*, Seminar
                     for Arabian Studies, London
Hazzidakis 1934   Hazzidakis: *Etudes Cretoises III*, Paris
Ibrahim 1982   M. Ibrahim: *Excavations of the Arab Expedition at Sar El-Jisr, Bahrain*, Bahrain
Kjærum 1980   Poul Kjærum: 'Seals of Dilmun-Type from Failaka, Kuwait', *Seminar for
                     Arabian Studies*, vol. 10, London
Kültépé I, 1952   Hrozny: *Inscriptions Cappadociens de Kültépé I*, Prague
Kültépé II, 1962   Hrozny: *Inscriptions Cappadociens de Kültépé II*, Prague
Lambert 1976   Maurice Lambert: 'Tablette de Suse avec Cachet du Golfe', *Revue
                     d'Assyriologie*, 70, 71–72
Lefébure 1906   E. Lefébure: 'Le Bucrane', *Sphinx*, 10, 67 ff
Legrain 1951   Leon Legrain: *Ur Excavations X*, Seal Cylinders, London
Matthiae 1978   P. Matthiae: *Studi Eblaiti I/* 9–12
Mortensen 1970   P. Mortensen: 'On the Date of the Barbar Temple', *Kuml*, 1970, 385 ff
Mughal 1983   M. R. Mughal: *The Dilmun Burial Complex at Sar*, Bahrain
Parpola 1974   Asko Parpola: Persian Gulf Seals and the Paradise Myth, D. C. Sircar
                     Felicitation Volume, Mysore (in manuscript)
Parpola 1984   Asko Parpola: 'New Correspondences between Harappan and Near Eastern
                     Glyptic Art', *South Asian Arch.* 1981, 176–195
Pettinato 1983   G. Pettinato: Dilmun nella documentazione di Ebla, *Dilmun*, (ed. Potts),
                     Berliner Beitr. zum Vorderen Orient, Berlin, 75 ff
Porada 1947   Edith Porada: 'Seal Impressions of Nuzi', *SSÖR* XXIV
Porada 1966   Edith Porada: 'Les cylindres de la jarre Montet', *Syria*, XLIII, 245 ff.
Porada 1971   Edith Porada: 'Remarks on Seals found in the Gulf States', *Artibus Asiae*,
                     CCCIII, 4, 331 ff
Rao 1963   S. R. Rao: 'A "Persian Gulf" Seal from Lothal', *Antiquity*, XXXVII, 96 ff
Ratnager 1981   Shereen Ratnager: Encounters. The Westerly Trade of the Harappa
                     Civilisation, Oxford
Roaf 1976   M. Roaf: The Work of the British Arch. Mission to Bahrain, 1976. Unpublished
                     report
Seyrig 1960   H. Seyrig: 'Les dieux de Hiérapolis', *Syria*, XXXVII, 233 ff
Ward 1910   W. H. Ward: *The Seal Cylinders of Western Asia*, Washington
Woolley 1955   L. Woolley: *Alalakh*, Reports of the Research Com. of the Soc. of Ant. of
                     London, no. XVIII, Oxford
Yale 1982   B. Buchanan: *Cylinder Seals*, Yale

Indus and Gulf type seals from Ur

T. C. MITCHELL

The excavations which were carried out for twelve years at Ur constitute one of the major operations of the twentieth century in Babylonia. Among all the artifacts of local style and manufacture, a few were discovered which throw light on, or at least give evidence of, relations with areas outside Mesopotamia.

In 1932 C. J. Gadd published a paper on a number of '*Seals of Ancient Indian Style Found at Ur*',[1] and these have featured in subsequent discussions, with others, both seals and impressions, found at Kish, Umma, Girsu (Telloh), Eshnunna (Tell Asmar), Ishchali, Susa, Tepe Gawra, Hamath in Syria, and more recently on the islands of Bahrain and Failaka in the Gulf.[2] Buchanan has sketched out the main lines of classification for these seals, namely: I, pure Indus style, though probably locally made since, in being circular, they differ from the standard Indus seals which are nearly always square; II, local, rather crude, imitations of the Indus style; and III a homogeneous group distinct from but related to I.[3] The backs of the seals of Type I usually have a high central boss with a single groove across it, at right angles to the V-shaped suspension hole, whereas in Type III the back boss is lower and broader and has three grooves at right angles to the V-shaped suspension hole, and on the boss four circles with central dots. The seals of Types I and III, and most of those of Type II, are made of steatite with a white surface, produced by coating the stone with an alkali and heating it.[4] In view of the number of seals of Types II and III known from Bahrain and Failaka, Buchanan has designated them 'Gulf Seals', II being the earlier, and III the later, or 'Tilmun Group' (Tilmun being at that date located in the Gulf, probably Bahrain). Here the name 'Gulf' will be reserved for Buchanan's Type III alone.

The purpose of this paper is to assemble the seals of these three types which were excavated by Sir Leonard Woolley at Ur, and to see what may be learned about their chronology from the details of their find spots, and at the same time to record the principal bibliography concerning each one. The inscriptions are all included in the Concordance of Koskenniemi, Parpola and Parpola under the provenance code 9001.[5] Seventeen seals were found, and these are listed here, together with the impression of a seal on a tablet, possibly from Ur,[6] according to their type. Under Types I and III the backs conform to the characteristics noted above, unless otherwise indicated. In each case the excavation number (U.), where known, and the Museum number (B=Baghdad, L=London, P=Philadelphia) is given after the dimensions.

I.   INDUS STYLE

1.   Bull to right below inscription in Indus script. Lower part broken away, fig. 106.
      Diam. 2.55, ht. 1.55 cm.
      Ur season VII (1928–29). L. BM. 122187.
      Provenance not traced.
      Gadd *PBA* 18 (1932), pp. 6–7, pl. I, no. 2.
2.   Bull to right below inscription in the Indus script, fig. 107.
      Diam. 2.3, ht. 1.5 cm.
      U. 17649. L. BM. 123208.
      From the upper filling of grave PG/1847, a burial of the time of the Third Dynasty of Ur, but containing objects of the Akkadian period.
      Gadd, *PBA* 18 (1932), pp. 13–14, pl. III, no. 16.
      Woolley, *Ur Excavations* II (1934), pp. 192, 333, 356, 593, pl. 211 no. 285.
      Buchanan, *JAOS* 74 (1954), p. 149.
      Nissen, *Datierung* (1966), pp. 68, 106, 191.
      Wheeler, *Indus Civilization* (1968), p. 117 no. 2.
      Woolley, *Ur Excavations* IV (1974), p. 50, n. 3.
3.   Bull to right, probably below inscription in the Indus script. Upper part broken away.
      Diam. 2.55, ht. 1.25 cm.
      U. 17341. P. 31-43-76.
      From Diqdiqqah. Though the bulk of the material from this site, which lies to the northeast of the main mounds, belonged to the Old Babylonian period,[7] the site also yielded remains from other periods ranging from the Third Dynasty of Ur and possibly earlier to the Persian period.[8]
      Gadd, *PBA* 18 (1932), p. 7, pl. I, no. 5.
      Legrain, *Ur Excavations*, X (1951), no. 630.
      Buchanan, *Studies Landsberger* (1965), p. 205, n. 8.
      Nissen, *Datierung* (1966), p. 68.
4.   Part of an inscription in the Indus script. Lower part broken away, fig. 108.
      Diam. 2.6, ht. 1.2cm. (as far as preserved).
      U. 17342. L. BM. 122946.
      From 'Ur'. No further information recorded.
      Gadd *PBA* 18 (1932), p. 7, pl. I, no. 3.
      Legrain, *Ur Excavations*, X (1951), no. 629.
5.   Fragment of an inscription in the Indus script. Lower and left hand part broken away, fig. 109.
      Length 2.1, ht. 1.25 cm.

106   Indus style seal: a bull facing right below an inscription in Indus script. The lower part has broken off

107   Indus style seal: a bull facing right and below an inscription in Indus script

108   Part of an inscription in Indus script

109   Fragment of an Indus script inscription whose lower and left hand part have both broken off

Ur season IX (1930–31). L. BM. 122188.
Provenance not traced.
Gadd, *PBA* 18 (1932), p. 7, pl. I, no. 4.

II.   LOCAL COPIES OF THE INDUS STYLE

6.   Circular 'button type' stamp seal of steatite. Bull to right below a scorpion (left) and other symbols, perhaps misunderstood signs from the Indus script, fig. 110.
Diam. 2.4 cm.
U. 8685. B.IM. 4022.
From tomb PG/401, which also included an earring (U.8684) of Royal Cemetery type 5,[9] probably to be dated in the Akkadian period.
Legrain, *MJ* (1929), p. 306, pl. XLI, no. 119.
Gadd, *PBA* 18 (1932), p. 13, pl. III, no. 15.
Woolley, *Ur Excavations*, II (1934), pp. 333, 363, 537, pl. 216 no. 370.
Nissen, *Datierung* (1955), pp. 54, 169.
Wheeler, *Indus Civilization* (1968), p. 117, no. 3.

7.   Rectangular stamp seal of dark steatite with pierced lug handle. Bull to left below cuneiform inscription SAG.KU(?).IGI.X or SAG.KU(?).P[AD] (?), fig. 111.
Length 2.7, width 2.4, ht. 1.1 cm.
U. 7683; BM. 120573.
From the surface soil beyond Diqdiqqah,[10] date uncertain.
Woolley, *AJ* 8 (1928), p. 26, pl. XI.2.
Legrain, *MJ* (1929), pp. 305–6, pl. XLI, no. 118.
Gadd, *PBA* 18 (1932), pp. 5–6, pl. I, no. 1.
Legrain, *Ur Excavations*, X (1951), no. 631.
Woolley, *Ur Excavations*, IV (1956), pp. 50, 174.
Nissen, *Datierung*, (1966), p. 68.
Wheeler, *Indus Civilization*, (1968), p. 117, no. 1.

8.   Cylinder seal of white shell. Bull to right, below a fish (?) and a trefoil design, facing a stylised tree. Below the bull's head is the 'fish' sign of the Indus script, fig. 112.
Ht. 1.7, diam. 0.9 cm.
U. 11958, B. IM. 8028.
From loose in the soil of the Royal Cemetery area (PG), date uncertain.
Gadd, *PBA* 18 (1932), pp. 7–8, pl. I, no. 7.
Woolley, *Ur Excavations*, II (1934), pp. 333, 363, 576, pl. 215 no. 367.
Woolley, *Ur Excavations*, IV (1956), p. 50 n. 3.

9.   Rectangular stamp seal of dark steatite with pierced lug handle.
Scorpion, fig. 113.
Ht. 1.4 × width 1.1 cm.
U. 11181; B. IM. 7854.
From grave PG/791, of the late Early Dynastic III to early Akkadian period.
Woolley, *Ur Excavations*, II (1934), pp. 327, 335, 336, 397, 568, pl. 192 no. 9.
Woolley, *Ur Excavations*, IV (1956), p. 50 n. 3.
Nissen, *Datierung*, (1966), pp. 68, 175.

III.   'GULF' SEALS

10.   Seated deity to right between two bull-men, each holding a staff surmounted by a crescent. Below is a bull.
Diam. 26, ht. 11 cm.

110   On this 'button type' steatite stamp seal there is a bull below a scorpion; above are some other symbols perhaps misunderstood signs from the Indus script

U. 7027; P.CBS. 16301.

From a 'grave outside city of Ur' (Field card).

Legrain, *MJ*, (1929), p. 299, pl. XXXVIII, no. 94.

Gadd, *PBA* 18 (1932), pp. 12–13, pl. III, no. 14.

Legrain, *Ur Excavations*, X (1951), no. 626.

Woolley, *Ur Excavations*, IV (1956), p. 173.

Woolley, *Ur Excavations*, VII (1976), p. 226.

11. Two men to left, one grasping the neck of a goat, and both carrying a small object between them, fig. 114.

Diam. 2.2, ht. 1.15 cm.

U. 6020; L. BM. 118704.

From 'loose surface soil of EH', 'EH' being an area in the south west corner of the Temenos with evidence of occupation going back to prehistoric times,[11] but since there was substantial evidence from the Larsa period,[12] this seems the most likely date of the seal.

Gadd, *PBA* 18 (1932), pp. 9–10, pl. II, no. 8.

Legrain, *Ur Excavations*, X (1951), no. 627.

Woolley, *Ur Excavations*, VII (1976), p. 220.

12. Man carrying two vessels suspended from a yoke, that on the left hanging over a stand (?), and that on the right next to another vessel on the ground.

Diam. 2.6, ht. 0.9 cm.

U. 16747; P. 31-43-75.

From 'upper rubbish Kassite (?) level over PUMP HOUSE.A.H.'. (Field card), Larsa to Kassite period.

Gadd, *PBA* 18 (1932), pp. 11–12, pl. II, no. 12.

Legrain, *Ur Excavations*, X (1951), no. 628.

Woolley, *Excavations at Ur* (1954), pl. 15.3.

Woolley, *Ur Excavations*, IV (1956), p. 185.

Woolley, *Ur Excavations*, VIII (1965), pp. 96, 97, 106, pl. 35.

Buchanan, *JAOS* 88 (1968), p. 537.

Wheeler, *Indus Civilization* (1968) p. 118 no. 11.

Woolley, *Ur Excavations*, VII (1976), p. 243.

13. Four female figures, each to left, at right angles to each other in quadrants defined by cross lines. The figures have outstretched legs and, alternately, they hold their breasts and extend their hands. One quadrant largely destroyed. Back much worn, fig. 115.

Diam. 2.25, ht. 1.05 cm.

U. 16181; L. BM. 122945.

From No. 1 Boundary Street, Room uncertain,[13] Larsa period.

Gadd, *PBA* 18 (1932), p. 10, pl. II, no. 9.

Legrain, *Ur Excavations*, X (1951), no. 624.

Woolley, *Ur Excavations*, IV (1956), p. 185.

During Caspers, *Persica* 5 (1970–71), p. 110, pl. IX.4.

Woolley, *Ur Excavations*, VII (1976), pp. 120, 236.

14. Four stylised bulls' heads (bucrania) in the quadrants of an elaborate quartering device which has a cross-hatched rectangle in the centre. Area of damage on the face, fig. 116.

Diam. 2.35, ht. 1 cm.

Ur Season VIII (1929–30); L. BM. 122841.

Provenance not traced.

Gadd, *PBA* 18 (1932), p. 12, pl. II, no. 13.

Woolley, *Ur Excavations*, IV (1956), p. 50.

111 A regular steatite stamp seal with a pierced lug handle. Below a cuneiform inscription is a bull facing to the left

112 A cylinder seal of white shell. A bull faces right and below is a (?) fish and a trefoil design. A stylised tree is at the centre

113 A rectangular steatite stamp seal with a scorpion

114 Two men facing left; one grasps the neck of a goat and between them they carry a small object

115 Four female figures at right angles to each other, each facing left. Each quadrant is defined by cross lines; one has been largely destroyed. The figures have outstretched legs and alternately hold their breasts and extend their hands

116 Four stylised bulls heads (bucrania) in the quadrants of an elaborate quartering device which has a cross-hatched rectangle in the centre

15. Long-horned ox below an uncertain object, possibly a quadruped and rider, at right angles to the ox (counter clockwise), fig. 117.

Diam. 1.8, ht. 0.9 cm.

U. 9265; L. BM. 120576.

From 'Loose soil, TTG' (Field card). Trial Trench G (TTG) was not further excavated. Date uncertain.

Gadd, *PBA* 18 (1932), p. 10, pl. II, no. 10.

Woolley, *Ur Excavations*, II (1934), pp. 333, 363, 543, pl. 216 no. 371.

Woolley, *Ur Excavations*, VII (1976), p. 232.

16. Scorpion.

Diam. 1.8 × ht. 1.05 cm.

U. 16397; P. 31-43-74.

'Brought in' (Field card).

Gadd, *PBA* 18 (1932), pp. 10–11, pl. II, no. 11.

Legrain, *Ur Excavations*, X (1951), no. 625.

Woolley, *Ur Excavations*, IV (1956), p. 185.

Woolley, *Ur Excavations*, VII (1976), p. 238.

17. Cylinder seal of steatite with white surface. Humped bull to left, feeding from bale of fodder, facing stylised tree, and followed by scorpion, both of them below a horizontal human stick figure, fig. 118.

Ht. 2.6, diam. 1.55 cm.

U. 16220; L. BM. 122947.

From a vaulted grave cut down into the Mausolea of the Third Dynasty Kings. Several graves answering this description were found during the excavations, and, of the main possibilities among these: a corbel vaulted recess cut down into Room 4 of the main (Šulgi) Mausoleum,[15] and; a chamber tomb cut down into Room 4 of the North West (Amar-Suena) Annex of the Mausoleum,[16] it now seems to me that the former, (a)=(d), is the more probable, in which case the seal would belong to the Larsa period.

Gadd, *PBA* 18 (1932), pp. 7–9, pl. I, no. 6.

Frankfort, *Cylinder Seals* (1939), pp. 305, 306.

Legrain, *Ur Excavations*, X (1951), no. 632.

Woolley, *Ur Excavations*, IV (1956), pp. 50, 185.

Woolley, *Ur Excavations*, VIII (1965), pp. 89, 96, 97, 106.

Nissen, *Datierung* (1966), p. 68.

Buchanan, *JAOS* 88 (1968), p. 537.

Wheeler, *Indus Civilization*, (1968), pp. 117–118, no. 10.

Brinkman, *Orientalia* 38 (1969), pp. 313 n. 1, 314 n. 1.

Mitchell and Woolley, *Ur Excavations*, VII (1976), pp. 236–237.

18. Impression of circular seal showing a bull's head (bucranium) between two seated figures drinking from two vessels through straws.
Diam. *c.* 2.5 cm.
YBC. 5447.
Possibly from Ur, dated to the tenth year of Gungunum of Larsa, 1923 B.C.

Hallo, *Studies Landsberger* (1965), pp. 199–203.

Buchanan, *Studies Landsberger* (1965), p. 204.

Wheeler, *Indus Civilization* (1968), p. 118 no. 13.

117   A long-horned ox below a design at right angles, possibly of a quadruped and rider

Of these seals only eight come from contexts which supply even the most general indication of date, and these, together with the sealed tablet (no. 18) are plotted on the accompanying chart, Table 1. From this it is clear that Type III, the 'Gulf' or Dilmun group, at Ur centres on the Larsa period, when indeed sea trade with the east is attested in economic texts from Ur.[17] The date ranges of nos. 11 and 12 are permissive and not restrictive, and do not militate against a Larsa period date which, indeed, is most likely, as has been mentioned above, for no. 11. The evidence on Type II, the local copies of Indus seals, is limited since no. 9 is a rather uncertain member of the group, but no. 6 is reasonably dated, so a range including the Akkadian period is acceptable. The datable examples of Type I, the Indus group, do not make a particularly useful contribution. This group is unlikely, on grounds of general probability, to be later than Type II, and examples from other sites appear to group round the Akkadian period. All that can be said is that the provenance of no. 2 does not conflict with this, and that the uncertainty of the evidence from Diqdiqqah may allow no. 3 to be dated to this time.

118   A steatite cylinder seal with a white surface. A humped bull, feeding from a bale of fodder, faces a stylised tree. He is followed by a scorpion. Above both is a horizontal human stick figure

PERIOD		TYPE		
		I	II	III
EARLY DYNASTIC	I II III	■	9	■
AKKADIAN	Early Middle Late	2	6	■
UR III	Early Late			■
ISIN		■		■
LARSA		3		11 12 13 17 (18)
OLD BABYLONIAN		■		■
KASSITE				■

1. *Proceedings of the British Academy*, 18, 1932, 191–210.

2. Sir Mortimer Wheeler, *The Indus Civilization* 3rd ed.; Cambridge, 1968, pp. 114–118; B. Buchanan 'A Dated "Persian Gulf" Seal and its Implications' in H. G. Güterbock & T. Jacobsen (eds.), *Studies in Honor of Benno Landsberger on his Seventy-Fifth Birthday* [Assyriological Studies 16] Chicago, 1965, 204–209, which supplies the main bibliography up to that date; and most recently, on the Seals from Failaka, P. Kjaerum, *Failaka/Dilmun. The Second Millennium Settlement, 1:1, The Stamp and Cylinder Seals* [Jutland Archaeological Society Publications, XVIII.1] Aarhus, 1983.

3. In Güterbock and Jacobsen, *Studies Landsberger*, 204–209.

4. Wheeler, *Indus Civilization*, 101.

5. S. Koskenniemi, A. Parpola and S. Parpola, *Materials for the Study of the Indus Script. I. A Concordance of the Indus Inscriptions* Helsinki, 1973 xvi.

6. W. W. Hallo 'A Mercantile Agreement from the Reign of Larsa' in Güterbock and Jacobsen, *Studies Landsberger*, 199–203.

7. R. Opificius, *Das Altbabylonische Terrakotterelief* Berlin, 1961, 16.

8. Woolley, *Ur Excavations*, VII, 81–87; T. Jacobsen, *Iraq* 22 1960, 179, 181–184.

9. Woolley, *Ur Excavations*, II, pl. 219, on which see R. Maxwell-Hyslop, *Western Asiatic Jewellery c. 3000–612 B.C.*, London, 1971, 23–24, fig. 15d.

10. Woolley, 'Excavations at Ur, 1926–7, Part II' *Antiquaries Journal*, 8, 1928, 26.

11. Woolley, *Ur Excavations* IV, 56–58, pls. 1, 70, 83, Pit F, falling within it.

12. Woolley, *Ur Excavations*, VII, 72–79.

13. See Woolley, *Ur Excavations*, VII, 236.

14. These are listed in Woolley, *Ur Excavations*, VII, 236, sub U. 16220.

15. Woolley, *Ur Excavations*, VII, 237–238, nos. (a)=(d), *Ur Excavations*, VI, 3–4, 10–11=*Ur Excavations*, VII, 210, no. LG/165.

16. Woolley, *Ur Excavations*, VII, 237–238, nos. (b)=?(f), *Ur Excavations*, VI, 32=?, *Ur Excavations*, VII, 167.

17. A. L. Oppenheim, 'The Seafaring Merchants of Ur', *Journal of the American Oriental Society*, 74, 1954, 6–17.

ABBREVIATIONS

Bibby, G.   *Looking for Dilmun*, London, 1970.
Brinkman, A.   Review of *Ur Excavations*, VIII, *Orientalia* 38, 1969, 310–348.
Buchanan, R.   'The Date of the So-Called Second Dynasty Graves of the Royal Cemetery
                               at Ur', *J.A.O.S.* 74, 1954, 147–153.
                               'A Dated 'Persian Gulf' Seal and its Implications', in Güterbock and
                               Jacobsen, *Studies Landsberger*, 1965, 204–209.
                               Review of *Ur Excavations*, VIII, *Journal of the American Oriental Society*,
                               88, 1968, 537.
During Caspers, E. C. L.   'Some Motifs as Evidence for Maritime Contact between Sumer and the
                               Indus Valley', *Persica* 5, 1970–71, 107–118.
Frankfort, H.   *Cylinder Seals*, London, 1939.
Gadd, C. J.   'Seals of Ancient Indian Style Found at Ur', *Proceedings of the British
                               Academy*, 18, 1932, 191–210.
Hallo, W. W.   'A Mercantile Agreement from the Reign of Gungunum of Larsa', in
                               Güterbock and Jacobsen, *Studies Landsberger* 1965, 199–203.
Kjaerum, P.   *Failaka/Dilmun. The Second Millennium Settlements. 1.1. The Stamp and
                               Cylinder Seals*, Aarhus, 1983.
Koskenniemi, S., Parpola, A and Parpola, S. *Materials for the Study of the Indus Script, I, A
                               Concordance of the Indus Inscriptions*, Helsinki, 1973.
Güterbock, H. G. and Jacobsen, T. (eds.), *Studies in Honor of Benno Landsberger on his Seventy-
                               Fifth Birthday*, [Assyriological Studies 16], Chicago, 1965.
Legrain, L.   'Gem Cutters in Ancient Ur', *The Museum Journal*, 1929, 258–306.
Legrain, L. and Woolley, C. L., *Ur Excavations*, X, *Seal Cylinders*, London and Philadelphia, 1951.
Maxwell-Hyslop, R.   *Western Asiatic Jewellery c. 3000–612 B.C.*, London, 1971.
Nissen, H. J.   *Zur Datierung des Königsfriedhofes von Ur*, Bonn, 1966.
Opificius, R.   *Das Altbabylonische Terrakottarelief*, Berlin, 1961.
Oppenheim, A. L.   'The Seafaring Merchants of Ur', *Journal of the American Oriental Society*,
                               74, 1954, 6–17.
Rao, S. R.   'A 'Persian Gulf' Seal from Lothal', *Antiquity* 37, 1963, 96–99.
Wheeler, M.   *The Indus Civilization*, 3rd ed.; Cambridge, 1968.
Woolley, C. L.   *Ur Excavations*, II, *The Royal Cemetery*, London and Philadelphia, 1934.
                               Ur Excavations, IV, *The Early Periods*, 1956. *Ur Excavations*, VI, *The Ur
                               III Period*, 1974. *Ur Excavations*, VIII, *The Kassite Period and the Period
                               of the Assyrian Kings*, 1965. 'Excavations at Ur, 1926–7, Part II', *Anti-
                               quaries Journal*, 8, 1928, 1–29. *Excavation at Ur*, London, 1954.
Woolley, C. L. and Mallowan, M. *Ur Excavations*, VII, *The Old Babylonian Period*, 1976. *Ur Excava-
                               tions*, IX, *The Neo-Babylonian and Persian Periods*, 1962.

Animal designs and Gulf chronology

ELISABETH C. L. DURING CASPERS

Any reliable interpretation of an ancient culture should be based on a well integrated documentation of both archaeological and textual data. Such a situation pertains, unfortunately, only to a limited number of culture areas, one of which is the island of Bahrain and its neighbouring coastal appendages. When applied with care, intelligence and common sense such datal documentation can provide tantalizing possibilities for a sensible and reliable reconstruction of the ancient past of Bahrain island and the nearby coastal strips of the Arabian mainland which are loosely termed the Dilmun culture.

For some unknown reason archaeologists working in the Gulf have ignored or perhaps been unaware of the existence of cuneiform records predating the well-known Early Dynastic IIIb account by Ur-Nanshe of Lagaš which reads: Ur^DNanše . lugal má . dilmun kur . ta gú . ğiš mu . ğál, 'King Urnanshe loaded Dilmun-ships with wood (as a tribute to him) from abroad'. Consequently, these earlier pre-ED IIIb cuneiform texts which mention Dilmun in one way or the other, have not been taken into account in the present re-evaluation of Gulf chronology which proposes a low, post-ED IIIb date for the cultural remains of Bahrain in particular.

Although these earlier cuneiform references to Dilmun do not provide an insight into the exact geographical, political and economic strength of this place, the mere fact that the name Dilmun occurs in these early, i.e. c. 3200–3100 B.C.,[1,2] cuneiform writings sufficiently warrants the supposition that its political and economic importance had already been well recognized. In the Early Dynastic I–III records of Mesopotamia, Dilmun apparently had already attained such prestige as a centre of international commercial fame that the Dilmun shekel was an internationally recognized standard weight. This fact gives further evidence of Dilmun's prime importance as an international emporium and an accepted, independent trading centre. Consequently, it can be surmised that the Dilmun market was no longer in its infancy and that around Early Dynastic III times its position as entrepôt was the result of a long experience probably dating back to the very beginning of the Early Dynastic period or even before that date in the late fourth millennium (c. 3200–3100 B.C.). These dates are supported by evidence in the archaic economic and lexical texts from Uruk which suggest the existence of trade, in particular in metals.[3] Whatever its exact geographical boundaries were we do know through the actual occurrence of its geographical name in the corpus of archaic Uruk texts that Dilmun already existed in Uruk III–IV times and maybe even earlier. Therefore, a likely Jemdet Nasr horizon in the coastal areas of Northeastern Arabia certainly gains considerable relevance when viewed in conjunction with possible references to Dilmun in the earliest documents available. For example we have the reported occurrence of Jemdet Nasr pottery wares from tombs and settlement sites near Dhahran and Abqaiq,[4] on Tarut Island, and the recovery of a Jemdet Nasr polychrome sherd in a layer north of the first Barbar temple[5] and an apparently re-cut hemispheroid Jemdet Nasr stamp seal (?) of limestone found in a grave at the site of Al Hajjar I.[6] The archaeological information just mentioned supports the possibility that in considering the enumeration of male and female servants in a Jemdet Nasr text,[7] there may well be signs which could be regarded as forerunners of the sign DILMUN as a geographical indication. Perhaps these are references to Dilmun as the native birth place of this particular servant or his or her relatives. Obviously, not only is it of prime importance that the name Dilmun already figures in the late Uruk and the Jemdet Nasr documents as a geographical reality, but this particular Jemdet Nasr text which may relate to a Dilmun servant amongst those from various Mesopotamian localities, could possibly allow future speculations regarding social and other contacts between Jemdet Nasr, Mesopotamia and Dilmun and the internal structure of this early third millennium Dilmun. A similar closer contact between Dilmun and Mesopotamia than that resulting through trade alone has been suggested by Nissen also for the archaic Uruk period[8] and Englund's reference to a 'tax collector of Dilmun'[9] certainly sustains this notion. Early Dynastic IIIb records from Lagaš refer to seafaring merchants and commercial agents, who should buy [urdu] a-ru$_{12}$-da = aruda-metal, most likely 'pure copper', on the Dilmun market. However, there is an absence of pre-Akkadian cuneiform references to Makkan, Sumer's foremost copper producer, now definitely associated with the rich copper bearing regions of Oman and to Meluḥḥa, the other Mesopotamian copper supplier mentioned in the Sumerian documents, the latter generally located in the Indo-Pakistan subcontinent of today. Nevertheless this pure copper may have been imported from Makkan and other copper mining areas. Recent archaeological discoveries by the German

Mining Museum at Bochum, Germany[10] have revealed large-scale copper mining and production areas in the mountainous regions of Oman and an analysis of copper ores and copper objects from Middle Eastern fourth and third millennium sites[11] now appears to show that a regular Mesopotamian copper trade should be dated as early as Early Dynastic II. Consequently, the Makkan copper producing centres in Oman also belong to the early part of the third millennium B.C. This adds a new dimension to the Early Dynastic III cuneiform information regarding Dilmun's international position in the metal trade via the Arabian Gulf. Therefore, these combined philological and archaeological facts strongly support the view that Oman-Makkan was already an active and prosperous trading centre well before its name officially entered the Sumerian registration system.

The Meluḫḫa trade has not been recorded either in pre-Akkadian times and we have, therefore, no direct evidence of Meluḫḫa copper entering the Mesopotamian scene before the time of Agade. However, Krispijn makes reference to lexical texts from Ebla/Tell Mardik in Syria[12] which are slightly earlier than the Early Dynastic IIIb texts from Lagaš and which mention, for example, the import of pure copper, (tin) bronze, tin and Dilmun tin as coming from Dilmun. We know from Gudea of Lagaš that during his reign tin was imported from Meluḫḫa and the Indian tin ore deposits in Rajasthan and Gujarat may have been exploited by the Meluḫḫaites.[13] We also know that the Indus Valley artisans used copper with a high arsenic content. In some cases this could still be regarded as a natural impurity in the copper ore, but in other instances it may well be an intentional alloy added to ensure a certain harder copper, termed 'low bronze'. I am grateful that Dr Krispijn has allowed me to mention his opinion that a trade in arsenic-copper, either conducted overland or by sea, must have preceded the one in pure copper and tin, which would have enabled the consumer to produce bronze in the proper sense.

On these grounds, a pre-Akkadian date for at least some of the Meluḫḫa trade with Mesopotamia appears perfectly legitimate. This would be in accordance with my long held view that a considerable span of time and complexity were involved in the establishment of trade connections between such widely separated regions as Meso-potamia and the Indus Valley. The existence of a sophisticated civilization with a well-organized economic structure would certainly be essential for the successful operation of such long distance trade.

The acceptance of an Early Dynastic II copper trade in the Arabian Gulf linking Sumer, Makkan, possibly Meluḫḫa and also other territories, must, by definition, lead to a reconsideration of the presently proposed low chronology for Bahrain,[14] if we want to suf-ficiently accommodate Dilmun's participation in, at least, this Early

Dynastic II commercial enterprise. The possibility that the name Dilmun already occurs in one (perhaps more(?)) of the Jemdet Nasr and late Uruk texts would guarantee Dilmun's existence during this time. In turn, this would be in accordance with the archaeological evidence for a subsistence pattern as known from Jemdet Nasr Mesopotamia which has been recognized in various localities of the Arabian littoral. Needless to say more than a thin scatter of readily identifiable ceramic traces is required before the philological and archaeological indications can satisfactorily merge into a clear picture of Jemdet Nasr Dilmun as a properly functioning social, economic and religious structure, operating within a well-defined geographical delineation.

We have seen that Urnanshe's statement of the Early Dynastic IIIb period, i.e. *c.* 2520 B.C., in which he (ordered) Dilmun-ships to be loaded with tribute wood from abroad is generally regarded as the earliest cuneiform reference to Dilmun. The fact that Krispijn, Englund and Nissen have gathered earlier references to Dilmun both as a geographical name and a non-geographical indication dating back to the archaic Uruk period and that, therefore, these earlier references from Sumer and Ebla/Tell Mardik leave no doubt that Dilmun was already in existence in pre-ED IIIb times, does not in itself necessarily preclude the possibility that at that time only the Arabian littoral was called Dilmun. What does militate against such a geographical restriction is that these records show that already in the Early Dynastic III period, Dilmun possessed an international standard-weight for metal, the Dilmun shekel, confirming Dilmun's position as an international mercantile centre at this time. Also of importance in this context is the reference in an Early Dynastic II text to a 'Dilmun harp' which reminds us of the representations on two Dilmun seals from Failaka of a harp with a two-register sounding box consisting of two superimposed typical 'Persian Gulf' bulls with short horns, dot-in-circle eyes and ringed necks. The harp has apparently three strings and is played by a seated person clad in a garment similar to a kaunakes robe.[15]

It may be remembered that in prehistoric times people used to travel with their musical instruments and the reference to a Dilmun harp and also to the one from Mari in this particular text may well indicate that even in this early period (*c.* 2700–2600 B.C.) Dilmun's characteristic features were already so well-known that their musical instruments could be immediately distinguished and recognized as being typically Dilmunite. Of great value is Englund's reading of Uruk III records as dilmun . tùn = 'Dilmun axe'[16] and Nissen's opinion that this reference would be regarded as a 'Dilmun-type axe'[17] bears much relevance to the present context.

In view of the textual evidence it is difficult to continue to restrict Dilmun's location in pre-Sargonid times simply to the Arabian littoral. Therefore we venture to propose that this international trading centre virtually occupied the same regions throughout its existence.[18] This view is in opposition to the present opinion that Bahrain island has not yet been able to furnish any evidence for a pre-Akkadian occupation, whereas the Arabian mainland including Tarut Island lying opposite Qatif has already shown clear Early Dynastic I–III occupational traces. However, we feel confident that when all relevant arguments for a short chronology of Bahrain are placed next to the textual evidence from Mesopotamia, the north wall pottery sequence of the Qal'at al-Bahrain on which this chronology hinges will be brought into a better, more objective perspective. The cuneiform records we have presently been dealing with picture Dilmun as an important, international trading and transit centre from at least the Early Dynastic II period onwards. It was apparently geographically and morphologically so well situated that merchants and businessmen from places other than Mesopotamia came with their merchandise to Dilmun to trade their goods for a variety of products brought from places here and beyond the Arabian Gulf. This consequently implies that Dilmun had facilities for the anchorage of the Dilmun fleet as well as for the ships coming from abroad, accommodation for the storage of the local and foreign goods and merchandise and last but not least, possibilities for housing the foreign merchants during their stay in Dilmun. One could hardly compare the Arabian mainland appendages with a 'Great Dilmun' and even the island of Tarut would not satisfactorily fit this description despite its prominent position as the only Gulf producer and supplier *par excellence* of carved steatite vessels in Early Dynastic times.[19] In our opinion, only Bahrain could have been a 'Great Dilmun' or the main Dilmunite centre because of its favourable geographical location, suitably positioned halfway down the Gulf, its harbour facilities and its abundant fresh sweet water supplies from springs and wells in the north and northwest part of the island and offshore. In addition we have to be prepared to search for a reflection of this eminent position in Bahrain's archaeological remains because the cuneiform records unfortunately do not supply us with any helpful assistance in this respect. It seems improbable that the Early Dynastic sites on the Arabian mainland or even Tarut Island were regarded as the main centre(s) of the Dilmun Civilization in pre-Akkadian times, without being intimately associated and incorporated with a larger, more important cultural and economic entity, which had its own standard weight used in the international Gulf trade traffic whilst in close vicinity, the more suitable island of Bahrain remained unmentioned and unnamed in the texts until Akkadian times.

As we now understand it, Dilmun was a country with its own

distinctive character, whose origin cannot yet be traced and whose name does not appear to have a proper, recognizable Sumerian meaning. This is another point in favour of discarding the proper solitary Early Dynastic sites in northeastern Arabia as having been Dilmun on their own without having been incorporated into a larger socioeconomic structure. The low chronology, recently proposed, implies that none of the archaeological remains of Bahrain can be ascribed to a pre-Akkadian date and yet in all marshalled respects it would appear to have been the perfect place for the international Early Dynastic trading centre and metal market of the Sumerian documents.

It may, therefore, be proposed to describe the third millennium Bahrain populace as a conglomerate of several different cultural and possibly also various ethnic elements, consisting of an original substratum associated with the burial mounds, and the Mesopotamian-Oman-Indian features deriving from flows of recurrent newcomers adapting themselves to live amongst the long-established traders and the whole intimately interlinked by strong mercantile liaisons. We may not be far from the truth in regarding the Bahrain society of that time residing on the island and in the nearby littoral appendages as a melting pot both in a cultural and an ethnic sense. Traders and businessmen coming from various localities, e.g. Mesopotamia, the Indus Valley, Iran, other Arabian regions, Egypt and even possibly Crete, as I have recently[20] tried to verify negotiated and concluded trade transactions both with each other and with the mixed populace in permanent residence. Therefore, we may well have to visualize a Bahrain population in the third millennium B.C. consisting of different grades of cultural and mercantile involvement, associated one way or the other with local, inherent populace groups. The expansion of the late third-early second millennium Dilmun culture towards the west coast of Qatar and to Failaka island, seems a natural development of a rapidly growing mercantile concern which in the throes of overshadowing its former trade partners has become Mesopotamia's only supplier of Gulf products in the early centuries of the second millennium B.C.

As far as the Dilmun Civilization is concerned we would like to suggest that this is, in fact, a subsistence pattern in which several different ethno-social elements co-existed. The third millennium Barbar period may represent nothing less than the final outcome of a 'hybrid' society, which originated on the island of Bahrain most probably from an earlier, local or semi-inherent substratum. Developing within its own cultural confines it was confronted by a continuing influx of foreign, non-local Arabian elements. These in turn may be shown to have caused a mutual effect on all parties concerned, and to have set into motion an amalgamation of religious ideas and cultural concepts perhaps resulting eventually in a multifarious, multi-ethnic, closely knit complex of accumulated cultural and religious inheritance elaborately, if not implicitly, graded. The predictable ingredients of this cultural melting pot may be found in the elements from important civilizations such as Mesopotamia, Iran and the Indo-Pakistan subcontinent added to local Arabian interference. Bahrain with its convenient geographical location and the early formation of a centre for shipping, trade and marketing, leads to the conclusion that it was a suitable place for harbouring, sustaining and unifying such an interracial and multicultural distribution.

A short reference should here be made to a recent article by Edith Porada[21] dealing with a small female statuette of lapis lazuli from Hierakonpolis in Egypt and which, in her opinion, may well have been manufactured outside Egypt proper. She bases her view on the fact that this standing lapis lazuli figurine combines Egyptian features with non-Egyptian characteristics shown in the crossed hands placed on the abdomen above a well-indicated pubic triangle and the head, which is fitted separately onto the female statue and which shows a face, characterized by large oval-shaped and now empty eye-sockets, a flat, broadly based nose and tight lips, and a hair-do consisting of rows of little, tight ringlets representing curls. Porada considers the possibility of its place of origin to lie 'somewhere within the Iranian sphere of influence, perhaps in a locality in the area of the Persian Gulf'[22] and furthermore that '. . . the only certain fact is that a relatively large piece of lapis lazuli reached Egypt before 3000 B.C. from the most eastern region of Western Asia. Such imports may have come not through overland trade but via the sea-route . . .'[23]

In the light of the present discussion and my recent contribution at the Conference for South Asian Archaeologists in Brussels 1983[24] one may perhaps wonder whether this fine piece of artistry could not have been carved in one of the Arabian localities of the Gulf, e.g. in Dilmun, to subsequently reach Egypt via the searoute along the Arabian peninsula.[25]

An early blending of Egyptian iconographic traits with features inherent in another cultural environment, most likely as a result of mutual contacts, may also be present in a squattish cylinder seal made of steatite and found in Moenjo-daro in the Indus Valley.[26] Neither the shape of the cylinder, which is not inherent in the Indian cultural sphere of influence, nor the device depicting two short-horned animals, one with a upturned spiky tail,[27] with birds above their backs, and interspersed by a small spiky tree and a gigantic erect snake with prey in its mouth, are recognizably Harappan characteristics. By dint of its mere presence at Moenjo-daro an early third millennium date, for example, would militate against the present chronological conventions regarding the Mature/Late Indus

Culture dates. Yet a tenuous liaison with the Early Dynastic I Scarlet Ware from the Diyala region in Mesopotamia and a surprising likeness of this Indus concept to a representation on an ivory comb of late predynastic Egypt equally showing in the top register of one of the two sculptured sides a procession of elephants and intervening rampant snakes, their tails also forming the base line of the picture, is worth registering. The basis concept behind both examples seems also to conform to an, as yet, ill-defined contact between early Egypt (*c.* 3000 B.C.) and areas across the Arabian Sea. What role Dilmun could have played in this suggested intercourse is not at all clear, but it may well pay to record these observations in the light of a much earlier existence of Dilmun according to the cuneiform records than the present archaeological tolerance seems to permit.

Animal representations in the round in the Gulf are neither frequently encountered nor peculiar to Bahrain. Those few examples of animal representations made available to us through publications will constitute the second part of this paper.

In 1954 the Danish Archaeological Expedition briefly explored the southeast corner of the stone-walled spring called by the Arabs Umm es-Sejur at Diraz, a small village situated in the fertile northwest of the island of Bahrain. This southeast corner of the Diraz spring enclosure consisted of a well-chamber with a ramp and a roofed staircase set at right angles to one another. Bibby[28] suggests that the well-chamber may have had a domed roof, no traces of which remain at present. The structures are built of stone set in plaster, and the walls themselves are surfaced with plaster on each face. Pottery unearthed from between the edges of the well-head stone and the sides of the chamber of the well date to the Barbar culture which in the 1950s was estimated to encompass the greater portion of the third millennium B.C.

Bibby, who excavated the complex in 1954, mentions that an empty pedestal was found at the head of the staircase on either side. Each pedestal was just large enough to accommodate one of the two limestone statues of kneeling rams, 21 cms and 20 cms in height respectively, figs. 119, 120, 121, and each with the head struck off. One was discovered on the staircase and the other in the well-chamber below. They are rudely carved in stone, apparently quarried on the island of Jiddah off the coast of Bahrain, and unfortunately the severed heads have not been recovered.

The width of the ramp running eastwards and of the associated staircase which descends from a sharp corner in a southerly direction, is about one metre. The small well-chamber itself measures only 1.48 m × 1.40 m. The significance of these measurements is immediately apparent, when one considers that the bases of the two rams measure 15½ × 28½ and 16½ × 29 cms respectively. The

119   Frontal view of two limestone kneeling rams from Diraz, Bahrain. Photograph J. C. M. H. Moloney. Courtesy Department of Antiquities, State of Bahrain

121   Rear view of two limestone kneeling rams from Diraz, Bahrain. Photograph J. C. M. H. Moloney. Courtesy Department of Antiquities, State of Bahrain

pedestals are no longer *in situ*, but, should one gauge their platforms to have measured only 20 cms in width and the orientation of their siting to have lain alongside the wall, then the passage-way for traffic on a right-angled elbow, would have been reduced to 60 cms. Had the pedestals and their statues been standing at right angles to the wall then the path is further reduced to a mere 40 cms. The bases of the ram statues do not show visible traces of a means of securing them in any way to the missing pedestals. This is a strange factor when we consider that other reclining rams from Iran, to be discussed shortly, do show holes in this flat base to accommodate a kind of plinth or pedestal. We can then recapitulate as follows: 'at the time of the existence of the well, two limestone statues of reclining rams, 21 cms and 20 cms in height respectively, apparently sited upon pedestals, had stood watch at the head of the staircase.' This appears to justify the assumption that the well-chamber with its staircase and well-head formed an entity centring on a water cult. However, to risk elaboration on this interpretation would unfortunately involve conjecture. The right-angled position of the ramp would guarantee privacy and this could, therefore, imply a rather secluded nature of any religious practice performed within the architectural unit. Moreover, the narrowness of both ramp and staircase, each only one metre in width, excludes almost certainly the participation of a large number of people in the rites at any one time. It is, of course, possible that the small dimensions of the well-chamber restricted its use to a selected few rather than that it was in constant use by the inhabitants of the adjacent village of Barbar date, the ruins of which lie over a seemingly large and much quarried area, in the immediate vicinity of the hollow. Only a small area of this village site has been excavated by the Department of Antiquities of the State of Bahrain, up to the time of writing.

In addition to its modest overall measurements the stairway was even further restricted in width by the presence of the ram statues on their pedestals at the head of the staircase and on a right-angled turn from the ramp. Moreover, the staircase and well-head was roofed and the resulting lack of daylight would limit activity to some extent. Thus, in my opinion, the possibilities that this well was used as a public washing and bathing place can be excluded.

Both the entrance to the 'well-temple' of the three super-imposed Barbar temples, and the well-chamber of the Diraz enclosure, were flanked by cult objects or statues and these must surely have borne a direct relationship to the ritual acts, or cere-monial cleansings or washing, performed at a lower level, in or near the spring itself. In neither case, can we, unfortunately, be more specific, without entering the realm of pure speculation, but it does seem justified to stress that the presence of sweet spring water played its part in the religious rites of the inhabitants of Dilmun.

The modelling of the two Diraz rams, figs. 119-121, is, to say the least, rather rudimentary. This could be put down to an unfamiliarity with working in the medium of limestone, or it may be speculated that the artist reserved his finest creative effort for the now missing heads. On the other hand, the clear adze or chisel markings may imply that we are dealing with unfinished products of the workshop. Whatever the reason, the workmanship is poor indeed.

The lack of anatomical understanding is most obviously apparent in the rendering of the folded legs of these reclining animals. The upper part of the forelegs is indicated by crudely drawn, shallowly chiselled lines which lack both proportion and suggestion of muscular development. The lower parts of the limbs stand out rather more in relief where the surface of the stone has been cut away to form the chest and the curve of the belly. The hindlegs are even less distinctly indicated, and consist merely of a horizontal ridge

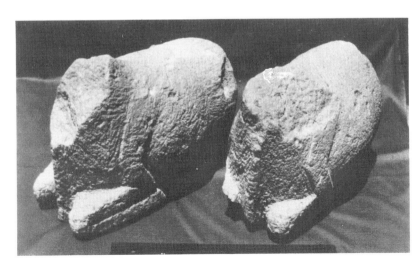

120 ¾ side view of two limestone kneeling rams from Diraz, Bahrain. Photograph E.C.L. During Caspers. Courtesy Department of Antiquities, State of Bahrain

abutting the sagging curve of the animal's body. The rear end is, in both cases, shown as completely flat, with no indication of the shape of the hindquarters. The only prominent feature of this aspect is the flattish triangular tail, cut in low relief. The other distinguishing characteristic is a well marked wedge-shaped ridge, which runs from the place where the heads were struck off, down the entire length of the chest to the base between the knees of the rams. Neither animal has any surface treatment other than on this ridge down the throat and chest, which is vaguely marked by horizontal grooves as if to indicate a frontal hair growth.

Curiously, the two characteristic features which mark the headless animal representations as rams, are the only two outstanding details, the short fat tail which is supposed to be an indication of a domesticated breed and the hairy chest, which appears to be one of the characteristics of wild species, along with erect ears, an absence of fleece and curling horns, fig. 122.[29]

Although it cannot be taken as proof that the Barbar pottery found in such close proximity to the two ram statues is indeed contemporary with the latter, yet there is no overriding argument for any substantial opposition and we have, therefore, to turn to other culture regions with an approximate date for possible comparisons.

As I have previously pointed out, between the end of the fourth and the beginning of the third millennium B.C., Near Eastern

122 Top register of alabaster vase from Uruk-Warka, Mesopotamia. Courtesy E. Strommenger, *Fünf Jahrtausende Mesopotamien*, 1962, Abb.21

iconography shows two breeds of mouflons or sheep which appear to have disappeared by the Akkadian period. They represent maned sheep with short tails and either pointed and erect ears, or the long and pendant type.

Agnes Spycket has pointed out in her excellent and well-documented oeuvre *La Statuaire du Proche Orient Ancient* (Handbuch der Orientalistik 1er Band der Alte Vordere Orient, Zweiter Abschnitt . . . B. Hrouda (Ed.) . . . Brill, 1981) p. 39 ff. that regarding the proto-historic animal representations 'C'est encore d'*Uruk* et de Suse que provient l'essentiel de la documentation animal protohistorique. Les espèces les plus souvent représentées sont celles du troupeau, telles qu'on le voit défiler sur les cylindres-sceaux de l'époque ou sur le registre inférieur du grand vase d'albâtre de Warka. Il s'agissait de faire fructifier le cheptel qui appartenait aux dieux et en particulier à la déesse Inanna, dont le rôle était d'assurer la fécondité. Son troupeau sort de bâtiments identifiés par la hampe bouclée, symbole de la déesse'.

In conclusion we can say that in Mesopotamia towards the close of the fourth millennium B.C. representations of wild sheep or mouflons occur in which the males have a hairy chest, shown as a well-marked, hatched ridge running from the upper part of the throat downwards towards the forelegs. This type of ram with its pronounced hairy chest seems to be no longer represented in the Early Dynastic and Akkadian periods, possibly as a result of breeding with species, resulting in the cross-breeds which we occasionally see in Akkadian times.

As detailed reference has already been made to the occurrence of Jemdet Nasr and Early Dynastic cultural influences in northeastern Arabia and Tarut Island no further elaboration is needed here. It may suffice to recall Rashid's publication of a male limestone statue from Tarut Island in a typically, locally made, Early Dynastic II tradition.[30]

The two rams from Diraz may appear to belong to the same local Gulf production. Allowing for a certain lapse of time for an artistic concept to travel from its original Mesopotamian homeland, to be followed by the rendering of that idea in its new environment, in this case Bahrain, the transference of this idea most likely falls within the span of time in which the particular concept is still in vogue in its own homeland or in an intermediary area. In Mesopotamia the portrayal of wild sheep characterized by pronounced frontal hair-growth and powerful horns had their floruit before the beginning of the Early Dynastic period and despite the regrettable absence of the heads and horns of the Diraz animals, the hairy chest, the short tail and the apparently short-haired body would appear to safeguard us from mistaking them for other and later breeds of sheep.

Although it would, therefore, seem reasonable to assume that the ram statues from Diraz are likely to have been manufactured in the first centuries of the third millennium B.C., one cannot exclude the possibility of transmission of Mesopotamian artistic concepts through the medium of an intermediary cultural area to the Arabian coastal region. This could account for a discrepancy in the date between the original prototype and its final recreation in Bahrain, because its arrival there could then be said to have occurred in stages.

A magnificently sculptured quartzite(?) recumbent mouflon, now in the Metropolitan Museum of Art, N.Y.[31] and said to have come from Iran certainly falls within this category of reclining sheep or mouflons. It is dated approximately *c.* 3200–3000 B.C. and bears testimony to a longstanding experience in modelling animals in the area of its provenance.

This quartzite(?) animal measures 28 cms long and represents a couchant ram. A disproportionately small triangularly-shaped head juts forward from between two well conceived down swept horns. The one which is still intact shows limited ribbing nearest to the head and presented by short vertical strokes. Because the other side of the head is considerably damaged, little detail is discernible. Close to the updrawn outer corner of the almond-shaped eye lies a loop-like protuberance, resting, as it were, against the exceptionally thick neck. The reason for the exaggeratedly heavily modelled neck of the animal and for the entire frontal aspect on this side, can be found in the stance of the ram. When it is viewed from behind it is seen to be seated in the typical sagging posture of a reclining animal at ease. A mere impression of a triangular tail, modelled softly, can be seen to disappear into the almost surrealistically conceived back side of the animal's body.

The front legs are schematically rendered and their upper body merges gently into the soft bulge which lies across the shoulders and which is carried up across the neck to produce the ridge of skin caused by holding the head erect. The hindlegs are even more just an outline and the right hand one is only shallowly modelled, consisting merely of a horizontal ridge abutting the sagging curve of the animal's body. The left hindleg has not even been indicated, but a curiously light-coloured loop-like configuration in the stone at this location admirably replaces its omission. Indeed, one could even wonder whether this effect was not achieved intentionally.

Comparable to other representations of this mouflon type the ram under discussion also shows the well-marked wedge-shaped ridge running from the chin of the head down the entire length of the chest to the base between the knees of the ram. In the present case, however, the ridge tapers gently towards the base between the ram's knees.

Obviously the Diraz ram figures are rendered with far less observation and actuality than the Mesopotamian examples and the ram from the Metropolitan Museum of Art, presently described, whose skilful and masterly portraits suggest that they must be based on direct knowledge and attention to detail, indicating their actual physical presence in these localities at the time of their manufacture, whereas the Bahrain environment can be better described as a typical goat country.

Despite Bibby's statement that at the time of excavation two empty pedestals were found on either side of the staircase, each just large enough to accommodate one of the ram figures, the bases of these ram statues do not show visible traces of a means of securing them in any way to the missing pedestals. The Iranian ram statue in the Metropolitan Museum shows a general likeness to the Diraz statues, not only in concept matter and in iconographical expression, but also in the fact that both the Diraz rams and the one in the Metropolitan Museum of Art represent a breed of ram or mouflon comparable to the ones encountered in Mesopotamian representations towards the end of the fourth millennium-early centuries of the third millennium B.C.

The base of the ram from the Metropolitan Museum shows one finished drill hole and another one still in an early stage of perforation, both situated along the longitudinal axis of the flat and polished base. Their presence can only be explained as a securing device in order to fasten this ram figure onto a pedestal or another support. Could the rudimentary modelling of the Diraz rams and the presence of clear adze and chisel markings perhaps imply that we are dealing with an unfinished product of a workshop, located in one of the Dilmun sites, possibly Bahrain itself where local as well as foreign craftsmen worked alongside each other? If this suggestion should prove acceptable as a working hypothesis, might we not assume, that among these foreign artists were also people from across the Gulf, i.e. Elam or perhaps, the Bampur-Yahya region, who had taken up residence in Dilmun. Consequently, might it not be possible to visualize the Diraz rams as unfinished products of an artist from outside the Dilmun cultural sphere, belonging to a locality across the Gulf, who did intend to supply the ram statues from Diraz with a similar securing device as that used for the Metropolitan mouflon after completion of the statue itself. For it seems a logical assumption that only after completion of the figures the artist would drill the holes in the finished bases of the statues for securing them onto a pedestal. This supposition might in turn explain the rough and unfinished appearance of the surface of their bases. On the other hand, the overall appearance and the clumsy and unnatural posture of the two reclining animals could be a point in favour of a product by a local artist, who was unfamiliar with the anatomical features and characteristics of this breed of animal which may not have been indigenous to the Dilmun environment.

The acceptance of a possible pre-Akkadian date for at least some of the Meluḫḫa trade with Mesopotamia, as just mentioned, may have considerable consequences for a Meluḫḫa-Dilmun contact during the first half of the third millennium B.C. Dilmun's position along the southern Gulf shores, with Bahrain as the main entrepôt and the fact that Dilmun possessed an international standard weight for metal, the Dilmun shekel, confirming Dilmun's position as an international mercantile centre in pre-Akkadian times, may well have resulted in an early settling of Indus Valley merchants and business-men in this part of the Gulf. Their subsequent involvement with other indigenous, as well as foreign, inhabitants, who had also taken up residence in these parts in order to facilitate their different trading affairs, would easily have resulted in a growing knowledge and under-standing of other existent cultural traditions prevailing in the areas on and around the Gulf in Early Dynastic times.

At this point it may seem pertinent to bring into the present discussion three stone statues from Moenjo-daro in the Indus Valley,[32] representing a reclining animal with a ram's body and with what has been often described as an elephant's trunk. Unfortunately, extensive damage to the heads and the fore-quarters, and the presently unknown whereabouts of two of the figures has so far prevented a definite hypothesis as to their true animal nature. At present the inaccurate and incomplete description of the statues in the old excavation reports allows only a discussion of the one animal figure on display in the Moenjo-daro site museum, Pakistan,[33] but when studying the descriptions and the old photographs of the other two in conjunction with the example in this museum, it appears that a great similarity in general outline and overall appearance exists. As detailed treatment of this stone animal statuary from Moenjo-daro will appear elsewhere,[34] it may suffice here to summarize the most unique points.

The animal illustrated in figs. 123, 124 is made of limestone and measures 25.4 cms. It represents a couchant animal with ram's horns and a ram's body in addition to a long appendage hanging from the head, which is generally regarded as representing the trunk of an elephant. The head, though badly broken, leaves no doubt as to its being that of a ram. The animal reclines on a plinth measuring 20, 32 cms × 15, 75 cms × 10, 79.5 cms. It is roughly shaped with slightly rounded corners and an unequal base.

When this animal statue is viewed from behind it is seen to be seated in the typical sagging posture of a reclining animal at ease. The curve between the bony structure of the shoulder and the foreleg, and the soft bulge of the belly is clearly shown on either side, and this is carried up across the back of the neck to produce the ridge of skin caused by holding the head erect. The cloven hooves of the ram are very clearly seen on both back and foreleg on one side, but on the other the back lower leg is not completed, but appears to melt into the plinth. When viewed from above, the creature is seen to have been carved askew on the rather high plinth, giving it a nonchalant and relaxed attitude. The plinth itself is rounded at the corners and is curved gently upward towards the foreparts of the animal.

A well carved, ribbed and downswept ram horn curves forward realistically to its tip on one side, but is rather broken on the other although it is still visible. The so-called elephant's trunk is prominently ringed but the form is badly rendered, becoming thicker as it descends, instead of being gradually tapered as in life. The tip is not shown and the trunk merges indeterminately into the plinth. What seems to be the remains of a small raised dependent loop, can be seen roughly where the eye of an elephant would be placed, if we were to decide upon the composite nature of this animal, but it is not easy to differentiate exactly. The shape and angle is wrong for a natural eye and it is too close to the so-called trunk. Likewise, it appears too small and badly situated to represent an ear.

At this point it may be pertinent to recall the head of the ram in the Metropolitan Museum, which also shows a similar small raised dependent loop placed within the sweeping curve of the horn and set behind the small pointed ram's face which juts out from above the

123 Side view of limestone kneeling ram from Moenjo-dara, Pakistan. Photograph J. C. M. H. Moloney. Courtesy Department of Archaeology, Pakistan

124 ¾ rear view of limestone kneeling ram from Moenjo-daro, Pakistan. Photograph J. C. M. H. Moloney. Courtesy Department of Archaeology, Pakistan

wedge-shaped ridge representing the frontal hairgrowth. The identification of all three animal statues from Moenjo-daro as being of a
composite nature is mainly based on the presence of the ribbed
frontal feature of the one seen in figs. 123, 124 and which is visible
under the damaged animal's head and explained as an elephant's
trunk.

Our description and illustration clearly indicate that this animal
from the SD Area in Moenjo-daro, and most likely also the other two
from this site, with which it shows so many closely parallelled details,
is a cloven hooved species with characteristics inherent to a breed of
ram and represented with a ribbed frontal appendage running from
the point where the head was struck off down the entire length of the
chest to the surface of the plinth between the knees of the animal.

Figure 123 clearly shows that this ribbed feature broadens
towards the point where the animal's folded frontlegs meet the
surface of the plinth and it merges into the surface without interruption. Rather than pursuing this notion of an elephant's trunk, could
we propose an alternative explanation based on the appearance of
this so-called trunk and aided by the other two statues from Moenjo-
daro, and the ram and mouflon portrayals from Diraz and in the
Metropolitan Museum, previously discussed.

If we can agree that, very likely, the artist did not intend to
portray an elephant's trunk, which may also be substantiated by a
comparison of this animal with the composite monstrosities on the
stamp seals from the Indus Civilization, then there appears to be little
objection to regarding this ribbed appendage as an ill-rendered and
misinterpreted frontal hairgrowth inherent to the early breed of rams
we have been discussing. Such an identification, if accepted, would
seem to be more fitting and would, moreover, place all three animal
representations from Moenjo-daro within the same category of
reclining rams or mouflons with down sweeping horns, a short fat tail,
which is clearly indicated in the case of the SD statue of fig. 124, and a
frontal hairgrowth. Whether and in which way they had originally
been attached to a support or a pedestal can, at present, not be
ascertained.

Although these three stone animal statues are relatively speaking, well modelled, when compared with the clumsy and ill-propor-
tioned seated human statuary, and despite the fact that the one from
the SD Area, in particular, shows a basic anatomical understanding
with a certain amount of sensitivity in the harmony of lines, yet this
remarkable group are not masterpieces of the stonecutters' art.

We have already indicated that the textual evidence from
Mesopotamia appears to suggest a possible Meluḫḫa trade through
the Arabian Gulf in pre-Akkadian times, leaving room for speculation
regarding the date of these three ram portrayals from Moenjo-daro.

Although lack of a proper stratigraphy of the ancient excavation material prevents us, at present, from being too categorical about a date for these statues, the recently revised view on the building history of Moenjo-daro[35] does not militate against a date which would be in congruity with the two stone rams from Diraz, even if they would seem to be later than the latter two. It may, then, suffice to recapitulate that in the lower town of Moenjo-daro in the Indus Valley three ram statues were found which show certain parallels with the two stone figures discovered at Diraz on Bahrain and with others, possibly of a still earlier date, and coming from Iran. Further research may lead to a more satisfactory definition of their appropriate place within the chronological framework of the Mature Harappan period. However, we have to keep an open mind for a possibly higher dating than we are, presently, willing to accept both for the chronology of the Indus Civilization and of Bahrain and for their mutual contacts which may have resulted in a much closer cultural intimacy than would appear from the isolated examples which have constituted the backbone of my speculations.

1. E. C. L. During Caspers, Krispijn, Th.J.H., Gulf Chronology and pre-Sargonid cuneiform records, Ed. Elisabeth C. L. During Caspers, *A Beatrice de Cardi Felicitation Volume* (forthcoming).

2. Robert Englund, 'Dilmun in the Archaic Uruk Corpus', ed. D. T. Potts, *Dilmun. New studies in the archaeology and early history of Bahrain* (Berliner Beiträge zum Vorderen Orient, Band 2), Berlin, 1983, 35–37; also Hans J. Nissen, The occurrence of Dilmun in the oldest texts of Mesopotamia, this volume.

3. Englund, 1983, 35.

4. C. M. Piesinger, Legacy of Dilmun: The Roots of Ancient Maritime Trade in Eastern Coastal Arabia in the 4th/3rd Millennium B.C., Unpublished PhD thesis, University of Wisconsin-Madison, 1983.

5. P. Mortensen, 'Om Barbartemplets Datering', *Kuml*, 1970, 389ff.

6. M. Rice, The Grave Complex at Al Hajjar, *Proceedings of the Seminar for Arabian Studies*, Reprint 1–3, 1970–73, p. 70 (1971 Meeting).

7. During Caspers & Krispijn (forthcoming).

8. Nissen note 2.

9. Englund, 1983, p. 35.

10. G. Weisgerber, . . . und Kupfer in Oman – Das Oman-Projekt des Deutschen Bergbau-Museums, *Der Anschnitt* 32, 1980, 62–110; Weisgerger, 'Archäologische und archäometallurgische Untersuchungen in Oman', *Allgemeine und Vergleichende Archäologie*, Beiträge, Deutsches Archäologisches Institute, Bonn, Band 2, 1980, 67–90; Weisgerber, 'Mehr als Kupfer in Oman – Ergebnisse der Expedition 1981', *Der Anschnitt* 33, 1981, 174–263.

11. Th. Berthoud, *Etude par l'analyse de traces et la modelisation de la filiation entre mineral de cuivre et objects archéologiques du Moyen-Orient (IVème et IIIème millénaire avant notre ère)*, thèse de docteur, Université Pierre et Marie Curie Paris VI, Paris, 1979.

12. During Caspers & Krispijn (forthcoming).

13. B. K. Thapar, 'The Harappan Civilization: Some Reflections on Its Evironments and Resources and Their Exploitation', ed. G. L. Possehl, *Harappan Civilization A Contemporary Perspective*, Warminster, 1982, 4–13.

14. C. E. Larsen, Holocene land use variations on the Bahrain islands, PhD dissertation, University of Chicago, 1980.

15. *Archaeological Investigations in the Island of Failaka 1958–1964*, Fig. (82), middle row right, Ministry of Guidance & Information, Department of Antiquity & Museums, Kuwait n.d.; P. Kjaerum, *The Stamp and Cylinder Seals*, Failaka/Dilmun – The Second Millennium Settlements Vol. I: 1 ('Danish Archaeological Investigations on Failaka, Kuwait'), Jutland Archaeological Society Publications XVII: 1, 1983, 114–115, nos. 267–268.

16. Englund, 1983, 35.

17. Nissen note 2.

18. B. Alster, 'Dilmun, Bahrain, and the alleged Paradise in Sumerian myth and literature', ed. D. T. Potts, *Dilmun. New Studies in the archaeology and early history of Bahrain* (Berliner Beiträge zum Vorderen Orient, Band 2), Berlin, 1983, 51.

19. J. Zarins, 'Steatite Vessels in the Riyadh Museum', *Atlal*, 2, 1978, 65–93.

20. Elisabeth C. L. During Caspers, A Possible Harappan Contact with the Aegean World, *South Asian Archaeology 1983* (forthcoming).

21. E. Porada, 'A lapis lazuli figurine from Hierakonpolis in Egypt', *Iranica Antiqua* Vol. XV, 1980, 175–180, Pls. I–II.

22. Porada, 1980, 180.

23. Porada, 1980, 180.

24. During Caspers 1983 (forthcoming).

25. Elisabeth C. L. During Caspers, 'New Archaeological Evidence for Maritime Trade in the Persian Gulf During the Late Protoliterate Period', *East and West*, N.S. Vol. 21, 1971, 34.

26. E. J. H. Mackay, *Further Excavations at Mohenjo Daro*, New Delhi 1938 (2 vols.), Vol. II, Pl. LXXXIX, no. 376.

27. Compare this spiky tail with S. Corbiau, (II) An Indo-Sumerian Cylinder, *Iraq* III, 1936, 100–103, Fig. 1.

28. T. G. Bibby, 'Tyrebrønden', *Kuml* 1954, 154–163; Bibby, *Looking for Dilmun*, London, 1970, 68; P. V. Glob, *Al-Bahrain – De danske ekspeditioner til oldtidens Dilmun*, Gyldendal, 1968, 70; Elisabeth C. L. During Caspers, 'Cultural Concepts in the Arabian Gulf and the Indian Ocean. Transmissions in the Third Millennium and their Significance', *Proceedings of the Seminar for Arabian Studies* Vol. 6, 1976, 8–39; During Caspers, 'Statuary in the round from Dilmun. Further Evidence for Trade Contact in the gulf', ed. J. E. van Lohuizen-de Leeuw, *South Asian Archaeology 1975*, Leiden, 1979, 58–75.

29. See During Caspers note 28.

30. Rashid, Subhi Anwar, Eine Frühdynastische Statue von der Insel Tārūt im Persischen Golf; Gesellschaftsklassen im alten Zweistromland und in den angrenzenden Gebieten – XVIII. Rencontre assyriologique internationale, Munchen, 1970, *Bayerische Akademie der Wissenschaften, Phil.-Hist. Klasse, Abhandlungen*, N. F. Heft 75, München, 1972, 159–166.

31. The photographs with which the Metropolitan Museum, N.Y. very kindly provided me, are, unfortunately, not meant for publication.

32. For a detailed description see my forthcoming paper More on the Stone Sculpture from Moenjo-daro in Aion.

33. The number is SD 1109.

34. See note 32.

35. *Forschungsprojekt DFG Mohenjo-Daro. Dokumentation in der Archäologie. Techniken Methoden Analysen.* G. Urban, M. Jansen (HRSG). Veröffentlichung des Geodätischen Instituts der Rheinisch-Westfälischen Technischen Hochschule Aachen nr. 34, 1983.

Eyestones and Pearls[1]

THERESA HOWARD-CARTER

In standard Old Babylonian texts from Mesopotamia the word for 'eye' is IGU;[2] this a survival from the earlier Sumerian. The word appears in Akkadian as *inu*[3] in the designation of stones and plants.

In 1936 Campbell Thompson proposed that the term IGI.KU$_6$ referred to the oyster pearl.[4] In 1954 Leo Oppenheim in a review of Ur texts largely from the Old Babylonian period revived the suggestion that IGI.ḪA be identified with the oyster pearl;[5] for the succeeding thirty years this notion has been widely repeated in archaeological literature.

The actual texts which need to be considered in this matter are the *ḪAR-ra=ḫubullu*[6] lexical lists or dictionaries which were composed by scribes to organize the language for teaching purposes in the second millennium B.C. Other pedagogical texts used fuller statements such as the following, taken from tablets found at Sultan Tepe:

1. The name of the stone which looks like a fish-eye is fish-eye stone.

2. The name of the stone which . . . looks exactly like gold, is fish-eye stone.

3. The name of the stone which looks like a snake's eye is snake-eye stone.

4. The stone which looks like the eye of a turtle-dove is love-stone.

5. The name of the stone which looks like a pig's eye is pig's-eye stone.[7]

It seems appropriate here to make reference to some actual biological illustrations:

1. The eye of a grouper fish from the Arab-Iranian Gulf, fig. 125.

2. The eye of an Angel fish from the Gulf.

125 The eye of a grouper fish

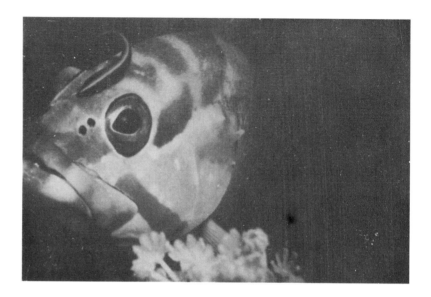

3. The eye of Abyssinian Roller bird from the Arabian Peninsula.

4. The eye of a Slevin's Ground Gecko, also from the Arabian Peninsula.[8]

From this small sampling it should be abundantly clear that none of the actual faunal eyes in any way resembles pearls. Thus we turn to geological possibilities which might be designated eye stones. An obvious suggestion is that natural beach stones in many places do resemble the composition of an eye, and when properly cut could well be referred to as eye stones.

Polychrome stones in the form of eyes occur on many sites in the Near East. These are natural stones, usually of the agate family. The nearest source of agate is in India, and the best gravels are at Ratanpur in Rájpipla, located approximately seventy-five km. from the Gulf of Cambay where trade in cut and polished agates began in an early period.[9] Agum-kakrime II, the ninth king of the Kassites in Babylon, dated after 1600 B.C. speaks of importing eye-stones from the land of Meluḫḫa to be included as gifts to the temple.[10] This suggests a very reasonable connection between Meluḫḫa to the east and the extended land of Dilmun on the west of the Gulf.

Another category of eye stones not identified with any specific fauna are those described by Wilfred Lambert.[11] These also are of banded agate, circular with brown or black pupil and white cornea. They were obviously highly valued objects often inscribed as amulets by kings, bearing dedications to deities, and found in temple votive deposits. It was once assumed that this type of inscribed eye stone was intended to be set into the eye sockets of cult statues, but none has ever been found in convincing circumstances.[12] Other eye stones have found their way into archaeological publications in the bead classification because they are frequently pierced transversely.

The following are a few examples of excavated eye stones, regardless of published classification:

1. Three eye stones among beads from Lothal, India, dated early second millennium.[13]

2. A varied group of eye stones from the temple at Tell al-Rimah in Northern Iraq dated to the Nuzi and Middle Assyrian periods,[14] fig. 126.

3. Eye stones from Failaka found in Bronze Age context.[15]

4. A group from The University Museum, Philadelphia, collected by Hilprecht, fig. 127, is probably from Nippur, as they are all inscribed with the names of Enlil and Ninlil. Also they are most likely to be of the Kassite period, as were the majority of the similar ones published by Professor Lambert.[16]

5. Of the twelve eye stones published from Babylon, three were inscribed with the names of Late Kassite and Neo-Babylonian kings. They formed a small part of a treasure hoard excavated in a Parthian house, but presumed to have been originally in the Esagila Temple.[17]

6. In the spring of 1983 the French Mission to Failaka discovered an important hoard of twenty-five assorted eye stones in a Hellenistic sanctuary by the sea. Here at least three types of natural eyes, fish, bird, and reptile, can be seen, figs. 128, 129.

7. Another striking assortment easily identified with wild life comes from the first century site Qaryat al-Fau in Saudi Arabia.[18]

128,129 Eye stones from Failaka excavations. (Photograph by Jawad al-Najjar)

126 Eye stones from Tell al-Rimah. (Photograph by author)

127 Inscribed eye stones from Nippur. (Photograph by Corethia Qualls)

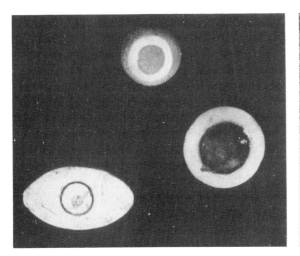

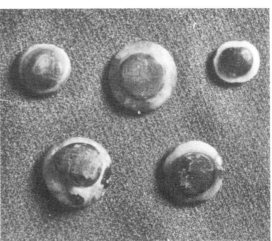

As for oyster pearls themselves,[19] their fragile nature does not give them a great chance of survival. Among the few extant examples are the following:

1. A small string of pearls from Warka dated to the Archaic period *c.* 3000 B.C.[20]

2. A small gilded bronze figurine from Gezer, Palestine, wearing a skirt and a low crown, has pearls set into the eye sockets.[21]

3. At Failaka three have survived in presumed Late Kassite contexts from the Ruler's Villa.[22]

4. Among the small finds from Nineveh, Layard published a gold earring in the form of a ridged barrel with three loops for suspension. A pearl is attached to either end of the barrel.[23]

5. Included among a variety of rich offerings in an Achaemenian bronze sarcophagus burial at Susa was a necklace in three strands of fine irregular pearls. The necklace consisted originally of 400–500 pearls combined with occasional gold disc spacer beads.[24]

CONCLUSION

The earliest textual reference to eye stones must be contained in the Akkadian version of 'The Descent of Ishtar' cited by Lambert; *viz.*, 'Her lap was full of eye-stones' and 'She filled . [. . .] with her eyestones'.[25]

However eye stones make their first appearance in archaeological context somewhat later in the early second millennium at Lothal, a site located appropriately near the finest agate source in the Old World.

Because many of the eye stones are perforated transversely, they were classified as beads, and have thus escaped their proper designation.

The ḪAR-ra=ḫubullu lexical lists compiled also in the second millennium indicate that eye stones were known materially to scholars at that time. It follows that the importation in quantity of eye stones into Sumer and Dilmun begins early in the millennium; this should be dated in the Middle Khalij I period (2100–1800) at the time of the most active commerce in the Gulf. By 1500 B.C. highly prized stones resembling the eyes of fish, bird, and snake as described in the texts are distributed in a number of Mesopotamian sites. The resemblance can be demonstrated by reference to actual fauna.

In the Late Kassite period at the end of the millennium, naturalism is sacrificed to standardization, and a round form with white cornea and brown or black pupil prevails. The preponderance of inscribed examples belong in this period.

As for the oyster pearls, they are found, although rarely, as early as the beginning of the third millennium in archaeological context. Inherent fragility and chemical composition constitute the obvious explanation for their almost complete absence from the corpora of excavated material.

Until now no satisfactory word has been found in cuneiform for pearl. However, more than eight hundred terms in the lexical lists of stones and gems remain to be identified.[26] There is yet hope that we shall find the true word for pearls of the Gulf.

1. In 1979 Åke Sjöberg explained to me the philological impossibility of the 'fish-eye' – pearl association, and I am most grateful for his continued encouragement in the pursuit of this subject.

2. *Chicago Assyrian Dictionary* I/J, p. 45, '*igu*, eye (Standard Babylonian) Sumerian loanword'.

3. *Ibid.*, p. 157, '*inu*, (Akk.) Used in names of stones, plants, and birds'.

4. R. C. Thompson, *A Dictionary of Chemistry and Geology* (Oxford, 1936), 53, n. 2.

5. A. L. Oppenheim, 'The Seafaring Merchants of Ur', *Journal of the American Oriental Society*, 74 (1954), 7, n. 6 (a review article of *UET* V). Oppenheim reasoned that because the word IGI.ḪA in the Ur texts did not include the determinative for stone (NA4) possibly the 'fish eyes' were of another material.

6. H.-h xvi D iii: 7.

7. STT 108: 28; STT 108: 29; STT 108: 31; STT 108: 40; STT 108: 30.

8. E.g. Peter Scott, *Wildlife of Arabia* (London 1981), 90, bottom; 87; 42; 55, middle, from which fig. 000 B reproduced.

9. *Encyclopedia Briannica*. 11th edit.

10. *CAD* I–J p. 158 'eye-shaped pebble (of precious stone)'; E. Unger, *Babylon* (Berlin 1931), 277, 1.39 NA4.IGI.MEŠ Meluḫḫa (VR 33 ii 39).

11. W. G. Lambert, 'An Eye-Stone of Esarhaddon's Queen and Other Similar Gems', *RA* 63 (1969), 65–71. Lambert discusses the Ashmolean acquisition of an Esarhaddon example together with four belonging to Kurigalzu and Kadashman-Enlil and one of Nebuchnezzar II, from the Louvre and previously unpublished. He cites the published corpus as one each from Ipiq-Adad II of Eshnunna, Warad-Sin, Shamshi-Adad I, Hammurabi, Abieshuh, and Sargon II. Sixteen additional Kassite examples belonging to Kurigalzu and Kadashman-Enlil listed are mostly from Nippur.

12. *contra* C. L. Woolley, *Alalakh* (Oxford, 1955), 56 in a description of the contents of a Level IX temple deposit: 'In the basin were found a gold bead, a lentoid agate bead, and the pupil, in white limestone and grey steatite, of the eye of a statue (AT/48/56–58), two small carnelian beads, one of jasper and one of shell, a clay sling-bolt, a fragment of bronze, a lump of lapis paste, and a small clay pot, much crushed'. *contra* also C. J. Gadd, *British Museum Quarterly* 16 (1951–2), 44 in an explanation of *BM.130829* described as an inlaid eye from a divine statue of Shamash.

13. S. R. Rao, *Lothal and the Indus Civilization* (New York 1973), pl. 29 E.

14. Th. Howard-Carter, *Tell al-Rimah: Catalogue of the Objects* (Philadelphia, forthcoming), TR 67, cornea grey, pupil black and raised (Nuzi period); TR 2410, cornea white, pupil orange and raised (Nuzi period); TR 2411, cornea grey, pupil brown and raised (Middle Assyrian period).

15. *KM 1676* (F–3 Settlement); *KM 1688* (F–6 Ruler's Villa).

16. *UM 1.29.442–445, L.29.447*, and no. 6 (without identification, inscribed ᵈEnlil). I am much indebted to Erle Leichty who introduced me to the Pennsylvania material and who, together with Hermann Behrens examined the inscriptions, which attempt to render archaic signs. However, the signs were incorrectly executed with a poor instrument, and actually should be dated in the Late Kassite-Neo-Babylonian period. Enlil is mentioned four times and Ninlil once, which suggests Nippur as a reasonable provenance. From University Museum records we know that at the time Hilprecht collected these eye stones, his excavations were principally in Kassite levels. More

recent excavations at Nippur (D. McCown *et al., Nippur,* vol. I: *Temple of Enlil, the Scribal Quarter, and Soundings,* OIP 78, pl. 30: 10) have added yet another eye stone dedicated to Enlil, this by the Kassite king Kurigalzu.

17. Friedrich Wetzel, Erich Schmidt, Alfred Mallwitz, *Das Babylon der Spätzeit Wissenschaftliche Veröffentlichungen der Deutschen Orient-Gesellschaft,* Leipzig, 62 (Berlin, 1957), 34–36, pl. 42: p. VA 8872; q. VA 8868; r. VA 8878 (inscribed); not inscribed: s, u, aa, ab, ac, ad, ae, af, ag.

18. A. R. al-Ansary, *Qaryat al-Fau: A Portrait of Pre-Islamic Civilisation in Saudi Arabia* (London 1982), 83 top.

19. The non-edible oyster *sp. Margaritifera,* inhabitant of salt water, produces the finest natural pearls. The pearl is formed as a reaction to irritation such as sand grains or miniscule worms which penetrate the bivalve. The animal attempts to protect itself by producing *nacre,* a substance composed of 85% calcium carbonate of the aragonite species, and the remainder organic *conchiolin.* The irritant factor becomes the nucleus for tiny flat pieces of aragonite in a matrix of conchiolin which form around it and also line the shell. The microscopic irregularity of this construction causes a light diffraction resulting in the lustre of the pearl. (Condensed from P. E. Desautels, *The Mineral Kingdom* [New York, 1968], 89–90.)

20. E. Heinrich, *Kleinfunde aus den Archaischen Tempelschichten in Uruk* (Berlin, 1936), 42 and pl. 37 (top).

21. R. A. Stewart Macalister, *The Excavation of Gexer* II (London, 1912), 334–5, fig. 458. I am very grateful to Suzanne Richard and William H. Dever who provided me with the date of Late Bronze II based on known parallels and comparable material.

22. These rare examples are from the uppermost level in the northwest corner of the building.

23. A. H. Layard, *Discoveries in Nineveh and Babylon* (London, 1853), 590, 597. The general provenance of the earring cited by Layard is 'earth and rubbish' in the mound of Kuyunjik. The earring undoubtedly belongs in the first millennium B.C., presumably the second half, but greater precision is scarcely possible.

24. J. de Morgan, 'Découverte d'une sépulture Acheménide à Suse', *Memoires de la Delegation en Perse,* 8 (Paris 1905), 51–52, pls. II, V.

25. Lambert, *op. cit.,* p. 71: CT 15, 47, rev. 52=48 27; rev. 54=48 29.

26. Hermann Behrens, personal communication, November 1983.

The Tarut statue as a peripheral contribution to the knowledge of early Mesopotamian plastic art

FIORELLA IPPOLITONI-STRIKA

The limestone male statue coming from Tarut, and dated to the Fara stage by Rashid[1] seems worthy of reconsideration in some detail. In fact it is so far the most remarkable example of Dilmun statuary in the round; while it demonstrates, with its expressively barbarian appearance, the existence of a local tradition, it may also contribute, thanks to the peculiarity of its style and iconography, to a better understanding of the formative period of Sumerian statuary itself. At the same time it seems that Rashid's dating is not indisputable, insofar as some peculiar features could allow us to date it as far back as the Jemdet Nasr period.

Such a working hypothesis is essentially originated by a feeling I had when I first saw Rashid's article, that there was a certain affinity between the Tarut statue and the prehistoric alabaster statuettes from Tell es-Sawwan; which I published in 1976.[2] I was struck by the fact that the Tarut statue, apart from being nude, seemed to be much more freely rendered than the comparable Early Dynastic Mesopotamian examples: in this respect it seemed to echo the more naturalistic stylization displayed by some nude statuettes from Sawwan. On the other hand, that feeling of similarity would not be significant were it not for the demonstrable evidence of a developmental line coming down from the earliest Mesopotamian stone sculptures of Sawwan to the late prehistoric and Early Dynastic plastic art. The archaism or archaicism of the Tarut state seemed thus able to throw some light on a little known period of Mesopotamian art.

Indeed my attitude is that inasmuch as the Gulf area was from prehistoric times one within a Mesopotamian sphere of interests, where Mesopotamian ideas and materials were probably blended with local peculiarities, and with non-Mesopotamian items,[3] a locally produced piece of art should be expected to answer some requirements of 'provincial art',[4] namely: 1) variation of the models, with a tendency towards simplification and sometimes to primitivism; 2) a certain delay in the reception of these models, plus a tendency to keep them, that means archaicism alongside conservatism; 3) keeping of substrata and easier reception of adstrata, that means the keeping of local ideas alongside a more dynamic attitude to receiving alien items; 4) tendency to eclecticism and contamination. These requirements seem to fit well the Tarut statue, but for a better understanding of it we should bear in mind as well that their contemporary occurrence in a single piece of art may lead to a very deceptive result on the stylistic and chronological point of view.

The above observations may explain why, on one side, Rashid's dating seems to hold good, especially for what concerns the comparison of the head with those of the Dudu and Sa'ud statues and with several isolated heads, all belonging to the realistic trend which succeeded the earlier abstract Early Dynastic style according to Frankfort: same aspect, same slightly raised position;[5] but on the other hand the head's details could fit also a much earlier dating, and the peculiarities of the statue as a whole plus its innovations compared to any Sumerian prototype are such, that considering it simply as a first example found of a nude statue of the Fara stage seems unsatisfactory. On the other hand we should underline that as a matter of fact none of Rashid's comparisons, preceding or contemporary to the Fara stage, seems close to it, including the nude statuette from the Nintu Temple VI at Khafajah, which is its closest though diverging parallel.[6]

On the contrary, if we hypothesize for it an echo of pre or protohistoric concepts, see points 2) and 3), or even a more ancient dating, which should not be impossible on the basis of present evidence from Mesopotamia and from Tarut itself,[7] the statue should become more easily understandable. Indeed while nudity seems new in a Fara context, it characterizes the Mesopotamian and related prehistoric and protohistoric statuettes. Incidentally, nudity seems an item much more important for comparative purposes, inasmuch as the greatest difficulty in comparing prehistoric and Early Dynastic human representations in the round is inherent in the possibilities given by the rendering of the naked body, against the restrictions imposed by the rendering of a dressed body, almost hidden behind the kaunakès and similar garments.[8] That also provides an obvious explanation for my impression that the Tarut statue was closer to the Sawwan statuettes than any Early Dynastic piece was, because it shares such pan-mesopotamian features as emphasized eyes and eyebrows/nose, baldness, bulging shoulders with arms in the attitude of worship, but it shares also the legs separately modelled in the round.

I should exclude an explanation of the statue's innovations (or archaicism?) in terms of local, accidental re-inventions, since I believe that the role of diffusion can never be stressed too much for what concerns the development of culture in the Near East. Accordingly, the old view, that early Sumerian statuary was created suddenly, without any indebtedness to the preceding tradition of clay figurines,[9] seems quite untenable, especially inasmuch as the iconographic links with such tradition acquire new light after the discoveries of Tell es-Sawwan.

It seems thus important for a better understanding of proto-Sumerian statuary as well as of the Tarut statue, to examine in some detail the development of human representations in the round, prior to the establishment of the Sumerian world, emphasizing the existence of a true school of stone statuary at Tell es-Sawwan, long before those known at Tell Asmar, Khafajah etc. indicating when possible the figurines which may represent intermediate stages of transmission.

As an anthropological background to support our artistic approach, we should bear in mind that we have so many clues to continuity in such important different fields as subsistence patterns, temple architecture[10] and possibly religious beliefs and rituals,[11] from prehistory through history in Mesopotamia, that a certain continuity of development in materials related to religious exigencies, as stone and clay statuettes demonstrably were, is accordingly to be expected.

As I have tried to point out,[12] the proto-sumerian character of the stone statuettes found at Tell es-Sawwan is so strong that they seem to represent a new *terminus post quem* for the development of stone sculpture in the round in Mesopotamia. First we should underline that they are not poor evidence: well over one hundred stone statuettes have been found within the graves belonging to the earliest pre-Samarran levels of the settlement, sometimes associated with beads, stone vases and bone implements.[13] Within the overlying buildings a few clay figurines were found, which are much more carefully done, than the average contemporary Mesopotamian clay figurines and seem related to the stone ones from the stylistic and iconographic point of view; a closely related cult value may accordingly be suggested for them.[14]

The stone statuettes, whose heights range from *c.* 3 to 15 cms, give the immediate impression of a fairly homogeneous group, in what concerns the material employed, a soft alabaster and some fundamental technical and iconographical devices,[15] and only with careful analysis do they show a certain variety with several different trends. In fact, alongside flattened squarish shapes we have more soft and rounded types, and even statuettes with a phallic profile (Sawwan nos. 3, 41, 68);[16] moreover, fairly naturalistic pieces occur together with abstract ones (Sawwan nos. 1–2, 14, 24, fig. 130, a, b), and pieces

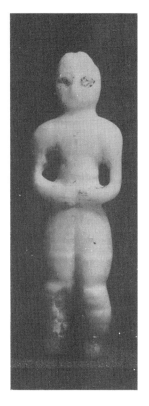
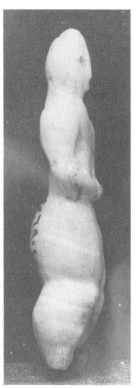

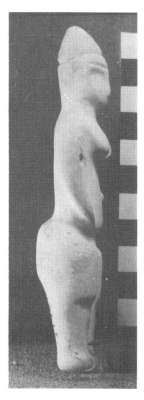

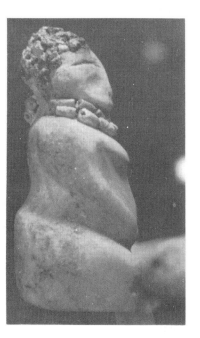

of good artistic quality, sometimes highly refined and polished, occur side by side with pieces which seem dull repetition of a given model, and instances of very poor craftsmanship (Sawwan nos. 46, 84; 18, 25, 33, fig. 131, a, b and 132, a, b, c).

The statuettes are all represented as naked and though the emphasis is on secondary sexual features only, we can share a wide typological range, going from the 'males' with arms bent at waist/breast in an attitude of worship (Sawwan n. 2), to the 'females', in the attitude of Venus (Sawwan n. 47), to ambiguous types (Sawwan nos. 18, 24), and types with arms set along the body, or fused with the shoulders (Sawwan nos. 67, 68; 5, fig. 133, a, b).

The stylistic and qualitative variations, plus the variations in the preservation of the statuettes (some statuettes are mended, some are fragmentary), favour the hypothesis of a fairly long period of use prior to their interment,[17] and remind us of deposits of the late protohistoric and Early Dynastic ages, including pieces of different quality and even broken and mended pieces or fragments, whose variations have been explained by several scholars as due to the intrinsic cult value of the sculptured piece, whatever was the actual outlook at the moment of their burial.[18]

Incidentally, with regards to the external relations of the statuettes, we should mention that, though showing several points of contact, especially with Anatolian and even with Greek materials, apparently transmitted through Jarmo,[19] they immediately characterize themselves as an all-Mesopotamian whole, thus representing real roots for the succeeding Mesopotamian stone sculptures, whose affinities can only partially be explained by the clay intermediaries known and by the employment of a similar material: we should therefore hypothesize missing links in stone still to be found.

In fact, as we go into a more detailed stylistic-iconographical comparative analysis, we notice that, notwithstanding the millennia intervening between the Sawwan statuettes and the earliest Mesopotamian stone sculptures known, we can trace several analogies, both concerning single details and general stylistic trends. I should point out first that an impressive feature shared with Early Mesopotamian plastic art is the 'monumentality' of some Sawwan statuettes: looking at a piece like Sawwan no. 5, it seems difficult to accept that it is a statuette of only 10 cms. It has been stressed accordingly by Porada that the monumentality of Early Mesopotamian sculptures, notwithstanding their reduced dimensions, is 'inherent rather than actual'.[20] Also common is the trend towards fine representations of the standing figure, while the sitting body poses some problems to the artist and is rendered more cursorily or in a seal-like manner.[21] The special meaning relating to cult and the pious preservation of mended or fragmentary pieces, could also be considered, as mentioned above, as a further point of comparison.

130a, b   Stone statuette, Sawwan no 1

131a, b   Stone statuette, Sawwan no 46

132a, b, c   Stone statuette, Sawwan no 84

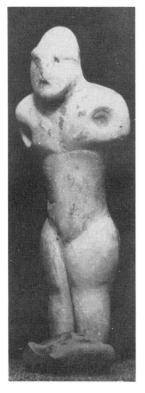 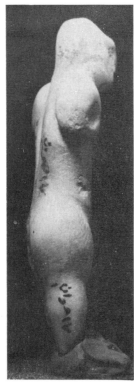 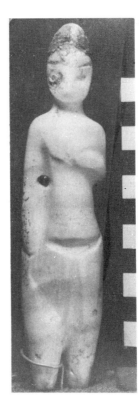 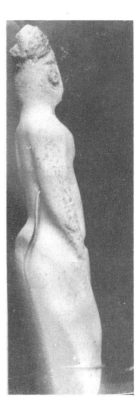

133a, b   Stone statuette, Sawwan
no 5

134a, b   Stone statuette, Sawwan
no 54

To descend to details, a strong thread of continuity is represented by some of the Sawwan heads, which show elaborate, usually bipartite hair-dos, sometimes simply incised, sometimes enriched by the applying of moulded bitumen (Sawwan nos. 86, 59, 54, 57, fig. 134, a, b), which are quite original with respect to any preceding or contemporary stone or clay statuettes.[22] Analogous elaborate bipartite hair-dos are witnessed at Choga Mami and go up until the Warka head and some Early Dynastic ones, while the use of moulded bitumen is witnessed in the Late Ubaid figurines and is a common practice in Early Dynastic statuary.[23] We have also a peculiar analogy in the conical bitumen cap of a Sawwan statuette and the strange conical cap of an Early Dynastic stone statuette of Eridu.[24]

An obvious thread of continuity is the tendency to inlay with bitumen the eyebrows or the eyes, or the rendering of the eyebrows-nose by a continuously drawn 'T' shaped ridge, while emphasizing the eyes by means of bitumen and stone or shell inlays seems a particularly meaningful analogy. Certainly, though the Choga Mami and Late Ubaid clay figurines show emphasized applied eyes in clay, the expressivity of the stone inlaid eyes is quite different and the comparison is thus more striking.[25]

A minor clue to continuity is perhaps given by the bitumen outlined beards of Sawwan stone and clay statuettes and the short beard
witnessed on the painted terracotta head from Kish which was
assigned by Langdon to the Jemdet Nasr period;[26] we may also recall
a short 'linear' beard on an archaic head from Susa.[27] Also of interest
is the semicircular beard carved on a Sawwan statuette, which
reminds us of the 'scheibenformige' beard of a gypsum figurine from
Warka, of late Uruk/Jemdet Nasr period.[28]

The treatment of the upper body of the 'male' statuettes from
Sawwan finds a close parallel in that of the Early Dynastic worshippers, which show a common stylistic and iconographic trend
towards emphasized bulging shoulders, drawing a quadrangular
pattern together with the elbows' angles, whose arms meet over the
waist at varying levels, while the fingers are indicated by horizontal
incisions.

At Sawwan sometimes a squarish abstract block is rendered,
armpit holes are sometimes indicated or, in the more realistic pieces,
there is a tendency to emphasize the armpits that leads as a consequence to the thinning of the waist, while the elbows are neatly
detached from the body.[29] Such a tendency, which has been already
pointed out by Portratz for early Sumerian sculpture,[30] leads to
similar results in both groups of stone sculptures.

It should be stressed that a very close stylization of the upper
body in a squarish block is found in a Jemdet Nasr alabaster statuette
from Telloh, and in gypsum and stone statuettes from Warka of
roughly the same age,[31] while the intermediate links for the more
naturalistic rendering are the fragmentary clay figurines of Samarran
age from Choga Mami and the late Ubaid ithyphallic clay statuette
from Eridu.[32]

As we come to the lower body we have the fundamental dif-
ference already pointed out between the prehistoric nudity of
Sawwan and the prevalence of clothed figures in Early Dynastic times.
The best analogies are thus with the few extant nude figures of the
late protohistoric and Early Dynastic ages including, obviously, the
Tarut statue.[33]

As far as the seated figures are concerned, it should be pointed
out that, though we have no exact parallel, we find an analogous trend
to the rendering of the lower body as an almost undifferentiated seal-
like mass, sometimes with crudely drawn crossed legs; close parallels
are to be seen between the foot-shaped figure Sawwan no. 75 and
several examples with the same peculiar rendering of the lower body:
namely the 'kneeling' archaic stone statuettes from Susa and the one
from Tell Agrab.[34]

Summing up, so close and so numerous and exact seem to be
the points of contact between the prehistoric statuettes of Sawwan

and the protohistoric and historic ones, that some sort of a continuous line of development should be implied. In fact nudity seems to be, aside from the obvious differences accumulated in the course of the millennia, a main item of differentiation, probably implying some kind of evolution in the religious-cult aims of the stone statuettes, and the Tarut male should be seen in this context.

In this connection we should point out that though none of the Sawwan stone statuettes bears evident primary sexual features (what can only partially be ascribed to the limits imposed by the material and seems an item of differentiation with the succeeding tradition of nude stone figures in Mesopotamia) we have in Sawwan the important evidence of a naturalistically rendered clay statuette, showing close relationship to the stone ones, but ithyphallic, which was found at the site in a closely related context. The 'red male' of Sawwan[35] apparently bears traces of a painted beard of the short type, leaving the cheeks free and as a distinctive feature he wears, aside from such ornaments as a necklace and bands at the arms and knees, a girdle, which certainly represents a distinctive trait of mythological naked creatures on seals, and has been rightly pointed out as a fundamental detail of the Tarut statue,[36] fig. 135, a, b.

The problem of the function of nude figures, as opposed to the dressed ones more commonly found in the temples, was pointed out several times by Frankfort. He stressed that some figures, bearded, long haired and wearing girdles, are not to be associated with the nude priests sometimes appearing on reliefs, who are beardless and bald, and a mythological meaning by analogy to the super-men depicted on seals is suggested.[37] Returning to the subject, with regard to the nude worshipper (*More Sculpture* n. 229) Frankfort acknowledges that 'statues of nude men were placed in the temple' and that there were also 'equally exceptional figures of naked women'.[38] Furthermore the problem of nudity is felt by Frankfort to be connected in some way to the clay and marble 'mother goddess figurines', for whom he hazards no interpretation,[39] and that seems important to me, since I believe that these figurines are to be interpreted as a prehistoric inheritance, and that the paucity and pecularity of the nude statues in Early Dynastic times should be interpreted in the same way. Indeed the male statue no. 229, and more particularly the unfortunately fragmentary female statuette (*Sculpture* no. 154), have a very archaic appearance and it is quite possible that they are more ancient than their find level.[40] The same applies to some peculiar pieces which look very like true 'fossils' (*Sculpture* nos. 153, 288–289).[41] As a matter of fact these last would fit better within the context of the Sawwan statuettes than in an Early Dynastic one.

Returning again to the Tarut statue, if its peculiar iconographic

135 The 'red male' from Sawwan

rendering can be considered as hinting either to archaism or to archaicism, we should not dismiss the importance of its extra size as a diagnostic item of archaism. Indeed it has been stressed that the late Uruk/Jemdet Nasr era was marked by the development of a monumental architecture as well as sculpture.[42] To this period belong several near lifesize fragments, including the Brak heads,[43] the Warka head and gypsum relief[44] and the Susa head.[45] Here, particular interest seems to attach to the dating of the 'Ishtar of Nineveh' to the Jemdet Nasr period, as suggested by Nagel,[46] since it is also about two-thirds natural size. At 94 cms the acephalic statue would come very near to the Tarut statue itself, which is 94 cms including the head, and moreover it is nude and shows that kind of rigid naturalism which is not far from the acephalic naked female statuette from Warka,[47] and from the rendering of the Tarut male.

Unfortunately, the originality of this out-sized, bald and clean shaven nude man, though it enriches our knowledge of early Mesopotamian sculpture, does not help much to solve the problem of nude figures, an uncertainty emphasized by its casual discovery. We can only state that since our present evidence shows that nudity was an archaic feature, as we can see in the stone and clay pre and protohistoric statuettes, we should consider the Tarut male as related to this early tradition.

Richer and more continuous evidence would be necessary to throw light on the meaning of nude figures, and their hypothetical prehistoric roots. It is the more regrettable that no assemblage of pre-historic stone statuettes, comparable to those of Sawwan, has been found in the succeeding Mesopotamian and related cultures, though we could argue that the late Ubaid clay statuettes, so similar to those of Sawwan and found likewise in a burial context, and in sacred areas, deserved similar meanings notwithstanding the employ of a 'poorer' or more easily available material. We might also suggest, since stone vessels continued to be in use, and considering that stone statuettes are an easily transportable item, that we just lack the discovery of some special place, such as the Sawwan cemetery certainly was, where similar statuettes may have been deposited after a certain period of use.

New discoveries are able to throw a different light on this subject, even if made in a non-Mesopotamian area, and the Tarut statue could certainly represent a step in the development of the representation of nude figures. In this connection, though it is not unfortunately the expression of a school but just a single find, the stone statuette found at Tepe Yahya in a neolithic layer seems very important.[48] This is akin to the flattened, slender elongated type of 'male' statuettes from Sawwan, and is as well represented with separately drawn legs. Such extra-Mesopotamian extension of the evidence seems important, especially when added to the evidence stressed above of contacts between the stone materials of Sawwan and those found in the 'archaic deposits' of the Susa acropolis, in a sacred area.[49]

We may suggest that these scanty analogies, though perhaps not compelling enough to establish a convincing case, are the visible part of the iceberg represented by religious traditions and related paraphernalia which certainly affected not only the Mesopotamian plain proper but a wide range of related cultures all around it. We may also wonder to what extent the Mesopotamian element was the determining factor and to what extent Mesopotamia itself was influenced and conditioned by the 'peripheral' areas.

In this wide cultural circulation the model I would choose is that of a Mesopotamian heart circulating ideas and materials in all directions and being in turn nourished by foreign ideas and materials. A modern analogy could be seen in the influence of the art and culture of 'primitive', resource-producing areas on industrialized countries. This makes much more relevant to the study of Mesopotamian cultures the analysis of the developments which occurred in the peripheral areas, inasmuch as they can preserve Mesopotamian items, undocumented in Mesopotamia itself, and were probably playing a formative role in the development of some basic Mesopotamian concepts, for instance those relating to death, fertility, music.

Returning to the Tarut statue, to employ the criterion of naturalism or abstraction, or to note the occurrence of single details as main chronological determinants seems inappropriate, since abstraction and naturalism and different 'fashions' in the rendering of head and body seem to have existed together since the very beginning of Mesopotamian art, to have alternated from period to period and even from site to site, and from piece to piece on the same site. We can thus see how a detailed analysis of the Tarut statue shows that, besides the Early Dynastic parallels pointed out, which are quite imperfect owing to its originality and possibly to its marginality, the rendering of most of its features (like shaven heads, eyebrows/nose, eyes, ears, shoulders/arms, girdle, ithyphallism, separated legs, with slender frontal view and somewhat plump profile) is already visible in pre- and protohistoric sculptures.

That is why, without rejecting Rashid's dating, I would also envisage the possibility that the statue could be dated earlier, and even to the Jemdet Nasr period, inasmuch as that was also an age of relative naturalism, with a concern for works of art of a comparatively large size. The possibility would be enhanced by the finding of other artifacts of the Jemdet Nasr period at Tarut Island.

1. S. A. Rashid, *Eine frühdynastische Statue von der Insel Tarut im Persischen Gold',* *Abhandlungen Bayerische Akademie der Wissenschaften,* München 1972, 159–166.

2. F. Ippolitoni-Strika, 'Le statuette in alabastro ti Tell es-Sawwan', *Aion,* 36, 1976, 25–53. We shall refer hereafter to the Sawwan statuettes as catalogued in this work.

3. A. Masry, 'A reply to J. Oates *et al.* "Seafaring merchants of Ur"?', *Antiquity,* LII, 1978, and references given p. 46, 47. On the importance of cultural diffusion and interactional patterns among Mesopotamia, the Gulf and the Iranian Plateau see C. C. Lamberg-Karlovsky, 'The Protoelamites on the Iranian Plateau', *Antiquity,* LII, 1978; P. Amiet, 'Archaeological discontinuity and ethnic duality in Elam', *Antiquity,* LIII, 1979; E. C. L. During-Caspers, 'Statuary in the round from Dilmun – Further evidence of trade contact in the Gulf', in J. E. Van Lohuizen de Leew, ed. *South Asian Archaeology 1975,* Leiden, 1978.

4. For a definition of provincial styles see *Provinciale Arte, Enciclopedia Universale dell'Arte*, vol. XI, 159–160.

5. Rashid 1972, 163; compare E. Strommenger–M. Hirmer *Fünf Jahrtausende Mesopotamien*, München 1962, Pls. 85, 86–87, 104; for the isolated heads see H. Frankfort *Sculpture of the third millennium B.C. from Tell Asmar and Khafajah*, Chicago 1939 (hereafter quoted as *Sculpture*), Pls. 40, 56, 58, 59, 94; ID *More sculpture from the Diyala Region*, Chicago 1943 (hereafter quoted as *More Sculpture*), Pl. 22.

6. *More Sculpture* Pl. 17. The general rendering is close and fairly naturalistic and the rough but expressive outlining of the eyes and of the raised eyebrows, while the beard and the hair-do are differentiating items. As to the nude body, though it shares several features with that of the Tarut statue, it has a different aspect since the legs are thinner in profile and not separated. Also the final aspect is quite different since the Tarut statue is more 'monumental', and shows a more geometrical, cylindrical style.

7. On the evidence of Jemdet Nasr, and perhaps earlier material from Tarut, see M. Golding, 'Evidence for pre-seleucid occupation of Eastern Arabia', *Proceedings of the Seminar for Arabian Studies*, 1974; D. Potts, 'The Jemdet Nasr culture complex in the Arabian Gulf *c.* 3000 B.C.', *Second International Symposium on Studies in the History of Arabia. Pre-Islamic Arabia*. Riyad 1979.

8. Ippolitoni-Strika 1976, 46.

9. A. Moortgat, *Die Kunst des Alten Mesopotamien*, Köln 1967, (hereafter quoted as *Kunst*), 15: 'Von diesem keramischen Stil der vorgeschichtlichen Rundplastik führt kein direkter Weg zum ersten Rundbild historischer Zeit in Mesopotamien'. Indeed apart from the Sawwan stone statuettes and the Choga Mami and Eridu hair-dos (see hereafter), at least the unnaturally protruding lips of several Early Dynastic sculptures are strongly hinting at clay techniques. Furthermore the painted terracotta head from Kish, so similar to the isolated Early Dynastic heads, suggests that there was a true 'sculpture' in clay, of a higher level than the average terracotta figurines, see L. Ch. Watelin, *Excavations at Kish*, IV, Paris 1934, 46 Pl. XXX.

10. J. Makkay, 'The origins of the "Temple-Economy" as seen in the light of pre-historic evidence', *Iraq*, XLV, 1983.

11. F. Ippolitoni-Strika, 'The cult of the Great Goddess from prehistory to Inanna-Ishtar', forthcoming publication.

12. Ippolitoni-Strika, 1976, 44–46, 53.

13. *Ibidem* 28–32.

14. *Ibidem* 39–40; J. Oates, 'The baked clay figurines from Tell Es-Sawwan', *Iraq*, XXVIII, 1966, 146–153.

15. Ippolitoni-Strika 1976, 35–38.

16. *Ibidem*, Diagram and Pls. I–XXVI.

17. *Ibidem*, 48–52.

18. E. Porada, 'The chronological position of steatite carvings', *Artibus Asiae* XXXIII (1971), 330; *Sculpture*, 16: 'In fact, the frequency of ancient repairs of statues . . . shows . . . that old and valued works were often retained along with recent acquisitions'; B. L. Goff, *Symbols of Prehistoric Mesopotamia*, 1963 (hereafter *Symbols*) 265 ff. n. 36.

19. Ippolitoni-Strika 1976, 40–42.

20. Porada 1971, 327; *ID*, 'Sumerian art in miniature', in D. Schmandt-Besserat ed. *The Legacy of Sumer*, Malibu 1976, 107. If we compare, for instance, Sawwan n. 5 and the proto-Elamite lion-Atlas statuette (see E. Porada, *JAOS* 70, 1950, 223–226), we can feel, notwithstanding the iconographical differences, and the small size of both, a similar trend to express power and strength, resulting in a 'monumental' impact.

21. *Sculpture*, 34–36; *More Sculpture, 9*: 'In Mesopotamia, in contrast with Egypt, the seated pose is not appreciated, nor its plastic possibilities exploited'. Compare e.g. *ibidem*, Pl. 45 A–B, and Moortgat, *Kunst*, Pls. 105–108, with the seal-like Sawwan statuettes nos. 80, 82, 86. Incidentally it seems that the squat Sawwan statuette n. 80, with its peculiar cuneiform-like incisions underneath the base, is giving an early

parallel for the amulet/seal in human shape of the Newell Collection, dated to the Jemdet Nasr period (Goff *Symbols*, n. 425).

22. Ippolitoni-Strika 1976, 41–43.

23. J. Oates, 'Prehistoric investigations near Mandali, Iraq', *Iraq*, XXX, 1968, 5–8, Pls. I–III; ID. Goddesses of Choga Mami, *Illustrated London News*, no. 19 (1969). I would also point out that a bipartite hair-do simply outlined by incision (a device often used at Sawwan) is witnessed on an otherwise 'bald' head from Sin Temple IX, *Sculpture*, Pl. 40 C–E: if we accept Frankfort's suggestion, *ibidem* p. 26, that it 'originally may have possessed locks molded in bitumen', and if we consider that several 'plain' heads at Sawwan bear bitumen traces, then we could infer that other 'bald' heads could have worn wigs or some kind of painted hair-do. For an early witness of peculiar stone 'wigs' see P. Matthiae, *Journal of Near Eastern Studies*, 39, 1980, 249–273.

24. Compare Sawwan n. 83 with F. Safar-M. A. Mustafa-S. Lloyd, *Eridu*, Baghdad, 1981, fig. 150–151.

25. G. F. Dales, *Mesopotamian and Related Female Figurines*, 1960, 202, quotes the God Abu as an example of cultural continuity, for the tendency to emphasize the eyes.

26. Ippolitoni-Strika 1976 n. 68 and p. 39. For the Kish head see above note 9.

27. P. Amiet, 'Contribution a l'histoire de la sculpture archaique de Suse', *DAFI*, VI, 1976, Pl. XI 1–2, p. 57 note 47. Though Amiet rightly stresses that short 'linear' beards are never found in Mesopotamia and point to Eastern relations, I should suggest, on the basis of the above quoted examples, that a short beard could have been once depicted with bitumen on some now 'shaven' statues.

28. Sawwan n. 75 and Moortgat *Kunst* Pl. 5.

29. Sawwan nos. 1–6 and *More Sculpture* Pl. 6.

30. J. A. H. Portratz *Die Menschliche Rundskulptur in der Sumero-Akkadischen Kunst*, Istanbul, 1960, 11.

31. G. Cros *Nouvelles Fouilles de Tello*, Paris, 1910, 78; Moortgat *Kunst* Pls. 3–5 and J. Schmidt, *Baghdader Mitteilungen*, 5, 1970, p. 72 fig. 22 a–b. This last statuette, which was found in Uruk levels, spoiled by Seleucid intrusion, is very close to Sawwan's seated statuettes.

32. J. Oates *op. cit.; Eridu op. cit.*, fig. 115 A–B.

33. Rashid 1972, 161–163 and references given. Compare also the fragments from Susa: *Amiet* 1976, 63, Pl. XIX 1–3.

34. *Ibidem*, p. 62, Pl. XVIII 1–6; *More Sculpture* Pl. 45 n. 289.

35. Ippolitoni-Strika 1976, 39–40.

36. Rashid 1972, 161 note 15.

37. *Sculpture*, 11–12.

38. *More Sculpture*, 9, 11-12, Pls. 19–20, 56; *Sculpture* Pl. 91 n. 154.

39. *More Sculpture*, 9 and references given to *OIC*, 17 fig. 63, *Oriental Institute Chicago Monographs*, 19 figs. 24, 28, *OIC* 20 fig. 57. It should be stressed, apart from the Cycladic links suggested by Frankfort *ibidem*, that these hyper-stylized, sometimes fiddle-shaped figures find a counterpart already in Halaf time at Arpaciyah, M. E. L. Mallowan–J. C. Rose, 'Excavations at Tall Arpachiyah', *Iraq*, II, 1935, 99, Pl. Xa.

40. See above note 18. Especially archaic seems the acephalic fat lady n. 154: her armpits are drilled roughly like Sawwan n. 1; also her squarish breasts have an archaic appearance. On the problem of archaism/archaicism of early Susa sculptures see *Amiet* 1976. Also on the subject of the chronology of early sculptures see E. Porada, *Journal of American Archaeology*, 72, 1968, 303, concerning the nude servant from Sin Temple VII: 'it shows a continued tradition of craftsmanship from the Uruk and Jemdet Nasr periods, but with a more lively and interesting posture, greater reliance on outline, a minimum of articulation, and slenderness of forms'. In fact the 'nude servant' finds a close parallel in the above quoted seal from the Newell collection (Goff *Symbols* n. 425).

41. *Sculpture* Pl. 91 K, L; *More Sculpture* Pl. 45 A–B, E.

3333333333

42. Porada 1976 *op, cit.* p. 107.

43. Moortgat *Kunst*, 23–24, Pls. 27–28.

44. E. Strommenger–M. Hirmer 1962, Pls. 30–31; E. Strommenger, 'Kunststeinfragmente aus dem "riemchengebäude" in Warka', *Baghdader Mitteilungen* 6, 1973, 19 ff.

45. Amiet 1976, 61, Pl. XVII 1–2.

46. W. Nagel, 'Frühe Grossplastik und die Hochkultur Kunst am Erythräischen Meer', *Berliner Jahrbuch für Vor- und Frühgeschichte*, 6, 1966, 53–54, Pl. XIV. I should mention that, though Porada, *Artibus Asiae*, 1971, 327 note 20 finds difficult to accept Nagel's early dating for the Ishtar of Nineveh and for the Lion of Eridu, Nagel's dating seems confirmed by comparison with the acephalic female statuette from Khafajah (*Sculpture*, Pl. 91 n. 154) which shows similar high waist and flat breasts, and the body of the Ishtar of Assur (Moortgat *Kunst* fig. 11) is also similar to the Nineveh statue in profile. Also the early dating of the lion of Eridu seems confirmed by J. Schmidt, 'Ein Frühsumerischer Löwe', *Baghdader Mitteilungen*, 9, 1978, 22–24.

47. B. Hrouda, 'Zur datierung frühsumerischer Bildwerke aus Uruk-Warka', *Baghdader Mitteilungen* 5, 1970, 44 Pl. 13.

48. C. C. Lamberg-Karlovsky–R. H. MEadow, 'A Unique Female Figurine', *Archaeology*, XXIII, 1970, 12 ff.

49. Ippolitoni-Strika *Peculiar foreign affinities of Tell es-Sawwan*, forthcoming publication.

Commerce or Conquest: variations in the Mesopotamia-Dilmun relationship

JULIAN READE

Mesopotamian involvement in the affairs of the central Gulf has been a recurrent historical phenomenon, but the further back in time we go, the hazier our records naturally become.[1] The interlocking personal, political and commercial interests behind the involvement, in antiquity, cannot be disentangled without much more documentation than we yet possess. These are far too many variables.

For instance, if we review the physical communications between Mesopotamia and the areas to its east and south, there are three routes which may be followed: by land through Iran, by sea through the Gulf, and by land through Arabia; or there is a combination of two or more of these routes; and, within these broad divisions, many choices may be available at one and the same time. Lapis lazuli from Afghanistan and myrrh from Yemen may have arrived in Mesopotamia from virtually opposite directions by land or may have travelled, side by side, on Gulf ships, Critical factors, besides the obvious necessity both for supplies of goods and for satisfactory markets, include the relative security of different routes, the political relationships between different authorities controlling parts of the routes, and the variable rates of local taxation on goods in transit.

There are specific patterns which recur from time to time, one such being that documented by the excavations at Qal'at al-Bahrain where periods of pre-Islamic settlement correspond broadly to periods of prosperity in Mesopotamia. This is hardly a coincidence, since if there is one thing of which we may be confident in Gulf archaeology, it is that people went on living and working in the Gulf states, with their own indigenous traditions and culture, even at periods when Mesopotamia itself was not prosperous and when contacts were minimal. Evidently, in periods of closer contact, Qal'at al-Bahrain had natural advantages as a commercial or strategic centre. Its prosperity was partly dependent on events in Mesopotamia. Yet it was not the only such place, and many unpredictable circumstances will have controlled which town or harbour was the most important at any particular time.

I wish, then, to look briefly at some of the ways in which contacts between Mesopotamia and Dilmun were established and maintained in periods before the first millennium B.C., stressing some of the alternatives to the straightforward and well-attested pattern of sea trade by merchants. I shall assume that the name Dilmun, applied primarily to Bahrain, was as flexible in its connotations as Bahrain itself has been, embracing at different times a greater or lesser area inland along the southwestern shores of the Gulf. I shall use the so-called Middle Chronology (Hammurapi, 1792–1750) for the second millennium B.C.; this is the normal practice in Mesopotamian studies, but it may well be wrong by over half a century.[2] Dates for the late third millennium are still more uncertain, and for periods before about 2500 B.C. they are based on little more than guesswork.

It is appropriate to start with a reference to the Ubaid period, say 6000–4000 B.C., because Ubaid pottery has been found both in Mesopotamia and far down the Gulf. Radically different interpretations of this evidence have been put forward by Masry (1974: 197–205) and Oates (1977: 232–4): large-scale interaction between the two areas, as against a much smaller scale of Mesopotamian enterprise. One could also adopt an intermediate position, and simply insist that prehistoric cultures, like historic ones, are seldom entirely isolated from their neighbours. It is strange, however, whatever kind of explanation we prefer for the Ubaid phenomenon, that there has not yet been any unequivocal archaeological evidence for Mesopotamian penetration of the Gulf around 3500 B.C., during the Uruk period. Settlements with the distinctive material culture of Uruk Mesopotamia and Khuzestan have been found on the Iranian plateau, in northern Iraq, and on the central Euphrates in Syria, in places where it had certainly not developed locally. Perhaps it is only a matter of time before we have something comparable from the Gulf, and it seems that the philological evidence is already pointing in that direction.[3]

Be that as it may, our evidence for contacts during the early third millennium is plain: for instance, the Jemdet Nasr pottery from the United Arab Emirates (Potts 1981: 35–6). The status of Enzag, god of Dilmun, in Sumerian mythology, may even imply that Sumerian or a related dialect was spoken by some Gulf communities at this time, possibly because it was one of the aboriginal languages of the Gulf area, before the waters rose. If so, an island such as Bahrain would have been one of the likeliest places for it to have survived longest; the odd ancient traditions associating the islanders with Phoenicians or Nabateans (Palgrave 1865: II, 199), while obviously not credible as they stand, may be remote echoes of other linguistic anomalies in later antiquity. At this stage I should like to draw attention also to the work of Mynors (1983). She has studied pottery from the Early

Dynastic Mesopotamian site of Abu Salabikh and the sites of Hili and Umm an-Nar in the United Arab Emirates, using neutron activation for the identification of trace elements, and thin-sectioning for petrographic analysis. Both techniques led to the conclusion, already suggested in some cases by typological considerations, that a significant proportion of the Hili and Umm an-Nar pottery must have come from Mesopotamia. The sherds studied belong to jars, not particularly well made. As Mynors says, 'the implication is that the pottery was not traded for its intrinsic value, but rather that it reflects a large-scale organisation of trade in those commodities which might be supposed to be suitable for transport in pottery containers.' Most of her sherds were of Early Dynastic III types, though some may have been Jemdet Nasr or Early Dynastic I.

The Early Dynastic period ended in chaos in Mesopotamia, around 2400 B.C., and there were further periods of chaos around 2200 and 2000 B.C. Between them we have the more prosperous Akkadian and Neo-Sumerian empires, during which sea trade through the Gulf is well attested and some political involvement is a possibility. The changes in Mesopotamia were presumably reflected in events on Bahrain, in City I at the Qal'ah and possibly early City II. It is after 2000 B.C., however, during what we take to be the main period of City II, that we begin to have more circumstantial evidence on the complexities of the Mesopotamia-Dilmun relationship (see map, fig. 136).

Between about 2000 and 1794 B.C. southeastern Mesopotamia was mainly ruled by kings of the cities of Isin and Larsa; then, until 1763, by Larsa alone. The existence of a flourishing sea trade between the Larsa state and Dilmun is recorded in documents found at Ur, a natural port of entry for goods from the Gulf. Yet there were other states in Mesopotamia, notably Babylon to the northwest. From unobtrusive beginnings about 1900 B.C. Babylon grew into a major power which finally, in 1763, incorporated the Larsa kingdom.

The period during which Isin, Larsa, and Babylon co-existed was not always a peaceful one: there seems to have been a constant process of manoeuvring for position, shifting of alliances, and recourse to war. These circumstances did not prevent inter-city trade, but there must have been periodic difficulties. Yet the demand for Dilmun goods was not restricted to the southern state of Larsa. Babylon, and states yet further north and west, will have been interested too. There was therefore an opportunity for the development of a trade-route which by-passed southeastern Mesopotamia and went straight from the central Gulf either to the kingdom of Babylon or even to other states, such as Mari, further up the Euphrates.

It is in this context that we should view a letter sent by Yasmah-Addu, viceroy of Mari, to Hammurapi, king of Babylon, somewhere

136   Mesopotamia and the Gulf

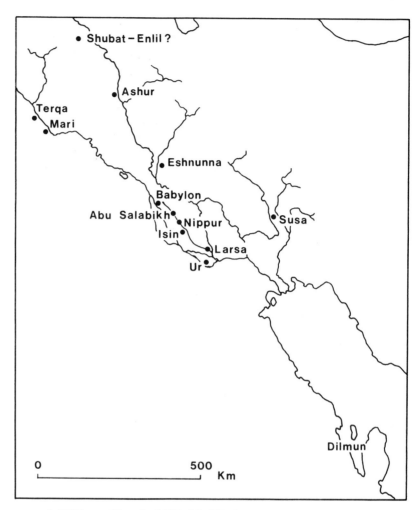

around 1785 B.C. (Dossin 1952: 28–31). It refers to a caravan, sent by Yasmah-Addu[4] to Dilmun, which had been detained on its return journey; it goes on to propose, after a break, that what is apparently the same caravan should proceed to Babylon and remain there until Yasmah-Addu sends for it. One of the men involved is probably a Sutean, a member of a pastoral tribe that seems to have been very widespread (Heltzer 1981). It is clear that a land caravan from Mari to the Gulf must either have passed through Babylonian territory, or through the desert southwest of Babylonia. In either case, when problems arose as they had done on this occasion, it is understandable that the ruler of Mari should have been obliged to rely on the co-operation of the Babylonian king.

There is also another letter of about the same date (Dossin 1950: 50–3) addressed to the same Yasmah-Addu by his father,

Shamshi-Addu, whose capital was at Shubat-Enlil in northeastern Syria and who controlled the great caravan trade from Mesopotamia to Anatolia. This letter refers to messengers from Dilmun, who are being sent back to Mari. Shamshi-Addu is giving instructions to ensure that they are well treated, and return home with a favourable impression. It seems evident that these messengers were interested in more direct contacts between Dilmun and Shamshi-Addu's north Mesopotamian empire, and they are likely to have come by land since Larsa, controlling the port of entry by sea, must have viewed any such developments with serious concern, as detrimental to its own business interests. Moreover, if Mari was sending caravans to Dilmun, whether or not this developed into a regular trade, it is hardly conceivable that Babylon, more conveniently sited, was not doing the same; I do not know of specific evidence for this, however, at this period.

Not being personally familiar with the countryside, I will not propose a precise route by which a caravan of merchants may have travelled from the central Gulf to the central Euphrates, but there are certainly no insuperable obstacles. As a partial parallel, from antiquity, we have the reputed trade between Gerrha and Palmyra, and in more recent times there is the route taken by many European merchants travelling from Aleppo to Basra. Their caravans, in the eighteenth century, went the entire way through the desert, under the protection of the Arab tribes who profited from the deal. It was apparently far better to travel in this way than to risk the exactions and inconveniences of what we may see as the obvious route down the heavily populated Euphrates valley.

If we now turn to Dilmun, at the other end of the land route, we find a situation comparable to that in Mesopotamia. We do not know anything about internal politics in the Gulf area, but we can see that land caravans were potentially bad business for the island of Bahrain, just as they were for Larsa. There was no point in landing goods on Bahrain, whether from Arabia or further east, if they were to be put on ships again for transfer to the Arabian mainland a little further to the northwest. Even if both Bahrain and the mainland were under one ruler, there might have been no obvious objection to two ports, which would then have competed for the long-distance transit trade.

In 1763, thus some twenty years after the Mari caravan, Hammurapi of Babylon captured Larsa and incorporated south-eastern Mesopotamia into his own kingdom. We cannot be sure that this change affected Ur's status as a trading port; the lack of documents may be a chance of excavation. A little later, however, there was a far greater change. In 1741 there was a rebellion against Babylon throughout the south, led by a new king of Larsa. During the suppression of the rebellion, about 1740, Ur was sacked and virtually depopulated; so, apparently, were other cities of the south, and they did not recover. A major tool in the suppression of the rebellion seems to have been water-control (Stone 1977): Babylon, upstream, was in a position to divert the main branch of the Euphrates which flowed through Larsa, but it seems to have been less easy to divert the river back afterwards. This was achieved once, but about 1720, after another rebellion, even the great city of Nippur in the central alluvium seems to have been virtually abandoned. The Babylonian kingdom was reduced in size to what it had been before the southern conquests of Hammurapi. Southeastern Mesopotamia fell into the hands of the so-called Sealand dynasty, a succession of kings of whom very little is known. There is next to no evidence for building activities in any of the old major cities, and it may well be that, as in the ninth century A.D., improvident tinkering with the rivers had transformed the landscape, creating Sealand marshes over a much wider area than before.

These developments are likely to have been disastrous for the sea-borne trade between Mesopotamia and the Gulf. They would not have made it impossible, but there was a great difference between trading out of a prosperous city, Ur, with established communications and contacts, and re-establishing relations after political and socio-economic crises had left the land impoverished and the river routes, probably, very insecure. So here again we have an incentive for land trade, direct to the kingdom of Babylon. Leemans (1960: 141–2) cites a Babylon text of 1729 which refers to some rations issued to men of Dilmun, but its context is unclear.

There may even be evidence for the entry of oriental goods into Mesopotamia as late as about 1700–1600 B.C. This comes from Terqa on the central Euphrates, in the shape of a pot containing cloves; the identification of these spices was announced by G. Buccellati at the 1982 *Rencontre assyriologique internationale* in London. It has been argued, however, that the Terqa material should be dated substantially earlier in the second millennium (Tubb 1980); this matter, important as affecting the entire chronological placement of the Hana dynasty in Terqa, will eventually be settled by further consideration of the associated finds.

The presence of these cloves, whatever their exact date, serves to underline the impressive range of Indian Ocean trade in the early second millennium. Of course there are two methods of long-distance distribution: direct contacts, for instance by sea, and indirect contacts through what can be a host of middlemen. When as here we have surprising botanical specimens, we have to reckon with the additional possibility that they have not grown in the area where the plant is or is thought to be native, but in an area to which it has spread, through human intervention or otherwise. Nonetheless these cloves are, in some degree, evidence for direct or indirect contact between Mesopotamia at one end and, at the other end, the place where cloves are native, the latter being according to the botanists not India or Africa where they are commercially grown now, but the Maluku islands of Indonesia, the Moluccas. We are reminded of the eastward spread of sorghum from Africa to India. Although the tangible evidence is still meagre, there seems no intrinsic reason why there should not have been coastal traffic all along the shores of the Indian Ocean, from Africa to Indonesia, in this period, with the Gulf trade as one tributary. It is not inappropriate to mention here the remarkable fact that the language and aspects of the traditional culture of the Malagasy Republic, the great island of Madagascar, are Indonesian too; the language has its only cognate in the Moluccas. No one knows when that migration happened, except that it must have been an extremely long time ago; but even if we cannot push it back to 2000 B.C., it is remarkable as an example of what can happen. Now, it is interesting to note that the place named Meluḫḫa, in Mesopotamin records of the third millennium B.C., is an area reached through the Gulf, whereas in the first millennium it is beyond Egypt. It has been thought that this seeming contradiction, as with Ethiopia in Greek, results from the fact that Africa and India were both exotic places, with dark inhabitants and tropical goods. Yet we might more broadly think of Meluḫḫa as meaning the lands of the Indian Ocean, from as far away as the Moluccas even perhaps to Malagasy, as we ourselves use increasingly vague nomenclature as we refer to places that are further and further away from home. For Europeans the term 'Indies' came to mean anywhere between the Caribbean and Indonesia, and there may have been no greater inconsistency in Mesopotamian usage of the term 'Meluḫḫa'.

If now we return to Qal'at al-Bahrain, and compare the archaeological evidence from that site with what we know from Mesopotamia, we find that City II is abandoned some time in the first half of the second millennium, about 1750 according to Bibby (1970: 378). Clearly we cannot date the abandonment with any precision, but it does fall within a period during which, it seems, there was no particular reason for merchants from abroad to visit Bahrain at all. Any revival would tend to be dependent on the exploitation of Bahrain's special insular position, and that implies a revival of trade or other activities by sea. This brings us to the Kassite involvement in the Gulf, which took an entirely different form to that of the Larsa kings.

The Kassite kings of Babylonia, who probably originated in the Zagros region, overthrew the Sealand dynasty and gained control of southeastern Mesopotamia in the middle of the fifteenth century B.C. or a little later. Our earliest evidence for a revival of the area's prosperity comes from the reign of Karaindash, who built at Uruk around 1415; another king, Kurigalzu I, about 1400, restored buildings at Ur, and this city remained part of the Kassite dominion into the twelfth century. A Kurigalzu also worked at Eridu, near Ur, a city whose only importance by this time was as a cult-centre of immemorial antiquity. These activities mark a deliberate attempt to reconstruct the southern cities and integrate them into the Kassite empire. In the process of eliminating the Sealand dynasty, the Kassites will also have come into contact with its southern neighbours, and will have had their attention focussed on Dilmun.

Archaeological evidence for Kassite involvement in the Gulf is now accumulating. The Danish excavations at Qal'at al-Bahrain produced, in City III, besides some texts that remain unpublished (see Glob 1968: figure facing p. 94), pottery that was distinctively Mesopotamian Kassite in shape and ware (Bibby 1970: 137). Recently we have had the excavation of a purple dye factory in Qatar, and there too we are told of Kassite pottery. If Kassites did establish outposts in the central Gulf, they presumably came first by sea and started with island sites; that is a logical procedure. On the other hand, specific textual evidence for Kassite rule in the area has been lacking, and there has been no satisfactory evidence for the date of their activities. While Cornwall (1952) suggested that the Kassites did gain political control, Oppenheim (1954: 16) was dubious whether the two texts cited by Cornwall were evidence for anything more than commercial relations.

There is, however, a cylinder-seal in the British Museum, fig. 137: BM 122696,[5] which has long remained unpublished though occasionally mentioned in public, and which helps add substance to Cornwall's proposal. The seal has a long text giving the name and ancestry of a man called Ubalisu-Marduk, son of Arad-Ea, grandson of Ushurana-(. . .), and great-grandson or possibly a more remote descendant of Usiananuri-(. . .) who bore the title *shakkanakku*,

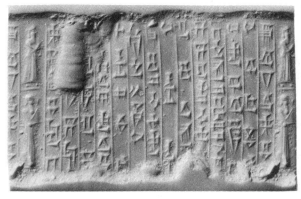

137 Seal (BM 122696), with seal impression, naming a Kassite viceroy of Dilmun. Length 4.2 cm

viceroy, of Dilmun. The seal-owner, Ubalisu-Marduk, held an office under a king named Kurigalzu, and one might hope that one could date him approximately. There is no internal evidence, however, to tell whether it is Kurigalzu I, about 1400 B.C., or Kurigalzu II, about 1332–1308, or even a Kurigalzu III whose existence has sometimes been mooted though it seems decreasingly probable (Brinkman 1976: 205). The name Ubalisu-Marduk, either son of Arad-Ea or belonging to the Arad-Ea family, occurs on other documents too (Lambert 1957: 112), but we cannot be sure we are dealing with the same man. We therefore have to fall back on general considerations, and find that, if Ubalisu-Marduk was a contemporary of Kurigalzu I, then his forebear was viceroy of Dilmun four or even five generations previously; at twenty years per generation, that would take him back to 1480 B.C., long before the Kassites even controlled southeastern Mesopotamia. On the other hand, if Ubalisu-Marduk lived under Kurigalzu II, then his forebear was viceroy of Dilmun in a period that may have centred around 1420–1410. This is, in broad terms, the very time that Karaindash was building at Uruk and Kurigalzu I at Ur: a period of triumph and expansion, during which, for example, we have the first evidence for diplomatic correspondence between the Kassites and the rulers of Egypt. It was probably in this phase, then, that Usiananuri-(. . .) ruled Dilmun, with the grand title of *shakkanakku* implying control of a very important area. We may observe that, like many officials under the Kassite dynasty, he and all the members of his family had local Mesopotamian names, in the Akkadian language.

With Usiananuri-(. . .) in mind, we may now turn back to Cornwall's two texts. They are letters addressed to one Ililiya, governor of Nippur during part of the reigns of Burnaburiaš II (1359–1333) and Kurigalzu II (1332–1308) (Landsberger 1965: 76–7). The letters, of which only an unsatisfactory translation has been published, are from a man named Ili-ippashra. He addresses the governor of Nippur as 'brother', which implies equal status, and the letters are partly concerned with high state affairs. The greetings formula invokes Enzag and Meskilag, gods of Dilmun, which implies that that is where they were written. So we probably should accept Ili-ippashra as governor of Dilmun. How long he retained this position is questionable, as he is much concerned about enemies carrying off all the stores of dates, and wonders whether they will overrun all the settlements. Here the evidence from Qal'at al-Bahrain is again pertinent, since Bibby (1970: 346) refers to a radiocarbon date from a storeroom full of burnt dates in the Kassite level. The date, apparently uncalibrated, is 1180 ± 110; by current calibration this would lie, with 95% probability, in the range 1670–1120 B.C., but obviously points near the middle of this range are the most probable, suggesting the fifteenth or fourteenth century. In fact, from about 1300 B.C., the Kassite dynasty encountered various difficulties, and may well have lost its Dilmun province before then.

Nonetheless this would not necessarily have meant that all contact between Dilmun and Mesopotamia was broken. One passage in one of Ili-ippashra's letters mentions sending a Sutean woman across the sea, apparently, direct to Babylon, and a land route could well have been operating. If Qal'at al-Bahrain was the Kassite provincial capital, then the trading centre is likely to have moved elsewhere when the Kassites left. That some degree of contact persisted, even through the twelfth-ninth centuries B.C. when Mesopotamia was again, and repeatedly, in a state of chaos, is suggested by a list of goods available in the southern marshes in 850, when an Assyrian king collected them as tribute: silver, gold, tin, copper, elephant tusks and hides, ebony, and sissoo wood (Hulin 1963: 55–6). There are uncertainties about the translation of the woods, but these things, whatever their ultimate origin, were certainly not all local products.

Thirty years ago we knew next to nothing of Gulf archaeology. Today we have a rough chronology, and the Mesopotamian correlations have been vital in establishing it. Yet there are deficiencies in the Mesopotamian record too, and we are perhaps reaching a stage when archaeological work in the Gulf will help us to understand what was happening in Mesopotamia itself. The relationship between the two areas was an exceedingly complex one, and we have to be careful in our generalizations. We need to know much more, for instance, about the blank periods, when the evidence fails us; but, given the quality and quantity of archaeological work now in progress, in Bahrain and elsewhere, we may not have to wait too long for some more answers.

1. This article is, with minor changes, the same as the one distributed at the conference.

2. Thus the latest study (Huber 1982) opts for Hammurapi, 1848–1806; but, in view of the long history of this question, it is difficult to believe that we have yet heard the last word.

3. See the paper by Hans Nissen in this volume.

4. Butz (1983: 144) supposes that the caravan was sent by Ishme-Dagan, the brother of Yasmah-Addu, and presumably therefore that it came from the Ashur region rather than from Mari. Certainly Ishme-Dagan will have been interested in trade; but the term *ahuka*, 'your brother', in line 4 of this Mari letter, may be understood more naturally as referring to Yasmah-Addu himself rather than to Ishme-Dagan.

5. I am much indebted to J. A. Brinkman for permission to make use of his transliteration of the text on this seal; I have also had the benefit of discussing it with W. G. Lambert.

The occurrence of Dilmun in the oldest texts of Mesopotamia

HANS J. NISSEN

Almost from the beginning of the excavations in the ruins of the old city of Uruk in Lower Mesopotamia in 1928, work has concentrated on uncovering large parts of the temple area of that city, the holy district of Eanna. The centre of this area was marked well into the first millennium B.C. by the presence of a stage-tower with presumably a temple on top, a so-called Ziqqurrat. Such stage-towers, or raised platforms, were the landmark of nearly every major Babylonian town from the end of the third millennium B.C. on. As elsewhere in Uruk the sacred tradition is older at that particular place since we know of a succession of older terraces at the same spot dating to the earlier centuries of the third millennium B.C. Still earlier, the same area was occupied by a large assemblage of buildings and open spaces, undoubtedly of cult importance. Thus from the archaeological evidence the cult tradition can be traced back to the second half of the fourth millennium B.C.

In spite of this continuity, at one particular point the configuration of the area was altered dramatically, when around 3100 B.C. the complex was transformed from the situation of wide-spread cult installations on ground level to that of one temple on top of a raised platform. We do not have the faintest idea of the reasons for this complete renewal but we can follow the actual procedures. Special efforts seem to have been made to transform the entire area formerly occupied by cult installations outside what was to serve as building ground for the new terrace into a moderately even tract. After the old buildings were torn down the remaining wall stumps were filled in with rubble from the old buildings, while in other places courtyards, building remains and open spaces were filled up with large amounts of rubbish which was brought in from somewhere else, probably still from within the temple area.

It was in these various layers and accumulations of debris covering large parts of the Eanna district that over the years more than four thousand clay tablets and fragments were found. Their surface was covered with archaic looking signs, consisting of incised or imprinted lines which soon proved to be the ancestors of the later cuneiform script.

With the exception of a handful of tablets, unfortunately no tablets have been found in definite relation to specific buildings, nor can they be assigned to specific building levels on the whole. Only in few cases is it possible to decide on the date of the deposit of the rubbish containing the tablets. This date then would give us a *terminus ante quem* for the tablets found in that context. Since we cannot determine the span of time which elapsed between the use of the tablets and the final deposit we cannot be sure about the date when these tablets were written.

There are some exceptions to this general rule. In the course of the re-organization of the Eanna district by the end of the so called Late Uruk period one of the early buildings with a large courtyard, the so called but wrongly named 'Red Temple', had been torn down apparently with the intention that it should be replaced by a new one. In the course of the widespread raising and levelling mentioned before, the area over the remains of the 'Red Temple' was raised by *c.* 2 m before that new building was erected. The raising was accomplished by the deposit of debris containing among other items several hundreds of discarded clay tablets. The time of the deposit thus can be dated safely to have anteceded the oldest building phase of Level III in Eanna, or Jemdet Nasr period. That means that those tablets had been written some time before the re-organization of Eanna. If we put that into our chronological framework this means that the tablets certainly must be older than the Jemdet Nasr period. Just how old they are we cannot be sure, but it may be a good approximation if we assign these tablets a date of around 3200 B.C.

These are the oldest texts recovered from Babylonia, and they antedate any other kind of writing in any part of the world. There are strong indications that in fact they do represent the oldest stage of writing, meaning that for also Babylonia they should be considered the absolute beginning.

The texts found in the deposit just mentioned show a strong internal consistency in the shape of the signs. They set themselves apart from another large group of tablets which by comparison show more developed forms of signs. Also these exclusively come from layers of debris and thus cannot be dated stratigraphically. But the more developed forms of signs indicate that they are to be considered younger. We can thus distinguish two chronologically distinct groups of texts within the corpus of the Archaic Texts from Uruk, which we attribute to the latest phase of the Late Uruk period and the Jemdet Nasr period respectively.

When it comes to the contents of the texts we are still at a stage when we can speak only in approximate terms. To be sure, we now have reached a point at which we can identify over 70% of the signs of the Archaic Texts from Uruk with signs of the later cuneiform script; thus we can try to 'read' some of these tablets to some degree. But since these texts should be compared more with scrap notes, noting only catch words without indicating the syntactic relations, rather than to real texts, the sense of the texts still eludes us in most cases. One distinction concerning their contents can be made, however, which is obvious from the different organization of the tablets. The majority invariably show preceding the sign or signs within one case, or compartment, a number of round or elongated-round impressions. They so much resemble in shape and usage the numerals of the cuneiform system that it has long been recognized that they represent numbers. Something is counted and its result is written down. This cannot be anything but a clear indication that these tablets belong to the economic sphere in the widest sense. Such tablets account for more than 80% of the whole corpus of the Archaic Texts from Uruk, and they are found in both chronological groups of texts.

There are no texts which display no numerical signs at all at the opening of each case. Yet, in distinction to the tablets just mentioned, which I will refer to as administrative or economic texts, there are a large number of texts each case or line of which is preceded by the sign for '1'. Not only is it highly unlikely that they should be economic texts as well, but from later periods we know that this is the way all kinds of lists were written, including lexical lists. In fact, in many cases it can be shown that this category of texts have their exact duplicates in later texts of the middle of the third millennium B.C., and indeed can be classified as lexical lists. According to internally meaningful categories words, titles or names are enumerated and arranged according to principles which more often than not still elude us. Among those lists we note a list of titles and professions, of metal objects, of tree names, of textiles, of city names and various kinds of animals.

Some parts of these lists are found already among the tablets of the older group, while the majority belongs to the younger group. Although with some marginal variations these lists show a remarkable consistency throughout the long time of their existence; one has to assume that from the beginning the concept of such enumerations did exist and that they existed even before they were put in writing.

If we now turn to the question of whether and in what context the name of DILMUN is attested in the Archaic Texts from Uruk we have to bear in mind the old age of the lists. As has been discussed elsewhere[1] the question of the identification of the sign for DILMUN has been answered positively. The sign occurs in three lists and in eleven administrative documents. Except one administrative text and one fragment of the professions list they all belong to the younger group of tablets.

In the Archaic Professions List DILMUN appears in line 85 in connection with the professional name ZAG, or enkux, for which a meaning of 'tax collector' is proposed. The lines 82–85 give composites with enkux, starting with gal.enkux, perhaps 'head of the tax collectors', followed by the 'harvest tax collector' and the 'tax collector of the land(?)'. Finally, we find the 'tax collector of DILMUN'. Dilmun here stands in parallelism to things on which taxes could be levied. Does it stand here for 'foreign relations'? On the other hand, the lists often can be shown not to be logical; the parallelism need not be significant.

In the Archaic Metals List we again find DILMUN in a line which due to a common denominator proves to be part of an internally cohesive group of entries. The entire list starts out with a sequence of metal vessels and continues with metal tools and weapons. This group opens with a sequence of various daggers, continues with various groups of unidentified objects and from line 23 on shows five entries with the common denominator tun2, 'axe'. The lines read in tentative translation: 'big axe', 'two-handed axe', 'one-handed axe', 'x-axe' and 'Dilmun axe'. Here most likely the differentiation bears on differences in shape, size or function; the 'two-handed axe' may mean a double-edged axe, for instance. Again, if seen as a coherent context DILMUN may be used here as equivalent to 'Dilmun-type axe'. I do not think it could just refer to the provenance of an axe but rather to specific qualities.

The third occurrence could have been the most interesting one, if the text were fully preserved. It is contained in what was a compilation of geographical names. Unfortunately, the text is very fragmentary and badly preserved. One other line of the text may be reconstructed to have mentioned the name of the city of Zabalam. The context in which DILMUN appears is destroyed. Yet, it is clear that DILMUN here is used in a geographical sense.

Unfortunately, also the administrative documents containing the sign for DILMUN are mostly very badly preserved. Thus in five texts the sign is either barely recognizable or without recognizable context. One additional text has DILMUN in contact with the sign for copper, without further specification since the rest of the text is broken off.

Even if the context were better preserved, however, we could not be more precise. For instance, three texts clearly are dealing with textiles but only one of them has a context which might be interpreted; tentatively it reads '1 bale of DILMUN garment'.

Another text is almost completely preserved but is of limited accessibility because it contains only three cases. According to the subscript it deals with a distribution of food-stuff: 30 x-Dilmun are given to, or taken from some official. The meaning is unclear.

The last text to be mentioned here again deals with the distribution of food items. Among other commodities distributed we find a section dealing with the distribution of milkfat. Six officials are mentioned as recipients with only their titles given. Far from being able to understand the entire context it is highly interesting that as the title following the one containing the sign for DILMUN we find the composite sign for *namesda*, the title of the opening line of the Archaic Professions List. It is supposed that this title represents the highest official. Probably without all connotations of the terms 'ruler' or 'king' it nevertheless should be fairly close. The preceding line contains a number of signs which if translated literally could mean 'the prince of the good Dilmun-house (or temple)'. The exact meaning is elusive. To sum up, from our texts we do not get an adequate picture of the relations of Babylonia, or the city of Uruk, with Dilmun. On a general level, however, we can conclude that not only did such relations exist already by the end of the fourth millennium B.C., but that these contacts apparently were not restricted to trade. To be sure, the exchange of metal and textiles may represent the main ties, but the existence of titles containing Dilmun in their name in normal Babylonian contexts like the Professions List point to much closer mutual contacts that would be sustained by occasional trade. The same is suggested by the existence of DILMUN in generic designations for kinds of textiles or metal tools. We certainly are entitled to assume that these relations had existed long before the emergence of writing.

Unfortunately, the paucity of occurrences of DILMUN in the Archaic Texts from Uruk will not allow us to be more specific even if one day we can master the reading of the early administrative texts. But the sheer existence of this geographical term in the oldest written documents is meaningful enough.

1. Robert K. Englund, 'Dilmun in the Archaic Uruk Corpus', in *Dilmun*, D. T. Potts (ed.), Berliner Beiträge zum Vorderen Orient Band 2, 1983.

This article is based on the files of my project 'Decipherment and Edition of the Archaic Texts from Uruk' which has been supported by the German Research Society, the Volkswagen Foundation and the Free University of Berlin. I am indebted to my former and present collaborators, Dr. M. W. Green and Mr. R. K. Englund.

A complete sign list and an edition of the lexical lists will be published in the near future. For particular problems see: M. W. Green, 'A Note on an Archaic Period Geographical List from Warka', *Journal of Near Eastern Studies*, 36, 1977, 293ff.; M. W. Green, 'Animal Husbandry at Uruk in the Archaic Period', *Journal of Near Eastern Studies*, 39, 1980, 1ff., M. W. Green, 'The Construction and Implementation of the Cuneiform Writing System', *Visible Language* XV, 1981, 345ff.; H. J. Nissen, 'Bemerkungen zur Listenliteratur Vorderasiens im 3. Jahrtausend', *La Lingua di Ebla*, L. Cagni (ed.). Istituto Univ. Orientale Napoli, Series Minor XIV 1981.

The Deities of Dilmun

KHALED AL NASHEF

The cuneiform sources mentioning the deities of Dilmun are quite varied, both in respect of their nature and of their provenance. On the one hand, these deities are found both in Mesopotamian texts of various types, beginning in the Ur III period and in the very few sources originating from the area of Dilmun itself.[1] On the other hand, they appear in yet another area, namely Susa. Hence a study of these deities requires a critical approach in dealing with different traditions reflecting a complex process of interaction and transmission of cultural elements. Though this study does not claim to stand up fully to this difficult requirement, it hopes, nevertheless, by marshalling a complete corpus of the material involved and by scrutinizing opinions expressed on the subject to date, to be a modest contribution to the study of the intricate question of religious syncretism.[2]

It is clear that one should take as a point of departure the sources coming from Bahrain and Failaka, since these two islands – the latter to a lesser degree – represent the two most important centres of Dilmun known to us. The most significant source from Bahrain is undoubtedly the basalt stone found there in 1879. The stone bears an inscription (No. 1) dated to the Kassite period, in which a palace of a certain Rīmum – presumably a local governor – is mentioned. Rīmum refers to himself as the 'servant of Inzak of Agaru'. The deity 'Inzak of Agaru' occurs in a similar manner in one of the seal inscriptions from Failaka (No. 15). Agaru, designating most probably a geographical region,[3] would have been, from a Dilmunite point of view, the original home of the deity Inzak. The toponym Agaru has already been identified with medieval Hağar in the area of al-Hasā in Eastern Arabia.[4] Further support for this identification is presented below.

As for the stone inscriptions from Bahrain, one has also to mention a small fragment bearing an inscription of a priest in the service of a deity, whose name is not preserved (No. 2). Among the clay tablets found at Qal'at al-Bahrain there is one from the Ur III or

Isin-Larsa period, which mentions four Amorite personal names (No. 3),[5] which do not contain theophoric elements. Another tablet from the Kassite period seems to refer to two divine titles: 'Lady of Bread' and 'Lady of Drinking' (No. 4). We do not know to whom these titles refer.

A late copy of an Old Babylonian inscription, which may have originated on Bahrain or Failaka, seems to mention Inzak of Dilmun (No. 5). The inscription – if its reading and interpretation should prove to be correct – is to my knowledge the only evidence from Dilmun itself defining explicitly Inzak as the deity of Dilmun.

The other Dilmunite texts I know come from the island of Failaka.[6] Almost exclusively the texts represent inscriptions on stone or clay vessels and seals. It is difficult in some cases to ascertain the date of these inscriptions, but it seems that the majority of them date to the Kassite period. Possibly of an early date (Isin-Larsa) is an inscription on a red Barbar sherd mentioning the deity Inzak (No. 6). One inscription contains a reference to the 'Great House of Insak' (No. 7). This piece of information allows us to conclude that the main temple of Failaka was dedicated to the deity Inzak.[7] A similar inscription seems to refer to the same temple, but the occurrence of Inzak therein is unclear (No. 8). A person, whose name or title seems to contain the theophoric element ^{d}in-za (sic), is mentioned on a steatite bowl possibly dedicated to the god Enki (No. 9).

Turning to the inscribed seals, we have a circular stamp seal whose owner was presumably a priest of 'Inzak of Agaru' (No. 15). A certain Riqqatum (?) dedicates his stamp seal to the god Enki (No. 16). This is relevant to the question of the relation between Inzak and Enki as we shall see later. A difficult seal inscription published only in transliteration allegedly contains a reference to Inzak, as well as a dubious mentioning of Muati, a Nabû name connected with Dilmun according to a later lexical list (No. 17).[8]

The inscriptions on cylinder seals mention the following deities known to us from Mesopotamia: Enki (No. 28), this deity with his spouse Damgalnuna (No. 19), Marduk (Nos. 23, 25), and finally Adad (No. 27). The mere occurrence of these deities on seals from Failaka does not mean of course that they were also worshipped there. The case of Enki and Damgalnuna is, however, different. The question of the relation between Enki and Inzak will be dealt with below.

Let us now consider references to Dilmunite deities in Mesopotamian sources. Despite the fact that Dilmunite deities are already mentioned in early sources, I shall begin with relatively late references (OB, Kassite), which are in a way directly related to Dilmun, and could be taken as reflecting an authentic Dilmunite tradition.[9] A certain Insak-gāmil is mentioned among Dilmunites receiving deliveries of barley according to a document from Lagaba

(No. 29a). Another Dilmunite with the name *I-din-*^{d}*Nin-In-za-ak* (No. 30) occurs in two OB texts from Ur, a city not far from the general area of Dilmun. As we are dealing here with Dilmunites, it is not surprising to find the writing *In-za/sa-ak*, which we know from indigenous Dilmunite sources discussed above. I cannot offer a convincing explanation for the combination nin[10] with DN, that is, 'Lord Inzak'. The combination may reflect an attempt towards assimilating a foreign deity by adding nin, a common element in Mesopotamian divine names.

We now turn to the two famous Kassite letters originating from Dilmun. I do not have to point to their historical importance, as P. B. Cornwall has dealt with them extensively, and confine myself therefore to the main points relevant to the question of Dilmunite deities. Ilī-ippashra, the writer of the two letters, informs Ilīya in his first letter of certain raids conducted by groups of Ahlameans. What concerns us here is the greeting formula, found in both letters: 'May Inzak and Meskilak, the gods of Dilmun, protect your life' (Nos. 31.1, 32). As is well known from Mesopotamian letters, the place referred to in the supplication of the addresser is the place (city) where the addresser is. The locality, here Dilmun, most probably refers to a city.[11] No matter where this city is located, the greeting formulae give us clear evidence that the main deities of Dilmun were Inzak and Meskilak. This conclusion is obviously enforced by the occurrences of the male deity Inzak in Dilmunite sources, as well as by those later Mesopotamian references mentioning Inzak and the female deity Meskilak side by side. In addition to this significant information, the first letter makes allusion to a certain goddess, whose temple was old and in need of repair. Ilīya seems to attribute the attacks of the Ahlameans to the anger of this goddess over the neglected temple. The name of the goddess begins with the element nin 'Lady' (No. 31.2).

Another piece of evidence from the Kassite period should also be mentioned at this point. It is the woman's name Baltī-Inzak (No. 33), probably of foreign origin.[12] It is nevertheless difficult to decide whether this woman, if a prisoner of war, originally comes from Dilmun since, as we shall see later, Inzak is also attested in Susa already in the OB period. The latter possibility appears more likely in view of the writing *En-za-ak*, which is the same as that occurring in a royal inscription from Susa (No. 77), although one expects the writing *in-za-ak* or similar, as appears in Elamite personal names.

The remaining references to Dilmunite deities in Mesopotamian sources come exclusively from literary and lexical texts.[13] One must therefore look at the evidence derived from these texts with caution, since, generally speaking, literary compositions are influenced by the ideological tendencies of the age in which they appeared or were composed. The oldest reference is contained in Gudea Cylinder A, in a passage listing different raw materials brought from foreign countries. In this context we hear of Gudea boasting of having given orders to the god Ninzaga and the goddess Ninsikila to bring copper and wooden beams, respectively, to be used in building the Eninnu (No. 38). Though the two deities are mentioned without reference to Dilmun, they obviously must be connected with that country, since this section immediately follows that dealing with Makkan and Meluḫḫa. But how can we relate philologically these two names to Inzak and Meskilak?

At this point one has to look closely at earlier interpretations of the names Inzak and Meskilak, for it was just these occurrences in the Gudea passage which, in part, influenced those interpretations. For practical reasons, I shall start with the name Meskilak. S. N. Kramer has made the suggestion[14] that it represents a phonetic writing of the divine title Nin-me-sikil-ak, which may be translated as 'The Lady of the Pure Divine Powers'.[15] Accordingly Meskilak would have developed from that title after dropping the initial syllable nin. In support of this explanation Kramer refers to the DN Inšušinak, usually explained as rendering an original form such as Nin-Šušinak 'The Lord of the City Šušin'.[16] It should, however, be noted, that in Inšušinak not nin but the initial n is dropped. Apparently this difficulty has led P. B. Cornwall to suggest an alternative solution, according to which Meskilak has developed from the divine name ᵈNin-sikil-la (cf. the Gudea passage) by assuming that the latter stands for a genitive construction, that is, ᵈNin-sikil-ak.[17] Furthermore, a change of nin to min is assumed to have taken place.[18] The difficulty in this interpretation is the change n to m which cannot be justified on philological grounds, and not the occurrences of the name Ninsikila without the genitive sign ak (Cornwall), which is not expected anyhow.[19] Turning now to Inzak, we note that A. Falkenstein derived the name from ᵈNin-zà-ga, known from the Gudea passage, suggesting that a change took place similar to that in the case of Inšušinak.[20] It should be nevertheless observed, that the genitive sign here, as opposed to the alleged original form of Meskilak, has dropped completely from the name explained by Falkenstein as a genitive construction.

The above mentioned explanations share one common assumption, namely that the deities Inzak and Meskilak are of Sumerian origin. Though one may accept the meaning given to Ninzaga and Ninsikila as they appear in the Gudea inscription, that is, 'The Lord of the Sanctuary' and 'The Lady of the Pure',[21] it is difficult, for various reasons, to accept these names as the original forms of Inzak and Meskilak. The analogy with Inšušinak in the case of Inzak seems convincing, but the dropping of the genitive sign -ak, kept nevertheless in the alleged Ninsikila > Meskilak, has still to be accounted for. Discarding then the argument based on analogy to Inšušinak, one has to ask why the Dilmunite sources consistently write the name Inzak with the sign *in* and not *en*, i.e. 'Lord'.[22] In fact we have at least four instances from Bahrain and Failaka, in which the name is written with the initial syllable in. It must also be pointed out that the Mesopotamians knew other deities bearing the names Ninzaga and Ninsikila, which must be distinguished from the deities of Dilmun.[23] It can therefore be concluded that Inzak and Meskilak do not represent Sumerian deities. The Dilmunite deities are attested in Mesopotamian sources at least from the Ur III or Isin-Larsa period onwards, but their names were altered as they were assimilated into the local pantheon. That in this process of assimilation only Ninzaga (later Enzag(a)) and Ninsikila were affected may be explained as being due to certain ideas on Dilmun common in Mesopotamia. I tend, however, to consider the changes taking place in the names as a popular etymology, and exactly these altered forms were responsible for the rise of specific ideas on Dilmun reflected in Sumerian mythology.

The background of the Sumerian myths or mythical passages related to Dilmun is now fully discussed by B. Alster.[24] He rightly observes that there is no connection whatever between the seemingly unique burial mounds on Bahrain[25] and the picture of Dilmun as expressed in Sumerian mythology. Furthermore, Alster puts forward the challenging idea that a 'paradise' motif, whether related to Dilmun or not, does not exist at all in Sumerian thought. To quote this scholar: 'The unique position of Dilmun as a prosperous trade centre gave the island a unique place in Sumerian literature, one comparable to Delos, . . .' (p. 59). One can only agree. Leaving aside the question of the validity of applying a 'paradise' motif to some passages from Sumerian compositions, it is clear that these compositions, as they stand, represent the result of diversified mental processes and are hardly the right source in the first place for gaining some historical information on Dilmun. Yet, as they explicitly mention deities related to Dilmun, they must be dealt with. I shall not, however, go beyond trying to find possible relations between the deities as known in the Sumerian myths and as they appear in the Dilmunite sources.

I shall begin with a section from the myth 'Enki and the World Order', which describes the works of Enki and how he assigned to different gods their functions. Ninsikila was the goddess whom he appointed to be responsible for Dilmun (No. 44). The passage concerned with Dilmun in 'Enki and the World Order' relates to, and probably summarizes, a major theme in the myth 'Enki and Ninhursag'. The hero of the latter myth, the events of which take place in Dilmun, is again Enki, the god of the sweet waters. Dilmun is described as pure and holy, probably as a result of Enki's coition with Ninsikila, his wife (No. 45.1). In reply to the wish of Ninsikila (No. 45.2), Enki brings sweet waters to Dilmun, where, after a series of actions in which the goddess Ninhursaga is involved, different deities were born. One of these deities is Ensag (No. 45.3), whom Enki appoints to be the lord of Dilmun (No. 45.4).

Different points could be made here. Ninsikila is related to Dilmun, only in so far as it is a modified form of the name of the original female deity of Dilmun, i.e. Meskilak. This alternation already took place in the Ur III period (cf. the Gudea passage). The aspect of 'purity' and 'holiness' ascribed to Dilmun constitutes a part of the so-called 'paradise' motif, and probably originated as an attempt to explain Ninsikila as the goddess of Dilmun.[26] The relation between Ninsikila and Ninhursaga should also be considered. These two deities are nowhere in the myth explicitly identified with each other. It is, nonetheless, to be assumed, though not easily,[27] that they denote one deity in the myth. Yet exactly this discrepancy makes one suspect that the plots dealing with Ninsikila and Ninhursaga represented or were originally part of separate myths.[28] Whatever the case may be, Ninhursaga cannot be taken as representing a deity of Dilmun, as is sometimes considered,[29] on the basis of the myth 'Enki and Ninhursag' alone. Turning now to Ensag himself, the name (written ^{d}En-sa$_6$-ag) seems again to be a modification of the original Inzak. Aside from a possible interpretation of the name as 'The Sweet Lord', the modified name, by using the sign SA$_6$ = GIŠIMMAR 'date-palm' hints at the relation between the deity and the date-palm (cf. below). Furthermore, this altered form is yet another indication that the name of the main Dilmunite deity is not of Sumerian origin. For how can one reconcile the two names with each other, that is, Ninzaga in the Gudea cylinder on the one hand, and Ensag here on the other, having different meanings?

The myth 'Enki and Ninhursag' raises the question of the relation between Enki and Dilmun. Except for the seals from Failaka mentioning Enki, there is to my knowledge, no philological evidence (or archaeological for that matter)[30] justifying the postulation of an Enki cult in the area of Dilmun. The seals from Failaka, which are probably not older than the OB period, should be, however, accounted for. The proximity of Failaka to Eridu in particular and to Mesopotamia in general may, in a way, explain the existence on that island of seals mentioning Enki, the patron deity of Eridu, along with other Mesopotamian deities. One of the seals mentioning Enki (No. 16) represents a type of seal intimately connected with the Dilmunite culture,[31] and was dedicated to Enki according to its inscription. This may be an indication that Enki was worshipped on the island. It is, however, preferable to assume that Enki, as well as Damgalnuna,

represent merely two names of Inzak and Meskilak, the spouse of
Inzak mentioned in other sources. In other words, when the
Dilmunites use the names Enki and Damagalnuna they mean their
deity pair Inzak and Meskilak. This supposition is enforced by the fact
that the emblem of the date-palm engraved beside the inscription of
Rīmum (No. 1) is also found on the circular seal dedicated to Enki.
The emblem in question cannot be related to Enki, but to the
Dilmunite deity Inzak (cf. below).

Returning now to the myth 'Enki and Ninḫursag', one can safely
assume that the association of Enki with Dilmun occurred only after
Mesopotamia and Dilmun became bound to each other through long-
distance trade.[32] This is dated by B. Alster to the Ur III period. But, if I
understand Alster correctly,[33] he also seems to assume that, as a
result of these contacts, the cult of Enki was established in Dilmun.
However, from the perspective of Dilmun, this assumption raises
some difficulties. How could the Dilmunites dismiss so easily their
own cult, that is Inzak, in exchange for the cult of Enki? Or is it
possible that two main cults co-existed at the same time? Or is it
assumed here that the cults of both Enki and Inzak (and eventually
Ninsikila) were imported from Mesopotamia? It seems to me safer to
assume that the identification of Inzak, an indigenous Dilmunite deity,
with Enki, was achieved in Dilmun. Only then, being aware of this
identification, could the Mesopotamians speculate on the relation or
relations between Enki and Inzak, and consequently Dilmun. This
speculation is reflected in the myth 'Enki and Ninḫursag',[34] but it does
not necessarily mean that Enki was the object of a major cult in
Dilmun (whether Bahrain or Failaka).

It is appropriate at this point to dwell upon the question of the
nature of the deity Inzak. I believe that Inzak probably represented
the deity of the date-palm. This is indicated in the first place by the
date-palm branch engraved on the left side of the Rīmum inscription
(No. 1). The symbol can only be related to the deity mentioned in the
inscription, that is, Inzak. The same inscription, as well as another
from Failaka (No. 15), specify Inzak as Inzak of Agaru. Although the
connection of Inzak with Agaru has not hitherto been clarified, the
latter toponym has already been identified with medieval Haǧar in al-
Hasā in eastern Saudi Arabia, both linguistically and on the grounds
that this area has long been known for its flourishing date-palm
gardens and quality dates.[35] Another indication of the intimate
relation of Inzak to the date-palm is the writing of the name in the
myth 'Enki and Ninḫursag' already alluded to above.[36]

The remaining references to the deities of Dilmun come from
later sources, i.e. from those of the late second and first millennia B.C.
The list of divine names known as An-Anu-ša amēli mentions two
deities of Dilmun: Muati and Enzag. The names are included among

names of Nabû (No. 49). It is difficult, however, to explain the occurrence of Muati as a deity of Dilmun. It seems nevertheless reasonable to assume an error here, as has been suggested by W. G. Lambert,[37] since we know from three similar lists containing Enzag and Muati, but only the former is referred to as Nabû of Dilmun (Nos. 50, 51.2, 52.2).[38] There are, furthermore, lists containing names of Nabû which mention only Enzag, but not Muati (Nos. 53.2, 54, 55, 56.1). In regard to the names of Nabû one has to mention the name of Laḥamun, which the lists explain as Sarpanītu (i.e. spouse of Nabû) of Dilmun (Nos. 51.1, 52.1). We cannot decide whether Laḥamun represents another name of Meskilak, the main female deity of Dilmun, but Nin-Dilmuna 'The Lady of Dilmun', a title occurring in the great list An-Anum (No. 56.2), may refer to the latter deity.

As we have seen, Enzag and Laḥamun were, in the eyes of the Babylonian scribe, the main deity pair of Dilmun, for he characterizes them as Nabû and Sarpanītu of Dilmun. The identification of Enzag with Nabû relates of course to a specific process, by which the latter deity gained a special position in the late second and first millennia B.C. This in itself does not however explain why such a basically minor deity as the Dilmun deity was chosen to be identified with Nabû. The explanation must be sought elsewhere. In a group of liturgical texts[39] related to the cult of Nabû, the god is glorified by mentioning, among other things, his attributes, cities, and domiciles, as well as his different names. We find among the latter Enzag or Enzaga, without reference to Dilmun (Nos. 64, 65, 66, 67, 68), but obviously meaning Enzag, Nabû of Dilmun, in light of the lexical texts already mentioned. A clue towards understanding the problem of the identification of the Dilmunite deity with Nabû may be found in the same group of texts. Two of them (Nos. 66, 67) characterize Nabû as the one who gave birth to the city of Eridu. Accordingly, the deity identified with Nabû was probably Enki and consequently his Dilmunite equivalent. In an Eršemma text Enzag is furthermore identified with Marduk (Nos. 69, 70). The equation of Enzag with Marduk, though isolated, represents perhaps the original tradition, back to which the identification of Enzag with Nabû can be traced. It was actually Marduk, father of Nabû, who was exalted to a higher position in the Mesopotamian pantheon.[40] Further occurrences of the Nabû name Enzag or Enzaga do not add any further substantial information (Nos. 71, 72, 73).

The late Babylonian literary tradition is nevertheless aware of Enzag and his spouse Meskilak. In a hymn to Nanaya, this goddess is called Šuluḫḫitu who is at home in the temple Ekarra, and characterized as the spouse of Enzag *and* Meskilak (No. 74). Dilmun is certainly meant here. We know Ekarra as a temple in Dilmun from another source (No. 75).[41] In addition to the occurrence of Enzag and

Meskilak, the toponym Dilmun itself is probably also mentioned (cf. notes to text reference No. 74). But who is Šuluḫḫîtu? In spite of the reservations of Erica Reiner, the editor of the hymn, I believe that Šuluḫḫîtu is an Akkadian translation of the name Ninsikila. I assume furthermore that the scribe knew three divine names connected with Dilmun, that is Ninsikila, translated into Akkadian as Šuluḫḫîtu, Enzag and Meskilak. The latter two names were combined to give the appearance of one name standing for the male spouse of Šuluḫḫîtu. This may be explained as resulting from the piety of the scribe, and not necessarily as a misinterpretation of a transmitted tradition. In yet another text we find Enzag and Meskilak mentioned together as a male and female deity (No. 76).

Finally we should consider the material from Susa. Inzak was certainly worshipped in Susa as can be shown from a building inscription of the OB period (No. 77). The deity is mentioned together with Inšušinak and Ea. Leaving aside for the moment the fact that Inzak is also a Dilmunite deity, the occurrences from Susa suggest that Inzak was an indigenous deity in that area. To start with, the DN occurs in the above-mentioned inscription as *En-za-ak*, that is, partly syllabic. The use of the syllable en here may be explained as a result of the name's occurrence in a genre susceptible to literary influences. The other testimonies for the DN are found exclusively in personal names of the same date (Nos. 78, 79, 81, 82). The form of the DN in these names is more like that known to us from the Dilmunite sources. This does not, however, permit the conclusion that the cult of Inzak was transmitted from Dilmun to Susa, even if one of these names most probably refers to a Dilmunite (No. 78). Yet one is struck by the relatively high number of personal names with the theophoric element Inzak. It should also be pointed out that in the royal inscription mentioned above Inzak figures as a personal deity in Susa. It has, therefore, to be said that Inzak, at least within the periods under discussion here, represents a local deity both in Susa and Dilmun. The question cannot be pursued further without having more evidence.[42]

I may finally summarize the basic conclusions reached here. At least from the Ur III and Isin-Larsa periods onwards Inzak and Meskilak were worshipped in Dilmun as the main deity pair. These names are most probably not Sumerian.[43] The Dilmunites identified these two deities with Enki and Damgalnuna, the main deity pair of Eridu, notably the Mesopotamian centre nearest to Dilmun. In Mesopotamia, however, the Dilmunite deities were normally known under the names of Ninzaga (Enzaga) and Ninsikila, probably reflecting an attempt to assimilate the two foreign deities into the Mesopotamian pantheon. Independent of any Mesopoptamian influence, Inzak was also worshipped at Susa. In which direction the transmission of the cult of Inzak took place, that is from Dilmun to

Susa or vice versa, cannot at the moment be decided, though it probably took place in prehistoric times. Finally, it should be noted that the Dilmunite deity Inzak was in all probability responsible for the date-palm.

1. Different scholars now share the opinion that the topographic designation Dilmun has undergone certain shifts from period to period. Cf. D. Potts, *Dilmun* II (1983) 15–19; P. L. Kohl, in this volume; K. Kessler, BBVO 2, 154f. A single topographic definition of Dilmun cannot therefore be given. I wish in this respect, however, to stress the following points:

1. Our concept of Dilmun comes basically from Mesopotamian sources. How the population of the area concerned designated themselves, their land, and their cities is another matter. It seems, generally speaking, that from a Mesopotamian point of view Dilmun meant, beginning in the Ur III period (cf. D. Potts, *loc. cit.*), a loose topographic area covering both Bahrain and Failaka, as well as some parts of the mainland facing the island of Bahrain. I do not believe, however, that in the Kassite period there was a shift of importance from Bahrain to Failaka (cf. the hesitant view of D. Potts, *loc. cit.* 17). The greeting formulae of the two Kassite letters found in Nippur (here Nos. 31.1, 32) could easily be explained as referring to the centre of the area (that is, Bahrain), even if they were actually sent from Failaka. However, the possibility that they originated on Bahrain should not be excluded.

2. Again from a Mesopotamian point of view, Dilmun denoted a city (cf. here Nos. 31.1, 32 with fn. 12, and No. 45.2; cf. also one reference quoted in RGTC 5, 261), from which the area derived its name. The best candidate for this city is undoubtedly the impressive site of Qal'at al-Bahrain (for a plan of the site see now Monik Kervaran/Arlette Negre/M. Pirazzoli t'Sertsevens, *Fouilles à Qal'at al-Bahrain, 1ère Partie (1977–1979),* Bahrain 1982, p. 8).

3. From a Dilmunite point of view, the mainland facing the island of Bahrain was probably called Agaru (cf. the discussion in this paper concerning the deity Inzak of Agaru). This article is a modified version of the lecture delivered in Arabic at the conference. It has been published in its original form in *Bahrain through the Ages Conference 3–9 December: Collection of Papers Submitted '1'.* Bahrain 1983, Arabic Section p. 170–199. For the benefit of Assyriologists who cannot read Arabic I have modified the paper and published it in *Akkadica* 38 (mai – août 1984) 1–33, unaware that the conference papers would be published in English, as Mr. M. Rice later informed me. This then is the paper as it was published in *Akkadica* with a few modifications and corrections of printing mistakes. In modifying the article, I have profited from the different papers delivered at the conference, as well as from the contributions on Dilmun now in BBVO 2. At the time I was preparing my paper for the conference, I was aware (courtesy Dr. K. Kessler) of two contributions for that volume, those of K. Kessler and F. Vallat. Lively discussions with Dr. P. Kjaerum in Bahrain have elucidated some points, which will be mentioned in the text accordingly. Finally I wish to express my sincere thanks to Dr. D. Potts, who read the manuscript in its final form and made corrections and additions. In the meantime, J. J. Glassner has kindly sent me the manuscript of his edition of the Failaka inscriptions. In view of this new edition some minor modifications would have to be made, but I will return to these on another occasion.

2. Numbers mentioned in the text denote text references relevant to the subject of this paper. They are listed separately in the 'List of Text References' below. Dr. G. McEwan had kindly provided me with some references, of which I had not been aware. These are marked with an asterisk.

3. Agaru may mean here one of the places where the deity Inzak was worshipped. Cf. e.g. Ištar-ša-Ninua, Ištar-ša-Arbail. Cf. RGTC 5 s.v. Ninua and Arbail. The lack of

determinatives ki and URU does not, however, favour this possibility. For the use of toponyms in the sense of regions cf. the analogous Amurru and Aramu (cf. RGTC 5, s.v.).

4. Dr. D. Potts has provided the following comments on the question of Agaru/al-Haǧar. The identification of Agaru with medieval al-Haǧar and Strabo's Agraioi was first suggested by F. Hommel, *Ethnologie*, p. 552, n. 2. Cf. also P. B. Cornwall, *JCS* 6, 1952, 141 and H. von Wissmann, *Sammlung Eduard Glaser* 13, 1975, 12. For critique (now retracted) see C. Robin, *Semitica* 24, 1974, 102–111. For review of various suggestions put forward, see D. Potts, *Northeastern Arabia in the Later Pre-Islamic Era*, in R. Boucharlat and J.-F. Salles, eds., *Arabie Orientale, Mésopotamie et Iran Méridional de l'Age du Fer au Début de la Période Islamique*, Lyon, 1984, Table 6.

5. These names as well as some scattered names from OB sources (collected by E. E. Knudsen, *JCS* 34, 1982, 1–18: Nos. 3645a, 4591a) possibly reflect a foreign background. Nevertheless, the Amorites must have been integrated into Dilmunite society, and the possibility of a local DN occurring in their names should not be excluded. For the name quoted under No. 4591a cf. 37. The whole question of the relation between the Amorites and Dilmun is now discussed by J. Zarins, *MAR-TU and the Land of Dilmun*: in this volume.

6. I list here all the texts from Failaka known to me, regardless of whether they contain occurrences of DN. Stone or clay fragments: Nos. 6–12; seals: nos. 14–28. Some of the texts from Failaka have been mentioned by Theresa H. Carter, *RlA* 6, 389ff. These texts quoted only in part and without signature numbers, will not be referred to in the present documentation.

7. A temple of the Bronze Age (three stages) has been uncovered in the site designated as F 3 (Tall Sa'd). Cf. the plan in *Failaka* p. 19 and Theresa H. Carter, BASOR 207 (Oct. 1972), p. 17.

8. But cf. fn. 37.

9. On the question of the concentration of Amorites in Ur in the OB period and the relation of that city to Dilmun in general cf. now J. Zarins, in this volume.

10. For nin and en cf. below fn. 22.

11. This follows from the use of toponyms in greeting formulae as well as from general considerations related to the definition of local pantheons in Mesopotamian religion. The city Dilmun mentioned in the greeting formulae of the letters would mean then Qal'at al-Bahrain. Cf. also fn. 1 above.

12. This and similar names were usually carried by female slaves. Cf. J. J. Stamm, MVAG 44, 307f.

13. Up to No. 34 the texts are listed in chronological order, but note that under 'Later Sources' the references from the Middle Assyrian period are also included. These come from the MA copies of the lists An-*Anum* and An-*Anum-ša amēli: Nos. 49, 56, 57, 61, 63*. Also included are references from literary and non-literary texts which, although not related to the deities of Dilmun, are relevant to the discussion. Cf. fn. 23.

14. Mentioned by P. B. Cornwall, *JCS* 6, 1952, 141f.

15. S. N. Kramer refers to the phrase in VS 2, 5 ii 27: Dilmun (MÍ.TUK) kù-kur me-e sikil-la [. . .] 'holy Dilmun, the land of the pure divine powers . . .'. He connects the phrase with kur-me-sikil-la, said of Aratta (cf. BASOR 96 Dec. 1944 21 (17). In kur-me-sikil-la, however, kur stands for 'mountain'. Cf. Adele Berlin, *Enmerkar and Ensuhkešdanna* p. 75. But cf. Gertrud Farber-Flügge, *Der Mythos 'Inanna and Enki'*, p. 125, with note 138, who does not seem to find a difference between the two phrases.

16. On this deity cf. W. Hinz, *RlA* 5, 117–119.

17. *JCS* 6, 142[54].

18. It is superfluous to say that this is what is meant here, although Cornwall refers to a reading of the sign NIN aš/min/, mentioned in one list. The attempt to adhere to a reading NIN = /min/ (similarly A. Falkenstein, ZA 56, 77) has to be rejected, since a reading min in the first syllable of the DN [d]Nin-sikil-la, as it is known from the Gudea passage, makes the name devoid of meaning, and consequently annuls its assumed

Sumerian character. This contradicts the basic assumption behind the interpretations of Cornwall and Falkenstein, that the name of the Dilmunite deity developed from an original Sumerian form.

19. Cornwall mentions the instances in 'Enki and Ninḫursag' (cf. Nos. 45.1–2). One does not, however, expect the appearance of the genitive sign in its full form (that is ak), neither in the instances of 'Enki and Ninḫursag' nor in those of the Gudea Cylinder (No. 38). For the genitive sign before the comitative sign -da cf. A. Falkenstein, AnOr 28, 93f.

20. ZA 56 (1964) 77.

21. A. Falkenstein, AnOr 30, 107 and 109: 'die Herrin des Reinen' and 'Herr des Heiligtums' (zà[g] = aširtu). It is further stated by Falkenstein (p. 109), that Ninzaga came to be known later as ᵈEn-za-ak. The later form, however, does not exist, and Falkenstein seems to give here a mixed form between ᵈIn-za-ak (the two letters of Nippur: Nos. 31.1, 32) and the forms beginning with en in later literary texts. But cf. the form En-za-ak occurring in a Kassite personal name (No. 33) and in a royal inscription from Susa (No. 77).
The latter writing ᵈIz-za-ka for Inzak instead of the expected Enzag (No. 76) gives support to the assumption that Ninzaga and consequently Enzag/Enzaga represent genitive compounds, giving away to *Inzaga>Izzaka.

22. As is the case in later sources, which regularly write the name as Enzag/Enzaga, that is, replacing the earlier element nin with en. On the question of nin and en, both meaning 'lord' in divine names, cf. E. Sollberger, TCS 1, 158 and most recently A. Westenholz, Early Cuneiform Texts in Jena, Copenhagen, 1975, 13.

23. Deities not related to Dilmun: 1) Ninsikila, the spouse of Lisi of Nina (cf. A. Falkenstein, AnOr 30, 107¹⁰): Nos. 41 (OB), 42, 43.4 (OB), 43a (OB), 46–48 (MB), 57–60 (later sources); 2) Enzaga as a name of Nuska: No. 43.1 (OB), 61–62 (later sources). The following deity should be in any case kept apart from the deities of Dilmun: Ninš/saga of Nippur: Nos. 39–40 (OB).
Isolated references: 1) Ninzag(a): No. 34 (Fara), 36 (uncertain; pre-sargonic), 83 (Susa, OB); 2) Ninsikila: No. 37 (Ur III), 53.1 (?, later sources); 3) EnPA: No. 35 (Fara); 4) Inninš/saga: 43.3 (OB: but cf. fn. 37), 63 (?, later sources); 5) Ninš/saga: No. 85 (Susa, OB).

24. BBVO 2, 52ff.

25. That the number of burial mounds on Bahrain is not out of proportion with respect to the size of the ancient population of the island had been demonstrated by B. Frohlich, Dilmun 11, 1983, 5–9 and in his article in this volume.

26. Attributing the concepts of 'purity' and 'holiness' to Dilmun is basically a case of etiology. The statement in 'Enki and the World Order' 239 ('He installed Ninsikila in its sanctuary (zà)', No. 44) can also perhaps be explained on these lines (compare the DN Nin-zà-ga).

27. Compare however B. Alster, BBVO 2, 59.

28. From a thematic point of view the myth can be easily divided in two parts exactly at the point where Ninḫursaga or Nintu takes part in the action. Cf. the analysis of the myth given by B. Alster, UF 10, 1978, 16ff. Note furthermore that Damgalnuna also figures in the myth as the wife of Enki.

29. Cf. fn. 36.

30. Cf. fn. 36 below.

31. Seals of the so-called Dilmun-style. Cf. P. Kjaerum, PSAS 10, 1980, 45–53.

32. One has to mention, though, that certain relations between the two areas go back to the Ubaid period.

33. BBVO 2, 59: 'It is the astonishing presence of fresh water on Bahrain itself, and the fresh water sources in the very Gulf round Bahrain, which made the Sumerians associate Dilmun with Enki. The interest was undoubtedly aroused at a time when the Dilmun trade had grown to become important enough for a ramification of the cult of Enki to be established on Bahrain – as we shall see by providing a genealogy in which Enzak, the god of Dilmun, was the son of Enki, ultimately with Ninsikila, the goddess of Dilmun.'

34. It should be noted in this respect that the myth does not consider Ensag as the son of Enki, but that he – in mythological terms – was born to Enki as a counterpart of the aching body member ag. In the same passage other deities were created, including Ninti (corresponding to the rib of Enki), which brings to mind of course the creation of Eve (cf. W. G. Lambert, *Theologische Realenzyklopädie* Bd. V, Lieferung 1/2, p. 72).

35. Cf. fn. 4 above and K. Butz, *BBVO* 2, 118 with literature (N. 9 and 23). The connection between Inzak and the palm tree gives strength to the assumption that Dilmun also denotes the mainland facing the islands of Bahrain (cf. N. 1), though this assumption was partly based on invalid arguments (i.e. the occurrence of 'Dilmun-dates' in Mesopotamian sources). Cf. K. Kessler, *BBVO* 2, 152f.

36. It is noteworthy here to point to a study by Elisabeth C. L. During Caspers in *East and West 23*, 1973, 75ff. concerning two circular structures from the site of Barbar at Bahrain. These structures, which belong to Temple II, have measurements of 1,80 and 2,60 m for the inner and outer diameters, height not stated (probably not exceeding one metre). The author suggests that palm trees were planted in the structures for cult purposes. H. H. Andersen, in his recent study of the Barbar site (this volume), speaks of a 'double circular altar'. On account of the existence of a basin enclosing fresh water (Temple II) with features reflecting a water cult, these structures were connected by Andersen with Enki and Ninḫursag. As I have mentioned above, Ninḫursag – except in mythological terms – has nothing to do with Dilmun. As for Enki, the correlation of the basin of fresh water in Barbar Temple II on the one hand with ideas concerning Enki on the other – if not defined in clear chronological and spatial terms – is not feasible. If there is any transmission from Mesopotamia to Dilmun, then it would be the cult itself as it is exhibited in the Barbar temple. Yet we do not have exact parallels for such a cult in Mesopotamia. Furthermore, Inzak must be accounted for, which is difficult under the assumption that Enki was the main deity in Dilmun. The attempt to connect Inzak with Barbar Temple III, which shows architectural changes over the previous temples, becomes accordingly less convincing. Turning now to the circular structures in the Barbar Temple II, one should note that the suggestion of During Caspers is tempting indeed, but the evidence offered by her is very thin. The question should be left open, though the suggestion coincides in a striking way with the idea presented in this paper, that Inzak was the deity of the date-palm.

37. MIO 12 (1966/67) 47f. Note however the occurrence of Muati before In-nin-ša$_6$/sa$_6$-ga in an OB list of divine names (No. 43.3). There is, however, no relation between Inzak and the latter deity, which may be an expanded form of an original goddess name Innin. Nevertheless it is possible that the later list, which goes back to the OB list (cf. W. G. Lambert, RIA, 3,475), took In-nin-ša-ga (understood as ^{in}In$_g$-ša$_6$-ga or ^{in}In$_g$-ša$_6$ga) to stand for Inzak or the modified form En-zag/Enzaga. Cf. also reference No. 73, where Nanaya is characterized as the wife of Muati and the beloved of Enzag. A possible occurrence of Muati in one of the Failaka seals (No. 17) is too uncertain to be considered here. Accordingly, the Dilmunite name *me-a-ti-a-nu-um* (UET 5, 716, 8) must be kept out of the discussion (assumed as possibly containing the DN Muati by E. E. Knudsen, JCS 34, 1982, 17: No. 4591a).

38. For other references from lexical lists to be kept apart from Enzag of Dilmun, cf. fn. 23 above.

39. Cf. W. G. Lambert, in: *Near Eastern Studies*, 335ff. These texts were known under the name uktin-ta eš-bar til-la. They are quoted here according to the order established by W. G. Lambert, *loc. cit.* 336 (Nos. 64, 65). Nos. 66, 67 belong to the group, but their position in it has still to be determined. No. 68 belongs to a similar group (cf. S. Langdon, in: *Gaster Anniversary Volume* 335ff.).

40. On the exaltation of Marduk cf. recently W. G. Lambert, *Theologische Realenzyklopädie* Bd. V, Lieferung 1/2, p. 78).

41. The so-called *Šagnamsar temple (P. B. Cornwall, JCS 6, 1952, 142[58]) does not exist at all. Cf. now A. Sjöberg, MNS 56, 14.

42. F. Vallat, *BBVO* 2, 93–100 explains the inclusion of the main Dilmunite deity among the deities of Susa as being due to the strong influence exercised by the Elamite concept of the other world on Susa in the period of the Sukkalmaḫ. In this respect F. Vallat refers to the special role water played in funerary rites. It is concluded by F. Vallat, that Inzak was imported to Susa through Mesopotamia, bearing in mind the association of Dilmun to paradise, and its connection with Enki/Ea, the god of sweet waters. Apart from the arguments presented above for considering Inzak as an indigenous deity in Susa, I wish only to remark here, that even if one accepts the existence of a paradise motif in Sumerian literature (whether this refers to a certain locale or not, is beside the point), the concept of paradise on earth is different from the concept of life after death. On the other hand, one must postulate a certain knowledge of the myth 'Enki and Ninhursag' on the part of the Susians, which may have been possible (cf. reference No. 84); the transmission of some elements of that myth into a cult is nevertheless difficult to accept.

43. R. Zadok, *Elamite Onomasticon*, p. 4, who mentions some of the personal names with the theophoric element Inzak from Susa, seems to allude to the possibility of an Elamite origin of the deity Inzak. R. Zadok argues in vague terms, whereas only two of the relevant references (Enzag as Nabû of Dilmun, cf. Nos. 49.1, 52.2) are mentioned. It is clear from the evidence presented in this paper, that neither Inzak of Dilmun nor Inzak of Susa are of Sumerian origin. This evidence alone is, however, not enough to assume an Elamite origin of the deities Inzak and Meskilak. Strictly speaking this can be shown only through philological arguments within the Elamite language itself.

ABBREVIATIONS

Abbreviations according to R. Borger, *Handbuch der Keilschriftliteratur* I, Berlin 1976; II, Berlin + New York, 1975. In addition note the following:

BBVO 2 = D. Potts (Ed.), *Dilmun: New Studies in the Archaeology and Early History of Bahrain*, Berlin, 1983 (= Berliner Beiträge zum Vorderen Orient 2).

C. A. Benito, *'Enki and Ninmaḫ'* = C. A. Benito, *'Enki and Ninmaḫ'* and *'Enki and the World Order'*, Dissertation, University of Pennsylvania, 1969.

Adele Berlin, *Enmerkar and Ensuhkešdana* = Adele Berlin, *Enmerkar and Ensuhkešdanna*, Philadelphia, 1979.

G. Bibby, Dilmun = G. Bibby, *Dilmun. Die Entdeckung der ältesten Hochkultur*, Reinbek bei Hamburg, 1973.

East and West = East and West (Roma).

Failaka = Archaeological Investigations in the Island of Failaka 1958–1964. Kuwait.

Gertrud Farber-Flügge, *Der Mythos 'Inanna und Enki'* = Gertrud Farber-Flügge. *Der Mythos 'Inanna und Enki' unter besonderer Berücksichtigung der Liste der me*, Roma, 1973.

Festschrift Kraus = Zikir Šumim-Assyriological Studies Presented to F. R. Kraus on the Occasion of his Seventieth Birthday, Leiden, 1982.

Festschrift Matouš 2 = B. Hruška/G. Komoróczy (Eds.), *Festschrift Lubor Matouš II*, Budapest, 1978.

Caster Anniversary Volume = B. Schindler (Ed.), *Gaster Anniversary Volume*, London, 1936.

P. V. Glob, *Al-Bahrain* = P. V. Glob, *Al-Bahrain. De danske ekspeditioner til oldtidens Dilmun*, Denmark, 1968.

P. Kjaerum, *The Stamp and Cylinder Seals. Plates and Catalogue Descriptions*. Aarhus, 1983 (= *Danish Archaeological Investigations on Failaka, Kuwait; Failaka/Dilmun. The Second Millennium Settlements* Vol. 1:1).

R. L. Litke, *Reconstruction* = R. L. Litke, *A Reconstruction of the Assyro-Babylonian God-Lists. AN: ᵈA-NU-UM and AN: ANU ŠÁ AMĒLI*, Dissertation, Yale University, 1958.

Near Eastern Studies = H. Goedicke (Ed.), *Near Eastern Studies in Honor of William Foxwell Albright*, Baltimore + London, 1971.

F. Pomponio, *Nabû* = F. Pomponio, *Nabû. Il culto e la figura di un dio del pantheon babilonese ed assiro*, Roma, 1978 (= *Studi Semitici 51*).

PSAS = *Proceedings of the Seminar of Arabian Studies* (London, 1970–).

RGIC 5 = Kh. Nashef, *Die Orts- und Gewässernamen der mittelbabylonischen und mittelassyrischen Zeit* (= *Répertoire Géographique des Textes Cunéiformes 5*), Wiesbaden, 1982.

R. Zadok, *Elamite Onomasticon* = R. Zadok, The Elamite Onomasticon (in press) (= *Supplemento agli AION*, 1984).

LIST OF TEXT REFERENCES

1. Durand, JRAS 1880, plate opposite p. 193 (copy):
É.GAL ^{2}*Ri-mu-um* ^{3}ÌR ^{d}*In-za-ak* ^{4}*šá A-ga-rù* 'Palace of Rīmum, servant of Inzak of Agaru'
Notes: A basalt stone found out of original context on Bahrain in the year 1879. The stone, which came into the possession of the Durand family in London, was probably destroyed during World War II (Elisabeth C. L. During Caspers, in: J. E. van Lohuizen-De Leeuw (ed.), *South Asian Archaeology 1975*, Leiden 1979, 60[6]; quoted by K. Butz, BBVO 2, 123, n. 29). The inscription has found frequent treatments, most recently by K. Butz, BBVO 2, 117–118. The important new reading of šá instead of LÚ in line 4 made by K. Butz and J. Renger has already been referred to in my RGTC 5,339. Accordingly, the inscription has to be dated in the Kassite period. However, the implication of this reading has been overlooked by K. Butz, *loc. cit.*, since, influenced by earlier interpretations, he still takes Agaru as referring to a tribe. This assumption, though not clear in the translation on p. 117, is implied by the commentary on p. 119 as well as by the unnecessary reference to a certain occurrence of the particle ša (surely elliptic). The latter is taken to mean that the original object on which the inscription was engraved was manufactured by the tribe of Agaru. Leaving aside the fanciful suggestion to which this explanation led, (i.e.: the stone representing the foot of a statue or vessel presented to Rīmum as a gift from the tribe of Agaru), it is clear that *ša* in *Inzak-ša-Agaru* is simply a determinative pronoun expressing a usual genitive construction. This explanation is enforced by the occurrence of the same syntagm in one of the inscriptions of Failaka (No. 15). It should also be noted that *-aš* put forward by K. Butz as an alternative reading for RUM should now be excluded in view of the variant *-ru* in the Failaka inscription. The date-palm branch engraved on the left side of the inscription can only be the emblem of the deity mentioned in the inscription, that is, Inzak of Agaru.

2. Bahrain Museum Room No. 1, glass case No. 2, piece No. 1:
É [. . .] ^{2m}*la-ak*-[. . .] ^{3}ÌR ^{d}[. . .]
Notes: A steatite (?) fragment exhivited in the Bahrain-Museum seen there by the author. The name in line 2 is probably Amorite.

3. R. H. Brunswig, Jr./A. Parpola/D. Potts, BBVO 2, Pl. III: Fig. 12 (copy):
l *I-a-bi-na-im* ^{2}l DINGIR-*mi-il-kum* ^{3}l *I-zi-ta-am-bu* ^{4}DUMU *I-a-bi-na-im*
Notes: Transliteration and commentary with previous literature ibid. 107. Tablet found in Qal'at al-Bahrain and to be dated according to the script in the post-Ur III or Isin-Larsa period.

4. P. V. Glob, Al-Bahrain p. 95 (photo):
Notes: This is one of four tablets exhibited in the Bahrain-Museum (seen by the author). Apparently all of them are from Qal'at al-Bahrain. It is not clear whether the two photos published by P. V. Glob represent two tablets or the obverse and reverse of one tablet. In one of the photos (possibly the reverse) a Kassite date can be read: *x* MU *Kaš-til-ia$_4$-šu*. However I am not able to read the remainder of the text from the unclear photo. According to P. V. Glob, who summarized the text (p. 94), it is an economic document listing foodstuffs delivered to the 'Lady of Bread' (NIN.NINDA) and 'Lady of Drinking' (NIN.NAG).

5. W. M. Leake, Trans. of the Royal Society of Literature, Vol. 4 (1853) 258 (copy):
Notes: Royal inscription on a small polished white stone found in Kythera, which allegedly mentions Inzak of Dilmun. The awkward copy may be attributed to the fact that it was effected at a time when Assyriology was in its beginnings (see Th. Jacobsen, DIP 43, 139). Accordingly any inference to be derived from this inscription should be considered as highly tentative. The inscription is now dealt with by K. Butz, BBVO 2, 119ff., and hence the text and the problems involved will not be repeated here. The

attention to this inscription in connection with Dilmun was drawn after E. Unger, RIV 13 (1929) 313, had thought he could discern the names Anzak and Dilmun in the first two lines respectively. K. Butz offers for these lines the reading: *a-na* ᵈ*In-za-ak* ²*ša Dilmun* (NI.TUK)ᵏⁱ.

6. 881-ACJ (transliteration):
[ᵈ]*In-za-ak*
Notes: From F 2. Mentioned by B. Alster, BBVO 2, 42. A sherd of red-ridged Barbar ware. For dating the red-ridged Barbar ware to the Isin-Larsa period cf. R. H. Brunswig, Jr./A. Parpola/D. Potts, BBVO 2, 2,108.

7. 881 Hu (G. Bibby, Dilmun p. 271: Photo):
[Ć].GAL ᵈ*In-za-ak* 'The Great House of Inzak'
Notes: Signature mentioned by B. Alster, BBVO 2, 67, fn. 26. Steatite fragment found in F 3. For the use of é-gal in the sense of 'temple' cf. CAD E p. 55.

8. P. V. Glob, Al-Bahrain p. 134 (photo):
[. . .É].GAL ²[. . .] EN⁷ x ³[. . .] x x ⁴[. . .] IR ⁷ ⁵[. . .] A⁷ R[I . . .]
Notes: A translation of this text is not possible. B. Alster, BBVO 2, 42 offers the following reading: [. . .]-gal ²[. . .]en(?) dilmunᵏⁱ (?) ³[. . .]x y ⁴[. . .]-ni ⁵[. . . in]-za-a[' <] ⁶[. . . mu-na-]n[i-dím]. The restoration of the DN in line 5 is, of course, uncertain.

9. 87 B (transliteration):
ᵈ*In-za*
Notes: A fragment of a steatite bowl from F 3. B. Alster, BBVO 2, 42, who mentioned the fragment, writes: 'as part of the name or title of the giver'.

10. Failaka Fig. 53 (photo):
ᵐ*Šu-x* [. . . DUMU] ²ᵐ*Ia-mi ú* ³*ša Uš-x* [. . .]
Notes: Fragment of stone bowl. The toponym in line 3 (*Uš-x*) should be added to my RGTC 5, if the text is to be dated in the Kassite period.

11. A. J. Ferrara, JCS 27 (1975) 232 (copy):
Notes: A large limestone door sill, which bears a one line inscription of Nebuchadnezzar, king of Babylon. According to J. A. Ferrara, this store was probably brought to Failaka from another area, to be transported at a later date to Babylon. Cf. also Theresa H. Carter, RIA 6, 395. Dr. P. Kjaerum (personal communication) believes, however, that the stone originated on Failaka itself, possibly belonging to a small governor's palace on the island from the NB period.

12. Failaka Fig. 32 (photo):
[. . .] ŠEŠ⁷ x x DINGAIR NIN⁷ GAL⁷ ta [. . .] ²[. . .] x x É x ra⁷ [. . .] TIL⁷.LA.NI [. . .] ⁴[. . .] x MUN BI [. . .] ⁵[. . .] DINGIR [. . .]
Notes: A fragment from a steatite bowl found in the southern side of temple under the walls of the Greek fortress in F 5. It is difficult to recognize with certainty any divine names in this fragment.

13. 881-GT:
Notes: Mentioned by B. Alster, BBVO 2, 68 fn. 28. A tablet with a list of personal names. The DN Ninsikila previously read in the tablet (J. van Dijk by M. Weitmeyer, AcOr 26 [1965] 206') should be now eliminated according to B. Alster, *loc. cit.*

14. P. Kjaerum, Seals p. 127: Fig. 311:
É⁷ RI UD ²Ù PA GA ŠU⁷ NA⁷
Notes: From F 3. Nos. 14–16. 18–28 are read from photographs as published by P. Kjaerum, *Seals*.

15. P. Kjaerum, Seals p. 153: Fig. 336:
KIŠIB ᵐx ᵈx x ³DUMU⁷ ᵐ*Zu-x-x-an* ⁴ÌR ᵈ*In-za-ak* ⁵*šá A-ga-ru* 'Seal of . . ., son of . . ., servant of Inzak of Agaru'.
Notes: From F 6. Judging from the use of the sign *šá* instead of *ša* in line 5, one may date this seal to the Kassite period. The reading in line 5 is thanks to Dr. K. Kessler. B. Alster, BBVO 2, 42, No. 7 gives this inscription but leaves *šá A-ga-ru* in line 5 unmentioned. For the combination Inzak-ša-Agaru cf. notes on text reference No. 1.

16. P. Kjaerum, Seals p. 143: Fig. 350:

a-na ^d*En-ki* ²TIL.LA.A.NI.IR ^{3m}*Ri-iq*[?]*-qá-tum* 'To Enki, for his life: Riqqatum[?]'.

Notes: A photo of this seal was published in *Failaka* Fig. 82: No. 5; P. V. Glob, *Al-Bahrain* p. 133; P. Kjaerum, PSAS 10 (1980) p. 51: Fig. 11. It was found in F 3. A precise date for this seal cannot be given. The name of the deity in line 1 is mentioned by P. V. Glob as 'Insak'. In view of the new photo given by P. Kjaerum this reading is untenable. The seal cutter has abbreviated the sign *ki* in ^d*En-ki*, as it came on the edge of the seal. Arguing on the same lines, the reading Enki has also been offered by B. Alster, BBVO 2, 42. The older reading of PN in line 3 (*Ribbatum; accepted by E. E. Knudsen JCS 34 [1982] 17) is certainly wrong. The reading has been retained by B. Alster, who considers also ^m*Ri-ib(!)-qa-tum* as an alternative possibility.

17. 881-GS (transliteration):

é-ušumga[l] ^{2m}*Engar-*^d*Mu-a-t[i]* ^{3d}*En-za-[ak]*

Notes: A seal of greenish stone. Text referred to by J. van Dijk, in: M. Weitmeyer, AcOr 28 (1965) 206. The transliteration given here is according to a reading of J. Laessoe mentioned by B. Alster, BBVO 2, 42. According to Alster the reading of Muati is doubtful, as in Enzak to judge from the transliteration.

18. P. Kjaerum, Seals p. 155: Fig. 368:

Nam-ḫa-ni ²dumu Inim-kù 'Namhani, son of Inimku'

Notes: This seal was published in *Failaka* Fig. 64 and P. Kjaerum, PSAS 10 (1980) p. 50: Fig. 1 found in F 6. Judging from the typical Sumerian names Namḫani and Inimku, the text is probably to be dated to the Ur III or Isin-Larsa period.

19. P. Kjaerum, Seals p. 155: Fig. 370:

^d*Enki* ^{2d}*Dam-gal-nun-na*

Notes: Photo of this seal was published in *Failaka* Fig. 46. Found in F 3, and dates according to glyptic in the OB period.

20. P. Kjaerum, Seals p. 257: Fig. 376:

kur-ba-šu ^{2d} x x ^{3d}AMAR.UTU-⁴*ni*[?]*-x(-x)* 'Bless him, O . . .; Marduk- . . .'

Notes: From F 3. The phraseology of this and the following seal inscriptions is typical of Kassite seal inscriptions. The name of the seal owner is probably mentioned in both lines 3 and 4 (cf. the following inscription and H. Limet, *Légendes* No. 5.6). The personal name has theophoric element Marduk (Marduk-nišu is a possible restoration). I am not able to read the divine name in line 2.

21. P. Kjaerum, Seals p. 159: Fig. 379:

kur-ba-šu ²*x ki*[?]*-lil*[?] ³DINGIR É ŠU-⁴*ri-me-ni*[?] 'Bless him, O . . .; . . .-rimēni'

Notes: From F 3. The cutting of signs on the seal is awkward.

22. P. Kjaerum, Seals p. 163: Fig. 397:

. . . *ru* NI+TUK[?]

Notes: From F 3. Only two signs are preserved. If the reading of the second sign should prove to be correct, it would be the first attestation of Dilmun from Failaka. For possible attestations from Bahrain cf. Nos. 5 and 8 above.

23. P. Kjaerum, Seals p. 163: Fig. 399:

^dMES UMUM DIM₄ ²DINGIR ŠÀ.LÁ.SÙ ³SAG[?]-^dUTU[?] ⁴DUMU[?] x x 'O Marduk, great lord, merciful: Rēš-Šamaš[?], son of . . .'

Notes: From F 3.

24. P. Kjaerum, Seals p. 165: Fig. 401:

Notes: From F 3. Inscription is badly eroded.

25. P. Kjaerum, Seals p. 167: Fig. 405:

^dMES UMUM DIM₄ ²DINGIR ŠÀ.LÁ.[SÙ] ³DU₁₀(SAG ?)-^dUTU ⁴ DUMU x x 'O Marduk, great lord, merciful: Tāb(Rēš?)-Šamaš, son of . . .'

Notes: From F 3. Cp. No. 23.

26. P. Kjaerum, Seals p. 137: Fig. 406:

Notes: From F 3. Inscription badly eroded.

27. P. Kjaerum, Seals p. 167: Fig. 408:

ᵈIŠKUR *be-lu* GAL ²DINGIR *ri-me-nu-ú* ³*tab-ni u-*? ⁴*šu-ul-lí-im* ⁵ÌR *pa-*₂*li-iḫ-ka* ⁶*Ki-im-ru*
⁷DUMU *Ke-eš-gal:* 'O Adad, great lord, merciful, you have created; – sur^ur – protect,
keep healthy your servant who fears you: Kimru, son of Kešgal?'
Notes: The reading of line 3 instead of my older reading m-bi-ib² is due to Dr. W.
Sommerfeld. The readings of the names in lines 6 and 7 are uncertain.

28. P. Kjaerum, Seals p. 167: Fig. 407:
ᵈ*EN-ki* ²*be-lu* GAL? *x* ³AD AD? NU? ⁴DINGIR *x pa a nu* ⁵*Za-ra-qum* ⁶DUMU *Ba-an-Be x* 'O
Enki, great lord . . .: Zaraqum, son of Ban . . .'
Notes: From F 3.

29. 'unpublished Failaka F 3. cp./881. XR' (or XRR ?):
Notes: Mentioned by E. E. Knudsen, JCS 34 (1982) 16–17 sub Nos. 1799a and
3878a/6280a. The text (seal ?) contains two names: *gu-ur-da ? [-x]/x* and *ia/wa-ta-ra-[x].*

29a. TLB 1, 160, 7:
ᵐᵈ*In-sa-ak-ga-mil*
Notes: On this text cf. W. F. Leemans, *Trade* 141f.

30.1 UET 5, 286, 9*:
[I-di-i]m?-ᵈ*Nin-In-za-ak*
30.2 UET 5, 526, 2*:
*I-din-*ᵈ*Nin-In-za-ak*
Notes: In both texts the same person (a Dilmunite) is meant. Cf. W. F. Leemans, *Trade* p.
24 and 31.

31.1 Ni 615 (A. Goetze, JCS 6 [1952] 143):
ᵈ*In-zak_x* (SAG) *ù* ᵈ*Mes-ki-la-a[k]* ⁵DINGIR.MEŠ *ša* NI.TUK^ki ⁶*na-ap-ša-ti-ka li-is-s[u-r]u*
31.2 ibid. lines 18–22:
i-na li-t URU.KI *ša ú-[. . .]* ¹⁹*i-na* ᵈ*30-nu-ri ki-i* [. . .] ²⁰*ù* É DINGIR *ša eš-[. . .]* ²¹É ᵈ*Ni n-*
[. . .] ²²*ù* É *la-bi-[ir . . .]* 'On the outskirts of the town . . . As to what I have heard from Sîn-
nūri concerning . . . and the house of god . . . That temple is for the goddess Nin- . . . The
temple is old . . .'
Notes: For the remainder of the text see the translation and commentary of A. Goetze.

32. Ni 641 (A. Goetze, JCS 6 1952 143) 7–19:
ᵈ*In-za-ak* ⁸*ù* ᵈ*Mes-ki-la-ak* ⁹DINGIR.MEŠ *ša* NI.TUK^ki ¹⁰*na-ap-ša-ti-ka* ¹¹*li-is-su-ru*
Notes: The writing of the divine name as *In-za-ak* indicates that in Ni 615 SAG should be
read as /*zak*/. In the MB syllabary ZA and *sa* are usually differentiated.

33. CBS 4596:
ᶠ*Bal-ti-En-za-ak*
Notes: This name has been listed by A. T. Clay, YOSR 1, 62 (reference courtesy Dr. K.
Kessler). It means: 'Inzak is my dignity'. Dr. K. Kessler has pointed also to the name *In-
za-ḫu-da-ak* CBS 3646 (A. T. Clay, *loc. cit. 90*). The name is included by K. Balkan,
Kassitenstudien 1, 56 among Kassite names having the elements *inza* and *ḫudak*.

Sources Prior to Ur III Period

34. A. Deimel, Inschr. Fara 2, Nr. 1 IV 10*:
ᵈNin-zag
Notes: Between ᵈNin-gi-x and ᵈNin-ki-[(x)]

35. A. Deimel, Inschr. Fara 2, 61 III 3:
ᵈEn-PA
Notes: Cf. fn. 23.

36. F.-M. Allotte de la Fuÿe, DP 53 VIII 10:
ᵈNin-x-zà-ga
Notes: Presargonic; uncertain.

Ur III Period

37. E. S. Speleers, RIAA 174 III 19:
Lú-Ḫu-rìm ¹⁹gudu₄ ᵈNin-sikila 'Lu-Ḫurìm, the gudu₄-priest of Ninsikila'
38. Gud. Cyl. A 15, LL-18:
ᵈNin-zà-ga-da à mu-da-àg ¹²urud-da-ni še-maḫ túm-a-gim ¹³gù-dé-a lugal é-dù-a-ra

[14]mu-na-ab-ús-e [15d]Nin-sikil-a-da á mu-da-ág [16gis]ḫa-lu-úb-gal-gal [gis]esi [gis]ab-ba-bi
[17]énsi é-50-dù-ra [18]mu-na-ab-túm-e

'He (Gudea) gave instructions to Ninzaga: He brought his copper to Gudea, the king, the builder of the temple, as if he were bringing large quantities of barley. He (= Gudea) gave instructions to Ninsikla: She brought large oak beams and beams of the esi- and ab-ba trees to the ruler, the builder of the Eninnu'

Notes: For the translation of this passage cf. A. Falkenstein, AnOr 30, 184. In his personal copy of TCL 8, now in the possession of the Altorientalisches Seminar, Tübingen, A. Falkenstein refers for line 12 to OECT 1, p. 14 IV 11 (hymn of Enlil-bāni of Isin; cf. now A. Kapp, ZA 51, 82). S. Langdon, OECT 1, p. 14[3] had already interpreted maḫ in še-maḫ here and in the hymn of Enlil-bāni in the sense of 'much'. For maḫ = *mādu* cf. CAD M/1, p. 20b.

Old Babylonian Period

39. PBS 8/2, 146, 16.29*:

[d]Nin-ša$_6$/sa$_6$-ga

Notes: Document from Nippur mentioning prebends of a gudu$_4$-priest connected with different deities. Cf. J. Renger, ZA 59 (1969) 151; *id.*, HSAO 151.

40. A. Goetze, JCS 4 (1950) 106: YBC 4973, 7*:

1 udu É [d]NIN-<<x>>-ša$_6$/sa$_6$-ga

Notes: This is probably a reference to the temple of Ninš/saga in Nippur (cf. A. Goetze, *loc. cit.* 90f.) and not Larsa (correct J. Renger, HSAO 147).

41. CT 8, 44, 19:

[d]NE-GÙN[?]-*na-lu[?]-mu-di* [19]DUMU LÚ [d]Nin-sikil-la

Notes: PN, as the patronymicon indicates (Lisina-lū-mudi?), refers to Ninsikila, the spouse of Lisi(n)/Lisina (for the full form Lisina, cf. S. N. Kramer, *Festschrift Kraus* 137[10]).

42. YOS 9, 33, 2:

[d]Li$_9$(NE)-si$_4$(GÙN) [2d]Nin-sikil la

Notes: Royal inscription of Rim-Sîn of Larsa.

43.1 TCL 15, No. 10 (Pl. 26) 133:

[d]En-zà-ga

Notes: As has been pointed out by R. L. Litke, *Reconstruction* 70[255] this deity must be distinguished from Enzag, Nabû of Dilmun (Nos. 49–55.1 . . . etc.). The DN occurs here (note lines 130.135) among names of Nuska (cf. Nos. 61, 62). The name means probably 'Lord of the Right Hand'.

43.2 TCL 15, No. 10 (pl. 26) 139:

[d]MES-ki[?]-la-ak[?1]

Notes: This possible occurrence of the name Meskilak has been mentioned by P. B. Cornwall, JCS 6, 142[55].

43.3 TCL 15, No. 10 (pl. 29) VI 277*:

[d]In-nin-ša$_6$/sa$_6$-ga

Notes: Between Kaškaš and Mú-a-ti. Cf. fn. 37.

43.4 TCL 15, No. 10 (pl. 30) VIII 357:

[d]Li$_9$-si$_4$
[d]Nin-sikil-la

43.a W. Förtsch, MVAG 21 (1917) 22ff. Tf. V 10:

[d]Li$_9$-si$_4$
[d]Nin-sikil-la

44. Enki and the World Order 238–241:

238 F 10 [kur]-MÍ[?1].TUK-na mu-un-ši-x[. . .]
　　　G 12 [　　　　. . . n]a mu-un-sikil mu-un-zalag
239 F 11 [. . . [d]N]in-sikil-la zà-ba-[. . .]
　　　G 13 [　　　. . . si]kil-la zà-ba nam-mi-in-gub

240 F 12 [. . .]x-AB-nun-šè ba-an-sum ku₆-b[i . . .]

    G 14 [. . .-nu]n-šè ba-an-sum ^{15}[. . .]-bi ì-kú-e

241 F 13 [^{giš}gišimmar] gán-zi-šè ba-an-sum zú-lum [. . .]

    G 16 [. . .] ba-an-sum ^{17}[. . .] kú-e

    K 1 [. . .] gán$^?$-zi-šè ba-an-sum zú-lum-n[i ì]-kú-e

    'He cleansed and purified the land of Dilmun

    He installed Ninsikila in its sanctuary

    He gave to the princely . . . . . ., in order that (Dilmun) can eat their fish

    He gave to the righteous fields palm-trees, in order that (Dilmun) can eat their

dates'

Notes: The latest edition of this myth is to be found in C. A. Benito, 'Enki and Ninmah' 82ff. The relevant section is on p. 98. The versions for this pasage are: F = Ni 4554 (I. Bernhardt/S. N. Kramer, WZJ 9 [1959/60] TF. 6); G = Ni 9805 (I. Bernhardt/S. N. Kramer, *loc. cit.* Obv 1; K = PBS 12, 48 (see WZJ 9, 256).
A transliteration and translation of this passage is now offered by B. Alster, BBVO 2, 60f. I differ in my translation from his only in minor points. For line 240 I would suggest the following restoration: 'He gave to the princely Abzu ([Z]U.AB-nun-šè) [fish-traps?], in order that (Dilmun) can eat their fish'. For the fish-traps in Bahrain known as 'hadhra' cf. now Angela Clarke, *The Islands of Bahrain: An Illustrated Guide to their Heritage.* The Bahrain Historical and Archaeological Society 1981, p. 115f. For fishing and fish-traps in Bahrain, cf. R. B. Sergeant, BSOAS 31 (1968) 486–514 (courtesy Dr. D. Potts).

    45.1 Enki and Ninhursag 7–12:

7 A dili-ni-dè Dilmun (MÍ.TUK)^{ki}-a ú-bí-in-ná

  B dili-mu-dè Dilmun (MÍ.TUK)^{ki} ù-bí-ná

8 A ki ^{d}En-ki dam-a-ni-da ba-an-da-ná-a-ba

  B ki ^{d}En-ki-ke₄ dam-a-ni-ta ba-da-ná-a-ba

9 A ki-bé sikil-àm ki-bé zalag-ga-àm

  B ki-bé sikil-la ki-bé zalag-zalag-ga

10 A dili-ni-dè

  B dili-mu-dè Dilmun (MÍ.TUK)^{ki} ù-bí-ná

11 A ki ^{d}En-ki ^{d}Nin-sikil-la ba-an

  B ki ^{d}En-ki-ke₄ ^{d}Nin-sikil-la ba-da-ná-a-ba

12 A ki-bé sikil-àm

  B ki-bé sikil-la <<a>> ki-bé ba-da-ná-a-ba

'As he (i.e. Enki) had lain down alone in Dilmun

The place, in which Enki had lain down with his wife,

This place is clean, this place is pure.

As he (i.e. Enki) had lain down alone in Dilmun

The place in which Enki had lain down with Ninsikila

This place is clean, this place is pure'

Notes: The myth 'Enki and Ninhursag' was published by S. N. Kramer, BASOR Suppl. Studies 1 51945. The pertinent versions for the present passage are: A = PBS 10/1, 1; B = UET 6, 1. The relevant passages from this myth are given now in transliteration and translation by B. Alster, BBVO, 2, 61ff. The references quoted here basically follow this edition. For the expression dili-ni-dè 'he (quite) alone' (dili-mu-dè: 'I (quite) alone' in B is a mistake) cf. C. Wilcke, *Lugalbanda* 116; D. O. Edzard, ZA 62 (1972) 20; A. Sjöberg, ZA 65 (1976) 240. In version A the scribe has abbreviated the lines 10, 11, and 12 after dili-ni-dè, ba-an, and sikil-àm respectively.

    45.2 Enki and Ninhursag 29–35:

^{d}Nin-sikil-la a-a-ni ^{d}Enki-ra gù mu-na-dé-e

uru mu-e-sum uru mu-e-sum nam-mu-sum-ma-zu

Dilmun (MÍ.TUK) uru mu-e-sum uru (me-e-sum nam-mu-sum-ma-zu)

[. . .] mu-e-sum uru (mu-e-sum nam-mu-sum-ma-zu)

[a(-x)] íd-da nu-un-tuku-a
[uru] mu-e-sum uru (mu-e-sum nam-mu-sum-ma-zu)
[uru-mu a-íd]-da (nu-un-tuku-a)
'Ninsikila spoke to her father Enki
"You have given me a city, you have given me a city, but as you gave it –
You have given me Dilmun, the city, you have given me a city, but as you gave it –
You have given me . . ., you have given me a city, but as you gave it –
It lacked [water] in its rivers.
You have given me a city, you have given me a city, but as you gave it
It lacked [water] in its rivers"'
Notes: In line 31 a-a 'father' is used here in an honorific sense (cf. S. N. Kramer, BASOR
Suppl. Studies, 1, 23 note to line 31).
     45.3 Enki and Ninḫursag 267f.
šeš-mu a-na-zu a-ra-gig ag-mu [ma-gig]
^{d}En-sa$_{6}$-ag im-ma-ra-an-[tu-ud]
'My brother, which part of your body is hurting you? My . . . is hurting me.
Then Ensag was born for you'
Notes: Text: PBS 10/1, 1 III 40f. The meaning of the body part ag is unknown to me.
     45.4 Enki and Ninḫursag 277:
[^{d}En-sa$_{6}$-a]g en-Dilmun (MÍ.TUK)-na ḫé-a
'Let Ensag be the lord of Dilmun'
Notes: Text: PBS 10/1, 1 III 38. It is clear that the divine name should be read as ^{d}En-sa$_{6}$-
ag instead of ^{d}En-ša$_{6}$-ag. Cf. F. Pomponio, *Nabû* p. 176[110]. The scribe, who intended
probably writing the name syllabically, used the sign SA$_{6}$ or ŠA$_{6}$, which also has the
meaning 'sweet, good'. He could have used the sign alone – having then the reading
ŠAG$_{5}$ – without adding the latter sign, a reading ša$_{6}$ instead of sa$_{6}$ is eliminated.
Furthermore the choice of the sign GIŠIMMAR (= SA$_{6}$), representing in a way a
'gelehrte Schreibung', should also be noted. On the one hand a syllabic writing of the
DN is offered, while on the other the relation between the deity and the date palm is
indicated. It is also possible that the name has been interpreted as meaning 'The Sweet
Lord'. The same writing is possibly attested in a school text from Susa (No. 84).
Middle Babylonian Period
     46. R.S. 20.121 (Ugaritica, 5, 411) I 9:
^{d}Li$_{9}$-si$_{4}$
^{d}Nin-sikil-la
Notes: For Nos. 46.5, 47, 48 cf. transliteration *loc. cit.* p. 212.
     47. R.S. 20.195A (Ugaritica 5, 413) line 9:
^{d}Li$_{9}$-s[i$_{4}$]
^{d}Nin-sikil-MA-la
     48. R.S. 23.459 (Ugaritica 5, 413) line 10:
^{d}Li$_{9}$-si$_{4}$
^{d}Nin-sikil-MA-la
Later Sources
     49. An-Anu-ša amēli lines 117–118:
Notes: This section (cf. R. L. Litke, *Reconstruction* p. 257) is preserved in two copies:
     49.1. K 4349 (CT 24, Pl. 42) 106–107:
^{d}PA^{ti}MIN (= ^{d}AG) *šá* NI.TUK^{ki}
^{d}En-zág(PA) MIN (= ^{d}AG) *šá* NI.TUK^{ki}
'Muati' „   (= Nabû) of Dilmun
Enzag   „   (= Nabû) of Dilmun'
     49.2. YBC 2401 (R. L. Litke, Reconstruction pl. XLVI) col. XII 40:
[Dil]-mu-un
Notes: Only the right side is preserved in this text, but it is clear from the preceding and
the following lines that only one line deals with Nabû of Dilmun. This gives support to

the suggestion of W. G. Lambert, that the scribe of 49.1 has made a mistake. Note the
syllabic writing of Dilmun (cf. R. L. Litke, *Reconstruction* 257[117]).

50. 5 R 43 lines 15–16:

^d*En-zag* ^dAG NI.T[UK^{ki}]

^dPA^{a-ti}[MIN]

'Enzag Nabû of Dilmun

Muati [„ (= Nabû)]'

Notes: Transliteration and translation of the text (lines 13ff.) are given by A. Pomponio,
Nabû 155ff. For the missing right section cf. 51.2.

51.1. Rm 610 (CT 25, pl. 35) Obv. 12:

^d *La-ḫa-mun* MIN (= ^d*Sar-pa-ni-tum*) NI-TUK^{ki}

'Laḫamun „ (= Sarpanitu) of Dilmun'

51.2. lines 20–21:

^dEn-^{za-ag}zag ^dAG NI.TUK^{ki}

^d ^{mu-ú-a-ti}PA MIN

'Enzag Nabû of Dilmun

Muati „ (= Nabû)'

52.1. K 29 (CT 25, pl. 36) Obv. 11:

[*La-ḫa-m*]un MIN (= ^d*Sar-pa-ni-tum*) NI.TUK^{ki}

'Laḫamun „ (= Sarpanitu) of Dilmun'

52.2. lines 19–20:

[. . .)^{za-ag}zag ^dAG NI.TUK^{ki}

[. . .] ^{ú-1-ti}PA MIN

'[En]zag Nabû of Dilmun

[Mu]ati „ (= Nabû)'

Notes: K 29 duplicates Rm 610 quoted under 51.

53.1. O. Neugebauer, Exact Sciences Pl. 14: No. 500 Vs. 10:

^dNin-sikil-la

Notes: The name of the goddess is mentioned between Irragal and Manītu. It is not
possible to decide whether this Ninsikila refers to the goddess of Dilmun, in spite of the
fact that the tablet lists on its reverse some names of Nabû. Cf. F. Pomponio, *Nabû* p.
156[40].

53.2. O. Neugebauer, *loc. cit.* Rv. 10:

^dEn-zag

Notes: Mentioned among names of Nabû (cf. notes on No. 53.1).

54. 5 R 43 Rev. 29:

^d*Umun-zag* ^dAG EN *a-šá-ri-du* 'Umunzag Nabû the foremost lord'

Notes: The name occurs among names of Nabû. Cf. F. Pomponio, *Nabû* p. 175[105]. The
name is written in Emesal.

55. STT 382 I 15*:

[^d*En]-zag*

Notes: Section deals with names of Nabû (cf. line 11': [^d]AG . . . etc.).

56.1. An-Anum Tablet II 244:

^dEn-sag MIN (= ^dMarduk-ke₄)

'Ensag (= minister) of Marduk)'

Notes: I quote this list according to the edition of R. L. Litke, *Reconstruction* p. 116. The
relevant text is YBC 2401 (cf. R. L. Litke, *loc. cit.* pl. 13 IV 6). The name is mentioned
among names of Nabû.

56.2. An-Anum Tablet IV 18:

[^dN]in-NI.TUK^{ki} ŠU

Notes: I quote this list according to the edition of R. L. Litke, *loc. cit.* p. 169. Relevant
text: YBC 2401 (R. L. Litke, *loc. cit.* pl. 23, line 57).

57. An-Anum Tablet II 71:

A ^dNin-sikil-lá dam-bi-sal

B ᵈN[in-sikil]-lá dam-bi-sal
'Nin-sikila his wife (i.e. the wife of Lisi)'
Notes: Cf. the edition of R. L. Litke, *loc. cit.* 55 (A = CT 24, 26, 113; B = YBC 2401 = R. L. Litke, *loc. cit.* pl. 9, 33).

58. KAV 63 I 9:
ᵈLi₉-si₄
ᵈNin-sikil-lá

59. KAV 65 I 9:
ᵈLi₉-si₄
ᵈNin-sikil-lá

60. MSL 4, 6, 37:
[ᵈ]Gašan-sikil-lá ᵈNin-sikil-lá   dam-ᵈ Li₉-si₄
'Cašan-sikila, Ninsikila, spouse of Lisi'
Notes: For this section two copies are available:
    A = K 171 + K 2112 (2 R 54, 2)
    B = Bu 91-5-9 (CT 25, 43) + Ki 1904-10-9, 14 (King, *Cat. Suppl.* No. 51, 23–47)
K 171 has been published in various older publications, among which is 2 R 59. I quote the section according to the edition in MSL 4. Gašansikila is Emesal of Ninsikila.

61. An-Anum Tablet I 254:
ᵈ [En-zà-]ga MIN (= Nuska)
Notes: Cf. R. L. Litke, *Reconstruction* 70 (YBC 2401; cf. pl. 5, line 43).

62. MSL 4, 4, 13–14:
[ᵈUmun-mu]-ú-a ᵈEN-PA(zág) ᵈNuska
ᵈUmun-mu-du-ru ᵈEn-PA (zág) ᵈNuska
Notes: For this section two copies are preserved: A = K 171 (2 R 59) + K 2112 (2 R 54, 2); D = CT 25, 45. For A cf. No. 60. I quote the section according to the edition in MSL 4. The two names of Nuska are in Emesal.

63. CT 24, pl. 50: K 4349N + Col. II 12*:
ᵈIn-na-ša₆-ga [...]
ᵈIm-gal-edin-na [...]
šá Ì.DU₈
Notes: Cf. N. 23.

64. SBH No. 12 Rev. 12:
ur-sag ᵈMu-zé-eb-ba-sa₄-a kala-kala-ga: umun ᵈEn-zà-g[aʔ ...]
'You, the warrior Muzebbasa, the mighty one: Lord Enzaga ...'
Notes: The title ᵈMu-ze-eb-ba-sa₄-a is in Emesal and corresponds to ᵈMu-du₁₀-ga-sa₄-a; which means: 'The One Called with a Fair Name'. Cf. F. Pomponio, *Nabû* p. 7f.

65. W. G. Lambert, in: Near Eastern Studies 346 line 9:
umun ᵈEn-zà-ga urú-ni-a na
'The Lord Enzaga, who decreed a good destiny in his city'
Notes: The sign na is an abbreviation of the phrase na-ám zé-eb ba-an-tar-re occurring in line 6.

66. K 9312 (Th. J. Meek, BA X/1, p. 97: No. 18):
1 ᵈMu-zé-eb-ba-s[a₄-a ...]
  ᵈAg dumu nun-na[...]
  ibila É-sag-íl-l[a ...]
  ᵈEn-zag ki-túš [...]
5 ama ᵈBa-ba₆ gašan úru-k[ù ...]
  e-lum umun na-ám zu ka-mag-[ga ...]
  kab-tum be-lum mu-du-u ši-mat ma- ti [...]
  alim-ma   ur-sa [g-gal ...]
  [ur]-sag-gal   umun-ᵈE[n-zag]

10 [umun-TI]N.TIR^{ki} umun-É-[sag-íl-la]
 [alim]-ma   umun-[Bàd-si-ab-ba]
 [umun] É-zi-da   umun [. . .]
 [umun É-t]e-me-an-ki [. . .]
 [umun É -d]àr-a-an [. . .]
 [^dAG] dumu-nun-na [. . .]
 [a-a tu)-ud-da Úru-zé-eb-ba[^{ki}-ke$_4$ . . .]
 [dumu] nun-gal [a-a ^dEn-zag . . .]
 [d]ìm-mer-er [maḫ-a mè šen-šen-na ti-na ba-gub-ba]

'Muzebbasa [. . .]
Nabû, son of the prince [. . .]
The heir of Esagila [. . .]
Enzag, residing in [. . .]
Mother Baba, lady of the holy city . . .
The revered one, the lord who knows the destiny of the land (Akkadian translation)
The honorable one great warrior
Great warrior   lord Enzag
Lord of Babylon   lord of Esagila
[The honorable one] lord of Borsippa
[Lord] of Ezida   lord [. . .]
[Lord] of Etemeanki lord [. . .]
[Lord] of Edarana   lord [. . .]
[Nabû], son of the prince [. . .]
[The father], who gave birth to Uruzebba [. . .]
[The son] of the great prince [father Enzag]
[The supreme] one [among the gods, the one rising fiercely to battle]

Notes: The same text has been published before by D. Macmillan, BA V/5, No. 28. F.
Pomponio, *Nabû* p. 175[106] completes line 4 as ki-túš [Dilmun ?]. The restoration is,
however, uncertain. The name of Eridu in line 16 is written in Emesal. For lines 16–18
cf. the following text reference.

  67. Rm 272 (Th. Meek, BA X/1, 98: No. 19) 3–5:
[^dAG dumu nun ga]l ki-túš [. . .]
[a-a tu]-ud-da Úru-zé-eb-b[a^{ki}-ke$_4$]
[dumu n]un-gal a-a ^dEn-[zag]
[dìm-me-e]r maḫ-a mè šen-šen-na ti-na ba-gu[b-ba]
[. . .]x DINGIR.MEŠ *šá AŠ qab-lim u ta-ḫ-zi da-ap-niš iz-[za-zu?]*
'Nabû, son of the great prince, residing in [. . .]
The father, who gave birth to Uruzebba
The son of the great prince, [Father Enzag]
The supreme one among the gods, rising fiercely to battle'

  68. K 11652 (BL No. 28) 4f.:
^dMu-zé-eb-ba [. . .]
umun ^dEn-zag [. . .]

Notes: This text is related to Nos. 64–67, but does not belong to the same group (cf. W.
G. Lambert, in: *Near Eastern Studies 351*). It duplicates BM 78878, published by S.
Langdon, in: *Gaster Anniversary Volume* 337f. and p. 348. BM 78878 mentions in the
Akkadian translation Nabû instead of Enzag:
^dMu-zé-eb-ba-sa$_4$-a [Úru]-zu mè ma-an-gi-la(?)
^dNa-bi-um [a-al]-ka ta-ḫa-zu il-[ta-mi]
'Muzebbasa/Nabium, your city which the battle has besieged'

  69. STT 155, 13f.*:
[umun]^dEn-zà-g[a] ^dŠid-dù-ki-šár-ra
be-lum [^d]En-[zag] pa-qid kiš-š[a-t]i
'Lord Enzaga, who looks after everything'

Notes: Eršemma-song for Marduk.

70. CT 51, 189 Obv. 10f.*:

umun En-zà-ga [. . .]

be-lum ᵈMIN [. . .]

Notes: Duplicate of No. 69.

71.1. KAR 23 II 1–2:

ᵈ AG EN   [. . .]

ᵈ*En-za[g* . . .]

71.2. LKA 40 Obv. 7–8:

[. . .] *me-riš-ti mu-diš-šú n[u* . . .]

[. . .a]mʾ-luʾ [. . .] UN.MEŠ *ta-* [. . .]

71.3. LKA 57 Obv. 10–11:

ᵈAG En *mi-riš-t[i* . . .]

   ᵈ*En-zag   ma-am-lu k[ul-lat* . . .]

71.4. LKA 40a Obv. 9–10:

ᵈAG EN *mi-riš-ti x-šu-u nu-uḫ-ši*

ᵈ*En-zag ma-am-lu kul-lat UN.MEŠ ta-pa-qid*

Notes: The texts mentioned under 71 belong to the group Šu-íla, published by E. Ebeling, AGH. The pertinent section is to be found on p. 16, lines 9–10:

'Nabû, lord of the plants, making fertility abundant

Enzag, the brave one, who looks after all the people'

72. W. G. Lambert, Festschrift Matouš 2, 84, 8f.*:

ᵈ*En-zag šu-pu-ú AN [(x) b]a-nu-ú ma-al-ku-tú*

[. . .] *x x* [. . .*m]u-al-lid ab-ra-atú [šá ku]l-lat DINGIR.MEŠ i-ḫi-tu*

'Enzag, resplendent . . . who creates kingship;

. . . begetter of mankind, who watches over the gods'

Notes: Translation according to W. G. Lambert, *loc. cit.*

73. K 3600+ D.T. 75 (D. Macmillan, BA V/5, 627: No. 4) II 3*:

ḫi-rat ᵈ*Mu-u₈-a-ti na-ram-ti* ᵈ*En-z[ag* . . .]

'The wife of Muati, the beloved of Enzag . . .'

Notes: Hymn to Nanaya.

74. Erica Reiner, JNES 33 (1974) 225, lines 12–14:

12 A [Ú-r]a-al-la Ú-ra-al-la-ka *šu-a-ab-dil-e-*[ne]

   C [. . .] (traces)   *šu-a-*[. . .]

13 A *ina É-kar-ra* ᵈ*Šu-luḫ-ḫi-tum DAM* ᵈ*[EN]-zag ù Mes-ki-lak*

   C [. . .] (traces)*-tu al-ti* ᵈ*Mes-ki-lak* [. . .]

14 A [*x x*] *x šá be-x i-qab-bu-u-ni ana-[ku-ma]*ᵈNa-n[a-a]

'(obschure)

In Ekarra, Šuluḫḫîtu, the wife of Enzag and Meskilak,

[the inhabitants ?] of Dilmun(?) call me, but I am Nanaya'

Notes: For this section there are two texts available: A = K 3933 (Erica Reiner, *loc. cit.*, translation); C = LKA 37. Line 12 is obscure. It contains the toponym Ù-ra-al-la, which I am not able to explain. At the beginning of line 1' there is most probably mention of the inhabitants of Dilmun: [UN]. MEŠ *šá Dil-mun(?).* Cf. the description of sign traces given on p. 231 (line 14), which fits the suggested restoration. Erica Reiner (p. 234) states that it is not possible to ascertain whether Ninsikala is the Sumerian version of Šuluḫḫîtu. She asserts furthermore, that Meskilak in the present instance represents a male deity, and accordingly cannot be considered the spouse of Enzag. However, the greeting formulae of the Nippur letters (Nos. 31.1, 32) speak strongly in favour of considering Meskilak a female deity. Even if we assume on the basis of the present text, that Meskilak stands for a male deity, then we have to justify the existence of two male deities in Dilmun, which is difficult. It is clear, on the other hand, that Ninsikila is a female deity, that is, the wife of Enki, according to the myth 'Enki and Ninḫursag (No. 51). According to the hymn of Nanaya Šuluḫḫîtu is certainly a female deity and the spouse of two male deities. It has, therefore, to be assumed that the scribe considered Enzak-Meskilak as a unity standing for one name. Moreover Šulubḫîtu stands most probably for Ninsikila as understood in Akkadian, that is: 'The One Related to Purification Rites'.

75. KAV 84A, 6a f.:

[. . .] *Dil-mun*^{ki}*: iš-ḫa-a* [. . .]

[. . .] *É-kar-ra É* ^d *x* [. . .]

[. . .] *Dil-mun*^{ki d} *x* [. . .]

Notes: The name of the temple means: 'The Quay Temple'. It may be interpreted as giving a hint that the main temple of the city Dilum (in Bahrain ? Failaka ?) was situated at the quay of the city.

76. AfO Beih. 11, 41, 37:

A ^dEn-zag ^dMes-ki-lak

B ^d*Iz-zi-ka u* ^d*Mes-ki-lik*

Notes: The pertinent section occurs in Tablet 8 of the incantations series Šurpu. Four texts have the section in question (two are available in copies: A = S. A. Smith, MAT line 20; B = UET 6, 408, 23*). The latter text offers the interesting variant ^d*Iz-zi-ka* and ^d*mes- ki -lik*. The writing Izzika may be taken as further indication that the name was understood as a genitive compound by local Mesopotamian tradition.

Sources from Susa

77.1. MDP 28, p. 10: No. 7:

a-ana ^dMUŠ. EREN ^{2d}*É-a ù En-za-ak* ³*be-lí-šu a-na ba-la-at*

⁴*Ku-te-er-na-aḫ ḫu-un-di*⁵*ù Te-em-ti-a-gu-un* ⁶ *sa-al-mu*[?]*-sú*

i-du-ul ⁷*É.DÙ.A ù ma-la-kam* ⁸*[š]a e-pi-ir-tim i-pu-uš*

77.2. MDP 6, p. 25 (plate 7: No. 4):

1 *[. . .] ù En-za-ak be-lí-šu a-na ba-[la]-at [. . .]*

2 *ù Te-em-ti-a-gu-un sa-al-[mu]-sú*[?]

3 *[i-du-ul-m]a É ù ma-la-kam ša e-pi-ir-tim i-pu-uš*

'To Inšušinak, Ea, and Enzak, his lord, for the life of Kuter-Naḫḫundi and <his life> . . . Temti-agun . . . built all the temple and the entrance of baked bricks'

Notes: The inscription of the brick No. 77.1 is also published by V. Scheil, RA 29 (1932) 69. No. 77.2 is similar to No. 77.1. The translation offered here is according to 77.1. The present inscription comes from the reign of the monarch Šilhak-Inšušinak and represents a copy of an older inscription of Temti-agun and his father Kuter-Naḫḫundi from the OB period. The inscription is partly obscure and requires further study. Cf. for the moment W. F. König, AfO Beih. 16, 88⁶; W. Hinz, *Das Reich Elam*, Stuttgart 1964, p. 82. The personal pronoun *-šu* in *be-lí-šu* refers to Temti-agun, which implies that Enzak was the 'personal god' of this ruler.

78. M. Lambert, RA 70 (1976) 71–72:

Mi-il-ki-el DUMU ⁵*Tè-em-*^d*x-za-ak*

Notes: That the present text is the same as the one published in MDP 28, 436, has been referred to by Grazia Bianchi (cf. F. Vallat, BBVO, 2, 93, fn. 10). The sign read here as x is not clear in the copy of the text. M. Lambert has read the sign in question as *en*. The possibility of a reading *in* cannot however be excluded. The tablet carries a seal impression of the so-called Gulf type. Consequently Tēm-Inzak has to be considered a Dilmunite, as well as some of the other persons mentioned in the tablet with typical Amorite names (cf. fn. 5). Hence Inzak represents in this case, strictly speaking, the deity worshipped in Dilmun. Connections between Susa and Dilmun certainly existed in the OB period, as can now be shown by the mentioning of a Dilmunite (Ti-il-mu-ni-i) in a tablet which can be dated to the reign of Kuter-Naḫḫundi I., (for the text cf. L. De Meyer, *Orientalia Gandensia* 3 [1966] 165ff.).

79. MDP 28, 434, 4:

I-din-In-za-ku

Notes: This name has been mentioned by W. F. Leemans, *Trade* 142². Cf. also R. Zadok,

Elamite Onomasticon p. 57. The DN is in the nominative case.

80. MDP 28, 423, 8:

Ku-un-In-za-ki?

Notes: The last sign can possibly be read as *ak*. The name has been mentioned by F. Vallat, BBVO 2, 93 and R. Zadok, *Elamite Onomasticon* p; 4. *ku-un* may be related to Akkadian *kūnu*. The syllable may represent, however, an Elamite word as has been pointed by R. Zadok, *loc. cit.* (cf. p. 23 under 105a).

81. MDP 22, 146, 20:

In-za-ki

Notes: Mentioned by R. Zadok, *Elamite Onomasticon* p. 57. It is an abbreviated name.

82. MDP 28, 550, 7:

Wa-tàr-In-za-ak

Notes: Mentioned by R. Zadok, *Elamite Onomasticon* p. 58. The name is Akkadian and means 'Inzak is Preeminent'.

83. MDP 28, 10, 1:

^{d}Nin-zag

Notes: A female deity according to the context. It has to be at any case kept apart from the male deity Ninzaga of the Gudea cylinder (No. 38).

84. MDP 27, No. 165*:

En-sa$_{6}$-ag

An-zag ba na sag

Notes: School text. Though the reading suggested here for the first line seems to be plausible (*cf. No. 45.3*), the second line remains difficult.

85. MDP 27, No. 161:

[^{d}]Nin-giš-zi-d[a]

[^{d}]Nin-šag$_{5}$/ša$_{6}$/sa$_{6}$-[ga]

Notes: School text. Cf. n. 23 above.

The lands of Dilmun: changing cultural and economic relations during the third to early second millennia B.C.

PHILIP L. KOHL

While the general identification of Bahrain with the Sumerian land of Dilmun is secure, questions remain as to how great an area Dilmun actually encompassed and whether or not this geographical referent applied to different regions at different periods of time. That is, Dilmun may have only been centered on Bahrain during specific periods. D. Potts has recently reviewed the archaeological evidence supporting such separate identifications and concluded that the earliest references to Dilmun, which extend from protoliterate Jemdet Nasr to numerous Early Dynastic texts, do not refer to Bahrain but possibly to the eastern Arabian mainland near Abqaiq and to Tarut island (1983b: 16). Potts also argues that a shift occurred during late Early Dynastic or early Akkadian times which made Bahrain the center of an enlarged Dilmun that encompassed al-Hasa or part of eastern Arabia and further suggests that roughly towards the end of the Third Dynasty of Ur Dilmun expanded north to incorporate Failaka island. Subsequently during Kassite times, Failaka may have become the center of a new Dilmun displaced northwards, just as the focus of Mesopotamian civilization during the second millennium also shifted to the north (*ibid*. 17).

Although Potts' arguments are exclusively based upon a far from complete archaeological record, they are consistent with the known evidence and persuasive. This paper focuses on one corpus of data, carved stone vessels, which support the earliest identification of Dilmun with Tarut island or what Golding (1974:26) describes as 'the capital of the Eastern province' during the Early Dynastic period or roughly the first half of the third millennium B.C. It also attempts to place the hypothesized shifts in Dilmun's location in a broader 'international' context which can be justified, of course, by consideration of Dilmun's essential function as a center or emporium for long-distance interregional trade.

The major reason against identifying the earliest Dilmun with Bahrain is the apparent hiatus between the al-Markh terminal

Ubaid/Qatar assemblages and the earliest City I occupation on the Qal'at. One cannot presume that Bahrain was unoccupied during the late fourth and early third millennia, but the lack of substantial remains dated to this period, particularly when compared to the spectacular discoveries on Tarut, which largely came to light as the accidental by-product of construction work, is striking and cannot be explained as due to insufficient exploration on Bahrain. This admitted, however, one still should not totally ignore the puzzling Jemdet Nasr sherd from the Barbar Temple and should recall the once-felt certainty of a pre-2700 (cf. Mortensen 1971: 300) date for Barbar I on the basis of this sherd, conical goblets, and stylistic parallels of objects, such as the bull's head, with Early Dynastic statuary (cf. During Caspers 1971b: 222; 1973: 128; 1979). Although most scholars now believe that the earliest pre-Barbar levels on the Qal'at date at most to late Early Dynastic or Akkadian times (cf. Larsen 1980: 48–49, 275) and place the initial construction of the Barbar Temple in the late third millennium (Potts n.d.: 23–24), it must also be admitted that several supposedly diagnostic ceramic wares, such as red-ridged and snake-cordoned-ridged wares, may have been utilized over a considerable period of time. Thus, it is hazardous to pinpoint absolute dates to relative sequences established on the presence or absence of such wares.

Chronologies must be based upon different types of archae-ological data and even, when possible, consider negative evidence. As Potts (n.d.: 21–22) also has noted, an additional argument in favor of a low or late third millennium chronology for Barbar and the Qal'at sequences is the absence on Bahrain of soft-stone vessels carved with easily recognizable motives which define what has been termed the Intercultural Style (hereafter I.S., cf. Kohl 1978; 1979). This absence suggests that the materials from Barbar I and from the pre-Barbar levels on the Qal'at postdate the E.D. II–IIIa or Fara period when nearly every excavated Sumerian temple contains vessels or vessel fragments carved in this style. Not only is their absence from the Barbar Temple, in particular, best explained in terms of the building's later construction, but the occurrence of hundreds of I.S. fragments in graves on Tarut (Burkholder 1971; Zarins 1978b) demonstrates that these vessels were traded in the Gulf presumably at the time that they were popular in Sumer or roughly during the middle of the third millennium B.C.

Negative evidence, in short, seems less problematic than usual, but this argument still cannot be pushed too far since some soft-stone vessels with related designs have been found on Failaka island in contexts apparently contemporary with Dilmun seals or which should date substantially later than the earliest pre-Barbar levels on Bahrain. The Intercultural Style corpus itself exhibits considerable variety which can be explained both as an inherent feature of the handcrafted production of the carved vessels and, more problematically, as a product of regional and/or chronological variation. Although the well-stratified examples from the Sumerian sites of Ur, Khafajeh, Nippur, Mari, and possibly Kish (*cf.* Kohl 1974: 242–257; for Kish *cf.* Herz 1965: 168–169; Moorey 1978: 56) suggest that this style was most popular during the E.D. II–IIIa period, the dates of the more numerous examples in this style from Tarut and Tepe Yahya are less clear.

The fragments from Tarut are most troublesome since their context has been destroyed and since other recovered materials, particularly the ceramics, range in date from Early Dynastic I to Ur III times. While the discovery on Tarut of two figurines, one rough limestone statue (Rashid 1972: 162; Saudi Arabia 1975: 149) and a tiny (3.5 cm high) lapis lazuli example with a drill hole for mounting (Golding 1974: fig. 4, 11) suggest an E.D. II–III date consistent with the Mesopotamian dating for the I.S. vessels, the occurrence of more than fifty stone vessels decorated with simple dot-in-circle designs, which de Miroschedji (1973) has demonstrated are later and labelled 'série récente', equally supports the broad chronological range of the materials from Tarut suggested by analysis of the ceramics. Moreover, investigations in the Maysar-related or Wadi Samad sites in Oman (Weisgerber 1981: 211–218) have shown that it is possible to distinguish later from earlier 'série récente' vessels decorated with dot-in-circle designs, both of which are present in the Tarut corpus (Potts n.d.: 28). The later 'série récente' bowls, found particularly at Maysar 9 and Hili 3 and 8, period IIIb (Wadi Suq period), should date to the first half of the second millennium and thus extend the range of the Tarut materials at least from the early third (excluding possible Ubaid sherds (Bibby 1969: 380; 1973) to the first half of the second millennium B.C.

Unlike at Tarut, the Yahya carved vessels have been found in stratified contexts and can therefore be dated with greater precision. The vast majority (*c.* 80%) of the carved fragments have been found in Yahya period IVB levels which postdate the proto-Elamite IVC construction of a large building which can be firmly dated by the presence of proto-Elamite tablets and on comparative stylistic grounds to the first two centuries of the third millennium. Potts (1980) has attempted to define six phases of levels within period IVB at Yahya and, although details of this division cannot be examined here, it should be noted that most of the Yahya I.S. fragments, indeed the bulk of the Yahya chlorite corpus, were found in the later IVB levels or what has now been called Yahya IVB4–1, particularly IVB4–2. Radiocarbon dates for Yahya period IV range too broadly within the third millennium (*cf.* Kohl 1974: 232–235) to provide a precise absolute determination for the later Yahya IVB levels, and detailed comparison of Yahya IVB ceramic types with stratified wares from Mesopotamia, southwestern Iran, and the Iranian plateau suggest a possible 'time span of over a millennium for the Yahya IVB assemblages' (Potts 1980: 325; *cf.* also p. 534). Apparently diagnostic or, at least, rarer early Yahya IV ceramic types, such as bevel-rim bowls, conical cups, low-sided trays, and knobbed ware (*ibid.*: 263–263; 211), show considerable continuity between Yahya IVC and early Yahya IVB (IVB6–5) which, by itself, casts doubt upon Amiet's assumption (1974; 1976: 2, 8) of a substantial chronological gap between Yahya IVC and IVB, a belief based upon his stylistic dating of Yahya IVB stamp and cylinder seals to Akkadian times. The chronological discrepancies for dating the later Yahya IVB levels cannot be fully resolved, radiocarbon determinations and ceramic comparisons are not helpful, and one can either opt for an earlier E.D. II–IIIa date based upon the stratified occurrence of I.S. vessels in Mesopotamia, as I prefer (Kohl 1974: 242–271); a later Akkadian date based upon the glyptic evidence, as Amiet argues; or a considerable range for these production levels, extending from E.D. II–IIIa down to Akkadian times (*cf.* Potts 1980: 534–538).

The Tarut corpus deserves more careful consideration. X-ray diffraction analyses of 375 soft-stone specimens (Kohl, Harbottle, and Sayre 1979: 138–139, table 3) from southwestern Asia have shown that the stone vessels from Tarut were made from several distinctive minerals, including relatively pure chlorite, talc, a talc-chlorite mixture, chlorite-quartz, chlorite-andradite, phlogopite, and, apparently muscovite schist (Potts n.d.: 12–13, reported as personal communication from M. Golding). It should be noted, however, that only one talc fragment from Tarut (CTO3) of the analyzed non-relatively pure chlorite examples together with single talc fragments from Mari and Kish and twelve specimens from Bismaya were carved in the Intercultural Style. This evidence, coupled with the lack of appropriate soft-stone deposits on Tarut, suggests that the Tarut materials came from several separate sources. The apparently later, stylistically anomalous vessel fragments from Failaka also exhibit considerable compositional diversity, a fact which suggests that both islands, possibly at different periods of time, imported their soft stone materials from a variety of sources. J. Zarins' catalogue (1978b) of the Tarut corpus shows unworked lumps of chlorite (pl. 75b, 605), unfinished fragments (pl. 72b), including, significantly, two partially worked combatant snake I.S. vessels (nos. 110 and 251), and lathe-turned plain vessels, a production technique never employed in the Yahya IVB levels. Zarins (1978b: 66) also accepts the division between an earlier carved and plain green soft-stone corpus and a later grey 'Omani steatite' corpus decorated with the ubiquitous dot-in-circle designs and implies that limited stratigraphic work on Tarut confirms the association of Early Dynastic pottery with the former and Akkadian/Ur III materials with the latter. Thus, it seems clear that Tarut did not obtain all its I.S. vessels from the only documented production center, Tepe Yahya, and, indeed, probably produced them themselves and/or trans-shipped unworked and/or partially finished vessels to the consumption markets of Sumer. Finally, worked and unworked lapis lazuli fragments, alabaster vessels, and metal objects also were found on Tarut, suggesting that soft-stone vessels were not the only luxury goods traded by this early Dilmun.

Proof of the existence of multiple production centers may help explain some of the chronological difficulties surrounding the *floruit* of the I.S. vessels. If, as Braudel (1982: 344–349) considers axiomatic for pre-sixteenth century Europe, pre-industrial production for purposes of long-distance trade was, by its very nature, sporadic and short-lived, then separate, fairly remote production centers, like that at late Yahya IVB, may have succeeded each other relatively rapidly (after one or two generations ?) depending upon local conditions for production and accessibility to broader interregional exchange networks. That is, it is not only conceivable, but even likely on *a priori* considerations that stylistically similar vessels were produced in different places at slightly different or in successive periods. Unfortunately, this hypothesis will be difficult to prove given not only the previously discussed chronological ambiguities of the stratified evidence, but also considering the tremendous stylistic diversity of soft stone decoration on vessels from the single documented late Yahya IVB workshop. For example, snake bodies at Yahya can either be carved in low or high relief or incised. Deeply cut oval holes or inlay may decorate the bodies of the vessels carved in high relief, but the scales on other vessels may be indicated by small punctate, triangular-shaped impressions and/or crudely incised oval holes (Kohl 1974: 151–155, pls. XXVIIIa–c, in particular). The hut or architectural facade fragments from Yahya, likewise, show considerable diversity in terms of the herringbone, bevelled square, imbricate, or stepped designs which accompany the primary sagging lintel motif (Kohl 1974: 177–186).

Such diversity simply is characteristic of handcrafted production and makes it extremely difficult to establish regional and/or chronological variants on the basis of fine stylistic distinctions, as illustrated, for example, by al-Gailani's overly ambitious attempt (1975) to define two chronological styles marked respectively by deeply cut figured and more shallowly carved geometric motives. On the other hand, the very existence of multiple production centers suggests regional variations and chronological developments. Several commentators, including al-Gailani (*ibid.*: 43) and Herz (1965:

119), have noted the flatter, almost 'imitation' style of the latest E.D. IIIa or IIIb stratified examples from the Ishtar Temple at Mari, and de Miroschedji (1973: 21, 25) suggests that some designs, like the bull-man on the Khafajeh vase (Frankfort 1935: 48, fig. 54–55), were more characteristic of Sumerian than Elamite iconography, indicating possibly local production within Mesopotamia or the Diyala valley. De Miroschedji (1973) also argues that three fragments from Sargonid levels at Ur (Woolley 1956: pl. 36, U.231, U.7072, and U.224), as well as a carved snake fragment (VA5298) now in East Berlin inscribed 'Rimush, King of Kish, Conqueror of Elam and Barahsum' (Klengel and Klengel 1980: 50), prove that the carving of vessels in the Inter-cultural Style continued down to Akkadian times, if not later. Stratigraphic evidence (de Miroschedji 1973: 38) suggests little chronological discontinuity, if not some overlap, between the latest 'série ancienne' and the earliest 'série récente' vessels and incised grey wares. The latter soft-stone imitation wares are known from Bampur V–VI and several sites on the Oman peninsula, including Amlah, Bat, Hili, and Umm an-Nar (cf. de Cardi et. al. 1976: 120–121, figs. 15–16).

Despite inherent difficulties with this carved soft-stone corpus, the evidence for some stylistic development is compelling and probably best illustrated by the unique figured fragments from Ur with their flat, non-rounded or almost squared-off relief, concave bands for snake scales, and unique horned demon. However, the argument for a lower dating or continuation of the style is not supported by the inscriptions of the Akkadian king Rimush. The two inscriptions were placed on the inside of the vessels, not as part of the design, but some time after they had been produced. They represent booty taken back from a successful campaign in the East and indicate only the high value accorded such luxury vessels by Mesopotamian rulers (Klengel and Klengel 1980: 51). In fact, all the inscriptions on the I.S. vessels, which include an inscription to Mesilim of Kish (Delougaz 1960: pl. IXa–b) on a fragment from Bismaya and an ideologically charged reference to 'Inanna and the Serpent' on the famous inlaid vessel from Inanna Temple VIIb at Nippur, appear to have been placed on the vessels after their production and, in this respect, contrast with the inscription on the carved chlorite fragment from Failaka (Bibby 1969: pl. XX) which mentions the 'Temple of the God Inzak.' The Failaka inscription seems to have been carefully and deeply cut between two figures wearing full-length robes and forms part of the design.

Unless there is something drastically incorrect with the dating of the earliest levels on Failaka, the figured chlorite and other soft-stone vessels from the island, some of which depict hut or archi-tectural facade designs, probably represent the latest manifestation of the Intercultural Style and can be dated to post-Akkadian times. Until this material is adequately published, however, I can only mention my superficial impression from examining some of the Failaka materials in Aarhus in 1972 that the carvings, in general, were unique and not stylistically comparable to the earlier, more widely distributed 'série ancienne' or Intercultural Style vessels found on Sumerian sites and at Susa, Yahya IVB, and Tarut (*cf.* also Kuwait 1964: figs. 48–52).

Although chronological ambiguities remain, the following observations deserve emphasis: the clustering of stratified I.S. vessels from Mesopotamian elite contexts in Early Dynastic II–IIIa levels; the lack of carved vessels on Bahrain and their virtual absence (save for one carved fragment from Umm an-Nar *cf.* Cleuziou forth. a: 23) from the Oman peninsula; the discovery of numerous I.S. fragments in contexts suggesting local production in later Yahya IVB levels and the infrequent, generally later appearance of 'série récente' dot-in-circle fragments at Yahya; and, finally, the tremendous variety of soft-stone vessels on Tarut. The remainder of this paper will attempt to determine what historical significance, beyond chronological considerations, is implicit in these observations.

The carved I.S. vessels, which are not found on Bahrain, primarily, though perhaps not exclusively, predate the earliest pre-Barbar levels on the Qal'at. Their virtual absence from the third millennium Hafit and Umm an-Nar horizons in Oman not only has chronological significance, but also suggests that the earlier green Tarut carved fragments were not imported from Oman, which was a later source, as excavations at Maysar 1, in particular, have demonstrated, for many of the grey 'série récente' bowls with dot-in-circle designs. Presently, no proven sources or production centers from the Arabian mainland are known for the earlier green Tarut chlorites, a fact which might imply that most, if not all, of the I.S. vessels from Tarut were imported from separate production centers on the Iranian plateau. This hypothesis is consistent with the generally accepted view of art historians (*cf.* Herz 1965: 138–143; de Miroschedji 1973: 22) that nearly all the major design elements of this style were related to or most strongly influenced by Elamite iconography. Moreover, as Lamberg-Karlovsky repeatedly and correctly has emphasized (*e.g.*, 1975: 362–363), the design motives represent complex symbols, laden with ideological force, and their broad distribution from Sumerian temple and elite burial contexts across the Iranian plateau suggests the diffusion and sharing of highly specific myths and deities. Conversely, their striking absence from roughly contemporaneous sites in the Oman peninsula suggests that the latter region, the future Makkan, did not participate in this far-ranging, syncretic ecumene. Excavations at the slightly later site of Maysar 1 (Weisgerber 1980;

n.d.) have documented ceramic and metal parallels to Harappan materials, and the discovery of a prismatic, three-sided seal with zoomorphic motives, including a humped bull (Weisgerber 1980: 86, Abb. 15), suggests that Makkan's closest cultural and possibly ideological relations were with the Indus Valley or related cultures to the northeast. Such an eastern connection, probably in a more attenuated form, also is evident on Bahrain where the Indus-based Dilmun standards and a similar prismatic seal with an Harappan inscription have been found (Weisgerber 1981: 219, Abb. 54; *cf.* also Bibby 1969: 361).

In addition, archaeological remains from the Early Dynastic center of Dilmun on Tarut seem to differ from those characteristics of the later 'Dilmun Civilization' that stretched from Failaka to Bahrain. The Intercultural Style vessels found in Tarut were imported into Sumer and stored in temples and royal graves. Some were kept for centuries and taken as booty on military campaigns and inscribed with rulers' names and titles. A luxury good *par excellence*, these vessels constitute only the best archaeologically documented example of numerous such elite materials which were imported into Sumer in finished and unfinished form during Early Dynastic times. The later 'international' trade at the end of the third and beginning of the second millennia B.C., which was channeled through a Bahrain-focused Dilmun, is documented archaeologically by different types of archaeological remains, primarily seals and weights. There is no indication that the broadly distributed 'série récente' bowls, some of which undoubtedly came from Oman, if not Maysar 1 itself, were considered luxury goods. Their dot-in-circle designs, formed by simple hollow tubular drills, required much less time and skill to produce than was necessary to finish the highly crafted, generally hand-smoothed I.S. vessels which had been widely traded centuries earlier.

The question is whether or not such a difference in the archaeological indices of long-distance trade is meaningful in historical terms or merely the accidental expression of a fragmentary archaeological record. As argued for chronological purposes, negative evidence sometimes is important, and it is suggested that the absence of seals from Tarut, particularly when compared with the more than three hundred characteristic Dilmun stamp seals found on Failaka (Kjaerum 1980: 45), implies a difference in what was exchanged or in the nature (as well, possibly, as the mechanics) of trade between Early Dynastic, on the one hand, and Ur III to later times, on the other. Specifically, it is during the latter periods that textual evidence refers to seafaring merchants from Sumer, the *alik Telmun*, plying the waters of the Arabian Gulf to trade principally textiles for metals, both tools and ingots. Trade in luxury goods continued, including, as Oppenheim (1954: 11) stressed, finished and unfinished ivory objects, but possibly may have decreased in importance relative to the increasingly essential exchange of mass-produced textiles for Makkan copper.

This reconstruction does not argue that all trade in the early and mid-third millennium was focused on less essential luxury goods. A trade in luxuries may only have characterized that maritime exchange controlled by the early Tarut-centered Dilmun. As Sargon's famous boast implies, other maritime trade with distant lands may have been direct, and Sumer and its rival, Susa, may have obtained some of the essential resources that they lacked from closer sources on the Iranian plateau. Later, as recent archaeological work in Oman is at last demonstrating, Makkan and Dilmun benefitted from trading both with Mesopotamia and the Indus Valley. Oppenheim's Mesopo-tamian-centered reconstruction (*ibid.*: 14) of a gradually restricted geographical horizon for commercial relations with the East is con-sistent with an early Harappan presence in (*cf.* also Tosi n.d.) or, at least, relations with Oman. The collapse of the Indus Valley civiliza-tion, which also is more thoroughly understood today as a result of recent archaeological investigations in Pakistan (*cf.* Costantini 1981; and Jarrige and Meadow 1980), clearly reverberated throughout this system and probably is related to the suggested northward displace-ment of Dilmun to Failaka during Kassite times.

Trade and cultural contacts between Bahrain and India in the third and second millennia B.C.

S. R. RAO

Among various items of Dilmun trade, copper, ivory, gemstones, beads and wood are important for the purpose of considering trade contacts between Bahrain and the cities of the Indus Valley (Harappan) Civilization. With the discovery of a true Bahrain seal in the port city of Lothal[1] situated at the head of the Gulf of Cambay, it is now abundantly clear that Lothal was an important partner in Bahrain trade. It has a well-designed tidal dock which could receive shipping and a large warehouse where the cargo used to be examined, sealed and where perhaps the collection of taxes was also undertaken.[2] The Lothal seal of Bahrain origin carries the motif of two jumping gazelles or ibexes flanking a doubleheaded dragon. There is no inscription at all, fig. 138. The Indus–Bahrain trade is further attested by six Bahrain type seals bearing Indus motifs or script. These are listed along with Bahrain seals (found in Bahrain and Oman) by Mughal,[3] Weisgerber[4] and others.[5] Gadd has also listed eighteen seals from Ur which he called Indian-style seals. In the thirties no Bahrain Civilization had come to light. Now those Ur seals (circular in shape) which bear Indus script or motifs or both have been rightly considered as Bahrain type seals belonging to Indus merchants residing in Ur.[6]

It must be said to the credit of Bahrain rulers that, while insisting on the use of circular seals to maintain the identity of the island, they permitted the Indus merchants residing in southern Mesopotamia and India but trading with Bahrain, Oman etc. and those residing in Ur but trading with other countries, to use their own script and motifs on circular seals.

The Indus writing on Bahrain seals 6 to 9 illustrated by Brunswig et al.[7] are from Bahrain–Failaka sites and show cursive writing of the second millennium B.C. Besides these there are some seals (circular ones) of Bahrain type among those illustrated by C. J. Gadd.[8] They are from Ur. We know now that they are mostly Bahrain type seals used by Indus merchants in Mesopotamia who

138 The Bahrain type seal from Lothal

must have had trade contacts with Bahrain–Failaka–Oman region. The earliest Bahrain–Oman seals on which any script as such can be traced are those using the Indus script which Ali Akbar H. Bushiri assigns to 2400 B.C.[9] The Bahrain seals with Indus script or motifs from Ur, Duristan and other places referred to by Briggs Buchanan[10] and Brunswig are of the second millennium B.C. The script is in the pure cursive writing of the Indus people as distinct from their hieratic script on two of the seals illustrated by Gadd.[11] The circular seal from Moenjo-daro (Marshall Pl. CX, 309) also carries the hieratic writing with a scorpion to which auxiliary signs are attached, fig. 139. But the tiny circular seals/sealings of Harappa (Vats Pl. C, 552–666) may not be of Bahrain origin, fig. 2–6. The larger circular Harappan seals/sealings (Vats Pl. XCIII and XCV) no. 317, fig. 7, 372, 373, 378, 379, 380, fig. 8–12, carrying Indus cursive inscriptions seen to be of Bahrain affinity though they are not exactly of Bahrain type. The inscription on seal 378 is not clear except for the first letter *pat* 'Lord or chief'. The inscription on 373 reads *śa-śā-pav* 'Sasa pure' and *tra'* 'saviour', while the one on seal 379 reads *paha* '(seal) of protector'.[12] *Pat, pa* and *tra* are meaningful phonenes in Old Indo-Aryan (OIA). Another interesting testimony to close cultural contact between the Indus and Bahrain civilizations is the Fire God motif on the circular seal 317 from Harappa, fig. 139, closely resembling the deity in an arch of flame. The inscription in the former is not clear. In the latter it reads *bhag-rk-a* 'Lord Arka'. Arka stands for sun as well as fire in OIA. Here it is a fire god who is referred to, fig. 140.[13] Yet another seal, fig. 141, depicting a goat behind a devotee kneeling before the Fire God in an arch of flame has an inscription reading *pa-eka-ka-ppra-tr-a* 'protect

139 Circular sealings from the Indus sites: some are of Bahraini origin (no. 1 = 309; 2-6 = 662, 663, 664, 665; 7 = 317; 8-12 = 372, 373, 378, 379, 380).

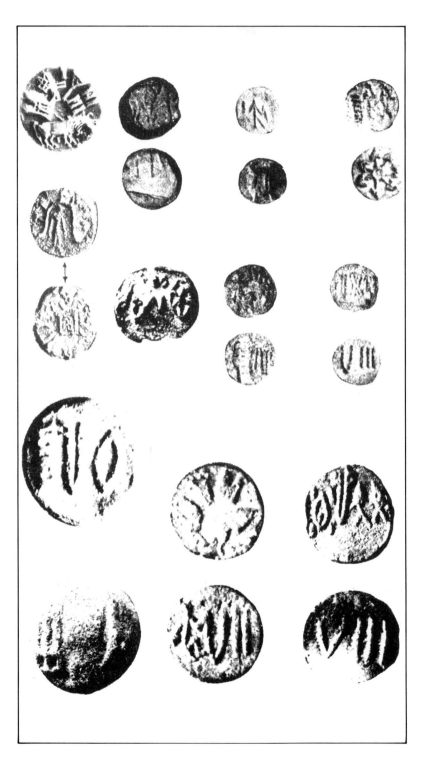

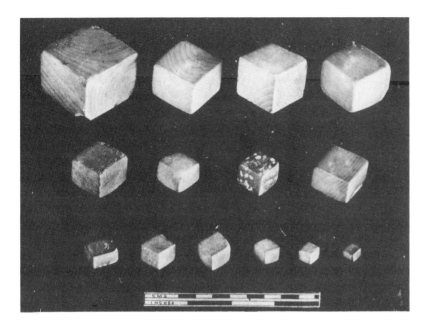

singularly great saviour'. The fire cult and offering of sacrifices were common to Bahrain and Indus people. Sacrificial altars and animal remains have also been found in Kalibangan, the Barbar Temple complex,[14] and Lothal.[15]

Another important mechanism of trade common to the Bahrain and the Indus merchants is the tetrahedron weight of chert, agate, etc., fig. 142. The Dilmun standard of 1370 gm is five times the Lothal weight 274.4096 gm.[16]

The cargo list of Dilmun merchants included copper, ivory, gemstones and beads. The carnelian and varieties of beads from Sar burials are of Indus origin, especially Lothal. May be some are from Chanhudaro. Lothal has a large bead factory from which eight hundred beads of carnelian in various stages of manufacture were recovered.[17]

Ivory was another item of Dilmun trade which came from the Indus cities. Lothal was a major ivory-working centre as is evident from the ivory-workshop laid bare on the Acropolis. A large variety of ivory articles including sawn-pieces used for making boxes, combs and inlays have been found along with gamesmen, seals, linear scales, antimony rods and ornaments of ivory.[18]

Copper seems to have been purified in the Lothal workshops and exported in the form of bun-ingots. One of them found at Lothal is of 99.81% purity and it is arsenic-free unlike the Moenjo-daro ingot. Hitherto it was believed that arsenic-free copper was obtained by the Lothal smiths from Oman: but Weisgerber[19] has shown that Oman

140 Seal from Harappa; "deity with a trident-like headgear in an arch of flame". The inscription reads (from left to right) bhag-rk-a-bhaga-Arka, 'Lord Arka'. Arka refers to the sun as well as fire in the Rigveda

141 Seal with a goat behind a devotee kneeling before the Fire God in an arch of flame

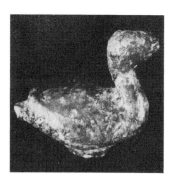

143 Copper bird: the rod beneath it is broken

copper is not arsenic-free. In this connection it may be recalled that Ea-Nasir's letter refers to 'good copper' and 'ordinary copper'.[20] Perhaps ordinary copper was not purified while pure copper meant one like that of a Lothal ingot absolutely free from arsenic and other impurities. If that is so, it is Lothal which could have supplied 'pure copper' of 99.81% purity. The re-smelting and other processes for purifying copper were adopted at the Lothal coppersmiths' workshops situated at the northern end of the Lower Town.[21] Out of three hundred copper objects analyzed by Dr. B. B. Lal, Chief Archaeological Chemist, not one contained arsenic. A unique copper object found at Lothal[22] is the 'bird', fig. 143, which closely resembles the 'bird' (perhaps a peacock) from Temple III of Barbar.[23]

From these details it should be obvious that the Indus Civilization and Bahrain Civilization had very close trade and cultural contacts.

A word must be said about the 'Sumerian Paradise of Dilmun'. 'Paradise' is an abstract concept to most of the ancient, and even to modern, civilizations. It is also associated with the 'creation of the world' and 'Flood' theories. Both are in vogue in ancient Hindu mythology. Bendt Alster has taken into account all the evidence available from Bahrain, Oman and Failaka (archaeological as well as epigraphical) to see if any particular island or littoral of Arabia could be definitely identified with Dilmun. Though he says that 'denying the possibility of the existence of a paradise in the beginning of time in Sumerian mythology is not an attempt to underestimate the richness of these early resources' and 'that the whole story takes place in the marshes, in the Mesopotamian setting, rather than in Dilmun itself', he cannot resist supporting the popular feeling that Bahrain might have been the Paradise of the Sumerians.[24] It must however be remembered that Dilmun lay to the east of Sumer, while Bahrain and Failaka lie to the south. The clean cities referred to in the Sumerian Epic are not to be found on either site. In fact, well-planned and clean cities noted for underground drains were built in the Indus Empire. Secondly, a much larger settlement than the one found in Ras al-Qal'a, accounting for a large population suggested by 150,000 or even 300,000 burials in the small island of Bahrain must have existed here. It seems to have been submerged subsequently by the sea in the latter half of the second millennium or still later. This is not a wild guess. Curtis E. Larsen observes: 'Another suggestion for later high relative sealevel stand is also preserved at Qala-at-al Bahrain. Wave-rounded potsherds of Kassite date are found between 63 and 74 m from the present shoreline. These occur at about 1.25 m above high tide, but in an uncertain context. They are overlain by Hellenistic and medieval Islamic occupation levels. Neo-Assyrian and Neo-Babylonian pottery is absent. . . . Such waveworn pottery may have been refuse discarded on the nearby beach during Kassite or later times, but the absence of the first millennium B.C. occupation levels tentatively argues for a postulated higher sealevel that reworked earlier Kassite deposits. Subsequent retreat of the sea allowed the northward spread of later settlements onto the recently exposed intertidal zone'.[25]

In the Gulf of Kutch also a similar rise in sea-level during the latter half of the second millennium B.C. which was responsible for the submergence of the ancient port-town of Dwarka[26] has come to light as a result of underwater exploration and excavation by the Marine Archaeology Unit of the National Institute of Oceanography, Goa, under the author's direction. It is most likely that the pre-Kassite period city at Qal'at al-Bahrain was also submerged by the sea. Instead of propounding attractive theories[27] about depositing the bodies of those who died elsewhere in the Bahrain tombs and that 'the fractional burials were deposited at various times of pilgrimage in order to allow deceased family members access to the land of paradise', it would be more scientific to look for the habitational settlements in the shallow waters of Qal'at al-Bahrain and recon-struct the true history of Dilmun.

1. Rao S. R. (1973) *Lothal and the Indus Civilization*, New York, Pl. 121, 162, 165.

2. Rao S. R. (1982) 'Indus Cities: Planning for Perfection', in *Science Today*, (Bombay) June 1982, 13–19.

3. Rao S. R. (1979) *Lothal – A Harappan Port Town*, MASI 78, New Delhi, 113–14: Fig. 18A.

3. Mughal M. R. (1983) *The Dilmun Burial Complex at Sar* (Bahrain) Pls. XLV–XLIX.

4. Weisgerber G. (1981) 'Mehr als Kupfer in Oman–Ergebnisse der Expedition 1981', *Der Anschnitt* 33, 174–263.

5. Tosi M. (1982) 'A possible Harappan Seaport in Eastern Arabia: R's Al Junayaz in the Sultanate of Oman' paper read at the *First International Conference on Pakistan Archaeology*, Peshawar.

5. *The Temple Complex at Barbar* (Ministry of Information, Bahrain), 3–9.

7. *Dilmun – New Studies in the Archaeology and Early History of Bahrain* Ed. Daniel T. Potts, Berlin 1983, Pls. I–III.

6. Gadd C. J. (1932) 'Seals of Ancient Indian Style Found at Ur', *Proceedings of the British Academy*, VIII.

7. Brunswig R. H. *et. al.* (1983) 'New Indus Type and Related Seals from the Near East' *Dilmun*, 1983 (Ed. Daniel T. Potts), 101ff., Pl. I–II.

8. Rao S. R. (1973) *op. cit.* 121: also Gadd (1932) *op. cit.*

9. Busheri, Ali Akbar, "Tatawwur al-kitaba al-Dilmuniyya bil-idmāj" Al-Watheekah 'Bahrain Through the Ages' Conference, Volume 3 pp 122–189.

10. Buchanan B. (1965) 'A dated Persian Gulf Seal and its Implications', *Studies in Honor of Bruno Landsberger on his Seventy-fifth Birthday, AS* 16, Chicago, 204–209

11. Gadd C. J. (1932) *op. cit.* pls. I & II.

12. Rao S. R. (1982a) *The Decipherment of the Indus Script*, Bombay, 82.

13. Rao S. R. (1981) *Presidential Address, Seventh Annual Congress of the Epi-graphical Society of India*, Calcutta, 26.

14. *The Temple Complex at Barbar*, 31.

15. Rao S. R. (1973) *op. cit.*, 139ff.: Pls. XXVIB to XXVIIB.
Rao, S. R. (1979) *op. cit.*, 216ff.: Pls. XCIIIB, XCIV & XCVA.
16. Powell M. A. (1983) 'The Standard of Dilmun' in *Dilmun* ed. Daniel T. Potts, 141.
Rao S. R. (1982) *op. cit.*, 16–17.
17. Rao S. R. (1979) *op. cit.*, Pls. XC–XCI.
18. Rao S. R. (1973) *op. cit.*, Pl. XXXIIA.
Rao S. R. (1982) *op. cit.*, 17.
19. Rao S. R. (1973) *op. cit.*, 80ff. Pl. XVIIIA and personal communication from Weisgerber.
20. Oppeneheim A. L. (1954) *Journal of the American Oriental Society*, 7–14.
Bibby G. S. (1970) *Looking for Dilmun* (Pelican).
21. Rao S. R. (1973) *op. cit.*, Pl. LIV.
22. Rao S. R. (1973) *op. cit.*, 87: Pl. XIXc.
23. Rice, M., *The Temple Complex at Barbar*, 33.
24. Alster B. (1983) 'Dilmun, Bahrain and the Alleged Paradise in Sumerian Myth and Literature', in *Dilmun* (Ed.) Daniel T. Potts, 58ff.
25. Larsen C. E. (1983) 'The Early Environment and Hydrology of Ancient Bahrain', *Dilmun*, ed. Daniel T. Potts, 11.
26. Rao S. R. (1983a) 'Sunken Ships and Submerged Ports' *Science Today*, Bombay, September 1983. Rao S. R. (1984) 'Submergence of Dwarka is a fact' *Jnana Jyoti*, Bangalore (Ed. S. R. Rao).
27. Alster B. (1983) *op. cit.* Lamberg-Karlovsky C. C. (1982) 'Dilmun, Gateway to Immortality, *Journal of Near Eastern Studies*, 41, 1982, 45–50. Frohlich B. (1983) 'The Bahrain Burial Mounds', *Dilmun, Journal of the Bahrain Historical and Archaeological Society*, 11, 1983, 5–9.

Bahrain and the Indus civilisation

AHMAD HASAN DANI

New light can be thrown on the Bronze Age history of Bahrain if a more definitive statement can be made on the westward trade of the Indus Civilisation. A comparative study of the archaeological and literary evidence under the title 'Dilmun, Where and When'[1] has provided a chronological frame for fixing the geographical locale of Dilmun in one or the other Gulf sites on the basis of the excavated material, but this is based on the assumption that the available evidence is highly suggestive, though not perhaps final. However, no attempt has so far been made to assess the role that the Gulf area may have played in advancing the trade prospects of the Ancient World during the Bronze Age. It is possible that more archaeological work in the years to come, if properly directed, may provide a better perspective.

Indus contact with Bahrain has been established by Professor T. Geoffrey Bibby, who, in his various contributions,[2] has dilated on the 'Ancient Indian Style' seals from Bahrain. Sir Mortimer Wheeler[3] has distinguished three types among them and talked in terms of a wider perspective: 'Enough is known of them to indicate that in bulk they must in future, as 'Persian Gulf Seals', be considered with Gadd's group in terms of a varied but related extension of the great Indus series, made largely in and around the Persian Gulf for use in connection with long-range Indus trade.' C. J. Gadd[4] was the first to describe 'Seals of Ancient Indian Style found at Ur', but that was in the different contexts of providing a comparative view of the Indus Civilisation against the background of Mesopotamian archaeology.

Both these aspects of contact have expanded in the years that followed these early discoveries. Of greatest importance is the discovery of S. R. Rao[5] 'of a Persian Gulf seal' at Lothal – an Indus Civilisation site on the bank of the Sabarmati river in Gujarat on the western coast of India. According to Rao, 'The material of which the Lothal seal is made is steatite of a light grey colour with a creamy surface. Its diameter is 2.25 cm. and the thickness at the center 1.2

cm. At the back is a perforated boss covering almost the entire surface and divided by triple lines between four circles with a central dot. On the face are two jumping goats or gazelle-like animals looking behind and flanking a double-headed dragon. Both in motif and shape this seal is entirely different alike from the normal square seals of the Indus Civilisation and from the Sumerian cylinder seals. It bears no script of any kind. On the other hand, it has a resemblance to the circular seals of steatite found in the excavations at Barbar and Ras-al-Qala in the island of Bahrain in the Persian Gulf. Comparable circular seals found in the excavations in Failaka, a little island near Kuwait, are assigned by Dr. Bibby to the Sargonid period. They are identical in almost every detail, except for the variation in size, with the Persian Gulf seal from Lothal, and, in so far as a single 'Document' is valid, indicates that the Lothal merchants traded with the Persian Gulf in the latter half of the third millennium.'

Although the date of this particular seal in the archaeological context of Lothal is uncertain, as it is a surface find, its very presence on an Indus site on the western coast of India speaks of some kind of trade relation between the Indus-land and Persian Gulf. Another important find is reported from the Indus level at Balakot on the Makran coast by Professor G. Dales.[6] 'One pottery vessel is, however, almost certainly a Near Eastern import. Its high center of gravity, carinated shoulder and black painted geometric decoration are non-Harappan and point to southern Iran and the Persian Gulf, especially to Umm an-Nar in Abu Dhabi'. Professor Dales has also drawn attention to pottery having distinctive Kulli and other Baluchistan characteristics, excavated from burial cairns on the island of Umm an-Nar[7]. More finds of similar pottery can also be compared and studied in this background.[8] Special reference has also been made to 'a most distinctive type of male terracotta figurine', only three in number, that 'come from the current series of excavations at the holy city of Nippur in southern Iraq.'[9] On these figurines the remarks of Professor Dales are pertinent: 'Thus we are confronted with a small group of atypical figurines in southern Mesopotamia, found in contexts dating to the period of presumed Sumerian international seafaring activities. Is it merely coincidental that we find almost identical fat male figurines at Harappan sites where they are typologically and stylistically at home? The basic concept of animated figurines with movable heads and arms is widely manifested among Harappan figurines as is the popularity of grossly exaggerating the roundness of the human body. There is a large corpus of Harappan figurines, both male and female, whose bodies are blown up into round balls.'[10]

Notice has also been taken of the find of Harappan-type cubical dice from Mesopotamian sites.[11] It will be relevant here to quote an important context in which such a find was made. 'The most significant discovery was that of 'broken clay dice' in a 'Hoard' found in a pottery vessel buried beneath an Akkadian period house floor at Tell Asmar in the Diyala region of central Iraq. It was in this and other 'hoards' from Akkadian houses at Tell Asmar that etched carnelian beads, bone inlays, stamp seals, a cylinder seal, and a distinctive type of knobbed pottery – all these with strong Harappan stylistic parallels – were found.' About this hoard of objects Professor C. C. Lamberg-Karlovsky remarks: 'If anywhere in Mesopotamia we have evidence for Indus Direct Contact Trade it would be best supported at Tell Asmar.'[12] Another type of information is noted by Briggs Buchanan,[13] who, in the Yale University Babylonian collection, found a seal impression on a tablet recording a mercantile agreement of the Larsa period, i.e. second half of the twentieth century B.C. This is the impression of a typical 'Persian Gulf Seal', suggesting that such seals were in actual use in the entire region from Mesopotamia to Lothal in Gujerat. To this group must be added an Indus seal impression on a pot-sherd found in Oman by M. Tosi. Such seal impressions have also been reported from other sites in the Gulf.

It is in the light of these archaeological discoveries that Old Babylonian texts should be re-examined, place names like Dilmun, Makkan and Meluḫḫa should be understood in their true geographical context and trade relations determined on the basis of possible routes followed for imports and exports. Enough has been written on the goods that were traded. It has also been shown that such items of trade related to raw material, like copper ingots, carnelian, ivory, shell, lapis, pearls, spices and wood. That these items could have come from as far away as the Indus Valley Civilisation sites has also been well argued. But some of the material could equally well have come from other regions, e.g. copper ingots from Oman. Such a possibility cannot be ruled out. However, the crucial issue is the two-way traffic. It is here that the Indus Civilisation zone diminishes in importance as the material imported from Mesopotamia into the Indus Valley is almost insignificant. Even if we note the presence of Gilgamesh and Enkidu figures on Indus seals found here, they cannot be taken as objects of trade. In view of these facts the identification of Makkan and Meluḫḫa with Makran and the Indus Valley respectively has been doubted. This is mainly because direct trade relations between Mesopotamia and the Indus Valley have been sought and archaeologists have been looking for objects of direct imports and exports in the two regions. Not much importance was placed on the intermediaries or 'middle-men' who could have managed the trade because not much was known about the archaeology of intermediate countries. That position no longer holds good. It was C. C. Lamberg-Karlovsky who first drew attention to this possibility by discussing the details of trade mechanism. Of the three types propounded by him he has rightly emphasized 'Central Place Trade' – a viewpoint that comes closest to indirect trade as suggested by other scholars. But the importance of this indirect trade could not be fully realised as it lay hanging between two pulls, one by land route across Baluchistan and Iran over to Elam and Mesopotamia, the other by sea past the Gulf states. This position, I believe, could now be clarified.

There has been considerable improvement in our perception of Indus Civilisation since the days when C. J. Gadd presented his material on the 'Indus Type Seals' found in Mesopotamia. At that time the main consideration was to build up the chronology of the main phase of the Indus Civilisation. Today that stage is past. We have now at our disposal enough material to show progressive development in the Bronze Age cultures of the Indus Valley. The most significant is the realisation of at least two main phases – the earlier pre-Indus phase, recognised for the first time by Dr. F. A. Khan[14] as the Kot Diji Culture, links of which have been found throughout Panjab[15] and also in the Gomal[16] and Bannu[17] plains, at Mundigak in Afghanistan,[18] at Sahr-i-Sokhta in eastern Iran[19] and as far as Turkmenistan[20] in the U.S.S.R., as has been shown in excavations by Professor V. Masson. As has been aptly pointed out by Dr. M. R. Mughal,[21] in this period the land connection with the northerly and westerly sites was very well established. Excavation at Bampur by Miss de Cardi[22] has also shown inter-relation between the cultures of this period in Baluchistan and those of eastern Iran. The new excavations conducted by Professor Dales[23] at Balakot has extended the Baluchi cultural pattern as far south as the Makran coast. The central place of Tepe Yahya, whose contacts have been so well established by Professor Lamberg-Karlovsky, should be traced to this phase of the Bronze Age cultures of the Indus region. It is precisely for this reason that he has argued for an early date for Tepe Yahya, period V A, referring it to 3400–3200 B.C. It is in this level that Nal pottery of pre-Harappan phase was recovered. Tepe Yahya has also yielded the evidence of working steatite mines some twenty-five km. away – raw material which continued to be imported later in the mature Indus phase. Later in Tepe Yahya IV B, dated to the beginning of the third millennium B.C., a Persian Gulf type seal was also found. Such a rich connection of pre-Harappan date is sufficient proof to show the landward contact, possibly through the Central Place of Tepe Yahya, westward in the pre-Indus phase of the Bronze Age cultures of the Indus region.

When we come to the mature Indus phase a southward shift of such trends has been long noted[24] but its significance has hardly been realised. Similarly Professor Dales[25] has well argued for the commercial activity of the Indus people along the western coast by his discovery of port towns as far west as Sutkagen-dor in the Dasht valley. He has also noted that while along the Makran coast the advance of the Indus Civilisation has been observed far away, on the landward side the Indus Civilisation hardly penetrates into the western hills, except as trading colonies.[26]

What is the meaning of this picture? A proper understanding of the mature Indus phase must be based on a wider archaeological contextual frame in which the literary evidence about Dilmun, Makkan and Meluḥḥa along with the new discoveries in the Gulf region should be properly focussed. The so-called 'Persian Gulf Seals', and particularly the Indus weight found in the 'Custom House' at Bahrain[27] must be taken as strong evidence for Central Place Trade in the mature Indus phase. It is only such contacts, if pursued further, can throw more light on the new trends seen in the mature Indus Civilisation. We have so far been looking in vain for direct contact with Mesopotamia. But the very fact that the 'Persian Gulf Seals' emerged, were actually in use for trade agreements and have been found in Mesopotamia, Tepe Yahya and as far east as Lothal, is sufficient evidence to prove the existence of middle men for trade – a trade relationship that must have enriched the Indus people on the one hand and on the other given an opportunity to the people in the Gulf area to play a decisive role in building up the whole mechanism of trade. It is only when this trade contact and its requirements are fully grasped that we can understand the development of new trends in the Indus Civilisation as distinct from those seen in the pre-Indus phase. It is possible that the chronology of the Indus Civilisation and the Gulf trade is inter-related. How far the prosperity and decline are mutually related remains to be proved by future work.

1. *Dilmun, Journal of the Bahrain Historical and Archaeological Society*, no. II, 1983, 15–19.

2. See *Ancient Cities of the Indus*, ed. by G. L. Posshel, New Delhi, 1979, under Bibby, T. Geoffrey for Bibliography, 372. (Henceforward abbreviated as *Posshel*.)

3. *The Indus Civilization*, 3rd ed., Cambridge, 1968, 115–116.

4. Reprinted in *Posshel*, 115–22.

5. Reprinted in *Posshel*, 148–50.

6. 'The Balakot Project. Summary of Four Years Excavations in Pakistan', in *South Asian Archaeology, 1977*, ed. by M. Taddei, Naples, 1979, 265–66.

7. See *Posshel*, 140.

8. *Archaeology in the United Arab Emirates*, Vol. I, II–III, for Hili see 8–13.

9. See *Posshel*, 141–43.

10. *Ibid.*, 142.

11. *Ibid.*, 141.

12. *Ibid.*, 132.

13. *Ibid.*, 145–47.

14. *Pakistan Archaeology*, No. 2, 1965, 11–85.

15. See M. R. Mughal, 'New Archaeological Evidence from Bahawalpur', in *Indus Civilization – New Perspectives*, ed. by A. H. Dani, Islamabad, 1981, 33–42.

16. Ahmad Hasan Dani, 'Excavations in the Gomal Valley', in *Ancient Pakistan*, Vol. V, 1972.

17. F. A. Durrani, 'Evidence West of the Indus', in *Indus Civilisation New Perspectives*, ed. by A. H. Dani, Islamabad, 1981, 133–38.

18. J. M. Casal, *Fouilles de Mundigak*, Paris, 1961.

19. See M. Tosi in *East and West*, Vol. XVIII, 1968, 9–66, and vol. XIX, 1969, 283–386.

20. See Masson and Sarianidi, *Central Asian: Turkmenia before the Achaemenids*, New York, 1972.

21. See his paper 'The Present State of Research on the Indus Valley Civilization,' reprinted in *Posshel*, 90–100.

22. 'The Bampur Sequence in the third millennium B.C.', in *Antiquity*, Vol. 41, 1967, 33–41.

23. 'Reflections on Four Years of Excavations at Balakot', in Dani, *Indus Civilization, New Perspectives*, 25–32.

24. See Mughal's article reprinted in *Posshel*, 90–100.

25. See *Posshel*, 139–40.

26. See Louis Dupree, 'Notes on Shortugai', in Dani, *Indus Civilization, New Perspectives*, 103–15.

27. See Bibby, T. Geoffrey, *Looking For Dilmun*, New York, 1969.

Dilmun's further relations: the Syro-Anatolian evidence from the third and second millennia B.C.

DANIEL POTTS

The strong mercantile connections which existed between Dilmun and Ur during the Old Babylonian period have been discussed at length by a number of authorities (e.g. Oppenheim 1954, Leemans 1960, Butz 1979, Neumann 1979). Yet perhaps less easily documented in either the archaeological or cuneiform sources is a connection between the Gulf area in general, Dilmun in particular, and the Syro-Anatolian region. The southern gateway of this region can be identified for our purposes with Mari, while the northernmost area which comes into question is the heartland of Anatolia itself. Here sites such as Açemhöyük and Kültepe bear witness to the contact which shall be discussed below. The intensity of that contact, as with the intensity of Dilmun's contacts with southern Babylonia, probably peaked during the Old Babylonian era, yet it was of an antiquity undoubtedly greater and lasted considerably longer, as both archaeological and written records attest.

THE ARCHAEOLOGICAL EVIDENCE
We can point to a number of signs of contact noted between the Syro-Anatolian area and the Gulf which have accumulated in the archaeological literature over the last two decades. Taken together, they amount to a growing body of data suggestive of a significant relationship between the two areas. Chronologically speaking, we can trace the beginnings of an awareness of this connection in the realm of glyptic art back to 1965, and follow it up to the present day. Let us briefly review the evidence thus accumulated.

I. In 1965 Briggs Buchanan noted that elements of so-called 'Persian Gulf' glyptic – namely the bucranium and the drinking scene – were common on Syro-Cappadocian and Syrian cylinder seals of the period *c.* 2100–1800 B.C. Buchanan wrote, 'The Syrian connection thus suggested by both the bucranium and the drinking scene makes it seem possible that around 2000 B.C. the Persian Gulf merchants had a relationship, other than one involving trade, with some ethnic element in Syria (merchants or colonists?)' (Hallo and Buchanan 1965: 207).

II. In 1971 Edith Porada noted further parallels between Gulf and Syro-Anatolian glyptic. Specifically, she pointed to the comparability of protomes emanating from a circular hub on Gulf seals from Bahrain and Failaka, and on a sealing from Açemhöyük near Konya. Further, she pointed to the similarity between figures with streams of water emanating from them on a Gulf seal from Ur and one in the Pierpont Morgan Library collection of Syrian style (Porada 1971: 335).

III. In 1975 Pierre Amiet re-published a cylinder seal-impressed sherd from Umm an-Nar island, which shows close parallels with similar impressed sherds from Tell Chuera (pre-Sargonic) and Hama J (cf. Wäfler 1979). Amiet dated the sherd to, at the earliest, ED I. Noting that the practice of impressing pottery with cylinder seals was largely a Syro-Palestinian one, not widely practised in Elam or Mesopotamia, Amiet wrote, 'The most striking fact, undoubtedly, is that this impression forms the southernmost piece of evidence at present known of a trade flow emanating from northern Syria and corresponding to one that, in a probably later age, brought chlorite vases originating in eastern Iran at least as far as Mari' (1975: 426).

IV. In 1978 Poul Kjaerum published a preliminary report on the glyptic of Failaka. There he noted (Kjaerum 1980: 47):

a. the presence on many seals of the 'serpent monster held by the gods flanking it'. Declaring this to be 'absolutely non-Babylonian', Kjaerum nevertheless wrote, 'while definitely local, they recall the motif of serpent monsters with bull or stag heads from Anatolia and Nuzi'.

b. the presence on some Failaka seals of 'two bulls on altars, each with a fowl above their heads . . . flanking a man', about which he wrote: 'It is tempting to interpret these bull figures as idols (and) to compare them with the Syro-Anatolian bull altars'.

c. the presence of standards on the Failaka seals, including 'the local net square or double volutes like Syro-Cappadocian standards'.

d. one seal on which 'a palm tree stands in the centre of a composition consisting of symbols only, placed on a platform. The symbols are protomes, well known from several Dilmun seals, heads or masks on poles, which are unique here but known from the Syrian group'.

e. the depiction of tables 'with a curved top and a shaped pedestal dividing into bulls' feet in the fashion of the Syro-Cappadocian tables depicted on seals and ivory carvings'.

f. the presence of drinking scenes, already compared by Buchanan and Porada to Syrian glyptic, with, in one case, the insertion of 'the animal throne which is a common Anatolian feature'.

In conclusion, Kjaerum wrote of 'strong influence on the Dilmun pictographical repertoire from the Syrian-Anatolian cultural sphere, an influence not indicated by the direct evidence' (Kjaerum 1980: 48–49).

Aside from the glyptic repertoire, one should also point out the well-known finds of chlorite and steatite belonging to the 'série ancienne' or 'Intercultural Style' which have such a wide distribution in the Near East in the second half of the third millennium B.C. Specifically, it appears on the basis of recent analyses, that certain soft-stone objects, made of a true talc, i.e. steatite, or talc-chlorite, from Mari, were fashioned from stone probably quarried in Arabia c. 150–200 miles southwest of Riyadh (Kohl, Harbottle, and Sayre 1979). That these pieces, or the raw stone from which they were manufactured, reached Mari via the Gulf, is indicated by the distribution of examples of like composition. These have been found on Tarut, most probably the Gulf outlet for the stone if indeed it did come from the Arabian hinterland, on Failaka, and at Bismaya, in addition to Mari. The analytical results complement the stylistic observations of several scholars, most notably Edith Porada, who pointed to the 'vase with a spread lion-headed eagle' from Tarut, which she felt was 'obviously related to one from Mari', and to the presence of chlorite or steatite 'curls of a male beard' from Tarut, similar to objects of the same form in lapis lazuli from Mari (Porada 1971: 329, 331, cf. now Zarins 1978b, where the soft-stone corpus from Tarut has been published in full).

THE CUNEIFORM EVIDENCE

I. EBLA

At the moment, the earliest references which attest to contact between Dilmun and the Syrian region are to be found in the corpus of texts from Tell Mardikh/Ebla. A complete study of all of this material has recently been published by G. Pettinato (Pettinato 1983: 75–82), and it is thus unnecessary to repeat his work here. To simply summarize the main points of Pettinato's important article, the attestations of Dilmun have been brought together in Table 1.

Of greatest interest are the attestations of Dilmun copper and tin. Despite the relative nearness of the Anatolian copper sources, it would seem that copper from the south was also known here in northern Syria. H. Waetzoldt, in discussing the terminology of the metals industry at Ebla, suggests that tin was imported to Mesopotamia from Dilmun as early as c. 2500 B.C. (Waetzoldt 1981: 367). One further note of interest is the use of the so-called 'Dilmun-shekel' at Ebla (Pettinato 1981: 182, cf. generally De Maigret 1980, and Pomponio 1980: 173, and n. 4). While it is not entirely clear whether

Table 1

DILMUN IN THE EBLA TEXTS, AFTER PETTINATO 1983

Dilmun as a Toponym	Text
d i l m u n^{ki} = 'Dilmun'	MEE 1, n. 2095
	MEE 3, n. 44

Dilmun as a Qualifying Particle	
g i š - d i l m u n = 'Dilmun tree (palm?)'	VE, 1. 409a
	MEE 1, n. 1861 r. X 37
b a p p i r - d i l m u n = 'Dilmun beer-bread'	MEE 3, n. 44 r. VIII 14
n a g g a - d i l m u n = 'Dilmun tin'	MEE 3, n. 44 r. I 6′
u r u d u - d i l m u n = 'Dilmun copper'	MEE 3, n. 59 v. II 9′
d i l m u n - b a l a g = 'Dilmun harp'	MEE 3, nn. 45–46 r. X 9
g í n - d i l m u n = 'Dilmun shekel'	MEE 1, n. 48 r. III 1

Dilmun as an element in professional titles	
DILMUN	translation uncertain
GAL.DILMUN	translation uncertain
DILMUN.ZÀ	translation uncertain
DILMUN.KUR$_6$	translation uncertain
DILMUN.KU$_5$	translation uncertain

this is meant to be understood as the 'shekel of Dilmun', or, more generally, as a 'noble shekel', it nonetheless demonstrates quite clearly that the name Dilmun had recognized connotations in mid-third millennium Syria. The use of 'Dilmun' as an adjective or appellative meaning 'noble' is otherwise attested in southern Babylonia as well (cf. Kutscher 1975).

II. THE MARI CORRESPONDENCE

Three letters in particular should be mentioned. The first of these (ARM I 21) was sent by Šamši-Adad (1813–1781 B.C.) to his son Yasmaḫ-Adad. In the first part of the letter, Šamši-Adad reprimands his son for not having sent on to him a messenger from Dilmun. In fact, as the letter tells us, the Dilmunite had been beaten as a result of his having broken into the home of a merchant and stolen a palm-wood box or trunk. Yasmaḫ-Adad had apparently used this incident as an excuse for not sending the man on to his father, but as the text shows, Šamši-Adad was not amused. I translate roughly from the original French edition of the text (Dossin 1950: 59):

ARM I 21
1 To Yasmaḫ-Ad(ad)
2 say this:
3 thus (speaks) Šamši-Adad,
4 your father.
5 Regarding the Dilmunite messenger,
6 of whom you wrote me in these terms:
7 'He entered the house of a merchant and there stole
8 a palm chest and someone beat him.
9 Therefore, until now, I have not sent him.'
10 There's what you wrote to me.
11 Perfect! So someone beat him! Can't he climb on an ass?
12 Why, till now, haven't you sent him to me?
13 According to my decisions, in truth, you should have sent him twenty days ago.
14 (Why) don't you send him?

Here the text breaks off, and the second section concerns a separate matter, namely the receipt and treatment of a shipment of copper which does not concern us. While the text gives no indications as to the mission of the Dilmunite messenger, another letter (ARM I 17) from Šamši-Adad to his son provides details of a setting which could well be similar to that which lay behind the letter just considered. In this letter, Šamši-Adad gives his son specific instructions concerning the preparations he must make so that a passing caravan from Dilmun can continue on its way in comfort and on schedule.

ARM I 17
1 To Yasmaḫ-Adad
2 say this:
3 thus (speaks) Šamši-Adad,
4 your father.
5 The second day after (the receipt)
6 of my tablet, the messengers
7 Dilmunite, from Šubat-Enlil
8 will depart. Ten labourers
9 who will be with them for their . . .,
10 that the nobles (?) promised for them,
11 and that, due to their promise, they permit to live with their people,
12 so that they'll leave contented.
13 You will thus receive the nobles (?)
14 but, as soon as the caravan will be moved, receive no more nobles.
15 30 sheep,
16 30 *qa* of excellent oil, 60 *qa* of sesame, which are to be poured into the grease jars,

17 3 *qa* of berries of juniper and boxwood;
18 for 10 men and for the young Dilmunites,
20 1 skin per person, 2 (pairs of) sandals per person;
21 for the 5 servants . . ., 1 skin per person and 2 (pairs of) sandals per person;
22 for 7 artisans
23 1 skin per person, 2 (pairs of) (sandals) per person;
24 for the 10 men who, on leaving (Šubat-Enlil)
25 will be with them,

Rev.
26 (1) skin per person, (2 pairs of sandals per person);
27 for 10 pack asses . . .;
28 in all 52 skins,
29 64 (pairs of) sandals;
30 1 large leather bag
31 10 leather thongs of 1½ *gar*;
32 which, according to the terms of my tablet,
33 (all this material) shall be prepared exactly.
34 As these messengers,
35 upon their arrival, were detained,
36 whereas previously they could go (freely),
37 I have spoken to Lâ'ûm in the following terms:
38 'As Ḥammi-tilû is waiting at Mari'.
39 Now, write
40 that someone will lead Ḥammi-tilû to you
41 and that he will await the messengers at Mari,
42 after which he'll go with them,
43 upon their arrival.
44 Furthermore, the provisioning which they will demand of you,
45 give it to them.

The detailed attention which Šamši-Adad gives to the Dilmun caravan clearly underscores the importance that must have been attached to this traffic.

In another letter (ARM V 14) Yasmaḥ-Adad writes to Ḥammurabi concerning a caravan which Išme-Dagan has sent to Dilmun from Mari, but which, on the return journey, was held up by a certain Ili-Ebuḥ, due to 'claims concerning a well'. This sounds as if the caravan had violated their water rights, perhaps by watering themselves at a well which they had no permission to use. Whatever the circumstances may have been, Yasmaḥ-Adad sends out two men to lead the caravan safely to Babylon, where it is to remain until receiving orders to depart.

ARM V 14

1 To Ḥammurabi

2 say this:

3 thus (speaks) Yasmaḥ-Adad.

4 Previously, your brother sent a caravan

5 to Dilmun. Now, this caravan, on its return,

6 due to claims concerning a well,

7 has been (held) at Ili-Ebuḥ's.

8 But, with this caravan

9 ....

10 ....

11 ....

Rev.

....

1 And.........your.......

2 who.....................

3 that your (heart) has no anxiety.

4 Now,...............igriya

5 and Img(urrum(?)) I send to you.

6 They will lead intact

7 this caravan to (Baby)lon, to you.

8 This caravan, up to the day when your brother writes to you that it leaves,

10 will be held down there.

The text ends by saying that all is well in Mari, Išme-Dagan is well, the town of Êkallâtum is well, and the author, Yasmaḥ-Adad, is likewise well.

One final Mari text which deserves mention is of an entirely different nature. It is part of the text destined for a victory stele of Zimri-Lim to celebrate his ascension to the throne, but it is not the stele itself, rather a copy or draft of the text preserved on a normal clay tablet (Dossin 1971: 2). Although poorly preserved, it is of interest because, after describing his defeat of Yasmaḥ-Adad, and the booty he seized, Zimri-Lim mentions several place-names including Tilmun (1. 20). Although the sense in which Tilmun occurs here cannot be determined, it is nevertheless important to note its occurrence. One could well imagine that the reference may relate to tribute, booty, or homage from Tilmun.

III. THE ITINERARIES

The Mari texts give an interesting glimpse into the overland caravan traffic between Dilmun and the Middle Euphrates. Yet this was hardly a self-contained circuit, routinely followed, without wider ramifications. Rather, it constituted quite clearly part of a much larger network with branches extending both further south and west. It is well known that the bulk of Dilmun's exports came not from Dilmun itself (cf. Potts 1982b: Table III), but rather from southern sources such as Makkan and Meluḫḫa, hence implying the existence of further lines of supply extending into the Arabian peninsula and the Indo-Iranian sphere. In the same way, Mari was in no way the penultimate endpoint of the supply network in question, but rather should be visualized as a particularly important point on that route into which, it is true, many goods flowed, but out of which, as well, caravans emanated northward and westward. From the south, we have testimony of a route in use during the Old Babylonian period which led from Babylon to Mari via Sippar and Rapiqum, continuing on from Mari to Hazor, either via Qatna, or via Emar, Aleppo, and Qatna (Hallo 1964: 87). The first part of this route could well be the same as that followed by the caravan sent to Dilmun for the distance from Mari to Babylon. A route linking Mari with Ugarit via Aleppo is also known (Dossin 1970: 98), so that we must reckon with the possibility of a very wide diffusion for goods originating in the Gulf or beyond within the Syrian area. Undoubtedly it was via such routes that the strong contact between Ebla and the south was maintained, and that the name Dilmun came to be known among Ebla's scribes.

One particularly interesting text (Millard 1973: 212) which documents the convergence of both the southern spur of the network, originating in the Gulf, and the northwestern spur, originating in the Mediterranean, is a list (WHM 114046) of metal objects dated to the fifth year of Samsuiluna, c. 1745 B.C. There we find, in what is uncontestably a Babylonian context, the mention of refined copper from Alasia, i.e. Cyprus, alongside that of Tilmun. This text thus nicely demonstrates the extended nature of the network which could bring Dilmunite copper as far north as Ebla, or Cypriot copper as far south as Babylonia.

IV. AḤLAMU AND SUTEANS IN DILMUN

Thanks to the work of A. Goetze and P. B. Cornwall, the Nippur letter Ni 615 has long been known (Goetze 1952, Cornwall 1952). The letter, dating to the time of Burnaburiaš II (c. 1359–1333 B.C.), mentions members of two West-Semitic groups whose homelands were in the Syrian steppe region. One of these groups, the Suteans, is well known from the Mari archives (cf. most recently Heltzer 1981: 87). We read in the letter that Ili-ippashra, writing from Dilmun to Ililiya, an official in Nippur, has directed a Sutean woman ((Su)-te-tu) to go to Babylon. The second group, namely the Aḥlamu, are said to be carrying off dates from Dilmun. Once thought to be the same as the Arameans, it is now most likely that the Aḫlamu represent a separate tribal group (for refs. cf. Gibson 1961: 231). Thus, for whatever reasons, we have the attestation of members of two largely nomadic, West-Semitic groups in Dilmun in the fourteenth century B.C.

V. AN INSCRIPTION OF TUKULTI-NINURTA I (1243-1207 B.C.)

An alabaster tablet (TA 94 = B.M. 115692) found at Tulul 'Aqir, ancient Kar-Tukulti-Ninurta, which is now in the British Museum, contains several interesting references to Tilmun which might suggest that it may have been, in the thirteenth century B.C., under Assyrian control. Whereas Tukulti-Ninurta I is known to have used the general title 'King of the Lower Sea' in several other inscriptions (e.g. Assur 19735, B.M. 98494, and TA 350 = VA 8253), this is the only one in which he calls himself 'King of Tilmun and Meluḫḫa' (1. 15). We cannot be sure, however, whether, in this case, the Assyrian king had truly won control of Tilmun, or whether this was merely a case of taking on yet another royal title. The latter seems, in fact, the more likely possibility.

VI. A PALMYRENE SATRAP OF THE *THILOUANOI*

The final reference which links the Syrian realm with Dilmun is neither written in cuneiform, nor does it date to the period of our concern. Yet is is appended here simply as an interesting detail attesting to the longevity of the contact we have been discussing. The text in question is a Greek inscription from Palmyra, written in the year 131 A.D. (Seyrig 1941: 253). It mentions Yarhai, a satrap who is qualified as *Thilouanôn*, 'of the Thilouanoi', and identifies him as Palmyrene. The actual toponym was probably *Thilouos* or *Thiloua*, as my colleague G. W. Bowersock kindly informs me, and the connection between the ethnic name here and Tilmun/Tylos was made by E. Herzfeld (Herzfeld 1968: 62) in a posthumously published note. R. Zadok has recently discussed this text anew (Zadok 1981/1982: 139), although he mistakes the term in question for a noun as toponym when it is in reality an ethnic. In any case, the connection between Palmyra and Thilouos is particularly interesting in light of the presence of Palmyrene merchants at Charax whom we know sailed the Gulf as far as India (Seyrig 1941: 251ff), and in view of the presence of Palmyrene tombs on Kharg island in the Gulf (cf. most recently Haerinck 1975).

CONCLUSION

This review of the evidence pointing to longstanding contact between the Syrian realm and Dilmun was intended, in part, to provide an historical setting for the parallels which have so often been noted between Dilmun glyptic and the glyptic of the Syro-Anatolian region.

In so doing, it has exceeded temporally the bounds of the Dilmun glyptic tradition, both by beginning in the context of the Ebla-Dilmun connection, and by ending in the second century A.D. Those examples which fall outside the *floruit* of the Dilmun seals, i.e. outside the Old Babylonian period, were included simply to demonstrate the longevity of the tradition of contact between the Gulf and the Syrian area. What has not been discussed, however, is the problem of Dilmun in Anatolian sources, and thus the historical background for the presence of Anatolian motifs in Gulf glyptic. Monolingual Hittite texts never mention Dilmun as a place-name (cf. del Monte and Tischler 1978). K. Kessler has recently pointed out, however, that a trilingual (Sumerian, Akkadian and Hittite) version of the literary text known as the 'Message of Lú-dingir-ra to his Mother' from Ras Šamra/Ugarit, and a duplicate of the same from Bogazköy/Hattuša, contains reference (1. 39) to 'a sweet Dilmun date' (Kessler 1983: 153, 159, n. 68). In the Hittite versions from Ras Šamra and Bogazköy Dilmun is rendered as *Tal-mu-na-aš* and SAL.KAB.NUN.N[A-aš], respectively. A Hittite translation of Dilmun from the Sumerian or Akkadian, however, need not imply any contact between the Hittite area itself and the Gulf. The glyptic motifs which indicate contact between the two regions may, therefore, for the moment, be interpreted as bearing witness to a distant and indirect connection via the overland routes discussed above.

Tylos and Tyre: Bahrain in the Graeco-Roman World

G. W. BOWERSOCK

From the fourth century B.C. at the latest until the incorporation of Graeco-Roman traditions in Byzantine sources over a thousand years afterwards, the two islands of Bahrain and Muharraq in the Arabian Gulf were known as Tylos and Arados. Occasionally the spelling Tylos was corrupted, in both Greek and Latin, into the form Tyros, but the confusion of the liquids *l* and *r* is not uncommon in foreign words (such as Rhinocolura/Rhinocorura and Athloula/Athroula), and in this instance it reflects the fame of a well known city on the eastern Mediterranean coast. The legitimacy of the form Tylos for Bahrain is established by the most authoritative source we have for the Graeco-Roman period, namely an admiral who served under Alexander the Great in the late fourth century B.C., Androsthenes of Thasos.[1]

Androsthenes went to Bahrain in 324 B.C. while the forces of Alexander were returning from India.[2] He identified the island as Tylos and wrote an account of the plant life and pearl-fishing of the area as part of an overall narrative of his travels in the gulf under the title Παράπλους τῆς Ἰνδικῆς ('Voyage Along the Indian Coast').[3] Regrettably the work of Androsthenes does not survive, but since it was obviously the one thorough eyewitness account of Bahrain to which Greeks and Romans had access, it was studied and excerpted repeatedly in antiquity. The geographers Artemidorus and Eratosthenes used it in the Hellenistic age, the philosopher Theophrastus cited it at length in his botanical writings, and the historians of Alexander turned to it for evidence on naval expeditions. Under the Roman Empire the antiquarian Athenaeus found Androsthenes a precious repository of details on pearling; and the testimony of Androsthenes, sometimes at second had through Artemidorus and Eratosthenes, continued to be quoted in the excerptors of the Byzantine era. The only Graeco-Roman evidence for Bahrain that is not manifestly dependent upon the report of Androsthenes is the registering of Tylos and Arados among the islands of the Arabian Gulf in the *Geography* of Claudius Ptolemaeus from the second century

A.D.,[4] but even here an ultimate debt to Alexander's admiral is likely.

The actual words of Androsthenes are quoted, among surviving writers from classical antiquity, only in Theophrastus, Strabo (borrowing from Eratosthenes), and Athenaeus. We may begin with the first two authors and return later to Athenaeus. Describing the beneficial effects of salt water on plants, Theophrastus invokes Androsthenes, ὑπὲρ τῶν ἐν Τύλωι τῆι νήσωι τῆι περὶ τὴν Ἐρυθρὰν θάλατταν ('concerning the things in Tylos, the island in the Red Sea').[5] In another passage, clearly drawing again on Androsthenes, Theophrastus locates Tylos ἐν τῶι Ἀραβίωι κόλπωι ('in the Arabian Gulf').[6] Red Sea was a general term that, as can be observed here, was in use for the Arabian Gulf as well as for what is known today as the Red Sea.[7]

Strabo, in his geographical work composed under the early Roman principate, explicitly cites Eratosthenes, who, in turn, gives a quotation from Androsthenes. After this Strabo provides information about Bahrain that was undoubtedly part of Androsthenes' account.[8] The text of Strabo as transmitted gives the name Τύρος (Tyros) instead of Τύλος (Tylos), but there can be no doubt that this is an error: we have not only Τύλος in Theophrastus' *verbatim* quotation of Androsthenes but also in the statement in Stephanus of Byzantium as follows: Τύρος . . . νῆσος πρὸς τῆι Ἐρυθρᾶι θαλάσσηι, ἣν Ἀρτεμίδωρος Τύλον διὰ τοῦ λ καλεῖ ('Tyros . . . island in the Red Sea, which Artemidorus calls Tylos with an Γ').[9] We know that Artemidorus based his treatment of the Arabian Gulf on Androsthenes.[10]

The passage in Strabo is of the greatest interest and importance: πλεύσαντι δ᾽ἐπὶ πλέον ἄλλαι νῆσοι Τύρος καὶ Ἄραδός εἰσιν, ἱερὰ ἔχουσαι τοῖς φοινικικοῖς ὅμοια· καὶ φασί γε οἱ ἐν αὐταῖς οἰκοῦντες τὰς ὁμωνύμους τῶν Φοινίκων νήσους καὶ πόλεις ἀποίκους ἑαυτῶν ('As one sails on farther other islands are Tyros (i.e., Tylos) and Arados, with temples like the Phoenician ones; and those who live on the islands say that the Phoenicians' islands and cities of the same names were colonized by them').[11] Any knowledgeable geographer in antiquity would certainly have been impressed by the curious coincidence that two islands in the Arabian Gulf happened to have essentially the same names as two of the principal cities on the Phoenician coast – both of which were also islands. The names in both cases were Semitic, not Greek. Arados represents Arad, a name which survives in modern Muharraq; the other place kept the names in the forms of Arvad and Rouad. Tyros or Tylos represents what is even today the name for Tyre in Arabic, صور. The confusion of a *sad* with Greek *tau* poses no difficulty, and, in the case of صور, something similar may have also occurred in Arabic, if we may assume that طور (like Syriac ܛܘܪ) is the same word (meaning 'mountain'). In any case, two island cities so far apart called Arados and two called Tylos/Tyros, صور / طور must inevitably suggest some kind of relationship. Androsthenes declared that the sanctuaries on the Gulf islands resembled those in Phoenicia and, furthermore, that on those islands there was a tradition of colonization in Phoenicia. With that wilfulness that occasionally blemished late nineteenth-century western scholarship some writers assumed that Androsthenes, and through him Eratosthenes and Strabo, had given exactly the reverse of the truth.[12] The amazing coincidence of names and temples they believed had to be explained by Phoenician colonization in the Gulf, instead of by Gulf colonization in Phoenicia.

But in fact there is nothing inherently implausible about Androsthenes' report, and there is good evidence to support it. Over a century before the expedition of Alexander the Great the historian Herodotus had visited Tyre on the Phoenician coast. In Book II he notes that he was told in Tyre that the city had been settled 2,300 years before (ἔφασαν γὰρ ἅμα Τύρωι οἰκιζομένηι . . ., εἶναι δὲ ἔτεα ἀπ' οὗ Τύρον οἰκέουσι τριηκόσια καὶ δισχίλια).[13] Calculating back from approximately 450 B.C., we obtain a date from Herodotus of 2750 B.C. or so for the foundation of Tyre. Later, in Book VII, the same historian reports of the Phoenicians generally that long ago, as they say themselves, they once dwelled on the Red Sea (οὗτοι δὲ οἱ Φοίνικες τὸ παλαιὸν οἴκεον, ὡς αὐτοὶ λέγουσι, ἐπὶ τῆι Ἐρυθρῆι θαλάσσηι), and from there they migrated through Syria to the Mediterranean coast.[14] Accordingly we can recover from Herodotus a tradition among the Phoenicians themselves that they came originally from the Red Sea, which – as we have already seen – is a perfectly normal Greek way of referring to the Arabian Gulf. In other words the local Phoenician tradition of the fifth century B.C., as reported by Herodotus, exactly matches the local tradition in the Gulf itself a century later, as reported by Androsthenes. Both traditions make the Gulf the homeland of the Phoenicians. Obviously the concordance of these traditions is strengthened by the parallel names of the cities of Tylos and Tyre, and of Arados and Phoenician Arados. Knowledgeable readers will be reminded of other well known parallels of nomenclature between Phoenicia and the Gulf, such as Jubail (Byblos) and the Sūr in Oman. For the dispatch of colonists from Bahrain to the Mediterranean Herodotus provides an approximate date of 2750 B.C.

Although it would be foolish to put any weight on Herodotus' precise date (it is the tradition that counts), excavations on Bahrain itself as well as discoveries in Mesopotamia have now established that Bahrain was undoubtedly a more important place by the early third millennium than had formerly been surmised.[15] It appears to have been a trading station for traffic between Babylonia and the

Indus valley, and it has been suggested that financing of these far-flung operations came from Ur.[16] There is nothing at all improbable about a colonial emigration from the mercantile center of Bahrain to the eastern coast of the Mediterranean in this period, and there is the remarkable unanimity of the traditions in the two parts of the world in so-called classical times to support it. As for Phoenician itself, we have, by the end of the fourth millennium, no contradictory evidence, as far as I am aware. 'Aucune ville en Phénicie n'est attestée avant cette époque (i.e., la fin du IVᵉ millénaire), mais elles vont naître, nombreuses.'[17]

In another passage Strabo takes up once again the current belief that Phoenician Tyre and Arados were colonized from the homonymous islands of the Arabian Gulf. At the end of Book XVI he cites Homer's *Odyssey* (IV.84), Αἰθίοπάς ϑ' ἱκόμην καὶ Σιδονίους καὶ Ἐρεμβούς ('and we came to the Ethiopians and the Sidonians and the Eremboi').[18] This line is part of Menelaus' account of seven years of wandering, and the references to the Ethiopians and Eremboi allude without any doubt to coastal territories on the Arabian Sea, most probably the Somalian territory of East Africa.[19] It would be odd therefore, as Strabo immediately recognizes, for the Sidonians mentioned in this Homeric verse to refer to the natives of the Phoenician city of Sidon.[20] Furthermore, Menelaus had already covered Phoenicia in the preceding line, along – reasonably enough – with Cyprus and Egypt.[21] Accordingly Strabo raises the possibility that Homer's Σιδόνιοι are not the people of Sidon (who, in any case, are Σιδώνιοι, with an omega) but are rather the inhabitants of the Arabian Gulf whom the ancients knew under the general appellation of Sidonians. Strabo asks, εἴτε τινὰς χρὴ λέγειν τῶν ἐν τῶι Περσικῶι κόλπωι κατοικούντων, ὧν ἄποικοι οἱ παρ' ἡμῖν Σιδώνιοι, καθάπερ καὶ Τυρίους τινὰς ἐκεῖ νησιώτας ἱστοροῦσι καὶ Ἀραδίους, ὧν ἀποίκους τοὺς παρ' ἡμῖν φασιν ('whether we should understand – by Sidonians – some of those people who inhabit the Persian – i.e., Arabian – Gulf, of whom the natives of our own Sidon are colonists, just as writers speak of island dwellers on Tyre and Arados there, of whom our own Tyrians and Aradians are said to be colonists').

It is clear that in this passage Strabo alludes explicitly to a broad colonization of Phoenicia from the Arabian Gulf, of which the settlement of Tyre and Arados was only a part. And in referring to this tradition, which he reasonably assumes to be a familiar one in his own day, he forms a close link with the tradition reported by Herodotus nearly four centuries earlier. We can now state with certainty that rightly or wrongly the Graeco-Roman world accepted a tradition that ascribed the settlement of Phoenicia, several millennia before, to colonists from the Arabian Gulf. We can state further, without certainty but with some degree of probability, that this tradition may, in fact, accurately reflect patterns of migration in the distant past when the Gulf was already a vital commercial area and Tylos (Bahrain), in particular, a major trading station.

Special interest in the colonization of Phoenicia, especially Tyre and Arados, appears not to have been confined to Strabo during the early Roman principate. The emperor Augustus' grandson, whom he had adopted as his son and heir, Gaius Caesar, embarked on an Arabian campaign in about 1 B.C.; and although the details of his objectives and movements are still obscure to us, we do know that knowledgeable scholars of the time studied the sources in order to equip the young Gaius with the necessary background material for his operations. The strongly hellenized and highly literate king of Mauretania, Juba II, is known to have composed a handbook on the Roman East for Gaius' edification.[22] This work evidently described the islands of the Arabian Gulf, as we can readily see from a reference in Book XII of the *Natural History* of the elder Pliny.[23] There *Tylos insula* is described as full of forests (*repleta silvis*) and wool-bearing trees (*lanigerae arbores*), and Muharraq is also mentioned as *Tylos minor*. Pliny then names Juba as his source for cotton growing on the islands. Juba can thus be seen to have disposed of detailed information about Bahrain at that time, and he may be presumed to have had access to Androsthenes' work. Like Androsthenes he calls the island Tylos, not Tyros (a form which has intruded into Pliny's text of Book VI in a passage also expressly drawn from Juba on pearl-fishing in the Gulf).[24] But Juba's designation of Muharraq as *Tylos minor* instead of Arados is notable. It points to a source, written or even oral, quite distinct from Androsthenes.

One may be justified in concluding, therefore, that the nature and history of Bahrain had a certain contemporary relevance to the foreign policy of Augustus at the end of the first century B.C. The testimony of Strabo and Juba, taken together, is proof enough. Even the cultivated elite of the Arab world itself at that time may have played a role in educating the young Roman prince. It seems that a native of Charax, at the mouth of the Tigris in the northern corner of the Arabian Gulf, composed another work for the instruction of Gaius. Pliny's *Natural History* gives this local scholar the name of Dionysius, although it is tempting (if unnecessary) to assume a textual corruption concealing the well known geographer Isidore of Charax.[25] Pliny says of this author, whether Dionysius or Isidore, *quem ad commentanda omnia in orientem praemiserat divus Augustus ituro in Armeniam ad Parthicas Arabicasque res maiore filio* ('whom the deified Augusts sent in advance to the East to write a full account when his elder – adopted – son was about to go to Armenia to launch Parthian and Arabian campaigns'). After taking due note of this writer Pliny is then careful to explain that he prefers to follow, in his own treatment, Juba of Mauretania instead of the man from Charax. Overall, however, it is apparent that the Arabian Gulf probably received more attention under Augustus than at any time since Androsthenes in the days of Alexander.

The only other identifiable quotation from Androsthenes' *Paraplous* occurs in Athenaeus, whose dazzling erudition is mirrored in his vast miscellany called 'The Sophists at Dinner' (*Deipnosophistai*) from the late second century A.D. In Book III of this work Athenaeus excerpts some lines of the *Paraplous* on the subject of pearling in the Arabian Gulf.[26] Androsthenes notes that the shellfish that produced pearls was highly prized throughout the whole region, and he reports that the native word for this creature was *berberi*: ἓν δὲ ἴδιον ὃ καλοῦσιν ἐκεῖνοι βέρβερι, ἐξ οὗ ἡ μαργαρῖτις λίθος γίνεται ('one particular kind – of shellfish – is what those people call *berberi*, from which the pearl stone is made'). This precious testimony, cited from an authoritative work of the fourth century B.C., has been largely ignored. And yet the native Gulf word *berberi* should excite curiosity in view of the emergence under the Roman Empire of the word *barbary* (Βαρβαρία) to cover the coastal areas of the Arabian Sea and Gulf, precisely where the pearl-fishers flourished.[27] Stephanus of Byzantium was sharp enough to recognize that Βαρβαρία as an ethnic designation was different from Βάρβαρος, meaning 'barbarian.' Strictly the adjective for the former should be Βαρβαριακός and for the latter βαρβαρικός, although this distinction was not regularly observed.[28] In any case, Androsthenes' evidence for the word *berberi* deserves a place it has never yet had in discussions of the origins of Greek βαρβαρία, not to mention Arabic بربر . The village of باربار in the north of Bahrain, where Danish excavators have uncovered an important temple,[29] may well preserve that word which Androsthenes heard on the lips of residents there over two thousand years ago.

In late antiquity, less than two centuries before the Prophet, the Greek epic poet Nonnos, from Panopolis in Egypt, gives us a tradition about the settlement of Tyre that is wholly different from that which Greeks and Romans had inherited from Androsthenes. By this time, with the new empire already well established at Byzantium, the Tyrians had evidently constructed an elaborate and otherwise unattested foundation legend proclaiming themselves as indigenous inhabitants of the region. In Book XL of his *Dionysiaca* Nonnos, who is singularly well informed about local traditions in the East, makes the god Heracles of Tyre tell the visiting god Dionysus that the people of the city sprang from the unplowed earth and built upon the rocks of the island in the immemorial past.[30] They are said to be autochthonous. There is no trace whatever in Nonnos of immigration from the Gulf – unless, by chance, it is to be found in the name of a local water-nymph, who is invoked in a description of the site of Ras al-cain at Tyre. She is called ʼΑβαϱβαϱή (Abarbarē),[31] and one cannot help wondering whether here in this strange name there is perhaps an echo of the people who long before, in the Arabian Gulf, had fished for *berberi*.

1. For testimonia and fragments, see F. Jacoby, *Die Fragmente der griechischen Historiker* III. C. no. 711 (Androsthenes von Thasos). The name of Tylos and virtually all the evidence discussed in this paper are unknown to the author of the article ʼal-Bahrayn' in the *Encyclopedia of Islam*, vol. I, 1960, 941–42 (purportedly covering the pre-Islamic history of the islands).

2. Arrian, *Anabasis*, 7.20.6–7. Cf. *Indica* 18.4.

3. For the title, Athenaeus, *Deipnosoph.* 3.93.

4. Claud. Ptolem., *Geograph.* 6.7.47: ἐν δὲ τῶι Πεϱσικῶι κόλπωι – ʼΑπφάνα νῆσος, ʼΙχάϱα (now identified as Failaka), θαϱϱώ, Τύλος, ῎Αϱαδος.

5. Theophrast., *Die causis plant.* 2.5.5.

6. Theophrast., *Hist. plant.* 4.7.7.

7. For discussion of the term Red Sea, see G. W. Bowersock, 'The Greek-Nabataean Bilingual Inscription at Ruwwāfa, Saudi Arabia', in *Lexmonde grec: Hommages à Claire Préaux*, 1975, 518–19 (on *rubrum mare*), with other bibliography cited there. Cf. Steph. Byz., *s.v.* ῎Αϱαδος – νῆσος Φοινίϰης· ἔστι ϰαὶ ἑτέϱα τῆς ἐϱυθϱᾶς θαλάσσης.

8. Strabo, *Geograph.* 16.3.2–4, 766C.

9. Steph. Byz., *s.v.* Τύϱος. The σατϱάπης Θιλουανῶν in a Palmyrene inscription of A.D. 131 (H. Seyrig, *Syria* 22 [1941], 253, No. 21) must refer to a govenor of Bahrain, as E. Herzfeld acutely observed in a note published in the posthumous volume entitled *The Persian Empire*, 1968, 62–63. (I am grateful to Daniel Potts for referring me to Herzfeld's note.) Θιλουανῶν is not, however, the genitive of a place-name Thilwana, as Seyrig thought, but of a people, the Thilwani. The place is certainly Tylos, appearing in the Palmyrene ethnic as Thilwos. Herzfeld sees this as a form of Tilmun/Dilmun.

10. For Artemidorus see F. Jacoby, *Die Fragmente der griechischen Histoker* III. B. no. 438. Note, in addition, Arrian's spelling in his report on Androsthenes' voyage: Τύλος δὲ αὐτῆι (*sc.* τῆι νήσωι) εἶναι ὄνομα (*Anab.* 7.20.6) and μέχϱι μὲν τῆς νήσου τῆς Τύλου (*Anab.* 7.20.7).

11. Strabo, *Geograph.* 16.3.4, 766C.

12. Cf., for example, Pauly-Wissowa, *Real-Encyclopädie* II.1, col. 372, *s.v.* Arados (2): 'Auch behaupten wenigstens ihre Bewohner, die gleichnamigen Inseln und Städte der Phoinikier seien Ansiedelungen von ihnen (das Umgekehrte dürfte wohl richtig sein, dass sie in früher Zeit von Phoinikien aus colonisiert worden sind).' In the *Encyclopedia of Islam*, vol. I, 1960, 941, the reverse of what the ancient sources say is advanced as a hypothesis of early excavators on Bahrain and then rejected. Nothing is said there of the real ancient tradition.

13. Herod., 2.44.

14. Herod., 7.89.

15. For a valuable summary of the Danish excavations, with references to the reports of the excavators (P. V. Glob and T. G. Bibby) in *Kuml*, see A. Grohmann, *Arabien*, 1963, pp. 255–67, especially for the situation c. 3,000 B.C., 255, 266. See also H. Schmokel, *Ur, Assur und Babylon*, 1955, 9, cited by Grohmann.

16. P. V. Glob, 'Bahrains Oldtidshovedstad', *Kuml* 1954, 169.

17. M. Dunand, *Supplément au Dictionnaire de la Bible*, vol. 7, 1966, col. 1155.

18. Strabo, *Geograph.* 16.4.27, 784C.

19. See James D. Muhly, 'Homer and the Phoenicians', *Berytus* 19, 1970, 19–64, especially p. 50. For Eremboi see particularly D. A. Russell and N. G. Wilson, *Menander Rhetor*, 1981, 292–93.

20. Muhly also points out this difficulty in his article, cited in the preceding note, p. 50: 'Sidon seems curiously out of place.' For *Sidonioi* as a people in the Arabian Gulf, see the discussion by J.-P. Rey-Coquais, *Arados et sa Pérée aux époques grecque, romaine et byzantine*, 1974, 93–94.

21. *Odyss.* 4.83: Κύπρον Φοινίκην τε καὶ Αἰγυπτίους ἐπαληθείς.

22. Pliny, *Nat. Hist.* 6.141 (*Iubamque regem ad eundem C. Caesarem scriptis voluminibus de eadem expeditione Arabica*); 12.56 (*Iuba rex iis voluminibus quae scripsit ad C. Caesarem Augusti filium, ardentem fama Arabiae*); 32.10 (*Iuba in iis voluminibus, quae scripsit ad C. Caesarem Aug. f. de Arabia*). Juba appears in F. Jacoby, *Die Fragmente der griechischen Histoker* III. A. no. 275.

23. Pliny, *Nat. Hist.* 12.38–40.

24. Pliny, *Nat. Hist.* 6.148 (141 shows that this part comes from Juba).

25. Pliny, *Nat. Hist.* 6.141. For Isidore of Charax, F. Jacoby, *Die Fragmente der griechischen Histoker* III. C. no. 781.

26. Athenaeus, *Deipnosoph.* 3.93.

27. See Paul-Wissowa, *Real-Encyclopädie* II.2, cols. 2855–56, *s.v.* Barbaria (1), article by Tomaschek. Cf. *Periplous Maris Erythraei* 5 (βαρβαρία), 7 (βαρβαρικὰ ἐμπόρια), 12 (βαρβαρικὴ ἤπειρος). It should be noted that the *Encyclopedia of Islam* has no entry for Barbary.

28. Steph. Byz., *s.v.* βάρβαρος – οὐχ ἀπὸ ἔθνους, ἀλλ' ἐπὶ φωνῆς ἐλαμβάνετο . . . εἴρηται παρὰ τοῖς νεωτέροις ἐθνικῶς, ἀφ' οὗ βαρβαρία. ἔστι δὲ χώρα παρὰ τὸν Ἀράβιον κόλπον βαρβαρία, ἀθ' οὗ καὶ βαρβαρικὸν πέλαγος. τὸ δὲ βαρβαρικὸς οὐκ ἀπὸ τοῦ βαρβαρία, ἀλλ' ἀπὸ τοῦ βάρβαρος. ἦν γὰρ βαρβαριακός.

29. P. V. Glob, 'Templer ved Barbar', *Kuml* 1954, 142–53. See the report in German by E. Weidner in *Archiv für Orientforschung* 17 (1956), 432.

30. Nonnos, *Dionys.* 40.429–573.

31. Nonnos, *Dionys.* 40.363 and 542.

A three generations' matrilineal genealogy in a Hasaean inscription: matrilineal ancestry in Pre-Islamic Arabia

JACQUES RYCKMANS

In a Hasaean funerary inscription from Thāj, recently published,[1] a woman gives her matrilineal ancestry reaching up to the third generation (great grandmother). The translation of the text runs as follows : 'Tombstone and grave of *Gdyt*, daughter of *Mlkt*, daughter of *Šbm*, daughter of *'hdt*, (she) of the family *Ynḫ'l*. Since this inscription is so far the only pre-Islamic text from Arabia which explicitly lists a genealogy of three successive female ascendents, it has a particular significance in the discussion about the importance of what is nowadays described as 'matrilineal system of filiation' (instead of the former term 'matriarchy') in pre-Islamic Arabia, and about the relevance of certain uses, past or present, as evidence to the possible existence and persistence of a former (partial) matrilineal system of filiation in the social structure of various populations of Arabia.

Nearly a century ago, following the publication of a book by A. G. Wilken[2] on 'matriarchy' among the ancient Arabs, W. Robertson Smith presented in his book *Kinship and Marriage in Early Arabia* (1885) a study of all the pre-Islamic data on various forms of kinship and marriage in Arabia. The whole work aims at arguing that the traditional patrilineal Arabic genealogies are an artificial reconstruction reflecting a situation which had emerged only in Muhammad's time, with the disruption of the old pagan order; that a matrilineal system of kinship (as we would call it now), was 'originally the universal rule of Arabia, and that the kinship through males [which is observed in Islamic Arabia] sprang up in polyandrous groups of kinsmen which brought in wives from outside but desired to keep the children of these alien women to themselves' (p. 151).

The theory put forward in such a categorical form was immediately subject to criticism, for instance from the great scholar T. Nöldeke[3] who objected to dogmatic constructions of such an extent, and to the risky undertaking of pretending to identify the unverifiable and slow transformations of prehistory, through analogies, the application of which may not be justified, and through remnants of dubious meaning. Nöldeke insisted also (p. 149) that many of the data put forward by W. R. Smith to prove his point could be explained in a different way. For instance, many female names intervening as female eponyms in the genealogies seem to be mythical and later personifications of an original feminine tribal name.[4] But this could not alter the fact, which T. Nöldeke acknowledged, of the existence of the 'matriarch' among the Semites (p. 149).

Strangely enough, in an Appendix to his book *Muhammad at Medina*, published in 1956, W. Montgomery Watt, while opposing (p. 272 f.) the evolution reconstructed by W. R. Smith, still declares (p. 388): 'The essential point is the composition of the group which owns and inherits property. Until the later sixth century, we assume, the group was a matrilineal one, and the property was held communally, or at least as a trust for the common good. It would normally be administered by the uterine brothers of the women concerned'. To that W. Caskel rightly replied that none of the cases put forward could justify such conclusions.[5]

As a result of nearly a century of discussion, it is now more or less generally accepted that while the passage from a matrilineal to a patrilineal system of kinship is possible and attested in many cultures, the reverse sequence of evolution is not possible.[6] It is also admitted that both patrilineal and matrilineal forms of kinship exist side by side in many primitive societies[7] without such a situation necessarily postulating an evolution from a former exclusively matrilineal system.

To the arguments in favour of the predominance of a patrilineal form of kinship in the historical period of pre-Islamic Arabia, it should be added that the past hundred years or so that have elapsed since the first edition of W. R. Smith's book have brought to our knowledge some tens of thousands of pre-Islamic inscriptions and graffiti which conclusively prove that throughout the Arabian territory, from the North of the Syrian desert to the coast of the Indian Ocean, patrilineal kinship was the 'normal' situation, as early as can be ascertained from epigraphic evidence.[8] Some Safaitic texts, for instance, give long genealogies, many being from 6 to 12 successive (male) generations in length.[9] A great number of cross references between the many Safaitic genealogies make it even possible to reconstruct larger and more ramified family trees which, being based on authentic and contemporary inscriptions, prove clearly that in spite of the numerous manipulations to which they were subjected, the traditional Arab genealogies follow at any rate a well attested pre-Islamic pattern.

Aside from the general observation that some denominations of tribal subdivisions originate in names of parts of the female body, such as *batn* or *rahīm*,[10] there are a number of other features generally assumed to be associated with a system of matrilineal ancestry – or its remnants.[11] Among the principal ones are: the use of metronyms instead of patronyms; the role of the maternal uncle; the mutual free choice of the partner in marriage; a greater social and sexual freedom of women; and finally – although those features are less cogently linked with matrilineal ancestry –[12] the location of the residence of the married couple with the family of the woman (matrilocality or uxorilocality), and polyandry.

The present paper aims at fitting the pre-Islamic epigraphic evidence, such as could point to the existence of a matrilineal system of kinship, into the broader picture resulting from the relevant date from the classical writers and the Arabic tradition, as well as from modern information on customs observed mostly in the southern part of Arabia.

The accent laid by the Thāj inscription on the female ascendants of the woman mentioned is apparently supported by another Hasaean epitaph[13] and is not without parallel in ancient Arabian epigraphical evidence. Some Nabataean dedications of tombs in Madā'in Sālih, in northern Hiğāz, stress in fact both the independent position of women – who have their own tombs, with an impressive façade carved into the rock, built for their own use – and some sort of privileged matrilineal relation expressed through the fact that they state their feminine ancestry (up to the second generation: grandmother), and insist in several cases that the tomb is also destined for their daughter with her own offspring.[14] In the text CIS,I, no. 198, for instance, a woman named Kamkam, daughter of Walat, granddaughter of Huram, together with her daughter Kulaibat, builds a tomb for both themselves and for their offspring.

The existence of such matrilineal genealogical sequences, in inscriptions from the Hiğāz and the Hasā, though it does not necessarily imply a matrilineal system of kinship, obviously imposes a certain revision of some views on the question. For instance, it has been observed that matrilineal features in present-day Arabia are nearly exclusively concentrated in South Arabia. Even some features cited in the Arabic tradition for Madina, were in fact observed among southern tribes emigrated there.[15] There has been a tendency among scholars to project this situation back into the pre-Islamic past, and to suppose that pre-Islamic matrilineal features were restricted to the southern tip of the peninsula.[16] The newly published Hasaean evidence corroborates the Nabataean; they jointly testify to the fact that even in the northwest and northeast of pre-Islamic Arabia a tradition of a certain matrilineal kinship was not absent.[17]

While the evidence of Hasaean and Nabataean inscriptions on matrilineal features remains rather scarce, that of the ancient South Arabian texts is somewhat richer and more varied, for the following reasons. Firstly, the epigraphical material is considerably larger and more detailed than in other parts of the Arabian Peninsula. Secondly, the inscriptions merely confirm a fact already made clear through the modern evidence, and that gathered by the classical writers and by the Arabic tradition about the Jāhiliyya, namely that matrilineal features in the kinship system were and are more important in South Arabia.

Although the South Arabian inscriptions give no extensive genealogies comparable to those of the Safaitic texts, there is no question that patrilineal ancestry was the general rule. But some South Arabian inscriptions show the existence of matrilineal features similar to those of the texts cited above.[18] The relevant inscriptions were quite recently gathered together and commented upon by A. F. L. Beeston in his article 'Women in Saba'. In each of the two texts Fakhry 3 and 76,[19] a Sabaean king decrees that a number of people of one given family will forthwith be fully incorporated into a larger noble lineage. The remarkable thing about the procedure involved is that while it is declared that Such-and-Such men, mentioned by name, will become part of the lineage in question, 'with their brothers, sons and (male) relatives', the same is said for Such-and-Such women of the same family, mentioned by name, 'with their sisters, daughters and (female) relatives'. We are confronted here with a privileged matrilineal relationship linking together the females within what appears to be a broader system of kinship of patrilineal type. The same can be said of the Nabataean texts and of the Hasaean inscriptions, since in both cases the other texts of the same provenance show that the dominant pattern of kinship was patri-lineal. It is however not easy to get a clear idea of the practical implications of this coexistence.[20] At any rate there are no modern examples of matrilineal succession over more than one generation.[21]

A situation quite similar to that described in Fakhry 3 and 76 appears in the inscription Iryani 34,[22] in which three women of the same family and 'their' daughter, who describe themselves collec-tively as '*lt Grhmm*, (females) of the clan Gurhum',[23] dedicate one male and three female statues for 'their' (probably the daughter's) children (one boy and three girls, according to the names men-tioned), who are collectively called *bnt 'lt grhmm* 'female offspring of the clan Gurhum'.[24] The text might possibly[25] be considered an exact matrilineal counterpart to many South Arabian texts in which the respective offspring of two or more brothers, in the first and second generations (respective sons and nephews, grandsons and great-nephews) are collectively designated by 'their sons'. It is further to be remarked, on the same inscription, that – whatever the status may be of the females qualified by the term '*lt grhmm* – the term *bnt 'lt grhmm*, applied to their descendants, cannot strictly speaking but designate females *born*, not married into the clan. If this distinction is

really significant, it would have important implications for the inter-
preatation of the status of the women mentioned in CIH 581, which is
another text having matrilineal connotations. According to the
interpretation given by A. F. L. Beeston to this text, two childless
women, married into the same family, accept having intercourse with
a man – not mentioned by name – and thank the god for the fact that
one of them has become pregnant. In his three successive treatments
of the text, Beeston gives slightly different interpretations of the
procedure involved. In one of these,[26] he considers the union as a
temporary marriage (*mut^c a*) of childless married women to obtain a
child by a passing stranger. In the next one[27] he alludes specifically to
what the Arab lexicographers call *nikāh al-mubtadā^c*. This is in fact a
form of marriage mentioned under the name *nikāh al-ibtidā^c* in a
tradition of al-Bukhārī,[28] where it occupies the second place in a list
of four kinds of marriages allegedly in use among the Arabs before the
Islam. According to that tradition, that form of union was used by a
man who desired illustrious offspring: he sent his wife to another man
to have intercourse with him, while he abstained from sexual
relations with her until she was with child.[29] But Beeston[30] remarks
that in our South Arabian text the motivation for this procedure is
that the marriage with the husband had proved childless, and that the
initiative is taken by the woman, not the husband. This feature, it
appears, while illustrating the independent status of women, as
Beeston rightly underlines, would preclude a strict comparison with
the *nikāh al-ibtidā^c*, but would favour instead a comparison with a
form of pre-Islamic marriage mentioned among the Saracens by the
classical writer Ammianus Marcellinus.[31] This was a sort of temporary marriage, *mut^c a*, but in which the decision to end the
relationship belonged to the woman. The comparison seems the
more plausible that, in view of the remark made above on the
expression *bnt 'lt X*, it seems that in line 2 of CIH 581, the expression
bnt 'lt thy^c z indicates that the two female authors of the text were not
married. It should also be observed here that the family name *Thy^c z*
is a typical formation for a female name ('May she live, O ^cUzzā!'),[32]
and could therefore bear evidence to the existence of female clan-
eponyms.

In his last treatment of the text, Beeston[33] still considers that
the mother of the child is married, the father being the man *Mhdb bn
Wdm*, qualified as *mr'* of the mother of the child. The second woman
mentioned could be the maternal aunt of the child. He compares the
case with some modern customs recently reported by J. Chelhod[34]
among the Humūm, a bedouin tribe in Hadhramaut. There a woman
can, without any social discredit, have extra-marital relationships
with a man; her kinsmen may then call on the man to marry her, but if
he refuses, he has to assure for some time the subsistance of the

mother and of the offspring.[35] The child will bear the name of the mother or of the maternal uncle. So far Chelhod's testimony. Similar customs had already been reported for Dathīna by Landberg,[36] and more recently among bedouin neighbours of the Humūm by R. B. Serjeant,[37] according to whom the child, while belonging to the tribe of the mother, does not take her name, but is nicknamed *am-Zanū*, 'the Bastard',[38] without this implying any social disgrace for him.

The above-mentioned facts must be put against the background of other observations, medieval or modern, and mostly South Arabian, already used in part by W. R. Smith, which give evidence to the liberty of the woman to take the initiative of putting an end to her marriage or to a relationship.[39] The greater social and sexual freedom of women, and the acceptance of the consequences in the tribal sphere[40] certainly explain[41] in part the larger number of bastard children among the bedouin tribes of Hadhramaut, and consequently, it seems, the more frequent appearance of metronyms. W. Dostal, while recording a high percentage of metronyms among the bedouin tribes which are the next eastern neighbours of the Humum,[42] makes no attempt at explaining the frequent occurrence of such names – nor does he record customs of the kind mentioned above.

Other observations, medieval or modern, which however bear little or no relevance to our subject – loose morals have no direct relation to matrilineal ancestry[43] – put forward evidence on the custom of *tawrīd*, or guest proxenetism, attested by medieval Arab authors as well as modern or contemporary travellers in some parts of Yemen and Hadhramaut,[44] along with isolated cases of promiscuity or prostitution in South Arabia or in Oman.[45]

In three further South Arabian inscriptions A. F. L. Beeston[46] detects evidence of matrilocality (or uxorilocality) of the residence of the married couple. This is another of the features, previously mentioned, that could be related to a matrilineal system of kinship. The first text is Iryani 24, in which, according to Beeston's interpretation, a man thanks the god because he has been enabled to marry (*hkrbn*) and bring home (*hklln*) a bride into his own household. Beeston[47] remarks that the last would hardly have been worth saying if a bride invariably moved into her husband's household. He therefore infers that there were fairly frequent cases of an uxorilocal arrangement, and he quotes from Chelhod a passage of Ibn Battūta[48] in which it is remarked that while the women of Zabīd were quite willing to marry strangers, they on no account ever consented to leave their city. According to W. Dostal,[49] uxorilocality is still prevalent among the Mahra, the Manāhil and the Awāmir tribes of eastern Hadhramaut.

In another text, RES 4233,[50] the expression *hkrbn glmtn*, translated 'to marry the girl', is preceded by the verbal form *l'db*. Beeston[51] compares this to the context of Hebrew *ʿāzab*, 'to leave' in Genesis 2,24, where it is used in the sense of leaving the parental roof to get married, and he concludes that if the possibility of the coalescence in Sabaean of the two different roots *ʿzb* and *ʿdb* is admitted, the whole phrase would mean that the man entered a marriage arrangement implying an uxorilocal residence. This interpretation[52] would give sense to a third text, MAFRAY Qutra 1, 3–4,[53] a decree found in a place which was formerly called *Mtrt*, prohibiting 'to *ʿdb* any of the girls of the city of *Mtrt* into another place'. According to Beeston,[54] the decree clearly aims at prohibiting giving away (in marriage) women of *Mtrt*, except on the basis of uxorilocal marriage arrangements. This, again, would prove that other arrangements were also possible.

A last subject, polyandry, should be dealt with in this paper since former evolutionist theories, such as that of W. R. Smith quoted above, consider this form of marriage as a stage of evolution towards patrilineal ancestry.[55] The principal sources on the existence of polyandry in Arabia are a tradition from al-Bukhārī, already mentioned above (note 28), on the forms of pre-Islamic marriage, a text of al-Bīrūnī, which probably depends on the source of al-Bukhārī, and a passage from Strabo.[56] Except for the third form of marriage listed by al-Bukhārī – a small group of men cohabit with a single woman who, after the birth of the child, designates the man of the group to whom the child will belong – the interpretation of those texts as pieces of evidence in favour of the existence of polyandry remains controversial.[57] Former interpretations of Minaean inscriptions of a type similar to that of the Sabaean text Jamme 705 (see note 25) as evidence for the existence of polyandry in South Arabia,[58] are now definitely put aside.[59] But W. W. Müller, in his article *Polyandrie*, recently interpreted some Sabaean texts of the same type, but in which the child is said to have been born to 'their wife So-and-So', as evidence in favour of the existence, on a limited scale, of polyandry in ancient South Arabia. My own opinion[60] on this interpretation is rather negative: in the first place, because the contexts in question usually express gratitude for the birth of the child, a circumstance which contradicts the malthusian motives put forward[61] to explain the existence of polyandry in South Arabia. Secondly, the odds are that in such texts the term 'their wife' means 'their (viz. of the dedicants) *respective* wife, sister-in-law, daughter-in-law, niece', etc., exactly as 'their son' in these texts means 'their *respective* son, nephew, grandson, great-nephew' etc., in other words, that 'their wife' designates the wife of one of the men mentioned, considered in her function of mother of a child whom the agnates of the family (grandfather, father, uncles etc.) will collectively call 'their son'.[62] In conclusion: the only reliable non-epigraphical evidence on polyandry in ancient Arabia, that of the third type of marriage quoted by al-Bukhārī, does not seem so far to be confirmed by the epigraphical material.

1. In an anonymous chronicle in *Atlal*, 6 (1402 H.-1982 A.D.), 139–140 (English section), 137–138 (Arabic section), and pl. 124 A.

2. *Het Matriarchaat* and *Das Matriarchat*.

3. Review of W. R. Smith, *Kinship*.

4. *Op. cit.*, 149; W. Caskel, *Ǧamhara*, I, 56. R. B. Serjeant, *The 'White Dune'*, 81, suggests, from examples in Hadhramawt, that the occurrence of women's names in the genealogies can partly be explained in the case of the untimely death of the father of a very young boy, who is then brought up by his mother, and called after her. See also J. Henninger, *Die Familie*, 146, n. 25.

5. Review of W. M. Watt's book, col. 1071–1072. See also the negative appreciations of J. Henninger, *Altarabische Genealogie*, 864, 868, and J. Chelhod, *Du nouveau*, 98.

6. See G. P. Murdock, *Social Structure*, 190, 218, cited by J. Haekel, *Zum Problem*, I, 305 and n. 4; W. Dostal, *Die Beduinen*, 143.

7. W. M. Watt, *Muhammad at Madina*, 373; J. Henninger, *Altarabische Genealogie*, 868.

8. See also J. Henninger, *La société bédouine* 92, who stresses the basic identity between the recent and the pre-Islamic bedouin family.

9. F. V. Winnett and G. L. Harding, *Inscriptions from Fifty Safaitic Cairns*, Toronto, 1978, 20–21.

10. W. R. Smith, *Kinship*, 33–34; Th. Nöldeke, 151; W. Caskel, review of W. M. Watt's book, col. 1072.

11. An elaborate list in J. Haekel, *Zum Problem*, I, 305 and note 4; see also J. Henninger, *Die Familie*, 145–157; W. M. Watt, *Muhammad at Madina*, 373–385; W. Caskel, *Ǧamhara*, I, 52–57; W. Dostal, *Die Beduinen*, 144.

12. J. Henninger, *Die Familie*, 84–85, 153; G. P. Murdock, *Social Structure*, 213–215, cited by J. Haekel, *Zum Problem*, I, 306; W. M. Watt, *Muhammad at Medina*, 388; W. Dostal, *die Beduinen*, 144.

13. Among more than two dozens previously known Hasaean inscriptions [listed by Chr. Robin, *Monnaies provenant de l'Arabie du nord-est*, in *Semitica*, 24, 1974, 112], the number of women mentioned in epitaphs is relatively high (as in the Sabaean epitaphs) but only in Ja 1048 [published by A. Jamme, *Sabaean and Hasaean Inscriptions from Saudi Arabia*, Rome, 1966, 74–75] the matrilineal genealogy would reach up to the grandmother, if one accepts the reading *mtmt bn[t] sbt bnt ʿhns d't* . . . proposed by Robin, *loc. cit.*, 113.

14. I. Sh. Shifman, *Gosudarstvo*, 67; both facts were already observed by W. R. Smith, *Kinship*, 313 (note 6 of p. 236), on basis of the same inscriptions, then just published in J. Euting, *Nabatäische Inschriften aus Arabien*, Berlin, 1885.

15. See J. Chelhod, *Du nouveau*, 98–99.

16. See J. Henninger, *Die Familie*, 151–152; J. Chelhod, *Du nouveau*, 77, n. 1.

17. One could in that context point to the prominent position of women in ancient North Arabia, as appears from the mention of several North Arabian queens in the *Annals* of the Assyrian kings of the end of the IInd and the first half of the Ist millennium B.C., describing their campaigns in Arabia; see already W. R. Smith, *Kinship*, 275 (note 12 of p. 104). A similar remark has been made, I cannot remember where, on the frequent appearance of queens in the Nabataean coinage.

18. Attention was first drawn to the presence of matrilineal features in the South Arabian inscriptions in my article *Himyaritica*, 4, 494.

19. Published in G. Ryckmans, *Epigraphical Texts*, 3–8 and 50–53. A corrected

reading of Fakhry 76 is given, from a photograph, in A. Jamme, *Sabaean Inscriptions*, 334–335. I identified the suffix -*hn* in Fakhry 3 as a fem. pl. possessive (not previously recognized as such in various commentaries of this context), in *Un rite d'istiqâ*, 381, n. 2. See on those texts A. F. L. Beeston, *Some Features*, 118–119, and *Women in Saba*, 8.

20. A probable feature of transmission of property from female to female in South Arabia is the custom of *tarh*, now called *rifd* (or *rifda* or *naqt*: Landberg, *Etudes*, II/2, 858), in Yemen (cp. J. Chelhod, *Du nouveau*, 89), and in Soqotrā (cp. V. V. Naumkin and V. Ja. Porhomovskij, *Očerki*, 97), and already mentioned by Ibn al-Muǧāwir, *Ta'rīh al-mustabsir* [ed. O. Löfgren, 86], cited and translated from his own manuscript by Landberg, *Etudes*, II/2, 827–829, and quoted by J. Chelhod, *Du nouveau*, 89: it is a sort of wedding loan given by women to the parents of the bride, to be reciprocated at the wedding of a daughter of the loaner. But in Mekka, according to the description of Ibn al-Muǧāwir (Löfgren's edition, 7), cited and translated by Landberg, *Etudes*, II/2, 859–861, the *tarh* gift was made to the groom (and was therefore a men's affair).

21. Cf. J. Henninger, *Die Familie*, 146 and n. 26.

22. Published in M. al-Iryani, *Fī ta'rīkh*, 174. See my commentary in *Himyaritica*, 4, 493–499; J. Chelhod, *Du nouveau*, 100. A. F. L. Beeston, *Women in Saba*, 9, minimizes the significance of the text from the point of view of matrilineal filiation.

23. The term *'lt X* is unmistakably a plural (feminine) of the singular *dht X*, which is considered to express the relation of a married woman to the family of her husband, cf. W. W. Müller, *Polyandrie*, 131, and *Ein Grabmonument*, 152; Chr. Robin, *Les hautes-terres*, II, 51; A. F. L. Beeston, *Women in Saba*, 11, 13. But that interpretation is not quite consistent with that of *bnt dt X*: see the next note.

24. Contrary to A. F. L. Beeston's interpretation in *Women in Saba*, 9 [but which he has abandoned since – personal communication], *'lt* is not an oblique case of the common gender plural, but a plural feminine nominative in apposition (and not in a state of annexion, as in J. Ryckmans *Himyaritica, 4*, 493) to *bnt*. Cp. the use of *'lt* with feminine subjects in Jamme 722, 2–3 (*bnt X 'lt Y 'mh 'lt Z*), and CIH 581, 2 (*bnt 'lt Thy^cz*), in the nominative (the restoration *bnt 'lt T* with a singular in line 1 seems faulty). In the last text *bnt 'lt Thy^cz* seems to be parallel to *'mh(hw) 'lt T* of lines 6–7 and 18. See also *'mh 'lt X* in Ja 722,3, and 734,4, and cp. further *bnt dt X* in the singular, in Jamme 738,9, which Chr. Robin, *Les hautes-terres*, II, 51, and W. W. Müller, *Polyandrie*, 132, consider to apply to a married woman (but see the preceding note). Chr. Robin, *Compléments*, 177 and 179, makes a rather inconsistent difference between the interpretation of *'lt* respectively in *'lt Grhmm*, 'du lignage de [of the lineage] *Grhmm*', and *bnt 'lt Thy^cz*, 'du lignage [of the lineage] *'lt Thy^cz*', in which *'lt* appears to be considered part of a proper name. In Iryani 34 one expects the offspring of the female dedicators to be unmarried and born into the clan; they are called *bnt 'lt Grhmm*. Finally, in his last treatment of CIH 581, Beeston, *Women in Saba* 10, considers at least one of the women jointly called *bnt 'lt Thy^cz* to be a married woman.

25. If the women were sisters. – For the Sabaean texts alluded to in that phrase, see the commentary on Jamme 705 in my article *Un parallèle*, 289–290.

26. *Temporary Marriage*.

27. *Some Features*, 121–122.

28. *Al-Ǧamī^c al-Sahīh*, Kitāb al-Nikāh, bāb 36, Cf. W. R. Smith, *Kinship*, 110; text and translation in Landberg, *Etudes*, II/2, 843–846; translation lastly in J. Henninger, *Neuere Forschungen*, 129–133. The third and, much less likely the fourth, of those types of marriage present a form of polyandry, see below and n. 58.

29. J. Chelhod, *Du nouveau*, 86 (without the technical name).

30. *Some Features*, 122.

31. See already W. R. Smith, *Kinship*, 67, and Landberg, *Etudes*, II/2, 935–936.

32. See my article *Himyaritica, 4*, 498.

33. *Women in Saba*, 10.

34. *Du nouveau*, 82.

35. The kind of relation described, more or less reminiscent of the *nikāh al-ibtidā^c*, is called in Hadhramawt *iktisāb* (Chelhod, *Du nouveau*, 82), from the word *kasb*, 'profit', which designates the offspring – a word also noted in a similar social context among bedouin tribes in Hadhramawt by R. B. Serjeant (personal communication).

36. *Arabica*, 4, 25–28; *Etudes*, II/2, 943–944. The child may have been conceived as a result of *tawrīd*, see below.

37. *The 'White Dune'*, 80–81.

38. Cp. Landberg, *Arabica*, 4, 26; *Etudes*, II/2, 944, on the same term, and J. Chelhod, *Du nouveau*, 83, on the comparable nickname *al-farh*.

39. Cf. W. R. Smith, *Kinship*, 65, 69–70; J. Chelhod, *Du nouveau*, 92.

40. Such, according to R. B. Serjeant, *The 'White Dune'*, 82, is not the case with the people living in houses in Abyan, who do not follow the custom of the bedouin tribes to the east of Shuqrā, but give an abortifacient to an unmarried girl who has become pregnant, and keep the matter concealed.

41. Cp. J. Henninger, *Die Familie*, 146; J. Chelhod, *Du nouveau*, 83.

42. *Die Beduinen*, 144, n. 190, and fig. 41, 145. See J. Chelhod, *Du nouveau*, 81, for the Humūm themselves.

43. See Landberg, *Etudes*, II/2, 933 f.; J. Henninger, *Die Familie*, 152–153; W. Dostal, *Die Beduinen*, 144, n. 191.

44. See a summing up of the subject in J. Henninger, *Die Familie*, 44–46. The principal Arabic text is about ^cAsīr in Ibn al-Muğāwir, *Ta'rih* [ed. O. Löfgren, 53 f.], already quoted by W. R. Smith, *Kinship*, 276–277 (note 4 p. 117); text, translation and commentary in Landberg, *Etudes* II/2, 909 ff., and 943–944; translation and commentary in J. Chelhod, *Du nouveau*, 90 ff., with further references for North Yemen. R. B. Serjeant, *The 'White Dune'*, 80, also mentions *tawrīd* in the tribal mountain territory of Hadhramawt.

45. See J. Henninger, *Die Familie*, 43–46; Landberg, *Arabica*, IV, 27–28; *Etudes*, II/2 826–829, 907 ff., 911 ff., 925 ff.; J. Chelhod, *Du nouveau*, 88–91.

46. *Women in Saba*, 11. See already his article *Two Epigraphic South Arabian Roots: HY^c and KRB*, in *Al-Hudhud*, 27–29.

47. *Women in Saba*, 11.

48. J. Chelhod, *Du nouveau*, 93. Ibn Battūta, *Rihla*, Bairut, 1960, 248.

49. *Die Beduinen*, fig. 41, p. 144. – In Soqotrā, according to V. V. Naumkin and V. Ja. Porhomovskij, *Očerki*, 97, the residence is patrilocal or neolocal.

50. Revised reading in K. Mlaker, *Die Hierodulenlisten von Ma^cin*, Leipzig; 1943, 56.

51. *Women in Saba*, 11.

52. The syntax is at any rate rather strained, since the two infinitives, linked in the same chain, are followed by an object related to the second verb only.

53. See Chr. Robin, *Mission archéologique et épigraphique française au Yemen du Nord en 1978*, dans *Comptes Rendus des Séances de l'Académie des Inscriptions et Belles-Lettres*, octobrè 1979, Paris, 1979, 184–190. Text republished by A. Jamme, *Pre-Islamic Arabian Miscellanea*, in *Al-Hudhud*, 106–107, where *^cdb* is translated 'to castigate'.

54. *Women in Saba*, 11.

55. J. Henninger, *Polyandrie*, 317.

56. See the commentary of the texts in J. Henninger, *Polyandrie*, 314–320, and partly in W. W. Müller, *Polyandrie*, 134–135, and (al-Bukhārī and Strabo) in J. Henninger, *Neuere Forschungen*, 128–135. The text of al-Bīrūnī is in *Ta'rīkh al-Hind*, ed. Sachau, London, 1887, 51 f., 91. J. Henninger, *Polyandrie*, considers that this text, so far away geographically and historically from ancient Arabia, cannot have a value of indepen- dent source, and that it summarizes the description of the 3rd and 4th forms of marriage of al-Bukhārī. – The text of Strabo, *Geogr.* XVI, 4, 25 (translation in Henninger, *Polyandrie*, 316, and *Neuere Forschungen*, 133–136), contains the story of a king's fair daughter who tried by a trick to escape the attention of her 15 brothers and lovers: a

fairy tale which probably is at the origin of the 'information' on the fact that in Arabia Felix the members of a tribe shared a single wife, as Hartmann, *Die arabische Frage*, Leipzig, 1909, 199, has argued (quoted by J. Henninger, *Polyandrie*, 318, who mentions the opposite opinion of Tkač, *ibid.*, 319, n. 55).

57. The more so, because of the confirmation some scholars meant to find in the South Arabian inscriptions. See the discussion in J. Henninger, *Polyandrie*, 317–321, who finally states that the anecdote in Strabo presupposes a context which is similar to that contained in al-Bukhārī's description, and could even serve to confirm it. He concludes that the existence of polyandry in Arabia is neither proved not probable, but that it would be hypercritical to put in doubt the possibility of its having existed. W. Dostal, *Die Beduinen*, 146, considers Strabo's information as very enlightening, from an ethnological point of view.

58. See the discussion in J. Henninger, *Polyandrie*, 317–320; W. W. Müller, *Polyandrie*, 136–137.

59. Henninger, *loc. cit.*, 320; W. W. Müller, *Polyandrie*, 137.

60. *Un parallèle*, 289–290.

61. W. W. Müller, *Polyandrie*, 137.

62. A similar view had been expressed by M. Höfner, in a personal communication quoted by J. Henninger, *Neuere Forschungen*, 137. Henninger himself takes no side in the discussion of the Sabaean epigraphic evidence, but stresses the unanimous opinion that if polyandry was ever attested in ancient South Arabia, it must have been a rare phenomenon.

Bahrain and its position in an eco-cultural classification-concept of the Gulf: some theoretical aspects of eco-cultural zones

WALTER DOSTAL

From an anthropological point of view, it has always been a fundamental question as to what extent there are regularities in cultural phenomena in a given geographical region. This refers to the concept of 'culture area', which is very generally defined in terms of the distribution of culture material in an environmental unit.[1] The elaboration of such areas is important regarding their use as descriptive and classificatory devices. However, the concept of 'culture area' only seems to be applicable after the relationship between culture and environment has been unfolded.[2] Firstly, therefore, I shall discuss this relationship in general, and secondly, I shall suggest specific 'eco-cultural zones' (E.C.Z.) in the geographically limited area of the Arabian Coast of the Gulf.

For the first, my starting point is a model of the eco-cultural interactions system.[3] This model, conceived as a basis for eco-cultural interpretations of a culture, emphasizes that no general assertion on cultural developments may be derived from this specific kind of interpretation alone. From this, the limitations of eco-cultural conclusions become evident and within this frame of validity the following theoretical concept has to be placed. The model is an approach in systems theory, established within a cybernetic system.

The decision to make use of a cybernetic system was mainly determined by the fact that with this system of theoretic formula one can study conditions and behaviour which are organized in one way, in order for their better understanding. The problem is to single out the determining and directing factors. In a cybernetic system, all elements chained together by the input and output couplings, are so coherent that they enable the processes of optimization and self-organization to tend toward stability. Just these processes of optimization and self-organization gave us the opportunity for qualifying and interrelationships between culture and environment. For this reason both processes – optimization and self-organization – are the constitutive elements of the model.

My theoretical reflections are based on the following axioms:

1. The relations between the natural environment and culture are perceived as an interrelationship.

2. This eco-cultural interrelationship represents a partial process only in the history of a culture. Therefore, other factors situated outside this eco-cultural interrelationship have to be considered in order to explain the total cultural formation.

3. The natural environment is referred to as being socialized, which is expressed by the term 'anthropological environment'. The definition of this term is based on the assumption that the spatial distribution of a culture is a function of the political territory of the culture-bearer-unit. This factor determines the spatial dimension of environment with all its attendant physiotope and biotope units. In other words: only the dīrah of a tribe has to be considered as the 'anthropological environment'. In a very simplified notation this term can be transcribed as

$$E_a (X_k) = (\{X_o\}, \{I\})$$

$$
\begin{aligned}
E_a &= \text{anthropological environment} \\
X_k &= \text{socio-cultural system} \\
X_o &= \text{eco-system} \\
I &= \text{set of relation here concerning the political territory} \\
(\ ) &= \text{ordered pair} \\
\{\ \} &= \text{set}
\end{aligned}
$$

According to the characteristics of a cybernetic system as mentioned before, the processes of optimization and self-organization tend towards stability. I will call this stability the 'eco-cultural stability', which should be understood as a hypothetical abstraction. I define this stability as a situation in which the balance between input and output remains temporarily unchanged by the needs of the society and the exploitation of resources, so that the re-cycling processes of the natural environment are ensured, and the ecological conditions of the society's existence are thus guaranteed.

We must now examine the processes of optimization as 'adjustment' and self-organization as 'adaptation'.

The processes of adjustment (optimization) are understood as reactions of the social-cultural structure towards the general conditions of the physical and biotopic units of the natural environment. These processes are directed and determined by the following variables: subsistence production and production of material culture (technology, implements, etc.), the reciprocal and redistributive forms of circulation of goods and the relevant socio-political institutions, juridical regulations and religious beliefs and institutions combined with the first mentioned variables.

The notation of adjustment processes:

$$E_a \leftrightarrows (\{SP\}, \{MP\}, \{GC\}) \circ (\{S\}, \{P\}, \{J\}, \{R\})$$

SP = subsistence production; MP = production of material
      culture;
GC = goods circulation/reciprocity, redistribution;
S = social institution; P = political institutions; J = juridical
      regulations; R = religious beliefs and institutions.
o = chaining together; $\leftrightarrows$ = Bijunction

The processes of adaptation (self-organization) are conceived as
reactions of specific parts of the socio-cultural structure towards
specific formations of the physical and biotopic units of the natural
environment. These processes of adaptation tend towards the
stability of the eco-cultural interrelationship. I regard the main
variable determining these processes as the transactions concerning
the exchange of external goods, connected with the relevant social
and political institutions, the juridical order and religious beliefs and
institutions. In the notation I shall write these processes as

$$E_a \leftarrow (ExT) \circ (\{S\}, \{P\}, \{J\}, \{R\})$$

ExT = good exchange transactions
$\leftarrow$ subjunction

The dynamics of the two processes in the foregoing discussion reflect
the eco-cultural interrelationship. We are unable to deduce the
totality of the socio-cultural development. It follows from this that
only within these limitations are eco-cultural interpretations possible; they refer only to a given stage in the cultural development
stage. In the following I will exemplify an eco-cultural interpretation
of some features of the Shiḥūḥ culture in the Rās al-Khaimah
territory.[4]
    Geographically the Shiḥūḥ area is divided into two zones:
1) The zone of limestone mountain-range, with wadis oriented
towards the coast and filled with limestone debris. The vegetation is
very limited, and most of the area shows symptoms of severe erosion.
2) The coastal zone, a deposit with a steppe-like girth before the
coastal sands.
    Now the question arises: What specific features have to be
singled out as the determining environmental factors of these two
zones? As for the mountain zone it is important to note that no wells
can be sunk in this area, whether in the mountains or in the wadis.
The population is therefore entirely dependent on rain water, which
is collected in cisterns and in the fields – agriculture here is com-

pletely rain-fed. In contrast to this situation the coastal zone is favoured by the stream of groundwater flowing along the mountain edge. This circumstance offers man the possibility of constructing wells and thus of irrigation. These antagonistic features characterize the environment of the Shiḥūḥ and have strong influence on their economic and social life. In the mountains only barley and wheat is cultivated on terraced fields, in the coastal zone we find a remarkable date-palm cultivation. Both areas offer the facilities for goat breeding.

What is the position of the two agricultural branches? The barley and wheat crops are only sufficient for the subsistence purposes of the household. Therefore, the circulation of goods with these crops is limited to the households of a segment and take place on the basis of the mutual support between neighbours or relatives on the principle of reciprocity. Regarding the date palm cultivation it should be noted that this is the only form of production which regularly produces a relative surplus and offers the Shiḥūḥ the possibility of exchanging dates in the market places outside Shiḥūḥ territory. In the market exchange, goats are also included.

Now we should have a look at social life. It is remarkable to discover that the environmental conditions already described force the Shiḥūḥ to a seasonal movement, which follows the pattern of winter and summer residence. In winter time they live in the mountains, where they have their hamlets, occupied by one or more segments, which are mostly in isolation over the vast mountain range. After the harvest of barley and wheat in spring time the population migrates to the coastal fringes, where they have their date palm gardens. During their stay for the whole summertime some groups are also occupied in fishing. The settlement pattern in the coastal fringe shows a trend to nucleation in which various local groups are temporarily integrated. We should now ask how the Shiḥūḥ manage their complex economy. To answer this question I choose the rules governing the division of labour within the house-hold, because I regard them as a key for understanding their economic activities. Male labour responsibilities include land-tilling, date palm cultivation and fishing. Incumbent upon the woman are the processing of agricultural and animals products, whereby only she takes care of the goats. By these rules man has enough time to look after his date palm gardens, as he has time between the sawing and harvesting of the barley and wheat crops in the mountains, fig. 144.

How we can give an eco-cultural interpretation of the selected features? In my understanding of the Shiḥūḥ culture I refer to the seasonal migration, the rain-red agriculture in the mountains, the date palm cultivation and fishing on the coastal fringe as adjustment (optimization) phenomena, whereas the intensity of date palm culti-vation connected with the rules governing the division of labour and

144   The seasonal migration of
the Shihuh (Ràs al-Khaimah)

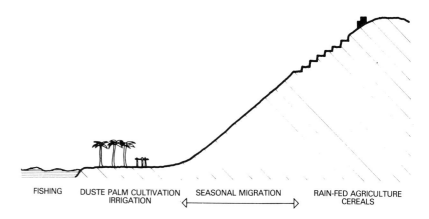

FISHING   DUSTE PALM CULTIVATION   SEASONAL MIGRATION   RAIN-FED AGRICULTURE
            IRRIGATION   CEREALS

the external exchange of dates and goats are understood as phenomena of the adaptation (self-organization) processes.

I have limited myself to some selected features to demonstrate
the necessity of a concept that mediates between ecological and
cultural contexts for the desired explanatory tasks. Whether or not
one prefers the system approach, the facts remains that we need a
basic concept for understanding the complexity of the inter-relation-
ship between environment and culture.

From the perspective of the aim of this paper we should now
discuss the 'eco-cultural zone' concept as the postulated pre-
requisite for cultural areas. In the foregoing discussion the concept of
the 'anthropological environment' was conceived as the basic unit for
eco-cultural investigations. Contrary to the restricted validity of the
term 'anthropological environment' a definition of the term 'eco-
cultural zone' must take into account a spatial extension. I suggest
confining the spatial dimension of this term to an environmental area
with significant regularities in the processes of adjustment and
adaptation. In the proper sense an 'eco-cultural zone' represents an
extension of a number of 'anthropological environments' within the
same environmental area. It is certainly plausible to propose that this
is a concept by which the field of study is approximated and
abstracted to facilitate understanding and explanation.

Let us now turn to the application of the eco-cultural concept
as exemplified on the Arabian Coast of the Gulf. Because of the lack of
ethnographic data of that region – one should realize that ethno-
graphically the Arabian Peninsula belongs to one of the most
unknown areas of the world – this attempt is a very tentative one. I
shall now proceed to emphasize the hypothetically worked out eco-
cultural zones, which are marked on the map, fig. 145.

The available ethnographic data allow the establishment of six

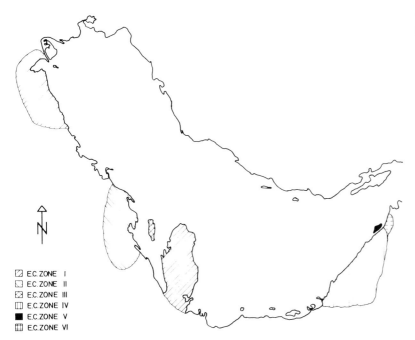

E.C. ZONE   I
E.C. ZONE   II
E.C. ZONE   III
E.C. ZONE   IV
E.C. ZONE   V
E.C. ZONE   VI

elaborate eco-cultural zones (E.C. Zone) on the Arabian side (from Kuwait until Rās al-Khaimah) of the Gulf.

I. The E.C. Zone (I) is patterned through the co-existence of two economies, nomadic and settled.[5]
The former is represented by camel, sheep and goat breeding; the economy of the latter comprehend the following main branches: only a few sporadically distributed agricultural centres (date-palm cultivation, cereals, vegetables), whose production is not sufficient to satisfy the local needs; on the coastal fringe some settlements with fishing and pearl-fishing; in the settlement with a sea-port trade-centres, pearl-fishing and fishing.

The phenomena of adaptation worth mentioning in connection with the nomads are their caravan services (inland trade), whilst those relating to the settled population are the trade activities with particular emphasis on long-distance trade and pearl-fishing.

II. The E.C. Zone (II): with similar features as E.C. Zone I, but differentiated by the spatial concentration of agricultural centre with flourishing date palm cultivation; in this area lies the inland-market place.[6]
In addition to the adaptation phenomena of E.C. Zone I the export of dates is a dominant factor.

III. The E.C. Zone of Bahrain is patterned by different economic branches of the settled population:[7] agricultural centres with mainly date palm cultivation, further fishing and pearl-fishing; in the sea-port settlement a long-distance trade centre. As significant adaptation phenomena the following have to be considered: long-distance trade, pearl-fishing and (to a lesser degree) the export of local dates.

IV. This E.C. Zone shows similarities, regarding the economic co-existence between nomads and sedentary population, with E.C. Zone I.[8] Within the latter we found a sharper distinction between the coastal population and the population of the oases. On the coast the inhabitants are engaged in fishing, pearl-fishing and trade; especially in the coastal settlement with sea-ports long-distance trade activities have been developed. The oases are spread over the hinterland; their date production satisfies only to a lower degree the subsistence needs of the coastal inhabitants.

The notable adaptation phenomena are the following: in addition to those of the nomads in E.C. Zone I, the temporary engagement of nomads in pearl-fishing.[9] For the settled population are to be mentioned fishing (fish drying), pearl-fishing and long-distance trade.

V. The pattern of the E.C. Zone of the Island of Ḥamrā (UAE) is marked only by the following economic activities: fishing, pearl-fishing and trade.[10] The inhabitants possess some date-palm gardens in the oases on the mainland, but with insufficient production. They use these gardens as summer residences. The characteristic adaptation phenomena are fishing and pearl-fishing, whereas the trade activities have a secondary role.

VI. This E.C. Zone is marked by the mixed economy of the inhabitants:[11] rain-fed agriculture (cereals) in the mountains, date-palm cultivation at the coastal fringe, goat breeding and fishing.

From the adaptation phenomena I refer to the rules governing market-exchange of dates and goats at the external markets.

In any case, the concept of 'Eco-cultural Zones' must be treated as a heuristic assumption in the study of the interrelationship between environment and culture. The elaborated concept represents an approach in its very beginnings and is, of course, afflicted with all the deficiencies of this stage. In summary, it can be stated that:

1. It is not the aim of this concept to comprise the cultural totality of such areas with their culture historical implications or to explain all relations of the cultural variables. With it, we strive for an explanation in a wider spatial dimension in contrast to the spatial limitation of an eco-cultural study of a single culture.

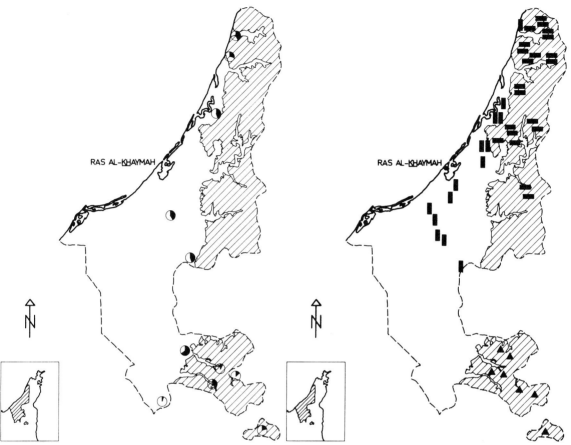

146 The spatial distribution of the 45 date palm varieties (black marked) in Ràs al-Khaimah

147 Distribution of selected house forms in Ràs al-Khaimah

2. Only a few characteristics have been established, but a number of significant eco-cultural patterns remain neglected, mainly the result of lack of ethnographic data. In concluding this paper I would like to use two examples to demonstrate what quality of data material is required. The first example concerns the date palm cultivation. For estimating the significance of this farming branch in each 'eco-cultural zone' we would like to have data for comparison available, whereby not only the number of the palm varieties but also the number of the varieties of a high exchange value could serve as criteria. During a survey carried out in Rās al-Khaimah it became clear that there is a qualitative difference in the date palm cultivation between the oasis belt and its border area, fig. 146. In the former, forty-five varieties are cultivated with a remarkable percentage of those varieties having a high exchange value. The quantity of both was found to be less in the border area mentioned.[12] From these findings I would imagine that were similar data from the other Gulf regions available one might derive basic material by comparative studies for the qualification of date-palm cultivation in the 'eco-cultural zones'. The same may be produced for the house forms. Here we would need distributional studies from the different regions, for which I append a map of the Rās al-Khaimah territory as an example,[13] fig. 147. Such samples for outstanding data could be quoted in a random number. In connection with the problems of data quality I would like to emphasize that the eco-cultural approach requires further ethnographic investigation.

1. cf. I. Rouse, 'The Strategy of Culture History', in *Anthropology Today* (ed. by A. L. Kroeber), Chicago 1953: 68 passin. For criticisms of these concepts cf. H. E. Driver, 'Cross-Cultural Studies' in: *Handbook of Social and Cultural Anthropology* (ed. by J. J. Honigmann) Chicago 1973: 353 passim, and idem in *Comparative Studies by H. E. Driver and Essays in his Honor* (ed. by J. G. Jorgensen) Hraf Press New Haven, 1974: 154 passim, 205 passim. M. Harris: *The rise of Anthropological Theory*, New York 1968: 340 passim, 374 passim.

2. For a summary of eco-cultural studies cf. J. N. Anderson, 'Ecological Anthropology and Anthropological Ecology' in *Handbook of Social and Cultural Anthropology* (ed. by J. J. Honigmann) Chicago 1973: 179–239. M. Harris *op. cit.*: 654 passim.

3. W. Dostal, 'Theorie des öko-kulturellen Interaktionssystems', *Anthropos*, 69, 1974, 409–444; further the same with L. Reisinger: 'Ein Modell des öko-kulturellen Interaktionssystems', *Zeitschrift für Ethnologie*, 106, 1981, 54–50.

4. For a preliminary report on the Shiḥūḥ cf. W. Dostal, 'The Shiḥūḥ of Northern Oman: A contribution to Cultural Ecology', *The Geographical Journal*, 138, 1972, 1–7.

5. Cf. H. R. P. Dickson: *Kuwait and her Neighbours*, London 1956; the same author: *The Arab of the Desert*, London 1959: 473 passim, 484 passim; J. G. Lorimer: *Gazetteer of the Persian Gulf, Oman and Central Arabia*, Calcutta 1908, 1915, IIB:1048 passim; W. Dostal: unpublished field notes from Kuwait (1956). In British statistics Kuwait figures for the first time in the year 1905/06 among pearl-fishing participants of the Gulf, which is conclusive regarding the beginning of this branch of the economy in that region (J. G. Lorimer: *op. cit.* Vol. I. Pt. II: 2253). In 1907 Kuwait had 461 boats for pearl-fishing (Lorimer: *op. cit.* Vol. I. Pt. II: 2259). For the insufficient date palm cultivation cf. J. G. Lorimer: *op. cit* Vol. I. Pt. II: 2297. For Qatar cf. J. G. Lorimer: *op. cit.* Vol. IIA: 487 passim Vol. IIB: 1505 passim. In 1907 the total number of pearl fishing boats in Qatar was 817 (J. G. Lorimer: *op. cit.* Vol. I. Pt. II: 2257); for the minimal date palm cultivation the same: *op. cit.* Vol. I. Pt. II: 2296.

6. For al-Ḥasā cf. J. G. Lorimer: *op. cit.* Vol. IIA: 642 passim. For the date palm cultivation cf. Lorimer: *op. cit.* Vol. I. Pt. II: 2297, further T. S. Vidal: 'Date culture in the oasis of al-Hasa'. *Middle East Journal* (1954): 417–428, the same: 'The Oasis of al-Ḥasā', *ARAMCO*, Arabian Research Division 1955: 149 passim. H.-J. Philipp: 'Geschichte und Entwicklung der Oase al-Ḥasā (Saudi-Arabien)'. Bd. 1 in: *Sozioökonomische Schriften zur Agrarentwicklung* 23, Saarbrücken 1976. For 1907 167 pearl-fishing boats in al-Hasa are mentioned (J. G. Lorimer *op. cit.* Vol. I. Pt. II: 2259).

7. For Baḥrain cf. J. G. Lorimer: *op.cit.* Vol. IIA: 212 passim. Regarding the cultural change cf. F. I. Khuri: *Tribe and state in Bahrain. The transformation of Social and Political Authority in an Arab State* Chicago-London 1980; for date palm cultivation cf. J. G. Lorimer: *op. cit.* Vol. I. Pt. II: 2296 with information on the date-export. For fishing cf. R. B. Serjeant: 'Fisher-Folk and fish-traps in al-Bahrain'. *Bulletin of the School of Oriental and African Studies*. Vol. XXXI (1968): 486–514. Pearl-fishing became evident by archaeological proof from 700 B.C. cf. E. C. L. During Caspers: 'Corals, Pearls and Prehistoric Gulf Trade' *Proceedings of the seminar for Arabian Studies* Vol. 13 (1983):

23. In 1907 917 pearl-fishing boats were registered in al-Baḥrain (J. G. Lorimer: *op. cit.* Vol. I. Pt. II: 2258).

8. For the UAE cf. J. G. Lorimer: *op. cit.* Vol. IIB: 1425 passim and the relevant principalities there; K. G. Fenelon: *The Trucial States. A Brief economic survey*. Middle East Economic and Social Monographs 1. Bayrut 1969[2]. In 1907 the total number of 1,215 pearl-fishing boats were registered, Abu Dhabi with 410, Dubai with 335 and Shardjah with 183 boats (J. G. Lorimer: *op. cit.* Vol. I. Pt. II: 2256). For the date palm cultivation cf. J. G. Lorimer: Vol. I. Pt. II: 2296.

A matter for further discussion might be the approximate configuration of this eco-cultural zone in the 3rd Millennium B.C. as is seen from S. Cleuziou: 'Hili and the beginning of oasis life in Eastern Arabia'. *Proceedings of the Seminar for Arabian Studies*. Vol. 12 (1982): 15–23, essp.: 20.

9. W. Dostal: *op. cit.* 1974: 435 passim.

10. The inhabitants are of the Za'ab tribe *The tribes of the Trucial States* Confidential Report, 1958: 24; J. G. Lorimer: *op. cit.* Vol. IIB: 1936. In 1907 in Djazīrat al-Ḥamrā 25 pearl-fishing boats had been registered (J. G. Lorimer: *op. cit.* Vol. I. Pt. II: 2256).

11. W. Dostal: *op. cit.* 1972; J. G. Lorimer: *op. cit.* Vol. IIB: 1805 passim.

12. Own field material now in print.

13. W. Dostal: *The Traditional Architecture of Rās al-Khaimah (North)*. Beihefte zum Tübinger Atlas des Vorderen Orients. Reihe B. (Geisteswissenschaft) Nr.54, Wiesbaden 1983. There are some valuable single studies, but outstanding are distributional investigations cf. J. Coles-P. Jackson: 'A Wind-Tower House in Dubai', *Art and Archaeology Papers*, London, June 1975; Cl. Hardy-Chr. Lalande: *La Maison de Shaykh Īsā a Baḥayn*, Recherches sur les grandes civilisations. Memoire Nr.8 Paris 1981.

Dilmun and the Late Assyrian Empire

DAVID OATES

My purpose here is to consider the relationship between Dilmun and the Late Assyrian Empire, taking into account both literary references and the buildings excavated at Qal'at al-Bahrain and assigned to this period by the Danish Expedition. All the archaeological information I have used obviously derives from their work and particularly from Mr. Geoffrey Bibby's *Looking for Dilmun*, but the comments of an archaeologist who has been particularly concerned with Late Assyrian history and architecture may be of some interest.

With regard to the general history of the 'palace' site, close to the lip of the ditch surrounding the Qal'a itself, it is interesting that there are substantial gaps in occupation even at this relatively central point on the mound in the second and first millennia B.C. The Kassite domination had a character unique in the history of Bahrain, in that the pottery found in this level is recognisably Mesopotamian (Bibby, 1970, 137) and two letters of this date from Nippur demonstrate that Dilmun's affairs were in the hands of officials with Akkadian names reporting to the governor of Nippur itself (Cornwall, 1952, 137 ff.). This phase came to a violent end, presumably at or before the fall of the Kassite dynasty in the early twelfth century B.C. Then there is apparently no intervening building level until the 'City IV' stratum, in which the 'palace' walls are said in some cases to rest directly on their Kassite predecessors, and occasionally even to incorporate them. We are presented with the picture of a massive building abandoned for some five centuries with its walls still standing, and then replaced by a complex of structures which the excavators assign approximately to the seventh century B.C. These in turn were deserted, though apparently not violently destroyed since their floors had been completely cleared of occupation material, and at some time before the collapse of their upper walls three burials in terra-cotta 'bath-tub' coffins were inserted beneath the floor of the stair-well in Building B, and a hoard of silver was buried at some unspecified point within the complex. These clearly provide a *terminus ante quem* for the end of level IV and their possible date is discussed below, but before turning to the archaeological evidence it may be useful to review the evidence provided by written sources.

DOCUMENTARY SOURCES

References to Dilmun in Assyrian royal inscriptions as well as earlier Mesopotamian documents have been previously recorded, but it is worth re-examining their implications for political history. The first Assyrian mention occurs in an inscription of Tukulti-Ninurta I (1244–1208 B.C.), in which he claims to be king of Dilmun and Meluḫḫa. This probably means little more than a nominal suzerainty which he inherited by his defeat and capture of the Kassite ruler Kashtiliash IV, and it is interesting that this text, as noted by Grayson (1972, 120, n. 250), is unique among Assyrian royal inscriptions in its use of a formula common in Babylonian royal titularies 'shēmû ilānishu', 'obedient to his gods'.

Dilmun does not reappear in Mesopotamian records for another five centuries, which may reflect their incomplete nature but is at least an interesting coincidence when we remember the long gap in occupation on the 'palace' site. It is striking, however, that when it is mentioned by Sargon II (721–705 B.C.) and his successors on the Assyrian throne their claim to suzerainty is again closely linked with the establishment of their authority in Babylonia. Assyrian campaigns in the late ninth century had done much to destroy stability in Babylonia, and in particular to undermine the authority of the native Babylonian monarchy. The way was left open for the assumption of effective control by the Chaldaean tribes whose territory, the 'Sealand', lay on the lower courses of the Tigris and Euphrates and around the head of the Arabian Gulf. Increasingly in Late Assyrian records the Chaldaeans appear as their principal opponents and the champions of Babylonian independence. Foremost among them, in prestige if not in size, was the tribe of Bīt Yakin, whose homeland was on the upper shores of the Gulf and whose rulers frequently held the throne of Babylon when it was not occupied by an Assyrian king or his nominee. In the period with which we are concerned the greatest of these rulers was Marduk-apla-iddina II, Merodach-Baladan of the Old Testament, who reigned in Babylon from 721 until he was ousted by Sargon in 710. Sargon's entry into Babylon was marked by the receipt of gifts from Upēri, the ruler of Dilmun. In 709 he performed the ritual duties of kingship at the New Year Festival in the city, and conducted a second campaign against Merodach-Baladan, sacking his capital Dur-Yakin. In this year he records the 'subjugation' of Upēri, who sent an ambassador offering submission and bringing tribute and gifts, but in the context this cannot imply an actual conquest of Dilmun, since all references to the extent of his direct control of territory refer to Bīt-Yakin 'up to the borders of Dilmun', implicitly excluding Dilmun itself.

The same tributary relationship without direct Assyrian administration seems to have persisted at least intermittently during the next two reigns. After Sargon's death there was renewed resistance to Assyrian rule in Babylonia, which forced his successor Sennacherib to campaign against the Chaldaeans, especially Bīt-Yakin, and their allies in the kingdom of Elam in S.W. Iran. Sennacherib's patience was finally exhausted, and in 689 he captured and sacked Babylon. The debris of the ruined city was cast into the Euphrates, and he claims that its earth was carried as far as Dilmun. At all events the occasion was marked by the despatch of 'treasures' from Dilmun to the Assyrian king, accompanied by builders and other artisans with examples of their craft, 'a copper chariot, copper tools and vessels of the workmanship of their land'. Obviously again Dilmun sent gifts or tribute to the Assyrian king when he was in undisputed control of Babylonia, and presumably to other rulers at other times as the price of uninterrupted trade. The reference to copper objects clearly of considerable value, as the workmanship of their land, shows that Dilmun at this time was not merely an entrepot for Gulf trade and a producer of dates, important though these may have been, but a centre of craftmanship in its own right.

In the inscriptions of Esarhaddon, Sennacherib's son and viceroy in Babylon until he succeeded to the throne in 681, there are only two references to Dilmun (LAR II, 572 and 668). One text is very broken and uninformative, while in the other Esarhaddon describes himself as 'king of the kings of Dilmun, Makkan and Meluḫḫa', obviously implying suzerainty but not direct rule. Dilmun appears for the last time in Assyrian sources in the reign of Ashurbanipal (668–627 B.C.) whose later years saw the beginning of Assyria's final decline. On a foundation cylinder from Uruk (LAR II, 970) he claims 'I established my rule over Tyre in the midst of the Upper Sea and Dilmun in the midst of the Lower Sea, and they drew my yoke'. The inclusion of Dilmun in a list of Assyrian provinces at this time, albeit in the Babylonian section (Forrer, 1921, 53), might suggest a more direct form of administration, but this cannot be regarded as conclusive in view of two documents which are worth discussing in some detail.

In the first years of Ashurbanipal's reign his brother Shamash-shum-ukin was king in Babylon, though Ashurbanipal claimed and, to a degree, exercised overall authority. This led to the rebellion of Shamash-shum-ukin in 652, supported by Elam and from 651 by Nabu-bel-shumate, son of Merodach-Baladan and ruler of the Sealand. The Chaldaean tribes were brought back under Assyrian control in 650, when Ashurbanipal sent Bel-ibni to the Sealand as his representative, while Nabu-bel-shumate fled to Elam. The Assyrian king demanded his extradition in 646, whereupon Nabu-bel-shumate and his shield-bearer killed each other. Two letters from Bel-ibni to Ashurbanipal, found at Nineveh, relate to affairs in Dilmun and should apparently be dated between 650 and 646, the first at least before the Assyrian capture of Babylon which ended the revolt in 648. This states (RCAE 458) 'Idru the rival of Hundaru, with the tribute of Dilmun in his hands, I have sent to the palace'. The existence of two rival rulers of Dilmun is most probable when the issue of the conflict in Babylonia was still in doubt, and we may suppose that Idru was the pro-Assyrian claimant while Hundaru had not yet abandoned allegiance to Shamash-shum-ukin.

In the second letter (RCAE 791) we have more but tantalisingly broken details of an apparent sequel. Idru is not mentioned, but there is a reference to Nabu-bel-shumate in connection with property belonging to him which had been removed from Dilmun, including the considerable quantity of twenty-six talents of copper. His name is qualified by a formal curse as an enemy of Assyria, but there is no indication that he is already dead, nor do we know whether the property was taken to Assyria or to Elam. Its presence in Dilmun does not imply that he was ever resident there, but as former ruler of the Sealand he would presumably have accumulated a share of the profits of the copper trade which passed through his territory to Mesopotamian markets. It is possible, though this is conjecture, that his agent in Dilmun was one Nishur-bel, whose name is linked with his and whose scribe was sent by Bel-ibni to Ashurbanipal, an action reported in the text immediately after the reference to his property. Bel-ibni also mentions Hundaru, first apparently in connection with a visit to Elam by Hundaru himself or another person whose name may have occurred in a broken passage. Hundaru is also being sent to Nineveh to be questioned by the king, who is asked to decide whether he should be punished. The offence is not specified but can hardly have been more than a failure to change sides in good time, for in more serious matters Assyrian rulers were accustomed to execute the culprit first and ask questions afterwards. If he was not to be punished, Bel-ibni proposes that he should be required 'to confirm Nergal-uballit in the king's presence'. There is no other clue to the identity of Nergal-uballit except that he is to report in detail to the king concerning Nabu-bel-shumate and Nishur-bel, and was obviously a trusted Assyrian official with knowledge of local affairs. The stipulation that he must be officially recognised by Hundaru suggests that he was to be Assyrian Resident in Dilmun to supervise the conduct of the ruler, but that the actual administration of the kingdom was to be left in Hundaru's hands. This would have been a prudent arrangement, particularly at a time when Ashurbanipal was preparing to settle accounts with Elam, and might justify the inclusion of Dilmun in the list of Assyrian provinces noted above, but it still fell short of establishing a formal provincial administration.

So we may conclude that under Sargon and his successors Dilmun was never an Assyrian province in the full sense, although its rulers accepted the Assyrian kings as overlords and paid them tribute when their control of Babylonia rendered this desirable for the maintenance of the all-important Gulf trade route. Dilmun's relations with Mesopotamia did not end with the fall of Assyria. Nebucha-drezzar, the greatest king of the Neo-Babylonian (Chaldaean) dynasty which briefly inherited much of the Assyrian empire, lists dates and prickly pears from Dilmun among the supplies for a New Year festival in Babylon, and a governor of Dilmun is mentioned in an admini-strative text of the eleventh year of Nabonidus (555–539 B.C.) whose reign ended with the conquest of Babylon by Cyrus, founder of the Achaemenid Empire. It is, then, within these chronological limits – c. 710 to 539 B.C. – that we should attempt to date the remains of City IV at Qal'at al Bahrain.

THE BUILDINGS

Little can be said about the buildings of City IV exposed in the 'palace' area until we have a fuller description of them and their contents, including later deposits, in the long-awaited final report, but some observations on their character and function can be based on the plan published in *Looking for Dilmun* (Bibby, 1970, 344), and on scattered descriptions in the text of that volume and preliminary reports in *KUML*. The plan shows the existence of four separate units, clearly contemporary since they interlock with one another. Of these the most extensive are Units A and B, referred to by the excavators as 'palaces', although it would seem more likely that Unit A had a secular and administrative, Unit B an essentially religious function. One must remark, however, that the two units are closely connected and the distinction between secular and religious functions reflects a comparatively recent European attitude which is probably irrelevant to ancient Near Eastern society. The known entrances to both open off a 'street' some 2 m. wide, leading to the doorway of Unit B at its eastern end. Despite its fine ashlar construction and massive stone sill (Bibby, 1970, Plate 12), I would suggest that neither this nor the entrance to Unit A on the north side of the 'street' was the main means of access to either complex.

Let us examine the two buildings in turn. The focal point of Unit A is clearly the group of rooms A1 to A5, with A1 as its most important reception room, A2 a more private but still large chamber behind it, and two vestibules A3 and A4 opening off it at either end. A3 has a second doorway on the north leading into what was, judging by the existence of another door jamb continuing the line of the west wall of A1, a further unexplored room or range of rooms, marked A6 on the plan. A4 similarly had a door in the north wall, though here there is no evidence of a corresponding range of rooms. On the south it gave access to A5, which was equipped with two drains concealed behind a flimsy screen. The function of these 'lavatories' will be discussed below, but the immediately relevant fact is the obvious similarity between this reception suite and well-dated Mesopotamian models. The same layout can be observed as early as the ninth century B.C. in the arsenal palace known as Fort Shalmaneser in the southeast corner of Nimrud (Kalhu), the first capital of the Late Assyrian Empire. The plan again incorporates a large reception chamber (S17), a second more private room behind and parallel with it (S30), and a small lobby at its eastern end (S18) linking it with a lavatory (S19). This was probably the reception suite of a high official, reproducing in its essentials but on a smaller scale the royal throne room and its appurtenances (Oates, 1959, 116). The layout may have had an earlier origin for which there is no excavated evidence, but it certainly persisted into the sixth century, for Woolley's report on the Neo-Babylonian houses at Ur reveals the same plan (Woolley, 1962, 41 ff. and Plates 70 and 71) varying only with the importance of the individual house which prescribes the number and size of the rooms.

The feature of Mesopotamian plans of this type which is most relevant to our understanding of Unit A is that the principal reception room faces north to avoid the direct rays of the sun, and is entered from an outer court, the *babanu* or courtyard of the gate, usually surrounded by rooms in which the public business of the establishment was transacted. It seems probable that, in view of the striking similarities of layout, the Dilmun 'palace' was organised in the same way, that A1 was preceded by a courtyard and that the main public entrance to the whole complex lay on the north or the northeast. This would confirm the opinion expressed above that the east-west 'street' was in fact a service entrance to both Units A and B, and suggests that Units C and D on its south side were domestic quarters for the two major buildings. The lack of occupation material on the floors makes it unprofitable to speculate further on the function of other subsidiary parts of the complex, but it may be worth suggesting that the structure west of the reception suite, incorporating at least one small courtyard, A7 on the plan, might have been in Mesopotamian terms the *bītanu* or residential area. It was obviously accessible by a passage from the 'street' and, through the vestibule A3, from both the courtyard and the principal reception room A1.

In the case of Unit B there is on the available evidence little to add to Bibby's published comments. Room B1 was apparently a shrine, B2 a covered area with a roof or possibly a second storey, supported on massive pillars and approached by a stairway, B3. We against suggest that the main entrance to B2 lay not through the doorway from the 'street' but through the two ante-chambers B4 and B5, probably from a northern courtyard B6. The plan bears no resemblance to that of any contemporary Mesopotamian building and presumably reflects the requirements of local ritual, by contrast with Unit A where business and ceremonial evidently followed an international pattern. A striking feature of the building is the number of lavatories, no less than eight in two groups of three and one pair, adjoining what we have suggested was the main entrance to the shrine through B4 and B5. It seems likely that these were lavatories in the most literal sense, ablution areas for those entering the temple, rather than purely functional urinals which would hardly have been needed in such numbers. One is reminded of the close association between the sacred area and an ablution tank at the very much earlier Barbar temple. Cornwall (1952, 142, n. 59) calls attention to a text in which the goddess Inanna is said to bathe her head in a fountain of Mount Dilmun, and it seems likely that the waters of Dilmun played a significant part in its religious tradition.

CHRONOLOGY

We have seen that the layout of the reception suite in Unit A has close parallels in Mesopotamia from the ninth to the sixth centuries B.C. Historical evidence shows the existence of rulers of Dilmun in contact with Mesopotamia from the late eighth to the mid-sixth centuries, and it seems plausible that the 'palace' existed in the time of Upēri and probably before, though whether it was the royal residence remains an open question. The date of its abandonment is problematic, since no occupation material remained on the floors. Certainly a considerable interval elapsed before the Hellenistic settlement of City V, during which the rooms were filled with the collapsed debris of the roofs and upper walls. But before the collapse occurred three 'bath-tub' burials were inserted beneath the stairwell of Unit B, and a silver hoard was buried at some point in the same building. Bibby relies on the presence of a signet ring in this hoard, said to be of Phoenician workmanship, to date it *c.* 650 B.C., but in a collection of scrap material presumably destined for re-use or as currency (Potts *et. al.*, 1983, 163) such an object provides only a *terminus post quem*. Woolley, on the other hand, states firmly that at Ur terracotta bath-tub coffins with one round and one square end belong to the Achaemenid and not to the Neo-Babylonian period (Woolley, 1962, 67). It seems most likely on present evidence that the end of City IV came with the Persian conquest of Babylonia, which must have dealt a severe blow to Dilmun's laboriously maintained trading connections, and perhaps opened the way for rivals on the Gulf's eastern shore.

Some notes about Qal'at al-Bahrain during the Hellenistic period

RÉMY BOUCHARLAT

The successful researches of the Danish Expedition at Qal'at al Bahrain have shown the importance of the Hellenistic settlement. G. Bibby found Hellenistic remains in several places on the site, especially under the Islamic Fort and at the South of the Fort, in the so-called 'Hundred Meters Section'. In these soundings, the Hellenistic levels were more than two metres thick. In the middle of the Portuguese Fort, another sounding also provided Hellenistic objects.

This occupation was dated from the last four centuries B.C. A date as early as the fourth century was given by a few Greek imported sherds, but they could be dated from the third century B.C. according to J-F. Salles. G. Bibby pointed out other pottery imitating Greek shapes, and others in Mesopotamian/Oriental shapes, both dating to the Seleucid/Hellenistic period, i.e. third to second centuries B.C. Some examples of this pottery are displayed in the National Museum.[1]

In his study, C. Larsen mainly deals with the pottery discovered by the Danes inside the Portuguese Fort. From this excavation, he was able to offer a chronological sequence going down as late as the Late Parthian and Sasanian periods.

The new French excavations on the Islamic Fort provide us with fresh information on the Hellenistic levels under the Islamic Fort, but raise several questions. The following notes are based upon a preliminary study of the pottery excavated by Monik Kervran, Head of the French Expedition. I would like to thank her for allowing me to undertake such a study. This article deals with three points:

– Below and beside the Hellenistic levels, M. Kervran found some pottery belonging to the mid-first millennium B.C., a little known period at Qal'at al Bahrain.

– According to these excavations, there are defensive walls under the previously known Islamic Fort. The general plan of these walls is still unknown, but they could be partly built on the same plan as the latest ones. The bulk of the pottery found in the corresponding levels can be dated from the third and second centuries B.C., but, in my opinion, includes some later shapes, as late as the first century A.D. These discoveries raise the question of the first construction of the Fort.

– Whatever the date is for the construction of the earliest Fort (or the defensive walls) it is clear now that some parts of Qal'at al Bahrain have been settled without any major gap from the Neo-Babylonian period down to the first centuries of the Christian era.

Beyond these archaeological notes, we can suggest some questions about the function of Qal'at and Bahrain island during these periods, at a time when Bahrain played a prominent part in interregional, rather than in international trade.

THE SOUNDINGS

The location of the four soundings which provided us with the pottery presented here is shown on the plan, fig. 148. Two (nos. 2 and 3) yielded good stratigraphy: the layers were sealed with an Islamic plastered floor. Apart from these four soundings, M. Kervran was able to discover some burials in which interesting unbroken vessels were found. This East Trench is not shown on the plan.

In *sounding 1* which was dug in the centre of the Fort no floor has been found. Level 8 (see also Kervran 1982, 19 and fig. 9) provided us with some pottery probably dating from the pre-Hellenistic period, which in Bahrain chronology means the Neo-Babylonian period (or Late City IV at Qal'at).

In *sounding 2*, one metre under the Islamic floor, another floor was connected with the outer wall of the Fort, according to the excavator. Many typical 'Hellenistic' sherds have been found on this floor.

In *sounding 3*, outside the Fort and close to the North-West tower, a pit whose diameter is 1.30 m and height 1.80 m has been discovered, yielding many sherds. This very regular pit was plastered. The plaster covering the wall spreads as high as the lower part of the tower. With such a connection between the pit and the tower, the Hellenistic pottery found in the pit must be of the same period as the tower or even later.

In *sounding 4*, near the Eastern wall, many Hellenistic sherds were found with two coins of Alexander type. They could have been struck by a local mint, maybe Gerrha. As usual, they present Alexander's head covered with the lion's skin. The reverse shows Zeus with an eagle. Beside these coins a small gold sheet 2 cm high has been found. It shows a human figure.

In the *East Trench*, by the seashore, one of the burials yielded three complete pots: a jar appears to be dated to the mid-first millennium B.C.; the other two are covered with a pale yellow glaze occurring from the sixth century down to the third–second centuries.

148 Qal'at al-Bahrain. The Islamic Fort. Location of M.Kervran's soundings which yielded pre-Islamic pottery

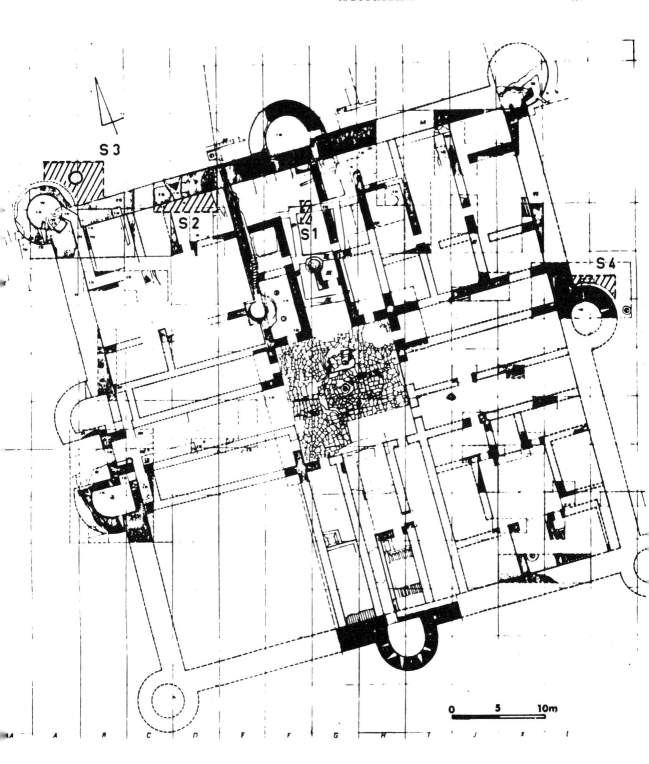

S 3

S 2

S 1

S 4

0   5   10m

149 Qal'at al-Bahrain.
Neo-Babylonian and Achaemenian
pottery from sounding 1

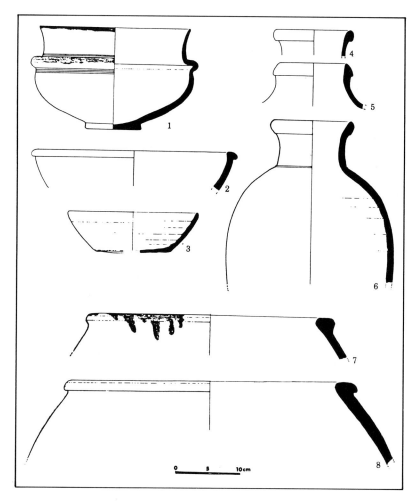

1. MID-FIRST MILLENNIUM SETTLEMENT

This period, poorly known in Bahrain, is usually classified as City IV Period which is the Neo-Assyrian and Neo-Babylonian Period according to G. Bibby (1970, Table p. 122 and p. 166, 178). Some pottery shapes from Qal'at al-Bahrain show that this period could include the Achaemenid period. Therefore there is probably no gap from the Neo-Babylonian period down to the Hellenistic one. We would agree with C. Larsen (1980, 328–336) who has produced evidence for the links between the Achaemenian and the Hellenistic periods.

Unearthed from sounding 1, several shapes can be compared to the assemblage offered by C. Larsen (1980, fig. 56–57). For instance a bowl with a fold (fig. 149; 1; Kervran 1982, fig. 10). A small jar with a thickened rim (fig. 149, 4) necks of jugs with a rib, and large bowls. In

Mesopotamia the long life of such a Neo-Babylonian tradition in pottery is evidenced on several sites (Ur, Nippur, Abu Habbah) down to the fifth and fourth centuries B.C.

In the East Trench, the unbroken pots found in a grave (not illustrated) clearly show the long life of the necropolis or more likely of the pottery shape. Besides the previously quoted Neo-Babylonian jar with a rounded bottom, two small pots are in also the Mesopotamian tradition, going by their shape (Neo-Babylonian and Achaemenid) and their glaze: it is very decayed to-day and appears as a yellow powdery surface. Such a glaze has been evidenced elsewhere in various contexts: for instance, in Susa, it has been found from the sixth century down to the third–second centuries B.C. (Boucharlat and Labrousse 1979, 76–77). In Failaka, it is known in the lower level, third–second centuries B.C. (Hannestad 1983, 12). On both sites, this glaze covered Achaemenian shapes or Hellenistic ones. At Qal'at, we suggested a late period for these pots since another grave provided us with a fish-plate, greyish-black clay, with an incised spiral in the centre.

The main problem of this period concerns the type of occupation: apart from the graves we have no trace of settlement (such as walls, floors, pits, etc.), connected with the pottery.[2] We may suggest that the settlement was further from the seashore and we may put forward two observations: a large pit dug south of the large moat yielded a huge quantity of 'City IV' pottery; many of the sherds may be as late as the fifth century B.C.; Kervran's soundings west of the Fort provided us with very poor pre-Hellenistic layers, without any structure, as Sounding 1 inside the Fort did. From this evidence one cannot deduce a poor mid-first millennium settlement in Qal'at. According to the findings, it does exist and it has to be found elsewhere.

II. THE DATE OF CONSTRUCTION OF THE 'ISLAMIC FORT'

The excavator (Kervran 1983, 12) stated that the plan of the Islamic Fort is partly that of a Hellenistic fortification. According to the stratigraphy the North wall (sounding 2), the N.W. tower (sounding 3) and the East tower (sounding 4) are to be dated from the levels yielding Hellenistic pottery and not a single Islamic sherd.

So we are facing two series of questions: the first concerns the stratigraphy and the second the chronology of the objects. I shall not discuss the first problem, since M. Kervran will publish the data concerning the structures and their stratigraphical relations. I shall only deal with objects here.

As far as the pottery found in these last three soundings is concerned, we note that the bulk of the sherds clearly dates from the third and the second centuries B.C., by comparison with Mesopo-

150　Qal'at al-Bahrain. Hellenistic pottery from soundings no 2 and 3. Glazed ware (no 1-8), Red washed ware (no 9-12, 14), and Western imports (no 13 and 15)

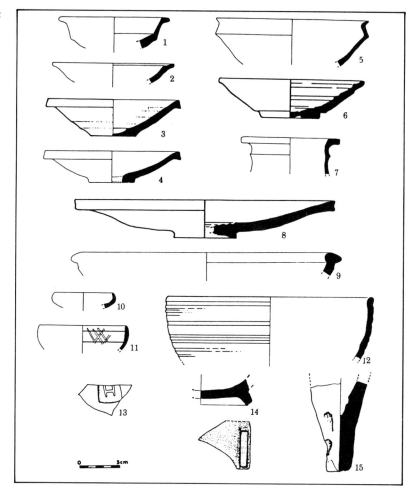

tamian pottery and Failaka pottery. For instance, there are several glazed and unglazed fish plates (fig. 150: 3, 4, 8), sometimes with inside concentric circles; glazed plates with thickened interior rim (fig. 150: 2); glazed and unglazed bowls with flaring side and offset lip (fig. 150: 5 and 150: 3); cooking pots, etc. All of them are very similar to the shapes of the Failaka pottery.[3] From the same Failaka assemblage, we can notice some rare shapes in Qal'at, for instance bowls with incurving rim, despite fig. 151: 1–2, and some missing shapes: bowls with angular profile and outturned rim (Hannestad 1983, Pl. 3, 24–29, Pl. 3, 30–34). These last two shapes are very characteristic of this Hellenistic period. At Qal'at, we can also recognize some red-washed Arabian ware (fig. 150: 9–12, 14) equally found in Failaka in third–second century levels, but the egg-shell ware is missing or very rare. Apart from a stamped sherd (fig. 150: 13)

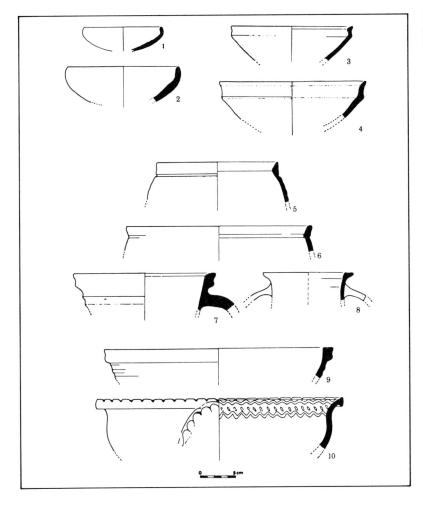

and the bottom of an amphora (fig. 150: 15) we note the lack of Greek imported sherds showing that such imports were very scarce. G. Bibby found a handful of these black glazed sherds in his Hundred Meters Section.[4]

The problem arises from some other sherds: they were all found in the same precise stratigraphical context in soundings 2 and 3, but they belong to a later period; provisionally, I would say first century B.C.–first century A.D. To cite but a few, there are a bowl with an everted rim showing a rich incised decoration (fig. 151: 10), and large bowl with a thickened flat rim (fig. 151: 9). In my opinion they fall into Larsen's Late Parthian-Sasanian assemblage (Larsen 1980, fig. 61–62) if we restricted the date to the Late Parthian period. The new French excavations in Janussan provide us with similar shapes (Lombard and Salles 1984, figs. 46, 40 and 143).

As usual in archaeology, we should date the earliest construction of the Fort according to the latest sherds found in it, *i.e.* the very beginning of the Christian era. We are facing two problems: a. The bulk of the pottery belongs to the third–second centuries B.C. (the actual Hellenistic period), while the sherds certainly dating from the later period are very few, but they occur. One must remember that several Hellenistic shapes (*e.g.* fish plates, carinated bowls with everted rim, . . .) last for a long time from the third century B.C. down to the first century B.C. or even later. b. The Fort was presumably reinforced with round towers, a very distinctive feature in the Near Eastern fortification from the third century A.D.

During the Hellenistic and Parthian periods, the usual shape is the square tower, for instance, near Bahrain, in the Failaka fortress (Hannestad 1983, fig. p. 10). This feature is still in use later in the Roman *castella* and in Mesopotamia too (for instance Dura Europos). As far as fortifications in southwest Asia are precisely dated, we may assume that the earliest round towers do not occur before the first century A.D. – for instance in Nippur, where an irregular round tower is associated with a square one (Keall 1977, fig. p. 82) but they are not numerous before the third century A.D. (Bishapur and Firuzabad in Southern Iran, Kish in Mesopotamia, and along the Roman *limes*). In Saudi Arabia too, we know another square fort with round towers at Qaryat al-Fau, dated to the third century A.D. by al-Ansary.[5] According to these examples, the fortification of Qal'at with regular round towers, including regular loopholes could not be built much earlier than the third century A.D. Unfortunately the soundings along the walls did not provide us with any pottery of this period.

We will now try to summarize the two solutions: a. The earliest Fort had been built during the late Hellenistic period, in the first century B.C. or first century A.D. according to the latest sherds. In such a case it would be among the very earliest examples of round towers. b. The Fort was built in the third century A.D. or much later (including even the Middle Islamic period). In this case the sherds recovered from the lower floors came from a filling brought from another area, and no objects dating from the building period are preserved. This hypothesis seems quite plausible to me, considering sounding 2 and sounding 3 (especially in the pit sounding 3 the filling of which contains pottery covering several centuries). As M. Kervran pointed out, this hypothesis is not valid in relation to sounding 4: there, the layers yielding the Hellenistic pottery rest partly against the East wall of the Fort.

Such is the actual state of the problem which still remains to be solved. The only conclusion concerns the date of the Hellenistic period which must be extended down to the first century A.D. It would be more accurate to call this later period Parthian.

III. PROBLEMS OF OCCUPATION AT QAL'AT AL-BAHRAIN

The pottery recovered from the new excavations covers a long period, about seven centuries. The third and second centuries are well illustrated. The other periods are less in evidence on the site of the Fort. There, all of them are connected with very few architectural remains (a floor, a pit, some graves and questionable defensive walls are recorded) and we still wonder whether these levels correspond to building phases or to fillings. As for the mid-first millennium settlement, we may suggest that the main occupation was located outside the Fort area. For instance, concerning our 'Parthian' period, we may mention some evidence provided by M. Kervran's soundings near the Portuguese Fort. There, the pottery of the upper (Pre-Islamic) layers fits perfectly with Late Parthian-Sasanian assemblage (Larsen 1980, fig. 61–62). The sherds are not numerous but they show that this area was inhabited in these periods.

From these findings we get an idea about the evolution of the settlement at Qal'at, which is very similar to the settlements previously studied in Mesopotamia: it is possible to recognize an important Neo-Babylonian period; the Achaemenian one is almost unknown, although we think this latter does exist in Bahrain (Level IVb of Qal'at City according to J-F. Salles 1984, 156). As it appears in Mesopotamia, in the better known Hellenistic/Seleucid period, the pottery clearly shows a Western influence, as well as a strong local or regional tradition. For instance in both areas, the percentage of Western and local shapes is roughly the same and glazed pottery is recorded in the same proportions. Western importations, such as amphorae and stamped sherds and black glazed pottery, are very scarce. Such imports are usually published, because they are very distinctive: we are able to identify them and to date them. Apart from the red or black-washed pottery, all other kinds of pottery have parallels in Mesopotamia. The situation is roughly the same in Failaka, except for the temple and the Greek inscriptions which show stronger Greek influence and maybe a Greek settlement, I would say a Seleucid one. Even the decreasing quantity of pottery after the second century B.C. can be paralleled on several Mesopotamian sites (for instance Larsa, Susa). But there, we can partly explain such an evolution, since new sites replaced the Seleucid ones. In Bahrain, such Parthian and Sasanian sites are still to be found (see Salles 1984, 156–157).

What can we state about Bahrain in the periods under review? Bahrain is certainly no longer, as Dilmun was in the second millennium B.C., a prominent international trade centre. Qal'at cannot be compared with Gerrha. The comparison with Failaka is rather difficult: both sites yielded roughly the same pottery, but at Failaka function is usually emphasized because of the temple and Greek inscriptions. From another point of view, there is a great difference between Failaka or Gerrha and Bahrain: Bahrain has local resources, mainly agricultural goods, fruit, pearls, maybe wood, according to the Classical authors (Theophrastos, Pliny, Arrian). There was probably no Greek settlement in Bahrain, where the activity could be two-way: trade and export of local goods. Such items could be sent into the neighbouring areas. If we adopt this view, it would be wiser to distinguish three levels of study: local, regional and maybe international, rather than only two: local and non-local.

Another question concerns the post-Hellenistic occupation: an explanation has to be found for the decrease of objects after the second century B.C. and the gap between the third century A.D. and the Middle Islamic period. Such a general evolution can hardly be paralleled with the political events: for instance, the powerful Achaemenid empire does not seem to correspond with any very important activity in Bahrain. The unsteady Parthian empire is well illustrated in Bahrain, but mainly in the necropolis with many objects (pottery and glass which are displayed in the National Museum; see also During Caspers 1980; Lombard and Salles 1984). The well organized Sasanian empire only left a few sherds in Bahrain, according to C. Larsen and the recent discoveries by M. Kervran. We only observe a good parallel in the Seleucid period, when strong administration is connected with a wealthy period at Qal'at.

1.Very few are published: Cat. No. 96 (al Wohaiby 1981, fig. 29); 97 (Bibby 1966, fig. p. 84); 111 (Bibby 1957, fig. 5); 112 (Bibby 1957, fig. 4 left); 12 (Bibby 1957, fig. 11); 127 (Bibby 1970, fig. p. 128, 13). The other pots found at Qal'at are 95, 98, 123, 246, 247, 284. No. 124 and 125 belong to the Pre-Hellenistic period.

2. G. Bibby found some complete pots of this period in the Hundred Meters Section, such as a jar displayed in the National Museum, Cat. No. 125.

3. These types are common in Mesopotamia apart from the cooking pots which are known mainly on Failaka (Hannestad 1983, Pl. 61–62).

4. Some Greek sherds which have been found by G. Bibby are displayed in the National Museum (Cat. No. 123).

5. Information given in his lecture delivered at the Bahrain Through the Ages Conference.

The Janussan necropolis and late first millennium B.C. burial customs in Bahrain

JEAN-FRANÇOIS SALLES

Two seasons of excavations have been carried out in 1980 and 1981 on the site of Janussan, Bahrain, thanks to the support of Shaikha Haya al Khalifa, Director of the Department of Antiquities and Museums, and thanks to the helpful support of the French Foreign Relations Ministry. The aim of such excavations was to provide us with some tentative explanation of the high sand dunes of Janussan, which are a rather unusual and even unique feature on the northern plain of Bahrain. They are the only signficant relief in a fairly flat area which has been occupied for millennia by palm-groves and gardens; on the other hand, as far as their external appearance and their filling is concerned, they look noticeably different from the funeral *tumuli* of the central plateau (for example the necropoleis at Ali, Sar, Umm Jidr, etc. . .) and from the first millennium B.C. cemeteries at al-Hajjar, Shakhoura, Jidd Hafs, or on other sites of the northern plain of Bahrain.

The Janussan hills, or 'Mounds' as they have been called by the English-speaking people, have been visited several times, and some archaeological work has even been carried out, though no thorough exploration has yet been undertaken. They were mentioned by Captain Durand (Durand 1979, § 62) and by Prideaux (Prideaux 1912: 66), and they have been surveyed many times by the Danes (Bibby 1970: 85). In 1969, a rescue excavation was undertaken by the Department of Antiquities of Bahrain, under Dr al-Takriti's direction (McNicoll and Roaf 1976, note 21). The British Expedition directed by T. McNicoll and M. Roaf took some interest in these Mounds and carried out a dig on a neighbouring hill, close to the sea (McNicoll and Roaf 1976). During the twenties, Major Daly, who was the British Resident, may have opened several trenches on one of these Mounds: that is what may be understood from Mackay's report (1929: 29).

1. THE SITE
The site is a line-up of high sandy hills following a southwest/north-

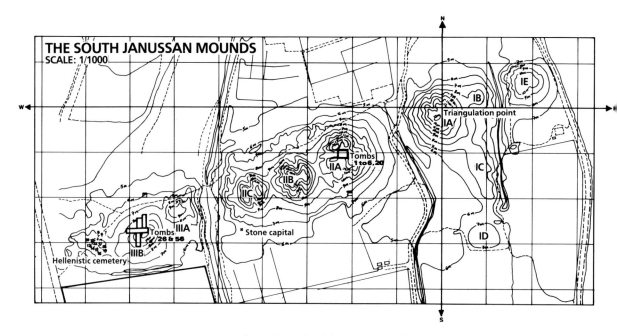

152 General layout of the Janussan Mounds (drawing: Jean Gire)

east orientation; the highest mound is more than 14 m high, fig. 152. Three main groups can be distinguished; they are separated one from the other by narrow stream-beds, and each group includes several hills. Mound IIA was selected for the 1980 excavations as it was Major Daly's presumed place of digging, and Mound IIIB for 1981; it was on Mound IIIC that the Department of Antiquities had carried out excavations in 1969, and the French Mission at Janussan cleared out a tomb on Mound IIIA in 1981. The mounds of group I, close to the Janussan village, are covered by Islamic cemeteries, and a triangulation point of the National Survey is set on the highest. As can be guessed from the numerous trenches which have been cut on the slopes, all the mounds seem to have been plundered: this fact has been confirmed by excavation.

It is possible to restore the building-process of these mounds as follows, as it appears from the dig itself and from the geomorphological studies carried out in the field by John Sceal, Roland Paskoff and Paul Sanlaville:

a. during the second millennium B.C., that is Dilmun time, there was no hill in this area. We have found some Barbar pottery sherds at the bottom of Mound IIA: they show that this place had been at least visited, if it was not also inhabited by Dilmun people.

b. it seems that after 1800 B.C. sandy hills rose at that place, partly by natural building (Mound IIA), partly artificially (Mound IIIB). It can be at least assumed that, at the time of the agricultural revival of the Iron Age in the earlier centuries of the first millennium B.C., people piled up there rejected soils from the clearings of the surrounding gardens and palm-groves: the area itself was actually uncultivated and covered by sand. Nevertheless, we may state that one of the main reasons for the mounds is the heaping up of soil thrown away from the neighbouring cultivated areas (Weisgerber 1982).

c. during the first millennium B.C. cemeteries were sited on the Janussan Mounds: they contributed to raising the height of the hills. These cemeteries are the subject of the present study.

d. after the first millennium B.C., and even nowadays, this area was used as a large dumping place for unwanted earth. This fact is shown by the overdigging of the surrounding gardens and irrigation channels, and by the numerous pottery sherds which have been collected on the surface: on this uncultivated and long deserted place, all these remains of human origin can only come from the surrounding gardens.

Nevertheless, it is worth noting that in spite of intensive surveys and despite several architectural findings not *in situ* (a door-socket by Captain Durand, a decorated stone-capital by the French Mission), it has been impossible to spot any settlement in the close neighbourhood of the necropolis. It could be that a former village might have been destroyed by some extension of the cultivated areas, or might lie under the actual village of Janussan. But it could equally be that the settlement might not be in the close vicinity of the cemetery: we will come back to this point later.

Eight burials have been found in the Mound IIA sounding, and the same number in Mound IIIB; a sketch-plan of Mound IIIC has been drawn. All these burials can be divided into four groups, which show good parallels in the other cemeteries of the island. The study will lay stress on the tomb typology and the burial customs, leaving aside the funerary material which has been thoroughly studied in the final report (Lombard and Salles 1984).

2. THE BUILT TOMBS

A monumental built tomb, *T 1*, was discovered in 1980 on Mound IIA fig. 153. It is composed of an internal burial-room built with dressed stones and of an external complex filling.

THE BURIAL CHAMBER

The burial chamber is 2.65 m long and 1.18 m large; the stone-worked walls are 1.10 m high, but the full height of the chamber under the covering slab was 1.65 m. The floor of the chamber is paved with irregular slabstones which are not strictly joined: they are laid

straight on the sand. The walls are set on a pebble-bed of small
stones, the level of which lies under the central pavement; they are
built with white limestone dressed blocks, carefully worked on their
inside face. Actually, the lower course of blocks seems to be less
regular than the upper one. The blocks are set as stretchers, although
they are of unequal size: in some cases, the joints are filled with a
plastered coating. Although the building is not strictly regular and
does not follow precise rules, it is nevertheless very carefully built,
and the inside view of the burial chamber is outstanding.

THE EXTERNAL FILLING

The chamber is externally held up by deep pilings of stones and sand
mixed with mortar; this grey mortar, locally called *juss*, is made of
plaster, ashes, small stones and sand. The external walls, *i.e.* the
pilings of mortared stones, lie on a wide and thick (0.20 m) bed of
juss and they are about 1 m wide; alternated courses of unworked
stones, *juss* and small stones can be seen in their build-up. The
external walls are themselves held up by heaps of sand which can be
seen in the eastern section of the sounding.

The tomb was covered with a huge slab, 2.81 m long × 1.65 m
wide × 0.45 m thick, which had to be removed with a scraper. This
heavy monolith was not lying on the top of the inside dressed walls
but on a thick support 0.50 m high; it consisted of several layers of
juss and small stones.

COMMENTS

The process of building this tomb can be clearly understood. It was not dug into the sand, but built above the floor. The burial chamber was first raised with dressed blocks, and then held up with pilings of stones and *juss*, here called the external walls; from the beginning of the building process, there was a large enclosure of sand heaps. At the time of the burial – the tomb was certainly prepared some time before the buried person's death – the covering slab was laid down on a rather plastic support in order to protect the burial chamber; then, everything was covered with a sand mound. This way of building is quite similar to that of the Dilmun *tumuli*, as described by Mackay (1929), by Cleuziou (Cleuziou, Lombard and Salles 1981) and by Ibrahim (1982): it seems to be a typically Bahraini way of building.

THE BURIAL

The tomb had already been plundered at the time of Major Daly's discovery, but the fall of the covering slab inside the burial chamber prevented Major Daly from excavating a thin earth level on the pavement, in which some material was found in 1980. Among the findings, we must mention a tubular gold bead, several iron or bronze arrowheads, an iron spearhead, and remains of a scaled piece of armour. Such findings, connected with the size and the careful building of the tomb, could suggest that the buried individual might be an important personage, maybe from the army.

Another tomb, *T 31*, was discovered on Mound IIIb, fig. 154: it is built with dressed blocks, but is of smaller size than T 1 (1.85 × 0.55 m; height 0.50 m). One of the blocks was evident on the slope of the mound, and we thought it would be useful to clear out this structure. The burial chamber is built with only one course of dressed stones set out as stretchers, and it was doubtlessly covered with a large slab sealed on a *juss* bedding which is still visible. In the eastern section of the sounding, it is possible to see a filling of stones and sand which was the mound of the tomb. The building method is the same as that of T 1, although on a smaller scale. The tomb had been thoroughly plundered, and no material was discovered.

In the center of Mound IIIB, there is a large robbers' pit which had most probably previously contained a tomb similar to T 1: it shows similarities to T 1 in its large size and in the external filling made with *juss* and small stones. The funeral chamber had been completely looted, and only some remains of the central pavement and the foundations have been cleared out.

This first type of tomb in the necropolis of Janussan is quite original: dressed blocks, external filling and sand mound. It is not possible to know whether the blocks were dressed only for the tomb

154 Smaller built-tomb T 31 (Mound III A)

or were picked up elsewhere: if the latter were so, the settlement or the cemetery where they come from remains undiscovered.[1]

COMPARISONS

Two other similar tombs have been found in Bahrain.

Sar. The first one was excavated by the Department of Antiquities and is still visible at the southwestern end of the village. It is quite similar to T 31 of Janussan and it is built in the same way, with parallelipedic dressed stones set out as stretchers. It is not possible to know whether there was a covering mound or not, but it seems quite likely there was one. According to Shaikha Haya al Khalifa, the funeral offerings were numerous and valuable.

Barbar. At Barbar village, while building a new school, another built tomb was discovered: there are no remains of it, and it is only referred to in a report by F. Tarawneh (1970). According to this archaeologist, the dressed stones were inscribed with Greek letters so as to give the builder the order of construction. This noticeable comment could suggest two hypotheses:

● since no inscribed stones have been found at Sar or at Janussan, we could think that the Barbar tomb is the oldest one of this type. It would have been necessary, when this type of tomb was first introduced in Bahrain, to give instructions to the builders; later, at Sar and at Janussan, the now skilled builders did not need these instructions any longer.

● the writing of these instructions in Greek might suggest that this type of tomb, and the people for whom they were intended, were foreign to the island. We have already mentioned that tomb T 1 at Janussan could be the tomb of a high-ranking military personage (see the armour); according to Shaikha Haya al Khalifa, there was a gold ring with a Parthian royal seal in the Barbar tomb. Could we interpret these tombs as those of official and foreign personages, maybe some 'rulers' of the island who came from a more hellenized area? Answers to these questions can only be brought out by the full publication of the already excavated tombs and, with some luck, by the discovery of an unlooted tomb of this type.

These Bahrain tombs can be compared with the Ain Jawan tomb, in Eastern Arabia (Bowen 1950: 22–23). On that site, a monumental tomb built of dressed blocks was buried under a mound of sand and earth. Nevertheless, a quotation of Bowen's report will reveal the differences:

> The tomb had a central chamber about six feet wide by eight and one-half feet long, which was over 20 inches higher than the entrance or niches, themselves all of the same height. The tomb

had four niches located in the ends of the central chamber . . . The tomb . . . had entrance passages from both east and west . . . each of the four niches had pits sunk into the floor, as well as shelves above the pits, so that multiple burials seemed to be indicated. The roof of the central chamber was supported by cantilever blocks. (p. 23).

According to Potts (1984: 120) the Ain Jawan tomb is to be dated to the Late Hasean period, that is the first centuries of the Christian era (first–fourth centuries A.D.), although some ceramics from a close sounding seem to be slightly earlier. At Ain Jawan, besides the built-tomb, there are several tombs of a different type: cist tombs built with dressed blocks dug into the floor.

The similarities between the tombs at Ain Jawan and in Bahrain could lead to assigning them a similar date. No easily datable material has been discovered inside the built-tombs at Janussan, but all the evidence coming from the site suggests a date between the first century B.C. and the second century A.D. for this type of burial.

To summarize, this type of tomb is quite unique in Bahrain, and the fact it is to be found in Eastern Arabia too is a strong illustration of the cultural unity which links these two areas of the former Bahrain. The finds in Bahrain could suggest that these tombs were intended for high personages, maybe foreign military local rulers. But for a more satisfactory interpretation it will be necessary to study the relations between the Parthian empire and the Arabian Gulf more closely, and more precisely, between the Gulf and the Characene province.

3. THE CIST-GRAVES

Most of the tombs at Janussan are a type rather common in Bahrain, the cist-grave. They are found on each mound, but we will give only two examples, *T 4* on Mound IIA and *T 29* on Mound IIIB, and we will then compare these findings to other cemeteries in Bahrain.

T 4: 2×0.48 m; height: 0.50 m, fig. 155. Rectangular cist, made with eight roughly dressed white limestone slabstones; the inside faces are smoothed, but the outside reverse of the blocks is hardly worked. There is no plastered joint between the slabs, nothing on the floor.

A thick coating of mortar is laid around the top of the cist-walls, outside the tomb: on this mortared layer which lies straight on the sand, the limestone capstone was put down.

The burial was intact: according to Karen Højgaard's studies, it was a male about thirty years old. The body was lying on its back, arms stretched along the body; the head pointed to the East. In the sand filling, a few bronze beads were found, mixed with charcoal fragments, small shells and remains of bitumen. There was a bowl on the sand, near the left foot of the skeleton. Another bowl was partly hidden under the covering capstone, inside the sandy mound over the tomb.

T 29: 1.90 × 0.50 m; height: 0.50 m, fig. 156. The covering stone is a fine limestone slab broken in four pieces at the moment it was laid down: the breaks were filled with mortar. The rectangular cist was slightly trapezoidal in section; the walls are made with oolithic limestone slabs, irregular in size, set down on edge on the sand floor. There is a thick plastered coating inside the chamber. A mortar soil is laid on the sand around the cist, at the top of the cist-walls: in some places it is 0.60 m wide, and the capstone was put down on this mortar sill.

The cist was in a pit dug in the sand: a filling of small stones and mortar was inserted between the side of the pit and the walls of the cist.

The burial was intact: it was an individual about thirty years old, according to Karen Højgaard. The position of the body is the same as in the previous example. Traces of a shroud coated with bitumen were observed. A bronze pin and a bone disc were found in the sand filling. Outside the tomb, on the capstone, a bowl was discovered: it was turned upside down.

Many other similar tombs have been found at Janussan, all of which can be compared to the Hellenistic cemeteries in Bahrain, Shakhoura, Bu Asheira, al-Hajjar, Umm al-Hassam, etc. . . . . A few dominant features can be observed.[2]

USUAL ARCHITECTURAL PATTERNS

a. No obvious rule concerning the orientation of the tomb emerges: it is most frequently east-west, or close to this axis, but any orientation is to be found in the large necropoles, at Bu Asheira or at Umm al-Hassam for example (see the plans which are displayed in the Bahrain National Museum).

b. The outline of the funeral cist is always rectangular, and the size of the cist is matched to the size of the deceased (see the small cist-graves for children in Janussan Mound IIIC or in Shakhoura). In a few cases, the funeral cist is dug into the rock (al-Hajjar), but it is usually built on the ground and then covered with a small earth or sand mound. The walls of the cist can be built with standing slabs, or with small stones mixed with mortar (*i.e.* T 5 at Janussan), or even with mortar only (*i.e.* T 2 at Janussan, Mound IIA). These differences in the way of building seem to be due only to local conditions: at Shakhoura for example, Tarawneh noticed that it is 'easier to build on

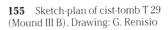

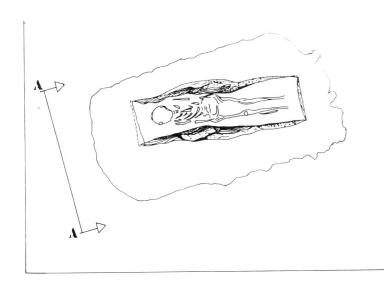

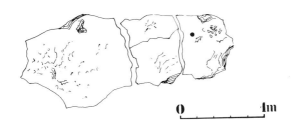

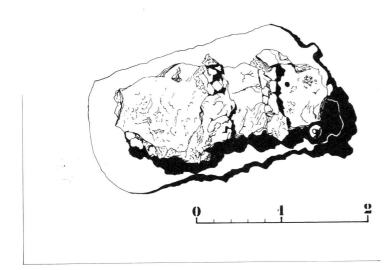

T.29

156 Cist-tombs of Mound II A, under built-tomb T 1 level.

the rock than to dig into the rock'. At Janussan, there are only a few stones; the cultivated surroundings, and the use of mortar, *juss*, seems to have been more widespread than in the other cemeteries.

c. At the time of building the funeral cist, heaps of earth or sand were piled up around the walls to strengthen them; at the time of the burial, the cist was closed with capstones and then the grave was covered by a mound. Except for the previously mentioned T 1 at Janussan, it does not seem that the Hellenistic tombs were built in advance and followed precise standards of construction, as was the case for the Dilmun *tumuli*: the Hellenistic tombs were built when death occurred, according to needs and the means.

d. One detail of the building process is worth emphasizing: in several cases, maybe the majority, a layer of *juss* was laid around the top of the cist-walls. This largely overspreading layer is a kind of sill on which the covering slabstones are sealed; they are usually roughly cut large slabs. We must equally notice that the inside walls of the funeral cist are very often covered with a plastered coating, more or less regular and thick, more or less carefully made; sometimes, a similar coating is laid on the floor.

e. The fact of arranging numerous individual tombs side by side, each one covered by a small mound, gives the Hellenistic cemeteries the typical aspect of a rather flattened large hillock, such as al-Hajjar, Bu Asheira, Umm al-Hassam 'mounds'. At Janussan, the piling up of these individual tombs one above the other contributed to increase the height of the site.

USUAL BURIAL CUSTOMS

f. Burials are usually single: there is only one individual in each cist-grave. A few examples of multiple burials are mentioned at Bu Asheira: this might be simultaneous burial. The body lies on its back, fully extended, rarely crouched, arms usually stretched along the body. Tarawneh mentions traces of dress (that is organic material), and we have observed traces of a shroud coated with bitumen at Janussan.

g. The funeral offerings are scarce: ceramic vases, common or glazed ware, personal ornaments (beads, pins, ivory combs . . .), some small glass bottles, some weapons. A bitumen-coated basket is mentioned at the Moon Plaza Hotel cemetery, in Bu Asheira, and an incense-burner was found at Shakhoura. All these offerings constitute the minimum kit for an after-death life, and they do not provide us with much information about funeral beliefs: the dead was given his personal objects (weapons, ornaments), with perfumes (glassware) and a few dishes for the life after death. Such beliefs are widespread in the Oriental world. More noticeable among the offerings are the figurines: the terracotta figurine of a woman was found at Bu Asheira, a Bes figurine at al-Hajjar, and three plaster figurines at Janussan (T 5), to which we must add the plaster figurine of a woman which came from Major Daly's excavations and which is kept in the British Museum.[3] They could be depictions of deities, or votive figurines, or just funeral offerings. Such a custom is found in Mesopotamia, at Warka for example (Loftus 1857: 214).

h. Some more remains could help us understand the beliefs in the hereafter, which have already been illustrated by the reference to deities. In several tombs, animal bones were found, and even the sacrifice of a camel is mentioned (Bibby 1954: 140): are these bones from a pet animal buried with the dead, a sacrifice, or more prosaically the remains of a funeral meal? These animal bones should be analyzed for an answer. There is no evidence of a similar custom at Janussan.

i. A bowl is frequently found outside the burial cist: it is turned upside down, near the capstone, and it contains ashes or organic material (Janussan, Shakhoura, Bu Asheira, al-Hajjar . . .). It must be an offering at the funeral ceremony, as it is found inside the earth mound which covers the grave (*i.e.* after the cist had been closed, before the mound had been built over): but what was put in these bowls: food, incense . . .?

j. Finally, at Bu Asheira, small channels and holes dug into the floor seem to be associated with the graves; at Shakhoura, similar remains have been cleared out (Petocz 1981) on a platform which did not contain any tomb. Is it possible to associate these findings with libations or with a funerary cult?

MORE ELABORATE GRAVES

Beside these common graves, some outstanding graves have been discovered.

At Shakhoura there were two sealed and unlooted tombs; neither contained any skeleton: there were only offering vases. In Mesopotamia of the Hellenistic period (Negro-Ponzi 1968–9) and in Bahrain of the Dilmun period there were similar finds.[4] We could imagine it might be the tomb of somebody who died far away from his village and whose body could not be brought back home (sailor? soldier? . . .). The grave would then be intended to honour his memory and for the good of his life after death. It can hardly be supposed that the skeletons should have completely decayed.

At Bu Asheira, a large tomb was dug into the rock: the access is a slope which leads to a subterranean room where three niches contained benches on which skeletons were laid; there was a column in the middle of the room. This plan is reminiscent of the Ayn Jawan tomb, but no comparison is possible until a sketch-plan of the Bu Asheira tomb is published.

At al-Maqsha, Sir Charles Belgrave found a tomb with an enclosure made of big dressed stones: it has not yet been explained. The Department of Antiquities may have excavated a large multiple burial with more than twenty-five skeletons in the same area (personal communication from Daoud Yousof Folath).

To summarize, the tombs and the burial customs of Bahrain are quite similar to those which have been evidenced in Eastern Arabia (see recently, Potts 1984), and are close to those which have recently been studied in Oman (Vogt 1984); they can be compared with the tombs and the burial customs of southern Mesopotamia during the same period (Negro-Ponzi 1968–9). But it is impossible to find evidence of strong Hellenistic influences in Bahrain such as those which can be seen in Mesopotamia: there is no lamp in the tombs of Bahrain, nor any coin (Charon's obol) or eye-covers . . .[5] The burial customs of Bahrain come within the scope of the Dilmun *tumuli* local tradition (same process of building, same kind of offering . . .), even if some differences are noticeable between the second millennium B.C. and the Hellenistic burial customs, and even if the funeral beliefs seem to have been enriched by some foreign influences at that later time.

4. THE BURIAL-JARS

These occur frequently during the Hellenistic period, mainly for child-burials. Some examples have been found at Janussan, on Mound IIA and Mound IIIB, and some more are mentioned at Shakhoura or at al-Maqsha. But we must remember that we can find child burial-jars associated with child cist-graves at the same time: such is the case in Janussan or in Bu Asheira.

Other interesting remains have been found at Janussan, in the levels which are under the Hellenistic tombs of Mound IIIB. Several commonware burial-jars have been discovered, buried in the sand, lying down or standing up. They were closed with sherds of large containers (*pithoi*), with *juss* lids, or even with the piece of a covering roof, fig. 157. T 34 was not a jar, but a round basin made of local *juss*. Some of the burials contained bones of very young children, but it is clear that the empty jars were just as much tombs, the very fragile skeletons having completely decayed. Karen Højgaard has identified five children in T 28, of an age from one month to two years, and fourteen children in T 34, ranging from birth to thirty months old. There is no satisfactory explanation for these mass burials.

The funeral offerings are scarce in these jars, and do not include any pottery vessels for the life after death: only personal ornaments were found, amongst them bronze or iron bracelets or rings, beads and one real pearl.[6]

This type of burial-jar is not found in Bahrain, at least to my knowledge;[7] no similar jars are mentioned in the Hellenistic pottery catalogues or in earlier pottery assemblages. But quite similar shapes have been found in Mesopotamia, where comparable jars are used for burials, the *Topfgräber*, at Babylon, at Uruk, at Ur, at Nippur. The Mesopotamian findings are dated from the end of the seventh/sixth century B.C., and we must attribute a similar dating to the Janussan burial-jars. The latter are certainly locally made.

At the same time, rock-cut tombs are found at al-Hajjar (Rice 1972), with built facing-walls; bath-tub coffins are found at Qal'at al-Bahrain, and child-burials in bowls or in jars of a different shape (Glob 1956); re-uses of earlier tombs are mentioned at Ali or at Diraz. The markedly unique nature of the Janussan burial-jars and their very close resemblance to the above-mentioned Mesopotamian finds lead us to suggest that these tombs might belong to some foreigners who came from Babylonia to settle in Bahrain. We must recall the old tradition according to which Gerrha, on the eastern coast of Arabia, was founded by Chaldeans exiled from Babylonia (Strabo, *Geography*, XVI, 3).

157   A burial-jar (Mound III B).

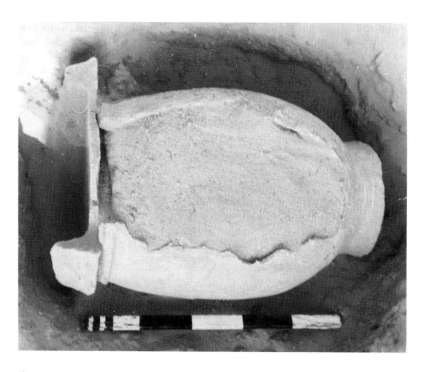

5. THE PLAIN BURIALS
Several simple burials, a body buried in the sand, have been discovered on Mound IIA and on Mound IIIB at Janussan. Similar burials
are mentioned in other cemeteries of Bahrain (Budayiah Road,
Shakhoura, Jidd Hafs . . .) and at Qal'at al-Bahrain. All are pre-Islamic
burials.

CONCLUSIONS
We have described the main types of tombs which have been found at
Janussan. Each of them is quite comparable to the other cemetery
types in Bahrain, and it has been pointed out that the burial customs
and beliefs belong to a strong Bahraini tradition.

A few precise remarks about a chronology of the end of the first
millennium B.C. can be made. The burial-jars at Janussan can be dated
from the end of sixth century B.C., that is the Iron Age as it has been
defined for Bahrain (see Pierre Lombard's article in this volume). No
remains from the fifth and fourth centuries B.C. have been found; these
centuries are not illustrated by any findings at Qal'at al-Bahrain, nor
in any other necropolis of Bahrain. This gap could suggest a period of
abandonment on the island, without settlements or cemeteries: but
nothing in the already known history of Bahrain could argue this two
century gap between the rather prosperous Iron Age and the
Hellenistic period. An attractive solution would be to draw the end of

the Iron Age period down to the end of fourth century B.C.; this Late
Iron Age would then come just before Level Va at Qal'at al-Bahrain,
Hellenistic-Seleucid (Salles 1984: 157). It must be emphasized that no
intermediate level can be seen at Janussan between the burial-jars
cemetery (Late Iron Age) and the Hellenistic necropolis, and it must
be remembered that this kind of burial-jar in Mesopotamia was still in
use during the fifth and the fourth centuries B.C., for example at Ur
(Woolley 1962).

The material which comes from the Hellenistic tombs at
Janussan is mainly pottery – complete vases from the unviolated
tombs or sherds from the looted ones and from the filling of the
mound. The extreme dates of this pottery are the third century B.C. at
one end (green-glazed Seleucid pottery) and the first century A.D. at
the other end (Thadj-type bowls). The necropolis of Janussan would
illustrate phase Va and beginning of phase Vb of the archaeological
sequence of the Hellenistic period in Bahrain (Salles 1984: 160);
several other cemeteries would rather illustrate phase Vb and Vc.

The two soundings on Mound IIA and Mound IIIB do not allow
us to give a complete interpretation of the whole site (more than six
mounds), but it seems sensible to infer from the findings that the
whole site of Janussan is a large necropolis. New excavations on the
unexplored mounds would bring results similar to those described
above.

The most intriguing problem is the lack of any settlement which
could be associated with the necropolis. No traces of a dwelling site
could be found in the surroundings, although some occasional finds
definitely come from a built settlement (a stone capital, certainly
coming from a large building; a door-socket; pieces of plastered
roofing . . .). The only site which is known for this period is Qal'at al-
Bahrain, about four miles westwards. A closer study of the layout of
the Hellenistic remains and cemeteries would suggest three main
inhabited areas in this northern part of the island, fig. 158:

a. the first one is to be located around the ancient city of Souk
al-Khamis, previously known as the chief town of Bahrain. Due to
recent urbanization, the site has completely disappeared, and the
only preserved remains are the necropoleis at Bu Asheira, Umm al-
Hassam and Isa Town (Hellenistic period).

b. the second one is the Qal'at al-Bahrain area, densely settled
from the earliest periods down to the Portuguese phase, with its
Hellenistic cemeteries at al-Hajjar, al-Maqsha and Jidd Hafs.

c. the third one, eastwards, is well-known during the Dilmun
period (Barbar and Diraz sites) and during the Islamic era; it is
illustrated by the Hellenistic necropoleis at Shakhoura, at Budayiah
Road and Janussan, or by the built tomb at Barbar (*see supra*). No

doubt that we must look for an inhabited Hellenistic site near Barbar and Diraz, a city which used to bury its dead at Janussan.

This paper is based on the Janussan excavations final report, edited by Pierre Lombard and Jean-François Salles, and submitted to the Department of Archaeology and Museums, Ministry of Information, State of Bahrain in August 1983. See bibliographical references, Lombard and Salles 1984.

1. Mr Brian Doe thinks that several dressed blocks at Janussan might come from the Barbar Temple.

2. Most of the Hellenistic cemeteries in Bahrain are not yet published; descriptions of the tombs with difficulty hardly available in the files of the National Museum, in restricted reports or in local newspapers and magazines. The present study seemed an opportunity to list the less common documentation and to briefly state results which are not available until they are published.

3. New discoveries have been made in recently excavated cemeteries, at Shakhoura or at Karranah, near Qal'at al-Bahrain; among other items, they include Parthian

158　Hellenistic sites and areas in Northern Bahrain

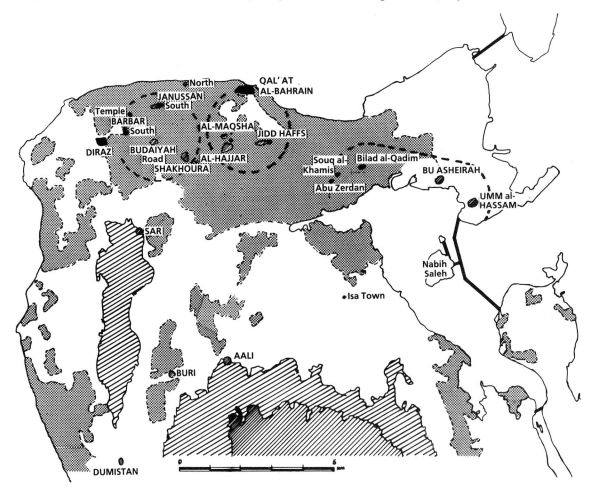

elaborated jewellery and stone-sculptures. I am deeply indebted to Judith Littleton for this information.

4. About the empty Dilmun *tumuli*, see Lamberg-Karlovsky's article in this volume.

5. A very recent find could contradict this restrictive statement about Hellenistic influences in Bahrain: it is a funeral stele inscribed in Greek discovered at Karranah by Khaled al-Sindy and Judith Littleton. I am deeply indebted to Shaikha Haya al-Khalifa for the opportunity she gave Dr Jean Marcillet-Jaubert and myself to study this inscription.

6. Maurizio Tosi has mentioned a real pearl coming from a second millennium B.C. child-burial in Oman. See his article in this volume.

7. But new excavations at Karranah, under the direction of the Department of Antiquities, have brought out similar burial-jars. Information kindly provided by Judith Littleton.

BIBLIOGRAPHY

Belgrave, C. D. 1937: article in *The Times* May 1937.

Belgrave, J. H. D. 1953: *Welcome to Bahrain*, The Augustan Press, Bahrain.

During-Caspers, E. C. L. 1974: "The Bahrain Tumuli", *Persica*, VI, p. 131-156.

Loftus, W. 1857: *Travels and researches in Chaldea and Susiana*. London.

Macnicoll, T. and Roaf, M. 1976: *Expedition to Bahrain*. Unpublished mimeo, Department of Antiquities, Bahrain.

Negro-Ponzi, M.M. 1968–9: "Sasanian glassware from Tell Mahuz (North Mesopotamia)", *Mesopotamia*, III-IV, p. 293-314.

Petocz, D. and Hart, S. 1981: *Report of the Australian team working for the Bahrain Department of Antiquities, 1979–1980*. Unpublished mimeo, Department of Anitiquities, Bahrain.

Potts, D. 1984: "Northeastern Arabia in the Late pre-Islamic era" in *AOMIM*, p. 85-144.

Tarawneh, F. 1970: *Preliminary report on Shakhoura excavations*. Unpublished mimeo, Department of Antiquities, Bahrain.

Tarawneh, F. 1971: *The al-Hajjar Excavations*. Unpublished mimeo, Department of Antiquities, Bahrain.

Vogt, B. 1984: "1st millennium B.C. graves and burial customs in the Samad area (Oman)", in *AOMIM*, p. 271-284.

Weisgerber, G. 1982: "Mechanics of Falaj irrigation", paper delivered at the Réunion de travail, Lyon, Maison de l'Orient.

Qal'at al-Bahrain: a strategic position from the Hellenistic period until modern times

MONIK KERVRAN

For archaeologists, the difficulty of relating archaeological discoveries to textual data is a source of much frustration. Yet at the same time this difficulty is a justification for their efforts, for when the texts are absent or silent, then the earth and stones may be able to speak, and it is from them we may extract the information that the texts refuse to deliver.

In Bahrain this situation is particularly true because we have spectacular archaeological relics for periods where there is a real scarcity of narrative or epigraphic material. An example of this is the fortress complex of Qal'at al-Bahrain and its immediate surroundings, which together make up one of the most attractive sites in the entire Gulf for any visitor interested in the past.

For more than a quarter of a century it has been known that between the monumental medieval fort, incorrectly known as the Portuguese Fort,[1] and the seashore, there lies another fortress, smaller in size, square in plan, with round towers at its corners and in the middle of each of its sides.[2] This building has yielded only one precise date, that of its occupation during the thirteenth century A.D. But it has emerged, after six seasons of excavation inside the building and around it, that the fortress had been erected centuries before. By examining these two periods of the building, we can ask ourselves what they signify in the history of Bahrain.

The construction of the fort seems to have taken place in the very last years B.C. or at the beginning of the Christian era, fig. 159. It is only after some years of doubt that it has been possible to arrive at this dating. It was noted that the ground plan of the fort is connected with a tradition of Graeco-Roman forts, whose final appearance during the Umayad times, was in castles in Syria and Jordan (late seventh/early eighth century). Two other elements, however, made one inclined to suggest a 'pre-Islamic' date for the fortress: the presence of pre-Islamic material in a lower level of the fortress,[3] and the presence in its eastern wall of a pink coloured mortar which is

159 The Hellenistic Islamic fortress at Qal'at al-Bahrain

characteristic of the Hellenistic period at Qal'at al-Bahrain.

While carrying out a number of trial excavations to try to obtain confirmation of the Hellenistic date for the fortress, one seemed to provide evidence to the contrary: it brought to light, under the flagstone paving of the courtyard which was deliberately lifted, the presence of Islamic ceramics of the twelfth/thirteenth century. These ceramics were found in abundance and to the exclusion of all others on the floors of the fortress.

Then a discovery made in January 1983 brought an end to all speculation: a pit, or silo was discovered, whose internal plaster extended up and out over the floor level in which it had been dug and then continued up the base of the tower of the west corner of the fortress. The cut stone blocks of this tower bonded perfectly with the stones of the north wall. Thus, it was established without doubt that the silo, the tower and the north wall were all contemporary. Significantly, the silo contained only pre-Islamic material.[4]

Thus the fortress, with its towers, its external and internal walls, was for the most part constructed before Islamic times; while certain interior alterations, such as the paving of the courtyard, had been carried out during a later re-occupation of the fort, during the thirteenth century.

The historical context of the building of the fortress and the reasons for its construction around the beginning of the Christian era are poorly known: not a single inscription has been found within the fort, and there are no references to its construction in historic or narrative sources.

While leaving it to my colleagues in those periods to throw some light on the pre-Islamic history of Bahrain, let me note in passing a reference in Tabari that mentions the existence of a fort in Bahrain at the beginning of the third century A.D., that is to say during the Sassanid epoch, when a king named Satirun took up position there in the face of the victorious advance of the Persian sovereign Ardeshir, who finally took possession of the fortress and left it to his son Shapur the First as regent.[5]

It is far from certain that the fortress mentioned by Tabari is the fortress of Qal'at al-Bahrain: at the time when the Arab historian was writing, the beginning of the tenth century, the name Bahrain was applied to an area very much more extensive than today: it covered all the eastern part of Arabia around al-Qatif and al-Hasa, as well as the archipelago which today comprises Bahrain, together with the principal islands of Awal and Muharraq. Equally, the fortress where Satirun took up his position could well have been situated on the mainland: either at al-Hasa or at al-Qatif where the sovereigns of Bahrain, whether the Qarmats or the 'Uyunids, usually resided.

Apart from the construction itself, the occupation of the pre-Islamic period has left no trace in the fortress, having been obliterated by the thirteenth century occupation.

The long gap which separates these two periods of occupation calls for some explanation: two hypotheses can be advanced to explain this vast interval.

First: the citadel was abandoned after its first occupation, for no trace of either Sassanid ceramics, nor of early Islamic ceramics has been found in the immediate area. Nevertheless it would be astonishing if, after such a long period of neglect, the building was in a good enough state of repair to have been restored in the thirteenth century.

Second: the fortress underwent either continuous or intermittent occupation for nearly a thousand years, but all trace of this occupation was wiped out by the major occupation during the thirteenth century. This phenomenon is quite well known to archaeologists and I can cite another instance: the Achaemenid palace at Susa (Shush) in Iran, where one finds no trace of the original occupation, only the ceramics of the Parthian epoch when the palace was re-used.

Logic would lead one to favour the second hypothesis. And indeed it would be surprising if a fortified position so carefully constructed, located at a place which during so long a period was considered exceptional, was not utilised during an interval of maybe a thousand years between its construction and its final occupation. Several times the narrative sources, without mentioning the fortress, relate events which are certainly connected with its existence. In the period when the island, along with the mainland part of Bahrain, was under the rule of the Qarmats Awal, the main island, served several times as a place of refuge or retrenchment: three times during the tenth and eleventh centuries supporters or members of the Qarmathian dynasty were banished or fled to Awal. At the time of the troubles which marked the end of Qarmat domination, Awal was once again the scene of events which it would be difficult to imagine taking place except in relation to a fortress: I refer to the rebellion which Abu'l Buhlul b. Muhammad b. Yusul al-Zajjaj fermented against the Qarmats living on the island. These he destroyed, and expelled their governor, but himself fell victim to the attacks of Zakariyya b. Yahya b. al-'Ayyash, conqueror of the Qarmats on the mainland.[6]

It was the 'Uyunids, with the help of a Seljuk army, who reaped the benefit of these victories over the Qarmats. But their rule, which lasted more than one hundred and sixty years, was also marked by violence, in particular the troubles instigated by the descendants of 'Ali and Dabbar al-Uyuni, who had been denied power in favour of their eldest brother al-Fadl.

At some unknown date in the twelfth century, Bahrain became a possession of the emirs of Qais. Then at the beginning of the thirteenth century, it passed to the Salgharid atabegs of Fars, without losing its local dynasties, the 'Uyunids and later the Usfurids.

Possibly it was under the 'Uyunids that the old fort was restored: it is known that the third sovereign of the dynasty, Abu Sinan Muhammed ibn al-Fadl, decided to live on Uwal. It was he who ordered the rebuilding of the Friday Mosque (the Suq Al-Khamis).[7] This could reflect this ruler's interest in architecture.

On the other hand the fort could also have been restored, a little more than a century later, on the orders of the powerful governor of Fars, the Salgharid Abu Bakr, when he integrated Bahrain into his possessions. In and around the fortress has been found a considerable number of coins bearing the name of this ruler and his descendants who maintained their sovereignty over Bahrain until the last years of the thirteenth century, when they were replaced by the al-Tibi, the merchant princes of al-Qais.[8]

The rebuilding stayed faithful to the original design of the fort. The arrow slits were remade, wherever it was necessary, in exactly the same spot as the Hellenistic arrow slits. The defences were strengthened by the building of a bastion wall which, extending out from the North-West angle of the fortress, followed the coastal defences westward. From this period, a stock of naphtha-covered pebbles have been found, intended as projectiles against attackers coming from the sea. A small celadon pot, found among these projectiles, dates them to the end of the thirteenth century.

Despite the care lavished on the construction of the fort at Bahrain, at the date which can be placed between the end of the eleventh and the beginning of the thirteenth century, the building was not used for any length of time. Perhaps it was considered to be too small or too old. Above all, it suffered from being situated too close to the sea. Indeed its North-East tower, when it was excavated in 1976–77, already appeared to have been badly damaged by marine erosion at an earlier date.

It is known that the height of sea level was appreciably lower during the Hellenistic period, and that the level has continued to rise since then. One might therefore suppose that, when the fort was constructed around the beginning of the Christian era, it was placed well away from the shoreline so as not to be exposed to severe storms or very high tides. Centuries later this was no longer the case, and doubtless the collapse of the North-East tower of the building before the attack of the sea led to the fort being abandoned, and the construction of a new fort some distance inland.

The construction of the second fort of Qal'at al-Bahrain is among the least known episodes in the history of the island. Nevertheless, when in 1956 Danish archaeologists undertook the exploration of the site, Sheikh Suleiman explained that the 'Portuguese fort' was only the reconstruction of an old Arab fort, and in due course the Danes found certain traces of this older building.[9] Investigations carried out last spring have revealed the outline of the earlier fort and the design of its towers, fig. 160.

The exact date of its construction is not precisely known. It falls between the abandonment of the shoreline fort (perhaps towards the middle of the fourteenth century) and the Portuguese alterations which are dated by an inscription: 1004/1586.[10] The Portuguese entirely covered the preceding fort with new masonry, and gave its towers and bastions a particular form which had recently been developed in Western Europe. Nothing remains visible of the older building. Thus those who are unaware of the history of Bahrain are accustomed to think of the fort as purely Portuguese.

By about the fifteenth/sixteenth centuries, Qal'at al-Bahrain had ceased to be regarded as the only position of strategic value in the immediate area: another fort had been constructed on the island of Muharraq, the fort of Arad, the ancient name of the island, fig. 161. This construction took place at a particularly dramatic period in the

160   The Islamic Portuguese
fortress at Qal'at al-Bahrain

161   The Arad fortress

history of Bahrain, when the Ottomans, Persians and Portuguese were contesting control of the Island, at that time held by the Banu Djaber. It became important to have a base from which to reconquer Bahrain and its fortress, and Arad was chosen, as it was accessible to deepwater shipping. The fortress, as shown on Portuguese miniatures, is depicted as having a double enceinte: traces were found a few years ago under the present Arad Fort.[11] This present fort, which dates from the very beginning of the last century, was no more than a reconstruction of the inner enceinte of the old fort.

The double-enceinte fort at Arad was in existence at the end of the Portuguese stay in Bahrain, for it is shown in the 'Book of the Fortresses of India'[12] (dated to 1635), and two fortresses are mentioned in the text with the drawing. But it seems that it was not already built by 1559 when Turks besieged Qal'at al-Bahrain: no fortress can be seen on Arad island in the anonymous miniature showing these events.[13] On the other hand, neither in 1521, when they made a landing in order to punish Bahrain for not having paid the tribute which was imposed by the Princes of Hormuz, nor in 1514, when they came to the island for the first time, did the Portuguese mention Arad fortress: this one seems to have been built between 1559 and 1635.

This brief archaeological summary of the military architecture of Bahrain shows how, throughout its history, Qal'at al-Bahrain retained a particular importance for the island as well as for the archipelago. If in earlier times cities appear to have succeeded one another, the main construction since the beginning of the Christian era has been the fortress, restored and reconstructed several times over the centuries, but always guarding, until recently, this section of the north shore of the island.

In the pre-Islamic period, the construction of the fort was helped by the abundance of good quality material which was ready to hand: many carved quarried stones were re-used in the stonework of its walls (one with an inscription of the Kassite period).[14]

It appears that during the twelfth and thirteenth centuries the fort's purpose was more that of a fortified storehouse, judging by the very many traces of trade with Southeast Asia that have been found there (Chinese coins and porcelain). Bahrain, however, does not appear to have participated directly in long-range trade: its traditional role was to redistribute foreign products within the Gulf.[15]

Later, the role of the fortress was purely strategic, its possession being identified with control of the island. The response was the building of another fortress, Arad, in a position that was evidently more suitable because it gave direct access to deep water without the need for lighterage.

1. See below.

2. This fortress was discovered in 1955 by the Danish Expedition at Bahrain, but properly excavated by the French Expedition between 1977 and 1983.

3. A preliminary study of this material seems to give a date between the last two centuries B.C. and the first three centuries A.D.: see R. Boucharlat, 'Some notes about Qal'at al-Bahrain during the Hellenistic Period', in this volume.

4. *Idem.*

5. These events are quoted by A. T. Wilson, *Persian Gulf*, London, 1928.

6. On these events, see Ibn al-Muqarrab, *Diwan*, compiled by M. J. de Goeje, 'La fin de l'empire des Carmathes du Bahrain', in *Journal Asiatique*, 1895, and *Mémoire sur les Carmathes du Bahrain et les Fatimides*, Leide.

7. The name of this ruler appears on one of the two inscriptions of Suq al-Khamis mosque.

8. On the Al-Tibi of Qais, see J. Aubin, 'Les princes d'Hormuz du 13è au 15è siècle', in *Journal Asiatique*, Paris, 1953, p. 77–128.

9. G. Bibby, *Looking for Dilmun*, New York, 1969, p. 76.

10. Arabic inscription in the quarry of Jidda island, west of Bahrain.

11. Those soundings, carried out in 1978 by the Museum of Bahrain and the French Expedition will be published soon.

12. See a good copy of the page of this manuscript in *Dilmun, Journal of the Bahrain Historical and Archaeological Society*, 11, 1983, middle pages.

13. This anonymous miniature was shown at the International Conference 'Bahrain Through Ages': see the papers of Prs. A. Dias Farinha, *New Portuguese Documents on Bahrain History in the 16th and 17th centuries*, and A. Tazi, *An unpublished Document on Bahrain*.

14. This inscription will be soon published by B. Andre-Leiknam, Curator at the Musée du Louvre.

15. A preliminary report has already been published on the first seasons of excavation of this fortress: M. Kervran, A. Negre and M. Pirazzoli, *Excavation of Qal'at al-Bahrain*, 1977–1979, Publication of the Ministry of Information, Bahrain, 1982. The final results of the excavation of the fortress as well as its surroundings will be published in 1985/1986.

The presentation and conservation of archaeological sites in Bahrain

BERNARD M. FEILDEN

Free standing and excavated ruins are structures in an advanced state of decay and are therefore more vulnerable to all the slow causes of destruction than structures in use. They are particularly exposed to climatic elements such as wind, rain and blown sand and gravel which can be particularly destructive. Other factors such as ground water and dissolved salts can be destructive and any changes in ground water level generally have an adverse effect. The water level is lowered by industrial pumping which may draw in salt laden water or raised by irrigation and sewage disposal schemes. There are also long term geological changes in level to consider. The macro-climate determines to a large extent the techniques needed for the preservation of ruins.

The basic problem of conserving archaeological remains is how to minimise the action of destructive agents. There is no final solution, all we can do is to aim at reducing the rate of decay. In many cases it is not feasible to conserve excavations and in such cases they should be back-filled.

In Bahrain the most obvious causes of decay are crystallisation of ground water salts due to evaporation due to high air temperatures and wind. The chemical composition of the salts should be analysed and their sources traced. Borings should be made to see if impermeable strata exist at a reasonable depth in which case it should be possible to isolate the monument from contaminated ground water. Subject to the underlying geology it might also be possible to pump in pure water to displace the contaminated water. Unfortunately it is not possible to insert an effective horizontal damp proof membrane under such large monuments as the important Sumer, Akkadian, Kassite, Assyrian, Hellenistic and Islamic ruins and Portuguese Forts at Qal'at al-Bahrain, but it should be possible to do this with the historic houses at Al Muharraq Town, where walls are generally not more than 1 m thick.

Building materials and lime mortar in particular are subject to damage by most ground salts and also when impregnated with these salts the level of dampness rises with time. It is not good trying to plaster over this dampness and it only makes matters worse to use a cement based mortar as this prevents evaporation and merely drives the moisture further up the wall to destroy a further section of plaster and weaken the basic masonry.

Here I should repeat the warning given in my book *Conservation of Historic Buildings* that Portland cement is the enemy of historic buildings. Portland cement, in its various specifications, is a magnificent material for modern structures which require its strength and quick setting qualities. It is useful in reinforced concrete, with suitable aggregates, to strengthen and consolidate the structure of an historic building under professional guidance. Because it is modern, efficiently marketed by advertising and is readily available, and because it is indispensible to the modern building industry, many people think that Portland cement is ideal for historic buildings and sites, but to sum up – unless it is correctly used Portland cement mortar is the enemy of historic buildings. Portland cement is not designed for use in mortars or plaster on historic buildings, which do not require its specific good qualities, but which suffer from its defects and side effects on traditional materials. Its disadvantages are:

1. Its use is not reversible. To remove it damages all historic building materials, which cannot then be recycled.

2. It is too strong in compression, adhesion and tension, so that it is not compatible with the weak materials of historic buildings. It is a paradox that such weak materials have the greatest durability.

3. Because of its high strength it lacks elasticity and plasticity when compared with lime mortar, thus throwing greater mechanical stresses on adjacent materials and hastening their decay.

4. It is impermeable and has low porosity, so it traps vapour as well as water and prevents evaporation. Consequently it is no good for curing damp walls. In fact, the reverse is true, for if used it only drives moisture upwards. When used as mortar its impermeability accelerates frost damage and increases internal condensation.

5. It shrinks on setting, leaving cracks for water to enter, and because it is impermeable such water has difficulty in getting out. Therefore, it increases defects caused by moisture.

6. It produces soluble salts on setting which may dissolve and damage porous materials and valuable decoration.

7. It has high thermal conductivity and may create cold bridges when used for injections to consolidate walls.

8. Its colour is 'cold' grey and rather dark. The texture is too often smooth and 'steely'. These characteristics are generally judged aesthetically incompatible with traditional materials.

Portland cement should not be used alone for mortars or plasters in historic buildings, but as a last resort a small proportion of Portland cement, preferably white cement, although this costs more, should be added to the lime, but not more than 10% of the volume of the lime should be added without expert advice.

The traditional methods of burning and slaking lime are best, but have been lost in many countries. Traditionally, lime mortars in the mix of 1 part lime to 3 parts of coarse sand were used. The sharper and more varied the size of its particles, the better the sand; its colour determines the ultimate colour of the mortar. Its texture can be improved by light spraying to remove 'laitance'.

In thick walls and to accelerate setting, some pozzuolanic material should be added. Some countries like Italy and Germany have natural pozzuolana; in others, it is possible to crush broken brick and tile to obtain this material, which is added as part of the sand proportion to improve the setting characteristics of lime.

162 The Burial Mounds of Bahrain form a unique complex worthy of UNESCO's World Cultural Heritage accolade. To preserve the *genius loci* with all the messages of prehistory is a formidable task, yet unless this is done skilfully the unique aspects of the complex may be damaged or destroyed

Wind and rain have to be combated, which means paying attention to the tops and surfaces of walls be they built of stone, burnt brick or earthen materials. Rain can have a devastating effect on mud brick structures if their roof copings and rain water disposal are not in good order. In the case of ruins the effect is even more damaging as they lack the regular maintenance of occupied structures and in desert countries there is also the danger of flash storms and floods at rare intervals. No satisfactory chemical treatments have been found yet for preserving mud brick.

The tops of masonry walls have to be made weather proof and self draining. This often means lifting the top courses of stone or brick, first carefully recording their position, and removal of all humus and plant growth, down to the very roots. A chemical weed killer may be used to prevent future growths; this is best brushed on as spray may blow away and kill valuable plant life nearby. After careful preparation the original materials are replaced in their original position using a traditional mortar mix. The original mortar should be analysed and care taken to match the mix and the sand itself. If this is not possible the new work should use slightly darker and slightly coarser sand. When the mortar has set it should be brushed and lightly sprayed to bring out the coarser grains of sand. In countries where *juss* (calcium sulphate) is used, special care must be taken to follow traditional practices. Juss mortars can prove to be durable in arid climates.

It is very difficult to combat the problem of blown sand in desert countries as it has an abrasive action on masonry and fills excavated sites. Here attention to the microclimate and possibilities of landscape architecture may be helpful.

Having appreciated some of the causes of decay let us now consider planning of archaeological excavations.

The *genius loci*, as classical writers described the landscape characteristics of a site, is most important. The thousands of burial mounds south of Sar in Bahrain are a unique antiquity of world cultural heritage status and for them the *genius loci* is a vital consideration as intrusive modern developments could destroy the visitor's appreciation of these unique monuments, fig. 162. So landscape planning must be introduced at the beginning of an archaeological excavation. One problem common to all excavations is where to dispose of the spoil. It must go into the right place as nobody wants to move large quantities of earth twice. If mechanical plant be used, great care has to be exercised because of the damage machines do to ground surface and flora. The scars last for years or even centuries.

Advance planning is essential to efficient operations in any field. The archaeologist planning an excavation should consult a landscape architect about the *genius loci*, an architect about structures and an engineer about soil conditions and safety of excavations, (too many archaeologists are lost due to the sides of deep excavations collapsing.) Water levels also effect excavations and any pumping should be from outside whatever is of value. Ideally a conservator should be a member of the archaeological team, which could also include a medical anthropologist if many burials are anticipated. In planning, the position of huts and lavatories and the disposal of waste in a suitable way need careful thought.

In planning excavation the difficulty of forecasting what may be found should be recognised, but plans must be made for short term and long term preservation of artifacts which may have existed in a state of equilibrium for thousands of years. Excavation immediately changes this state of equilibrium and exposes the object to a new syndrome of decay. The underground environment was characterised by the lack of light, the presence of soluble salts, contact with soil, often corrosive, a stable temperature and extremely stable relative humidity which is the most important factor for preservation of the object. Ground temperature at a depth of 5–6 m varies by $\pm 1°C$ annually. Relative humidity underground varies according to the nature of the soil and depth, that in the tomb of Queen Nefertari in the Valley of the Queens, Luxor, Egypt being 30% while the tomb of Nefer at Saqqara has a relative humidity of 66%. The relative humidity of buried objects in Bahrain is probably even higher making them more vulnerable to the sudden change caused by excavation.

In order to retain the 'message' of the object as intact as possible it is essential from the moment of discovery to take a series of measurements which will prevent the object already damaged by its stay underground from being more so by being brought to light. Gael de Guichen of ICCROM has prepared a summary table indicating the risk to the object and recommended actions which is given as Appendix I. Wood, ivory, ceramics with salts and metals are most vulnerable.

A site laboratory for the resident conservator on large excavations is highly desirable as is a drawing office and facilities for inventorying, labelling and storing finds. In planning, the need for this building should be foreseen and its subsequent use to provide visitor facilities should be considered, together with its landscape implications. Piecemeal excavations with *ad hoc* decisions are more expensive than those with well co-ordinated planning. It is also important to retain control strata for future reference. However, these may conflict with the presentation of the site and may have to be removed at a later stage.

After excavation the site should be evaluated and the policy for its presentation and conservation can then be finally decided. The initial budget foreseen before excavation should have made suitable provision for this activity as a site cannot be left unprotected with valuable artifacts lying on the ground as I have seen myself. To decide the presentation policy, first the objective must be defined, then all the values in the site considered and put in order of priority, and in this process the contribution of the historian and archaeologist is of crucial importance as there may be conflict between the presentation of different periods on a site which has been occupied over a long period of time. For instance in the case of the Barbar temples, Temple II has been emphasised in presentation. There is need to interpret the complicated issues of cultural influences, mythical and historical events as well as the economic, technological and political factors which have been the cause of the rise and fall of the site, and explain this to the future visitor. It is a good idea to surround the site with temporary railings and establish view points with explanatory material as has been done by Dr Doe at Barbar, fig. 163.

In multi-disciplinary work involving academics and professionals with different backgrounds, perhaps having different objectives and different values, it is inevitable that there will be conflicting views. These should be exposed in a good natured way in order to find creative solutions. In conservation there is no best solution. It is wise to examine all the alternative solutions that are practicable, bearing in mind the capital and annual costs. Then one should choose the 'least bad' solution in the light of conservation theory but this may involve a sacrifice on the part of one or more of the experts involved. This means we all have to learn the arts of communication and compromise.

It should again be stressed that conservation of ruins and archaeological sites only buys time, it cannot stop decay totally, it can only reduce the rate of decay. Bearing this in mind the best method of preserving some archaeological sites is to back-fill them after all recording has been done so reinstating their stable environment after a short (but damaging) exposure. In England one site that has been recovered is opened up every ten years for scholars to study. P. Mora recommends the procedure for recovering an excavation given in Appendix II. Another alternative is to build a cover over the archaeological site and this has been used, in some cases successfully, to give an outline of the original structure but there is always a danger that the relative humidity will be altered by the covering structure and that it will make the attack by evaporation of ground salts more aggressive. Restraint in the architectural design of covering structures and indeed in any building on a historic site is essential so that the *genius loci* be respected. Anastylosis and reconstruction are full of dangers and generally should be made only in model form for the instruction of visitors. Re-erecting fallen columns can, however, help one appreciate the architectural spaces and volumes of a ruined site.

THE VISITOR

The needs of the visitor need careful consideration in the presentation plan. Visitor circulation should be in harmony with the historic layout of the site, that is, the same as for the original inhabitant; then the visitor can imagine more easily the functioning of the site and how the inhabitants lived in time past. Often a site or a ruin needs protection from visitors who may cause damage by walking over ancient walls or wear out valuable pavings, so tactful control should be applied. A good example is the way in which the temples at Barbar are protected by railings and significant view points are defined for the visitor who can read an explanation of what he is looking at, fig. 164. All these measures enhance the sacred character of ancient sites. The visitor needs education with literature, and models of reconstruction of the various phases of the site. Video presentations can be prepared to explain the significance of each phase. He may even wish to take away tangible evidence of his visit, so it is best that he should take away a good replica of some object rather than find something for himself. In fact vandalism is an increasing anxiety for the guardians of the historic sites and this danger increases if the sites become too crowded. Each site has its maximum visitor capacity beyond which proper supervision can not be maintained and physical damage and wear and tear become excessive. In addition to interpretation facilities, visitors also need car parking space, toilets and refreshments.

As has been said, each site has its own *genius loci* and in this respect the landscape architect has a major contribution to make to achieve a significant presentation. Nobody can appreciate the past if their eye is offended by the debris and litter of the present age – even though it may be the archaeological material of the future – so landscape considerations extend beyond the site as far as the eye can see. If something is intrusive it is best to plant trees to screen it at least, but the landscape architect has a positive contribution using gardens, water, carefully selected plant material, but avoiding large rooting water-loving trees and ivy, to enhance the *genius loci* of the site. He can improve the microclimate and assist in preventing wind blown sand from accumulating by skilful planting. The function of the historic site plan can be made clear by the use of different textures on the ground. There are no standard treatments as the *genius loci* will dictate what is appropriate.

The objective of conservation and presentation of historic sites is to educate the citizen and visitor about the history of Bahrain through the Ages, making him aware of its importance and significance.

164 The site of the second millenium city at Qal'at al-Bahrain shows the difficulties of presenting sites with many levels of occupation and of preserving the exposed ruins. A presentation policy has yet to be developed for this complex historic site, which is full of opportunities to show the sequence of the expansion of Bahrain's role up to the sixteenth century AD

163 The site of the Barbar temples was re-excavated in order to show the evidences of occupation of this site, related to a unique fresh water spring. The visitor is guided by footpaths to significant view points where he is given a graphic description of the site. All the elements of presentation and interpretation are reversible

APPENDIX I

SUMMARY TABLE BY GAEL DE GUICHEN ICCROM

What is buried	What is found	What is the risk	What is recommended
Wood	the imprint	none	make a mould
Wood	wood	any variation in R.H.	maintain the same R.H.
Wood	waterlogged wood	any drying out which will make the material collapse	keep underwater or at 100% R.H. before treatment
Leather (see wood)			
Textiles	the imprint	none	make a mould
Ivory	damaged ivory	crystallisation of salts	avoid all variation in R.H. before treatment to remove salts
Ceramic	ceramic		
Ceramic	ceramic with salts	a crystallisation through drying out	avoid all variation of R.H. before treatment by desalination – with water or paper compress
Stone (see ceramic)			
Glass	weeping glass	loss of transparency	some recommend a R.H. of 44%
Metal	metal	none	
Metal	metal with stable corrosion	none	
Metal	metal with unstable corrosion	activation of the corrosion, will happen if R.H. above 50%	keep at a R.H. below 45% before chemical treatment
Metal	metal with corrosion	crystallisation of salts	desalination in fresh water

APPENDIX II

For the re-covering of built structures the following sequence is proposed (see fig. 165):

1. *plastic net,* with fairly tight mesh (e.g. for protection against hail), spread over the pavement and applied liberally over all the vertical surfaces to be protected

2. *an upright partition* to contain vermiculite, placed upright on the pavement parallel to the surfaces to protect

3. *expanded clay* 15–20 cm deep in a horizontal stratum

4. *plastic net,* laid down over the expanded clay outside the upright partition

5. *vermiculite* to fill the spaces between the decorated surfaces and the partition

6. *earth* to fill in partially the excavation, treated with adequate biocides

7. *bentonite* (clay) in horizontal layers, to prevent direct penetration of rainwater

8. *earth,* for final filling in of the trench to higher than the surrounding ground level (depth of trench plus 5–10%)

9. selected planting of shallow-rooted plants

The plastic nets (levels 1 and 4) are designed to make it easier to remove the backfill material; these can be omitted if the excavation is to be filled in for ever.

Before spreading the expanded clay (level 3), upright partitions to contain the vermiculite should be provided, at 20 cm distance from the vertical surfaces. The partitions can be made of expanded polystyrene sheets about 2 cm thick, with support footings of the same material. Expanded polystyrene, even in the long term, will never have a negative effect on the decorated surface.

After spreading the stratum of expanded clay over all the pavement, including the part of the pavement within the partitions, a second plastic net (level 4) will be put down. Then the space between the partition and the wall will be filled with vermiculite (level 5) while the rest will be filled with earth (level 6).

At this point, naturally, care should be taken that the space within the partition be filled at a similar rate as the rest of the area being filled with earth. In this way the process of filling continues until the vertical sides are completely covered with earth, and the space within the partitions filled entirely with vermiculite.

The conservation intervention on the subject and the protective backfill will not be sufficient for preservation unless future inspections are planned. This is because after a certain time, the natural animal and plant life of the earth will begin to establish itself as before, with results that cannot be foreseen but that will be similar to those that occurred before the excavation.

Author's Note: Figure 165 is based on figure 1 in 'Conservation of excavated intonaco, stucco and mosaics' by Paola Mora, published in *Conservation on Archaeological Excavations*, ICCROM, 1984, 97–107.

165

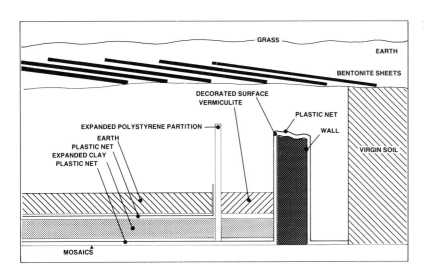

The Barbar Temple site in Bahrain: conservation and presentation

BRIAN DOE

The recent re-excavation of the Barbar Temple was intended to provide a permanent monument for Bahrain. This involved not only its preservation and conservation but also required consideration for visitors viewing the monument and its presentation in an understandable manner.

The initial work was simplified by the availability of detailed plans of the excavation. This enabled the more interesting and significant parts to be displayed, and for the unexcavated portions to remain preserved for future investigation. An important feature of the monument is that these are the remains of three temples built one above the other.

At the outset it was decided to reveal the remains of Temple II, as providing the more interesting monument, and Temple I, lying below the platform of Temple II would therefore remain as it was left by the excavators.

Of Temple III built above Temple II there were only the remains of foundations, entrance piers and the circular well head above the well of Temple II and it was decided these would remain on view as part of the whole monument.

The collapse of the north wall of the Apsu during its cleaning, for it had been used as a tip, presented an unforeseen problem. At the time all that could be done was the lowering of high ground on the north side and the retrieving of a few of the stones of the collapsed wall. Strutting was also placed against stones above the steps leading into the Apsu.

It is just possible that the eventual collapse was caused by the vibration of a pump placed on the top of this wall during the first excavation, which may have affected the stability of the sub-soil, in addition to pressures from an apparent rise in the water table. Another factor may have been the weight of sand piled high behind the wall which was perhaps aggravated by the transport of soil from elsewhere across the top level.

The collapse occurred shortly after pumping out the Apsu to floor level and the cleaning of the walls. In this event the pump was placed some twenty metres northwest of the Apsu. From the positions of lower (under-water) stones, one of which was sheared across, the collapse appears to have been caused by water pressure at the floor level of the Apsu forcing the lower stones inwards and the collapse of the upper part of the masonry.

During the reconstruction it was found that stones below the Apsu floor level had sunk, together with stones alongside the stone steps on the north side.

Fortunately 'foundation' stones were located below the 'floor' level of the Apsu and it became possible to rebuild on these, although fractured stone had to be measured and sections replaced during rebuilding on the bottom courses. With the lower courses established it was necessary first to complete the building of the wall around the northwest inlet opening for this feature determined the course levels of the remainder of the wall. The lintel stone was broken and had sheared at the bond with the west wall. It was decided to shore it up and manufacture a permanent steel frame support, leaving it exposed so that it would not be confused with the original building, fig. 166.

The ground behind this wall was excavated to below the water level and below the level of the floor of the Apsu and large loose boulders, left by the original builders and probably contributing to the collapse, were removed.

Galvanized sheeting was inserted as far down as possible, on the north side, and the wall length behind was then filled with mass

166 The reconstruction of the north wall of the Apsu, the positions of the main stones. The metal frame in position supporting the lintel still to be painted. The water level reduced to expose the hardcore base. The normal water level is indicated by the scum line.

concrete to form a pressure barrier. The galvanized sheeting was intended primarily to reduce seepage of cement into the Apsu, for water would return to this level during the initial set, and also to separate the concrete from the ancient stonework.

One of the problems was the identification of the individual stones for exact placement in the wall. The rebuilding was made easier and in fact possible in the time available by the photographs taken by the Danish Expedition so that a numbered sequence was possible before rebuilding. This stresses the need for careful photography at all times and stages of archaeological work.

It was found during rebuilding that the north wall foundations and the steps had sunk. Without disturbing the steps, which appeared secure although fractured, it was necessary to cut two replacement stones as 'fillers' to maintain the 'course' lines for the upper stones of the walls.

Before rebuilding the upper part of the north wall, the floor of the Apsu was laid with two layers of large hardcore, placed together to inhibit any lateral movement of pressure at subsoil level of well foundation stone. A wide tube was inserted vertically into this stone layer for a pump nozzle to reach floor level should the need to pump out be necessary in the future. The hardcore could then be lifted out if required.

The provision of small fish by the appropriate Ministry has been of value in keeping the water clean.

A solid concrete block wall, with vertical and horizontal cranked steel reinforcing bars was also built on the mass concrete

167 Fixing the galvanised wire mesh to the exposed face of excavation.

placed behind the north wall. Certain of the walling stones were pointed in cement/lime mortar to inhibit movement but otherwise the stones were relaid without mortar as originally built.

The round jar with holes originally found in the Apsu was placed upon a square slab on top of the hard core above its place of original discovery. The stone on which it was found remains in its original position.

Work on the remainder of the Temple site was concerned with its preservation for future archaeological work and conservation of the exposed portions, as well as its appearance. Facilities for visitors viewing the site were essential, but its protection was of equal importance.

The platform or floor of Temple II had been stone robbed in antiquity. This was artificially refronted on the original alignments on the south and west sides with a sloping wire mesh cover which was covered with a plaster finish, fig. 167.

This was necessary to preserve the platform shape and protect it from further erosion as well as to establish the height of the temple floor for the viewer and to emphasize the physical relationship of the three temples. Its masonry predecessor is suggested by an edging of square paving slabs.

Previously unexcavated faces and all other vertical faces of ground within the site area were covered with small gauge wire mesh netting pegged with 150 mm long metal staples.

This has been done to preserve the face of unexcavated ground from erosion. Other faces of previously excavated ground were also

168 Laying the paving for the pathway. The slabs are laid on building sand on levelled ground with a mortar to the joints. The sides of the pathway are haunched in mortar to reduced lateral movement.

covered to reduce the blown sand and keep the monument as clean as possible.

This factor is assisted by the provision of paved concrete paths and five viewing platforms, with a set route clockwise for the visitor to view the temple. Metal railings were erected to inhibit trespass on the unprotected surface of the Temple.

The paths are placed on prepared ground on a bed of fine building sand and only pointed in cement to reduce movement, fig. 168. They are removable in the event of future excavation. These tube railings are removable also as the tubes are merely inserted over metal bars set in the ground and within the mortar haunching at the edge of the pathways.

It is expected that the whole of the remainder of the site, which is all of archaeological importance, will be further protected by a boundary wall, with a single controlled entrance from the main road. Plans for this entrance, and also a high level viewing platform and store as well as a proposed site museum and office were also prepared for the future development of this area and for the protection of the monument.

A description of the site of the Barbar Temple as observed from the Viewing Positions and path has also been produced to assist the visitor.

The traditional architecture of Bahrain

RONALD LEWCOCK

To a connoisseur of architecture, the buildings of old Bahrain are extremely fascinating. Not merely do they represent an obvious response to local building materials and climate, but they have a splendid architectural character of their own: clear, logical statements of the structure in a system which is articulated and proportioned according to the principles of classical Islamic architecture a thousand years old. Furthermore, a number of styles occur – although it is not easy, immediately, to identify which is the earliest and which is the most recent.

After long acquaintance with the architecture, other characteristics become clear. The methods by which cool comfort is obtained in this hot humid climate are often very ingenious and varied. They affect the fundamental concept and use of the buildings; they affect the methods of building construction and ultimately the whole character of the architecture.

The architecture of Bahrain has links with that of many of the surrounding countries, but its essential qualities might be said to be unique. Although the few forts on the islands resemble those of the rest of the Gulf and elsewhere (naval and military affairs in the lands around the Indian Ocean ensured a certain homogeneity of influences on fortifications and the mosques bear resemblances to ancient mosques of Arabian, Mesopotamian, and Persian type, the domestic architecture has evolved along a pattern which is, in the main, distinctively Bahraini. No one knows how ancient this pattern of secular architecture may be. It evidently has some links with neighbouring countries, especially those north of the Gulf. But, with the exception of ancient Zubara, the only other possible sites where this architecture is thought to be found are Qais island, Linga, and Deyyer in Iran.

I propose to discuss here first the particular characteristics of the secular architecture, and where these may have come from, and to conclude with a brief discussion of the monumental architecture, the mosques and the forts.

THE CHARACTERISTICS OF THE SECULAR ARCHITECTURE

Bahraini palaces and traditional houses were essentially conceived as a series of pavilions around courtyards. Usually, there were two courtyards, one for the reception of men and the other for private living. Modest houses might be content with one courtyard, a practice which was also followed in some of the larger houses away from urban conditions. Where a family included many dependants, or was engaged in business, there might be other subsidiary courts.

The palaces and houses were organized in terms of seasonal migration. The most important pavilions for living and reception had a counterpart on the roof where the summer breezes could be caught to provide air movement over the surface of the skin in the worst conditions of the heat and humidity.

In order to provide screening in these upper pavilions, while permitting air movement, recourse was had to a number of ingenious devices which are briefly discussed below.

Two or three months of the year are cool enough for the Bahrainis to value the thick walls of the lower rooms in their old houses.

For the remainder of the year the weather tends to be unpleasantly close, with continual high temperatures and high humidity, posing a most difficult problem in the achievement of comfortable interior conditions by natural means.

The solution to this climatic problem was found in the construction of as much as possible of the upper part of each building as a framework of rough coral rubble piers, with the spaces between filled with large panels of coral rock. Apart from the fact that the coral itself is very porous and light-weight, the mass of the panels is reduced to a minimum, making them as thin as possible: they are seldom more than 4 cm thick. In the higher levels of rooms the panels are sometimes arranged in a two-leaf construction, with trapped air in between to reduce thermal conductivity when the sun shines on the outside walls. Because of their porosity, all the stone surfaces are sealed with a continuous skim coat of a mixture of lime and gypsum. This, too, is kept to a minimum thickness (about $\frac{1}{8}$ cm) to reduce weight, and thus reduce the capacity of the walls to store daytime heat into the evenings – when it might have been re-radiated at a time of high humidity to cause acute discomfort.

Although hundreds of fine examples of these houses survive in many parts of the islands, hardly any of them are maintained with the care that was traditionally lavished on them. Annual inspection and repair ceased several decades ago, in all but exceptional cases. Although the walls are finished with durable plasters (evolved over countless years of experiment), the core of the rough coral rock walls was built using only clay from the centre of Bahrain as a mortar. This clay has a soapy consistency and dissolves easily. The result of ceasing the annual repairing of cracks in walls and roofs before the winter rains has therefore been disastrous: much of the packing between the stones in the core of the walls has disappeared. Therefore, a structure which appears externally still to have a sound, often beautifully decorated, plaster finish, is actually lacking in structural strength and may even be on the point of collapse – a situation which could easily be avoided by regular maintenance using the traditional materials.

SOURCES FOR THE BAHRAINI SYSTEM OF PANELLED WALL CONSTRUCTION

The need to provide continuous cross-ventilation through rooms in hot, humid climates anciently led to a system of construction using piers with openings, or pierced panels, between them. Models which have been found in excavations of Assyrian times (c. sixth century B.C.) clearly show this kind of construction, which can be traced back further still to the structures of the Uruk VI–IV period (c. 3000 B.C.) at Warka and Uruk; the early buildings are also illustrated on cylinder seals of the period. The device of pier-and-opening construction was also favoured during the old kingdom of Egypt, and something extremely close to the Bahraini appearance of a building was achieved in ancient Ionia in Wesern Asia, in classical Greek times, (tombs in the shape of houses, at Xanthos). The same kind of construction was still in use in Sassanian Persia (third-seventh century A.D.), e.g. the palaces at Qaleh-i Dukhtar and Firuzabad. It is from this precedent that the principle must have been adopted by the Seljuks, by whom it was developed to be the high point of sophistication which is still exemplified in the traditional architecture of Bahrain as it is today.

Along the coasts of Bahrain it is possible to see occasionally a brushwood shelter which is a timber version of the same system of construction. That is, there are wooden uprights, made of rough poles: these carry cross poles acting as beams, sometimes tied up into an arch to give them greater supporting strength. Between these, a smaller lattice-work supports mats, or else the wattling between the posts is worked into a fine screen to provide some degree of privacy to people within the shelter. In this way, a screened enclosure is provided between posts which allows continuous cross-ventilation.

The plans of the houses, designed around large courtyards, may be likewise traced back to the period of 2000 B.C., where we find very large open courtyards surrounded on three or four sides by a single row of rooms, with the main halls being narrow transverse halls with a door in the centre of the long side (e.g. the palace of Mari, built under combined Western Semitic and Sumerian influence). The rooms had no windows; light penetrated through very tall doorways. Being inland, however, the ancient Mesopotamian house did not involve the seasonal migration up into roof-rooms, as happens in Bahrain. But the plans are similar in often having a separation of the house into different zones related to distinct activities, each focussed on its own courtyard: that is, a large house, such as Bayt Shaikh Isa al-Khalifa, might have a separate business court, living court, males' reception court, and kitchen court. This system of planning with units, each existing of a paved court surrounded by shallow rooms, can be traced back through Ur (palace of Urnammu, *c.* 2065 B.C.), to Tello, and to Akkadian Tell Brak (palace of Marim – Sin *c.* 2200 B.C.). It is possible, therefore, to argue that, in many respects, the traditional architecture of Bahrain is a historic continuation of ancient Mesopotamian architecture with roots in a building vernacular older than Ur and Sumer.

WIND-TOWERS AND WIND-CATCHERS (BADGIRS)

In the densely built-up Gulf towns the streets were purposely made narrow to ensure shade in the heat of the day; any natural movement of air was obstructed. Cooling breezes tended to be deflected upwards so that they passed over the rooftops without disturbing the air below, unless special devices could be introduced to deflect the air movement downwards. A wide variety of wind-towers and wind-catchers were employed in Bahrain in an endeavour to provide air movement over the bodies of the inhabitants within the buildings, thus encouraging evaporation and lessening the oppression created by the humidity.

The earliest known evidence of the use of ventilators to convey cooling breezes down into a room is to be seen on the numerous small models of houses found in Egyptian Old Kingdom tombs, which were intended to symbolise the living quarters of the deceased in their after-lives; these models date from approximately 2100 B.C. By the time of the Egyptian New Kingdom, wall paintings depict both the exterior of triangular wind-catchers on the roofs of houses and sections through bedrooms with angled ceilings above them, clearly representing angled wind-catchers of the type that survives down to modern times. The earliest evidence we have in Mesopotamia of the use of ventilators shafted down into a room below is from an inscription of Sargon II (722–712 B.C.). The wind-towers were found on all the largest houses in Bahrain by the mid-nineteenth century.

Three types of wind-catcher are common in Bahrain: wind-towers, mid-wall wind-catchers inside the rooms, and roof-top, parapet wind-catchers.

Wind-towers were themselves of two types. That of ancient Egypt and Mesopotamia was a single catcher, facing the prevailing breeze, with a shaft extending down below it to an opening less than two metres above the floor, usually above a bed or a sitting and working area. This kind of wind-catcher was occasionally built until recently in parts of the Gulf, but I know of none that now exist in Bahrain.

The second type of wind-tower has a square turret projecting from the top of the building, with open decorated arcades or grilles on all four sides. Internally, the turret is normally divided into four vertical shafts. This may be done in two ways. In northern and western Persia, Iraq and Kuwait, it seems normally to have been done by creating four rectangular shafts with cross walls built parallel to the outer walls of the wind-tower, the two vertical shafts facing the directions of the prevailing winds are often larger in cross-section than those facing in the directions at right angles. Alternatively, the turret is divided into four individual shafts of equal size by two diagonal cross walls. The shafts are carried down through the height of the building to the ceiling of the main reception room, so that cool breezes are admitted from the windward shaft at the same time as stale hot air is drawn out through the leeward shaft. Even more effective is the device of projecting the wind shaft down into the room, so that the opening is no more than 2–1.5 m above the floor; this is usually done against the back wall or in a corner. The turret using diagonal cross walls is common in the central and southern Gulf; a number of examples of it may be seen in Manama and Muharraq.

MID-WALL WIND-CATCHERS

Universally used in Bahrain, this type of wind-catcher relies on the pressure of wind against the large expanse of wall of a roof-room. A row of such wind-catchers is seen externally as a row of horizontal recesses mid-way up the height of the external wall. At the bottom of each recess there is a shuttered opening which can be closed or opened from the inside. The high air pressure on the windward side of the wall is thus captured and allowed to enter the room less than one metre above the floor, where it creates air movement across the body of people sitting inside the room. Internally there are a series of recessed niches each corresponding to one of the ventilator openings. Using this ingenious device the whole interior of a roof-room can have a constant flow of air moving across it at breast level to cool the inhabitants in humid weather, provided that there is a slight breeze blowing outside.

WIND-CATCHER PARAPETS

A variation of the above was the wind-catcher parapet. It is constructed of two flat planes which are staggered vertically. The outer plane is built of brick or rammed earth and forms the lower half of the parapet. The upper half is recessed behind an air gap and therefore has either to be supported on wooden beams, the traditional construction, or manufactured from reinforced material as a slab spanning the upright supports. A horizontal coping should complete the construction, but this is missing in some constructions. This parapet functions in exactly the same way as the mid-wall wind-catcher. The pressure of air in the recess diverts the wind down over the people sleeping on the open roof. In this case, however, there are no shutters closing the air space, as these are not judged necessary and would be an extra expense. It will be noticed that this parapet provides more privacy than the traditional open-screened parapet, while at the same time ensuring that the maximum air movement is obtained close to the surface of the roof.

The last two types of wind-catcher are almost entirely restricted to Bahrain and small areas under Bahraini influence. Early in this century they seem to have appeared for the first time in Dubai, and subsequently in Kuwait, in both cases apparently under Bahraini influence. They are one of the most characteristic and distinctive features of architecture in Bahrain.

DOORS

The entrance doors of Bahraini traditional architecture offer some of the finest examples of decorated woodwork in the Gulf. They are constructed of vertical planks, usually of teak, which are held together by vertical crossbars on the inside to which the planks are fastened by closely spaced nails, which have large dome-shaped bosses on the outside faces of the doors. A pair of handsome doors will have five horizontal rows of these bosses. In the centre, a boldly projecting cover piece between the two doors is richly decorated with carving. This decoration is sometimes composed of a series of diamond shapes, sometimes with curved sides, carved in shallow relief. In the centre of each diamond there may be carved a flower or a rosette. Another alternative has the raised decoration on the cover strip as a continuous band from top to bottom, varying in width from cartouches the whole width of the cover strip to narrow bands linking rosettes with diamonds and other shapes. The rosettes usually have a lotus pattern, very reminiscent of ancient Achaemenid work and ultimately traceable back to Uruk, 3200 B.C. Other doors belong to a type which was reputably favoured by one of the greatest of all Bahraini craftsmen in wood, who was at the height of his career about sixty years ago. This type of door is identifiable by a strictly geometrical cover strip with parallel notches arranged in steps.

Elaborate door frames have a chain or rope moulding on the face, edged by a row of classical darts.

Other types of doors which used to be found in Bahraini traditional architecture were ultimately derived from the styles introduced by the European factories in the Gulf. These doors were of six-pannelled or four-pannelled types and were also favoured by architects working under Turkish influence.

A remarkable aspect of the richly decorated doors of the vernacular architecture of the Indian Ocean is that it is rare to find the same pattern reproduced in two different geographical localities. Each town had its own fashion in door designs and in the decorated patterns that were used on them. Particularly characteristic of Bahrain was the stepped geometrical pattern described above. These doors are sometimes found in other places in the Gulf and it can often be established that they were from Bahrain. The flat faces on the cover strips of such doors had the traditional Islamic pierced screen patterns etched in bold relief. Bahraini doors are also often characterised by a curious scalloped decoration which is used on the face of the door frames.

It is known that the large projecting dome-headed bosses or nail-heads were used by the ancient Assyrians in the sixth–fifth century B.C., for some of them were excavated at Deim in the Dokan region of Northern Iraq and are now preserved in the Bagdad museum. Early texts of India describe elaborate doors with projecting bosses being imported to the Punjab in the third half of the twelfth century A.D.

PLASTER SCREENS

A characteristic feature of Bahraini architecture is the use of pierced and blind panels of decoration in the form of pierced geometrical screens. These are of a characteristic Islamic type, the use of which can be traced throughout history in many cultures and in many areas of the Islamic world. Although those of Bahrain are extremely beautiful, only a few can be identified as being particularly characteristic of work in Bahrain because of the frequency with which they are repeated.

One of these common screen patterns has a series of small interlocking rectangles which form a stepped pattern; it is closely aking to the pattern favoured for the Bahraini door cover strip described above. Whether its origin was indigenous, or it was derived from Oman or Persia, it has become so characteristic a feature that it must be regarded today as fundamentally Bahraini. Another pattern much favoured in Bahrain, and in some ways akin to the foregoing, is a pattern of overlapping circles and squares which produces an effect of interpenetrating rosettes. But there are countless other patterns, most of them very geometrical in character, which are popular as decoration.

Screens were also sometimes made of turned wooden pieces fitted together to make up a large area of patterned screening, exactly as in the 'mucharabies' of the Red Sea and Egypt.

CASTELLATIONS AND CRESTING

At the top of the walls, it was common for Bahraini buildings to finish against the sky with castellations or cresting. The castellations were composed of repeated finials, each finial having three or four steps. This was an ancient type of castellation occurring in Assyrian bas-reliefs. Closely allied to it is a cresting of spade or fleur-de-lye finials. The latter are believed to be Islamic in origin, dating back to Mamluk times in Egypt, that is, to the thirteenth century A.D.

THE STYLES OF SECULAR ARCHITECTURE IN BAHRAIN

At least three different styles are discernible in the design of the tops of the wall panels of Bahraini houses and palaces. These are: semi-circular-headed panels, square-headed panels and pointed-arch-headed panels. Variations on the latter may include a trefoil arch or an ogee arch. It is notable that this upper arch is sometimes contained within a rectangular frame and at other times the arch reads at the head of the frame itself. A full analysis of the significance of all these features and the development of Bahraini styles during the last two hundred years must await a more exhaustive study; but a few conclusions about stylistic preferences in relation to chronology may be given here.

The oldest datable building in Muharraq is Bayt Salman, originally Bayt Shaikh Abdulla, dating from c. 1800. This has semi-circular arches at the top of the frames, but not contained within rectangular panels. (The use of the semi-circular arch, which is surprising in an Islamic building, is probably derived from fashions then current in Turkish buildings in Bagdad and Basra: it is just possible that the fashion may be dated back to the European styles introduced by the Portuguese and Dutch into the Gulf in the seventeenth century.) Bayt Shaikh Hamad, dating from perhaps thirty years later, had trefoil and pointed arches at the top of its panels; these shapes also rise straight up from the ends of the piers and are not recessed in rectangular panels. Bayt Shaikh Isa, of roughly the same period, had the same characteristics; sometimes its pointed arches were set in rectangular panels. Many houses in Muharraq, which are known to be more recent, favour the device of setting the arched panel within a rectangular frame, or have a rectangular headed opening containing no shaped panel head at all.

It seems likely that the use of a pointed arch with straight sides, characteristic of many of the old doorways, is an ancient practice in Bahrain; there were until recently small houses near the suq in

Muharraq which had such arches above panels and appeared to be buildings of considerable antiquity.

MOSQUES

Two quite distinct types of mosques are found in Bahrain. The first, and undoubtedly the most ancient, is the *apadama* type, with high wooden columns carrying the wooden beams of the roof. The second has masonry arcades parallel to the qibla wall, which serve to support the roof beams. The oldest mosque in Bahrain, the Suq al-Khamis mosque, combines the two types in two different periods of erection. It appears to have been built in two main phases. The first structure was apparently a small mosque with timber columns supporting carved timber beams of Samarra III type. This building was ascribed by Diez to the tenth or eleventh century A.D. However, it should be noticed that Diez found an inscription on one wooden pillar (which has since disappeared) which would date that pillar at least to the period *c.* 1340 A.D. Three of the original beams from this mosque are now displayed in the museum, but all the pillars, two of which still existed in the old museum in 1965, have now disappeared.

The second phase in building the mosque seems to have been the addition of a number of rows of masonry piers, made up of squat single or double columns carrying simple pointed arches. All this masonry work is ascribed by Diez to the same date as that which he found included in the long inscription above the arches in the court-yard wall, i.e. 740/1339–40. Some fragments of this inscription are still in position in the building, others are in the museum, while still others have disappeared. Of two qibla stones which stood at the feet of the pillars on the west side of the courtyard, one has also dis-appeared. It should be noted that the corners of the surrounding wall had imitation circular bastions of a type which is known only from very early mosques of the seventh to ninth centuries A.D.

ABU ZAIDAN MOSQUE

This is a most beautiful mosque, with a three-arched loggia giving access to a long transverse prayer hall which has open double arcades on the sides. There is a fine scalloped niche recess as a qibla. In front of the facade of the loggia is an open, raised platform for prayer. The mosque is in a relatively good state of repair. The build-ing appears to date from the eleventh/seventeenth centuries, but could possibly be earlier. The Abu Muhara Mosque on the Budaiya Road contains an inscription referring to its building in the year 809/1406. The present appearance of the mosque, however, suggests that it was extensively rebuilt in the thirteenth/nineteenth centuries. It is a splendid old Bahraini mosque.

The Hālat Nu'aym Mosque (Hālat al-Naim Mosque) is a fine

example of the old kind of Bahraini mosque with timber columns supporting the beams of the roof. There is an outer portico and a long transverse room serves as the prayer hall.

Mosques of the columned hall, the *apadama* type, have high wooden columns carrying tall capitals. The latter often incorporate stalactite mouldings.

Traditional Bahraini minarets were slightly tapering masonry cylinders curving over into a rounded cone at the top. Only a few windows interrupted this form. Often there was no wooden balcony, the muezzin simply making the call to prayer through large arched windows. In the tallest minarets, however, like the Suq el-Khamis mosque, wooden balconies were added, which had lattice-work or turned balustrades.

FORTS

Bahrain is fortunate in having examples of many phases of fort building throughout its history.

Through archaeological excavation the well preserved remains of an ancient fort of Sassanian type have been uncovered. Its use continued throughout the early centuries of Islam until it seems to have fallen into disuse.

The fort is a perfect square with round corner bastions and a semi-circular bastion in the centre of each side, except the Western where two quadrant bastions flank the entrance. In the centre of the fortress there is a small square courtyard containing a cistern. The outer walls of the fortress are constructed of fine, coursed, square ashlar limestone blocks.

The full history of the great castle of Qal'at al-Bahrain is not known. The Portuguese ruled Bahrain for eighty years from *c.* 1517 A.D. But two factors in particular probably led to the creation of such a large fortress there. First was the uneasy hold of the Portuguese over the allegiance of the Bahrainis, second the increasing conflict with the Ottomans for hegemony of the Gulf after 1550 A.D. By 1590 Persian strength had grown so much that they, in turn, were posing a serious challenge to the Portuguese in Bahrain, finally taking the island in 1602. It is probable that the Portuguese merely extended and elaborated a Bahraini fortress which was already standing on the site to control the ancient port alongside it.

Portuguese drawings survive in the Archives in Lisbon showing a five-sided fortress in a somewhat simpler form than the surviving building, with three or four circular bastions, and several higher towers. Although these are said to date from the early seventeenth century, it seems likely that they represent the fort in the form it assumed after being strengthened *c.*1550, and before the final remodelling which all Portuguese forts in the east received under the direction of leading Italian and Spanish military engineers brought out for the purpose *c.* 1590. As far as is known, no Portuguese plan or drawing of the building in its final form exists.

After the Portuguese were driven off, the fortress continued to be used to defend the island until, with the silting up of the port which it sheltered, its use could no longer be justified except as a prison. As the Persian hold of the island loosened after 1750, it seems that maintenance of the fortress diminished, allowing the onset of the decay which destroyed the curtain walls and the interior courtyards. The great bastions, being composed of work done in ashlar under strict supervision of skilled military engineers, have fared better with time. There does not seem any evidence of post-Portuguese alterations to the bastions.

The fort is a large one, comprising three high, massive bastions in varying, but relatively good, states of preservation, parts of two higher central towers, and long stretches of the enceinte linking the bastions – which is now in a heavily decayed condition. The whole outline of the moat and of the castle within it is visible, but the towers on the eastern end are ruined. Enough shows above ground level to suggest that a careful clearing of the site might reveal the lower levels with many more walls, towers and possibly whole rooms.

Four rooms and three staircases within the bastions are well preserved in their entirety and can be entered by visitors today. The other rooms cannot be entered but can be observed from above through holes in the roof of the southwest bastion. Of the six rooms, five are roofed with domes on squinch arches above semidomes (one of the five has an elongated oval dome). The sixth room is roofed with a barrel vault carried on transverse arches. Each of the rooms has a large arched firing port, the actual opening in each case being reduced to a narrow square. The two rooms in the northern bastion have, in addition, divided firing ports to allow raking fire to left and right. The latter are especially well preserved.

In its final form, the fortress had its major defensive works in a roughly square plan on the western side, with a triangular outer bailey to the east. Entrance was apparently across an arched causeway from the south, through the outer bailey, and then through a gate in what is now almost the centre of the mound, facing west, and thus into a large central courtyard. The largest bastions are those on the northwest, the southwest, and in the centre of the south side. There was a further wide, but low, bastion at the eastern end of the outer bailey.

There is enough surviving evidence above ground for us to be able to see that there were three high points to the fortress on the southern side, which rose above the height of the great bastions. The first was immediately inside the southwest bastion; the second, the circular keep midway between the southwest and the south bastion, and the third a short distance to the east of the south bastion. There is evidence of a further strong tower in the centre of the eastern side of the main fortress, overlooking the bailey. This may have been one of a pair of towers flanking the gate, or the gate may have passed through it (in which case it may yet be possible to excavate the gate). The latter type of gateway was used in Fort Jesus, Mombasa, remodelled at the same time. A further high tower occurred to the north of this tower, being the northeast bastion of the main fortress, overlooking the outer bailey.

Most of the inner plan of the main fortress is indiscernible owing to the great mass of fallen rubble and sand which has filled it up as the walls collapsed. But the lowest part of the inner courtyard appears to have been that to the north. There is some evidence of the walls of buildings of medium height still remaining under the debris in the south central area of the courtyard, adjoining the greater masses of the high southern towers.

Several forts defended Muharraq Island. They were occupied at various times by the Portuguese, and one, Arad, was rebuilt by them with dual concentric surrounding walls and corner bastions separated by a space which contained buildings. In this form it is shown in the early Portuguese maps of Bahrain, such as that in the Bibliothèque Nationale in Paris. Around the outside of the whole fortification there was a wide outer moat, the presence of which has been confirmed through archaeological excavations. This fort was temporarily occupied by Omani forces during wars at the beginning of the nineteenth century. They appear to have strengthened the inner fort and demolished the outer one.

These forts would undoubtedly reveal many items of great interest upon detailed study and excavation. They remain as imposing monuments – albeit urgently in need of conservation.

Bibliography

Adams, R. McC.
1972 'Settlement and irrigation patterns in
      ancient Akkad' in M. Gibson 1972 *The City
      and Area of Kish*, appendix V, Field
      Research Publications. Miami.
1975 'The Mesopotamian Social Landscape: A
      View from the Frontier', in C. B. Moore ed.
      Reconstructing Complex Societies, 1–22.
      *Bulletin of the American School of Oriental
      Research*, supplement No. 20.
1981 *Heartland of Cities*, University of Chicago
      Press, Chicago.
Adams, R. McC. and Nissen, H. J.
1972 *The Uruk Countryside*, Chicago.
Adams, R. McC., Parr, P., Ibrahim, M. and
al-Mughannum, A.
1977 'Saudi Arabian archaeological reconnais-
      sance 1976', *Atlal* 1: 21–40.
Adams, W. Y.
1984 'The first colonial empire: Egypt in Nubia,
      3200–1200 B.C.', *Comparative Studies in
      Society and History*, 26: 36–71.
Agrawal, D. P.
1982 *The archaeology of India*, Scandinavian
      Inst. of Asian Studies, Copenhagen. Mono-
      graph Series No. 46.
Alayne Street, F. and Grove, A. T.
1979 'Global Maps of Lake Level Fluctuations
      since 30,000 yrs B.P.', *Quaternary Research*
      12: 83–118.
Alekshin, V. A.
1983 'Burial Customs as an Archaeological
      Source' *Current Anthropology*, Vol. 24, No.
      2, 137–150.

Altheim, F. and Stiehl, R.
1964–69 *Die Araber in der Alten Welt*, I–V/2,
         Walter de Gruyter, Berlin.
al-Ansary, A. R.
1982 *Qaryat Al Fau*, U. of Riyadh, Riyadh.
al-Gailani, L.
1975 'Steatite Stone Vessels from Mesopotamia
      and Elsewhere', *Sumer* XXI, (nos. 1–2),
      41–48.
al-Hudhud
1981 *Festschrift Maria Höfner zum 80.
      Geburtstag*, hrsg. v. R. G. Stiegner, Graz.
al-Iryani, M. A.
1973 *Fi Ta'rīkh*: Fī ta'rīkh al-Yaman, Cairo.
al-Muğāwir, Ibn
1951 *Ta'rīh*: Ta'rīh al-mustabsir, ed. O. Löfgren,
      Leiden, 2 vols.
al-Sayari, Saad S. and Zötl, Josef
1978 *Quaternary Period in Saudi Arabia*,
      Springer-Verglag, Vienna and New York.
al-Takriti, A. K.
1975 'The Diraz Excavations and its Chron-
      ological Position', *Dilmun* 8.
al-Takriti, W. Y.
      Forth. – *The Cultural Evolution of the
      United Arab Emirates during the 3rd
      Millennium B.C.*, Ph.D. dissertation,
      Cambridge.
al-Wohaibi, F.
1980 *Studio storico-archeologico della costa
      occidentale del Golfo Arabico in età
      ellenistica*. Roma, 'L'Erma' di
      Bretschneider.
Amiet, P.
1974 'Antiquités du desert de Lut', *Revue*

d'Assyriologie et d'Archeologie Orientale 68, (2), 97–110.

1975   'A cylinder seal impression found at Umm an-Nar', *East and West*, 25, 425–426.

1976   'Antiquites du desert de Lut II', *Revue d'Assyriologie et d'Archeologie Orientale* 70, (1), 1–8.

Amiran, R., Beit-Arieh, I and Glass, J.

1973   'The Interrelationship Between Arad and Sites in Southern Sinai in the Early Bronze Age II', *IEJ* 23, 193–197.

Anati, E.

1955   'Rock Engravings in the Central Negev', *Archaeology* 8, 31–42.

1962   *Palestine Before the Hebrews*. New York.

1968   *Rock Art in Central Arabia*, 2 volumes, Louvain: Institut Orientaliste Université de Louvain.

Angel, L. J.

1970   'Human Skeletal Remains from Karatas', *American Journal of Archaeology*, No. 74. U.S.A.

Angel, J. L.

1971   *The People of Lerna: Analysis of a Prehistoric Aegean Population*, Washington.

Arnaud, D.

1970   *Le Proche-Orient Ancien*, Collection Etudes Superieures Bordas.

Aro, J.

1970   *Mittelbabylonische Kleidertexte der Hilprecht Sammlung, Jena*, Sitzungberichte der Sachsischen Akademie der Wissenschaften zu Leipzig, Phil-Hist. Klasse Bd. 115(2).

Arrian

1933   *History of Alexander and India*, translated by E. I. Robson. Loeb Classical Library, vol. 2, Cambridge: Harvard University Press.

Archi, A.

1980   'Notes on Eblaite Geography', *Studi Eblaiti*, II/1, 1–16.

Bahrain, Government of

1975   *Results of the 1974 Agricultural Census (1 November, 1973–31 October, 1974)*, Budaiya: Ministry of Municipalities and Agriculture.

Bahrain National Museum

1976   *A summary Book of the Bahrain National Museum*, Directorate of Antiquities and Museums, Ministry of Education, Bahrain.

Beeston, A. F. L.

1979   'Some Features of Social Structure in Saba', in *Studies in the History of Arabia*, Vol. I, Sources for the History of Arabia, Part 1, Riyadh, 115–123.

1978   'Temporary Marriage in Pre-Islamic South Arabia', in *Arabian Studies*, 4, 21–25.

1983   *Women in Saba*: in R. Bidwell and G. R. Smith (eds.), *Arabian and Islamic Studies, Articles presented to R. B. Serjeant*, London/New York, 7–13.

Beit-Arieh, I.

1974   'An Early Bronze Age II Site at Nabi Salah in Southern Sinai', *Tel Aviv* 1, 144–156.

1981   'A Pattern of Settlement in Southern Sinai and Southern Canaan in the Third Millennium B.C.', *Bulletin of the American School of Oriental Research* 243, 31–55.

1983   'Central-Southern Sinai in the Early Bronze Age II and its Relationship with Palestine', *Levant* 15, 39–48.

Bent, J. T.

1890   'The Bahrain Islands in the Persian Gulf', *Proceedings of the Royal Geographical Society* 12: 1–19.

1900   *Southern Arabia*, London.

Berthoud, Th.

1979   *Etude par l'analyse de traces et la modélisation de la filiation entre minerais de cuivre et objets archéologiques du Moyen Orient aux IV et III° millénaires*, Thèse pour le Doctorat d'Etat, Université de Paris VI, Paris.

Betts, A.

1982   'Prehistoric Sites at Qa'a Mejalla, Eastern Jordan', *Levant* 14, 1–34.

1983   'Black Desert Survey, Jordan: First Preliminary Report', *Levant* 15, 1–10.

Bibby, T. G.

1954   'Fem af Bahrains hundrede tusinde gravhøje', *Kuml*: 116–41.

1957   'Bahrains oldtidhovedstad gennem 4000 år', *Kuml*: 128–63.

1958   'The "Ancient Indian Style" Seals from Bahrain', *Antiquity* 32, 243–244.

1958   'Bahrains oldtidshovedstad gennem 4000 år (the hundred meter section)', *Kuml*, 1957, 128–163.

1965 'Arabiens arkaeologi (Arabian Gulf archaeology)', *Kuml*, 1964, 86–111.

1966 'Arabiens arkaeologi (Arabian Gulf archaeology)', *Kuml*, 1965, 133–152.

1967 'Arabiens arkaeologi (Arabian Gulf archaeology)', *Kuml*, 1966, 75–121.

1969 *Looking for Dilmun*. New York: Alfred A.
Knopf.

1970 *Looking for Dilmun*, London.

1970b '... According to the Standard of Dilmun',
Kuml, 1970, 345–53.

1973 *Preliminary Survey in East Arabia 1968*,
Jutland Archaeological Society Publication
12, Copenhagen.

Binford, L.
1971 'Mortuary Practices: Their Study and Their
Potential', in J. A. Brown (ed.) *Approaches
to the Social Dimensions of Mortuary
Practices*, Society of American Archaeology Memoir, vol. 25.

Biscione, R.
1977 'The crisis in Central Asian urbanization in
II millennium B.C. and villages as an
alternative system', in *Le Plateau iranien
des origines à la conquête islamique*,
Colloques Internationaux du CNRS no. 67,
Paris.

Blalock, H. M.
1972 *Social Statistics*, second edition, New York.

Boehmer, R.
1972 'Die Keramikfunde im Bereich des Steinge-
bäudes', *Vorläufiger Bericht über die ...
Ausgrabungen in Uruk-Warka*, 26/27, 31–42.

Boucharlat, R. and Labrousse, A.
1979 'Le palais d'Artaxerzès II sur la rive droite
de Chaour à Suse', *Cahiers de la DAFI*, 10,
21–136.

Boucharlat, R. and Salles, J.-F.
1981 'The History and Archaeology of the Gulf
from the 5th Cent. B.C. to the 7th Cent. A.D.:
A Review of the Evidence', *Proceedings of
the Seminar for Asian Studies*, 11: 65–94.

Bowen, R. Le B.
1950 'The Early Arabian Necropolis of Ain
Jawan', *Bulletin of the American School of
Oriental Research*, Supplementary Studies
Nos. 7–9.

Braudel, F.
1982 *The Wheels of Commerce: Civilization and
Capitalism 15th–18th Century*, vol. 2, New
York.

Branigan, K.
1981 'Minoan colonialism', *Annual of the British
School in Athens*, 76, 23–34.

Brinkman, J. A.
1968 *A Political History of Post-Kassite Babylonia, 1158–722 B.C.*, Analecta Orientalia
43, Rome.

1972 'Foreign relations of Babylonia from 1600
to 625 B.C.: the documentary evidence',
American Journal of Archaeology, 76,
271–281.

1974 'The monarchy of the Kassite dynasty', in P.
Garelli (ed.) *Le Palais et la Royauté*,
Librairie Orientaliste de Paul Geuther,
Paris.

1976 *Materials and Studies for Kassite History*,
v. 1. University of Chicago Press, Chicago.

1983 'Istanbul A. 1998, Middle Babylonian
chronology, and the statistics of the Nippur
archives', *Zeitschrift für Assyriologie*, 73,
67–74.

Browning, I.
1979 *Palmyra*, London.

Brunsden, D., Doornkamp, J. C. and Jones, D. K. C.
1979 Natural Resources Survey of Bahrain, *Geographical Journal*.

Brunswig, R. H. Jr. and Parpola, A.
n.d. 'New Indus Type and Related Seals from
The Near East', unpublished ms.

Buccellati, G.
1966 *The Amorites of the Ur III Period*, Naples:
Studi Semitici.

Buchanan, B.
1965 'A Dated "Persian Gulf" Seal and its Implications', *Studies in Honor of Benno Landsberger on his Seventy-Fifth Birthday April
21, 1965*, AS 16. Chicago: The University of
Chicago Press, 204–209.

1967 'A Dated Seal Impression Connecting Babylonia and Ancient India', *Archaeology* 20,
104–107.

Bulliet, R. W.
1975 *The Camel and the Wheel*, Harvard University Press.

Burrows, E.
1928 *Tilmun, Bahrain, Paradise*, Rome: Scriptura
sacra et monumenta orientis antiqui,

pontifici instituti biblici, Rome

Butz, K.
1983   'Dilmun in altbabylonischen Quellen', in D.
        T. Potts (editor), *Dilmun New Studies in the
        Archaeology and Early History of Bahrain*,
        143–5, Berlin.

Butzer, K. W.
1959   'Environment and Human Ecology in Egypt
        during Predynastic and Early Dynastic
        Times', *Bulletin de la Société de Geo-
        graphie d'Égypte* 32, 43–87.
1971   *Environment and Archaeology: An Eco-
        logical Approach to Prehistory*, Chicago:
        Aldine Press.
1976   *Early Hydraulic Civilization in Egypt: A
        Study in Cultural Ecology*, The University
        of Chicago Press.

**Butzer, K. W., Isaac, G. L., Richardson, J. L. and
Washbourn-Kamau, C.**
1972   'Radiocarbon Dating of East African Lake
        Levels', *Science* 175, 1069–1075.

Burkholder, G.
1971   'Steatite Carvings from Saudi Arabia',
        Artibus Asiae 33, 306–322.

Burkholder, G. and Golding, M.
1971   'Surface Survey of Al Ubaid Sites in the
        Eastern Province of Saudi Arabia', in H.
        Field, ed., *Contributions to the Anthrop-
        ology of Saudi Arabia*, Field Research
        Projects, 50–55.

Butz, K.
1979   'Ur in Altbabylonischer Zeit als Wirt-
        schaftsfaktor', *Oriens Antiquus*, 5, 257–409.

Carbonell, V. M.
1958   The dentition of the Kish population 3000
        B.C. Thesis. University of Chicago.

Cardi, B. de
1968   'Excavations at Bampur, southeast Iran: a
        Brief Report', *Iran* 6, 135–55.
1970   'Excavations at Bampur, A Third Millen-
        nium Settlement in Persian Baluchistan,
        1966', *Anthropological Papers of the
        American Museum of Natural History*, vol.
        51 part 3, 233–355, New York.
1972   'A Sasanian Outpost in Northern Oman',
        Antiquity, 184, 305–310.
1974   'The British Archaeological Expedition to
        Qatar, 1973–74', *Antiquity* 47, 196–200.
1983   'Ubaid Mesopotamia Reconsidered', in the

Braidwood Festschrift, Chicago.

Cardi, B. de (Ed.)
1978   *Qatar Archaeological Report. Excavations
        1973*, Oxford.

Cardi, B. de, Colliers, S. and Doe, B.
1976   'Excavations and Surveys in Oman', *The
        Journal of Oman Studies*, vol. 2. Ministry of
        Information; Sultanate of Oman.

Cardi, B. de, Doe, D. B. and Roskams, S. P.
1977   'Excavation and Survey in the Sharqiyah,
        Oman, 1976', *Journal of Oman Studies*, vol.
        3 part 1, 17–34.

Carter, E.
1971   *Elam in the Second Millennium B.C.: the
        Archaeological Evidence*, Ph.D. disserta-
        tion, University of Chicago.

Carter, E. and Stolper, M.
1976   'Middle Elamite Malyan', *Expedition* 18(2),
        33–42.

Caskel, W.
1959   Review of W. M. Watt's *Muhammad at
        Madina*, in: *Deutsche Literatur Zeitung*, 80,
        col. 1066–1072.
1966   *Ǧamhara: Ǧamharat an-nasab*, Leiden, 2
        vols.

Chang, K-C.
1971   *The Archaeology of Ancient China*, Yale
        University Press, New Haven.

Chelhod, J.
1981   'Du nouveau à propos du "matriarcat"
        arabe', in *Arabica*, 28, 76–106.

Chisholm, M. D. I.
1962   *Rural Settlement and Land Use: An Essay in
        Location*, London: Hutchinson University
        Library.

Civil, M.
1961   'The Home of the Fish', *Iraq* 23, 154–175.

Clarke, D. L.
1968   *Analytical Archaeology*, London.

Cleuziou, S.
1977   *Archaeology in the United Arab
        Emirates*, Department of Tourism,
        al Aīn.
1978/79 'The Second and Third Seasons of
        Excavations at Hili 8', *Archaeology in the
        United Arab Emirates* II/III, Department of
        Antiquities and Tourism, al Aīn, 30–69.
1981   'Oman Peninsula in the Early Second
        Millennium B.C.', in H. Hartel (Ed.), *South*

Asian Archaeology V, Berlin 1979, D. Riemer, Berlin, 279–93.

1982   'Hili and the Beginning of Oasis Life in Eastern Arabia', *Proceedings of the Seminar for Arabian Studies* 13, 15–22.

Forth. a – 'Oman Peninsula and its Relations East- wards during the 3rd Millennium B.C.', in Lal, B. B. and Gupta, S. P. (Eds.): *A Sir Mortimer Wheeler Memorial Volume,* New Delhi.

Forth. b – 'The Fourth to Seventh Seasons of Excavations at Hili 8', *Archaeology in the United Arab Emirates,* Department of Antiquities, al Aīn.

Cleuziou, S. and Costantini, L.

1980   'Premiers éléments sur l'agriculture proto- historique de l'Arabie orientale', *Paleorient* 6, 245–51.

1982   'A l'origine des oasis', *La Recherche* no. 137, 1180–82.

Cleuziou, S., Lombard, P. and Salles, J. F.

1981   *Fouilles a Umm Jidr (Bahrain),* Recherch sur les grandes civilisations, Memoire 7. Paris: Editions A.D.P.F.

Cleuziou, S. and Vogt, B.

1983   'Umm an-Nar Burial Customs, New Evidence from Tomb A at Hili North', *Pro- ceedings of the Seminar for Arabian Studies* 13, 37–52.

Clutton-Brock, J.

1978   'Early Domestication and the Ungulate Fauna of the Levant during the Prepottery Neolithic Period', in *The Environmental History of the Near and Middle East Since the Last Ice Age,* W. C. Brice ed. new York, 29–40.

Cohen, R. and Dever, W. G.

1978   'Preliminary Report on the Pilot Season of the "Central Negev Highlands Project"', *Bulletin of the American School of Oriental Research,* 232, 29–45.

1979   'Preliminary Report of the Second Season of the "Central Negev Highlands Project"', *Bulletin of the American School of Oriental Research,* 236, 41–60.

1980   'Be'er Resisim, 1980', *Israel Exploration Journal,* 30, 228–231.

1981   'Preliminary Report of the Third and Final Season of the "Central Negev Highlands

Project"', *Bulletin of the American School of Oriental Research,* 243, 57–77.

Cornwall, P. B.

1943a   'Dilmun: The History of Bahrain Island
=1944   Before Cyrus' Ph.D. dissertation, History Department, Harvard University.

1943b   'The Tumuli of Bahrain', *Asia and the Americas,* vol. XLIII, 4, 230–44.

1946a   'On the Location of Dilmun', *Bull. of the American Schools of Oriental Research,* No. 103: 3–11.

1946b   'Ancient Arabia: Explorations in Hasa, 1940–41', *Geographical Journal,* 107, 28–50.

Cornwall, P. B. and Goetze, A.

1952   'Two letters from Dilmun', *Journal of Cuneiform Studies,* 6, 137–145.

Costantini, L.

1981   'Palaeoethnobotany at Pirak: A Contribu- tion to 2nd Millennium B.C. Agriculture of the Sibi-Kaachi Plain, Pakistan', 271–277 in *South Asian Archaeology 1979,* ed. by H. Hartel, Berlin.

Courtney-Thompson, F. C. W.

1975   'Rock Engravings near Madinah, Saudi Arabia', *PSAS* 5, 22–32.

Crawford, H. E. W.

1973   'Mesopotamia's invisible exports to the third millennium B.C.', *World Archaeology,* 5.2, 232–241.

1978   'The mechanics of the obsidian trade: a suggestion', *Antiquity* 52, 129–132.

Currelly, C. T.

1906   'Gebel Musa and the Nawamis', in *Researches in Sinai,* H. F. Petrie, New York, Chapters 15–18.

Delougaz, P.

1960   'Architectural Representations on Steatite Vases', *Iraq* 22, 90–95.

Dept. of Antiquities and Museums

1975   *An Introduction to Saudi Arabian Anti- quities,* Riyadh.

Dever, W. G.

1971   'The Peoples of Palestine in the Middle Bronze I Period', *Harvard Theological Review,* 64, 197–226.

Diester-Haas, L.

1973   'Holocene Climate in the Persian Gulf as Deduced from Grain Size and Pteropod

Distribution', *Marine Geology*, 14, 207–233.

Doornkamp, J. C., Brunsden, D. and Jones, D. K. C., eds.

1980   *Geology, Geomorphology and Pedology of Bahrain*, Norwich: Geo Abstracts.

Dossin, G.

1950   *Correspondance de Šamši-Addu et de ses Fils, Archives Royales de Mari*, Paris, vol. I.

1952   *Correspondance de Iasmah-Addu*, ibid., V.

1970   'La Route d'Etain en Mésopotamie au Temps de Zimri-Lim', *Révue d'Assyrologie*, 64, 97–106.

1971   'Documents de Mari', *Syria*, 48, 1–15.

Dostal, W.

1959   'The Evolution of Beduin Life', in *L'Antica Societa Beduina*, Rome: Studi Semitici, 1–34.

1977   *Die Beduinen: Die Beduinen in Südarabien* (Wiener Beiträge zur Kulturgeschichte und Linguistik, Veröffentlichungen des Instituts für Völkerkunde der Universität Wien, Bd. 16), Horn-Wien.

Dubertret, L. and Dunand, M.

1954–5   'Les gisements ossiferes de Khirbet El-Umbachi et de Hebariye (Safa)', *AAAS* 4–5, 59–76.

Durand, E. L.

1879   *Notes on the Islands of Bahrain and Antiquities: A Report Sent 1st May 1879 by the Political Resident, Buschire to the Foreign Department of India.*

1880   'Extracts from *Report* on the Islands and Antiquities of Bahrain', *Journal of the Royal Asian Society*, N.S. vol. 12, 189–201.

During Caspers, E. C. L.

1971a   'New Archaeological Evidence for Maritime Trade in the Persian Gulf During the Late Protoliterate Period', *East and West* 21, 21–55.

1971b   'The Bull's Head from Barbar Temple II, Bahrain: A Contact with Early Dynastic Sumer', *East and West*, new series 21 (3–4), 217–224.

1972a   'Etched Cornelian Beads', *Bulletin of the Institute of Archaeology*, vol. 10, 83–98.

1972b   'Harappan Trade in the Arabian Gulf in the Third Millennium B.C.', *Mesopotamia* 7, 167–91.

1973   'Sumer and Kulli Meet at Dilmun in the Arabian Gulf', *Archib fur Orientforschung* XXIV, 128–132.

1979   'Sumer, Coastal Arabia and the Indus Valley in Protoliterate and Early Dynastic Eras', *Journal of the Economic and Social History of the Orient* XXII (part II), 121–135.

1980   The Bahrain Tumuli, An Illustrated Catalogue of Two Important Collections, Nederlands Historisch-Archaeologisch Instituutte Istanbul XLVII.

1982   Review of Hartel, H. (Ed.) 'South Asian Archaeology 1979', *Bibliotheca Orientalis* XXXIX no. 3/4, 432–56.

1984   'Dilmun: International Burial Ground', *Journal of the Economic and Social History of the Orient*, vol. XXVII, part 1.

Edens, C.

1981   'Protohistory: excavations on Khor Ile', *Rapport d'Activité RCP 476*, 1981, 11–26.

1982   'Protohistory: excavations on Khor Ile', *Rapport d'Activité RCP 476*, 1982, 17–26.

n.d.   'Consumption and exchange: a history of the Gulf trade *c*. 3000–1500 B.C.' in preparation.

Edmunds, W. M. and Walton, N. R. G.

1980   'A Geochemical and Isotopic Approach to Recharge Evaluation in Semi-arid Zones, Past and Present', in *Arid-Zone Hydrology, Invesitgations with Isotope Techniques*, Vienna: International Atomic Energy Agency, 47–68.

Edzard, D. O.

1960   'Die Beziehungen Babyloniens und Ägyptens in der mittelbabylonischen Zeit und das Gold', *Journal of Economic and Social History of the Orient*, 3, 38–55.

Eigland, T.

1970   'The Twice Used Water', *Aramco World* Nov.–Dec., 22–29.

Evans, G., Kendall, V., Bush, P. and Nelson, H.

1969   'Stratigraphy and geologic history of the Sabkha, Abu Dhabi, Persian Gulf', *Sedimentology*, 12, 145–159.

Facey, W. H. D. and Martin, E. B.

1979   *Oman, a seafaring nation*. Government of Oman, Muscat.

Fairservis, W.

1967   'The origin, character and decline of an early civilization', *Novitates* no. 2302, 1–48.

Ferrara, A.
1977 'A Kassite cylinder seal from the Arabian Gulf', *Bulletin of the American Schools of Oriental Research*, 225, 69.

Field, H.
1960 *North Arabian Desert Archaeological Survey, 1925–50*, Cambridge: The Peabody Museum. Vol. 45.

Filov, B. D.
1934 *Die Grabhugelnekropolis bei Duvanlij in Sudbulgarien*, Sofia Staatsdruckerei, Bulgaria.

Finley, M. I.
1976 'Colonies – an attempt at a typology', *Transactions of the Royal Historical Society*, series 5, v. 26, 167–188.

Forrer, E.
1921 *Die Provinzeinteilung des assyrischen Reiches*, Leipzig.

Franke, J.
1978 'Area WB' in M. Gibson (ed.) *Excavations at Nippur, Twelfth Season*, Oriental Institute Communications 23, University of Chicago Press, Chicago.

Frankfort, H.
1935 *Oriental Institute Discoveries in Iraq, 1933/34: Fourth Preliminary Report of the Iraq Expedition* (Oriental Institute Communications, no. 19), University of Chicago Press, Chicago.

Frifelt, K.
1969 'Arkaeologiske undersogelser pa Oman palvoen', *Kuml*, 1968, 159–175.
1970 'Jemdet Nasr Graves in Oman' *Kuml* 1970, 355–83.
1975a 'On Prehistoric Settlement and Chronology of the Oman Peninsula', *East and West*, 25, 359–424.
1975b 'A Possible Link Between the Jemdet Nasr and the Umm an-Nar Graves of Oman', *Journal of Oman Studies* 1, 57–80.
1976 'Evidence of a Third Millennium B.C. Town in Oman', *The Journal of Oman Studies*, vol. 2, 57–74.
1979 'Oman during the 3rd millennium B.C.', in M. Taddei (ed.) *South Asian Archaeology 1977*, v. 1, Instituto Universitario Orientale, Seminario di Studi Asiatici, Series Minor VI, Naples.

Frohlich, B.
1982 'A Preliminary Report on the Human Remains from Bahrain Island, Excavated by the Arab Expedition, 1978–1979', in *Excavations of the Arab Expedition at Saar el-Jisr, Bahrain*. M. Ibrahim, editor. State of Bahrain.
1983 'The Bahrain Burial Mounds.' *Dilmun*, vol. 11.

Frohlich, B. and Ortner, D. J.
1982 'Excavations of the Early Bronze Age Cemetery at Bab edh-Dhra, Jordan, 1981, A Preliminary Report', *The Annual of the Department of Antiquities*, vol. 26.

Frohlich, B., Moghannum, A., VonEndt, D. and Chalinor, C.
n.d. 'Excavations of the Dhahran Burial Mounds, Eastern Province, Saudi Arabia, 1984', *Atlal* (in press).

Gadd, C. J.
1932 'Seals of Ancient Indian Style found at Ur', *Proceedings of the British Academy* 18.

Gabriel, B.
1978 'Klima- und Landschaftswandel der Sahara', in *Sahara 10.000 Jahre zwischen Weide und Wüste*, Koln, 22–34.

Garrard, A. N., Harvey, C. P. D. and Switsur, V. R.
1981 'Environment and Settlement during the Upper Pleistocene and Holocene at Jubba in the Great Nefud, Northern Arabia', *Atlal* 5, 137–148.

Garrod, D.
1960 'The Flint Implements, Chapter VIII', in H. Field, 1960, 111–123.

Gelb, I. J.
1961 'The Early History of the West Semitic Peoples', *Journal of Cuneiform Studies* 15, 27–47.
1968 'An Old Babylonian List of Amorites', *Journal of the American Oriental Society* 88, 39–46.
1970 'Makkan and Meluhha in Early Mesopotamian Sources', *Revue d'Assyriologie et d'archeologie oriental*, 64, 1–8.
1973 'Prisoners of War in Early Mesopotamia', *Journal of Near Eastern Studies* 32, 70–96.
1980 *Computer-Aided Analysis of Amorite*, AS 21, The University of Chicago Press.

Ghirshman, R.
  1954 'Village Perse-Achemenide', *Memoires de
        la Mission Archaeologique en Iran*, XXXVI,
        Paris.
Gibson, J. C. L.
  1961 'Observations on some Important Ethnic
        Terms in the Pentateuch', *Journal of Near
        Eastern Studies*, XX, 217–238.
Gibson, M.
  1972 *The City and Area of Kish*, Field Research
        Publications, Miami.
  1974 'Violation of fallow and engineered disaster
        in Mesopotamian civilization', in T.
        Downing and M. Gibson (eds.), *Irrigation's
        Impact on Society*, Anthropological Papers
        of the University of Arizona, n. 25, 7–20.
  1980 'Current research at Nippur: ecological,
        anthropological, and documentary inter-
        play' in *L'Archéologie de l'Iraq au début de
        l'epoque neolithique á 333 avant notre ère*,
        Colloques Internationaux du CNRS, nr. 580,
        Paris, 193–206.
Giveon, R.
  1971 *Les Bédouins Shosu des Documents
        Égyptiens*, Leiden: E. J. Brill.
Glassner, J.-J.
  in press 'Inscriptions cunéiforms de Failaka', in
        J.-F. Salles (ed.), *Fouilles françaises à
        Failaka, 1983*, Lyon.
Glob, P. V.
  1954a 'Bahrain – Island of the Hundred Thousand
        Burial Mounds', *Kuml*, 92–105.
  1954b 'The Flint Sites of the Bahrain Desert',
        Kuml, 106–114.
  1954c 'Temples at Barbar', *Kuml*, 142–153.
  1954d 'The Ancient Capital of Bahrain', *Kuml*,
        164–169.
  1955 'The Danish Archeological Bahrain–
        Expedition's Second Excavation Cam-
        paign', *Kuml*, 178–193.
  1956 'A Neo-Babylonian Burial from Bahrain's
        Prehistoric Capital', *Kuml*, 164–174.
  1957 'Snake Sacrifices in Bahrain's Ancient
        Capital', *Kuml*, 114–127.
  1958 'Alabaster Vases from the Bahrain
        Temples', *Kuml*, 138–145.
  1959 'Archeological Investigations in Four Arab
        States', *Kuml*, 233–239.
  1960 'Danish Archeologists in the Persian Gulf',
        Kuml, 208–213.

  1968 *Al-Bahrain*, Copenhagen.
  1971 *Denmark, An Archaeological History from
        the Stone Age to the Vikings*, Cornell
        University Press.
Glueck, N.
  1955 *Rivers in the Desert: A History of the Negev*,
        London.
Goellner, W. A.
  n.d. *The Exposure Pits of the Dead of Jebal
        Qurain*, HBH co, Jubail.
Goetze, A.
  1952 'The Texts Ni 615 and Ni 641, Istanbul
        Museum', *Journal of Cuneiform Studies*, 6,
        142–145.
  1965 'An inscription of Simbar-Šihu', *Journal of
        Cuneiform Studies*, 19, 121–135.
Golding, M.
  1974 'Evidence for pre-Seleucid occupation of
        Eastern Arabia', *Proceedings of the
        Seminar for Arabian Studies* 4, 19–32.
Goldstein, L.
  1976 Spatial Structure and Social Organization:
        Regional Manifestations of Mississippian
        Society, Ph.D. thesis, Northwestern Univer-
        sity, Evanston.
Government of Kuwait
  n.d. *Archaeological Investigations in the Island
        of Failaka 1958–1964*. Kuwait: Kuwait
        Government Press, Ministry of Guidance
        and Information.
Grayson, A. K.
  1972 *Assyrian Royal Inscriptions I*, Harrassowitz,
        Wiesbaden.
Greenberg, M.
  1955 *The Hab/piru*, New Haven: The American
        Oriental Society.
Griffin, J. B.
  1967 'Eastern American Archaeology: A
        Summary', *Science*. Vol. 156. American
        Association for the Advancement of
        Science.
Groneberg, B.
  1980 *Die Orts- und Gewässernamen der altbaby-
        lonischen Zeit, Repertoire Géographiques
        des Textes Cunéiform*, 3.
Grotewold, A.
  1959 'Von Thunen in Retrospect', *Economic
        Geography* 35, 346–55.

Gupta, S. R.
1982 'The Late Harappan: a study in cultural dynamics', in G. Possehl (ed.), *Harappan Civilization*, Oxford and IBH Publishing Co., New Delhi, 51–60.

Haekel, J.
Zum Problem: 'Zum Problem des Mutterrechtes', in *Paideuma*, 1950–1954, Part 1, fasc. 6, 298–319; Part 2, fasc. 7/9, 481–508.

Haerinck, E.
1975 'Quelques Monuments funéraires de l'île de Kharg dans le Golfe Persique', *Iranica Antiqua*, XI, 134–167.

Haggett, P.
1965 *Locational Analysis in Human Geography*,
=1966 New York.

Haggett, P., Cliff, A. D. and Frey, A.
1977 *Locational Models*, New York.

Hakemi, A.
1972 *Catalogue de l'exposition: Lut*, Premier Symposium Annuel de la Recherche Archeologique en Iran. Teherean.

Hallo, W. W.
1964 'The Road to Emar', *Journal of Cuneiform Studies*, 18, 57–88.
1965 'A Mercantile Agreement from the Reign of Gungunum of Larsa', *Studies in Honor of Benno Landsberger* . . ., 199–203.

Hallo, W. W. and Buchanan, B.
'A "Persian Gulf" Seal on an Old Babylonian Mercantile Agreement', *Assyrological Studies* 16, 216–230.

Hanihara, K. and Sakaguchi, Y.
1978 *Paleolithic Site of the Doura Cave and Paleogeography of Palmyra Basin in Syria*, Part I. University of Tokyo Press.

Hannestad, L.
1983 *The Hellenistic Pottery from Failaka. Ikaros, the Hellenistic Settlement*, vol. 2. Jutland Archaeological Society Publications, XVI, 2.

Hansman, J.
1973 'A Periplus of Magan and Meluhha', *Bulletin of the School of Oriental and African Studies* 36, 554–587.

Hassan, F. A.
1981 *Demographic Archaeology*, New York.

Hastings, A., Humphries, J. H. and Meadow, R. H.
1975 'Oman in the Third Millennium B.C.', *Journal of Oman Studies* 1, 9–55.

Haynes, C. V.
1980 'Geochronology of Wadi Tushka: Lost Tributary of the Nile', *Science* 210, 68–71.

Hawkes, J.
1974 *Atlas of Ancient Archaeology*, New York.

Helms, S. W.
1975 'Jawa Excavations 1973: A Preliminary Report', *Levant* 7, 20–38.
1976 'Jawa Excavations 1974: A Preliminary Report', *Levant* 8, 1–35.
1981 *Jawa: Lost City of the Black Desert*, Ithaca, New York.
1982 'Paleo-Beduin and Transmigrant Urbanism' in *Studies in the History and Archaeology of Jordan I*, ed. A. Hadidi, Amman: Department of Antiquities, 97–113.

Heltzer, M.
1981 *The Suteans*, Istituto Universitario Orientale, Seminario di Studi Asiatici, Series Minor XIII, Naples.

Henninger, J.
1943 Die Familie bei den heutigen Beduinen Arabiens und seiner Randgebiete (Internationales Archiv für Ethnographie, Bd. 42), Leiden.
1954 'Polyandrie im vorislamischen Arabien', in *Anthropos*, 49, 314–322.
1959 'La société bédouine ancienne', in L'antica società beduina, Studi (. . .) raccolti di F. Gabrieli (*Studi Semitici*, 2), Roma, 69–93.
1966 *Altarabische Genealogie*: Review of W. Caskel's *Ǧamhara*, in *Anthropos*, 61, 852–870.
1983 *Neuere Forschungen*: Neuere Forschungen zum Problem der Polyandrie in Arabien', in Meqor Hajjim, *Festschrift für Georg Molin zum 75. Geburtstag*, Graz, 127–153.

Henry, D. O., Hassan, F. A. and Cooper Henry, K.
1981 'An Investigation of the Prehistory and Paleoenvironments of Southern Jordan (1979 Field Season)'. *Annual of the Department of Antiquities of Jordan*, 25, 113–146.
1983 'An Investigation of the Prehistory of Southern Jordan', *Palestine Exploration Quarterly*, 115–124.

Herz, A.
1965 *A Study of Steatite Vases of the Early Dynastic Period in Mesopotamia*, unpublished M.A. thesis, Institute of Fine Arts,

New York University.

Herzfeld, E.
1968   'Tilmun, the Bahrain Islands in the Sargon
        Itinerary', in G. Walser, ed., *The Persian
        Empire*, Steiner, Wiesbaden, 62.

Hoch, E.
1979   'Reflections on Prehistoric Life at Umm an-
        Nar (Trucial Oman) Based on Faunal
        Remains from the Third Millennium B.C.', in
        South Asian Archaeology, 1977. Naples:
        Instituto Universitario Orientale, Series
        Minor VI, 589–635.

Hodder, I.
1982   *Symbols in Action*, Cambridge University
        Press.

Højgaard, K.
1980   'Dilmun-tidens tænder', *Tandlægebladet*,
        84, 548, 1980.
1981   'Det søde liv på Bahrain, *Sfinx*, 4, 136–138.
1982   'Dental Extractions on Bahrain 2000 B.C.',
        *Proceedings of the Seminar for Arabian
        Studies*, 12, 28 (Summary).
1983a   'Dentitions from Janussan (Bahrain)', in,
        Lombard, P. & Salles, J.-F., La Nécropole de
        Janussan (Bahrain). Maison de l'Orient,
        Lyon.
1983b   'Dilmun's Ancient Teeth', *Dilmun*, 11.
1984   'Dental anthropology in relation to the
        North-West coast of the Indian sub-
        continent in the third millennium B.C.',
        South Asian Archaeology, 202–204.

Højlund, F.
1981   'Preliminary remarks on the dating of the
        palace at Sa'd wa-Sa'ad on Failaka
        (Kuwait)', *Proceedings of the Seminar for
        Arabian Studies*, 11, 37–42.
1983   The 2nd millennium settlements on Failaka
        (Kuwait), ms.

Hötzl, H. and Zötl, J. G.
1978   '3.2 Climatic Changes during the Quarter-
        nary Period', in *Quaternary Period in Saudi
        Arabia*, Vienna, 301–306.

Holland, F. W.
1870   *Sinai and Jerusalem: Scenes from Bible
        Lands*, London.

Horowitz, A.
1980   *The Quaternary of Israel*, New York.

Howard-Carter, T.
1981   'The tangible evidence for the
        earliest Dilmun', *Journal of
        Cuneiform Studies* 33, 3–4,
        210–223.

Howell, N.
1979   *Demography of the Dobe, Kung*, New York.

Huber, P. J.
1982   Astronomical dating of Babylon I and Ur III.
        Occasional Papers on the Near East I, issue
        4, Malibu.

Huckreide, R. and Wiesemann, G.
1968   'Der Jungpleistozäne Pluvial-See
        von El Jafr und Weitere Daten zum
        Quartär Jordaniens', *Geologica
        Palaeontologica* 2, 73–95.

Huffmon, H. B.
1965   *Amorite Personal Names in the Mari Texts:
        A Structural and Lexical Study*, Baltimore.

Hulin, P.
1963   'The inscriptions on the carved throne-
        base of Shalmaneser III', *Iraq*, 25: 48–69.

Hunt, L. A.
1976   'Rock Carvings', in S. W. Helms 1976,
        24–29.

Huot, J.-L.
1978   'Larsa: Rapport préliminaire VIIe campagne
        et la première campagne à Tell el 'Oueili
        (1976)', *Syria* LV, 183–223.

Ibrahim, M.
1982   *Excavations of the Arab Expedition at Sar
        el-Jisr, 1978–1979, Bahrain*, Manama:
        Ministry of Information.

Inizan, M.-L.
1980a   'Site à potérie obeidienne á Qatar', in
        Barrelet, M.-T., ed., *L'Archéologie de l'Iraq*,
        209–21. CNRS, Paris.
1980b   'Premiers resultats des fouilles pré-
        historiques de la region de Khor', 51–59, in
        Mission archéologique française à Qatar I
        (Ed. J. Tixier).

Ingraham, M., Johnson, T., Rihani, B. and Shatla, I.
1981   'Preliminary Report on a Reconnaissance
        Survey of the Northwestern Province (with
        a note on a brief survey of the Northern
        Province)', *Atlal* 5, 59–84.

Italconsult
1971   *Water and Agricultural Studies in Bahrain:
        A Report Prepared for the Kingdom of
        Saudi Arabia and the Government of
        Bahrain*, Rome: Italconsult.

Jacobs, L.
1980   *Darvazeh Tepe and the Iranian Highlands in the Second Millennium B.C.* Ph.D. dissertation, University of Oregon.

Jacobsen, T.
1953   'The Reign of Ibbi-Suen', *Journal of the Cuneiform Society* 7, 36–47.
1970   *Toward the Image of Tammuz and Other Essays on Mesopotamian History and Culture*, Harvard University Press.
1976   *The Treasures of Darkness*, Yale University Press.

James, W. E.
1969   'On the Location of Gerrha', in Altheim and Stiehl V/2, 36–57.

Jamme, A.
1962   *Sabaean Inscriptions: Sabaean Inscriptions from Mahram Bilqîs (Mârib)*, Baltimore.

Jarrige, J.-F. and Meadow, R. H.
1980   'The Antecedents of Civilization in the Indus Valley', *Scientific American* 243 (2), 122–133.

Jouannin, A.
1905   'Les Tumuli de Bahrain', *Recherches Archeologiques Ministere de L'instruction Publique et des Beaux Arts*, Mémoires de la Delegation en Perse. Vol. VIII. ed., Ernest Leroux, Paris. 149–57.

Kapel, H.
1967   'Atlas of the Stone-Age Cultures of Qatar' *Reports of the Danish Archaeological Expedition to the Arabian Gulf*, 1, Jutland Archaeological Society Publications, 6.

Kassler, P.
1973   'The structural and geomorphic evolution of the Persian Gulf', in Purser, B. H. (ed.), *The Persian Gulf*, Springer Verlag, Berlin, 11–32.

Keall, E.
1977   'Political, Economic and Social Factors on the Parthian Landscape of Mesopotamia and Western Iran: Evidence from Two Case Studies', in L. D. Levine and T. C. Young (eds.) *Mountains and Lowlands: Essays in the Archaeology of Greater Mesopotamia*, Bibliotheca Mesopotamica 7. Malibu, 81–89.

Kemp, B.
1978   'Imperialism and empire in New Kingdom Egypt (*c.* 1575–1087 B.C.)', in P. Garnsey and C. Whittaker (eds.), *Imperialism in the Ancient World*, 7–57, Cambridge University Press.

Kervran, M., Negre, A. and Pirazzoli T'Sertsevens, M.
1982   *Fouilles a Qal'at al-Bahrain, 1977–1979*, Manama: Ministry of Information.

Kervran, M.
1983   'Deux forteresses islamiques de la côte orientale de l'Arabie', *Proceedings of the Seminar for Arabian Studies*, 13, 1–77.

Kessler, K.
1983   'Zu den keilschriftlichen Quellen des 2./1. Jahrtausends v. Chr. über Dilmun', *Berliner Beiträge zum Vorderen Orient*, 2, 147–160.

Kinsman, D. J.
1968   'AAPG Sponsored Research Project: Early Diagenesis of Carbonate Sediments in a Supratidal Evaporite Setting', *American Petrological Institute, Research Project No. 99.*

Kjaerum, P.
1980   'Seals of 'Dilmun-type' from Failaka, Kuwait', *Proceedings of the Seminar for Arabian Studies*, 10, 45–54.
1983   *Failaka/Dilmun, the Second Millennium Settlements v. 1(1): the Stamp and Cylinder Seals*, Jutland Archaeological Society Publications, no. 17, 1.

Klein, J., Lerman, J., Damon, P. and Ralph, E.
1982   'Calibration of radiocarbon dates', *Radiocarbon*, 24, 103–150.

Klengel, E. and Klengel, H.
1980   'Zum Fragment eines Steatitgefasses mit einer Inschrift des Rimus von Akkad', *Rocznik Orientalistyczny* XLI (2), 45–51.

Krader, L.
1981   'The Ecology of Nomadic Pastoralism', in *Change and Development in Nomadic and Pastoral Society*, J. G. Galaty and P. Salzman (eds.) Leiden: E. J. Brill, 499–510.

Kramer, S. N.
1944   *Sumerian Mythology*, New York.
1963   *The Sumerians*, University of Chicago.
1963   'Dilmun: Quest for Paradise', *Antiquity*, vol. 37, 111–115.

König, F. W.
1965   *Die Elamitischen Königsinschriften*, Archiv für Orientforschung Beiheft 16.

Kohl, P. L.
1974   *Seeds of Upheaval: The Production of
        Chlorite at Tepe Yahya and an Analysis of
        Commodity Production and Trade in
        Southwest Asia in the Mid-Third Millen-
        nium.* Ph.D. dissertation, Department of
        Anthropology, Harvard University, avail-
        able on University Microfilms, Ann Arbor,
        Michigan.
1975   'Carved Chlorite Vessels, a Trade in
        Finished Commodities in the Mid-Third
        Millennium B.C.', *Expedition* vol. 18 part 1,
        18–31.
1978   'The Balance of Trade in Southwestern Asia
        in the Third Millennium B.C.', *Current
        Anthropology* 19 (3), 463–492.
1979   'The "World Economy" of West Asia in the
        Third Millennium B.C.', 55–85 in *South Asian
        Archaeology 1977*, ed. by M. Taddei,
        Instituto Universitario Orientale, Naples.
Kohl, P. L., Harbottle, G. and Sayre, E. V.
1979   'Physical and Chemical Analyses of Soft
        Stone Vessels from Southwest Asia',
        Archaeometry 21, 131–159.
Kupper, J. R.
1957   *Les nomades en Mésopotamie au Temps
        des Rois de Mari*, Paris: Les Belles Lettres
        de Université de Liege.
Kutscher, R.
1975   *Oh angry sea (a-ab-ba hu-luh-ha): The
        history of a Sumerian congregational
        lament*, Yale Near Eastern Researchs 6,
        New Haven.
Kuwait, Government of
1964   *Archaeological Investigations in the Island
        of Failaka 1958–1964*, Ministry of Guidance
        and Information, Kuwait Government
        Press.
Lamberg-Karlovsky, C. C.
1970   *Excavations at Tepe Yahya, Iran, Progress
        Report I*, American School of Prehistoric
        Research 27, Cambridge (Mass.).
1972   'Trade Mechanisms in Indus Mesopotamian
        Interrelations', *Journal of the American
        Oriental Society*, vol. 92, No. 2, 222–30.
1975   'Third Millennium Modes of Exchange and
        Modes of Production', 341–368 in *Ancient
        Civilization and Trade*, ed. by J. A. Sabloff
        and C. C. Lamberg-Karlovsky, Univ. of New

Mexico Press.
1982   'Dilmun: Gateway to Immortality', *Journal
        of Near Eastern Studies*, vol. 41, No. 1,
        45–50.
Lamberg-Karlovsky, C. C. and Tosi, M.
1973   'Shahr-i-Sokhta and Tepe Yahya: Tracks on
        the Earliest History of the Iranian Plateau',
        East and West 23, 21–53.
Lambert, M.
1976   'Tablette de Suse avec cachet du Golfe',
        Révue d'Assyriologie, 70, 71–72.
Lambert, W. G.
1957   'Ancestors, authors, and canonicity',
        Journal of Cuneiform Studies, 11, 1–14, 112.
Landberg, C. de
1897   *Arabica*, IV, Leiden.
1909   *Etudes II/2: Etudes sur les
        dialectes de l'Arabie méridionale*, II,
        Datinah, 2 partie: commentaires des textes
        prosaïques, Leiden.
Landsberger, B.
1954   'Assyrische Königsliste und "Dunkles
        Zeitalter" continued', *Journal of Cuneiform
        Studies*, 8, 47–73.
1965   *Brief des Bischofs von Esagila an König
        Asarhaddon*, Amsterdam.
Lapp, P.
1963   'Observations on the Pottery of Thaj'.
        *Bulletin of the American School of Oriental
        Research*, 172, 20–22.
LAR II
        D. D. Luckenbill, *Ancient Records of Assyri
        and Babylonia II*, Chicago, 1927.
Larsen, C. E.
1980   Holocene Land Use Variations on the
        Bahrain Islands. Ph.D. Thesis. University of
        Chicago.
1983   *Life and Land use on the Bahrain Islands:
        the Geoarcheology of an Ancient Society*,
        University of Chicago Press.
Leemans, W. F.
1960   *Foreign Trade in the Old Babylonian
        Period*, Studia et Documenta ad Iura
        Orientis Antiqi Pertinentia VI, Leiden.
1968   'Old Babylonian letters and economic
        history', *Journal of Economic and Social
        History of the Orient*, 11, 171–226.
Lees, S. and Bates, D. G.
1974   'The Origins of Specialized Nomadic

Pastoralism: A Systematic Model',
American Antiquity 39, 187–193.

Lernau, H.
1978 'Faunal Remains, Strata III-I', in R. Amiran,
*Early Arad: The Chalcolithic and Early
Bronze Age City*, Vol. I. Jerusalem: The
Israel Exploration Society.

Lieberman, S. J.
1969 'An Ur III Text from Drehem Recording
"Booty from the Land of Mardu"', *Journal
of Cuneiform Studies*, 22, 53–62.

Littauer, M. A. and Crouwel, J. A.
1979 *Wheeled Vehicles and Ridden Animals in
the Ancient Near East*, Leiden: E. J. Brill.

Liverani, M.
1973 'The Amorites', in *Peoples of Old Testament Times*, D. J. Wiseman ed. Oxford,
100–133.

Lloyd, J. W.
1980 'Aspects of Environmental Isotope
Chemistry in Groundwaters in Eastern
Jordan', in *Arid-Zone Hydrology: Investigations with Isotope Techniques*, Vienna:
International Atomic Energy Agency,
193–204.

Lloyd, S. and Safar, F.
1948 'Eridu', *Sumer* 4, 115–27.

Lösch, A.
1940 *Die raümliche Ordnung der Wirtschaft*,
Jena: G. Fischer.

Lombard, P.
1981 'Poignards en bronze de la peninsule
d'Oman au lièr millenaire', *Iranica Antiqua*,
16, 87–93.

Lombard, P. and Salles, J.-F.
1984 *La nécropole de Janussan (Bahrain)*, Lyon,
Travaux de la Maison de l'Orient, 6.

Lowe, T.
1982 A Burial Mound at Buri. *Bahrain National
Museum*, Ministry of Information, State of
Bahrain (manuscript).

Lukacs, J. R.
1977 Anthropological Aspects of Dental Variation in North India: A Morphometric
Analysis. Ph.D. Thesis. Cornell Univ.,
Ithaca, New York.
1978 'Bio-cultural interaction in prehistoric
India. Culture, ecology and the pattern of
dental disease in Neolithic-Chalcolithic

populations', in, Vatuk, S., *American
Studies in the Anthropology of India*, New
Delhi.
1981 'Crown Dimensions of Deciduous Teeth
from Prehistoric India', *Am. J. Phys.
Anthrop.*, 55, 261–266.
n.d. Dental Anthropology and the Origins of
Two Iron Age Populations from Northern
Pakistan.
n.d. 'Crown Dimension of Deciduous Teeth of
Prehistoric and Living Populations of
Western India'.

McClure, H. A.
1976 'Radiocarbon Chronology of Late Quaternary Lakes in the Arabian Desert', *Nature*
263, 755–756.
1978 '2.6 Ar Rub "Al Khali"', in *Quaternary
Period in Saudi Arabia*, S. al-Sayari and J.
Zötl eds. Vienna, 252–263.

McCown, D. and Haines, R. C.
1967 *Nippur I*, Oriental Institute Publications 78,
University of Chicago Press, Chicago.

McNicoll, A. and Roaf, M.
n.d. Archaeological Investigations in Bahrain,
1973–1975. Manuscript; Department of
Antiquities, Manama, Bahrain.

Mackay, E. J. H.
1925 *Report on the Excavations of the 'A'
Cemetery at Kish*, Mesopotamia, I, Chicago.

Mackay, E., Harding, L. and Petrie, F.
1929 'Bahrain and Hamamieh', *British School in
Egypt*. Vol. XLVIII, No. 1. University College,
England.
1938 Further Excavations at Mohenjo Daro. New
Delhi.

Maigret, A. de
1980 'Riconsiderazioni sul sistema ponderale di
Ebla', *Oriens Antiquus*, XIX, 161–169.

Mitland, R. A.
1927 'The "Works of the Old Men" in Arabia',
Antiquity 1, 197–203.

Marks, A. E. and Scott, T. R.
1976 'Abu Salem: Type Site of the Harifian
Industry of the Southern Levant', *Journal of
Field Archaeology* 3, 43–60.

Marshall, John
1931 *Mohenjo daro and the Indus Civilization*,
London.

Masry, A. H.
1974 *Prehistory in Northeastern Arabia: the*
=1973 *Problem of Interregional Interaction*,
Miami
Maxwell-Hyslop, K.
1983 '*Dalbergia sissoo* Roxburgh', *Anatolian
Studies*, 33, 67–72.
Mellaart, J.
1975 *The Neolithic of the Near East*, London.
Mikesell, M.
1955 'Notes on the Dispersal of the Dromedary',
Southwestern Journal of Anthropology 11,
231–245.
Millard, A. R.
1973 'Cypriot Copper in Babylonia, *c*. 1745 B.C.',
Journal of Cuneiform Studies, 25, 211–213.
Miroschedji, P. de
1973 'Vases et objets en stéatite susiens du
Musée du Louvre', *Cahiers de La Délega-
tion Archéologie Française en Iran* 3, 9–80.
Monte, G. F. del and Tischler, J.
1978 *Die Orts- und Gewässernamen der
hethitischen Texte, Répertoire Géographique des Textes Cunéiformes*, 6.
Moore, A. M. T.
1979 'A Pre-Neolithic Farmer's Village on the
Euphrates', *Scientific American*, 62–70.
Moorey, P. R. S.
1978 *Kish Excavations 1923–1933*, Asmolean
Museum, Oxford.
Mortensen, P.
1956 'Barbartemplets ovale anlaeg', *Kuml*,
189–98.
1970 'Om Barbartemplets datering', *Kuml*,
385–98.
1971 'On the Date of the Temple at Barbar in
Bahrain', *Artibus Asiae* XXXIII, (4), 299–302.
Mughal, R.
1982 'Recent archaeological research in the
Cholistan desert', in G. Possehl (ed.),
Harappan Civilization, 85–96, Oxford and
IBH Publishing Co., New Delhi.
1983 *The Dilmun Burial Complex at Sar: The
1980–1982 Excavations in Bahrain*, Ministry
of Information, Bahrain.
Muhly, J.
1973 'Copper and Tin', *Transactions of the
Connecticut Academy of Arts and Sciences*
v. 43, New Haven.

Müller, W. W.
1978 *Ein Grabmonument*: 'Ein Grabmonument
aus Nagran als Zeugnis für das Frühnordar-
abische', in *Neue Ephemeris für Semitische
Epigraphik*, 3, 149–157.
1974 *Polyandrie*: 'Sabäische Texte zur Polyandrie', in *Neue Ephemeris für Semitische
Epigraphik*, 2, 125–138.
Mulligan, W. E.
1977 'When Jawan's Precious Objects Were
Unearthed', *The Arabian Sun*, July 27, 2–3.
Murdock, G. P.
1949 *Social Structure*, New York.
Mynors, S.
1983 'An examination of Mesopotamian
ceramics using petrographic and neutron
activation analysis', in A. Aspinall and S. E.
Warren (editors), *The Proceedings of the
22nd Symposium on Archaeometry*,
377–87, Bradford.
Naumkin, V. V. and Porhomovskij, V. Ja.
1981 *Očerki: Očerki po etnolingvistike Sokotry*,
Moscow.
Nashef, K.
1982 *Die Orts- und Gewässernamen der mittel-
babylonischen und mittelassyrischen Zeit*,
Répèrtoire Géographique des Textes
Cunéiformes Bd. 5. Beihefte zum Tubinger
Atlas des Vorderen Orient, Reihe B, nr 7/5.
Weisbaden.
Neel, J. V. and Weiss, K. M.
1975 'The Genetic Structure of a Tribal Popula-
tion; the Yanomama Indians', XII, Bio-
demographic Studies. *American Journal of
Physical Anthropology*.
Neev, D. and Emery, H. C.
1967 'The Dead Sea', *Bulletin of the Geologic
Survey of Israel*, Vol. 41.
Neumann, H.
1979 'Handel und Händler in der Zeit der III.
Dynastie von Ur', *Altorientalische For-
schungen*, VI, 15–67.
Nielsen, V.
1954 'Berømt for den mange perler', *Kuml*.
Nodelman, S. A.
1960 'A Preliminary History of Characene',
Berytus 13, 83–126.
Nöldeke, Th.
1886 Review of W. R. Smith's *Kinship*, in
Zeitschrift der Deutschen Morgenlän-

dischen Gesellschaft, 40, 148–178.

Nützel, W.

1976 'The Climate Changes of Mesopotamia and Bordering Areas, 14,000 to 2000 B.C.', *Sumer* 32, 11–24.

Oates, D.

1959 'Fort Shalmaneser – an Interim Report', *Iraq 27*, London.

Oates, J.

1960 'Ur and Eridu, the prehistory', *Iraq* 22, 32–50.

1968 'Prehistoric Investigations near Mandali, Iraq', *Iraq* 30, 1–20.

1976 'Prehistory in Northeastern Arabia', *Antiquity* 50, 20–30.

1978 'Ubaid Mesopotamia and its Relation to Gulf Countries', in de Cardi 1978, 39–52.

1983 'Ubaid Mesopotamia Reconsidered', in the Braidwood Festschrift, Chicago.

Oates, J., Davidson, T. E., Kamilli, D. and McKerrell, H.

1977 'Seafaring merchants of Ur?', *Antiquity* 51, 221–234.

Oppenheim, A. L.

1954 'The Seafaring Merchants of Ur', *Journal of the American Oriental Society* 74, 6–17.ˑ

1967 'Essay on overland trade in the first millennium B.C.', *Journal of Cuneiform Studies*, 21, 236–254.

Ortner, D. J.

1981 'A Preliminary Report on the Human Remains from the Bab edh-Dhra Cemetery', *American School of Oriental Research*, Vol. 46.

Ortner, D. J. and Putschar, W. G. J.

1981 'Identification of Pathological conditions in Human Skeletal Remains', *Smithsonian Contributions to Anthropology*. Number 28.

Ortner, D. J.

1983 'Bab edh-Dhra, City of the Dead', *Jordan* Vol. 7, No. 3. Jordan Information Bureau.

Palgrave, W. G.

1865 *Narrative of a Year's Journey through Central and Eastern Arabia (1862–63)*, London.

Palmer, E. H.

1871 *The Desert of the Exodus*, Cambridge: Deighton, Bell and Co.

Parr, P. J., Zarins, J. Ibrahim, M, Waechter, J., Garrard, A., Clarke, C., Bidmeade, M. and Badr, H.

1978 'Preliminary Report on the Second Phase of the Northern Province Survey 1397/1977', *Atlal*, 20, 29–51.

Perkins, D.

1969 'Fauna of Chatal Hüyük – Evidence for Early Cattle Domestication in Anatolia', *Science* 164, 177–179.

Perthuisot, J.-P.

1977 'Contribution à l'étude du Quaternaire marin de la péninsule de Qatar', 7, XIX, 5, 1167–1170.

Pettinato, G.

1972 'Il Commercio con l'estero della Mesopotamia mevidionale nel 3 millenio au. Cr. alla luce delle fonti letterarie e lessicali Sumeriche', *Mesopotamia*, 7, 43–166.

1980 *Materiali Epigrafici di Ebla, Vol. 2.* Naples: Instituto Universitario Orientale.

1981a *Testi Lessicali Monolingui della Biblioteca L. 2769*, (= Materiali Epigrafici di Ebla, Naples 1979, 3).

1981b *The Archives of Ebla*, New York.

1983 'Dilmun nella documentazione epigrafica di Ebla', *Berliner Beiträge zum Vorderen Orient*, 2, 75–82.

Pézard, M.

1914 *Mission a Bender-Bouchir*, Publications de la Mission en Perse 15, Paris.

Piesinger, C. M.

1983a 'The Third Millennium B.C. Settlement Patterns of Eastern Arabia'. Ph.D. University of Wisconsin.

1983b 'Legacy of Dilmun: The Roots of Ancient Maritime Trade in Eastern Coastal Arabia in the Fourth/Third Millennium B.C.', Ph.D. dissertation, University of Wisconsin-Madison.

Plattner, S. M.

1976 'Periodic Trade in Developing Areas without Markets', In C. A. Smith, ed., *Economic Systems. Volume 1: Regional Analysis*, pp. 69–89, New York: Academic Press.

Poidebard, A.

1934 *La Trace de Rome dans le Désert de Syrie*, Paris.

Pollard, A. M. and Højlund, F.

1983 'high-magnesium glazed sherds from Bronze Age tells on Failaka, Kuwait',

Archaeometry, 25, 196–200.

Pomponio, F.
1980   'AO 7754 ed il sistema ponderale di Ebla',
       Oriens Antiquus, XIX, 171–186.

Porada, E.
1971   'Some Results of the Third International
       Conference on Asian Archaeology in
       Bahrain, 1970', *Artibus Asiae* 33, 291–338.

Posener, G.
1940   *Princes et Pays d'Asie et de Nubie*,
       Brussels: Foundations Égyptologique Reine
       Elisabeth.
1971   'Chapter XXI – Syria and Palestine *c.* 2160–
       1780 B.C. Relations with Egypt', *CAH 1/2*.
       Cambridge, 532–558.

Possehl, G. L.
1977   'Pastoral Nomadism in the Indus Civiliza-
       tion: A Hypothesis', in *South Asian Archae-
       ology*, 1977, 537–551.
1980   *Indus Civilization in Saurashtra*, B.R.
       Publishing Co., Delhi.

Potts, D. T.
1978   'Towards an Integrated History of Culture
=1981 Change in the Arabian Gulf Area: Notes on
       Dilmun, Makkan and the Economy of
       Ancient Sumer', *Journal of Oman Studies*,
       vol. 4, 29–51.
1980   *Tradition and Transformation: Tepe Yahya
       and the Iranian Plateau During the Third
       Millennium B.C.*, Department of Anthro-
       pology, Harvard University, unpublished.
1982a 'Northeastern Arabia in the late pre-Islamic
       era' paper presented at Table ronde: Arabie
       orientale, Mesoptamie et Iran meridional
       de l'age du fer au début de la periode
       islamique, Lyon.
1982b 'The Zagros Frontier and the Problem of
       Relations between the Iranian Plateau and
       Southern Mesopotamia in the Third Millen-
       nium B.C.', in H.-J. Nissen and J. Renger,
       eds., *Mesopotamien und seine Nachbarn*,
       Berliner Beiträge zum Vorderen Orient 1,
       Berlin, 33–55.
1983a *Dilmun: New Studies in the Archaeology
       and Early History of Bahrain*, Berliner
       Beiträge zum Vorderen Orient 2.
1983b 'Dilmun: Where and When?', *Dilmun,
       Journal of the Bahrain Historical and
       Archaeological Society*, No. 11, 15–19.

n.d.   'The Chronology of the Archaeological
       Assemblages from the Head of the Arabian
       Gulf to the Arabian Sea (8000–1750 B.C.)', to
       appear in *Chronologies in Old World
       Archaeology* (3rd ed.) ed. Robert W.
       Ehrich, University of Chicago.

Potts, D., Ali, S., Frye, F. and Sanders, D.
1978   'Preliminary Report on the Second Phase of
       the Eastern Province Survey 1397/1977',
       Atlal, vol. 2, 7–28.

Potts, D., Krauss, R. and Lombard, P.
1983   'The Silver Hoard from City IV', in D. Potts
       (ed.), *Dilmun*, Reimer, Berlin.

Potts, D., Pedde, F. and Fanelli, J.
1984   'Preliminary Report on the First Season of
       Excavations at Thaj. Winter 1983', *Atlal*, 7.

Prideaux, F. B.
1912   The Sepulchral Tumuli of Bahrain, *Annual
       Report of the Archaeological Survey of
       India*. Government Printing Office, Calcutta,
       India.

RCAE
       L. Waterman, *Royal Correspondence of the
       Assyrian Empire*, Ann Arbor, 1930–36.

Rashid, S. A.
1972   'Eine Frühdynastische Statue von der Insel
       Tarut im Persischen Golf', *Bayerische
       Akad. d. Wiss., Phil.-Hist. Kl.*, NF 75,
       159–66.

Rawlinson, Maj. Gen. Sir H. C.,
1880   'Notes on Capt. Durand's Reports on the
       Islands of Bahrain' JRAS XII.

Reade, J. and Burleigh, R.
1978   'The Ali Cemetery: Old Excavations, Ivory
       and Radio Carbon Dating', *Journal of Oman
       Studies*, Vol. 4, 75–83.

Rees, V. C.
1929   'The Transjordan Desert', *Antiquity* 3,
       389–407.

Rentz, G. and Mulligan, W. E.
1960   Al-Bahrayn. *Encyclopaedia of Islam* 1, 941–
       44, Leiden: E. J. Brill.

Reuther, O.
1926   *Die Innenstadt von Babylon (Merkes)*,
       Wissenschaftliche Veröffentlichungen der
       Deutschen Orient-Gesellschaft 47.

Rhotert, H.
1938   *Transjordanien, Vorgeschichtliche For-
       schungen*, Stuttgart: Verlag.

Rice, M.
1972 'The grave complex at al-Hajjar, Bahrain', *Proceedings of the Seminar for Arabian Studies*, 5, 66–75.
1983 'The Temple Complex at Barbar', Ministry of Information, Bahrain.

Ripinsky, M.
1975 'The Camel in Ancient Arabia', *Antiquity* 49, 295–298.

Roaf, M.
1974 'Excavations at al-Markh, Bahrain', *Paleorient* 2, 499–501.
1976 'Excavations at al-Markh, Bahrain', *Proceedings of the Seminar for Arabian Studies* 6, 144–60.

Robin, Chr.
1982 'Les hautes-terres du Nord-Yémen avant l'Islam' (Publications de l'Institut historique-archéologique néderlandais de Stamboul, 50), II, Nouvelles inscriptions, Istanbul.
1983 'Complémente à la morphologie du verbe en sudarabique épigraphique', in *Matériaux arabes et sudarabiques, recherches en cours, 1983* (Publication du Groupe d'Etudes de linguistique et de littératures arabes et sudarabiques). Paris, 163–184.

Ronen, A.
1970 'Flint Implements From South Sinai – Preliminary Report', *PEQ* 102, 32–41.

Rouzic, Z. Le
1932 *Tumulus du Mont St-Michel, Vannes*, LaFolye et DeLamarzelle, France.

Rowton, M.
1974 'Enclosed Nomadism', *Jesho* 17, 1–29.

Rudenko, S. I.
1970 *Frozen Tombs of Siberia, the Pazyryk Burials of Iron Age Horsemen*, University of California Press.

Ryckmans, G.
1951 *Epigraphical Texts*: Vol. II of A. Fakhry, *An Archaeological Journey to Yemen*, Cairo, 3 vols.

Ryckmans, J.
1973 'Un rite d'istiqâ' au temple sabéen de Mârib', in *Annuaire de l'Institut de Philologie et d'Histoire Orientales et salves*, 20, 1968–1972, Bruxelles, 379–388 (=Mélanges Jacques Pirenne).
1974 *Himyaritica, 4*, in Le Muséon, 87, 493–521.
n.d. 'Un parallèle sud-arabe á l'imposition du nom de Jean-Baptiste et de Jésus', in *Al-Hudhud*, 283–294.

Sahlins, M. D.
1968 *Tribesmen*, Englewood Cliffs, N.J.

Shaffer, J.
1979 'Harappan commerce: an alternative perspective' in S. Pastner and L. Flam (eds.), *Anthropology in Pakistan*, 166–210, South Asia Occasional Papers, Cornell University.

Safar, F., Mustafa, M. A. and Lloyd, S.
1981 *Eridu*, State Organization of Antiquities, Baghdad.

Salles, J.-F.
1978–1979 'Note on the Archaeology of Hellenistic and Roman Periods in the U.A E.', *Archaeology in the U.A.E.*, *II–III*, 79–88.
1982 'Bahrain: introduction et ètat des questions', paper presented at Table ronde: Arabie orientale, Mesopotamie et Iran meridional de l'age du fer au début de la periode islamique, Lyon.
1984 'Bahrain "hellénistique": données et problèmes', in R. Boucharlat et J-F. Salles ed. *Arabie orientale, Mésopotamie et Iran méridional de l'âge de Fer au début de la période islamique*, Paris, ERC, 151–163.

Sarianidi, V. I.
1981 'Margiana in the Bronze Age', in P. Kohl (ed.), *The Bronze Age Civilization of Central Asia: Recent Societ Discoveries*, M. E. Sharpe, Armank, New York.

Saudi Arabia, Dept. of Antiquities and Museums
1975 *An Introduction to Saudi Arabian Antiquities*, Riyadh.

Saxe, A. A.
1970 Social Dimensions of Mortuary Practices Ph.D. thesis, University of Michigan, Ann Arbor.

Sayari (Al), S. S. and Zötl, J. G.
1978 *Quaternary period in Saudi Arabia. 1- Sedimentological, hydrogeological, hydro-chemical, geomorphological and climatological investigations in central and eastern Saudi Arabia*, Wien.

Schoff, W. H.
1912 *The Periplus of the Erythraean Sea*, New York: Longmans, Green & Co.

Schyfsma, E.
1978 '1.3 Climate' in *Quaternary Period in Saudi Arabia*, 31–44.

Serjeant, R. B.
1971 'The "White Dune", at Abyan: An Ancient Place of Pilgrimage in Southern Arabia', in *Journal of Semitic Studies*, 16, 74–83.

Seyrig, H.
1941 'Antiquités Syriennes 38. Inscriptions grecques de l'agora de Palmyre', *Syria* XXII, 223–270.

Shennan, S. E.
1975 'The Social Organization at Branc', *Antiquity*, 49, 279–88.

Shifman, I. Sh.
1976 *Gosudarstvo: Nabatejskoe gosudarstvo i ego kul'tura*, Moscow.

Sigrist, R. M.
1977 'Offrandes dans le temple de Nušku à Nippur', *Journal of Cuneiform Studies*, 29, 169–183.

Smith, C. A.
1976 'Regional Economic Systems: Linking Geographic Models and Socioeconomic Problems', in C. A. Smith, ed., *Regional Analysis. Volume 1. Economic Systems*, 3–63, New York: Academic Press.

Smith, C. H.
1890 'The Bahrain Islands in the Persian Gulf', *Discussion Proceedings of the Royal Geographical Society*, vol. XII, London.

Smith, G. H.
1978a 'Al-Da'asa, Site 46: an Arabian neolithic camp site of the fifth millennium', 53–75, in *Qatar Archaeological Report. Excavations 1973* (Ed. de Cardi).
1978b 'Two prehistoric sites on Ras Abaruk, Site 4', 80–106, in *Qatar Archaeological Report. Excavations 1973* (Ed. de Cardi).
1978c 'Stone tools from Bir Zekrit, Site 50', 107–116, in *Qatar Archaeological Report. Excavations 1973* (Ed. de Cardi).

Smith, W. Robertson
1885 *Kingship: Kinship and Marriage in Early Arabia*, Cambridge (1st edition).

Stève, M.-J., Gasche, H. and de Meyer, L.
1980 'La Susiane au deuzième millenaire: à propos d'une interpretation des fouilles de Suse', *Iranica Antiqua*, 15, 49–154.

Stol, M.
1976 *Studies in Old Babylonian History*. Leiden: Nederlands Instituut voor het Nabije Ooosten.

Stone, E. C.
1977 'Economic crisis and upheaval in Old Babylonian Nippur', in L. D. Levine and T. C. Young (editors), *Mountains and Lowlands: Essays in the Archaeology of Greater Mesopotamia*, 267–89. Malibu.

Strommenger, E.
1964 'Grabformen in Babylon', *Baghdader Mitteilungen*, 3, 157–173.

Stronach, D.
1961 'The Excavations at Ras al 'Amiya', *Iraq* 23, 95–137.
1974 'Acheminid Village 1 at Susa and the Persian Migration to Fars', *Iraq* XXXVI, 240–245.

Sumner, W.
1981 'The development of an urban settlement system in the Kur River basin, Iran', paper presented at the USA/USSR Archaeological Exchange, Cambridge, MA, November, 1981.

Tainter, J. A.
1975 'Social Influence and Mortuary Practices: An Experiment in Numerical Classification', *World Archaeology*, vol. 7, 1–15.

Taylor, J. M. C. and Illing, L. V.
1969 'Holocene intertidal calcium carbonate cementation, Qatar, Persian Gulf', *Sedimentology*, 12, 69–107.

Taylor, R.
1856 Selections from the Records of the Bombay Government, No. 24.

Thomas, C.
1894 'Report on the Mound Explorations of the Bureau of Ethnology', in *Bureau of American Ethnology. 12th Annual Report*. Smithsonian Institution.

Thompson, T. L.
1974 *The Historicity of the Patriarchal Narratives*, Berlin.
1975 *The Settlement of the Sinai and the Negev in the Bronze Age*, Wiesbaden.

Thünen, J. H. von
1875 *Der isolierte Staat in Beziehung auf Landwirtschaft und Nationalokonomie*, Berlin.

Tosi, M.

1974 'The Dating of the Umm an-Nar Culture and a Proposed Sequence for Oman in the Third Millennium B.C.', *Journal of Oman Studies* 2, 81-92.

forth. 'A possible Harappan Seaport in Eastern Arabia: Ra's al-Junayz in the Sultanate of Oman', paper delivered at the *1st International Conference on Pakistan Archaeology*, Peshawar, 1982.

Trumbull, H. C.

1883 *Kadesh Barnea*, New York.

Tubb, J. N.

1980 'A reconsideration of the date of the second millennium pottery from the recent excavations at Terqa', *Levant* 12, 61–8.

Tyráček, J. and Amin, R. M.

1981 'Rock Pictures (Petroglyphs) Near Qasr Muhaiwair Iraqi Western Desert', *Sumer*, 37, 145–148.

Ubelaker, D. H.

1974 Reconstruction of Demographic Profiles from Ossuary Skeletal Samples; a Case Study from the Tidewater Potomac. *Smithsonian Institution Contribution to Anthropology*. No. 18.

1878 *Human Skeletal Remains*, Aldine Manuals on Archaeology, Chicago.

Ungnad, A.

1923 'Schenkungsurkunde des Kurigalzu mâr Kadašman-Ḥarbe', *Archiv für Keilschriftforschung*, 1, 29–36.

Vidal, F.

1956 'A Pre-Islamic Burial in the Eastern Province', *al-Manhal*, Sha'ban 1375/April 1956, 546–553.

Van Beek, G.

1969 *Hajar Bin Humaid: Investigations at a Pre-Islamic Site in South Arabia*, Johns Hopkins Univ. Press, Baltimore.

Vine, A. R.

1937 *The Nestorian Churches; A Concise History of Nestorian Christianity in Asia from the Persian Schism to the Modern Assyrians*, London.

Vogt, B.

1981 'Maysar 9', in Weisgerber 1981.

n.d. 'Excavations at Hili, Grave M', *Archaeology in the United Arab Emirates*, Department of Antiquities and Tourism, al Aīn.

Wäfler, M.

1979 'Zur Datierung von Hama J', *Ugarit-Forschungen*, 11, 783–798.

Waetzoldt, H.

1981 'Zur Terminologie der Metalle in den Texten aus Ebla', in L. Cagni, ed., *La Lingua di Ebla*, Istituto Universitario Orientale, Seminario di Studi Asiatici Series Minor XIV, Naples, 363–378.

Wapnish, P. and Hesse, B.

1982 'In the Footsteps of Dumuzi: Pastoralism in Greater Mesopotamia', in: *The City in the Ancient World*, R. Marchese ed. in press.

Weber, A. F.

1899 *The Growth of Cities in the Nineteenth Century. Studies in History, Economics and Public Law*, vol. XI. New York. Reprinted, Cornell University Press, 1963.

Weidner, E.

1959 *Die Inschriften Tukulti-Ninurtas I. und seiner Nachfolger, Archiv für Orientforschung*. Beiheft 12, Graz.

Weisgerber, G.

1980 'Patterns of early Islamic metallurgy in Oman', *Proceedings of the Seminar for Arabian Studies*, 10, 115–126.

1980 'Archaeologische und archaeometallurgische Untersuchungen in Oman', *Allgemeine und Vergleichende Archaologie-Beitrage*, Bd. 2, 67–89.

1981 'Mehr als Kupfer in Oman – Ergebnisse der Expedition 1981', *Der Anchnitt-Zeitschrift fur Kunst und Kultur im Bergbau* 33 (5–6), 174–263.

n.d. 'Makkan and Meluhha – 3rd Millennium B.C. Copper Production in Oman and the Evidence of Contact with the Indus Valley', paper delivered at the Sixth International Conference of South Asian Archaeology, Cambridge, England, July 1981.

Weiss, H.

1975 'Kish, Akkad, and Agade', *Journal of the American Oriental Society*, 95, 434–453.

Wendorf, F. and Schild, R.

1980 *The Prehistory of the Eastern Sahara*, New York.

Wheeler, R. E. M.

1958 comments p. 246 in Bibby 1958.

Whitehouse, D. and Williamson, A.

1973 'Sasanian Maritime Trade', *Iran* 11, 29–50.

Wilken, A. G.
1884   *Het matriarchaat bij de oude Arabieren*,
        Amsterdam.
1884   *Das Matriarchat (das Mutterrecht) bei den
        alten Arabern*, Leipzig.
Willis, R. P.
1967   *Geology of the Arabian Peninsula: Bahrain*,
        U.S. Geological Survey Professional Paper
        560–E. Washington, D.C.: U.S. Government
        Printing Office.
Woolley, C. L.
1934   *Ur Excavations: The Royal Cemetery*, vols.
        I, II, Joint expedition of the British Museum
        and University Museum, Published by the
        Trustees of the Two Museums.
1954   *The Early Periods, Ur Excavations*, IV, The
        Old Babylonian Period (*Ur Excavations
        VII*).
1962   C. L. Woolley, *Ur Excavations IX, The Neo-
        Babylonian and Persian Periods*, British
        Museum, London.
Woolley, C. L. and Lawrence, T. E.
1914–15 *The Wilderness of Zin*, London: Annual
        of the Palestine Exploration Fund.
Worsaae, J. A.
1849   *Primaeval Antiquities of Denmark*, London.
Wright, E. P.
1967   *Report on the Groundwater Resources of
        Bahrain Island, Arabian Gulf*, London: U.K.
        Geological Service.
Wright, H.
1981   'The southern margins of Sumer: archae-
        ological survey of the area of Eridu and Ur',
        in R. Adams *Heartland of Cities*, University
        of Chicago Press, Chicago.
Zadok, R.
1981/1982   'Iranian and Babylonian Notes',
        Archiv für Orientforschung, XXVIII,
        135–139.
Zarins, J.
1976   The Domestication of Equidae in Third
        Millennium B.C. Mesopotamia. Ph.D.
        University of Chicago.
1978a   'The Camel in Ancient Arabia: A Further

        Note', *Antiquity* 52, 44–46.
1978b   'Steatite Vessels in the Riyadh Museum',
        Atlal 2, 65–94.
1978c   'The Domesticated Equidae of Third
        Millennium B.C. Mesopotamia', *Journal of
        Cuneiform Studies*, 30, 3–17.
1979   'Rajajil: A Unique Arabian Site from the
        Fourth Millennium B.C.', *Atlal* 3, 73–78.
1982   'Early Rock Art of Saudi Arabia', *Archae-
        ology* 35, 20–27.
1982   Review of J. Clutton-Brock, *Domesticated
        Animals from Early Times*, in, *Biblical
        Archeologist*, 45/4, 251–253.
Zarins, J., Ibrahim, M., Potts, D. and Edens, C.
1979   'Saudi Arabian Archaeological Reconnais-
        sance 1978: The Preliminary Report on the
        Third Phase of the Comprehensive Archae-
        ological Survey Programe – the Central
        Province', *Atlal*, 3, 9–38.
Zarins, J., Whalen, N., Ibrahim, M., Morad, A. and
Khan, M.
1980   'Comprehensive Archaeological Survey
        Program – Preliminary Report on the
        Central and Southwestern Provinces
        Survey', *Atlal*, 4, 9–36.
Zarins, J., Murad, A. and al-Yish, K.
1981   'Comprehensive Archaeological Survey
        Program – a. The Second Preliminary
        Report on the Southwestern Province',
        Atlal, 5, 9–42.
Zarins, J., Rihbini, A. and Kamal, M.
1982   'Comprehensive Survey of the Central Nejd
        – The Riyadh Environs', *Atlal*, 6, in press.
Zarins, J., Moghannum, A. S. and Kamal, M.
n.d.   'Excavations at Dhahran South – Tumuli
        Field (208–91), 1403 A.H./1983. A Prelimi-
        nary Report', *Atlal*, in press.
Ziegler, C.
1953   *Die Keramik von der Qal'a des Haggi
        Mohammad*.
Zohary, M.
1952   'Ecological Studies in the Vegetation of the
        Near Eastern Deserts', *IEJ*, 2, 201–215.

List of contributors

Amiet, Pierre
Département des Antiquités Orientales, Musée de Louvre, Paris

Andersen, H. H.
Forhistorisk Museum, Moesgård, Denmark

Bibby, Geoffrey
Forhistorisk Museum, Moesgård, Denmark

Boucharlat, Rémy
Maison de l'Orient Mediterranéan, Université Lyon 2 – Lyon, France

Bowersock, G. W.
The Institute for Advanced Study, Princeton, N.J., U.S.A.

Cleuziou, Serge
Centre de Recherches Archéologiques, U.R.A. No. 30, Paris, France

Dani, A. H.
Islamabad, Pakistan

de Cardi, Beatrice
1A Douro Place, Victoria Road, London W8

Doe, Brian
Beeley Old Hall, Beeley, Matlock, Derbys

Dostal, Walter
Institut für Völkerkunde, Der Universität Wien, Austria

During Caspers, E. C. L.
Institut Kern, Indologish Institut, Der Rijks-universiteit, Leyden, Netherlands

Edens, Christopher
Dept. of Anthropology, Harvard University, Cambridge, Mass. U.S.A.

Feilden, Sir Bernard
Stiffkey Old Hall, Stiffkey, Norfolk

Frifelt, Karen
Forhistorisk Museum, Moesgård, Denmark

Frohlich, Bruno
Conservation Analytical Laboratory, Smithsonian Institution, Washington, D.C., U.S.A.

Højgaard, Karen
Tuekaeret q, Dk 3520, Farum

Højlund, Flemming
Forhistorisk Museum, Moesgård, Denmark

Howard-Carter, Teresa
The University Museum, Philadelphia, U.S.A.
Chief Adviser, Kuwait National Museum

Ippolitoni-Strika, Fiorella
Dept. of Oriental Studies, University of Rome I 'La Sapienza'

Joshi, Jagat Pati
Joint Director General, Archaeological Survey of India, New Delhi

Kervran, Monique
Mission Archéologique Française à Bahrain et Oman; Université de Paris Sorbonne, Paris, France

al-Khalifa, Shaikha Haya
Director of Antiquities and Museums, the State of Bahrain

Kjaerum, Poul
Forhistorisk Museum, Moesgård, Denmark

Kohl, Philip L.
Dept. of Anthropology, Wellesley College, Wellesley, Mass. U.S.A.

Lamberg-Karlovsky, C. C.
Dept. of Anthropology, Harvard University, Cambridge, Mass., U.S.A.

Larsen, Curtis E.
U.S. Geological Survey, Reston, Virginia, U.S.A.

Lombard, Pierre
Maison de l'Orient Méditerranéen, Université Lyon 2, France

Mitchell, T. C.
Dept. of Western Asiatic Antiquities, The British Museum, London

Mortensen, Peder
Forhistorisk Museum, Moesgård, Denmark

Nashef, Khaled
Altorientalisches Seminar, Universität Tübingen, Germany

Nissen, Hans J.
Frei Universität, Berlin

Oates, David
Institute of Archaeology, 31–34 Gordon Square, London
W.C.1
Oates, Joan
Girton College, Cambridge
Paskoff, Roland
Université de Tunis
Potts, Daniel
Institut für Voderasiatisches-Alter-tumskunde, Free
University of Berlin
Rao, S. R.
National Institute of Oceanography, Dona Paula, Goa, India
Reade, Julian
Dept. of Western Asiatic Antiquities, British Museum,
London
Rice, Michael
1 Lowther Gardens, London, S.W.7

Ryckmans, Jacques
Collège Erasme, Université Catholique de Louvain, Louvain,
Belgium
Salles, Jean-Francois
Maison de l'Orient Mediterranéen, Université Lyon 2,
France
Sanlaville, Paul
Maison de l'Orient Mediterranéen, Université Lyon 2,
France
Tixier, Jacques
CNRS, Meudon, France
Tosi, Maurizio
Instituto Universitario Orientale, Naples, Italy
Weisgerber, Gerd
Deutsche Bergbau Museum, Bochum, West Germany
Zarins, Juris
Southwest Missouri State University, Springfield, Missouri,
U.S.A.

Index

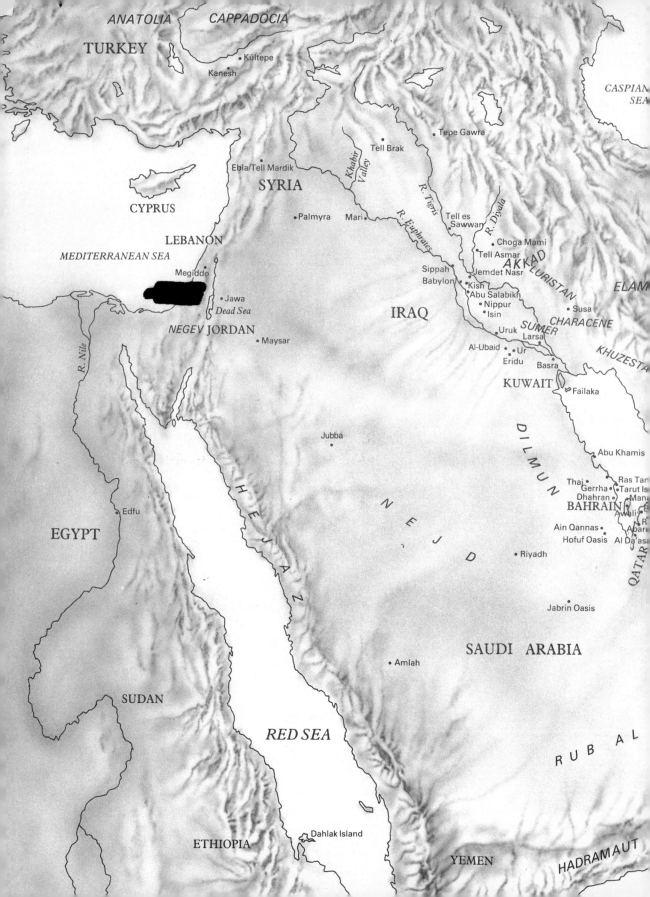

ANATOLIA   *CAPPADOCIA*

TURKEY

• Kültepe
Kanesh

CASPIAN
SEA

• Tepe Gawra

• Tell Brak

Ebla/Tell Mardik •

Khabir Valley

SYRIA

CYPRUS

R. Tigris

R. Diyala

MEDITERRANEAN SEA

LEBANON

Palmyra •   Mari •

Tell es
Sawwan •

• Choga Mami

R. Euphrates

Megiddo •

Sippah •
Babylon •

Tell Asmar •

AKKAD

LURISTAN

ELAM

• Jawa
Dead Sea

Jemdet Nasr •

Kish •
Abu Salabikh •

Nippur •

IRAQ

• Susa

NEGEV JORDAN

Isin •

CHARACENE

Maysar •

Uruk •

SUMER

Larsa •

Al-Ubaid •
Eridu •

• Ur

KHUZESTA

R. Nile

Basra •

KUWAIT

Failaka

EGYPT

Jubba •

DILMUN

Abu Khamis •

Thai • • Ras Tan
Gerrha • • Tarut Is
Dhahran •   Mana

BAHRAIN
Awali •

• Ras Tan

Ain Qannas •
Hofuf Oasis •   Al Da'as
Aparu

QATAR

N E J D

Edfu •

• Riyadh

SUDAN

Jabrin Oasis •

HEJAZ

SAUDI ARABIA

Amlah •

RED SEA

R U B   A L

Dahlak Island •

ETHIOPIA

YEMEN

HADRAMAUT